W9-BBD-510

DRINK AND THE VICTORIANS

The Temperance Question in England 1815–1872

by

BRIAN HARRISON

UNIVERSITY OF PITTSBURGH PRESS

Drink and the Victorians

1. Solomon King, arrested for drunkenness at Dunstable, 1866. Age 68. Previous offences: 1838, stealing potatoes; 1840, assault; 1847, want of sureties; 1848, ditto; 1849, ill-treating a dog; 1850, assault (twice); 1850, want of sureties; 1851, misbehaviour at workhouse (twice); 1853, assault; 1856, stealing turnip tops; 1857, assault; 1858, neglect of family. From *Register of Prisoners in Bedford County Gaol*, p. 70: Mr. K. V. Thomas, of St. John's College, Oxford, kindly referred me to this source.

First published in England
by Faber and Faber Limited

Library of Congress Catalog Card Number 70–141765
ISBN 0–8229–3223–7

Manufactured in Great Britain by Butler & Tanner Ltd, Frome

Preface

'The thing that most needs writing about is the temperance movement . . .'. I shall always be grateful to Professor H. J. Hanham, now of Harvard University, for his helpful letter of March 1961, and also for the generous help he has given me since. All historical books are co-operative ventures, and I have received generous help from many other people. From my former supervisor Peter Mathias, now of All Souls College, Oxford, I received many kindnesses, much penetrating comment, and endless patience. Temperance history has hitherto suffered from two contrasting defects. When written by temperance enthusiasts, it has been partisan and antiquarian: when written by outsiders, it has been patronizing and facetious. If this book has any success in steering between these two extremes, Peter Mathias deserves much of the credit. My former tutor Mr. Keith Thomas of St. John's College, Oxford, gave me the consistent encouragement, help and support which every research-student needs; he also introduced me to Solomon King. My friends Dr. John Walsh of Jesus College, Oxford, and Dr. Cormac Rigby of the B.B.C. have freely given time, ideas and trouble. St. Antony's and Nuffield Colleges were the two excellent Oxford institutions whose fellows had the imagination to see that here was a subject worth tackling; I can never repay them for emancipating me from distractions at a crucial stage.

Professor Asa Briggs and Dr. Kitson Clark gave me helpful initial guidance, and I have received generous help on detailed points from Lord Aberdare, J. M. Bestall of Sheffield University's department of extramural studies, M. G. Brock of Wolfson College, Oxford, W. H. Chaloner of Manchester University, Mrs. Christina Colvin, David Goodway of Birkbeck College, K. G. E. Harris, social science librarian, Bradford, Louis James of the University of Kent, Max Hartwell, Chelly Halsey and David Butler of Nuffield College, Oxford, Sir Hughe Knatchbull-Hugessen, Dr. Prys Morgan of University College, Swansea, Miss Felicity Ranger of the National Register of Archives, Raphael Samuel of Ruskin College, Robert Storch of Wisconsin University, Barrie Trinder of Banbury Historical Society, Professor John Vincent of Bristol University, and Dr. Theodore Zeldin of St. Antony's College. Mr. H. J. Bunker, Professor John Yudkin of Queen Elizabeth College, London, and my friend George Irons of Guinness's Brewery patiently initiated me into the mysteries of brewers' chemistry and dietetics; Robert

Bacon, now of Lincoln College, Oxford, and Dr. David Mayers of Oxford University Computing Laboratory rescued a historian distressed by an excess of statistics.

Many people made valuable comments on earlier drafts. Like so many Oxford students, I owe much to Philip Williams of Nuffield College, who vigorously criticized style, argument and presentation; I am also very grateful to several former Nuffield students, now scattered at universities throughout the country: José Chambers, Peter Dixon, Keith Harling, Patricia Hollis, Bob Morris, Tom Nossiter and Gill Sutherland. Three fellow-students of the temperance movement—Tony Dingle, Bill Lambert and Gerry Olsen—made valuable criticisms; Dr. Christopher Hill, Mr. Michael Hurst and Dr. Henry Pelling commented helpfully on early drafts of some chapters. I also greatly appreciate the help of two anonymous but shrewd and charitable publisher's readers, from whose criticisms I have profited considerably. My many other obligations have been acknowledged in the footnotes.

Although they will probably differ from many of my conclusions, I hope the many temperance reformers who generously and patiently helped me—particularly Mr. T. Garth Waite of the Alliance, Miss Daniel of the League, Mr. Mark Hayler and Mrs. Broadhurst—will not regret having done so; they made my research much easier and more pleasant than it might otherwise have been. The staff of the Bodleian Library typing room, of Colindale Newspaper Library, and of many public libraries have given the most painstaking and considerate service. Many others have helped in various ways—often unconsciously—but I am solely responsible for all remaining mistakes. My mother-in-law's help with the proofs was most valuable. My wife sustained me, and devoted many hours to helping me, amidst the agonies of checking footnotes and correcting proofs; I must end by thanking her and my mother most heartily for giving me ideal working conditions since I began my research. But I know that they will forgive me if I dedicate this book to my father: he consistently encouraged me in my academic work, and would have taken such pleasure in the book—despite its weaknesses—had he lived to see it.

Corpus Christi College
Oxford
November 1970

FOR MY FATHER

Contents

Contents

Illustrations

Tables

Figures

Figures

ABBREVIATIONS USED IN TEXT TO SHOW THE PRINCIPAL TEMPERANCE ORGANIZATIONS

B.A.P.T.	British Association for the Promotion of Temperance
B.F.S.S.I.	British and Foreign Society for the Suppression of Intemperance
B.F.T.S.	British and Foreign Temperance Society
B.T.L.	British Temperance League
C.A.S.S.I.L.S.	Central Association for Stopping the Sale of Intoxicating Liquor on Sundays
N.B.F.S.S.I.	New British and Foreign Society for the Suppression of Intemperance
N.B.F.T.S.	New British and Foreign Temperance Society
N.T.L.	National Temperance League
N.T.S.	National Temperance Society

NOTE

The Oxford English Dictionary prescribes 'teetotal', but 'teetotaller' and 'teetotallism': throughout this book I have preferred the spellings 'teetotaler' and 'teetotalism' because they possess the double advantage of consistency and of conforming to contemporary usage.

1
Perspectives

Solomon King caused infinite trouble in his day, and this book analyses attempts between 1815 and 1872 to reform him.* The campaign began when free traders, influential in government circles, tried to make milder and purer drinks more accessible by freeing the beer trade in 1830 and the wine trade in 1860. But by 1872 their remedy had been discredited, and to some extent temperance reformers† were responsible. Whereas free traders were never organized into a distinct free licensing organization, temperance reformers were at all times mobilized into a 'movement'. Originating in 1828, the temperance movement at first associated only abstainers from spirits. Teetotal societies soon grew out of this movement in the early 1830s, and at the end of the decade some teetotalers even adopted the 'long pledge' which banned the offering, as well as the consuming, of intoxicants. Though less patient with the continuance of drunkenness than the free traders were, the early temperance reformers did not immediately repudiate free licensing; they aimed at a temperance reformation through voluntary abstinence—a strategy quite compatible with abolition of licensing restrictions. Still, many early temperance reformers did suspect free trade, and feared the free traders' cheap gin introduced in the 1820s and their beerhouses introduced in 1830.

The real repudiation of free trade came in 1853, when the United Kingdom Alliance was founded to outlaw all trading in intoxicating drinks. This divided the temperance movement into 'moral suasionists' and 'legislative compulsionists': education versus prohibition. Prohibitionists, often free traders in every other sphere of life, gradually elaborated a full-scale critique of indiscriminate free trade, and pioneered among Liberals and nonconformists 'positive' attitudes to the state which later influenced other areas of social policy. Temperance pressure eventually forced the politicians to reverse their free trade policy and to revert in 1871–2 to the restrictive policy which had

* See Plate 1 (frontispiece).

† Strictly speaking, free traders and counter-attractionists were also 'temperance reformers', as were all those who tackled the nineteenth-century drink problem. However, I have followed convention by using the term to describe only those who joined the anti-spirits, teetotal or prohibitionist movements.

prevailed before the 1820s. 'While in some subjects,' said Gladstone in 1880, 'we trace in the mind of the country, and in the mind also of Parliament, a regular progress from the first beginnings of a conviction, along clear and definite lines, to the period of their maturity, this is a subject on which the course taken by Parliament—and, possibly, the public opinion of the country—have been attended by a marked irregularity, and even by a singular reversal . . . we have not yet got out of the stage of experiment in this matter.'[1]

The year 1872 did not see the complete victory of the temperance reformers, but it is a convenient stopping-point because it marks the end of the battle between free traders and restrictionists. The temperance crusade now moved into new areas—opposing the compensation of dispossessed publicans, the municipal management of the drink trade and the treatment of drunkenness as a disease rather than as a moral failing. Temperance reformers still had much life in them, but after the early 1870s their movement began to acquire the conservative outlook which has been steadily reducing its influence ever since. The change is reflected in the annual income of the two leading teetotal organizations: comparing the quinquennia 1856–60 and 1871–5, the annual real income of the British and National Temperance Leagues rose by 73% and 61% respectively—appreciably faster than the real national income *per capita*. After the early 1870s the position was reversed; whereas the real national income *per capita* rose by 57% between 1871–5 and 1895–9, the annual income of the British Temperance League in the same period rose by only 3% and that of the National Temperance League fell by 2%. A similar change affected the prohibitionist movement at the time.* Still more serious, from the early 1880s even the nominal income of these temperance organizations began to stagnate or decline: the fall in prices in the 1880s ensures that the figures for annual real income mask this decline [see Figure 1][2]. At the same time temperance reformers were coming under ideological attack. Between 1880 and 1914 the socialist critique of their movement was elaborated; this book must therefore attempt something which the late-Victorian temperance historians never attempted: it must set the temperance remedy against the background of the emergent labour movement. It will therefore conclude with a discussion of Teetotal Chartism and of the socialist/temperance debate.

These developments must be seen against the background of contemporary drinking habits. Drunkenness, like homosexuality, seems to be latent to a varying degree in all human beings, but except in cases of physiological or

* The temperance movement from 1872 to the first world war badly needs a historian. Mr. A. E. Dingle of Monash University is studying the United Kingdom Alliance from 1872 to 1895. Mr. Gerry Olsen of King's College, University of Western Ontario, Canada, is writing a history of the Church of England Temperance Society. Mr. D. M. Fahey of Miami University is studying the temperance movement from 1891 to 1908. Mr. David Wright of the University of Waterloo, Ontario, Canada, is studying the liquor licensing question in English politics, 1896–1910.

psychological disorder it affects day-to-day conduct only under special social conditions. Society can encourage or discourage the relieving of tensions through drinking. In many societies, individuals become helplessly drunk on special occasions—such as Saturday night, Whitsun, New Year, weddings or funerals—while remaining sober at all other times. For example, in June 1877 the metropolitan police arrested on average 141 people for drunkenness on a Saturday, and only 88 on each of the other six days of the week.[3] Drunkenness of this type is quite distinct from alcoholism, and requires some cultural or historical explanation. The alcoholic exists in all societies, whereas the occasional drunkard who—unlike the alcoholic—can choose when he wishes

FIG. 1

Annual real income of leading temperance organizations: 1830-1900

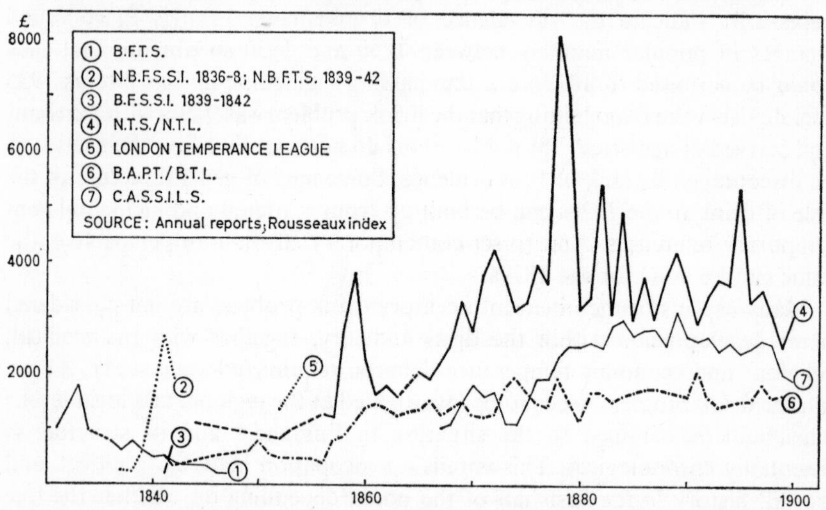

to drink, abounds only in a specific historical and cultural context. Although this book will discuss alcoholism in passing, its main concern is with the social, rather than with the physiological and psychological, factors affecting the incidence of drunkenness.

The Victorians often failed to distinguish between alcoholism, drinking and drunkenness. Temperance reformers argued that drinking inevitably led to drunkenness, and society at large failed to distinguish between drunkenness and alcoholism. The word drunkenness—'the state of being drunk'—has been regularly used by Englishmen at least since A.D. 893, whereas the word alcoholism—'the diseased condition produced by alcohol'—appeared only about 1860. Thomas Trotter, in his *Essay on Drunkenness* published in 1804, was among the earliest to describe habitual drunkenness as a disease: but he was unable to describe the condition in terms which were free from moral overtones. Not till the 1860s and 1870s did American experiments convince Englishmen that habitual drunkards required voluntary or compulsory asylum treatment, and that alcoholism was, as Chamberlain argued in 1877, 'more a disease than a crime'.[4] Some attempt is made to provide the essential background of Victorian drinking habits in Chapters 2, 14 and 15, and at the same time to consider the uncoordinated but important campaigns by isolated individuals to provide counter-attractions to the drinking place. These people included many temperance reformers, free traders and regulationists, but also many who took no definite stance on the drink question—even self-interested profiteers: railway promoters, coffee-house keepers and publicans.

'Drunkenness' is unfortunately not a scientific term: what was the reality which lay behind the temperance reformer's efforts before 1872? We have no reliable drink consumption figures for these years, nor would such figures necessarily indicate the prevalence of drunkenness. Francis Place found changes in popular manners between 1750 and 1830 so obscure that they could be surmised 'only from a few passing incidents', and as late as 1935 sociologists were complaining that the drink problem was 'beset with partisans and starved of statistics'.[5] Still, historians do not usually allow themselves to be discouraged by lack of firm evidence. Some sort of general picture of the role of drink in the 1820s can be built up from scattered and incidental contemporary references. And to set contemporary efforts into perspective, the same can be done for the 1870s.

Many aspects of the nineteenth-century drink problem are not considered here: developments within the drink industry, together with the medical, religious and economic temperance debates, require full-scale study. Above all, the drink problem needs to be investigated at the regional and local level.[6] This book is confined to the situation in England,* and its structure is essentially chronological. This entails a syncopation between 'political' and 'social' history in the first half of the book, depending on whether the free licensing movement (which operated from Westminster, at the political level) or the voluntary abstinence movement (which operated from the provinces, at the individual level) is being discussed. With Gladstone's budget of 1860, however, the two worlds began to come together; the narrative therefore becomes more exclusively political, and culminates in the licensing crisis of 1869–72. These years saw the legislature interacting at last with the social movement, and they therefore deserve more detailed attention. Yet the conventional distinction between social and political history is unreal: politicians operate within a social context which the political historian must describe. Even in the second half of the book, therefore, some attempt is made to assess

* The Scottish temperance movement is now being studied by Daniel Paton of Edinburgh University. See also W. R. Lambert, 'Drink and Sobriety in Wales 1835–1895' (University of Wales Ph.D thesis, 1969); I am most grateful for the author's permission to read this thesis.

the state of public opinion, and to estimate the effects of political action. As well as combining political with social history, this book combines a chronological with an analytical treatment—another unreal distinction, perhaps. To ensure that some of the underlying analytical points are not lost in the narrative, some of the most important are outlined in the rest of this chapter.

If Herbert Butterfield was correct in claiming that the historian's chief aim is 'the elucidation of the unlikenesses between past and present', the historian of nineteenth-century England could choose no better subject than the temperance question; for the subject abounds in unfamiliar arguments and forgotten attitudes. Referring in 1936 to the Edwardian period, R. C. K. Ensor spoke of 'the then monstrous evil of intemperance—how monstrous, it is perhaps difficult for the present generation to realize'.[7] The contrast does not lie solely in the prevalence of the evil: it also lies in the character of the agitation waged against it. Twentieth-century temperance reformers, like their predecessors, stress the dependence of national prosperity and good government on the morality of the individual citizen; yet nobody listens. For, as a recent report phrased it, 'the new psychology has . . . focused attention on immediate personal relationships, so that we now tend to think of the individual primarily as child, lover, friend or parent, rather than as citizen or creature with responsibilities to society at large and to God'.[8] Marx and Freud have shifted our perspective away from the nineteenth-century's concern for individual moral effort. Twentieth-century temperance reformers are also unfashionable in their fear of freedom: not for them the substitution of 'civilized' for 'permissive' in the term 'permissive society'! For like T. H. Green they know how easily 'the freedom of others' is neglected when the civilized society is 'based on the belief that different individuals will wish to make different decisions about their patterns of behaviour and . . . should be allowed to do so'.[9] The temperance reformers of the 1960s firmly opposed the new morality; recent scandals led them to support the abortive scheme in 1964 to found the *Daily Leader*, a paper whose trust-deed condemned the contemporary press for slipping 'into the way of emphasizing the dark side of life and human behaviour'. In August 1969 the *Alliance News*, a leading temperance organ, printed an interview with Malcolm Muggeridge and firmly stated its standpoint: 'we share the revulsion Mr. Muggeridge feels as he sees the Gadarene stampede of this generation over the edge of decency'.

These changes are partly a matter of fashion. But they also stem from a profound social transformation. Essential to an understanding of the nineteenth-century temperance question is the contemporary gulf—now rapidly vanishing away, or at least being recreated in a new form—between the 'rough' and the 'respectable' poor. Two 'incidents' illustrate this situation well. In a letter to *The Times* on 11 July 1872, 'three disgusted travellers' described how they had boarded a train at Cheshunt on a Sunday evening in

1872. Entering a first-class compartment, they were at first alone. Then at Lower Tottenham 'there was an ugly rush for places. Our compartment was instantly invaded and taken possession of by seven persons of an extremely offensive and noisy description without any remonstrance from porter or guard. During the remainder of our journey we were annoyed by having to listen to a succession of obscene and vulgar songs, interspersed with language of the lowest and most objectionable description, and in addition to this grievance the heat in our carriage, owing to the overcrowding, was almost overpowering. Judging from their slang and general demeanour, it will not be uncharitable to conclude that some at least of our companions belonged to the predatory classes. . . . On the collection of tickets, not a remonstrance was raised by the collector, and it was apparent that the third-class could do as they liked.' The second incident involved Mr. Pain, a respectable inhabitant of Banbury who lived close to the slums of Neithrop; he suffered great inconvenience from his situation, but felt helpless because the Banbury authorities were not empowered to police the suburb. 'In these parts', he said, 'are several beerhouses, much frequented by men and women of bad character, and at which there is frequently fighting and other disorderly conduct within the hearing of the borough police. . . . My house and premises are within the borough, but my back door opens into a lane in Neithrop, near to which is a beer-house, much frequented by boatmen and persons of bad character. Some time since there was a great disturbance at this beer-house—men fighting and women calling murder, and at the same time a borough policeman was walking in front of my house, but . . . I could not demand his interference.'[10] In these two incidents we glimpse the twin responses which the rough aroused in the respectable: disgust at a whole complex of behaviour—swearing, cruelty, drunkenness, vulgarity and violence: and an authoritarianism inspired by fear at the fragility of civilization. Several organizations tried to bridge this social gulf, and prominent among them was the nineteenth-century temperance movement.

Eyes accustomed to the very different class relations of the mid-twentieth century may see in organizations like the temperance movement mere attempts to impose middle-class manners on the working class. They will seize upon a personality like Rev. G. W. McCree—grocer's son, temperance advocate and presbyterian missionary of St. Giles' in London. At a dinner he organized for neglected children in the area, he noticed a child who had not begun his meal, and inquired why: the child did not know how to use the knife and fork. ' "Why", I said, "how do you eat your dinner at home?" "Oh!" said he, "off the edge of the table. My father cuts the meat, puts it on the table, and then I eat it with my fingers." "Oh!" I said; "that won't do here. We want you to eat like ladies and gentlemen." '[11] Patronizing and insensitive as this incident shows McCree to be, it will be argued in this book that McCree was helped in his civilizing task not only by many members of the middle class, but also by an élite of working men. The terms 'middle class' and 'working class' were of course coming into use in the 1830s when the temperance movement originated: but at that time they emphasized a social division far less important politically than the gulf which lay *within* the working class. McCree's knife-and-fork incident illustrates a second theme of this book: the fact that the social conscience of temperance reformers and others helped to prevent the polarization of English society which Marx in the 1840s forecast. McCree was acting as a broker between the classes, and information did not pass in only one direction; in the 1870s he was giving paid lectures—with titles like 'Day and Night in St. Giles' and 'Lights and Shades of Life in London'—to respectable audiences on the excitements of life in the slums they had never visited. The prohibitionist J. Ewing Ritchie played a rather similar role—publishing in the 1850s, together with temperance literature, his moralizing and rather prurient *Night Side of London* (1857). Like many pioneer teetotalers, Thomas Whittaker was exasperated at fashionable London's sudden 'discovery' of the East End in the 1880s; the pioneer teetotalers, he said, had been exploring the slums since the 1830s.[12]

If McCree epitomizes the middle-class benevolence channelled into the temperance movement, Whittaker [see Plate 15] epitomizes its resolute encouragement of working-class self-respect and self-realization. In the words of one old lady recalling for the author the late-Victorian Blue Ribbon temperance crusade in Oxford: 'all the decent people were blue'. The nineteenth-century working class always contained individuals who valued their self-respect without feeling the need to sharpen it by attacking their immediate superiors. R. C. K. Ensor recalled 'what a cruel and unescapable badge of inferiority clothes . . . constituted' until the improvement in ready-made clothing during the early twentieth century; the Whittaker brand of working man was distinguishable from other working men by his relatively smart personal appearance. He also shared many middle-class attitudes: a distaste for mobs, and a repudiation of the whole complex of behaviour associated with racecourses, fairs, wakes, brothels, beerhouses and brutal sports. He was more likely than his inferiors to vote Liberal, if only because his work-situation frequently fostered individualism, self-education and social ambition.[13] If he drank at all, he drank soberly, without neglecting his wife and family; he often took his recreation with them, and believed that the family should keep itself to itself. He was probably interested in religious matters—often a chapelgoer or a secularist. He was strongly attracted by the ideology of thrift, with its stress on individual self-respect, personal moral and physical effort, and prudence. He joined craft unions in their élitist mid-Victorian phase, read widely and often joined a mechanics' institute. His possession of capital—be it only in the form of working tools, a clock or a watch—he attributed largely to his regular habits and personal rectitude.

Eager to distinguish himself from the roughs, the Whittaker type of working man was in some ways a conservative influence: yet this is not to say that he was servile towards his betters. On the contrary, he cultivated an upstanding independence and integrity which made for radical attitudes. As one prohibitionist pointed out, the working man with savings 'need not care whether he sold his labour one day or another, but could wait and sell it to an eager purchaser instead of being a needy seller'.[14] By the high demands he made of life and by the exclusiveness of his unions, the Whittaker type of working man helped to keep wages high. His importance in nineteenth-century society sprang from his articulateness, his strong political and religious involvement, his relative affluence and his sheer numbers. For at this time the factory system was relatively localized, and political parties had not begun to adapt their policies in the face of his declining industrial importance. Estimates of the labour aristocracy's size from the 1840s to the 1890s vary considerably, but the lowest figure suggested for early Victorian London is about 10% of the work-force, and much higher figures have been suggested for other towns. Dissatisfaction with one's position within the working class was at that time politically much more important than dissatisfaction with the position of the working class in society at large.

Josephine Butler gave the best description of such men when she described working-class hostility to the Contagious Diseases Acts: 'I should say the temperance men almost always lead in this matter,—abstainers, steady men, and to a great extent members of chapels and churches, and many of them are men who have been engaged in the anti-slavery movement and the abolition of the corn-law movement. They are the leaders in good social movements, men who have had to do with political reforms in times past, and who have taken up our cause. They may not be the majority, but they are men of the most weight and zeal in their towns, and who have a considerable acquaintance with life, and large provincial experience, and they gather round them all the decent men in the place; when they start a movement they get all the rest to follow; and properly so, because they are men of character. They are secretaries of trades' councils, and presidents of working men's clubs, &c.'[15] In a modern society of hire-purchase, religious apathy, mass entertainment, immediate gratification and personal affluence—these are unfamiliar figures. Whereas the twentieth century idolizes 'heroes of consumption', the nineteenth idolized 'heroes of abstinence' and dietary habits followed from social status.[16] Social mobility could be attained through adapting one's style of life to the pattern adopted by one's immediate superiors. The social situation in Birmingham and even in some Lancashire mill-towns encouraged such conduct, for many of the employers had themselves risen from humbler origins.[17]

The expectation that before the privilege of property all other privileges would vanish was at least temporarily belied by movements like the temperance movement, whose fundamental social antagonism lay between aristocracy and trade. Such movements mobilized the reverence for property and the enthusiasm for thrift so widespread in both middle and working class, infused some of the nonconformist's righteous indignation, and contrasted this style of life with the image of the spendthrift aristocrat whose pension was filched from the public purse and whose lands had been stolen from the people at the Norman Conquest or at the Reformation. The occasional disruption of these reforming movements by schisms running along class lines reveals the simultaneous presence of a quite different social alignment in which middle and working classes took divergent roads; but this contrasting pattern was overlain, at least until the 1880s, by pan-class organizations like the temperance movement. If these movements—from anti-slavery to Josephine Butler—united the reformers, they also united their opponents. In the temperance movement, the respectable members of both middle and working classes united against the aristocrat who encouraged the worst recreational tastes of the poor. J. A. Hobson once described the 'lower leisure class whose valuations and ways of living form a most instructive parody of the upper leisure class'.[18] In both social groups he saw fighting, sporting and reckless waste [see Plate 17]; both displayed 'the same unaffected contempt for the worker, the same class camaraderie, often with a special code of honour, the same sex license and joviality of manners. . . .' In 1902 the King himself seemed to be patronizing such a moral code when he visited Burton breweries: 'it is no desire of his to be superior to the meanest of his subjects', wrote the prohibitionist *Alliance News* on 6 March: 'he patronizes dramatic art in the person of Dan Leno, placing himself on a level with any coster-monger at a music-hall. . . . Are we to have, after the noble Victorian era, dignity swallowed up in vulgar amusement, and high effort forgotten in gross materialism?'

Popular radicalism, it has been claimed, 'was the product of the leisure of Saturday night and Sunday morning, the pothouse and the chapel, not of the working week'.[19] Until the 1860s the Liberal party attracted working men by the radicals' free licensing movement, which defended beersellers—often themselves working men—against irresponsible and meddling magistrates: and which defended the honest consumer against a licensing system which allegedly feathered the nest of privilege, infringed popular liberties and enabled the rich brewer-monopolist to foist his adulterated beer on the public. And when, during the 1860s, free licensing fell into disrepute, another Liberal movement with working-class support—the temperance movement—was largely responsible. Although a few 'negative' Liberals like Henry Fawcett, Auberon Herbert and William Rathbone continued to champion the free trade remedy, the future lay with 'constructive' Liberalism pioneered by prohibitionists who taught many libertarians that the problem was, in the words of a modern politician, 'one of balance between individual freedom and social obligation'.[20] Apart from their educational influence, prohibitionists brought with them a formidable body of nonconformist and provincial support which galvanized the late-Victorian Liberal party in the constituencies. If the modern Labour party 'is a crusade or it is nothing',[21] still more can this be said of Gladstonian Liberalism. Moral reform crusades like the temperance movement enabled Liberalism to attract influential working men at least till the 1890s.

The comparative study of nineteenth-century social reform processes has recently been courageously and imaginatively pioneered by Professor Oliver MacDonagh, whose 'model' isolates the essential stages in the elimination of contemporary social evils. The model begins at the point where society pronounces an evil to be 'intolerable'—a trumpet-cry which 'no wall of either doctrine or interest could permanently withstand'. The state intervenes, inefficiently at first, but with increasing success after it has appointed officials who can provide it with accurate information. The whole process of extending state control is almost self-generating, and owes more to detailed empirical investigation of the evil in question than to outside and doctrinaire pronouncements on the role of the state.[22] For three reasons this model does not illuminate the history of the nineteenth-century drink question; firstly, it caters only for social evils which nineteenth-century society tackled through continuous state regulation. In this sphere there was no steady progress towards state intervention. On the contrary, the free licensing movement secured an abandonment of controls which were resumed only after 1869. Because they relied at first on voluntary action, early Victorian temperance and housing reformers differed from those who attacked evils on emigrant ships, and in mines and factories. Only during the 1860s did temperance reformers clash directly with free traders. Furthermore prohibitionism was a peculiar form of interventionism, quite different from that described by MacDonagh. It was never intended to operate through a body of inspectors, and it combined faith in the most drastic form of public control with an all-embracing belief in self-help.

Secondly, then, in this sphere MacDonagh's inspectors were never appointed. The 1853–4 public-houses committee, impressed by the success of the inspectors who enforced recent lodging-house legislation, urged the appointment of inspectors to supervise drinking places and restaurants. Yet even a moderate regulationist like H. A. Bruce, the home secretary from 1868, was prevented from acting on this recommendation; so the nineteenth-century temperance campaign was never enriched by detailed and expert knowledge of the problem it was tackling. Thirdly, MacDonagh's model begins too late in time, because it does not show how public opinion was awakened to the 'intolerability' of the evil. Social evils are not always apparent to those who suffer under them, until pointed out as such. George Orwell in the 1930s once asked a miner when the local housing shortage first became serious: the reply? 'when we were told about it'. The temperance movement forced society to recognize drunkenness as a serious evil, yet there is no place for it in MacDonagh's model. All this is an argument for extending the model, not for abandoning it: but this can be done only when our knowledge of voluntarist reforming movements has also been extended. Of these, the prohibitionist crusade is particularly interesting to the administrative historian, because in the middle of what Dicey described as a 'period of Benthamism or individualism' it was launched to promote the most drastic interference with individual freedom; and it was supported by two groups to whom Dicey attributed early Victorian *laissez faire* sentiment—evangelical Christians and Benthamite philosophers. 'Somewhere between 1868 and 1900', he wrote, '. . . changes took place which brought into prominence the authoritative side of Benthamite Liberalism'; yet in the United Kingdom Alliance from 1853, that authoritative side had never been concealed.[23]

For nineteenth-century temperance reformers, the 'two nations' of Anglican and nonconformist were more important than the 'two nations' of Disraeli. When Lord Rosebery attended one of Spurgeon's meetings in 1873, he came upon a world which was 'as completely unknown to the world in which I live as if it did not exist. Its aims are not our aims, its language is not our language, its aspirations and ideas are wholly alien to our aspirations and ideas.'[24] This nonconformist world was deeply influenced by seventeenth-century puritan and covenanting traditions, and ensured that—whatever happened in other countries—in England religion never uniformly opposed itself to radicalism. On the contrary, for the Liberal party's radical and nonconformist tail, the great landowners, the legal system, the Anglican church, the London clubs, the armed services, the magistrates and the great London brewers were constituents of a great Leviathan which obstructed social and political progress. Reforming movements attacked the monster from several directions. While the National Education League attacked aristocratic and Anglican control over popular education, the Anti-Corn Law League their self-interested manipulation of the economy, the Peace Society their military role, the Administrative Reform Association their capacity for government, the Liberation Society their influence over religion, Josephine Butler's movement their lax moral standards and their influence with the medical profession, and C. D. Collet their control over opinion—the temperance movement threatened their control over popular leisure, philanthropy, medicine, public order and over the framing of party policy. The temperance campaign threatened the moral platform of the philanthropic London brewers and the publican's traditional links with popular recreation. It denounced the political parties for resting upon local allegiances, emotive political symbols and personal rivalries rather than upon definite policies. It was no coincidence that the first general election to arouse real prohibitionist interest (in 1868) was also the first to be followed by the entry of a dissenter into the cabinet: or that the mounting self-confidence of mid-Victorian dissent and of late-Victorian Anglicanism should both be reflected in the mounting prosperity of their respective temperance organizations at that time. The sudden rise of the Church of England Temperance Society in the 1870s signalized the established church's winning of the initiative in the temperance world. The history of militant nonconformity in the nineteenth century has not yet been written, but no historian of the temperance question can afford to ignore it.

Yet the nonconformist world was in many respects isolated from the mainstream of English life. Political and industrial fluctuations do not coincide with fluctuations in the prosperity of nineteenth-century temperance organizations [see Figure 1]. Although temperance history lends some support to E. P. Thompson's interesting theory of an alternation over time between political and religious commitment—the temperance remedy being paraded during the 1830s and 1840s as a non-violent alternative to the violent solutions being produced for social problems—this theory cannot explain the contrasting fortunes of different temperance organizations in those decades; and it explains nothing at all about developments after the 1850s. For example, the continuous decline from 1835 to 1848 in the receipts of the British and Foreign Temperance Society reflects nothing except its defeat by teetotalism; the collapse after 1872 of the prohibitionist boom reflects nothing beyond the fact that temperance legislation, however feeble, had at last been won [see Figure 9]. Throughout the 1840s the two leading teetotal organizations, the National Temperance Society and the British Association for the Promotion of Temperance, pursued a steady and quiet existence unaffected by the dramatic political events of that decade. The peaks in the National Temperance League's fortunes in 1859 and 1879 reflect the visits of J. B. Gough the famous temperance lecturer—not involvement in the election campaigns of 1859 and 1880. During the 1860s the striking rise in the incomes of the Alliance and the National Temperance League does reflect the increasing political significance of the temperance question, but the boom period ended in 1872, not in 1874: with the 1872 Licensing Act and not with the 1874 general election. Although the funds of four temperance organizations rose before the 1880 general election, and although the funds of the two Leagues rose again in the early 1890s, these minor booms are insignificant when set beside the major rise and fall in funds which pivots on the 1872 Licensing Act. Even during its years of greatest influence with the late-Victorian Liberal party, the temperance movement lacked contact with political realities and national needs.

As for the economic sphere, there were of course connexions between fluctuations in the temperance and business worlds, particularly when—as in the early 1830s and 1870s—temperance reformers claimed to be able to expand the home market for textiles. Early Preston teetotalism owed much to the local industrial boom, the income of Bradford temperance organizations was badly hit by the depression of 1854–5, and the cotton famine held down the funds of the Lancashire-based Alliance and British Temperance League in the early 1860s. After December 1862, the League's newspaper, the *Temperance Advocate*, had to revert from weekly to monthly issues for this reason.

But whereas Beveridge's index of industrial activity shows a series of fluctuations lasting on average for eight years, the annual temperance receipts for the period show rather one large fluctuation, peaking at the early 1870s; beside this general development, all minor fluctuations are unimportant—nor do they always correspond with the peaks and troughs in Beveridge's index.[25] Even fluctuations in the frequency with which new temperance newspapers were launched, an aspect of temperance enterprise most likely to be affected by the national economic situation, correlate only partially with Beveridge's index.[26] The temperance community, like the political community, seems in general 'to live according to its own laws, different from the laws of the national community in which it is included; it has a personal rhythm of development'.[27]

The comparison is not too far-fetched, for many features of modern British political parties originated in Victorian moral reform crusades like the Alliance—which formulated electoral issues through its executive committee, disciplined M.P.s at the hustings and in the division-lobby through its parliamentary and district agents, mobilized the electors through its auxiliaries, and distributed propaganda through its public meetings, leaflets and periodicals. The temperance movement even helped to eliminate overt corruption from elections; it is curious that the historians of that development should have entirely ignored the one social group with a direct interest in electoral purity—particularly as corruption was eliminated by a shift in public opinion rather than by legislation.[28] Although the temperance movement's direct efforts to eliminate corruption may not have been very successful, its educational efforts helped to create the necessary shift in attitudes. 'To get purity at elections', wrote the National Temperance League's *Weekly Record* on 18 July 1857, 'we must begin, not with the M.P.s, but with the people, and to get them to take the matter up we must turn them into Temperance reformers.'

The temperance movement was, in fact, one of several transitional organizations channelling religious energies into party politics: like Miall's *Nonconformist*, 'instead of making Radicalism Christian it ended by secularizing Christianity'.[29] Throughout the nineteenth century, the movement tried to substitute a united moral reform crusade for the traditional concentration on liturgical, doctrinal and organizational questions. In the 1830s the teetotal lecturers, a band of secular friars, secularized the conversion-experience. And in the early Victorian period the teetotalers and prohibitionists directed attention away from an other-worldly paradise towards an earthly utopia, which would be realized after moral suasion or prohibition had teetotalized the world.

The gulf between Anglican and nonconformist is not the only social division highlighted by the study of the temperance movement which, like the Liberal party as a whole, was very patchy in its national coverage. It was a predominantly urban movement, strong in the northern industrial towns: its setbacks in southern rural areas were setbacks for the Liberal party. It could not fail to gain from any franchise extension which—like that of 1867—profited the north at the expense of the south. Above all, the movement was relatively weak in London and the home counties; militantly provincial, it saw itself as purging a corrupt metropolis of its Babylonian decadence and expediency. At prohibitionist meetings, popular and provincial innocence was often contrasted with the government's metropolitan guile. In retrospect Lloyd George's speech against compensating dispossessed publicans at an Alliance meeting in Manchester in 1890 has a certain irony: the drink traffic, he said, 'inflicted untold injury, misery, and wretchedness upon humanity, and accordingly, when there was a proposal to remove it from our midst, to . . . put an end to its ravage, you are told you must first of all compensate the people who provide the cause of all these ravages. I do not understand the principle of compensation. I am not a man of the world. I do not know its ways. I do not profess to understand its principles. I am a simple Welsh lad—(loud cheers)—taught ever since I first learnt to lisp the accents of my wild tongue that whatsoever a man soweth that shall he also reap.'[30]

Urbanization in modern Africa fosters the growth of voluntary associations similar—even in their titles—to the temperance societies which it created in nineteenth-century England. Town dwellers who have moved only recently from country areas have everything to gain from semi-recreational bodies which secure mutual protection, set standards of conduct, and evolve new criteria for assigning social status. They replace the close neighbourhood and kinship ties which formerly fulfilled these roles. According to one social anthropologist these associations serve 'as resocializing agencies in which aspiring young people taught themselves the principles of conduct in an achievement-oriented society'. Through their numerous honorific posts they distribute prestige, business experience and opportunities for self-expression. They 'express the idea that purposeful, organized social action to promote special interests is appropriate and possible'.[31] The parallel is close, though it may be no more than coincidental: but there is no doubt that the nineteenth-century temperance debate was really an argument about how leisure time should be spent.

While agricultural England had centred its recreations on seasonal festivals and on sports involving animals, urban England in the nineteenth century needed a different recreational pattern. Once brutal sports had been suppressed and seasonal festivals had lost their relevance to the working year, what could replace them? 'The village lad had two kinds of recreation open to him', wrote Joseph Arch, 'he could take his choice between lounging and boozing in the public house, or playing bowls in the bowling alley. That was all.'[32] By contrast the temperance reformer's vision of recreation centred on the home and the school: on self-improvement, sobriety and home-centred enjoyments. He did not foresee—any more than those old Chartists who regretted the frivolity of the late-Victorian working class—the striking development of the mass entertainment industry and of spectator sport during the late nineteenth century, if only because both these changes owed much to his rival the publican. Late-Victorian temperance societies were themselves forced to adopt a lighter touch, to the grumblings of older and more puritanical teetotal pioneers. They could hardly abandon their aversion to alcohol, however, or their pursuit of self-control; they were therefore doomed as recreational organizations for adults, and by the late nineteenth century had been forced into a stance which they have adopted ever since—that of helplessly lamenting the trend of the times.

The temperance movement was above all designed to alter public attitudes to diet, a subject which few historians have studied in depth. Some economic historians, however, are becoming increasingly interested in what Seebohm Rowntree called 'secondary' as opposed to 'primary' poverty—that is, poverty caused by inefficient expenditure rather than by inadequate income. One economic historian has even dared to ask 'how far is it possible to go along with those many Victorian critics who attributed want to improvidence?'[33] J. C. McKenzie stresses the irrationality of working-class food expenditure in the 1840s: in times of poverty, instead of cutting down only on the expensive foods, working people tended to reduce their consumption of *all* foods. Yet surely another irrationality—if food-value is the criterion—was their tendency to buy drink instead of food, for they could not always afford both. With them, as with some modern Africans 'other advantages sometimes seem preferable to a sufficiency of food';[34] drink could provide relaxation and sociability and could temporarily assuage hunger-pains. Faced with this situation, early temperance reformers aimed to switch expenditure from drink to food. Crawford and Broadley claimed in 1938 that 'only recently has the vital influence of diet on health been fully appreciated'. Yet teetotalers appreciated this in the 1830s; often in alliance with the vegetarians, they conducted a nation-wide educational campaign to alter dietary patterns, and in attacking the notion that fatness was a sign of health they strikingly anticipated modern attitudes, though not always of course for the right reasons. 'It is good food, my working friends,' said Joseph Livesey, depreciating beer in his famous *Malt Lecture*, 'good roast beef and barley pudding, from which you are to derive your strength.'[35]

Dietary reform is in fact a neglected aspect of the nineteenth-century 'self-help' movement, for it could enable the common man to avoid disease, and thus to emancipate himself from unexpected poverty and from medical rapacity. Most early teetotalers despised the doctors who shunned their movement. One prominent temperance reformer praised teetotalism for extending scientific knowledge: 'the whole matter rests much on an acquaintance with *the physical constitution* of man...', he wrote: 'the human intellect is here by set to work, to investigate chemically and philosophically into nature'.[36]

It is often said that industrialization required labour mobility; yet it also required dietary flexibility. Tea and coffee, imported in exchange for textiles and other exports, had to be consumed in larger quantities, and any dietary pattern which impeded punctual and accurate workmanship had to be discouraged. And in so far as the export trade needed to rest on a large home market, the wage packet had to be spent on manufactured articles rather than on drink.

The recent standard of living debate has been rightly condemned for its failure to acquire 'a serious sociological dimension':[37] but the criticism is difficult to follow up. For how does one precisely and objectively measure changes in 'qualitative' aspects of life like crime and disease, recreation and unemployment, housing and popular culture, prostitution and drunkenness? Still, if the debate does extend in these directions, it must certainly embrace a movement which educated working people in the concept of domesticity, and which encouraged husbands to spend their leisure-time with their families. And if the temperance historian cannot hope to analyse conclusively the impact of industrialization on drunkenness, he can at least illuminate the role of the reforming movement in nineteenth-century England. Pressure groups 'are not inimical to our parliamentary democracy', it has been claimed: 'they make it work'.[38] Pressure groups are too rarely seen in historical perspective; temperance history sheds light on their evolution. In 1838 the Speaker was already out of date when he insisted to Gladstone that parliament must 'shut out as far as might be all extrinsic pressure, and then . . . do what was right within doors'.[39] By the 1860s, reforming movements were so conspicuous that Taine likened them to snowballs, rolling about the country until large enough to force their way into parliament.[40] Radicals argued that they invigorated political discussion and were the Englishman's more efficient way of securing what Frenchmen obtained only through revolution. There could be 'no healthy political existence' without them, said Cobden in 1859: they were 'the very stay and bulwark of our national prosperity', said Joseph Cowen in 1876.[41] Gladstone, when formulating policy in later life, inclined his ear towards such movements in order to gauge the volume of their cries.

Reformers' claims for these movements should not be accepted uncritically, if only because their opponents were often shrewd and intelligent. Reformers liked to attribute purely self-interested motives to their opponents, but Dicey quite correctly saw the anti-reformer as 'in most cases . . . an honest man of average ability, who has opposed a beneficial change not through exceptional selfishness, but through some intellectual delusion unconsciously created by the bias of a sinister interest'. Dicey might have gone further, for he discusses only the opponents of *successful* reforming movements. Hitherto the anti-reforming case has often been allowed to go by default, but through discussing unsuccessful reforming movements, we can perhaps redress the balance. For every Anti-Corn Law League that succeeded there were several Complete

Suffrage Unions, Liberation Societies and Financial Reform Associations which failed. The temperance movement also failed, and by studying it we can see the confusion which such organizations imported into politics. One M.P. in 1846 shrewdly predicted that if ministers gave way to Anti-Corn Law League clamour 'they would have plenty of other leagues'; by 1876 W. S. Jevons, speaking of the prohibitionists, complained that the League's success had fostered the idea that any vigorously conducted agitation must eventually get its way with parliament.

The reformers made no allowance for skilful conservatives like Disraeli and Salisbury, who believed in defending the outworks: 'we have kept Church Rates alive thirty years and with our present numbers we can keep them alive ten years longer', said Lord Robert Cecil in parliament in 1861: 'at that rate we may keep tithes twenty years after that, and endowments twenty years longer still.... Who can tell what changes may have passed over England and the world when fifty years shall have elapsed?'[42] Nineteenth-century crusades were in fact a most inefficient way of securing reform: inflexible, unrealistic and often irresponsible—they used methods which unduly confused the situation. Their promoters exaggerated their representative character: their clamour diverted attention away from more serious problems, from better remedies: and their outlook discouraged serious social investigation. It is not even safe to assume that their prosperity bore any direct relation to the intensity of the evil they attacked; it is wrong for modern historians to assume that the temperance movement was a response to the factory system's accentuation of the drink problem, just as it was wrong for temperance historians to assume that their movement could be credited with every advance in sobriety. The Liberal belief that the best policy will emerge from a clash between rival pressure groups ignores the fact that agitations are recruited from individuals of a peculiar type or with special interests. The public good will not necessarily be promoted by a politician who aims simply to compromise between conflicting pressures—in this case, between prohibitionists and a militant drink interest. Political as well as economic voluntarism is now much criticized, and it is now widely accepted that 'laissez-faire pressure groups are as little likely to be conducive to the national interest as laissez-faire economics'.[43]

But it is the historian's business to explain, not to condemn. With temperance as with anti-slavery 'when a patient reacts with excessive vehemence to a mild stimulus, a doctor at once becomes suspicious of some deep-seated malaise'.[44] Before the conduct of Victorian teetotalers and prohibitionists can be understood, other contemporary movements need to be investigated, biographical and structural analysis must be conducted, and enemy criticisms scrutinized. The final theme, then, is the social reformer, who seldom tends to be studied comparatively. Although the narrative has stressed the social pressures acting on the individual, the biographical chapter on the teetotal leadership is designed to redress the balance. It will soon become clear that reforming campaigns, to be successful, must usually now be managed very differently from the teetotal crusade. The Webbs and other late-Victorians pioneered a new style of reforming activity. 'The growth of social reforms depends upon light even more than upon heat,' wrote one Fabian critic of the temperance movement.[45] Many reforms do not now need to be inspired by public agitations, for the idea of continuous change is built into the very structure of modern institutions. Instead of emotional, democratic, semi-religious public crusades against corrupt ruling powers, we now have debates within government circles between experts, in which the passion of a Josephine Butler or the wrath of a John Bright would be regarded as inappropriate.

Besides, we now have relatively few dissenters in Britain: hence the flight of disillusioned intellectuals into a conspiratorial élitism. Nonconformity has lost its bite, and even poverty has become relatively comfortable. There is no constituency for the mass reforming movement, nor is there now any wide sympathy with it. Rather the reverse: in the modern climate of opinion, 'the intellectual and emotional refusal "to go along" appears neurotic and impotent'.[46] It was not always so. Social reform movements in nineteenth-century England arose spontaneously and unpredictably—from energetic, eccentric and often charismatic individuals. In those days the entrepreneur was far more prominent in philanthropy and in business than he is now. Reforming activity was one aspect of the voluntarism in which the Victorians took such a pride: a consequence of a distaste for the state which has now greatly diminished. Reform now depends more on the group than on the individual, more on expertise than on indignation. These changes make it all the more interesting to investigate the temperance reformer's motives, environment and social attitudes: for this may enable us to understand that curious combination of sublime altruism and almost cynical calculation which motivates successful reforming leaders, that strange and self-defeating amalgam of sympathy and self-centredness which so often inspires their followers—not only in nineteenth-century England, but in all societies.

2

Drink and English Society in the 1820s*

In England and Wales, between 1831 and 1931, the number of on-licences per head of population fell by two-thirds, and in the United Kingdom the *per capita* consumption of spirits fell from 1.11 proof gallons to 0.22: that of beer from 21.6 standard gallons to 13.3. Such figures—which probably under-state consumption in the 1820s because so much liquor still flowed through illegal channels—provide an essential background to nineteenth-century campaigns against drunkenness.[1] Just as the widespread contemporary brutality and prostitution help to explain Victorian prudery and hypocrisy, so these statistics account for the somewhat censorious early Victorian approach to recreation, the fear that any increase in wages would be squandered, and that any extension of leisure-time would be misused.[2]

Why was drinking so widespread in the 1820s precisely among those social groups who could least afford it? Partly because of the extensive social functions performed by drink and drinksellers in those years. Alcoholic drinks were primarily thirst-quenchers. Even in the countryside, drinking water was unsafe and scarce, and when population concentration further contaminated supplies, it was natural for town-dwellers to rely increasingly on intoxicants whose water had been pumped from deep wells, or on beverages whose water had been boiled. London's problems in the 1820s epitomize those facing all rapidly growing towns. The Dolphin scandal of 1828 showed that the increased investment in water companies after 1805 had still not purified London's water. London hospitals wisely gave their patients alcoholic drinks, and in the 1840s Chadwick's inspectors were ridiculed by London slum-dwellers for supposing that the local water could ever be safe to drink. In the 1870s many Londoners still believed that water should not be drunk until purified with spirits.[3] It was difficult for a Londoner even to find drinking water in the 1820s; its scarcity created the profession of water-carrier. Even in upper-class households in the 1850s mains supplies were intermittent;

* In writing this chapter, I have often used evidence from earlier and later decades, but only where it seems safe to presume that the conditions described prevailed also in the 1820s.

only when iron replaced wooden pipes could cistern-storage remedy the defect. London brewers, anxious to prevent their own wells from drying up, opposed the sinking of deep wells for public supply; and London publicans were often the only slum-dwellers possessing their own water supply. London had few public pumps, and Pugin saw the contrast between the nineteenth-century's padlocked pump and a perhaps mythical free-flowing medieval fountain as a significant comment on the nature of industrial society.[4]

Milk was a dangerous drink even when fresh; and the relative anonymity of urban milk supply encouraged adulteration at just the time when more people were having to pay increased distribution costs. The quality of town milk suffered because cattle were kept in cramped suburban quarters and fed with poor-quality grain. At Lancing College in 1848 milk was double the price

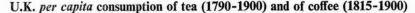

FIG. 2

U.K. *per capita* consumption of tea (1790-1900) and of coffee (1815-1900)

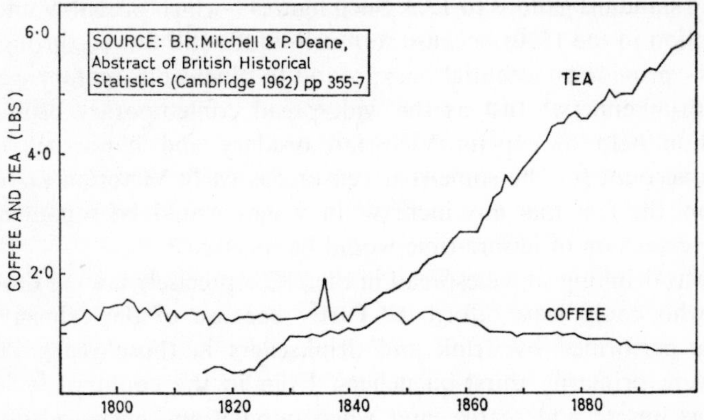

of beer.[5] In the northern industrial towns in the 1830s milk, though cheaper than in London, was 'but little used', and Manchester's milk was worse even than London's.[6] Few cordials were manufactured at this time: soda-water was not made commercially in England till 1790; ginger-beer was not sold in the London streets in summer till 1822; nor were Londoners served by the Parisian's itinerant 'limonadier'.[7]

Nevertheless, non-intoxicating drinks were cheapening in relation to alcoholic drinks, and in the 1820s it was becoming easier to obtain them outside the public-house. Although by the 1830s tea had fallen rapidly in price and had become virtually a necessity for working people,[8] it was the spread of the London coffee-shop after the tax-reduction of 1808 which impressed contemporaries; coffee soon completely supplanted its rival, 'saloop'. The popularity of tea in the late eighteenth century had closed many London coffee-houses, but from the 1820s to the 1850s *per capita* coffee consumption once more rose faster than that of tea [see Figure 2]. In 1815, London possessed not more than ten or twelve coffee-shops; in 1821 Lovett found 'comparatively few' for London working men, and had to eat in a tavern.[9] But the fall in coffee-duties under the 1825 budget prompted a rapid expansion. Feeling the competition, publicans quickly imitated their rivals by taking in newspapers. By 1830 coffee was cheap enough to rival beer.[10] Relatively little cocoa was imported. Van Houten invented modern cocoa only in 1828 and the name 'cocoa' was not widely used even in the 1830s. John Cleave advertised 'theobroma' in 1832 as a 'new beverage', but it could not yet seriously rival intoxicants. John Cadbury moved into his new warehouse for cocoa manufacture in 1831, but the Cadbury breakthrough in cocoa-essence did not occur till 1866.[11] Non-intoxicating drinks were still neither as cheap as alcoholic drinks, nor as accessible as they have since become. They were often adulterated, and many still thought them debilitating. The prevalence of smuggling caused statesmen to hold down the taxes on intoxicants; in 1830 a pint of coffee cost 3d. or 4d. whereas a quartern of gin cost only 3½d. and a quart of ale cost only 4½d. or 6d. In 1840, while Londoners could buy coffee for 1½d. a cup, tea for 2d. and cocoa for 4d., they could still buy porter for only 2½d. a pint. Furthermore, the drinkseller's many social roles made intoxicants more readily accessible than other drinks.[12]

Intoxicants were far more than mere thirst-quenchers. In the 1820s they were thought to impart physical stamina. On any occasion requiring extra energy, alcohol was employed. By drinking deeply one asserted one's virility; working men marked their sons' maturity by making them publicly drunk at a 'rearing'.[13] Stout-and-oysters was a popular aphrodisiac; home-brewed beer was thought essential to hospitality, health and good relations with servants. Until he became a teetotaler in 1843, the prominent Quaker J. J. Gurney was famous for the ale he supplied at Earlham Hall.[14] Alcohol gave extra energy and confidence to the public speaker—to the preaching parson, the perorating politician and even to the ranting revivalist. Intoxicants were closely associated with strenuous trades—with bellringers and blacksmiths, for instance. Whenever extra effort was needed, employers tended to distribute drink, and did not always give the early teetotalers the support they needed. Francis Place claimed in 1834 that almost all men in strenuous work believed that intoxicants gave them the energy they required.[15] Agricultural labourers long believed that it was impossible to get in the harvest without harvest beer. Nor were these beliefs entirely unfounded: though intoxicants were no better than food for providing energy, their stimulating effects could temporarily dull the fatigue resulting from long hours and hard labour.

Drinking was widespread also among trades where physical effort was less important—if only because the pressure of work could still be artificially varied. The drunkenness of self-employed craftsmen—early Victorian hatters, tailors and shoemakers, for instance—owed as much to voluntary idleness as to compulsory overwork. The accusation that the most educated working men were often the most drunken was, in the 1820s, not entirely unfounded; drunkenness and self-improvement were not at that time necessarily incompatible and at least one working man combined an interest in entomology with a taste for the drunken spree. An apprentice in a tailor's shop could be sent out for drink several times in one afternoon. It was among skilled craftsmen, with their exclusive initiation ceremonies, that drink customs had their strongest hold.[16]

The effects of industrialization on drinking habits are so complex that it is impossible to say whether it worsened the drink problem: in some ways it made sobriety more feasible. The change in methods of production at last created a class with a direct interest in curbing drunkenness. Traditionally, work-rhythms had fluctuated both within the day and within the week: idleness on 'Saint Monday' and even on Tuesday was followed by frantic exertion and long hours at the end of the week; at least a third even of London's factory employees celebrated 'Saint Monday' in the 1830s.[17] Essential but exhausting tasks had hitherto been accomplished largely through wielding the incentives of hunger or festivity, and the inseparability of drinking from customary recreations made it difficult to obtain precise and regular workmanship: yet the latter were precisely the requirements of the factory system. The frequency of early nineteenth-century protest against working-class drunkenness is as much an indication that the ancient inseparability of work and recreation had become inconvenient as that drunkenness had itself become more prevalent. Some early industrial employers were so impressed with the need to dissociate work from recreation that they tried to deprive work entirely of its traditional 'play' element. Their efforts were to some extent self-defeating, for later experience has shown that the complete dissociation of work from recreation actually *reduces* productivity. Still, early industrialists needed to create a smooth working rhythm and to induce employees to enter and leave their factories at specified times. Investment in complex and costly machinery placed the employee's precise and continuous labour at a higher premium than the spasmodic exertion of his crude physical energy. Once this need had arisen, customary drinking patterns had to change.[18]

Industrialization helped to reduce drunkenness in a second way: the factory's umbrella shielded an ever larger proportion of the population from the elements. Outdoor occupations exposed working people to extreme temperature fluctuations and even in the 1850s rain, wind and frost were 'many a labourer's natural enemies'. Climatic explanations were usually adduced to explain the relative prevalence of spirit drinking in Ireland and Scotland, and in the 1880s national rum consumption still fluctuated directly with the state of the weather. In the 1890s Londoners tended to switch from beer to spirits in the coldest periods of the year.[19] The heat endured by the harvester and the cold suffered by the serviceman created harvest beer and the rum ration: factory life required no such fortification against the elements. Nor was factory labour always as physically demanding as other types of work. The textile industries employed more women and children: a sign that less brute force was needed than in most contemporary occupations.

In other ways, however, industrialization actually increased the attractions of drink. If it curbed voluntary unemployment, it accentuated cyclical and technological unemployment; and with drunkenness as with prostitution, unexpected idleness was the gateway to sin.[20] Again, it created some new occupations—iron smelting for instance—which exposed some employees to new extremes of heat and cold. In many cases it substituted psychological for physiological strain by increasing the monotony of work. Finally, in nineteenth-century England as in twentieth-century India, industrialization fostered drunkenness by forcing migrant labourers into a strange environment and by weakening traditional sanctions on conduct.[21]

Alcohol was important in the 1820s as a pain-killer—if only because the poor tended to regard pain not as a symptom of disease, but as the disease itself.[22] It comforted the criminal about to be flogged, indispensably assisted dentists and surgeons before the days of anaesthetics, quietened crying babies as effectively as the popular Godfrey's Cordial, and 'kept up' the system against the ravages of child-bearing. In the 1850s Mrs. Cobden was unusual, as a nursing mother, in rejecting the aid of wine and porter.[23] Alcohol provided protection against the bad air resulting from poor sanitation and popular reluctance to open windows. 'Even the need for fresh air ceases for the worker,' Marx complained in 1844. Spirits were thought to cure indigestion—at that time, owing to bad or adulterated food, the commonest ailment of the poor.[24] They also gave protection against infection, and few working people were ever completely fit at this time. For doctors, alcohol was a godsend, in that it actually created several of the diseases it was supposed to cure. Even in the late-Victorian period, gout was so common that gout-rests formed part of the furniture of every West End club. Teetotal doctors were ostracized by respectable patients and medical prescriptions depleted temperance society membership. Mark Rutherford was but one of many patients who had difficulty in abandoning in health the alcohol which their doctors indiscriminately prescribed for them during sickness.[25]

Alcohol can relieve psychological as well as physiological strain. For Carlyle gin was 'the black throat into which wretchedness of every sort, consummating itself by calling on delirium to help it, whirls down . . . liquid Madness sold at ten-pence the quartern'. It calmed fears of social disapproval: in the southern counties in 1830 and at Newport in 1839, drink steeled the nerves of working men preparing to riot.[26] It calmed the murderer's fear of transgressing social norms, though temperance reformers too rarely allowed for the existence of malicious intent before the drinking; drinking is now regarded as a substitute for crime rather than as its cause.[27] Drink moderated the harshness of social isolation: it consoled the prostitute, the pauper and the rake. Temperance tales, often mistaking effect for cause, strongly emphasized the connexion between drinking and social downfall.[28]

Fear of strangers and enemies: Lord Shaftesbury probably antagonized many admirers by stressing 'how many quarrels and animosities have been made up by meeting at the convivial dinner-table'.[29] Through hospitality the landlord established good relations with his tenants, and reinforced his social prestige. Social anthropologists have described how, through drink exchange, members of some societies establish their mutual relationship without need for a written contract: and how, in societies where cash payment does not dominate economic relations, great importance is attached to the mode of greeting, and the whole question of food handling 'acquires tremendous emotional significance'.[30] Such attitudes seem to have survived in early nineteenth-century England, and explain the traditionalist Colonel Sibthorp's persistent resistance to abolishing treating and political dinners. In such a society, a teetotal movement which sought to eliminate the customary exchange of drinks between tradesmen and friends had revolutionary implications.

Drink helped to reduce the inhibitions of courting couples, who found privacy and recreation in the drinking place. They might even first have met at its 'cock and hen club', though by the 1830s such clubs in London had become disreputable.[31] The drinking place was 'neutral ground' in love as in business. The 'tiding' or drink gift symbolized good intentions in the marriage market, just as drink exchange between bargainers symbolized good commercial intentions. If a girl at an annual feast also agreed to enter the public-house with her partner, she had publicly declared her allegiance.[32] In the shape of 'fines and footings' drink enabled the outsider to gain acceptance in exclusive crafts whose work-group formed a small community. It would be quite wrong to regard nineteenth-century or even modern workshops solely as places of work: they have always been centres of social life and social relations. The newcomer to the workshop treated his fellow craftsmen in return for their instruction; this cost Lovett, entering the cabinet-making trade in the 1820s, at least a third of his weekly pay. 'Drinkings' marked the stages in apprenticeship, and even the most respectable occupations greeted newcomers thus. Yet the attack on fines had begun at least as early as 1795, when the coopers officially ended the system; the temperance movement, boasting many martyrs to shopfloor tyranny, merely continued the assault.[33]

Fear of society, fear of strangers, fear even of life itself could foster drinking, when prosperity seemed to be much more a matter of chance than of prudence. Drink was the refuge of working people whom catastrophe inevitably pursued, despite all their efforts as they drudged on 'in their hopeless state, unknown unheeded, quiet and composed'. It brought relief from 'preoccupazione', from the mingled fear, worry, anxiety and foreboding felt by peoples in all societies where the smallest setback means disaster.[34] Self-help ideologies, by attributing individual failure to personal inadequacy, did not help matters. The poor tended to share sorrows over a drink instead of giving more constructive mutual help. This was easily done, because drinksellers were more willing than other tradesmen to extend credit to distressed customers. But constructive aid was also sometimes given, through the whip-round in the drinking place; in remoter parts, organized 'drinkings' raised funds for the impoverished.[35]

Fatalistic escapism helps to explain the lavish drinking at funerals. Working men, if they saved at all, saved only for death, through the burial club. Temperance reformers strongly attacked funeral drinking customs—partly to promote sobriety, but also as part of their general assault on all unproductive expenditure; they advocated a saving for life rather than for death. There were regional variations: funerals in the north of England were relatively lavish, and Irish wakes, with their violence and joviality taking place beside a corpse exposed to raise funeral money seemed, to the fastidious Englishman, almost obscene. Drunken bearers of pauper coffins dropping their burden and accidentally exposing its contents helped to inspire philanthropic concern in sensitive observers like the young Ashley.[36] There were good reasons for the obsession of the poor with a 'decent burial'. Disease, disaster and death fascinate individuals unlikely to avoid any of the three for long. Drab lives acquired dignity in death. Again, relatives showed respect to the dead, as to the living, by ceremonially drinking. The lavish funeral enabled the bereaved to share their burdens; and it was one of the few occasions on which the poor had enough ready-cash to throw a party. Funeral drink customs also stemmed from the fact that all travellers required the accommodation and refreshment which only drinksellers could provide.

Besides moderating gloom, drink enhanced festivity. The close link between timekeeping and religious observance in agricultural societies lent a religious aspect to early nineteenth-century seasonal festivals. Drink, like the modern cigarette—which did not then exist—was a convenient, generally acceptable, easily consumed article of symbolic exchange and so featured prominently in the reaffirmations of social relationships which occurred at such times. Termly communion at Oxford in the regency period was a drunken occasion; dancing and drinking accompanied rural confirmation services, and one leading innkeeper—after Bishop Wilberforce's reforms—petitioned for compensation. The feasting which followed ordination services provoked the young Preston dissenter and future temperance leader Joseph Livesey to indignation, and Macaulay's Sunday school teachers at Little Shelford gave him wine once a week.[37] Festive and economic arrangements at weddings reveal how—in remoter areas—religion, drink and the agricultural interest were closely integrated: there were treats, or 'creeling' in Scotland: Welsh bridal couples were financed through the sale of bid-ale: and future Irish sons-in-law, whose lands were being inspected, lavishly treated prospective in-laws. These customs may sometimes have originated in the need to commute burdensome personal service into a more rapid and convenient form of exchange.[38]

Parsons—not infrequently themselves the sons of publicans—mingled socially with magistrates, brewers and farmers.[39] Clergymen with lavish treats promoted high bids at their tithe-auctions; in 1831, at what Samuel Wilberforce called 'a good Audit dinner', twenty-three people consumed 11 bottles of wine, 28 quarts of beer, 2½ of spirits and 12 bowls of punch 'and would have drank twice as much if not restrained'.[40] As the Anti-Corn Law League later realized, to attack heavy rural drinking was to attack the landed hierarchy. Vicars of Wakefield had always exhorted 'the married men to temperance, and the bachelors to matrimony' but in the 1820s the evangelical revival had only begun to elevate the clergyman into a moral exemplar by isolating him from parishioners' traditional social habits. Most parsons, when visiting, still accepted parishioners' offers of wine. Church and drinking place had not yet become rivals in providing consolation—their roles were complementary. Parsons felt no embarrassment in meeting parishioners and holding vestry meetings there; and like Crusoe, congregations travelling from afar readily took a dram and prayed. Naturally, much drunkenness resulted among the clergy. When archdeacon in the East Riding in 1841, Robert Wilberforce was much embarrassed by two notoriously drunken clergymen in the locality; and before Roman Catholicism could gain acceptance, the drinking habits of Irish priests in England had to be reformed. Publicans, as providers of meeting places, were indispensable to any religious group short of accommodation: to Catholics and even to nonconformist sects.[41] The close integration between drinksellers and the trading community moderated any temperance zeal nonconformist shopkeepers and ministers, drawn from behind the counter, might display. The watchdog committee of the Protestant Dissenting Deputies met regularly in a London public-house in the early nineteenth century.[42]

Thus alcohol the thirst-quencher, the reliever of physical and psychological strain, the symbol of human interdependence, was a formidable antagonist for temperance reformers to tackle. Early teetotalers, like pioneer vegetarians, sacrificed comforts which not only made life tolerable, but were actually thought to make life possible. Teetotalers resembled the secularists in presenting their contemporaries with a choice which had hitherto hardly existed. The bonds between drink and every aspect of life in a predominantly agricultural society had hitherto made teetotalers as rare as atheists. Indeed, in the early Victorian period, religion and drink were often abandoned together by the same individuals; early teetotalism strongly attracted the early secularists. The appearance of the teetotal movement in the 1830s symbolized the impending fragmentation of traditional social relations. 'I cannot describe the solemn terror with which I ventured for the first time to reject my customary allowance of porter, ale, or wine,' wrote Joseph Barker of his pledge-signing in the 1830s.[43] Peter Phillips clutched at his friend Richard Mee, who was about to sign the teetotal pledge at Warrington in 1834, exclaiming 'thee mustn't, Richard, thee'll die'.[44]

Sir William Harcourt argued in 1872 that 'as much of the history of England had been brought about in public-houses as in the House of Commons'.[45] The drinkseller's social roles were certainly extensive. Drinking places existed for all types of customer. In descending order of respectability there were the 'inn', accommodating the traveller, the 'tavern' catering for the casual drinker, the 'alehouse'—which unlike inn and tavern did not sell spirits and was not visited by magistrates—and the 'ginshop' which supplied gin to urban populations [see Plate 5]. All four categories depended on the magistrates for their licences, but the 1830 Beer Act created a fifth category—the 'beerhouse'—which, though drawing its customers from the same social level as the alehouse, was exempt from magistrates' control and drew its licence direct from the Excise. In the 1820s the first two institutions—run by licensed victuallers or publicans—were highly respectable and often barely distinguishable; the term 'public-house' applied to both.* They were usually divided internally to segregate their various grades of customer; private societies and discussion-groups were assigned one of the 'best rooms'. In the 1820s there were three ways of travelling long distances: the wealthy travelled in their own carriages, the middling ranks travelled on stage-coaches, and the poor used the slow-moving carrier's cart; some inns catered only for the occupants of private carriages. Alehouses, beershops and ginshops differed from inns and taverns by the articles they sold and by the lower social grade of their customers.

Although class segregation in drinking existed before the nineteenth century, it does not seem to have been so rigid in the eighteenth, when aristocrats occasionally drank with their social inferiors, squires with their villagers, landlords with their tenants, parsons with their parishioners, the Prince Regent in low London taverns with the humblest of his subjects. The Duke of Buccleuch entertained his friends at a low Middleton alehouse;[46] late eighteenth-century Manchester shopkeepers and London barristers, attorneys and tradesmen still spent their evenings in the drinking parlours which most publicans reserved for them; Irish tradesmen and some English yeomen-farmers and country professional men continued to do so in the 1830s. London tradesmen, however, were by then drinking at home, and private as opposed to public drinking was becoming a mark of respectability.[47]

* These definitions are very approximate, but are based on investigation of contemporary dictionaries. In this book I have tried to use these terms strictly, and to employ the term 'public-house' only for inns and taverns, and the term 'drinking place' as a general term to cover *all* premises licensed to sell intoxicating drink.

By the 1850s no respectable urban Englishman entered an ordinary public-house,[48] and by the late 1830s the village inn, where all classes drank together, had become a nostalgic memory—even if it had ever been as widespread as its admirers imagined.[49] Henceforth secrecy shrouded the shared recreation of different social classes: the excesses of the young Edward VII were less publicized than those of the Prince Regent. The casual 'tip' or gift of drink money was all that survived; few eminent Victorians imitated Macaulay in treating casual working-class acquaintances to a drink.[50] The reasons for this change are obscure: evangelical influences, the increasing comfort of *bourgeois* homes and an increasing class-consciousness which perhaps owes something to an increase in social mobility—these factors may have been responsible. The consequences were important. A social gulf was now interposed between those responsible for licensing regulation and those affected by it: indeed, statutory legislation after the 1830s was partly a substitute for the personal supervision of lower-class drinking which magistrates had exercised hitherto. A further consequence was inevitably a decline in the quality of the facilities the publican provided. The drinking place became less like a home, more like a shop. As customers gradually invaded what had once been the drinkseller's private quarters, the 'bar' was introduced. The righteous indignation aroused by the London gin-palace in the late 1820s shows that by that period this process had not gone very far.*

Drinking places mirrored the interests and needs of their localities; broadly speaking, their two main roles were as recreation centre and as meeting place. To begin with recreation: the working man's home was often cold, uncomfortable and noisy; he and his wife lived at too close quarters and his drink expenditure probably increased with the size of his family.[51] More important, his home had only begun to lose its machinery and was only beginning to acquire its comfortable furniture. It was only in the process of becoming a place of leisure rather than of toil, and was still 'oftener a place to fly FROM, than to fly TO'.[52] Temperance reformers wanted working men to improve the home by spending their money there. But until consumer-goods became more readily available—and until both the resources and the inclination necessary for the new style of living could be created—drinking was bound to remain a popular recreation.

Was it reasonable for reformers to deplore the male selfishness implied by such a recreational pattern? Drinking places on pay days were besieged by wives desperately anxious to feed and clothe the family; many married couples fought over the wage-packet, and many wives were kept ignorant of its contents. The nineteenth-century drinking place, like the twentieth-century expense account, encouraged men to enjoy better living standards than their wives.[53] To make matters worse, drunken husbands were often stung by the

* There are excellent accounts of internal arrangements in the drinking place in M. Gorham and H. M. Dunnett, *Inside the Pub* (1950), pp. 26, 64–5, 94–113.

wife's silent or open reproach into the wife-beating for which Englishmen were notorious abroad. Victorian sentimentality made the most of such situations, but music-hall songs emphasizing fear of the 'missus' suggest that some males fled from the home only because the female was dominant there; indeed domineering wives sometimes produced drunken husbands.[54] The fact that the drinking place was primarily a 'masculine republic' limited potential sources of conflict, and ensured that at least some houseproud women had no rivals in the home. Differentiation of social function between the sexes is no proof of personal subjection.[55] In other cases the home suffered from the wife's laziness or ignorance. By offering her outside employment, industrialization deprived her of time and energy for housework, and even caused a reversal of roles in which wives became wage-earners and husbands domestic drudges. If women were excluded from the public-house they had their own recreation in 'stair-head drinking clubs', chapel life and local gossip. Sometimes husbands, far from selfishly squandering the family income, came home to find that their wives had drunk away the furniture.[56] The picture is therefore complex, and even where—by modern standards—male selfishness did exist, there were good reasons for it.

By the 1820s retail specialization and the magistrates' policy of reducing the attractions of the drinking place were already beginning to cut down its ancillary functions—notably food provision.[57] Yet it still possessed many comforts absent from the poor man's home. Light, heat, cooking facilities, furniture, newspapers and sociability were then obtained by the poor only at the drinking place. The price of a drink was their entry-fee to comforts which the prevailing social situation enabled them to enjoy only communally. Unlike their social superiors, most working men could entertain friends only at the drinking place: perhaps the relative prevalence of solitary occupations enhanced the attractions of sociability. Outside the coalfields, and where wood-gathering was forbidden or impossible, the drinkseller could provide a warmth absent from the poor man's home. Coal later delivered at a hundred different homes was in the 1820s delivered at the drinkseller's coal-hole. Hence his influence with local coal-merchants and his close links with the London coal trade.[58] Temperance tracts of course emphasized how willpower could transfer the comforts of the drinking place to the private home, but they exaggerated the extent to which abstinence could or should have minimized the disadvantages of low wages and unavoidable idleness.

The drinkseller remembered the need for public lavatories at a time when housebuilders and parsimonious local authorities often forgot them. As early as the 1720s a scheme for 500 public lavatories in London was proposed, yet the need was still serious in the 1830s and George Jennings was still campaigning for them in the 1850s. Again, drinksellers provided lodgings for homeless or itinerant working men, and sheltered lodgers whose landladies allowed them on the premises only to sleep. London lodgers' substantial political influence later obstructed restrictive licensing legislation, and the lodger problem prompted the first experiment in state management of the liquor trade.[59] The drinkseller's influence with local tradesmen thus reflects the poverty of his neighbours, for which—if temperance reformers could be believed—he was himself largely responsible. Certainly the drinkshop's blaze of light gained effectiveness from the inadequacy of street lighting and from the darkness of homes where candles could not be afforded; and its lavish baroque façade was set off by the meanness of many surrounding slum dwellings. Yet the drinkseller was no parasitic villain: he responded to a genuine human need, and was a popular and respected provider of recreation and comfort to a world which would have been intolerably drab without him.

Foreigners from Montesquieu to Taine attributed English drunkenness to the depressing climate. Englishmen formed clubs and congregated in taverns, said Taine, because they needed to 'shut the door on the melancholy influence of a hostile nature'. Bad weather limited opportunities for outdoor recreation. Fine weather during leisure periods saw working people in the streets, in England as overseas; bad weather sent them into the drinkshop. Joseph Chamberlain in 1877 saw 'a closer relationship between climate and drunkenness than between any other two facts'.[60] Yet even in good weather, large towns lacked open spaces. Foreigners noted that the English, though commercially rich, were poor in recreations. According to contemporary radicals, enclosure virtually forced working people into drinking places for their recreation: 'when the village may-pole fell, and the commons were inclosed', wrote one, 'the fiend, intemperance, was ushered into birth'.[61] Some drinksellers themselves tried to remedy the lack of open space by attaching pleasure-grounds or deceptively named 'tea gardens' to their premises [see Plate 2], though these—by the 1830s—seem to have lost their respectability.[62] Public parks, where they did exist, were often closed to working people. Urban parks, originally designed to surround royal or aristocratic mansions, had only begun to assume their new function—that of enabling confined city-dwellers to breathe. Faucher likened English operatives to Israelites 'with the promised land before them, but forbidden to enter into it'.[63] The authorities feared their destructiveness. Surprised comment greeted the good conduct of operatives visiting the Crystal Palace, and the fear that crowds could not gather in public places without hooliganism and drunkenness survived into the 1880s and beyond.[64]

The fact that, before the railway age, working people seldom travelled for pleasure enhanced the drinkseller's recreational function. 'Resorts' scarcely existed, and holiday recreation was taken locally. Servants insisted on returning to their native villages for the annual feast, which naturally centred on the local entertainment centre. Outdoor sports, frequently involving the pursuit of animals, were readily sponsored by drinksellers. Taverns were centres of sports involving gambling or cruelty to animals, and the sporting print

2. RECREATION IN A LONDON SUBURBAN PUB. The Eagle Pleasure Gardens, Islington, one of many suburban pleasure-centres owned by early nineteenth-century publicans. The Eagle's Grecian Saloon, or variety hall, was one of the ancestors of the London music-hall. From Guildhall Library, London, Norman Collection, *London Inns & Taverns Vol. 3*, ref. no. I. 1.6. [see p. 49]

3. A MAJOR LONDON COACHING INN. The Bull and Mouth yard, c. 1820. By courtesy of the Mary Evans Picture Library, Lewisham. [see p. 51]

4. The public-house and the hiring fair. Pubs did a roaring trade on any occasion when large numbers gathered together. Before special registries appeared in the late Victorian period, servants were hired at statute hirings. These were semi-recreational occasions which—like wakes, fairs and feasts—marked out the phases of the agricultural year. This Warwickshire hiring fair is from *Illustrated London News*, Nov. 1872. By courtesy of the Mary Evans Picture Library, Lewisham. [see p. 55]

Bell's Life was always more popular than the more political papers among the drinksellers' customers. Tom Spring's Parlour—alias the Castle, Holborn—was a mine of gossip for early Victorian sporting men of all classes. Richard Nyren, innkeeper at the Bat and Ball, Hambledon, was prominent in the early history of cricket; and an advertisement for wines and spirits adorned the entrance to Thomas Lord's first cricket-ground, for he supplemented his income thereby. Nineteenth-century magistrates condemned many traditional recreations, particularly the fair and the wake, as superfluous and disorderly: yet such a response was self-defeating, and by the 1820s there were signs in some progressive circles of a more positive attitude towards recreation. George Combe's *Constitution of Man* taught many working men that all human faculties were intended for, and were capable of, good employment; and Robert Owen's social festivals provided 'rational recreation'.[65] Still, drink remained perhaps the most popular of all recreations. It displayed most of the characteristics of 'play': it was a voluntary activity, pursued in free time, in a special location, and in the secrecy bestowed by frosted glass and the 'snug'.[66] In many drinking places each customer had his own special seat reserved for him. What would early Victorian Londoners have done on Sundays without Marylebone's Yorkshire Stingo, Islington's Eagle and Rotherhithe's St. Helena Tavern? Such places brought temporary harmony into the disordered lives of many bored, exhausted or exploited individuals [see Plate 2].

Drinksellers themselves tackled the problem of cultural poverty, but in very different ways from the temperance reformer. By unconsciously pioneering commercialized entertainment, they were in the long term creating rival claims on the working man's surplus resources. Temperance reformers recognized the need for a change in recreational patterns but they did not correctly forecast its direction. Individual self-improvement and domesticity were their aims, not commercialized mass leisure. Only later did commercialized leisure compete seriously with drinking; in the 1820s the same individual profited from both. Itinerant professions, such as circus performers and actors, naturally attached themselves to the inns as transport centres which could also provide lodgings, together with yards or 'large rooms' for the audience. Harriet Mellon, the late Georgian 'star' made her stage début at the Sun, Hitchin, and the young Irving performed behind Watford's Wheatsheaf. Most leisure occupations, from amateur dramatics to pigeon-fancying, were pursued in the drinking place; so also were the less reputable sports, especially ratting and cock-fighting. Mayhew's sporting London publican bought 26,000 live rats a year[67] [see Plate 8]. The publican's rural connexions made him the natural provider of recreation, when so many sports involved animals. Retired prize-fighters often took London pubs and followed their clients with tents and booths to Epsom races and other sporting events.[68] Temperance reformers attacked cruel sports not only from humanitarianism but also because 'sporting men' were usually drinking men. The early meetings of the Preston Temperance Society, creator of the teetotal movement, were appropriately held in a converted cockpit [see Plate 9].

Temperance reformers often saw prostitution where none existed, but some drinksellers were as ready to cater for this local need as for any other.[69] Early Victorian London's underworld would have been a sorry affair without the Cyder Cellars, the Shades, the Coal Hole and Evans' Supper Rooms. 'Baron' Renton Nicholson presided over the salacious judge and jury societies right up to his death in 1861. The alliance between publican and prostitute was natural: the publican presided over a meeting place where human relations of all kinds were established, sold a powerful solvent of barriers between individuals, and was generally associated with recreation and gaiety. His house was as suitable a 'house of call' for prostitutes as for any other trade. Both prostitute and publican became scapegoats for social evils with much deeper roots: both had the same enemies—many prohibitionists supported Josephine Butler, just as several temperance leaders also campaigned against prostitution. Many nineteenth-century drinkers might have written of the publican what the sexual adventurer and author of *My Secret Life* wrote of the prostitute: 'to their class I owe a debt of gratitude . . . they have been my refuge in sorrow, an unfailing relief in all my miseries . . . I shall never throw stones at them, nor speak harshly to them, nor of them'.[70]

For all these reasons, then, the working man who abandoned the drinking place abandoned far more than drink alone. He was isolating himself from a distinct, vigorous, earthy culture—from a whole complex of recreational behaviour. 'To the poor and the unlettered . . .' wrote William James, drink 'stands in the place of symphony concerts and of literature'. Tea-meetings could never rival taverns in relaxing human strains. The teetotaler's self-denial, said Gladstone in 1867, 'demands and extorts from us the highest admiration';[71] it often required a complete change of friendships. Sociable pleasures were precious to working men for whom alternative recreations were scarce; to abandon drink was to abandon society itself, unless some alternative grouping were provided. Hence the tightness with which early teetotalers clung together for protection against a hostile world: 'I saw the hard struggle to give up all', wrote Mrs. Wightman, the Shrewsbury temperance reformer, of a working man taking the pledge in 1858, 'for I knew not till then, that, with the working man, signing the pledge involves nearly everything included in the world, the flesh, the devil.'[72]

The second of the drinkseller's two major social functions was to preside over the local meeting place. There were several reasons for this: perhaps most important was his transport connexion. In providing travellers with refreshment, lodging and stabling, the inn was the equivalent of the railway station, the siding and the engine shed. Great London inns like the George and Blue Boar in Holborn, whence ran the first direct coach to Glasgow, were predecessors of the great London railway termini; the Bull and Mouth in St. Martin's-le-Grand had stabling for 400 horses.[73] England also possessed many coaching villages dependent on travellers for their livelihood—long, narrow villages straddling a main road and well supplied with drinking places. The names 'Elephant and Castle' and 'Angel' still remain in London's transport system as a reminder of the inn's once universal role as transport-centre [see Plate 3]. The exhaustion caused by uneven roads and by long stage-coach journeys, the danger to health which was thought to result from their speed, and the cold endured by those who travelled outside the coach—all dictated a frequent resort to alcohol. Sale of spirits to travellers at nearly every toll-house constituted an important security for investors in Scottish turnpike roads in the 1840s. Drinking places were vital to itinerant trades; trade union lodges were usually held there and the tramping routes of particular groups of artisans seeking work can almost be plotted from inn signs bearing their craft name. Carters could scarcely pass a tavern without drinking, for they knew how directly their livelihood depended on the publican's goodwill. Some travellers even found it cheaper to move by coach rather than incur the drinking obligations imposed on pedestrians. The spread of the omnibus during the nineteenth century killed off many drinkshops *en route*.[74] Commercial travellers, itinerant nonconformist ministers and lecturers of all types also incurred great temptation. Teetotalers found this problem peculiarly embarrassing, and had to lodge with local supporters.[75]

Yet even before the railway there were signs of change. The faster the travel, the greater the dangers of insobriety: America realized this when motor-vehicle replaced ox-cart, just as England realized it when coach travel began to speed up during the eighteenth century. By 1740 moonlight coach travel had begun, and in the 1750s some stage-coaches were allowed to travel on Sundays. In 1784 night travel became more general, and by 1786 the journey from Edinburgh to London took only 60 hours as opposed to 85 at mid-century.[76] Coachmen—perhaps partly influenced by Arctic explorers' discovery that alcohol did not keep out the cold—began to moderate their notorious drinking habits long before temperance societies appeared. Drink suffered in a second way, for the stage-coach's increased speed reduced the frequency and duration of public-house stops. Sobriety in the nineteenth century probably owed more to faster travel than to temperance agitation.

Though there were fewer travellers in the 1820s than in the railway age, the relatively slow speed of travel demanded more lodgings per traveller. Some felt that accommodation of travellers was the publican's only rightful function: hence the importance of the '*bona fide* traveller' who later embarrassed temperance legislators. The inn's recreational functions grew naturally from travellers' need for diversion when lodging away from home. Itinerant working men, who normally lodged at ale- or beerhouses, found accommodation cheap but often sordid, and were usually expected to drink; W. E. Adams at the Black Bull, Kendal, in the 1850s had to share a bed with a drunken key-bugler. Some Northumberland and Durham miners on strike, who had been evicted from their homes in 1849, sheltered with the local publican and crammed his premises with their furniture. So important were the publican's lodging functions that temperance reformers soon founded temperance hotels.[77]

The drinking place also became a meeting place because it was the local news centre, at a time when most news travelled through personal encounter. It preserved 'old news' such as traditional songs and the ceremonial of trade unions and friendly societies. Just as the church preserved the tangible records of local history, so the drinking place preserved oral traditions: its customers often included amateur local guides, always ready to retail such information to travellers. New ideas entered a locality via the drinking place—witness the frequency with which co-operative societies, despite their early hostility to drunkenness, originated in public-house discussions.[78] The drinking place was 'for the operative, what the public squares were for the ancients'[79]—the centre for local gossip and sporting news, the window through which unadventurous local residents saw the world. It was also the mirror in which they saw themselves.

Written news arrived through the post and the press, both of which reached the public-house as soon as the coach arrived. If the public-house was the railway station of the 1820s, it was also the post-office. Twenty-eight coaches despatched the post to all parts of England in 1835 from leading inns in St. Martin's.[80] At public-houses, the literate working man read newspapers which he could never have bought for himself; the illiterate could hear them read aloud by hired readers, perhaps with added commentary. Some publicans hired out newspapers for a penny an hour. Dependence on public-house circulation caused most Chartist newspapers to fight shy of Teetotal Chartism. Radicals claimed that newspaper taxes fostered insobriety, and in the 1850s urged repeal on temperance grounds. Yet the newspaper was at least a painless distraction from the drink.[81]

Drinksellers reinforced their role by supplying local associations with 'large rooms'—often without charge—in the hope of extra custom. In Newcastle in the 1830s every political, musical, artistic and scientific club met in its own public-house.[82] Almost all nineteenth-century reforming campaigns, including a somewhat embarrassed temperance movement, occasionally met in public-houses. The Strand's Crown and Anchor accommodated some historic reform meetings. It was there that John Bright made his London début as an Anti-Corn Law League orator in February 1842. And according to Robert Owen, 'bigotry, superstition, and all false religions received their death blow' in the large-room of the City of London Tavern at his famous public meeting on 21 August 1817. Large rooms were, for the Reform League in 1865, 'a matter of necessity not choice'.[83] Licensing legislation was in fact originally designed largely to control opinion. Nineteenth-century drinking places accommodated election meetings and respectable political dinners, but also working men's debating societies. Early Victorian London's debating-halls, such as the Cogers and the Temple Forum, were the 'real little images of the British Parliament',[84] some of whose proceedings were even reported in the press. Publicans paid prominent working men to perform for the evening, and called for orders (not necessarily alcoholic) after each speech. W. E. Adams heard a decrepit Bronterre O'Brien speaking at the Shoe Lane Hall in the 1850s. Through these meetings and smaller less formal groups like the German Democratic Society of the 1840s, drinksellers did as much as any temperance society to educate working men for public speaking. The close link between the publican and working-class politics perhaps explains the relative political indifference of working men's wives.[85] It certainly affected the character of the temperance movement, because the alternative meeting places—schools, chapels and public buildings—could be used regularly only by reformers untainted by radicalism and irreligion.

Cheap facilities for meeting, the need to reinforce the incentives to thrift through communal festivity, the difficulty of safeguarding money at home, the absence of Post Office savings banks, the refusal of other banks to cater for small depositors, the absence of legal protection for the funds of working men's societies—all these factors sent working-class burial and savings clubs and friendly societies to the drinking place. Drinksellers were usually entrusted with the funds because they enjoyed access to small change, and were respected figures for whom, in the long term, honesty was the best policy; nine-tenths of Middlesex friendly societies in 1845 met in public-houses. These clubs were often ephemeral and, apart from burial clubs, promoted short-term saving for future and present extravagance rather than long-term saving for permanent security.[86] Joining such clubs to save money, said Bentham, was 'like choosing a brothel for a school of continence'.[87] Place wisely attended his benefit society in the 1790s only for the choosing of officers. Friendly societies had begun as groups of friends expressing personal concern for each other's welfare; the need for a more impersonal but less fallible system was realized only after generations of provident people had lost their savings.[88] Critics rightly conscious of the need for accurate accounting often ignored or despised the valuable social functions they performed.

Trade unions met in drinking places for similar reasons; the builders' union in 1834 even tried to use its drinking capacity as a bargaining-counter to force Combe Delafield the brewers into employing union labour. During industrial conflicts, some publicans sided with their customers and even contributed to strike funds.[89] Here, as elsewhere, they had to weigh up the relative advantage of deferring to the magistrates' licensing power or to their customers' money power. The presence of news, lodgings, travel facilities and trade unions at drinking places inevitably made them embryo labour exchanges. London trades kept employment-registers at their houses of call. Yet even at this time the public-house connexion was not universally acceptable. Some trades societies were stressing the need for sobriety as early as the 1750s, and Robert Owen and others resumed the campaign independently of the temperance movement in the 1830s. Most working men's groups in the 1820s were caught in a dilemma: if they shunned the drinking place, they would lose a free meeting-place, together with members eager for sociability: yet by meeting there they enabled hostile social groups (who really disliked them for other reasons) to attack them on moral grounds. Other interest groups were similarly attracted to the public-house; if the combers in the 1849 Keighley strike met in the Commercial Inn, their employers met in the Devonshire Arms.[90] Furthermore, because schools and public buildings were usually closed to working-class groups, alternative meeting-places were scarce. As the National Union of the Working Classes realized in 1833, meetings outside the public-house would 'be attended with a little difficulty, and probably a diminution in numbers'.[91]

Finally, the drinking place was a trading centre in its own right. Its role stemmed partly from the relatively high proportion of retailing still carried out by individual salesmen—by tallymen and hawkers. A sitting market in a benevolent mood and anxious not to appear mean could always be found there, especially in cold weather. Furthermore several trades lived directly off public-house customers: tradesmen brought foods for which drinkers had a special taste—shellfish, spicy foods or salty items—and were encouraged by the publican for obvious reasons. Again, bargains were ratified over a drink; there was a serious shortage of public trading centres, of exhibition-halls and corn-exchanges. To take one locality at random—mid-Victorian Banbury—a travelling exhibition of African pygmies was held at the White Lion in January 1851 and annual private vegetable shows were held at the Unicorn every October.[92] Public auctions invariably took place at public-houses; Holderness farmers were still tramping up and down the stairs of the Hildyard Arms with their corn samples in the 1830s, for lack of a public corn-exchange. The association between drinking and trading was perhaps closest, however, in the army canteen, still the general shop of the barracks in the 1880s.[93]

There were two further and more general reasons for the relative importance of the English drinkseller's social role in the 1820s. Drinking places, like religious institutions, nurtured many organizations—the music-hall, the friendly society, the corn-exchange, the trade union lodge—which later became independent. The process was gradual: all drinking places at first tried to cater for the need; later, individual drinking places specialized in catering for it; finally the links with the drinkseller were severed and even despised. Also relevant is the parsimony of the public authorities. A modern Englishman set back in the 1820s would immediately notice the lack of public buildings. The 'public-house' in the 1820s was one of the few buildings, apart from the church, which all could enter. Many individuals went to the drinking place—as to the chapel—simply because there was nowhere else to go.[94] Drinksellers temporarily accommodated people accidentally hurt or killed when away from home: Zachariah Coleman, wounded in a street-fight, was immediately taken to a public-house to get the wound sponged and strapped up.[95] Coroners held their inquests there, doctors interviewed their patients there, governments collected their taxes there, the authorities held their prisoners there, and publicans even sometimes acted as registrars of births and deaths. In the 'flash-house', police officers could bargain with criminals for information on wanted men.[96]

Publicans were also closely linked with the army. Although press-gangs no longer operated from London public-houses, some drinksellers—often themselves retired servicemen—accommodated recruiting sergeants and their 'bringers', even in the 1860s. One Thames-side publican gained great favour with the government during the Crimean War by going about in a small steamer with music playing and streamers flying, recruiting sailors for the Fleet.[97] At a time when army life was so unpleasant that potential recruits could see its virtues only through an alcoholic haze, radicals sometimes assumed that universal teetotalism could paralyse the government. Until the resort to railway transport and the Victorian outburst of barracks building, governments relied on publicans for billeting, so that the public-house came to be identified with the Englishman's traditional freedom from a standing army. It was no coincidence that the government troops who fired on the Newport Chartists in 1839 were positioned in the Westgate Hotel. As well as providing every conceivable service to the community, drinksellers in the 1820s were veritable maids-of-all-work for the authorities.

The drinkseller was only one member of a large complex of interests associated with the drink trade. In the 1820s the economic power of the 'drink interest' owed much to the persisting links between economic transactions and recreation. Drinksellers made large profits in the 1820s from seasonal fairs, statute hirings [see Plate 4] and feasts—veritable saturnalias which released contemporary social tensions at the same time as they promoted trade. On these occasions 'bush-houses' sprang up in all directions to take advantage of the traditional freedom, enjoyed by all, to sell beer. Not until 1874 was this right curtailed and replaced by the JPs' 'occasional licence'. The attack on these festivals was mounting—especially in the London area—some years before the temperance movement appeared, and many factory owners deplored the wake's disruptive effects on their work-force.[98] But a sense of friendship and personal responsibility still characterized many transactions: 'every bringer of a message or errand expects a pint of beer', wrote one Sussex vicar in the 1820s.[99] Economic relationships were continuous, not fleeting, and each transaction was only part of a sequence of mutual favours; cold cash payments, without drink-exchange, signified either the presence of an outsider, or a desire to conclude the relationship. To pay for personal favours, such as mutual assistance in ploughing, would have been a gross insult: 'with beer one thanks, but with money one pays'. Business was still not exclusively a search for better goods at lower prices: it was 'first of all a technique in social relations'.[100]

Where the aim really was to conclude a bargain, drink softened up potential purchasers by making sales-talk sound more plausible, and by increasing the pressures of goodwill: 'if an order be wanted,' said Joseph Livesey, the prominent teetotaler of the 1830s, 'when nothing else will answer, a few glasses will perhaps fetch it'. But drinking over a bargain was primarily a means of showing goodwill: teetotal tradesmen were often embarrassed when they were unable to please their customers in this way.[101] Drink exchange could also of course convey ill-will. The action of the Duke of Buccleuch who—in the presence of the Lord Advocate in 1803—refused to preface the drinking of a glass of sherry with the conventional address, was long quoted as an instance of ducal contempt. In 1858 when the Banbury Agricultural Society wished to advertise its contempt for the local bishop, it omitted its customary toast to the clergy.[102] Rivalry could be expressed through competitive drinking; status, through displaying alcoholic possessions. In short, through drinking, all types of human relationship were expressed without the need even for an exchange of words.[103]

Through truck payment, many employers saddled their employees with the task of retailing their products, just as—through the butty or the middleman—they delegated the management of their labour force. Cobbett noted an ancillary advantage of truck payment: it promoted sobriety, he said, by depriving the poor of ready cash—an interpretation which ignored the publican's willingness to give drink in exchange for truck. Even payment in beer was defended on temperance grounds; the purity of the 'home brewed' given to labourers in lieu of cash would prevent them from patronizing local beershops.[104] In the case of harvest-beer, there was a further motive for avoiding cash payment—lack of ready money. At harvest-time, farmers were still living on the proceeds of the previous year's crop, and unless they could sell their new crops unharvested, lacked ready cash.[105] Temperance reformers who condemned harvest-beer were attacking the farmer's capacity to pay his employees. Shortage of coin often causes alcohol, an article in universal demand, to become the medium of exchange—in the African slave trade, as in the early Australian colonies. The *Manx Herald*, short of small change in 1838, paid for G. J. Holyoake's first letter to the press with a roast chicken and a pint of port.[106]

The drinkseller's rapid turnover, cash sales and standard product made it easier for him than for most tradesmen in the 1820s to supply loans and small change to customers when they needed it most—especially to pawnbrokers and small London tradesmen on Saturday pay-nights. The mint had only recently acknowledged its responsibility for supplying the small copper coin demanded by the extension of weekly wage-payments and retail cash transactions.[107] Why should employers go to the expense and trouble of sending to a distance for their cash, or pay their bank to do so, when these small deposits of coin existed in every locality? Employees were therefore frequently paid in groups with a large banknote, and changed it at the drinking place for a small commission. Financial or blood connexion with a drinkseller, lack of suitable accommodation (widespread in the building and mining industries) or sheer desire to concentrate exclusively on manufacturing processes caused many employers to sub-contract all responsibility for wage-payment to a particular publican-paymaster. Both parties gained: the publican shed his excess small change and acquired customers: the employer shed worry, and established relations with a tradesman who might even discount his bills when necessary.[108] In some trades the publican managed the whole labour force. In the 1780s crews for slave-ships had been recruited by publicans, and even in the 1840s London coalwhippers could get work only by drinking. If a middle man were entrusted with arranging pay, he often came to a mutually profitable arrangement with a local drinkseller. Such relationships were common in the London docks and in Midland mining areas, and payees were kept waiting for long periods in the hope that they would drink. Public-house wage payment was attacked by Colquhoun and the Proclamation Society after the 1790s, and by the 1820s its disadvantages had become apparent in some mining areas; the system provoked vigorous complaint in 1834 from the spinner John Doherty.[109] For all these reasons it is hardly surprising that public-houses were placed in 1855 at all four corners of the central square in London's new cattle market at Copenhagen Fields.

The drink interest in the 1820s was allied with the powerful agricultural interest: this helps to explain the temperance reformer's political impotence in the 1830s, and the regional variations in the support for his movement. The nineteenth-century landed interest enjoyed immense political power; even today agriculture has more political influence than its mere voting power demands. Country gentry in the 1820s advocated cheap beer because 'agriculture must be supported' and farm labourers pursued temperance reformers with the cry 'Wot shall we du wi' the barley?'[110] The drink industry was closely integrated into most aspects of the rural economy; publicans and brewers were themselves often substantial landowners; beer and grain prices fluctuated together. The barley crop was most important to farmers, and without the distillers' demand for poor-quality barley, the lighter lands of Scotland and Ireland might never have been cultivated—hence the government's difficulties in mobilizing the local gentry against illicit stills. Malt cattle-feed was as important to the farmer as the manure obtained from the distillery and from the innkeepers' stables. London butchers stocked up from cattle fed on grains from London distilleries—as dismayed teetotal pig-breeders discovered. Housewives could hardly embrace teetotalism if it deprived them of the coveted publicans' yeast, and the temperance movement never prospered in the Home Counties, centres of malt and hop production.[111]

The structure of drink manufacture and sale demanded close co-operation from many other trades. Local brewers—restricted in the range of their sales by high transport costs—often invested surplus capital in other trades. The seasonal character of the brewing industry forced brewers into the banking and corn-dealing worlds during their inactive summer months. There were close links between brewers and bankers—often the only wealthy tradesmen in a locality. Much of the capital financing industrialization came from the food and drink industries. Beer—the 'temperance drink' before teetotalism—was often brewed by Quakers whose relatives were prominent in London banking circles. Most London brewing firms in the 1820s kept a banker or capitalist as a sleeping partner, and the rich banked with drink manufacturers just as the poor banked with drink retailers. Drinksellers deposited their customers' savings with the brewery at interest.[112] The temperance movement was thereby forced into connexions with the early building societies and other savings organizations outside the drinking place. The drinkseller's provision of communal comforts gave him great influence with local grocers, carpenters, drapers, newsagents and coaldealers. Pawnbrokers and drinksellers, usually situated in the same localities, were 'mutual assistants to each other'.[113] Birmingham had 63 pawnbrokers in 1830, as against 66 bakers and 194 butchers, and teetotalers disliked the pawnbroker almost as heartily as the publican.

In many towns of the 1820s drink retailers were as numerous as food retailers. A temperance reformer in 1836 claimed that a twelfth of Birmingham's total population—that is 11,000 people out of 140,000—was directly engaged in drink manufacture and sale. This figure included all occupants of public-houses but not individuals indirectly connected with the trade, such as coopers and cork-makers. The estimate may be near the truth. West's directory of 1830 lists 512 victuallers, 5 brewers, 56 retail-brewers, 14 innkeepers, 75 maltsters and 40 wine and spirit merchants—as against 66 bakers, 194 butchers, 12 fishmongers, 19 fruiterers, 393 grocers and 'shopkeepers'. 140 of the 881 'middle class' inhabitants of Vauxhall Ward Liverpool in 1842 were drinksellers. In the 1850s there were more drinksellers in London than fishmongers, dairy-keepers, cheesemongers, greengrocers, butchers, bakers and grocers combined.[114] Such figures emphasize the scale of the drinkseller's social functions in the 1820s, for so high a proportion of the retailing population could hardly have been occupied solely in selling drink. Apart from closing during Sunday morning service, many drinking places—especially in

London—opened almost continuously throughout the week. Opening hours varied in different licensing areas, so that in towns drink could usually be quite easily obtained at any time. Estcourt's Licensing Act of 1828 made matters worse because it left magistrates in doubt whether they could legally force public-houses to close at night. Until the Metropolitan Police Act of 1839 there was no statutory reason why London drinking places should not open continuously from Saturday night to Monday morning. After 1839 London publicans were forced to close on Saturday nights, but until 1864 there was no statutory hindrance to their opening all night throughout the week; outside London, in places which did not adopt these Acts, this freedom was not curtailed until even later.

The London brewers' almost legendary wealth, and the relative affluence of drink retailers and provincial brewers, lent social prestige to the drink interest.[115] First came the wine merchants, personal advisers to the aristocracy and plutocracy, as every student of Ruskin knows. Next came the London brewers, whose huge breweries symbolized England's industrial greatness; distinguished foreigners were still visiting them in the 1860s. Brewers' need for self-advertisement and public contracts attracted them into large-scale philanthropy which prejudiced magistrates in favour of their candidates on licensing day. When defending themselves against attack, publicans always made much of their famous charities. Before the days of welfare legislation, control over charity brought great power—a situation revealed to at least one teetotaler refused admittance to a lying-in charity.[116] Church Missionary Society subscription-lists of the 1830s feature Guinesses, Whitbreads, Buxtons, Hanburys, Barclays, Hoares and Perkinses. As soon as T. F. Buxton, the great opponent of slavery, agreed to become treasurer of the London City Mission in 1835, a flood of subscriptions resulted. Feasting and drinking were indispensable to the annual charity meeting; the contradictions between philanthropy and drink had not yet become apparent, if only because domestic social reform had not yet become the first concern of philanthropists—least of all of those who operated from Exeter Hall.[117]

In rural England brewers moved in the same circles as magistrates. If a young man of well-to-do family failed to enter the army, the church or a learned profession, brewing was one of the occupations he might well pursue.[118] The typical brewer-magistrate, said *The Times* in 1827, was 'a man of immense wealth', with 'a splendid mansion in the country, a park crowded with deer' and enough venison to bribe all whose votes might be useful on licensing day.[119] Irish and Scottish distillers, allies of the government in its fight against the illicit still, were often the only wealthy local industrialists. Publicans in their humbler sphere enjoyed as much social prestige as the brewer. 'There is scarce any common trade in which a small stock yields so great a profit', wrote Adam Smith.[120] Publicans were often the only literate and enfranchised individuals in their districts, and if selected for jury service, they were invariably chosen as foremen by the jurymen. Nineteenth-century working men dreamed of becoming drinksellers just as modern assembly-line workers long to own their own petrol station. 'Many men have an idea that to be a publican is a very easy matter,' said one observer in the 1850s: 'every man imagines that he can be a licensed victualler or a beer-seller; they rush into the trade'.[121] Some brewers actually supplied the necessary capital, but usually drinksellers already possessed capital and experience of other occupations before embarking on their trade. Many were retired soldiers, domestic servants or widows whom magistrates wished to keep off the rates. Service was 'the nursery . . . for both trades'.[122] One of the functions of the nineteenth-century licensing system, as of medieval monasticism, was to provide for individuals to whom the authorities felt obliged.

Industrial wealth, social prestige and influence with the landed interest would have made any interest-group formidable in the parliament of the 1820s, but there were special reasons why the drink interest should make use of its power. The motive was not that the drink interest needed to combat temperance pressure, for temperance reformers had little influence in parliament till the 1860s. It was rather that public authorities—the magistrate and the municipal council at the local level, the Treasury at the national level—were closely interested in the drink trade. While liquor taxes contributed a third of the national revenue [see Table 10] and accounted for so high a proportion of the wholesale price (47% of beer prices in 1812): while publicans performed so many official functions: while the size of the brewers' retail outlet depended so closely on licensing policy—the drink interest had to safeguard its profits by taking an active part in national and local government.[123]

Powerful on committees administering poor relief, closely supervising local licensing regulations, influential on most local bodies through their wealth and social prestige, members of the drink interest had great influence in local government—symbolized by the public-house feasts of so many unreformed corporations. In Newcastle-under-Lyme from 1835–71, in Leeds and Birmingham in 1839, the drink interest accounted for 9·4%, 7·8% and 3·1%, respectively, of the whole council.[124] Publicans and brewers were also well equipped for participating in national elections. Their wealth, business habits and the fact that—unlike many industrialists—they were not restricted to particular areas of the country by their raw materials or by localized demand, gave them great influence throughout the nation. In the public-house, the drink interest possessed a centre of political discussion and information in every community; in its *Morning Advertiser*, founded in 1794, it possessed an important national newspaper. And though its *Sunday Advertiser* failed in 1829, another publican paper, the *Manchester and Salford Advertiser* was founded in the same year, and the weekly *Era* followed in 1838.[125] Only religious institutions could rival the national coverage and political influence of the drink trade, but religion in the 1820s had not yet been captured by the temperance movement.

For several reasons the drink interest's full political potential was not realized in the 1820s; only the beginnings of trade organizations existed. The Incorporated Society of Licensed Victuallers was founded in 1794 as a mutual protection society, and in 1803 founded its school at Kennington. The first brewers' trade association—the Country Brewers' Society—was founded in 1822, but gained members mostly from small- to medium-sized firms in the south and east of England. Until 1871 it had less than 200 members, though its uniqueness lent it unobtrusive influence.[126] Publicans, brewers and distillers, though prominent in national politics, had not yet identified their trade interests with any one political party. Even enfranchised drinksellers' freedom of manœuvre was limited by their customers' freedom to withdraw their patronage, and by the magistrates' power to withdraw the licence. In Ireland the licensing power was used to control even the religious opinions of licensees.[127]

There was as yet no incentive for the drink interest to declare for any one political party. There was no temperance group in parliament, nor was there any clear party alignment on free licensing. In the 1820s and 1830s innkeepers and brewers leaned towards Liberalism, and beersellers towards radicalism. In August 1838 the Chartist Henry Vincent commented on the radicalism of Lancashire and Yorkshire: 'you have no idea of the intensity of radical opinions here. You have an index from the numerous public house signs—full length portraits of Hunt holding in his hand scrawls [*sic*] containing the words Universal Suffrage, Annual Parliaments, and the Ballot. Paine and Cobbett also figure occasionally.' But there was no political unanimity among drinksellers; coach travellers on the London–Leicester road noted the vigorous rivalry between Whig and Tory posting-houses, and at Shaftesbury in the 1840s all the inns were either Tory or Whig.[128] Only political setbacks could persuade publicans to tighten up their political organization. Even at the peak of temperance attack upon them in 1871–2 the drink interest's internal divisions persisted. It was as difficult to hold London and 'country' publicans together as with any other contemporary pressure group, let alone to resolve the divergent interests of publicans and brewers. Although there were thirteen respected and experienced brewer M.P.s in the 1820s, the debates on the Beer Bill revealed their divergent views.[129] And although the electorally powerful distillers strongly influenced members as distinguished as O'Connell,[130] there was bitter rivalry in the 1820s between Scottish and Irish whisky manufacturers. Thus in the 1820s the 'drink interest' was not really a united 'interest' at all. This was a testimony not to its weakness in national life, but to its unquestioned strength: though the licensing system had many challengers, no one yet challenged the drink interest's very existence.

The importance of the drink revenue increased the political prestige of the drink interest at this time. England relied far more heavily than continental countries on drink taxes for her national revenue [see Table 10]. Drink revenues were very elastic, and were therefore invaluable in wartime. Like his predecessors in the Napoleonic Wars, Gladstone responded to the Crimean War by raising the malt and spirit duties. Even now—when alcoholic drinks are no longer considered necessities—their consumption, unlike that of most other luxuries, does not decline rapidly with increased taxation. Another source of political influence: the drink interest gave employment to the agricultural districts, still regarded as the economic, military and political backbone of the nation. In 1822 Brougham denounced tea as tending 'not to the cultivation of one single acre of English land'.[131] Beer, for his contemporaries, was an evocative drink, and aroused a host of patriotic sentiments: John Bull and St. George, foaming tankards, contempt for the French, agricultural prosperity, 'no popery and wooden shoes' and the 'yeomen of England'. It was the 'good, sound, wholesome, constitutional beverage of the country'.[132] Its patriotic connotations were symbolized in the many inn signs depicting generals, admirals, dukes and kings, and their coats of arms. A similar alignment—between wine and patriotism—exists in France to this day. Sydney Smith expressed the British sentiment well in 1823: 'what two ideas are more inseparable than Beer and Britannia!'[133]

Stepping back for a more general view of the situation in the 1820s, it is clear that many social conditions which have now disappeared fostered drinking and drunkenness at that time. Yet certain social changes were easing the path for temperance reform even before the temperance movement appeared. The identification between work and recreation, festivity and religion, drink and economic exchange—was becoming incompatible with the industrialist's increasing need for punctuality and regularity in his employees. While the nineteenth-century volume of road transport reached its peak in the 1820s, its increased speed demanded sobriety from the coachman. While urbanization at first forced drinksellers to take on more functions, further expansion demanded specialized attention to such requirements outside the drinking place. The expansion in textile exports encouraged the importing of more tea and coffee, whose accessibility was increased by tax reductions. Industrialization, and an ideology of privacy and property, encouraged some sections of the population to brighten up the home in comparison with the drinking place.

Without the aid of these developments, the attack on the drink problem would indeed have been a daunting prospect. Teetotalers conceived of their foe as a great Juggernaut, to be opposed by every means in their power [see Plate 28]. Advocates of licensing reform and/or personal abstinence, like the opponents of the slave trade, were attacking men of substance in their localities. Yet it was perhaps precisely this that enabled the campaign to enlist radicals and idealists against the formidable powers of darkness. The early teetotalers were markedly optimistic, and envisaged that utopia—that 'good time coming', as one of their favourite songs put it—which is perhaps psychologically necessary to all campaigners who challenge customs and assumptions so deeply rooted.

3

Free Trade and the Beer Act: 1815–1830

The nineteenth century saw the rise and fall of several remedies for the drink problem. The first of these, rising into favour between 1815 and 1830, was the free trade remedy. Free licensers made no exaggerated claims: their policy would secure no immediate or dramatic decline in drunkenness; nor could it be effective unless buttressed by popular education. The free licensers' main inspiration lay not so much in concern about drunkenness as in their belief that free trade principles could be applied more widely. Drunkenness, for them, was a mere symptom of an underlying social injustice and could be eliminated only by indirect means. Their campaign was inspired by hatred and fear: by the free traders' hatred of privilege and by the general public's fear of an urban working class maddened by gin.

To the free licensers, the licensing system seemed a bastion of medieval irrationality and privilege. Licensing districts were at this time formed from the borough and from the petty sessional division of the county. Magistrates met once a year at the brewster sessions to consider applications for fresh licences, and jurisdiction was left to their absolute discretion. The law did not specify how many or which of the applicants should be granted this lucrative monopoly. Applicants had to fit up their premises without any guarantee that they would obtain a licence, but once the licence was granted the public had no claim to the resultant increase in the value of the property, nor were the magistrates bound to consider the wishes of the locality in question. Where brewers and magistrates were on good terms, such a system was bound to come under vigorous attack. Licensing sessions were often dominated by small groups of magistrates, whose frequent and unexplained dismissal of licensing applications seemed, to the free licensers, 'inconsistent with the spirit of the English Constitution'.[1]

Magistrates who demanded internal reconstruction before renewing a licence seemed to be favouring the brewer-proprietor, who alone could afford the consequent expense. Some London J.P.s seemed to be merely compensating for their own inferior birth by tyrannizing over all who came into their power. Speculative London housebuilders sometimes found their own applications

5. A LONDON GINSHOP IN THE 1830s. Engraving by George Cruikshank from *Sketches by Boz*. [see p. 66]

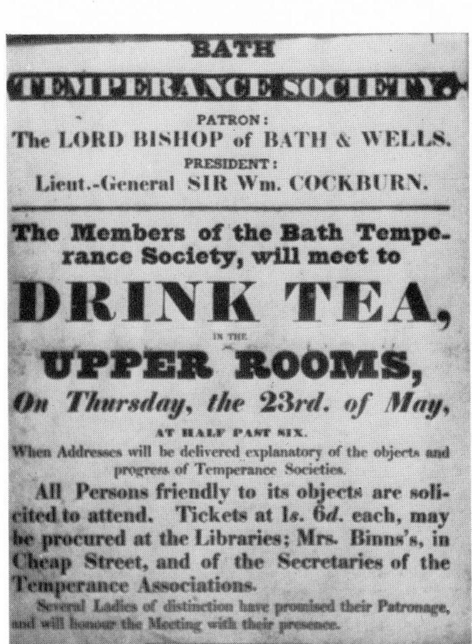

6. Advertisement for an early anti-spirits society meeting. Note the episcopal patronage, tickets at 1s. 6d. each, and the presence of 'several ladies of distinction'. Kindly lent by the Western Temperance League. [see p. 115]

7. The British and Foreign Temperance Society in decline. Store Street temperance festival, 23 May 1843. *Illustrated London News*, 27 May 1843. [see p. 115]

rejected in favour of inferior candidates allied with the great London brewers who controlled half London's public-houses. One-eighth of Barclay's publican-customers, one-seventh of Whitbread's and Hanbury's—managed public-houses owned by the firm.[2] In the case of Whitbread's a further three-sevenths were closely tied to their brewer with leasehold arrangements. Such ties ensured that certain areas of London were dominated by particular brewers—Whitbread's dominated Whitechapel, Hanbury's Bethnal Green, and Meux and Reid the West End. Most of London's suburban public-houses were owned by country brewers, and common brewers had only a small share of the market in the remoter parts—notably in the west midlands, Wales and parts of Lancashire and Westmorland. Common brewers had most influence in the home counties, the south-east, Durham, Yorkshire, Cumberland and parts of Westmorland and Lancashire. Managing one of England's first highly capitalized industries, and requiring an assured outlet for their highly perishable product, London brewers had to face much ill-informed hostility at this time; their enemies particularly disliked their meeting in private to fix beer prices.[3] The free licensing campaign thus constituted one branch of the general contemporary attack on the hated patronage system—one aspect of the general attack on the J.P.s' authority which began with the Licensing Act of 1828 and culminated in the Poor Law Amendment Act of 1834 and the Prisons Act of 1835.

The free licensing argument went something like this: government attempts to regulate the drink trade foster four related evils: high prices, adulteration, smuggling and drunkenness. High taxation and monopoly enable drink manufacturers to make large profits and to adulterate their product at the expense of the poor. Inefficient and corrupt government inspectors do nothing to improve its quality and fail to curb smuggling. Therefore, sweep away medieval sumptuary laws and monopolies, reduce taxes, and institute free competition! This will reduce prices, eliminate adulteration and smuggling, and curb drunkenness—which flourishes only when governments bestow artificial attractions on drink. If drink is made as accessible as bread and cheese, and as cheap as wine in France, it will be taken for granted, drunkenness will fall to the French level and supply will settle down to meet demand.[4] Even if governments could forcibly reduce drunkenness—and their disastrous attempts to curb spirit-drinking in the 1730s suggest that they cannot—it is not the business of the state to decide how much drink citizens shall consume. For citizens will never be securely sober until they have faced temptation and overcome it. If temptation did not exist, it would be necessary to invent it: so that the poor, 'being more frequently called to the practice of self-command, would have more scope for the acquisition of discreet habits'.[5]

In 1821 the government appointed a parliamentary inquiry. Its recommendations were embodied in an Act of 1823, which reduced the spirit duty—hitherto 6/2d. per gallon in Scotland and 5/7¼d. in Ireland—to 2/3¾d. in both countries. Free licensers then concentrated on equalizing the duties between England and Scotland. Hume in 1824 announced in parliament that he smuggled Scottish whisky into his own house and would continue to do so 'for if such foolish laws were made, they ought to be broken'.[6] In 1825 Robinson reduced the English spirit duty from 11/8¼d. to 7/– a gallon. The official statistics for gross and *per capita* consumption of spirits [see Figure 3] at once rose markedly. Many contemporaries assumed that this indicated a real increase in consumption, rather than a diversion of consumption from illegal to legal channels. The total United Kingdom spirits revenue jumped from under £4,000,000 in the early 1820s to over £5,000,000 in the early 1830s, despite the reduction in duty.

FIG. 3

***Per capita* wine and spirits consumption (United Kingdom): 1800–1880**

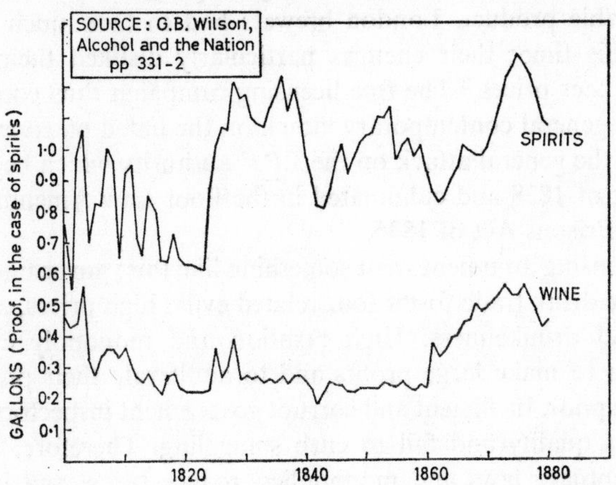

At the same time the number of spirit retailing licences rose faster than the population and the number of alehouses [see Figure 4]. Free traders of course denied that there had been any real increase in consumption, but fears of an impending 'gin panic' were reinforced by the spread of the 'gin-palace', lavishly decorated within and without [see Plate 5]. Though the actual term 'gin-palace' does not seem to have been used before 1834, licensed premises were being adapted for this purpose at least as early as 1815. Here too public alarm was largely misplaced; many gin-palace customers were collecting intoxicants for home consumption. The gin-palace was created, not by any *per capita* increase in spirits consumption, but by a retail revolution like that which had recently transformed London chemists, hosiers and tea-sellers, and which aimed to supply London's huge population more efficiently.[7]

Contemporaries might have been less alarmed if they had glanced at the figures for the consumption of non-intoxicating drinks. Though *per capita* tea

TABLE 1

Gross Consumption and Revenue Figures for Malt and British Spirits Charged with Duty in England and Wales: 1800-1872

YEAR	GROSS MALT CONSUMPTION (thousands of bushels)	RATE OF DUTY PER BUSHEL	GROSS SPIRITS CONSUMPTION (thousands of gallons)	RATE OF DUTY PER GALLON	TOTAL DUTY RAISED FROM SPIRITS (£1,000s).
1800	14,050	1/4¼d.	4,353	4/10¼d. 18/19	1,016
				5/4¼d. 6/19	
1801	18,006		2,556		622
1802	29,433		3,981		1,064
		2/5d.			
1803	29,562		5,370		1,467
				8/0½d. 1/10	
1804	21,854		3,691		1,499
		4/5¾d.			
1805	21,665		4,933		2,043
1806	26,652		4,095		1,690
1807	24,159		4,747		1,938
1808	21,726		5,391		2,213
1809	22,121		4,036		1,391
1810	23,546		4,788		1,586
1811	25,983		4,776		1,593
				10/2¾d. 7/19	
1812	18,093		5,242		2,588
1813	21,701		4,292		1,907
1814	25,321		4,957		2,485
1815	26,247		5,469		2,841
1816	21,158		4,745		2,447
		2/5d.			
1817	20,856		4,133		2,132
1818	24,630		5,260		2,681
1819	22,612		4,147		2,218
		3/7¼d.		11/8¼d. 10/19	
1820	23,884		4,285	11/8¼d.	2,511
1821	26,138		4,126		2,419
1822	26,689		4,694		2,749
		2/7d.			
1823	24,845		3,803		2,222
1824	27,615		4,393		2,567
1825	29,573		3,684		2,055
1826	27,336		7,407		2,593
				7/–	
1827	25,096		6,672		2,335
1828	30,518		7,760		2,716
1829	23,428		7,701		2,695
1830	26,901		7,732		2,857
				7/6d.	
1831	32,963		7,434		2,788
1832	31,670		7,282		2,731
1833	33,789		7,717		2,894

YEAR	GROSS MALT CONSUMPTION (thousands of bushels)	RATE OF DUTY PER BUSHEL	GROSS SPIRITS CONSUMPTION (thousands of gallons)	RATE OF DUTY PER GALLON	TOTAL DUTY RAISED FROM SPIRITS (£1,000s).
1834	34,450		7,644		2,867
1835	36,079		7,315		2,743
1836	37,197		7,876		2,953
1837	33,692		7,134		2,675
1838	33,824		7,930		2,974
1839	33,826		8,187		3,070
1840	36,653		8,278		3,184
		2/7d. +5%		7/10d.	
1841	30,956		8,167		3,199
1842	30,796		7,956		3,116
1843	30,891		7,724		3,025
1844	31,857		8,234		3,225
1845	30,509		9,076		3,555
1846	35,724		9,180		3,595
1847	30,270		8,409		3,294
1848	31,848		8,581		3,361
1849	33,161		9,054		3,546
1850	34,423		9,332		3,655
1851	34,638		9,595		3,758
1852	35,484		9,821		3,846
1853	36,246		10,350		4,054
1855*	30,577		10,852		4,249
		4/–			
1856	30,703		10,123		4,007
				8/–	
1857	36,314		11,386		4,555
		2/7d. +5%			
1858	38,016		11,634		4,654
1859	39,095		11,860		4,744
1860	40,715		12,904		5,166
				8/1d.	
1861	33,693		11,198		5,277
				10/–	
1862	41,314		10,728		5,364
1863	37,425		10,482		5,241
1864	43,569		10,721		5,360
1865	43,956		11,197		5,598
1866	45,190		11,258		5,629
1867	45,982		11,591		5,796
1868	43,609		11,562		5,781
1869	44,387		11,239		5,620
1870	45,352		11,592		5,796
1871	47,066		12,191		6,096
1872	46,318		13,036		6,518

SOURCE: *Parl. Papers* 1870 (82–I) XX, pp. 386–7, 395; *Parl. Papers* 1881 (C. 2979) XXIX, pp. 338, 343.

* From 1855, year ends 31 March.

consumption did not begin to rise till the 1840s, *per capita* coffee consumption was rising sharply in the 1820s—and its gross consumption more than doubled during the decade; in relation to the *per capita* consumption of beer and spirits, however, the *per capita* consumption of non-intoxicating drinks was still small—only 1·41 lb. of tea and 0·96 lb. of coffee per year, as opposed to 23·1 gallons of beer and 1·13 proof gallons of spirits in 1834 [see Figures 2 and 3].

Criminal statistics increased the prevailing alarm: between 1811 and 1827 criminal convictions in the London area quadrupled, but few were shrewd enough to attribute the increase to improved police efficiency. Both Londoners

FIG. 4

Population, and total retail liquor licences granted, in England and Wales: 1800-1900

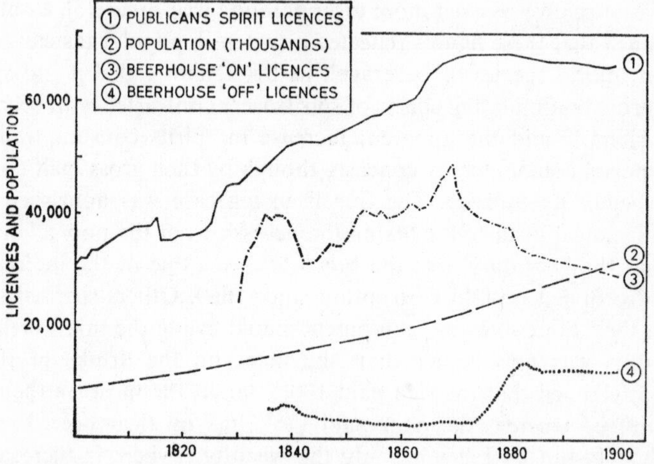

SOURCE: G. B. Wilson, *Alcohol and the Nation*, pp. 394ff; B. R. Mitchell & P. Deane, *Abstract of British Historical Statistics*, p. 6.

and Parisians at this time feared that such figures reflected a rapid increase in crime.[8] Several important inquiries into police and crime were held between 1815 and 1828, and though no causal connexion between gin and crime figures was or ever could be proved, the two were linked together in the public mind. Although the rates of increase in gross spirits consumption and in criminal arrests ran together in the 1820s, the figures did not entirely dovetail, and for other decades they clearly diverged. Sobriety was in fact essential for certain types of criminal, and criminal arrest statistics were useless as a guide during a period of varying police enforcement. Again, changing criteria for arrest, and even a changing catchment area, deprived early Victorian statistics for London drunkenness arrests of much value; impressive in gross, they made no allowance for persistent offenders; furthermore, many drunkards were arrested for disorderly behaviour rather than for drunkenness.[9] Nor could the figures indicate changing drinking habits within a particular social class, at a time when the police seldom arrested respectable drunkards.[10]

The fallacies lying behind these popular fears did not, however, prevent them from being politically influential in the 1820s: the sentiments which lay behind the introduction of the metropolitan police in 1829 also lay behind the Beer Act of 1830. For the twin branches of the free licensing campaign reinforced each other: once government had reduced the spirit duties in the hope of curbing smuggling, moral considerations made it the more necessary to reduce the taxes on beer. If hatred of privilege was important in reducing the spirit duties, the emancipation of the beer trade owed quite as much to fears of an impending 'gin age'. For some time there had been concern at the decline in the gross consumption of malt between 1790 and 1820, and *per capita* consumption was even more disappointing [see Figure 5]. Contemporaries assumed that these figures reflected a switch in popular taste away from beer—that 'moral species of beverage', as Brougham called it—to spirits.[11] The dangerously stimulating effects of spirits were contrasted with beer's more soporific effect,[12] and the apparent increase in spirits consumption in the 1820s deepened contemporary concern, though by then gross malt consumption had begun to improve. The free licensing case was nourished by the traditional radical distaste for taxing the necessities of the poor; Tom Paine argued that the beer duty, like the bread tax, was one of the indirect taxes which had propped up Old Corruption since 1660. Others stressed that the rich, with their home-brewing equipment, could evade the tax. Furthermore the beer duty was now higher than the taxes on the drinks of the rich. McCulloch claimed that the rich paid 100% tax at the most on their wines, tea and coffee—whereas the poor paid 175% tax on their beer. Free trade budgets had begun by relieving only the wealthy: 'where is there any free trade for the poor?' asked the *Examiner* in May 1829.[13]

The campaign to free the trade in beer had been active since 1815. Free licensers argued that if beer and spirits were sold separately, beer drinkers would be less tempted to switch to spirits; and that if the price of beer were reduced through licensing reform and tax reduction, the taste even of long-established gin-drinkers might alter—for at this time Londoners were paying 5d. a quart for beer and only 3½d. for a quartern of gin. Gladstone in 1866 claimed that his contemporaries eulogized the temperate qualities of beer 'as if it were positively an evangelizing power'; his remark applies equally to the free licensers of the 1820s.[14] The free trade campaign against the London brewers began during the Napoleonic Wars, but the failure of the Golden Lane brewery discredited commercial attempts at breaking their monopoly. Peace in 1815, as in 1918 and 1945, focused attention on domestic reforms, and in November *The Times* printed several letters advocating licensing reform.[15] The free licensing campaign seems to have gained momentum at just the moment when a striking reduction occurred in the rate of increase in publicans' spirit licences. From 1800–70, the rate of increase seems to have been almost constant, and more rapid than the rate of population increase, but between 1815 and 1824 the rate of increase was greatly reduced, though in the late 1820s it rose rapidly to restore the rate of increase established between 1800 and 1815 [see Figure 4].

The most active campaigner was J. T. B. Beaumont, a Middlesex magistrate who had unsuccessfully applied to get licences for houses he had built in suburbs to the East and West of London. Indignation was nourished by revelations that magistrates in the East End had been influenced by a magistrate named Merceron, a close friend of Hanbury the brewer. The parliamentary committee on the police of the metropolis issued a special report on the licensing question in 1817; it claimed that the law never intended magistrates to treat long-established licences on licensing day as though they were new applications to be rejected at will. To strip individuals of their property was unconstitutional, they felt, and they recommended that no established publican should lose his licence without trial by jury, except for clearly specified offences: that no person connected with the drink trade should act as a magistrate in the district where the breweries or distilleries were situated; and that more rigorous inquiry should be made into the character of applicants for licences.[16]

The Bill of Mr. Bennet, a prominent free licenser, embodied some of these suggestions. Introduced in June 1817, it did not pass; but the campaign was still very vigorous in 1818 when 14,000 Londoners petitioned against the brewers' monopoly. Beaumont held a public meeting in the Crown and Anchor, placards were pasted up all over London announcing the need for 'fair trade, and free trial', handbills were carried on poles, and petitions were left with shopkeepers for signature. Barclay the brewer told parliament that if free trade were introduced, the large brewers would probably gain, but the publican-proprietors would certainly suffer.[17] The select committee on public breweries in 1818 exonerated the brewers from charges of adulteration and profiteering. The tied-house system was far more restrictive in country areas than in London, though any future extension of the system might cause the public interest to suffer. In 1819 Bennet introduced another Licensing Bill; it aimed to tighten up the qualifications required of licensees, to limit magistrates' discretion by instituting a graduated scale of penalties for irregularities proved against a house, and to allow appeal against their decision to Quarter Sessions; but again the Bill came to nothing.

By 1822 Huskisson was defending free licensing in parliament; some licences should be transferred from tied to free houses, he said; now that brewing costs had fallen, brewers should cut their prices.[18] Bennet once again introduced a Licensing Bill; it included a provision enabling every owner of a house rated at £20 per annum to open a public-house; on the following licensing day, magistrates would be able to close the house if they saw good reason for doing so. Brewers' hostility to this clause forced Bennet to withdraw it, but the free trade movement had now acquired a still more prominent champion, Henry Brougham. He blamed taxation for reducing the consumption of beer, and introduced his own Licensing Bill in the same year. Supported by Huskisson, appealing to all who feared the return of a 'gin age', but opposed by Fowell Buxton, Brougham eventually had to withdraw his Bill. According to Buxton it was 'the first step towards an attack upon private property, and no man could tell which would be the last'. Brougham at this

FIG. 5

***Per capita* malt consumption (England and Wales) 1801-1880**

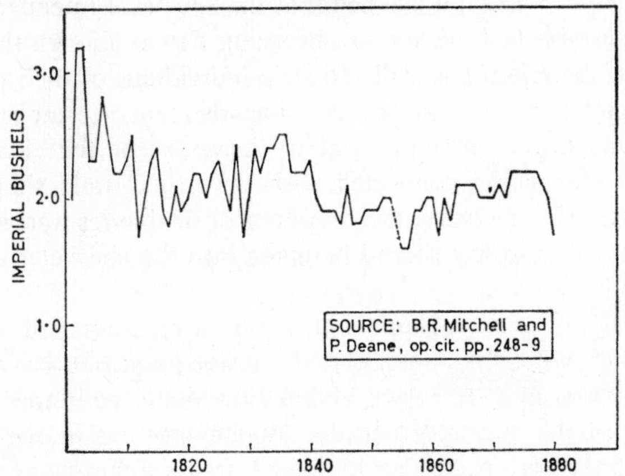

time seems to have envisaged only a gradual introduction of free trade in beer, so as to respect the capital embarked in the trade.[19]

So far the efforts of the free traders had been fruitless, but in 1823 Robinson introduced a new 'intermediate' grade of beer, coming between the table beer dutied at 2/– and the strong beer dutied at 10/– a barrel. It was to be sold only by individuals not already selling the other types of beer; they were to pay one guinea for an excise licence and were to be exempt from magistrates' control. Competition with existing publicans was minimized by confining the new beer to consumption off the premises. Fowell Buxton reluctantly acquiesced in the public demand, but the scheme was not a success.[20] By 1830 only seventeen survived of the 137 intermediate beer brewing licences taken out since 1823; in the year ending 5 January 1829, only 62,000 barrels of intermediate beer had been brewed, as compared with 6½ million of strong beer and 1½ million of table beer.[21] In 1824 Robinson made a second attempt to open up the beer trade, by allowing brewers to retail beer for consumption off the premises without a magistrate's licence. Once again the brewers Whitbread and Calvert opposed the Bill—not on their own account, they said, but because the publicans would suffer by free trade.[22] Once again the scheme failed. By 1830 only 960 survived of the 2,334 retail-brewers who had taken out licences since the Bill passed. Of the 6½ million barrels of strong beer brewed in 1829, only 215,000 were produced by the retail-brewers.[23] Furthermore, the new scheme flourished—not in areas where the common brewer was already influential—but in remoter areas like Cornwall, Staffordshire and Shropshire, where publicans tended to brew their own beer. Publicans in some areas went about trying to get their rivals convicted for allowing their product to be consumed on the premises.[24]

These disappointments by no means convinced the free licensers that the brewers' wealth stemmed from superior manufacturing processes rather than from privilege and corruption. *The Times* on 16 October 1824 insisted that the law of supply and demand must operate in this sphere: 'we know nothing more barbarous than the whole law of victuallers' licences.' The most influential item of free licensing propaganda appeared in 1826 from the pen of Sydney Smith; he wrote what the Webbs later described as an 'amazing' article in the *Edinburgh Review*, ridiculing the attempts of wine-drinking magistrates to gauge the number of houses which ale drinkers required. 'We *must* have a small massacre of magistrates,' he wrote privately in December: 'nothing else will do.'[25] *The Times* in October 1827 could hardly contain its wrath against the great brewers. Sydney Smith told Brougham in 1828 that the best way to check 'one of the most enormous and scandalous Tyrannies ever exercis[e]d upon any people' was to prevent small groups of magistrates from dominating the licensing sessions and to prevent magistrates from refusing applications except on specified grounds.[26]

Estcourt's Licensing Act of 1828—a consolidating measure which remained the basis of licensing law till 1872—embodied some of the free traders' ideas. During the committee on this Bill, the suggestion that it should embody free trade principles was strongly opposed by rural M.P.s. Two years later Charles Barclay recalled how the committee was willing to increase the number of public-houses in London and large towns, but that when it came to rural areas 'the members of the Committee got up individually and said, we cannot have it in our own neighbourhood; there would be a public house stuck up in such a village and such a hamlet; and that an open trade in beer must not be permitted in an agricultural district'. All proposals in a free trade direction were strongly supported by Hume,[27] and the Bill as finally passed did embody some of the suggestions made by Bennet and the other licensing reformers during the past decade. The licence-holder was no longer bound to enter into recognizances or to find sureties, and his licence was granted subject to the conditions specified upon it—that there should be no adulteration, no drunkenness or disorder on the premises, no unlawful games, no bad characters assembling on the premises, and no employment of illegal measures. All this limited magistrates' discretion. Houses were to close during Sunday morning church services, and the magistrates' authority was again curtailed when the Act allowed an appeal to Quarter Sessions against their refusal to grant, transfer or renew a licence. Furthermore, the sale of beer for consumption off the premises was entirely freed from magistrates' control.

Estcourt's Bill was generally regarded as finally settling the licensing question. The fear of disturbing public order gave Peel 'great doubts' in 1828 about the wisdom of enacting free trade in beer: 'we must take into consideration the *different effects* produced by the use of bread and cheese,' he said—rejecting the free traders' argument that beer should be sold like any other food.[28] The *Morning Herald* angrily recalled his words two years later—for in the interval a sudden and remarkable revolution in policy had occurred, and great concessions had been made to the free licensers.[29] 'I ask, if there ever was an instance, in which parties have been so completely turned round upon,' exclaimed Maberly in 1830. The change of policy resembled the more famous betrayal embodied in the Catholic Relief Act: 'in these days,' said Vyvyan, 'no man is obliged to abide by so antiquated a declaration as one of twelve months' standing.'[30] How was it possible for Wellington's government to risk such disruption of rural police, sacrifice such patronage and embark on a fiscal economy so drastic that even Gladstone a generation later regarded it with admiration?[31] Even contemporaries expressed surprise: 'how the deuce this Beer Act ever passed', exclaimed the *Chartist* in July 1839, noting the great power of the magistrates in parliament, 'we cannot very well comprehend.'[32] The answer lies in the peculiar political situation of the years 1829–1830. For heavy taxation was blamed for the prevailing depression, which was seen as the beginning of a permanent decline rather than as a temporary fluctuation.[33] The beershop plan had been lying for years in the excise office: only a serious crisis could make so great an innovation politically feasible. The beershops emerged from the excise office in 1830 as an irrelevant remedy for a dangerous economic and political *impasse*. 'Did you ever know or read of any popular movement for organic change', asked Cobden of Bright in 1851, 'when wheat was under 40s/- —to say nothing of cotton at 4d.?'[34]

Several county meetings were held in the south-eastern counties during winter 1829–30; many remedies were propounded for the economic situation —some wanted currency reform, most wanted tax reduction.[35] Somerset landowners, after getting a county meeting to recommend reduction in the beer and malt taxes, tried to do the same with a Bristol town's meeting. The Bristol townsmen—led by the maltster Herapath, soon to manage the Bristol Political Union—wanted cheaper tea, coffee, candles, soap and sugar, not cheaper beer. They also feared that money lost by reducing the beer taxes would be recouped through a property tax, which would favour agriculture at the expense of commerce. Their fears were justified: in a divided cabinet both Peel and Goulburn favoured an income tax. Bristol and Lincolnshire were both areas where urban and rural critics of Wellington's administration did *not* unite harmoniously,[36] but the south-eastern landowners, who at that time claimed to speak for the landed interest as a whole, sent out a trumpet call which no government could safely ignore.

Eldon in December 1829 considered it impossible that 'Measures of Consequence' should not be introduced early in the coming session.[37] Early in 1830 many provincial and national newspapers felt that the government must act to relieve the crisis. A mounting petitioning campaign reminded parliament of the existence of distress. 174 petitions against distress were received from almost all counties, with Kent, Suffolk, Sussex and Warwickshire particularly prominent among them. Several contemporary observers had already foreseen those great political changes of which the Beer Act was a mere foretaste. The opposition groups were recognizing their common interest now that Catholic emancipation had 'made reform respectable'.[38] Charles Arbuthnot advised Peel in February 1830 that the government should act, even if it had no faith in the efficacy of its actions: 'we ought I think to be the doers of what at least would be safe instead of leaving to others to do what w[oul]d be worse than unsafe.'[39] He went on to say that the Whigs were hostile to Wellington because he refused to take them into the ministry as a body; the High Tories had been alienated by Catholic emancipation, and the Canningites could not be relied on. If the government remained inactive, all three would unite against it.

Although Goulburn later denied that the Beer Bill had been inspired by the government's desire for popularity,[40] Wellington's government certainly needed reinforcement at this time: it had alienated many influential people by attacking the freedom of the press in 1829 and by aligning itself with the unpopular regime in France. The Beer Act was undoubtedly popular. Rugby schoolboys were praising it in their school songs a decade later; Cobbett described it as 'a sop to pot-house politicians', and during a reform debate of 1831 Peel adduced it as proof that the unreformed parliament could respond to public opinion.[41] To go further, however, and argue that it was 'the last desperate effort of a corrupt House of Commons to pacify a people who were asking for Parliamentary Reform' would be both to antedate the urgency of the reform demand in 1830, and to render inexplicable the Whig support for the Bill.[42] In reality Wellington, as a skilful political tactician, realized that a free trade measure could divide his opponents. 'Divide and conquer is a motto not unattended to by him,' wrote the Duke of Newcastle in August 1829.[43] Free trade in beer would be opposed by the High Tories but Whigs and Canningites could hardly fail to support it.

On 4 March 1830, Goulburn hastily appointed a parliamentary committee of inquiry which interviewed twenty-nine witnesses; these included four leading London brewers and several individuals connected with the London and provincial drink trade. Its report was regarded as a foregone conclusion, and the Earl of Falmouth complained that the views of the country gentlemen had been 'purposely excluded'. In his budget speech on 15 March Goulburn proposed to sacrifice £3,000,000 in revenue by repealing the beer and cider duties.[44] By removing restrictions on trade, this would benefit the public by a further £1,500,000—provided that the trade were opened up. Goulburn hoped to recoup his revenue through the anticipated increase in the demand for malt, whose tax he had left unaltered; to promote this and to attract support from the brewers he raised the spirit duty throughout the United Kingdom by sixpence a gallon. McCulloch, apprehensive of smuggling, strongly opposed such a course in January's *Edinburgh Review*; fifty years later no chancellor could have indulged in such favouritism towards the English national drink at the expense of Scottish and Irish spirits.

The parliamentary committee recommended that the excise supply beer retailing licences to anyone who paid the two guinea fee. On 8 April, before its report had even been printed, Calcraft its chairman introduced a Beer Bill embodying its recommendations—to enable the country to consider the measure during the Easter recess. Alderman Waithman recalled in July that the Bill had been received 'with more cheering and greater applause than any proposition I ever heard announced in this house'.[45] The response necessarily varied in different areas, if only because the effects of the licensing system were not uniform. Lancashire never suffered from London's grievances, and had been lukewarm even about earlier attempts at opening up the beer trade; during May 1830 it displayed 'a considerable degree of alarm and apprehension'.[46] Although there were no clear alignments, two types of regional conflict emerge from the discussion: London versus the provinces, and industry versus agriculture. Most of the arguments for opening the beer trade applied only to London and the Home Counties; and the free licensing agitation since 1815 had been based on London, whose inhabitants were enthusiastic beer-drinkers. London had supplied 22 of the 29 witnesses before the 1830 committee. It was the size of London's population which enabled it to support such huge breweries; some feared that the Bill might enable the London brewers to absorb the wealth of their provincial rivals, who had hitherto dominated the suburban trade.[47]

As for the contest between industry and agriculture, Cobbett pronounced the Bill a 'sop . . . to the sots of great towns, the Wen in particular'.[48] The Bill cheapened the common brewer's beer—primarily supplied to town populations—but did nothing for home-brewing, widespread in rural areas and also in some Yorkshire industrial towns. Yet as the *Spectator* pointed out, why should a family be encouraged to brew its own beer any more than to weave its own cloth?[49] Many urban Liberals welcomed any reduction of the drink taxes, for Liberalism had not yet been influenced by teetotal principles. The exciseman could pose as the champion of 'retrenchment, economy, Parliamentary reform' against the boroughmongers' 'good old cause'. Hitherto, aspiring licensees had first to purchase their freedom from the municipal corporation: the Beer Act greatly weakened the incentive to do so.[50] Nevertheless there was little demand among industrialists for reduction in the beer duty, and free traders were by no means united behind the Bill; Sir Henry Parnell actually considered the beer duty 'an exceedingly fair tax'. Many urban interests felt that better articles could have been selected for relief; reduction of beer taxes did little to increase mass purchasing power or to extend industrial employment by reducing the cost of raw materials.[51]

Rural areas were also divided: many who liked the tax reduction detested the free trade. Sibthorp, whose remarks are usually a good guide to the prejudices of the country gentry, strongly opposed free licensing. Rural magistrates feared a measure which would weaken their control over vagrants and public gatherings. Visions were conjured up of criminous beersellers in remote villages beyond magistrates' control: without an efficient rural police, the magistrate was solely responsible for public order. During the weeks before the Beer Act came into force, Dyott in Staffordshire was very apprehensive and believed, like the Norfolk magistrates, that crime would 'certainly increase'. Should excisemen, solely concerned with revenue and lacking the J.P.s' local knowledge, be the sole beerhouse licensing authority?[52] Such a measure would certainly weaken J.P.s' prestige and morale: 'on every side do we find that inroads are making upon old institutions', said one of the Bill's parliamentary opponents. The dilemma of many M.P.s in 1830 is epitomized in Sir Thomas Gooch's blunder which provoked a laugh at the time: 'I am as willing as any man to have a free trade in beer,' he said, 'but let us have some control over it.'[53]

How did the drink manufacturers respond? Hostile to Brougham's free trade efforts in the early 1820s, the London brewers were influenced in favour of the 1830 Beer Bill by the accompanying fiscal concessions to beer at the expense of spirits. Any monopoly which existed they blamed on the beer duty rather than on the licensing system, and were convinced that if given an equal start they could out-brew any home-brewer; said Barclay: 'we are power-loom brewers, if I may so speak.'[54] The views of the three leading London brewer-politicians diverged slightly. Barclay believed that his own firm would not suffer by free trade, and that the London brewers would be 'greatly benefited' by it; he at first feared that it would harm provincial brewers and also the publicans, whose investments Estcourt's Act had encouraged into the trade. Later he admitted that his fears had been exaggerated, but he wanted the full implementation of the Beer Bill delayed—as had occurred when protection had been removed from the silk trade.[55] T. F. Buxton rejoiced to be able to show his zeal for free trade even when it conflicted with his own interest; but he wanted the publicans treated leniently, for they could only lose by the measure. While he did not demand compensation for them, he wanted to assist them by preventing the new beersellers from allowing consumption on their premises.[56] Calvert was still more concerned for the publicans; while he too opposed compensation, he wanted the beer duty abolished for only a trial period and free trade instituted only if the duty reduction had not already succeeded in reducing the price of beer to the consumer. The Beer Bill would encourage smuggling, he maintained, and was 'an Act for the increase of drunkenness and immorality'. His relative eagerness to defend the publicans may have been influenced by the fact that he had more capital invested in public-houses than Barclay.[57]

The publicans were too disorganized to wield much influence, and the enactment of the Beer Bill shows them painfully dependent for protection on the London brewers. They appealed to public goodwill by pointing to their charities and to their personal frugality: to public fear, by saying that if the licensing system were modified without compensation, other monopolies such as the corn laws might follow, and other properties—such as those of the established church and the slaveowners—might also be invaded.[58] Publicans predominantly in the north and west co-operated with local common-brewers in promoting the 228 petitions against the Bill; only ten petitions, mostly from retail-brewers, appeared in its favour. In vain: petitions against the Beer Bill, like those against Catholic emancipation, were ignored by the government. The defeat of 1830 inspired the publicans to concentrate during the next decade on mobilizing their resources.[59] Their opponents in 1830 claimed that the licensing system was designed to protect the public, not to protect the publicans: and that all licences could be annually revoked by the magistrates. Private interest, it was argued, must bow to the requirements of progress, just as post-chaises had given way to stage-coaches. Publicans still retained their spirit monopoly and would profit from the Bill's discouragement of home brewing.[60] But the *Morning Advertiser* on 9 July was not convinced: 'the Licenced Victuallers, as a body,' it claimed, 'consider themselves to have been SOLD. . . .'

The Beer Bill's passage through parliament can now be briefly outlined. The session began with the arrival of 174 petitions against distress; many urged taxation repeal or currency reform. A petitioning campaign against the Beer Bill produced 228 petitions in all and culminated on 5 May when 53 hostile petitions were presented. Goulburn was embarrassed by the fact that only 10 petitions supported his Bill but he blamed the relative inexperience of labouring men in such methods of agitation. On 4 May Edward Portman, M.P. for Dorset, moved the Bill's rejection in a speech which Howick considered 'most absurd'.[61] The Bill passed its second reading by 245 votes to 29, and an attempt in committee to prevent beer from being consumed on beerhouse premises failed by 180 votes to 142, together with all attempts to impose rating qualifications and character safeguards for beersellers.

On 21 June Sir E. Knatchbull, the High Tory, again tried to prevent consumption on the premises, but was defeated by 138 votes to 108. Knatchbull detested Peel and regarded Roman Catholic emancipation as the great betrayal. He opposed free trade and parliamentary reform, and intrigued during 1829 with the Duke of Cumberland and Sir R. Vyvyan, another of the Beer Bill's opponents, in an attempt to supplant the Wellington ministry by a Church and King government. Most of the hard-core High Tories consistently opposed the Beer Bill, though without success. Vyvyan composed a list of 32 Tories who strongly opposed the government in October 1829. Ten of these were among the 29 who favoured rejecting the Beer Bill on Portman's motion of 4 May 1830; 18 were among the 108 who agreed with Knatchbull on limitation of the Bill on 21 June; and 15 favoured Maberly's motion for limitation on 1 July. Only 11 of the 32 fail to appear in any of the three divisions. G. I. T. Machin's list of 14 High Tories yields a similar correlation; 5 of them were in Portman's minority, 10 in Knatchbull's and 6 in Maberly's. Only 3 of the 14 fail to appear at all. If Wellington had continued during 1830 to defy the boroughowners in this way, his political reputation might now stand higher.[62]

Maberly tried unsuccessfully to delay the Beer Bill's enforcement and to limit its operation to villages with more than 300 houses; it passed its third reading without a division. Opposition in the Lords—led by the Earls of Falmouth and Malmesbury, and the Duke of Richmond—did not prevent the Bill from passing its third reading there on 12 July. The Bill did not entirely escape amendment, for to Hume's disgust the beershops were restricted in their opening hours [see Table 8]. 'This is called a Bill for the free sale of beer,' he said in 1830, 'but every clause limits its freedom.'[63] Henceforward, when opponents argued that the Beer Act had failed, free traders could reply that it had never applied free-trade principles to their fullest extent. After 1830, by paying two guineas a year, any householder assessed to the poor rate could obtain from the excise a licence to sell beer for consumption on or off the premises. The conditions of tenure, specified on the licence, were very similar to those for innkeepers, but closing-hours were much more strictly defined.

The Beer Bill had not passed smoothly through parliament. As late as 3 May the *Morning Advertiser* doubted whether the government would persist in allowing consumption on beerhouse premises. The government was accused of trying to force the Bill through by debating it late at night. How, then, did it get through the Commons? Sibthorp blamed the placemen, but these could never have passed it unaided. The *Morning Herald* claimed that Irish support saved the government from being defeated on the Bill; Huskisson supported it, but more important were the Whigs.[64] Fifty of those who normally opposed the government supported them on Knatchbull's amendment of 21 June; without their support the government would have been defeated. Sir E. Sugden even maintained later that the Beer Act had been 'forced on' Wellington's administration by the Whigs.[65] Only two of the 50 supported any form of restriction on the beerhouses. In 1830 Brougham, convinced by Calcraft and Goulburn that the beer trade should be unrestricted, opposed all attempts to limit the effects of free trade in beer and virtually claimed credit for the Bill, despite his assertion eight years later that he had 'strenuously exerted himself' in opposing it. Speaking in July at the general election in Yorkshire, Brougham heartily thanked the Wellington administration for its 'great measure of practical reform'. For it had deprived magistrates of a licensing power 'which is liable to be abused in crushing an obnoxious individual, who might choose to have his own opinion upon matters of state policy'. Of the 140 M.P.s who at various stages opposed the Beer Bill, 114 appear on Peel's list of political allegiances; 42 of these were 'friends', 33 'enemies', 13 'moderate Ultras', 12 'Violent Ultras', 6 'Bad Doubtfuls', 4 'Good Doubtfuls' and 4 'Doubtful Doubtfuls'. But the Ultras were by far the most prominent in opposing the Bill.[66] This cross-voting reflects the dislocation of parties at the time. Heron considered the session 'most extraordinary' and very undisciplined.[67] But the debates also reveal how in 1830 Wellington could expect Whig support and Tory hostility: he had become a national, rather than a party, leader. His peculiar situation enabled his government to push through the Beer Bill as the one substantial product of a barren session.

One of the prices Wellington had to pay was his increased unpopularity with publicans and even with some brewers. The *Morning Advertiser* on 1 July 1830 threatened that publicans would use their electoral power, particularly strong in the Home Counties, against any M.P. who supported the Beer Bill. At Great Yarmouth during the 1830 general election the brewers united with the High Tories to support two candidates whom the local pollbook described as 'the Brewers' Party in Lord Eldon's Gown'. In his nomination day speech at Bodmin in August, Sir R. Vyvyan attacked Wellington's administration for 'passing a Beer Bill which takes that branch of the police out of the hands of local magistrates, and gives it to excise officers'. Candidates anxious for publican support at this election, like Maberly at Abingdon, advertised their efforts to modify the Bill.[68] The Beer Act turned publicans against the unreformed parliament: 'who does not see . . . that a Reform of the Representation has become the general wish?' demanded the *Morning Advertiser* on 10 November 1830. The paper continued to denounce the Beer Act ('as pernicious as we prophesied') during 1831, and publicized complaints that beershops promoted agricultural unrest.[69] On 23 April 1831 the paper printed a correspondent's hopes that the Whig government would forbid the beershops to sell beer for consumption on the premises; and on 2 June 1832 a letter from another correspondent urged electors to return M.P.s pledged to repeal the Beer Act.

Publicans whose property had been sacrificed 'to gratify the ignorance of a Wellington Administration' were hardly likely to sympathize with boroughmongers' pleas for compensation.[70] The *Morning Advertiser* printed long lists of publican subscribers to the Loyal and Patriotic Fund, urged the fund's claims on its readers, and later emphasized 'how nobly the Licensed Victuallers and their friends have responded to our call'. A writer who in 1834 found it 'scarcely credible' that the Reformed Parliament should seek to modify so popular a measure as the Beer Act clearly had not been reading the *Morning Advertiser* between 1830 and 1832;[71] nor had he glanced at the pollbooks which reveal the extent of the publicans' gains from franchise extension in 1832. Only in the late 1830s, when the property qualifications required from them were stepped up, were beersellers in any number likely to possess the vote. And as providers of the drinking place used by the humblest members of the community, their influence over other electors was far less formidable than that of the publicans.

The Beer Act has so far received a bad press. How valid are the criticisms of it—particularly those of the Webbs in their *History of Liquor Licensing*? They are unfair to the free traders. The Webbs rightly maintained that the Beer Act was a 'leading case of legislation based on abstract theory . . . without inquiry into the existing facts'.[72] The parliamentary inquiry which preceded the 1830 Beer Act was certainly very cursory and tendentious, and several debaters in 1830 were remarkably ignorant. But this criticism fails to allow for the immense difficulty at the time of getting any reliable information on social problems. As McCulloch put it in 1835, 'almost all our legislation . . . is bottomed only on presumptions and conjectures'.[73] Again, the Webbs write as though the free traders were under some patently absurd delusion. Yet, given the conditions prevailing at the time, the free licensing argument was plausible, for the background to the whole campaign was fear of the smuggler. Reduction of the spirit duty in the 1820s seemed to show that high drink taxes fostered smuggling and illicit retailing; Chancellors of the Exchequer at this time were struggling to defend both the revenue and public order: 'we have but a choice of difficulties,' said Robinson in 1825. Twenty years after the Beer Act, unlicensed beershops were still common in the north of England. In Oldham in 1839 there were 200 of these, as against 343 licensed publicans and beersellers.[74] The beershop system after 1830 was a way of controlling houses which might otherwise have sold beer illegally.

Still less satisfactory is the Webbs' assessment of the Bill's consequences: 'it is hard to find a redeeming feature of this debauch,' they wrote.[75] Their narrative, written in 1903, has set the tone for all modern comments on the Beer Act. The Hammonds refer to 'that amazing piece of legislation', and W. L. Burn considers it 'arguable' that the Beer Act 'was more revolutionary in its immediate social consequences than any other of the reforming age'.[76] There is of course some evidence for this 'debauchery theory'. The Webbs and Hammonds cited figures for the number of beersellers created by the Act. While the number of public-houses rose only slowly in the 1830s, by 1833

35,000 beershops had appeared in England and Wales, and their number continued to increase till 1836. Not all of these were legalized versions of the hush-shops which had existed before 1830 [see Figure 4].

The Beer Act did temporarily increase drunkenness when it came into force. 'Everybody is drunk,' noted Sydney Smith on 24 October 1830: 'those who are not singing are sprawling. The sovereign people are in a beastly state.' At least one observer remembered the squalid consequences in his home town thirty years later.[77] Yet the many historians who have quoted Sydney Smith have failed to note three things: first, that free traders, including Adam Smith, had always *expected* a temporary increase in drunkenness until the people adjusted to the new situation. Furthermore Sydney Smith was writing only twelve days after the measure had come into force: beersellers and publicans at that time were still competing for custom by distributing free drink; the measure should be given a fairer trial than this. Finally Sydney Smith was a wit, and in this instance was indulging, as H. A. Bruce later stressed, in 'a huge hyperbole'.[78]

The statistical evidence in favour of the 'debauchery theory' is at best equivocal; the literary evidence for it is suspect. Statistics for malt and beer consumption, to which the 'debauchery theorists' unaccountably failed to refer, do not support the Webbs' interpretation. Unfortunately the abolition of the beer duty in 1830 makes it impossible to compare beer consumption on retail premises before and after that year. It also makes it impossible to isolate the effects of free trade from the effects of the accompanying tax reduction. Furthermore, statistics for the amount of malt used in common brewing are available only for the period after 1830. The period as a whole is covered only by the gross and *per capita* consumption figures for malt used for all purposes [see Figure 5 and Table 1]. However unreliable these figures may be for assessing changes in the total drink consumption, they can fairly be used for measuring the level of consumption in licensed premises. Gross consumption figures for England and Wales—the only relevant area, because the Beer Act did not apply in Ireland and Scotland—certainly do not prove that beer consumption 'greatly increased' after 1830.[79] They indicate a modest rise in gross malt consumption, which had levelled off by 1840, despite the continued existence throughout the 1840s of nearly 40,000 beerhouses. Gladstone in 1852 opposed Disraeli's attempt to reduce the malt tax: malt consumption after 1830, he said, had been insufficiently elastic to justify such a course, for although beer duty repeal had caused beer prices to fall by a fifth, gross consumption had risen by only 25% in the interval.[80] After a brief rise during the 1830s, *per capita* figures had actually fallen—from 2·0 bushels per head per annum in 1826–30 to 1·9 in 1841–5.

Figures for the consumption of taxed beer before 1830 show that gross malt consumption and gross beer consumption in official retail outlets were both rising throughout the 1820s—a process which would presumably have continued, Beer Act or no.[81] The Webbs might have strengthened their case by noting that the price of beer fell after 1830 by a penny a quart in London, and by twopence in the provinces—if figures for Bristol, Kendal and Boston are representative. Yet a London witness noted in 1834 that beerhouses there had had 'very little effects'.[82] Again, the Webbs tacitly assume that there was no switch from spirits to beer after 1830. Unfortunately statistics for imported spirits are not available for England and Wales alone, though gross figures for home-produced spirits (which accounted for over 80% of total spirits consumption at the time) do show a slight decline in consumption in the period 1831–3, whereas they had been rising markedly during the late 1820s. Too much must not be made of this though, as the reduction is only slight, and the English pattern does not diverge markedly from that of Ireland and Scotland where the Beer Act did not apply. But the Webbs were certainly wrong to accept uncritically the contemporary accusation that the publican's need to compete with the beershop had created the gin palace.[83] The gin palace had been evolving long before 1830, and was most common in London where the effects of the Beer Act were slight. Tax evasion, *lacunae* in statistics, and uncertainty about the quantity of malt required to brew a given volume of beer at different periods—all these factors make it impossible to generalize safely from statistical material. But the figures do not support melodramatic interpretations of the Beer Act's effects.

More damaging to the debauchery theorists is the bias in the literary evidence which they used. The beershop system cut across traditional patterns of rural life in several ways. It diverted resources from home brewing to the common brewer. Chains of rural beerhouses appeared, supplied by provincial common brewers who saw their battle to gain entry into a magistrate's locality as part of a crusade for progress and morality. Unlike previous drinking places, except to some extent the alehouse, the beerhouse lodged and entertained only the humblest type of labourer. It resembled a cottage rather than a public-house, and its owner was recruited from a lower social grade than the publican —from the 'half employed' coopers, farriers and carpenters whose wives supplemented the family income by running the bar while their husbands were at work. Butties or sub-contractors for labour often took a beershop, especially in mining districts. Critics too distant from the working class to perceive its subtle internal social distinctions doubted whether beersellers could keep order among their customers.[84] 'With respect to the beerhouse,' said a witness in 1853, 'the chief objection is to the character of the man who keeps it; we consider the ginshop to be more especially mischievous in what is sold.'[85]

The beershops were bound to upset many rural interests. Some brewers refused to supply them; some publicans even used *agents provocateurs* to convict them. Magistrates sometimes sympathized, for both they and the publicans had long been allies in promoting public order. It was not simply a battle for customers. Publicans with some reason feared that unscrupulous beersellers would use unruliness to force the magistrates into granting them a publican's licence, as the only means of controlling them. In this way they would attain a coveted social position without paying the customary entry-fee.[86] So it is essential to scrutinize closely any publican's testimony against the beershop: 'if there were no licensed victuallers,' said one M.P. in 1838, 'he was sure there would be no complaint against beer-shops.'[87]

The clergy were prominent among the opponents of the beershops after 1830. Many of them were more concerned about the beershops' recreational facilities than with increased drink consumption. Sabbath-breaking, gambling and cruel sports were the bugbears, for clerical criticisms embodied an attack on popular culture rather than a pan-class crusade for morality. In 1830 the evangelical *Record* wanted sabbatarian provisions inserted in the Beer Bill. It was gambling which prompted Zachary Macaulay and Wilberforce to complain to Brougham about the beershops; Brougham told parliament of Wilberforce's complaint during a Beer Bill debate of 1831.[88] The Bishop of Bath and Wells and his clergy blamed on beershops the 'alarming increase of immorality, pauperism, and vice, among the lower orders'; the bishops' efforts in 1831 to prevent skittle-playing in beershops brought them great unpopularity.[89] 'The Bishops seem to think that Satan has clothed himself in the New Beer Act,' wrote the *Examiner* on 7 August 1831. There was much to be gained from stressing the need for moral reform at a time of political and ecclesiastical danger, and for attributing popular discontent to conspirators and drink rather than to any genuine social injustice.

Equally biased were attacks from the magistrates, many of whom at this time were clergymen. In every year between 1830 and 1834 the petitions against the Beer Act outweighed the petitions in its support: in 1830 there were 10 for and 228 against: in 1831, 21 for and 35 against: in 1832, 5 for and 10 against: in 1833, 52 for and 211 against: and in 1834, 95 for and 115 against. There was less need for the free traders to whip up petitions when they knew they already had the politicians in their pocket; but as anti-beerseller opinion mounted in parliament after 1832, so the number of free trade petitions increased. London was the only area where petitions for greatly outweighed petitions against: it contributed a sixth of all the supporting petitions received in these years. The petitioners hostile to the Beer Act were more strongly regionalized than its supporters: Lancashire, Somerset, Staffordshire, Warwickshire and Gloucestershire were particularly prominent. Their attack was largely rural in origin. Petitions came primarily from churchwardens, landowners and magistrates, and the most vehement complaints came from remote villages previously free from drinking places.

Here too the attack largely reflected class prejudice, with perhaps a flavour of protectionist bigotry as well. According to C. P. Villiers in 1860, when beershops were accused of encouraging lawbreaking 'the crime that was always held in view . . . was poaching'—never accepted as a crime in the circles from which beersellers drew their custom.[90] While 'persons of property' disliked the beershop, small ratepayers generally favoured it, and by 1838 radical M.P.s were branding extended beershop restriction, which affected only working people, as class legislation.[91] From the magistrates' point of view, rural beershops resembled the dissenting chapels of an earlier age: they were potential centres of disloyalty. Police inefficiency, the ease with which suppressed beershops could be transformed into hush-shops, and informers' fear of retaliation—particularly strong in remote parts—made it difficult for magistrates to control them, especially as customers rarely co-operated in enforcing the law. The beershop destroyed the customary provision of one drinking place per village and made it more difficult to keep order, for magistrates could now no longer personally supervise lower class recreation. Exaggerating somewhat, the *Northern Liberator* on 4 April 1840 attributed these attacks on the beershop to 'the hatred of the Squirearchy to the labouring people, and the deep-rooted aversion they entertain against any enjoyment or social privilege they may by stealth obtain'.

Attacks on the beershop were often unfair and sometimes absurd. It was unfair, for instance, to prove the relative dishonesty of the beerseller by comparing statistics for publicans' and beersellers' infringements of the law. For the beerseller drew his customers from a class whose interests the law often neglected; furthermore his shorter opening hours and inability to sell spirits exposed him to temptations which publicans did not experience.[92] A naïve psychology inspired accusations that the beershops fomented rural lawbreaking. Some blamed the beershops for fomenting the riots in the south-eastern counties during 1830–1; one-sixth of the witnesses who gave reasons for these riots mentioned beerhouses to the poor law commissioners in 1834.[93] Even Brougham admitted in 1831 that many riots had begun in beershops, and though Melbourne and Althorp thought these complaints exaggerated, inquiries on the subject were made from the magistrates, and Melbourne unsuccessfully introduced a Bill to extend constables' powers. By 1832 however, fears of the new electorate had so transformed the atmosphere within the Commons, that Trevor could scarcely find a seconder for his anti-beershop proposals in that year.[94]

The social pathology which centred on the beershop was very ignorant. No direct evidence was produced that beersellers themselves participated in the riots, and some evidence indicates that they opposed them.[95] Beerhouses had been established throughout England and Wales, whereas rioting occurred only in the south-eastern counties and began some time before the Beer Act came into operation. Rev. John Clay and others made much of confessions extracted from prisoners; 'it was extraordinary', said the *Chartist* sarcastically in 1839, 'that all murders are committed upon beer—gin is quite a tranquillizing, humanity-teaching liquid.'[96] Admittedly many rioters in 1830–1 were intoxicated, and issued from beershops, which acted as unsupervised meeting-places where subversive literature could be distributed and riots planned.[97] But it was absurd, though convenient, to assume that drink or drinksellers had actually inspired the riots.

The Beer Act did not ruin the London brewers who, as they had always insisted, owed more to their great capital resources than to any licensing monopoly; unless the state were to regulate profits, nothing could be altered. After 1830 the battles between suburban contractors and licensing magistrates persisted, and during the 1850s the *Morning Chronicle* waged a campaign against the 'leviathan usurers of the brewing vat' which closely resembled *The Times*' campaigns before 1830.[98] The Beer Act, by fostering competition, actually accentuated the problem of adulteration, and undoubtedly gave a real grievance to some countrymen: 'almost nightly are we roused from our Beds by Quarrels and fighting', wrote one of Brougham's aggrieved correspondents in 1831.[99]

Yet there *was* a case for the beershop, though beersellers rarely found a voice to state it as publicly and as vigorously as did J. R. Stephens at a Lancashire beersellers' dinner in 1872.[100] Henry Solly, the promoter of working men's clubs, might describe the Beer Act as 'the most pernicious bill ever passed'; William Lovett might consider it a measure which 'introduced the means of intoxication and wasteful expenditure into almost every village and wayside hamlet in the kingdom'—yet for less puritanical working people the beerhouse helped to emancipate popular culture from upper-class control.[101] The *Morning Herald* on 11 June 1840 described the beershops as 'the consequences of that disruption of the whole framework of society, to which our modern manufacturing system, and the free-trade philosophy . . . have given rise'. Beershops' champions were 'the defenders of the factory system', for it is often forgotten that in the early nineteenth century 'the corollary of free labour was free leisure'.[102] The men who repealed the corn laws were also the advocates of free licensing and the 'free Sunday'.

The debauchery theory attracted the Webbs because of their sympathy with authority, their puritanism, and their distaste for popular culture. 'There are times when one loses all faith in *laisser-faire* and would suppress this poison at all hazards', wrote Beatrice of drunkenness in a London slum, in her diary for 1886.[103] Significantly, the Webbs' *History of Liquor Licensing* was reprinted by the prohibitionists in 1903. It began as part of the Webbs' work on local government, and its authors published it separately because, according to their preface, it 'might be specially instructive at this juncture'. 'We carefully abstain from pointing any moral or drawing any conclusions as to present day policy', they continued.[104] There was no need for them to do so, for the moral ran through every word of the book.

4

The Origins of the Anti-Spirits Movement*

Although some of its early leaders were apprehensive about the beershops in 1830,[1] the evangelical opinion which created the anti-spirits movement had no objection to beer, which at that time was seen as the temperance drink. The anti-spirits movement originated in Northern Ireland and Scotland, where the Beer Act did not apply, and the earliest anti-spirits societies were formed some months before the Beer Bill was announced. The evangelical *Record* on 18 March 1830 felt that the Beer Act would have 'happy effects . . . as . . . regards the morals of the people'. Brewers were prominent in evangelical philanthropy; some even supported the anti-spirits movement. When James Teare the pioneer Preston teetotaler in 1832 denounced beershops as 'vile and wretched establishments'[2] he gave great offence within the Preston Temperance Society. The policy of voluntarily associating abstainers could readily be reconciled with free licensing, for as Wilberforce noted—in relation to George III's proclamation against vice in 1787—only through voluntary associations 'can those moral principles be guarded, which of old were under the immediate protection of the Government'.[3] The early temperance movement naturally attracted free traders, for it attacked intemperance without invoking licensing monopoly or increasing the powers of Tory magistrates. Only when the temperance movement embraced legislative compulsion in the 1850s did temperance reformers clash with free traders, and even then both sides still had much in common.

Organized religion has attacked drunkenness at least since Anglo-Saxon times partly because of its pagan associations, partly out of humanitarianism. Dunstan, Wulfstan and Anselm were temperance reformers in their day.[4] Twelfth-century homilists and medieval friars described the drunkard's homecoming as luridly as any nineteenth-century teetotaler, and used many of his arguments, though they never recommended total abstinence.[5] Late fifteenth-

* To avoid repeating acknowledgements, I must note my general obligation to Mr. K. V. Thomas of St. John's College, Oxford, whose generous comments improved this chapter considerably. Dr. Christopher Hill rescued me from several errors in the early part of the chapter.

century Shene Carthusians had to abstain from all drinks except diluted wine, and during the Reformation period total abstinence seems almost to be a mark of the Catholic.[6] Yet Catholic asceticism, unlike the abstinence of nineteenth-century protestants, was other-wordly in its aims, and was confined to a spiritual élite. Prominent Reformation protestants made a point of distinguishing themselves from the Catholics by advocating moderation rather than abstinence, and Calvin argued that food and drink are given pleasant flavours 'because our Heavenly Father wishes to give us pleasure with the delicacies he provides'.[7] Asceticism characterized only the more radical protestant sects. The Hutterian Confession Brotherhood, for instance, forbade its members to become public innkeepers, and John Robins the Ranter trained his followers to reconquer the Holy Land on a diet of bread, raw vegetables and water.[8]

The puritans had no monopoly of temperance enthusiasm. English monarchs from Henry VII onwards enacted licensing legislation to promote public order and conserve grain. Elizabethan bishops—Barnes of Durham and Middleton of St. David's, for example—often attacked drunkenness; Raleigh denounced it on health grounds, Burghleigh on grounds of economy.[9] James I attacked the vice almost as energetically as tobacco smoking, and parliament before the civil war legislated against drunkenness quite as fiercely as any Commonwealth regime. Jeremy Taylor, chaplain to Charles I and from 1661 Bishop of Down and Connor, vigorously attacked drunkenness in his writings, and prescribed 'faith, hope, and charity', rather than total abstinence, as the best remedy.[10] Still, nineteenth-century temperance reformers liked to think only of the puritans as their predecessors; many of them took a pride in their puritan ancestry, and temperance periodicals sometimes reprinted puritan tracts.[11] The Cavaliers were painted as libertines whose triumph in 1660 led to a shameful reversal of the puritans' high moral standard. The prohibitionist F. R. Lees claimed that the puritans had failed only because English society was not yet ready for them; fortunately the nineteenth century could 'endure restraints in morals . . . that neither in Charles the Second's day nor in those of any of the Georges could have been borne, in the then lower and more depraved state of public opinion. . . . The fact is, we are in new times; the world has indeed moved upwards and is moving.'[12]

There were of course superficial similarities between seventeenth- and nineteenth-century puritans. Both used similar arguments and looked on recreation as for 'the repairing of nature, and fitting of our selves to all due employments'.[13] Both attacked drinking customs as infringements of individual liberty.[14] Both attacked drunkenness at both extremes in society, though seventeenth-century temperance tracts gave rather more emphasis to the sins of the rich.[15] There were even signs of prohibitionism in the seventeenth century: Milton dreamed of it, and so strong was the feeling against Somerset alehouses during the interregnum that J.P.s conceded local option to each village. The major-generals closed public-houses on Sundays and fast days, limited the number of alehouses in each parish, and also restricted the number of new licences issued.[16]

Yet these similarities are deceptive, for the major-generals were more concerned to prevent sedition than to promote temperance, and their motives hardly differ from those of the Tudors and Stuarts. The seventeenth-century temperance reformer's main objective was to discourage 'tippling' or drinking outside the home and outside mealtimes. A Tory M.P. in 1895 taunted Harcourt, the champion of local option, for admiring Cromwell—a man 'who . . . if reports were true, was not greatly in favour of a Local Veto Bill'. Cromwell had certainly not been an abstainer in youth, and later ridiculed the notion of promoting sobriety through prohibition.[17] No seventeenth-century tract demanded total abstinence, or repudiated the licensing system. Indeed they sometimes maintained, as no nineteenth-century teetotaler could, that intoxicants can be legitimately used for friendship and 'for honest delight'; Milton praised wine, and several puritans including Bunyan denied that the Bible forbids all consumption of alcoholic drinks. The puritan aim seems rather to have been the balanced life, requiring moderation in food as well as in drink.[18] No specialized temperance organizations appeared in the seventeenth century to attack drunkenness, despite the fact that seventeenth-century England was quite capable of mounting such large-scale reforming campaigns. The reason for this is probably that in the seventeenth century there was very little spirit-drinking, for it was hostility to these exceptionally strong drinks which first introduced the notion of total abstinence into Britain. There was alarm at the alleged increase after the Dutch wars in the taste for foreign wines and hopped beers, but gin-drinking did not become common till the end of the century. Furthermore there were at that time no cheap and palatable non-alcoholic drinks for use on social occasions. The first bag of coffee was not brought to England till 1652, and tea was a new drink for Pepys in 1661. Coffee, tea and chocolate in the late seventeenth century were drunk only by the relatively rich.[19]

Why, then, did no total abstinence movement appear in England during the eighteenth century? It is clear that gin and cheap tea or coffee were necessary but not sufficient conditions for its appearance. The 1670s saw the formation of Anglican religious societies aiming at the religious self-improvement of their members. As early as the 1680s there are signs of a link between temperance and the Whig party. The French wars fostered domestic moral reform, and in the 1690s there appeared philanthropic organizations similar in structure and scope to the nineteenth-century organizations based on Exeter Hall. Societies for the reformation of manners also appeared, and their marked resemblance to temperance societies was noted in the nineteenth century.[20] But the religious societies often met in public-houses, and never favoured total abstinence. And the Reformation Societies—though enthusiastic for temperance—sought the *legislative* suppression of vice, which was never the main platform of the nineteenth-century total abstinence movement. The Reformation Societies were élitist in character, and did not specialize in attacking any one vice; they generally sought to suppress tippling only on Sundays, and incurred Defoe's objection that 'in the Commonwealth of Vice, the Devil has taken care to level Poor and Rich into one class'.[21]

Even the gin riots of the first half of the eighteenth century could not create an anti-spirits movement founded on the voluntary association of total abstainers. Stephen Hales believed that habitual drunkenness was curable, but could think of no remedy beyond isolation from drinking company and dilution of the drink. A writer in 1770 stressed that 'there are some temptations, from which we cannot possibly escape without fleeing', and urged drinkers to abandon their drinking companions; but he did not go on to recommend societies of abstainers.[22] It is clear, then, that the anti-spirits movement of the 1820s differed from previous temperance campaigns in its specialization of function, its belief in total abstinence and its repudiation of public prosecution.

Why, then, did a temperance movement distinct from preceding attacks on drunkenness appear in the 1820s? Explanation can be sought at two levels: in terms of temperance personalities and in terms of their social situation. Nineteenth-century temperance historians wanted to demonstrate the long ancestry of their movement, and therefore did not emphasize its divergence from all previous temperance campaigns. If the problem had occurred to them, they would have sought a biographical explanation. Bred in the nonconformist tradition of the improving spiritual biography, admiring the courage of their predecessors and interested in their personalities, they compiled huge biographical dictionaries, hagiographical biographies and chronicles stuffed with personalities and starved of analysis. Hence the bitter controversies about who should gain credit for which particular innovation—paralleled in contemporary disputes over the origins of railways, Sunday Schools and anti-slavery effort.[23]

Yet social pressures cannot be ignored. 'We do not know how it sprang into life,' said Dr. Mary Gordon of the suffragettes' W.S.P.U.: 'no one explanation is entirely satisfactory, certainly not the theory that it was the work of "leaders". It began all over the country, even in silent lonely places. It was a spiritual movement and had fire—not form. . . . It released vast stores of unconscious energy. . . . It was not premeditated nor controllable—it *happened*.'[24] The same could be said of the temperance movement. The energy of the anti-spirits pioneers—Edgar, Dunlop and Collins—was significant. But their energy could take effect only in a particular cultural, social and political situation. Four factors emphasize the superficiality of a purely biographical explanation. Firstly, the anti-spirits movement appeared independently at the same time in several places. Secondly, it was only one of several contemporary attempts to propagate the middle-class style of life. The Lord's Day Observance Society was founded in the same year as the British and Foreign Temperance Society, and the Society for the Prevention of Cruelty to Animals had been formed only six years before. During the 1830s increasing pressure was exerted on working people to model their sexual conduct on the postponed and provident middle-class marriage. The *Monthly Review* in 1830 noted the 'striking circumstance' that friendly societies and provident institutions of all types were booming simultaneously; furthermore they were flourishing, together with mechanics' institutes and co-operative societies, in the same place: predominantly in Lancashire and Yorkshire.[25]

Thirdly, the anti-spirits movement arose at a time when drunkenness was already becoming unfashionable. 'No person who had lived so long as he had but must perceive that a greater degree of sobriety prevailed amongst the lower classes now than was formerly the case,' Huskisson told the Commons in 1822. Contemporaries placed the change at between thirty and fifty years previously, but it was consolidated no doubt by the wartime increase in the wine duties, and by wartime military experience of continental manners. It was certainly not the recently founded temperance movement which enabled the *Eclectic Review* in 1835 to pronounce drunkenness 'now a *vulgar* vice'; the change had begun long before, within small but influential groups in the worlds of fashion and labour.[26] These groups will not show up in the consumption statistics, but we know of them through literary evidence. One historian has dated the change from as early as the 1760s, with the appearance of the macaronis; a softening of manners was certainly in progress in Joshua Reynolds' time, and as early as the 1770s Adam Smith claimed that drunkenness was 'by no means the vice of people of fashion'.[27]

Finally, both religious and irreligious opinion-formers were campaigning for sobriety in the 1820s. Improvement in working-class sobriety began in the 1750s with the curbing of the gin mania; the number of spirit-retailers in London had declined markedly by the 1790s. Francis Place believed that between 1800 and 1830 a sober and self-improving aristocracy of labour had separated out. He claimed only that drunkenness had declined among a minority of working people; the change would not therefore affect the consumption statistics appreciably. Place was well-versed in London working-class life, and for many years collected material on popular morals; his assessment deserves respect. On this London working-class élite, the significant influences were not so much Wilberforce and Wesley as Hetherington, Place, Lovett, Godwin, Franklin, Owen and the rationalists. Jeremy Bentham, plotting the overthrow of the old poor law, favoured excluding beer from workhouse diets and reducing the number of alehouses—for purely secular reasons.[28] In the year when the anti-spirits movement first gained a hold on

Scotland and Ireland, William Lovett first petitioned parliament for the Sunday opening of the British Museum. Both religious and irreligious reformers were simultaneously moving in the same direction.

These intellectual pressures were not operating in a social vacuum. Four distinct influences prepared the ground for the temperance pioneers: doctors, coffee traders, evangelicals and industrialists. Several late eighteenth-century doctors championed sobriety. Dr. Trotter, the first scientific investigator of drunkenness, chose it as a thesis subject in 1788. He attributed drunkenness to psychological as well as physiological causes: doctors must know all the personal circumstances of the patient before a cure could be effected. 'Drunkenness', he said, 'carried to a certain length, is a gulph, from *whose bourne no traveller returns*'; the only cure was for the patient to abandon all alcohol, and for the doctor to establish a personal friendship with him.[29] Trotter's *Essay . . . on Drunkenness* was published in 1804, but by that time several other doctors were interested in the subject. In 1789 Dr. Lettsom, a Quaker influenced by the American Dr. Rush, published his 'Moral and Physical Barometer' which emphasized the health-giving properties of non-intoxicating drinks; in 1798 he wrote a tract on the serious effects of hard drinking. Erasmus Darwin—seeing the effects of alcohol on his patients, and fully recognizing the connexion between drinking and gout—conceived a medical rather than moral objection to intoxicants, and himself drank only well-diluted wine. Though he still sometimes prescribed alcohol, his influence was said to have promoted sobriety throughout Derbyshire.[30] Dr. Beddoes' *Hygeia* was also influential, and in 1814 Basil Montagu Q.C. published his *Enquiries into the Effects of Fermented Liquors*, which emphasized that total abstinence was quite compatible with a hard-working literary life. This was important preparatory work, but the temperance pioneers were inspired by moral rather than medical influences. Twenty years elapsed between Trotter's *Essay* and the appearance of the anti-spirits movement: the early temperance reformers seldom mentioned the views of Darwin, Beddoes, Lettsom and Trotter.

Of more direct importance was the new-found cheapness and accessibility of non-intoxicating drinks: hot drinks, not cold—for the quality of water was actually worsening at the time the temperance movement was founded. One coffee-house keeper in 1840 attributed the appearance of working men's temperance societies 'entirely to the establishment of coffee-houses, because a few years ago it used to be almost a matter of ridicule amongst working men to drink coffee; now they are held up to emulate each other'. Early temperance reformers encouraged tea- and coffee-drinking at their social gatherings; coffee-house keepers, of whom there were 2,000 in London in 1844, were prominent supporters of the early movement. Temperance reformers established close links with the manufacturers of non-intoxicating drinks, who were of course assisting the textile manufacturers by popularizing what was imported in exchange for their products.[31]

Evangelicalism was the third contributory factor, but not because evangelicals developed any new ideas or specialized institutions for combating drunkenness. Though they denounced the sin, they did not advocate total abstinence—even from spirits. Closely allied with the brewers, they enjoyed full cellars and a good table. Henry Venn deplored drunkenness because it deprived man of his reason and the poor of their food; but he never recommended total abstinence. And though for Thomas Scott the Christian was 'a stranger and a pilgrim upon earth', he was not expected to reject life's rational comforts.[32] Wilberforce and the second generation of evangelicals regarded the dinner-table as one of their chief recruiting-grounds. From strongly anti-Catholic evangelicals one would hardly expect what Bowles called 'an austere monkish system of harsh severity and rigid mortification'. If Wilberforce adopted some personal austerities, he kept them private; if evangelicals later joined the temperance movement, they were inspired more by thirst for souls than by any belief in abstinence for its own sake.[33]

The same applies to evangelicals outside the established church. Wesley vigorously attacked spirit drinking and excessive valuation of meat and drink, and some nineteenth-century temperance reformers even claimed him as their own.[34] Yet the Wesleyans were among the last of the denominations to embrace the abstinence principle. Eighteenth-century Quakers, allies of the evangelicals in many causes, banned the manufacture of spirits and began brewing beer, the contemporary 'temperance drink'. But although many of them individually abstained from spirits, they did not stint themselves in food and drink at mealtimes, and until the 1830s did not form abstinence societies.[35] Furthermore, evangelicals were slow to forsake the old authoritarian routes to moral reform. Typical of their approach was the evangelical vicar of Madeley, Rev. J. W. Fletcher. He made himself unpopular with local drink-sellers in the 1760s and 1770s by denouncing wakes as 'Bacchanals', public-houses as 'continual nurseries for sin', and Shropshire miners as drunkards who turned their 'enormous bellies into moving hogsheads'.[36] The temperance movement rested on far more than mere denunciation. Nor was it ever to favour the prosecution adopted by the evangelicals who, in the Yorkshire and Lancashire manufacturing areas after 1785, pressed magistrates to supervise alehouses more closely; besides, this campaign was also directed at gambling, cruel sports and sabbath-breaking, and did not isolate the temperance issue. The movement may have raised the respectability of the nineteenth-century working man, as the Webbs asserted, but it had no direct connexion with the temperance movement. Likewise the Vice Society, which many evangelicals supported, showed a zeal for prosecution, a concern with purely *public* vices and an inability to concentrate on any one of them—which disqualify it for any prominent place in temperance history.[37]

It was by lending impetus and technique to the humanitarian movement that evangelicalism made its most important contribution. The affinities between temperance agitation and the evangelical revival were close enough to make both contemporaries and subsequent historians express surprise that the temperance movement was so slow to appear in England,[38] for it was undoubtedly a child of late eighteenth-century humanitarianism. The link between Saturday's drunkenness and Monday's battered faces must have impressed many late eighteenth-century humanitarians as forcibly as it impressed the young William Lovett, watching Londoners setting off for work one Monday morning in 1821. The early temperance and humanitarian movements had the same friends—women, Quakers and evangelicals: and the same enemies—cockfighters, swearers, gamblers, tyrannical husbands, irresponsible drinksellers and sabbath-breakers.[39] Furthermore evangelicalism encouraged in the British aristocracy an involvement in moral crusading without which the anti-spirits movement could never have been launched as a nation-wide movement. In an age of war, revolution and rapid social change, the British aristocracy felt the need to prove its title to power by embracing a moral code more acceptable to its inferiors.[40]

Nor could the anti-spirits movement have made such an impact on the 1830s without the techniques of agitation perfected by evangelical humanitarians. A social movement can be launched only into a society accustomed to tolerate spontaneous and often mutually destructive crusades. The economical reform movement first linked sustained public agitation to specific items of policy, but in the anti-slavery movement evangelicalism built upon the long voluntarist tradition in English life to produce a new form of nation-wide reforming campaign. The contrast between the timidity of the anti-slave trade movement of the 1780s and the anti-slavery movement of the 1830s—with its processions, petitioning campaigns and permanent committees—indicates how much progress had been made. By 1829 the *Edinburgh Review* was complaining that no spiritual work now began spontaneously; the 'machinery' of public meetings, prospectuses and committees had first to be set in motion. Evangelicalism ensured that the notion of a parliament free from external constraint was replaced by a system of voluntarist pressure unparalleled except in Scandinavia and America.[41] The anti-slavery movement was long regarded as a model by temperance reformers, who met in the same premises, used the same arguments, attracted the same individuals: Richard Barrett, Captain Pilkington, and the Quakers J. J. Gurney, James Cropper, Samuel Bowly, R. D. Alexander, Joseph Sturge, R. T. Cadbury and many others. J. S. Buckingham, the first parliamentary advocate of temperance, had once resigned command of a ship rather than sail to Zanzibar on a slaving voyage. And both movements wanted moral considerations to set some limits on the complete freedom of trade; both campaigned to emancipate slaves from an evil 'traffick'.[42]

The fact that even irreligious influences were advocating sobriety immediately before the temperance movement appeared suggests that evangelicalism was not the only force at work. Place attributed the increased sobriety among the London working men partly to improved living standards after the Napoleonic Wars. This raises the important question of links between economic change and the appearance of the temperance movement. Several factors of time and place make it difficult to establish any simple link with industrialization. There were anti-drink crusaders long before the industrial revolution, and the anti-spirits movement appeared long after that revolution had begun. And although the temperance movement was from the start much stronger and more resolute in Lancashire and Yorkshire than elsewhere, it also attracted strong support in rural areas like Lincolnshire, Cornwall and North Wales [see Table 2]. It is true that accelerated urbanization and the need for precision and regularity of work made existing levels of drunkenness less tolerable. Yet with drink as with factory hours, humanitarian agitation against the evil began at a time when the evil itself had already begun to diminish—at least in fashionable society and among London working men.[43] Furthermore early temperance propaganda was usually cast in moral and religious, not in secular terms, and industrial employers did not always stand by their teetotal employees: teetotalers were sometimes dismissed for offending the employers' publican customers or for causing disputes among the work force by their refusal to co-operate in drinking customs.[44]

Yet in some areas there are signs of a link between textile manufacturing and the emergence of the anti-spirits movement. The earliest anti-spirits societies originated in the two textile manufacturing areas of Ulster and Glasgow, and spread through England from the textile centres of Preston, Bradford and Leeds. Henry Forbes, a worsted manufacturer, introduced the idea of anti-spirits association from Scotland into England, and the anti-spirits societies flourished first among the nonconformist trading and manufacturing classes in the northern industrial towns. Millowners occasionally agreed to chair temperance meetings in the 1830s; Leeds Temperance Society's ninth anniversary celebrations were held in Marshall's new Holbeck Mill; and several Bradford worsted manufacturers allowed their workpeople to leave the factory early on 14 June 1830—to boost attendance at the great inaugural meeting of Bradford Temperance Society, under its first president John Rand, the worsted manufacturer. Manchester millowners also gave encouragement, and textile manufacturers of all types featured prominently in the subscription lists of temperance organizations.[45] What advantages did the movement offer them? Broadly speaking, security of property, a disciplined work force and an expanded home market.

Every citizen with property gained from a movement which helped to maintain law and order. 'Are you CAPITALISTS?' asked Joseph Livesey in his *Malt Lecture*, the manifesto of teetotalism: 'what a comfort to live in the midst of a sober population! The Temperance Society is an insurance for the safety of every man's property. Drunkenness and disorder are sure to drive capital away. . . .' The movement sought to base public order on individual self-discipline: for Thomas Spencer, every teetotaler 'was a policeman engaged in repressing crime, and preserving the peace'.[46] To all ratepayers, the temperance movement offered a solution to the problem of pauperism; Chadwick told Thomas Spencer in 1841 that it was on the temperance societies that he rested his hopes for the recovery and permanent improvement of the labouring classes.[47] Yet the problem for the temperance movement—as for the anti-slavery movement—was that some types of property had to be attacked without antagonizing property as a whole. The hated trade was therefore branded as a crime or 'traffick', quite distinct from all other commercial activity. Nineteenth-century commercial and industrial capital was never monolithic: only recently it had been divided by the anti-slavery movement. In both campaigns industrialists turned against social groups whose capital had helped to launch the very process of industrialization.[48] The self-respect of a rising middle class strongly tinged with moralism demanded the purging of commerce from any disreputable connexions. The temperance movement contained many supporters—James Cropper, Titus Salt, Edward Baines, John Bright, to name only a few—with elevated notions of the dignity of commerce.

The temperance movement protected property in a less direct way: it helped to discipline the industrial work-force. Employers supported it for the same reasons that seventeenth-century J.P.s supported the attack on churchales in the textile manufacturing counties.[49] The textile industry was among the first to adopt a factory organization on a large scale: nowhere, said Ure in 1835, was the Gospel truth that 'godliness is great gain' more applicable than in administering a large factory.[50] There was in fact a peculiar need for efficiency in the work-force at just the time when the anti-spirits movement was launched in the industrial north. In the difficult years of 1827–32, the demand for cotton goods was rising more slowly than production. Cotton millowners were experiencing rising output but falling profits—a falling return on fixed capital; yet however low the ceiling price obtainable, high overheads demanded full-capacity output. The only possible remedies were further mechanization, reduced wages, improved manufacturing efficiency or enlarged consumer demand. In the woollen industry too, falling prices accompanied increasing output at this time, and both woollen and cotton industries were depressed during 1829, the year of the anti-spirits movement's successful launching in the textile districts of Northern Ireland and the Scottish Lowlands.[51] It may not be mere coincidence that the pioneer anti-spirits reformer John Dunlop made two unsuccessful visits to Glasgow in 1828, but found support there during his visit of August 1829. Or that November 1829 should be the date when Henry Forbes was converted in Glasgow by the anti-spirits movement which he established in 1830 at the wool-centre of Bradford, home of the first English anti-spirits society. By March 1830 trade began to improve in the textile districts, but the important steps had by then been taken.

The temperance movement was a valuable source of reliable men for key posts in the factory. During the nineteenth century a 'character' was more frequently required of industrial than of agricultural employees,[52] and among entrepreneurs 'character' could establish credit-worthiness. In Cobden's words, a shrewd capitalist would never back a man however wealthy without investigating his 'character, experience, and connexions'.[53] 'How often do you get drunk in the week?' Robert Owen was asked by a Manchester manufacturer from whom he was seeking employment. Blushing scarlet at the question, Owen replied that he had never been drunk in his life. 'My answer and the manner of it', he wrote, 'made, I suppose, a favourable impression; for the next question was—"What salary do you ask?"' Benjamin Franklin noted how the most trifling actions could affect a man's credit; what better way to demonstrate it, then as now, than through joining a reputable voluntary organization? Particularly when the temperance movement, like most religious organizations of the day, offered its members career openings and mutual help.[54] In this way the temperance movement could solve the problem of poverty for a small but influential group. Its ideology remained appropriate as long as property remained widely distributed and as long as it could plausibly be argued that poverty stemmed from personal inadequacy rather than from trade fluctuations and technological change.

The temperance movement expanded the home market for consumer-goods. Many industrial leaders combined the traditional advocacy of thrift with pleas for an expanding home market which have a more modern ring, and the Carlylean lament that 'cotton-cloth is already twopence a yard or lower; and yet bare backs were never more numerous among us' was often heard on temperance platforms.[55] Temperance pioneers boasted that they could release vast resources for expenditure on clothing, food and other consumer-goods; their tracts often listed the clothing which a year's drinking money could buy.[56] Joseph Livesey, the pioneer Preston teetotaler, wrote an address in the 1830s which urged local shopkeepers and tradesmen, if only from self-interest, to support the teetotal movement: 'nearly all the money spent at public-houses ought to be, and, if tee-totalism prevailed, would be, spent at YOUR SHOPS'.[57] During the crisis in the cotton industry of the late 1860s and 1870s, which in some ways resembled that of the 1830s, many prohibitionists and temperance reformers found the remedy in enlarging the home market.[58] Many nineteenth-century reforming movements found receptive audiences during times of depression,[59] but the temperance movement's remedy was more direct than some. The battle between the drink and textile industries, of which the temperance movement was in some ways an institutional outcrop, is seen at its crudest in the exchange of clothing for drink—in the 'doffing do', as Lancashire called it[60]—from which pawnbrokers made their fortunes. Excessive drinking had traditionally been restrained by low wages; but some industrialists believed that technological progress would introduce a high-wage economy. They naturally welcomed a movement which would not only accelerate economic growth, but which would also educate the masses in how to spend the proceeds.

The temperance ideology owed much to industrialization. Livesey admitted as much when he drew a direct analogy between moral and technological progress in an appeal for moral reform printed in his periodical *The Struggle*: '*A Better Moral Machinery Wanted*'.[61] Temperance zeal, like free trading enthusiasm, spread out from the towns, and temperance reformers saw their movement as part of a general attack on ignorance, feudalism and rusticity. This tendency was overlaid at first by the anti-spirits movement's eagerness to acquire the prestige of Anglican and aristocratic support: but with the triumph of teetotalism in the mid 1830s, it soon came to dominate the temperance crusade. Teetotalers were enthusiasts for industrial progress, for science, for education, for the railway (in which many of them invested) and for all humanitarian movements attacking traditional forms of recreation. Technological change required initiative and enterprise, and provided the rapid and cheap literature and travel which were needed by reformers challenging the old-fashioned ways. By copiously distributing their propaganda, temperance reformers hoped to secure a dramatic social transformation. 'The only rational way of dealing with erroneous opinions', said the temperance reformer Benjamin Parsons in 1851, 'was to talk and to write them out of people.'[62] Flexibility of outlook was now at a premium: the first parliamentary champion of temperance legislation, J. S. Buckingham, ridiculed Cobbett's argument that because drunkenness was a long-established vice it could never be eliminated.[63]

Industrialization also lent self-confidence to new groups in British society with new attitudes. It enabled moral initiative to be displayed independently of Westminster—and to some extent in criticism of it—by individuals for whom state intervention meant class domination. Tocqueville claimed that contemporary Frenchmen would never have attacked drunkenness by founding temperance societies; they would simply have pressed the government to supervise drinking places more closely.[64] At the Brussels International Philanthropic Congress of 1856, English temperance reformers were surprised to find their continental counterparts relying on the government to curb intemperance.[65]

Like many reforming movements the temperance movement was both a cause and a consequence of mounting sensibility to the evil it attacked. Though fashion still dictated a level of drinking at Christ Church in the 1830s which caused the youthful and sober Ruskin to pour claret down his waistcoat, it therefore seems that this was yet another sphere in which Oxford lagged behind the times.[66] As with the contemporary attack on the established church, the vehemence of the nineteenth-century attack on drunkenness does not seem to be closely related to the extent of the evil it attacked. 'Originality', John Morley wrote, 'may lie as much in perception of opportunity as in invention.'[67] The pioneer temperance reformer gave voice to ideas only half-formulated in many people's minds. Society in the 1820s was ready to welcome a new solution to the drink problem paradoxically because it had already begun to solve it.

In his fine study of *Capitalism and Slavery* Eric Williams confined his discussion of the actual campaigners against slavery to a small chapter at the end of the book. In the relationship between capitalism and drunkenness, perhaps the temperance reformers deserve just as little space. Yet however deeply indebted it was to a favourable environment, the temperance movement also owed much to the courage and energy of the anti-spirits pioneers. John Dunlop, while establishing the anti-spirits movement in Scotland, was haunted by the frightful evils of drunkenness: 'the subject was eternally present to my mind; I continually reverted to it', he wrote; 'if by chance my thoughts had been diverted a few minutes, they sprang back like the lock of a musket. I could as soon have left a leg or arm upon the road as have divested myself of the ever-enduring image.' One recalls the obsessive concern with the horrors of slavery which filled Clarkson's mind as he travelled, Wilberforce's dreams as he slept.[68] Joseph Livesey the pioneer teetotaler displayed an almost fool-hardy courage: in 1834, single-handed and undaunted by the size of London, he placarded the Bank of England and other public buildings with announcements of the public meeting at which he would explain his teetotal refinement of the anti-spirits movement, hitherto virtually unknown outside Lancashire. 'The fact is,' he declared thirty years later, 'I was so full of it, that I thought I was going to produce a revolution.'[69]

Four distinct groups created the temperance movement in nineteenth-century Britain: the individual abstainers who discovered the feasibility of abstinence: the American philanthropists who exported to Britain the idea of associating abstainers: the early leaders of the British anti-spirits movement: and the Quakers who provided them with so much money and support. Nineteenth-century temperance reformers boosted their self-confidence by unearthing predecessors in the remotest antiquity, but if the search is confined to Britain alone, water-drinkers existed long before the anti-spirits movement reached Britain.[70] There were at least three well-known Puritan teetotalers (also vegetarians) in the seventeenth century. One of these, Thomas Tryon, indirectly affected the nineteenth-century temperance movement because he influenced Benjamin Franklin, whose writings in turn influenced the pioneer teetotaler Joseph Livesey. In the 1720s Franklin preached teetotalism to his London fellow printers, and during the eighteenth century many Quakers showed the feasibility of abjuring spirits.[71] At least four M.P.s who were teetotalers in 1834—Buckingham, Joseph Brotherton, George Williams and Sir George Strickland—had begun to abstain before the temperance movement was founded. Several early temperance reformers decided to abstain some years before the movement appeared: J. S. Buckingham and Joseph Sturge, for example. There were even temperance missionaries in England before the temperance movement was launched in America in 1826. But these early abstainers were either isolated, and often eccentric, individuals; or they were associated for purposes more important than abstinence.[72] Crab, according to his epitaph, was 'separate from the giddy crowd';[73] Tryon was influenced by Behmen's mystical works, and neither he nor Henry Welbey had many followers. No abstainer before 1829 urged his personal practice on all members of society as a cure for the drink problem, let alone for other ills.

In the early nineteenth century, groups of abstainers were formed for several quite different reasons. After 1809 a small Manchester sect, the Cowherdites—some of whose members were later prominent in the prohibitionist movement—abjured meat and all alcoholic drinks. Joseph Brotherton, a leading Cowherdite, publicly recommended total abstinence in 1821 as the best way to combat drunkenness. But he did not suggest the association of abstainers; the principle of Cowherdite association was religious, not dietetic.[74] Many Lancashire radicals—including Cobbett and Hunt—abstained from wine and spirits after the Napoleonic Wars, but their motive was that of the Boston tea-party: to enhance radical solidarity and to weaken the government by depriving it of excise revenue, not to promote temperance for its own sake; the Manchester radicals did not hesitate to brew their own beer at Oldham wakes.[75] Many Quaker and radical opponents of the slave trade in 1791–2 banded together to abstain from sugar and rum, and their efforts impressed Cobbett, who in 1820 even suggested that 'little communities, little circles' be formed for abstainers from excised goods. Yet although he disliked wine and spirits, Cobbett was a devotee of home-brewed ale, strongly condemned tea and insisted that drunkenness could be cured only by the exertion of will power. When temperance reformers became prominent in the 1830s he denounced them as 'despicable drivelling quacks'.[76]

The literature on drunkenness published immediately before the temperance movement appeared shows no sign of the impending development. A writer in 1796 suggested that the drunkard wishing to be cured should draw up a resolution before a respectable individual to renounce spirits for a fixed period: the pledged man should impose on himself a voluntary penalty of subscribing to a public charity if he broke his pledge. In some respects this anticipated the anti-spirits pledge, but there was no hint that the pledged should associate in societies, or that the sober should take the pledge for example's sake. In 1805, a society was formed to repress drunkenness in Redruth, but it did not depart from the old pattern of upper-class enforcement of sobriety through police action. One of the last published attacks on drunkenness before the appearance of the temperance movement, by J. Yates in 1818, gives no hint of the forthcoming remedy.[77] By 1826, therefore, the idea of total abstinence from spirits had long existed; the fusion of the idea of association with the idea of abstinence was now required. This occurred in America in the first quarter of the nineteenth century.

The British feminist movement was preceded by many years of correspondence between individual feminist pioneers; by contrast, temperance principles appeared in England unannounced, and were propagated by a 'movement' almost from the start. The temperance and peace movements originated in Britain and America in the same way, among the same people and at the same time.[78] Both flourished on the close links between British and American philanthropists which had already created the agitation against the slave trade. The American anti-spirits movement was first mentioned in the evangelical *Christian Observer* in July 1826, and by May 1828 the periodical was urging London to participate. In 1830 the *Evangelical Magazine* doubted at first whether anti-spirits societies would be useful in England, where gin-drinking was less fashionable; but it later urged Englishmen to follow the American lead.[79]

Behind this exchange of ideas lay a whole complex of Anglo-American philanthropic activity. Though the English aristocracy disliked republican America, many English dissenters considered it 'the *ne plus ultra* of political perfection', and felt that they had more in common with Americans than with their own governing class.[80] Temperance, peace, anti-slavery, penal reform and Christian missions were all Anglo-American campaigns. For the nineteenth-century nonconformist moral reformer, as for the seventeenth-century puritan, America constituted a laboratory for social experiment. Nineteenth-century moral reform crusaders were pioneers of internationalism, and American temperance reformers frequently crossed the Atlantic in order to prevent their domestic campaign from being hindered by drunken immigrants. A British Temperance Emigration Society was founded at Liverpool in 1842, with Lawrence Heyworth as one of the trustees, to settle British emigrants in Wisconsin.[81] There was even a modest philanthropic rivalry between the two countries.[82] Anglo-American commercial ties fostered contact; the significant economic and religious frontier at this time lay in the Appalachian mountains rather than in the Atlantic Ocean.[83] Like Cobden, J. S. Buckingham, the prominent temperance pioneer, showed his faith in America by investing his money there, and like several English temperance reformers he also toured America. Francis Beardsall the Bible wine controversialist of the 1830s died in mid-Atlantic, *en route* for 'that land of liberty . . . where his mind would not be pained by a people's sufferings, the result of heartless oppression'.[84]

Americans helped to establish the British anti-spirits movement in several ways. American sea captains first introduced temperance principles into

Liverpool in 1829; American ministers influenced the two earliest temperance leaders—John Dunlop in Scotland and Dr. Edgar in Ulster—and also introduced temperance principles to Cork, soon to be Father Mathew's temperance headquarters. A letter from New York prompted the eccentric missionary G. C. Smith in 1829 to write the first English tract advocating the formation of temperance societies, and the Livesey–Delavan transatlantic correspondence in the 1830s reinforced enthusiasm on both sides of the ocean. Americans induced the first London temperance society to convert itself into a national temperance organization and supported extremist tendencies in the British temperance movement throughout the 1830s. Later they championed the more demanding 'long' pledge against the 'short', and generated enthusiasm through their literature and domestic legislation.[85] Lyman Beecher's *Six Sermons on Intemperance* and the annual reports of American temperance societies were very influential, as were the Bible wine researches of Eliphalet Nott and Beaumont's medical observations on Alexis St. Martin. The curtailing of spirit rations to the American services and, later, the Maine Law, set important precedents for the English temperance agitation. So close a link with America however—though invaluable in establishing the movement with English nonconformists and radicals—helped to prejudice the governing classes against it.[86]

The new movement also owed something to continental influences of a very different sort. John Dunlop had already heard of the American temperance societies before visiting Paris in 1828, but it was this visit which focused his attention directly on the temperance question: he asked himself how a nation 'of papists and infidels' could surpass in morals a nation with an 'upright confession of faith' and where the Bible was the 'test and spring of all ethical purity'.[87] Nineteenth-century Englishmen, apparently supreme in so many economic and religious spheres, suffered from an inferiority complex about their drinking habits. Hume in 1834 said that a man could land at Ostend and visit Brussels, Antwerp and Liège without seeing as many drunken men *en route* as he could see in London in half-an-hour.[88] Such contrasts lent impetus to a movement which claimed to be attacking English drunkenness at its root —though in practice temperance reformers took up two contradictory positions: when stirring up temperance enthusiasm in England they contrasted English drunkenness with French sobriety, but when refuting free licensers who argued that French sobriety proved the advantages of easy accessibility, they argued that the French were less sober than they seemed. As one teetotaler argued in 1839, 'the French, generally, are not drunkards . . . but they are *regular* drinkers'.[89] There was probably something in this argument, for even today the Frenchman's regular drinking contrasts with the intermittent but helpless drunkenness of a minority of Englishmen.

Protestant missions in France were discredited by drunken English navvies building French railways in the 1840s, and by reports of English habits brought back by French visitors.[90] Similarly the drunkenness of English colonists and the unscrupulousness of English traders embarrassed evangelical missions to the heathen. Chinese, Syrians and Kaffirs appeared on Exeter Hall platforms to rebuke the English for their sins. Visitors to the despised Arab populations, like the teetotalers Buckingham and F. W. Newman, were surprised to find them excelling the English in sobriety. Buckingham used similar arguments to launch the contemporary attack on animal cruelty.[91] If an avenging God bestowed material power only in return for superior morality, Englishmen must engage in temperance reform from motives of national defence. Temperance tracts often drew analogies between nineteenth-century Britain and Rome in her dotage: 'in proportion as a people become loose in morals', wrote a temperance handbook in 1847, 'they must sink in the scale of nations'.[92]

How did anti-spirits societies spread over Britain during 1829–30? In summer 1829 two simultaneous but independent movements appeared in Ireland and Scotland, both areas whose working people drank spirits rather than beer, and where there were complaints at the recent reduction in spirit duties. Influenced by the American Presbyterian minister Revd. Joseph Penney, Dr. John Edgar, Presbyterian professor of divinity at Belfast, hurled the family whisky out of the parlour window, and on 14 August appealed in the *Belfast Newsletter* against sabbath-breaking and intemperance.[93] Edgar was in his thirties—an energetic and eloquent minister and opponent of slavery. He later wrote much propaganda for the anti-spirits movement, but strongly opposed the move forward to teetotalism, and eventually retired from temperance work.

On the same day G. W. Carr, Congregational minister of New Ross, founded the first British anti-spirits society requiring total abstinence from spirits and moderation in other drinks; the event occurred at a Bible Society gathering in a Quaker meeting-house. Later claims that a similar society had been formed some years before at Skibbereen are irrelevant because this society, if it existed, wielded no influence outside its locality. By November 1829 the anti-spirits movement had been joined by Dr. John Cheyne, physician to the forces in Ireland, and by Rev. W. Urwick, a prominent Dublin Congregational minister. But though the Roman Catholic Archbishop of Cashel and the Bishop of Kildare lent their approval, Catholic fears of protestant proselytism hindered progress in Ireland until Father Mathew's campaigns of the late 1830s. Like Chartism, temperance suffered in Ireland from the bitterness of local religious rivalries. The Quakers were very helpful from the first, and by 1830 the Hibernian Temperance Society was distributing sophisticated tracts reconciling the anti-spirits movement with medical opinion, political economy and political prudence: the upper classes must sustain their threatened social position, it argued, by demonstrating their superior morality.[94]

Dr. Edgar almost immediately visited Scotland, but when he reached Glasgow in September 1829 he found that the evangelical, wealthy, serious-minded, well-educated socio-religious reformer John Dunlop had independently established an anti-spirits movement there. Dunlop's observations on his visit to Paris in the previous year had been published as a tract, and in August 1829—influenced by an American minister and by American literature—he agitated to establish a temperance movement in Scotland. Dunlop was inspired by his religious principles: Knox, Wesley, Wilberforce and Chalmers were his guiding-lights—despite Chalmers' failure to join the new movement till many years later. In October 1829, Dunlop walked 'in great fear and trembling' to his first public temperance meeting in Glasgow. Like Clarkson in 1787, catching his first view of the churches of Bristol—or like the pioneer feminists daring to make public the indignities they had long suffered in private—Dunlop was startled at his own temerity. The first Scottish anti-spirits society was established at Greenock in the same month. At that time, said Dunlop later, 'everything seemed against me'.[95] By June 1830 the *Temperance Society Record*, the first British temperance periodical, was able to list a total Scottish membership of 3,332 and an Irish membership of 3,500.

Scotsmen established the anti-spirits movement in England. Scottish temperance zeal for many years burned more brightly than English enthusiasm, and the Scottish religious atmosphere closely resembled that of New England, where the American temperance movement was born. Rich countries easily attract intellect and energy from nearby poor countries, and the temperance movement assisted the process. Scotsmen in fact helped to prepare the very ground in which the early anti-spirits movement took root, for evangelicalism itself owed much to the eighteenth-century diaspora of devout Scottish Presbyterians.[96] William Collins the publisher established the new movement in visits to London and Bristol. Many Scotsmen followed where Collins had led—John Dunlop, Robert Gray Mason, William McKerrow, Robert Rae, Francis Skinner, Robert Lowery, William Tweedie, James H. Wilson—men who, together with many other temperance leaders, converged on southern England from the remoter parts of Britain to promote its moral reform.

Despite G. C. Smith's pamphlet of 1829 and the efforts of three American sea-captains visiting Liverpool in that year, the first English temperance society was not established till February 1830. In November 1829 while on a business trip to Glasgow Henry Forbes, a Scottish worsted manufacturer aged 34 who had settled in Bradford, was won over by Scottish temperance reformers. Here, as in the wool trade, he became an excellent salesman of other people's ideas. Although according to his obituarist his views were often regarded as 'utopian and visionary' in Bradford, Forbes succeeded in establishing an anti-spirits society there. He later became an Anti-Corn Law Leaguer, espoused the cause of the Scottish seceders, was described by Bright in 1853 as 'very well informed', and became third mayor of Bradford. He was energetically aided by Dr. Beaumont, a surgeon of Wesleyan family, educated at Kingswood. Beaumont was a good speaker and became very active in local government after moving to Bradford in 1822; he eventually became one of the city's first aldermen.[97] John Rand, worsted manufacturer, Conservative and unsectarian Anglican philanthropist, became the first president. In June 1830 William Collins travelled down from Glasgow to speak at the new society's first meeting. The Dublin Quaker G. H. Birkett took the lead in founding the second and third English temperance societies—at Warrington and Manchester respectively.[98]

The early Bradford society strove to establish societies elsewhere, rather than to promote the cause locally. It inspired Edward Baines to recommend the new movement in his *Leeds Mercury* on 23 January 1830, and later in the year to help found the Leeds Temperance Society.[99] At the yearly meeting in May 1830, Quakers were already excited by the new movement; an irritated

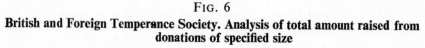

FIG. 6

British and Foreign Temperance Society. Analysis of total amount raised from donations of specified size

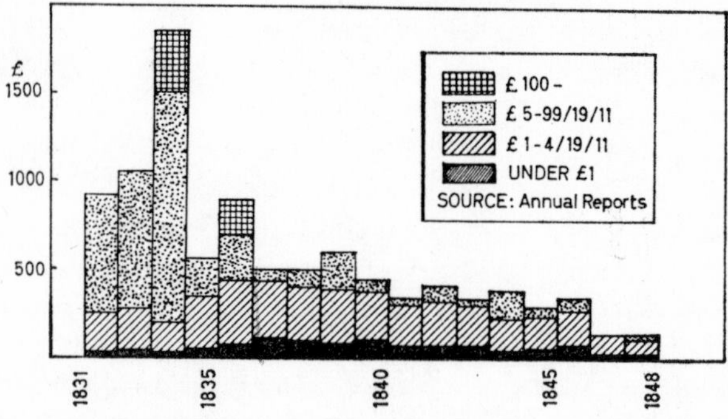

former wine- and spirit-merchant there complained of 'the strain of cant all set in one direction' and of a minute drawn up 'which will infallibly consign all us incorrigible publicans to moral outlawry'.[100] But William Collins, visiting London in summer 1830, found no temperance society there, and had great difficulty in founding one; this was the first sign of a metropolitan apathy which was to hinder the temperance movement, like most other reform movements, throughout the nineteenth century.[101] Wales was even slower than England to embrace the new movement, and the first two temperance societies for Welshmen—in Liverpool and Manchester—were not founded till 1831.

The London Temperance Society held its first public meeting in June 1831, but only when American influence had changed its title to 'British and Foreign Temperance Society' was the British anti-spirits movement safely launched.[102] These events, despite their great importance to temperance historians later, attracted very little attention in the contemporary press, even in the *Leeds Mercury*. Except for the *Monthly Review*, which in 1830 mentioned the 'most praiseworthy zeal and determination' of its leaders, the evangelical monthlies were the only London papers to pay any attention to the new movement.[103] In general, the newspapers in 1830 had more important things to write about.

5
The Origins of Teetotalism: 1830–1834

The British and Foreign Temperance Society was a London-based reforming society on the traditional evangelical model. It paraded great names, and within a year claimed the Bishop of London as president, with four peers and four bishops among its vice-presidents. In 1837 it secured the Queen's patronage. Clergymen contributed about one-twentieth of its funds, but non-conformist ministers like Dr. Pye Smith also gave their support. Quakers and women were prominent, the latter donating about one-tenth of the Society's funds. In some local branches, Anglicans co-operated with non-conformists. At Blackburn, for instance, the vicar was president, a Quaker, an Anglican and two Congregationalists were vice-presidents, and on the committee were Episcopalians, Presbyterians, Congregationalists, Baptists, Methodists and Quakers.[1] The Society's treasurer was Cornelius Hanbury, a Quaker minister related to William Allen and a friend of Richard Barrett. Rev. Owen Clarke was the Society's lifelong secretary and chief prop. Its supporters could be seen at the meetings of many other evangelical societies. Members pledged themselves to abstain from all spirits 'except for medicinal purposes' and to 'discountenance the causes and practice of intemperance'.[2] For the B.F.T.S. this meant moderate beer- or wine-drinking; teetotalers therefore labelled its members 'moderationists'.

The size of its subscriptions shows that the B.F.T.S. was financed by wealthy philanthropists, not by the *victims* of intemperance: benevolent paternalism was the Society's mood [see Figure 6]. Over £4,000 was raised in the first two years, mostly from donors of £5 or more. Total subscriptions continued to rise till 1833–4. Much came from Quakers—from the Manchester Crewdsons, the Lombard Street Gurneys, the Cirencester Bowlys, the Bristol Frys and the Birmingham Sturges. Quakers also gave time and energy to the early temperance movement. The Society had access to the banking-brewing complex and also to aristocratic evangelical ladies like Lady Olivia Sparrow and the Duchess of Beaufort: to admirals, generals and aristocrats like Lords Hervey, Bexley, Dover and Henley: and to two families long to shine in the temperance world—the Lawsons and the

Trevelyans. In the philanthropic world, self-effacement did not pay, and long subscription-lists advertising distinguished donors were appended to every annual report.

The B.F.T.S. concentrated on propaganda [see Figure 7]. Throughout its history, the temperance movement placed an exaggerated faith in the written appeal for sobriety. In a few instances, tracts or booklets deeply influenced individual readers: Mrs. Wightman's *Haste to the Rescue* strikingly influenced W. S. Caine, for instance. Yet in most cases, they missed their mark. This was partly because tract-writers often failed to appreciate what caused drunkards to drink, but more often because the problem was to make action accord with belief, rather than to inculcate the belief itself. Here the simple written appeal was insufficient. In three years the B.F.T.S.

FIG. 7

British and Foreign Temperance Society. Analysis of expenditure

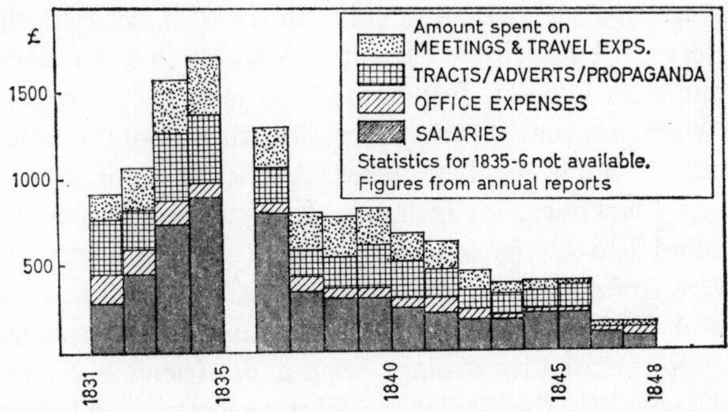

spent over a quarter of its income on printing and distributing over two million temperance tracts.[3] From 1832 it published periodicals filled with membership statistics, subscription-lists, American news and denunciations of spirits. During 1834 several temperance publications were presented to every M.P., and the Society tried to influence clergymen and doctors. By then there were 443 affiliated societies and the Society provided speakers for local temperance meetings all over England. In 1833 it had five agents at work—two years later, ten; but the Society never became strong enough to decentralize its agencies and failed, in 1834, to institute a county union with its own agent.[4] This was partly because the Society was not run by the most zealous individuals in the temperance movement—nor from the locality where the greatest temperance enthusiasm prevailed.

In 1834 the B.F.T.S. published membership figures which reveal its regional coverage. The B.F.T.S. was a London-based organization, and relied largely on clergymen for its local contacts. By contrast, the teetotal phase of the temperance movement depended even more firmly on support from the north, and from dissenters rather than from clergymen. Hence the regional pattern of temperance strength would have been rather different five years later. It would also have differed for another reason. By 1834 the teetotal message had not yet reached Wales, Northumberland and Lincolnshire; these areas later featured more prominently in the movement.

TABLE 2

B.F.T.S. Regional Strength in England and Wales in 1834

AREA	MEMBERSHIP	% OF TOTAL MEMBERSHIP	MEMBERS PER 1,000 POPULATION	RANK ORDER Col. 3	RANK ORDER Col. 4
Lancs	25,119	29·2	18·8	1	2
London/Middx/Kent/ Essex/Surrey	11,128	13·0	4·7	2	15
Yorks	9,493	11·0	6·9	3	9
Cornwall	7,550	8·7	25·1	4	1
Glos	3,579	4·1	9·2	5	5
Somerset	2,775	3·2	6·9	6	9
Durham	2,480	2·8	10·4	7	4
Cheshire	2,296	2·6	6·9	8	9
Devon	2,017	2·3	4·1	9	16
Warwickshire	1,700	1·9	5·0	10	14
Wiltshire	1,680	1·9	7·1	11	8
WALES	1,570	1·8	1·9	12	28
Cumberland	1,524	1·7	9·0	13	6
Northumbd	1,306	1·5	5·5	14	12
Berks	1,192	1·3	8·1	15	7
Staffs	1,098	1·2	2·7	16	22
Derbs	978	1·1	4·1	17	16
Suffolk	928	1·0	3·1	18	20
Hants	828	0·9	2·6	19	23
Bucks	790	0·9	5·4	20	13
Worcs	777	0·9	3·5	21	18
Notts	712	0·8	3·2	22	19
Salop	655	0·7	3·1	23	20
Norfolk	608	0·7	1·6	24	29
Westmd	606	0·7	11·0	25	3
Sussex	447	0·5	1·6	26	29
Oxon	382	0·4	2·5	27	24
Cambs	343	0·3	2·4	28	26
Dorset	330	0·3	2·1	29	27
Leics	312	0·3	1·6	30	29
Herts	185	0·2	1·3	31	32
Lincs	153	0·1	0·5	32	35
Hunts	134	0·1	2·5	33	24
Beds	100	0·1	1·1	34	34
Herefs	84	0·0	1·3	35	32
Rutland	—	0·0	0·0	36	36
Northants	—	0·0	0·0	36	36

SOURCE: population figures from B. R. Mitchell and P. Deane, *op. cit.*, p. 20; membership figures from British & Foreign Temperance Society, *Third Annual Report, 1833–34.*

The county membership figures can be profitably analysed in two ways: as a proportion of the total B.F.T.S. membership and as a proportion of the total county population. Column 3 immediately reveals the northern dominance which persisted throughout the nineteenth century, together with the prominence of the west of England. It also highlights the movement's weakest areas: only two of the twelve weakest counties were north of the Boston–Gloucester line. Column 4 shows how the northern rural counties—Westmorland and Cumberland—were far more strongly influenced by the movement than the agricultural counties further south. It also reveals the movement's relative weakness in the London area.

How did the B.F.T.S. regard parliament? The temperance movement prided itself on diverging from previous moral reform movements—for unlike them it did not advocate penal enactments against drunkards and drink-sellers.[5] Though less hostile to the licensing system than subsequent temperance reformers, the anti-spirits movement revealed its suspicion of state intervention by its attitude to the first parliamentary inquiry into drunkenness, chaired by J. S. Buckingham in 1834.* Hitherto identified with crusading for the free press and against slavery, Buckingham, an advanced radical, was elected M.P. for Sheffield in 1832. His lecturing connexions, his inflated oratory, his exaggerated self-confidence and his extreme radicalism alarmed and alienated the House. Convinced by his overseas travels that English drunkenness must be curbed, he had abandoned wine and spirits by 1826 and in the early 1830s joined the anti-spirits movement. Amidst much ridicule he worked up a petitioning campaign in the country during 1833–4, and induced parliament to appoint a parliamentary inquiry into drunkenness on 3 June 1834. Twelve of his supporters in the division were Tories, sixteen Liberals and thirty-one Whigs.[6] Nineteen of the thirty-six committee members had voted in favour of the inquiry; ten came from northern industrial towns; three were teetotalers. Other members included Knatchbull, High Tory opponent of the 1830 Beer Bill, Joseph Pease the Quaker, Edward Baines, Peel and Althorp—the two latter apparently not attending the committee. Later Sir Andrew Agnew the evangelical, very unpopular at the time for his sabbatarianism, was added to the committee. Fifty witnesses were interviewed in 22 days between 9 June and 28 July, and the report was presented on 5 August.

Accepting uncritically many of the statistics which had influenced the free licensers when campaigning for the Beer Act, the committee convinced itself that intemperance had declined at the top of society but was increasing at the bottom. It put the blame entirely on spirit-drinking and made no reference to beer-drinking. It clearly asserted the right of the state to intervene against

* I have discussed this committee fully in my 'Two Roads to Social Reform. Francis Place and the "Drunken Committee" of 1834', *Historical Journal* 1968; only a brief summary of parts of this article has been included here.

drunkenness. 'The *right* to exercise legislative interference for the correction of any evil which affects the public weal, cannot be questioned, without dissolving society into its primitive elements . . .,' it said: 'the *power* to apply correction by legislative means, cannot be doubted, without supposing the sober, the intelligent, the just and the moral portion of the community unable to control the excesses of the ignorant and disorderly'.[7]

As 'immediate' remedies, the committee recommended that all licences should be annually renewable under magistrates' supervision, and that their number should be related to the size and density of population. Closing hours should be uniform and earlier. Spirit-shops should be open to public view; the sale of spirits, except in the inn, should be entirely separate from the sale of other goods. Army and navy spirit rations should be abolished; benefit societies should not meet nor should wages be paid in public-houses. Parks, reading-rooms and libraries should be established, duties on reading matter, sugar and non-alcoholic drinks reduced, temperance societies encouraged and a national educational system established. As 'ultimate' remedies—to be applied when public opinion allowed—the report advocated the absolute prohibition of the manufacture, import and sale of spirits.

Unfortunately for Buckingham the ridicule persisted, and he was accused of guiding the committee towards his own opinions. The London papers were hostile, only the *Morning Herald* showing much sympathy; but the provincial papers were more favourable, and were surely correct in defending the need for such an inquiry—a need which the London press and many M.P.s disputed. Many of the committee's recommendations were remarkably imaginative for their day and far less sectarian than those later embraced by the temperance movement. For although the report anticipated prohibitionism, it did not repudiate continuous regulation and gradual improvement. Many of its suggestions reappear in later measures; H. A. Bruce in 1871 and the select committee on public-houses in 1853–4 both favoured relating the number of licences to density of population. In later years public-house opening-hours were progressively restricted, and by the 1872 Licensing Act they were also made uniform [see Tables 8 and 9]. When dangers of illicit distilling had receded, Gladstone in the 1850s gradually raised drink taxes to promote both morality and the public revenue; the taxes on tea, coffee and sugar were substantially reduced during the century. Alternatives were later provided for army and navy spirit rations, and although Gladstone in the 1860s reversed the tendency to separate the sale of drink from that of other articles, his experiment was later regarded as mistaken and was not pushed further. Benefit societies meeting in public-houses gradually became discredited and Shaftesbury's efforts helped to prevent wage-payment in drink shops.

Still more far-sighted, because reaching beyond nineteenth- to twentieth-century remedies for intemperance, were the report's positive proposals for public parks, public libraries and public education. For unlike many temperance reformers Buckingham was no mere negative restrictionist. It was not love of drink, he declared two years before his death, but a desire for a 'cheerful and friendly intercourse . . . with his fellow men' which first sent customers to the drinkshop.[8] Yet as a document designed to secure rapid political results, the report was faulty. It contained too many of Buckingham's excellent but at that time controversial ideas: it did not study the existing licensing system in sufficient detail: it was too eager to stir up public indignation: and some of its proposals were somewhat eccentric.

Burdened with Buckingham's formidable unpopularity, with its detested evangelical connexions, and also with the hostility of that arch-manipulator Francis Place, the project was doomed. At least 14 of the 50 witnesses came from evangelical circles, and it was no coincidence that one of the few prominent statesmen to recognize the report's value was the arch-evangelical Lord Ashley, who claimed in 1843 that it had 'never received a tithe of the attention so valuable a document deserved'.[9] Only two years after the committee had reported, evangelicals were using its conclusions on gin-drinking to raise funds for the London City Mission.[10] Like so many contemporary committees, this committee tended to interview only interested parties who could afford to send witnesses to London, instead of conducting a social survey of the functions of drink and drinksellers in working class life. The report should therefore be used only with extreme care.

Buckingham's attempt has a threefold significance. First, it provided the temperance movement with evidence (which it regarded as conclusive) against the drink trade. His report long remained 'the Text Book of every teetotal advocate—the source whence he drew his richest facts, his most important arguments',[11] and it supplied ammunition for teetotal textbooks like Grindrod's *Bacchus*, W. R. Baker's *Curse of Britain* and Burne's *Teetotaler's Companion*. Though soon forgotten at Westminster, the report was long praised on temperance platforms, and Buckingham remained a central figure in the movement until his death. Buckingham's efforts revealed, secondly, the powerlessness of the temperance movement at Westminster. Not only was the report ridiculed there: the very notion of inquiry had been scorned. Buckingham had gained publicity, but his licensing and public parks bills both failed. He remained a lone temperance voice in parliament till he retired in 1837; thereafter, the temperance movement lacked a parliamentary spokesman for a generation.

Thirdly, the episode revealed the political timidity of the B.F.T.S. It gave Buckingham 1,000 circular addresses encouraging petitions for inquiry, and it urged its supporters to make 'immediate exertions' for it.[12] But the Society refused to campaign for legislation, and its equivocal stance no doubt lent fire to a new development within the temperance movement: the emergence of teetotalism. At least as hostile to state intervention as the B.F.T.S., teetotalism was none the less much more resolute in its methods, much more confident that a dramatic change in national habits could be quickly secured. In many respects it was with teetotalism that the temperance movement really broke with previous patterns of moral reform.

Criticism of the B.F.T.S. had been rife almost from the first. It attracted less support than had been anticipated; few clergymen were prepared to set an example by taking the pledge, and London was difficult to rouse. The reports of the poor law commissioners in the 1830s at no point mention temperance societies as a possible remedy for poverty. The B.F.T.S. gave disproportionate attention to intemperance overseas, its secretary noting with pride at the 1842 annual meeting that very few persons present could read the Society's foreign language tracts.[13] The monthly *Temperance Magazine and Review*, published from March 1832, soon lost its initial admiration for the B.F.T.S., which it attacked for lack of energy and for its excessively refined outlook. Why, for instance, had it ceased to employ Mr. Cruikshanks, the Dundee carter? In its final number, for May 1833, it published the complaints of 'A.Z.' that the Society's members were 'calculating more upon *influence* to forward their cause, than upon the soundness of their principles'. The periodical praised provincial temperance effort, but without the aid of the leading London temperance organization no London-based paper could chronicle provincial activity. Further temperance progress could come only from outside London, and in fact came from teetotalers in Lancashire.[14] Even before the teetotal attack began, therefore, the B.F.T.S. was an ailing body.

Underlying teetotal attacks on the B.F.T.S. there existed a nonconformist distaste for its aristocratic and Anglican structure. The Society was closely wedded to the established church, and nonconformists were sometimes embarrassed at having to act under the local vicar.[15] The militant dissenter Joseph Livesey complained in 1835 that the Society had 'too long acted from EXPEDIENCY', and was 'seeking to please and secure the patronage and approval of the great... instead of the working classes'[16] [see Plate 6]. In a decade of mounting tension between Anglicans and nonconformists, internal friction in a pan-denominational protestant society was inevitable. The attack on the B.F.T.S. was formulated however, or perhaps rationalized, as a condemnation of its inability to reclaim the drunkard.

Four serious defects in the Society soon became apparent. Although William Wilberforce had expressly condemned any notion that virtue made milder claims on the rich than on the poor, the B.F.T.S. in spirit-drinking areas proscribed the drink of the poor while allowing the rich to retain their wine. This objection prevented Brougham from joining,[17] and the *Poor Man's Guardian* on 16 July 1831 urged the B.F.T.S. to begin its preaching at home. Again, it was soon found—especially in the north—that a mere switch from spirits to beer or wine did not necessarily promote sobriety, and that the intoxicating properties of these three drinks diverged less strikingly than many had hitherto supposed. Indeed, when some of their members became more drunk on beer than non-members on spirits, accusations of hypocrisy resulted.[18] Teetotalism gave the anti-spirits movement that precision of aim so necessary to a reforming movement. Teetotalers used the same arguments against anti-spirits societies which tolerated beer-drinking, as the anti-spirits societies themselves used against moderate spirit drinkers. The temperance movement was thus being launched on its path towards extremism—so that defects in the movement were remedied by attempts to close loopholes rather than by rethinking fundamentals, and the movement's original aim, the prevention of drunkenness, was subordinated to the pursuit of consistency.

Its failure to attack beer-drinking therefore prevented the B.F.T.S. from reducing drunkenness in beer-drinking areas of the country. So pronounced were regional variations in drinking habits that only a teetotal pledge could achieve in beer-drinking rural England and Wales what an anti-spirits pledge could achieve in spirit-drinking Ireland and Scotland. In the remoter parts, in Yorkshire and Staffordshire where home-brewed beer was highly prized, and also in the cider-drinking west, a mere anti-spirits pledge could achieve little. Yet the prominence of brewers in the London philanthropic world and even in its own branches prevented the B.F.T.S. from welcoming teetotalism. Finally the B.F.T.S. made no effort to reclaim the drunkard, whereas teetotalism paraded some striking reclamations. Anti-spirits branches were driven into embracing teetotalism by pragmatic rather than by theoretical considerations—by their need to insulate their members from temptation. Teetotalers challenged the traditional belief that drunkards were irreclaimable just as, in Josephine Butler's movement, many of them were to challenge the notion that prostitutes were beyond rescue. 'John's dispensation had passed away,' said Thomas Swindlehurst, a teetotal zealot, in 1836, 'and the true tee-total light had come into the world.'

Here teetotalers diverged from all previous temperance reformers, for many had hitherto shared the pessimism of a seventeenth-century tract writer: 'this sinne', wrote Younge in 1638, 'is like a desperate plague, that knows no cure; it may be called the Kings evill of the soule . . . for it cannot bee cured with the Balme of Gilead, nor by any Physitian.'[19] Teetotalism at first seemed a miracle:

> What has it done? Delightful things,
> Beyond our best imaginings:
> The Ethiop's white,—the lion's tamed,
> And hoary drunkards are reclaimed.[20]

During the dramatic debate at Leeds in 1836 between moderationists and teetotalers, the moderationist Rev. William Hudswell rashly likened his party to fosterbirds turned out of their nests by the young cuckoos they had unconsciously reared. The teetotal Crossley, the next speaker, at once pursued the metaphor, and amid loud cheering and laughter posed an embarrassing question: 'if there be any EGGS in the temperance NEST, (and I am happy to say there are) those eggs are the drunkards who have been reformed; and (turning to the moderation side of the platform)—how many of these eggs did *you* lay?'[21]

The question was of course unfair: teetotalers and moderationists differed in their aims. Like the evangelical movement as a whole, the B.F.T.S. preferred encouraging example-setting from above to generating self-help from below. It sought to confirm the sober in their sobriety rather than to reclaim the intemperate. Both in Britain and America, the propaganda of early anti-spirits societies explicitly sought to confirm the higher ranks in their superior station now threatened by the progress of mass education; their social position would be secure only if they took the lead in morally reforming their social inferiors.[22] By contrast, the early teetotal orator—although he often preached to the converted—also appealed to reprobates, many of whose lives he transformed. The early teetotal meeting was a theatre for dramatizing social mobility, whereas the anti-spirits meeting merely sanctified the existing social hierarchy. The anti-spirits movement's outlook had all the social divisiveness inherent in an organization aiming to 'do good to others'; attendance of drunkards at such meetings was unthinkable [see Plates 6 and 7].

For the moderationist, the drunkard had failed to exert his willpower and deserved denunciation; for the teetotaler the drunkard's will had been paralysed by alcohol, and he deserved sympathy. It was here that the teetotalers made a great step forward on all previous attempts to cure drunkenness. Seventeenth-century temperance reformers display none of the teetotaler's sympathy with the drunkard. The Petition and Advice suggested that drunkards should be disfranchised, and some seventeenth-century congregations excommunicated drunkards instead of assisting them. Seventeenth-century opponents of drunkenness concentrated on deterrence rather than on cure, and even the anti-spirits movement had not completely shaken off their outlook.[23] By contrast, teetotalers like Livesey and Whittaker could be seen walking through the streets arm-in-arm with drunkards whom moderationists spurned as an embarrassment to their cause. The unexpectedness of a teetotaler's kindly look 'went right to my heart', said J. B. Gough, the American reformed drunkard. Teetotal processions of reformed drunkards 'clothed and in their right mind' lent the early teetotal movement all the glamour of a rapid and dramatic panacea for social ills [see Plate 14].[24]

Once the temperance movement had adopted the reclaiming of drunkards as its leading objective it had to transform its local structure. Regular meetings alone could keep the drunkard out of the drinking place, provide him with the companionship he had sacrificed, and give him a shield against the ridicule faced by any working man who tried to rise out of his station. Only by regular visitation, by 'pairings off' with reformed drunkards, and by creating a new framework of life for its members could the teetotal movement secure the ground it had gained. Only by putting the reformed drunkard in office, by keeping him in good company, and by encouraging him publicly to announce his changed life could the incentives to sobriety be adequately reinforced. The early teetotal movement pioneered many of the remedies which have since been rediscovered by Alcoholics Anonymous.

For in contrast to the B.F.T.S.' the teetotal movement's aims were revolutionary and required great personal sacrifices from its members. To avoid losing them at times when the gulf between aspiration and achievement seemed too great, it had to eliminate cross-pressuring and reinforce the attractions of consistency by bringing personal considerations to bear: to encourage teetotalers to reduce their social connexions outside the movement and increase them within. Not only did this mean sectarianism: it also, in the situation of the 1830s, meant providing an alternative set of social institutions. Many of the teetotal movement's activities—the creation of temperance hotels, temperance friendly societies, temperance halls, temperance periodicals and building societies—were really attempts to enable teetotalers to survive in a drink-ridden society. The movement even developed a distinct set of entertainers, who gave temperance meetings the enjoyments which drinkers obtained at the public-house: the Poland Street handbell-ringers, the Shapcott and Edwards families of temperance musicians, and the teetotal singer Simeon Smithard, not to mention the many teetotal lecturers whose performances can hardly be distinguished from music-hall 'turns'.

The teetotal movement did not *initiate* the practice of teetotalism, for in both the seventeenth and nineteenth centuries individuals eagerly conducted dietary experiments on their own persons. One seventeenth-century temperance tract anticipated the nineteenth-century teetotaler's attack on obesity, and Thomas Tryon anticipated the nineteenth-century teetotaler's contempt for the professional doctor. Tryon's personal abstinence stemmed partly from his desire to extend his sphere of personal liberty by subordinating body to soul: extreme libertarian teetotalers in the nineteenth century, like F. W. Newman, did the same.[25] Adam Smith in the 1770s considered teetotalism feasible, Newman Hall's father independently realized about 1818 that teetotalism was the only remedy for his drink cravings, and by the 1820s many individuals later active in the teetotal movement had independently decided to practise water-drinking. The teetotal movement's achievement was simply to advertise teetotalism as a remedy for social evils.

Teetotal societies were formed in several places independently. Rev. W.

Urwick advocated organized teetotalism in tracts published in 1829; Paisley developed the first teetotal society in 1832. But although not first in the field, the Preston teetotalers were the first who vigorously propagated the new cause.[26] Their zeal originated partly in the peculiar political, social and economic situation of Preston in the 1830s. Orator Hunt's 1830 by-election defeat of the Stanleys marked Preston's repudiation of aristocratic patronage. The Stanleys showed that they realized this by severing their connexion with the town and destroying their family mansion, Patten House, which they had visited annually during the Preston races. In the early 1830s Joseph Livesey rented their cockpit, which had once housed the famous gamecocks of the twelfth earl, as a lecture hall for radical and moral reform causes[27] [see Plate 9].

Though not all Preston nonconformists supported Preston teetotalism, the prominent early Preston teetotalers all came from the Liberal/Radical nonconformist section of society, and were backed by the Whig *Preston Chronicle* against the Tory *Preston Pilot*. Livesey, a Scotch Baptist, supported Wood in the 1826 election and heckled Stanley in 1830. Thomas Swindlehurst, the most prominent Preston reformed drunkard, was a Methodist. Anderton the teetotal radical saddler versified for the Preston radicals, though he later split their ranks by campaigning against their public-house political meetings and by trying to sever their infidel connexions; he died in 1855 murmuring verses 1–3 of 14 *Revelation*. The first two nation-wide teetotal missionaries sent out from Preston—Teare and Whittaker—were both Methodist local preachers. James Teare was a shoemaker from the Isle of Man, and spoke with Bible in hand; Thomas Whittaker was haunted by his Methodist Sunday school teacher's vivid descriptions of hell. Preston Temperance Society's first public meeting, presided over by a Wesleyan minister, was held in a Wesleyan preaching-room; the second was held in a Primitive Methodist chapel.[28] Despite radical taunts, Swindlehurst and Livesey did not—by embracing teetotalism—change their political principles. The four teetotalers identifiable in the 1835 Preston pollbook all voted for Perronet Thompson: it was only their political tactics that had changed. Teetotalism was a convenient way of combining political and religious radicalism. In the Preston of the 1830s teetotalism never degenerated into a mere substitute for more radical reforms, as a brief description of Preston's most prominent teetotaler Joseph Livesey will show.

A self-made cheesemonger, who as a child had worked at the loom, Livesey was connected with most of Preston's Liberal causes. Though he supported the ballot and universal suffrage, he did not favour radical attacks on Whig reform bills; small mercies, he thought, should be gratefully accepted.[29] Individual moral reform was his road to social harmony. His monthly *Moral Reformer* (1831–3) attacked corn laws, absentee landlords, brutal sports and lazy parsons, and advocated temperance, forbearance, and free trade in commerce and religion. In the 1840s Livesey became a vigorous Anti-Corn Law Leaguer. He welcomed the railway, loved children and preferred working-class company to any other. An enthusiast for education, he helped establish the local mechanics' institution and promoted a mutual improvement society in his cockpit. His teaching methods were enlightened: Thomas Whittaker recalled seeing the whole class with their families joining hands in a ring to experience the effects of a shock administered by Livesey from a galvanic battery, and indulging, when the shock came, in 'dancing and prancing and grimaces' worthy of a Hogarth or Cruikshank.[30] Livesey was among Preston's leading opponents of the established church. As a youth he had denounced Anglican worldliness, and as an adult he admired the Quakers but joined the Scotch Baptists because he found them less introverted. By the 1830s he was describing the established church as 'a monopoly of the worst description' and his property was seized when he refused to pay Easter Dues.[31] He was a pioneer of that 'practical' religion which swept the country in the late-Victorian period and which substituted for theological and liturgical dispute a concern with moral and social reform.

Livesey's favourite role was that of mediator and peacemaker—whether it be in a street fight, a political squabble, or a dispute between mother and child. He found it difficult to identify himself with any one sect, and often quoted the text 'by their *fruits* ye shall know them'. He believed that many of the poor who lacked the respectable clothes necessary for church attendance would assuredly enter the kingdom of heaven.[32] Modelling his personal conduct on 'the kindly, benevolent, sympathizing, charitable, forgiving spirit of Jesus', he tried to mediate between middle and working class; he attacked vicarious charity, and urged Preston Christians to imitate the apostles by visiting the poor personally. He rebuked Robert Owen for not realizing that Christian principles could remove all social disharmony; they were, he thought, 'the best remedy' for the evils of the factory system.[33] To his credit, he tried to carry his principles into practice, and never used his Christian beliefs as a way of evading his social duties: on the contrary, they were the basis of his social conscience. He was the first to admit in 1830 that the state protected every form of property except that of the poor man; he energetically advertised the sufferings of Preston handloom weavers, impoverished by technological advance. He agitated against the new poor law on the local council and helped to prevent it from being introduced to Preston for decades. Though some Preston teetotalers exaggerated their case and maintained that only the vicious applied for poor relief, Livesey, from his personal visitation of the poor, knew better: 'it is not by charity, but by employment at competent wages', he wrote in 1830, 'that the people ought to be maintained.'[34]

The buoyancy of the Preston teetotalers in the early 1830s perhaps stems partly from the buoyancy of the local economy. The local cotton and flax-spinning trades were prosperous, and in the 1830s Preston grew faster even than Liverpool and Manchester. The *Preston Chronicle* in June 1834 had 'at no former period' seen such a building boom as had occurred locally during the previous two years. Just when teetotal zeal reached its peak, Preston was 'rapidly rising into a town of first-rate importance' for which, indeed, the teetotalers themselves claimed some of the credit.[35] Local tradesmen could not fail to profit from increased sobriety in their customers; and teetotalers, by promoting tea consumption, were also extending the popularity of imports brought from China in exchange for cotton-shirtings, a large proportion of which were made in Preston.[36]

Preston's attention was focused on the drink question by the Beer Act. The standard history of the temperance movement, relying on the Webbs, says that the Beer Act was 'calamitous in its consequences' and that it formed the 'immediate background' of the early teetotal movement.[37] One need not accept the Webbs' interpretation to realize that this measure undermined the exaggerated contemporary faith in the civilizing qualities of beer. By 1834 Preston supported 123 beerhouses as against 106 public-houses: 'we have beer-shops in every street,' Livesey told the parliamentary committee in that year.[38] Livesey had publicly attacked the Beer Bill in 1830 and sent a copy of his attack to Peel. A better way to relieve distress, he argued, was to provide employment and to expand the home market through instituting a minimum wage. He continued to attack the Beer Act during 1831, claiming that without further moral education the people 'should not be enticed by temptations which they cannot resist'; free trade principles could not be applied to so dangerous an article.[39] Here Livesey and the pioneer teetotalers diverged from many Preston Liberals; while the Tory *Preston Pilot* deplored the Beer Act's infringement of magistrates' authority, the Whig *Preston Chronicle* welcomed its cheapening of beer to the poor.[40]

Subsequent controversy cannot obscure the fact that Livesey, both in personal conduct and propagandist energy, was the pioneer Preston teetotaler. By 1826 he was issuing tracts against drunkenness, and by 1830 he was publicly declaring that no intoxicant was a necessity of life.[41] His *Moral Reformer* gradually transformed itself between 1831 and 1833 into the first teetotal periodical. In 1831, alarmed at the effects of a glass of whisky-and-water offered him in the course of business, Livesey and several other Preston acquaintances began to abstain from all intoxicants.[42] But he did not personally create the first Preston anti-spirits society. This was formed by a group of young men attending his cockpit adult school, though Livesey gave public encouragement and temperance tracts to its founder, an Anglican named Henry Bradley. Several outside influences expanded anti-spirits activity in Preston—notably John Finch, a Liverpool Owenite. Anxious to reclaim his drunken and nearly bankrupt debtor Thomas Swindlehurst, a Preston roller-maker, Finch in 1830 brought anti-spirits ideas and tracts from

Liverpool. These were distributed by John Smith 'a respectable chandler' and aroused so much interest that Teare, Livesey, Isaac Grundy (carpet manufacturer) and James Harrison (surgeon) wrote to the Bradford Temperance Society for aid.[43] Its agent, Rev. Mr. Jackson, gave 'two powerful lectures' in Preston, and on 22 March 1832 the Preston Temperance Society held its first public meeting. Also present were a Presbyterian minister and a Quaker from Blackburn, whose temperance society was the first to adopt a pledge forbidding entry to drinking places. This pledge was the model for the Preston society, which also forbade the offering of intoxicants to others. One further influence was that of William Pollard, a Wesleyan temperance advocate from Manchester, whose speech 'almost electrified the audience for a considerable time'.[44]

Who urged the Preston anti-spirits society forward to teetotalism? Several Preston teetotalers claimed the credit. The Anglican John Brodbelt apparently advocated a teetotal pledge even before the Preston Temperance Society was founded. Thomas Swindlehurst's personal experience independently showed him the inadequacy of a mere anti-spirits pledge at least as early as March 1832. James Teare later claimed that he had been convinced of the evils of beer by his visitation of the poor; he believed that in June 1832, by publicly urging the Preston society to adopt a teetotal pledge, he had anticipated Livesey's public adherence to teetotalism by several weeks. But even Teare admitted that in June 1832 he had been personally abstaining from all intoxicants for only six weeks, whereas Livesey had been a teetotaler for much longer. Teare also admitted that he owed to Dr. Harrison the realization that all intoxicants contained alcohol as their intoxicating principle. Such controversies are futile: the bitterness of the dispute between Teare and Livesey's supporters in the 1860s is paralleled in the anti-slavery movement of the 1830s by the controversy between Clarkson and the sons of William Wilberforce; in both cases, the role of individual inspiration was exaggerated. Preston's adoption of teetotalism was a communal affair, and by May 1832 several committee-members were abstaining for a trial period. Practical considerations forced teetotalism upon many of the Society's members independently but simultaneously.[45]

Unlike Livesey, Teare made no theoretical contribution to the transition from anti-spirits to teetotal association. Livesey's *Moral Reformer* in May 1832 published an unsigned article claiming that all intoxicating drinks contained alcohol, and citing Franklin's *Autobiography*—favourite reading for aspiring working men. Teare emphasized Franklin's influence on the Preston teetotalers, and it was from Franklin that Livesey 'got the first hint as to the trifling amount of nutrition contained in malt liquor'.[46] Livesey combined Franklin's hints with information provided by a brewer named Darlington, whom he met at Chester fair, and from these sources created the famous *Malt Lecture*, first delivered in Preston in February 1833. The scientific demonstrations which lent the lecture such popularity probably owed something to Benjamin Barton, a Blackburn chemist and Quaker, who was giving scientific demonstrations of brewing processes in Preston and Blackburn during the same year.[47]

The lecture deserves some attention, not only because it converted several individuals who later became prominent temperance reformers, but also because for the first time it gathered together the movement's apologia. 'LADIES AND GENTLEMEN!' he began, 'the greatness of a country consists not so much in its population, its wealth, or even in its general intelligence, as in its virtue.' Morals and material progress should advance together, yet intemperance was at present costing the country £100 million a year. The cause of intemperance was alcohol alone. Why did people drink it? From self-interest, because they were personally involved in the drink trade; from appetite; from fashion, because of drink customs; from ignorance, because of the 'great delusion' that alcoholic drinks were nourishing; and from 'deep depravity' because many, knowing this, still continued to drink.

To expose the 'great delusion' Livesey argued that 5d. worth (i.e. 6 lb.) of barley was used to make one gallon of ale costing 2/–. Taxation and brewers' and publicans' costs and profits were responsible for the difference between the two figures. Why not merely buy the barley—and consume it in the form of barley-pudding, soup or bread? At some temperance meetings, this point was driven home by free distributions of barley pudding. Livesey then explained the brewing process in detail. He claimed that the malting process produces saccharine matter and destroys about one quarter of the nutriment in the original 6 lb. of barley. In the second stage—mashing—the brewer throws the grist into a vessel of hot water at about 170° F. When the sugar has dissolved, the liquor is drawn off and used for other purposes until it ceases to run sweet; care is taken to prevent other parts of the grain—especially the starch—from coming off too. The mashing process destroys another third of the original barley content. At this stage the liquor is sweet and harmless. Only in the third stage—fermenting—is the damage done. Hop water and yeast are added, the temperature is adjusted, and the sugar decomposes to form carbon dioxide and alcohol. In the early version of the lecture, Livesey claimed that another quarter of the original barley content is destroyed at this stage owing to destruction of the sugar and overflow of barm (which is part of the barley). In the later version, he claimed that only one-sixth is lost at this stage, but he added a fourth phase—fining—in which he claimed that another eighth of the barley content is lost. In the earlier version he therefore maintained that 5 lb. of the original 6 lb. of barley is destroyed, and in the later version 5¼ lb. In the fining process, Livesey claimed that the brewer allows the liquor to settle, and draws off the barley residue at the bottom of the barrel for other purposes.

In the earlier version of the lecture, before audiences athirst for scientific knowledge, Livesey evaporated all the water and spirit from a quart of ale and found that this left only 2¼ oz. of barley residue, or 9 oz. per gallon. Weight for weight, he argued, wheaten bread gives more food value than this extract. Furthermore, you can get more than 9 oz. of bread for 1d. Therefore a pennyworth of bread contains more food value than one gallon of ale costing 2/–. In the later version of the lecture, Livesey abandoned the evaporation and merely quoted a chemist's analysis, showing that a quart of strong ale weighing 39 oz. contains 35 oz. water, 1¾ oz. alcohol and 2¼ oz. barley residue. In the earlier version Livesey gave another demonstration: he ignited the spirits obtained from evaporating a quart of ale and proved 'to the surprise and conviction of many who saw it' that it contained the same intoxicating ingredient as spirits. 'I find that the exhibition has a theatrical effect upon the meetings,' said a teetotaler who performed Livesey's lecture in Wales. Livesey denied that spirits have any nutritional value. 'Whiskey is the soul of beer, and no one can drink beer without drinking whiskey. . . .'[48] Alcohol resembles a bellows which 'blows up the fire, but does not add one single particle of fuel'. It burns the coats of the stomach, injures the liver, and produces 'a red-hot face and a nose covered with brandy blossoms'. It may stimulate in the short-term, but this is merely 'pawning the constitution' and using tomorrow's energy for the requirements of today. Livesey claimed that every quart of ale contains three-and-a-half gills of water: far better and cheaper to drink water in its natural state—or to flavour it with lemon, vinegar, ginger or burnt bread—rather than take it in beer! He then denied that alcohol is fattening by pointing to the large number of lean drinkers. But he also contested the contemporary view that fatness is a sign of health; 'strength of muscle is necessary for the working man; but to be what is called fat is really troublesome, and far from being conducive to activity'. Alcoholic drinks also cover the face with unsightly 'scratches and pimples'.

Livesey went on to refute several objections to teetotalism. It is impossible, he said, to consume alcohol 'moderately': the smallest amount of such a poison is excessive. As for those who claim that the Grace of God upholds their sobriety, he replied that 'the physical influence of liquor cannot be neutralized by any spiritual influence'. Even if no immediate harm results, the drinker sets a bad example to others. Nor does the Bible oppose teetotalism: 'do thyself no harm', 'love one another'—these are its messages. Livesey doubted whether Christ made intoxicating wine at Cana; but even if he did so, total abstinence might be necessary in another age and country. Livesey concluded by urging teetotalers to stand by their principles, and foreshadowed his brief support for prohibitionism in the 1850s when he claimed that magistrates were reluctant to ban public-houses because of 'the *legal* character they sustain in the eyes of the public, in consequence of their *license*'.

Even if discussion is confined to Livesey's scientific argument, several damaging flaws can be detected. In retrospect it is strange that the brewers never published a refutation of this basic document of teetotalism; for they possessed inside information which could have discredited many of its assertions about the brewing process. Even apart from the frequent loaded terms which make Livesey's 'science' look suspiciously like propaganda, six serious errors appear in his account: he wrongly claims that sugar is produced in the malting process; in reality it is produced at the mashing stage. The temperature of the hot water in the fermenting stage should be approximately 150° F not 170° F. Far from being dissolved at the mashing stage, sugar is actually *produced* then. Livesey wrongly assumes that starch remains in the wort when the beer wort is run off, whereas a brewer would not run off any liquid until he had tested to ensure that all starch had been converted to sugar. At the fermenting stage, Livesey wrongly assumed that all sugar content was destroyed, whereas in reality a varying proportion remains according to the type of beer in question. Finally, in his account of the fermenting and fining processes, Livesey seems to confuse yeast with barley-residue.

From the nutritional viewpoint, Livesey's whole concept of analysis is misguided. It is quite wrong to adduce weight-loss during the brewing process as proof that food value has diminished, for food value can actually be *increased* by a chemical transformation which involves a loss in weight; the correct procedure is simply to compare the nutritional value of ingredients and of end-product. Livesey was again wrong in assuming that one can speak so simply of the 'food value' of different items in diet. Their value depends very largely on the total dietary pattern: alcoholic drinks will be fattening, for instance, only if adequate calorific foods are already being obtained and if insufficient exercise is taken to compensate for the excess; no food is *in itself* 'fattening'. Again, the food value of an item of diet is a composite factor, involving assessment of calorific, protein, mineral and vitamin content. The brewing process probably actually created many vitamins—though it was of course unable to create minerals, and was likely to create only a negligible quantity of protein. A pint of modern beer (much weaker than beer in the 1830s) contains 10% of a man's daily requirement of calcium and 15% of his daily requirement of riboflavin. It is also energy-producing; Livesey assumed rather than proved its worthlessness as a food. And if high water-content can discredit a drink, milk would be abandoned as well as beer. Livesey's experimental process was entirely mistaken. A modern analyst would never evaporate the whole sample of beer, for—except for the mineral content—this would alter its very nature. He would take small samples from the original sample, and test for the presence of particular substances. Livesey assumed rather than proved that only the solid matter obtained from evaporating the ale contains food value; nor did he seriously investigate this solid matter. And he never investigated the food value of alternative drinks.

The *Malt Lecture* makes several unjustified psychological assumptions. Livesey assumes that if one consumes barley instead of the beer, the food intake will increase because of the barley's greater food value; this is to ignore the importance of diversifying diet. If a boring diet is merely increased, the individual may fail to increase his food intake till it is sufficient for his minimum needs: he may simply avoid hunger by cutting down on exercise. This would be to produce a type of personality quite the reverse of that cultivated by the teetotal movement! Beer-drinking rather than barley-eating might have increased the total food intake in three ways: by adding different nutrients, by encouraging—through its novelty—a larger intake of the food being consumed, and by itself producing appetite. A further argument: Livesey assumed throughout that the drinker who abandoned beer would obtain at least the equivalent amount of nourishment from eating extra barley. Yet the real alternative to one drink is another drink, and as alternative drinks Livesey recommended only water or mineral waters. These would be less nutritious than beer, and in an age of serious water pollution, positively dangerous. Although the churches during cholera epidemics claimed that only the immoral were afflicted, teetotalers who drank unboiled water at such times were extremely unwise.[49] Most teetotalers in fact drank tea, coffee, and later cocoa, instead of beer. The same quantity of tea, with milk and sugar added, would be slightly higher in calorific content: it would have more proteins and would contain less of some vitamins, more of others. In practice, the drinker who found non-alcoholic drinks less palatable than beer might consume far less of them, and his total food intake would fall.

Again, although no budgets survive from teetotal families before and after the pledge-signing, the drinking money saved might have been spent on other things besides food: perhaps on the clothes, furniture or books which temperance tracts so frequently recommend. Lastly, Livesey assumed throughout that beer was drunk largely as a result of a 'great delusion': from a belief in its food value. In reality, this was often a rationalization used by those who really drank beer for its many other delights—delights which bread and water could never provide.

If they had known the weaknesses in Livesey's nutritional argument, teetotalers would not have shut up shop, for what influenced them in favour of teetotalism was dismay at the prevailing moral degradation: they wielded the dietary argument merely in the hope that it would win over the whole population, and thus widely extend a practice initially adopted for other reasons. Nevertheless the dietary argument was more relevant in the 1830s—when many working men had to choose between eating or drinking—than it would be now; and although his argument was riddled with errors and unjustified assumptions, it is impossible to shake Livesey's two main conclusions. Given the need to abstain from alcoholic drinks, the drinker must logically give up his beer as well as his spirits. And given that food value is the objective, it is wiser to eat barley than to drink beer. Furthermore any flaws which the modern observer can detect in Livesey's arguments do not retrospectively justify his opponents, who usually concentrated only on the social and moral debate, and sometimes abandoned argument altogether in favour of sheer violence.

The *Malt Lecture* was not delivered outside Preston till February 1834, but thereafter its delivery helped to establish teetotalism in the north of England and even in America. It was published and reprinted as a tract many times; but its teachings took many years to gain wide acceptance and were not acknowledged in parliament till the 1870s. Before spreading the new doctrine, Livesey had to win over the Preston anti-spirits society. On 23 August 1832 John King—Methodist, and captain of one of the districts into which the temperance society had divided Preston—complained to Livesey that ale-drinking greatly hindered the temperance cause. Fearing to offend important elements in the society, Livesey suggested that they should both secretly sign a teetotal pledge. At a temperance meeting on 1 September, the 'seven men of Preston' publicly took the pledge experimentally for a year. The grouping was casual, many of the leading Preston teetotalers being absent; their significance was later exaggerated and John King even claimed later that two of the seven had recanted on the night of signing.[50] Livesey was the only prominent teetotaler among them, but they also included the Methodist plasterer Richard Turner [see Plate 10] who first applied the word 'teetotal' to total abstinence from all intoxicants: and Thomas Swindlehurst —later dubbed 'king of the reformed drunkards'. The professions of the 'seven'—cheesemonger, carder, clogger, roller-maker, plasterer, shoemaker and tailor—show how strongly the early teetotal movement attracted craftsmen and tradesmen. A list of 30 Preston reformed drunkards in December 1833 gives some idea of the groups the new movement attracted: it included six spinners, three weavers, three mechanics, three moulders, two plasterers, two shoemakers and one each of the following: joiner, fishmonger, tailor, sizer, sawyer, mole catcher, clogger, broker, roller-maker, cabinet-maker and shopkeeper.[51]

The Preston teetotalers' doctrinal innovation forced them also to innovate in propagandist techniques. The reformed drunkards were insulated from temptation by a round of singing, tea-parties, continuous meetings and counter-attractive recreations. Working men became increasingly prominent in the agitation; Livesey found them far more efficient as temperance workers than the temperance societies' original respectable patrons. Far from concealing their humble origins, reformed drunkards carried onto the temperance platform the symbols and working clothes of their trades. Teetotalism now required only its name: Preston provided this too when the stuttering Richard Turner told a meeting of the Preston Temperance Society in September 1833, amid great cheers, that he would 'be reet down out-and-out t-t-total for ever and ever'.[52] Preston could now embark on its most remarkable achievement—the education of the whole country in teetotal principles.

The origins of the national teetotal movement closely resemble those of the Anti-Corn Law League; in July 1833 several Preston teetotalers, including Livesey, travelled in a cart round the leading towns of Lancashire spreading their gospel.[53] As intoxicants at this time were thought to give public speakers the extra energy they needed, teetotal speakers were living refutations of the prejudices they attacked. In the same year Livesey sent a copy of his *Malt Lecture* to every M.P. His teetotal periodicals, tracts and lectures helped to convert the north and in 1834 he began the *Preston Temperance Advocate*, a model for all future teetotal periodicals. Unlike anti-spirits periodicals, it was designed primarily for the movement's beneficiaries, and included details of teetotal social functions, doctrinal debate, 'varieties' and a woodcut. The speakers traversed town and country spreading the news. Though the Quaker John Giles of Mile End was the first teetotaler in London,[54] Livesey in 1834 was the first vigorous teetotal propagandist there. Like Collins in 1830 he found London apathetic; he was obstructed by the B.F.T.S. and daunted by London's lack of community sentiment. Preston's methods of summoning a meeting were inappropriate in London, and serious teetotal activity did not begin there till 1835.[55]

Influenced by the reports of John Clay, chaplain of Preston gaol, teetotalers exaggerated the moral revolution they had wrought locally. In truth, they had not reduced the number of local beershops, nor did they ever number more than 2,000 individuals in a population of over 40,000. Preston was not a den of vice before the 1830s, nor was it a paradise of virtue afterwards.[56] Preston teetotalers are more important for their innovations in doctrine and for their missionary techniques. They displayed great energy in their propagandism—an energy which, in some cases, as with many reformers, owed something to childhood suffering: Joseph Livesey and Father Mathew were both sensitive as children, teased for their effeminacy.[57] They possessed an almost millennial faith in the completeness and rapidity of the impending social transformation. Their 'temperance reformation' would have social consequences quite as striking as Luther's sixteenth-century venture. The parallels with early Christianity were strong—particularly for men who knew their Bible: the miraculous conversion, the itinerant apostle, the band of adherents distinguished from ordinary men by their superior conduct and absence from the police-court, the success of a new cause among humbler social groups far from the centres of power—all these things had been seen before.[58] But it was not long before these enthusiasts felt the power of the scribes and the pharisees.

6

Moderationists Versus Teetotalers: 1834–1848

Close analysis of early teetotal meetings shows how inevitable was the schism between teetotalers and moderationists. The chairman and officers of the society normally sat on a raised platform, and the speakers stood between them and the members below. The audience usually sat in rows, as though in a theatre or in a religious congregation, with a few groups earnestly conversing in the aisles [see Plates 9 and 11]. Fortunately three quite detailed accounts of early teetotal meetings survive. The best is from Sir George Head who, touring the manufacturing districts in 1835, attended a teetotal meeting in a Bolton Primitive Methodist chapel.

By 8 p.m. the chapel was full. Several well-dressed women and some Quakers were present and the speakers gave addresses from beneath the pulpit. For the first fifteen minutes a stout man gave a 'prosing harangue' in the manner of a field-preacher, and introduced a reformed working man who recounted his past sins fluently for nearly half-an-hour. The stout man cut him off in the midst of a highly dramatic account of his teetotal conversion and introduced Harry Anderton, the Preston teetotaler. 'Up jumped Mr. Anderton, a little, dapper man, as lithesome as an eel, who plunged at once rhapsodically into the middle of his subject, in a speech more than an hour long, and remarkable for an energy and fluency really very uncommon; his utterance was distinct, yet he might be said to talk in demisemiquavers, for he never for an instant stopped, but continued incessantly to spit forth words and syllables with surprising volubility; at each inspiration inhaling breath to the utmost capacity of his lungs, he expended all, even to the last thimbleful, and then, but not before his voice had almost sunk to a whisper, did he refresh himself by a strong gulp, and . . . talk as fast again as ever. All the time he flung his arms about, stamped with his feet, butted with his head at the audience, tossed forward one shoulder, and then the other, striking (like Homer's heroes) the palms of his hands as hard as he was able against one, or both thighs together, and twisted a body, naturally unusually flexible, into many uncouth attitudes.' Sir George thought Anderton had talent, though he suspected that the address had been learned by heart. When Anderton got on to politics, his favourite theme, he grew too excited to hold Sir George's attention, but eventually roused him with a peroration which likened George Washington to Jesus Christ. Anderton's speech swelled with scraps of poetry and a style 'generally very superlatively redundant and inflated'. It was so congested with metaphor and allegory that 'long before he had finished, the pew-doors began to creak, and thick-soled shoes might be heard on their way out of the chapel'.

Like Rosebery's account of the Spurgeon meeting in 1873, this description gains excellence from the fact that Sir George and his readers were completely cut off from the culture of those described. Not all teetotal meetings were as enthusiastic or as political as this. Unlike Sir George, Joseph Taylor who wrote the second account was himself a temperance lecturer; but his memoirs show that he possessed a shrewd eye for significant detail. Describing the weekly teetotal meetings in Severn Street school-room, Birmingham, between 1836 and 1845, he notes that the working men present 'gave the meetings a strong compound odour of oil, sulphur, and japan varnish'. The meetings were enthusiastic, and cries of assent and dissent were allowed; although the masses gathered round the speakers were quiet and still, on the fringes there was 'a movement to and from the door, broken by criticism and debate'. Meetings were regularly attended by respectable individuals like the Cadburys or Joseph Sturge, who had not themselves experienced the horrors of drunkenness. These men 'were helpful by their presence more than by the sympathy of words: they were like pillars in the temple of public improvement'. The remaining two-thirds of the meeting knew the evil at close quarters, and 'did often carry on a warfare, apart from the general proceedings, in groups about the meeting'. There were visiting speakers—like the eloquent Edward Grubb, as high-flown and rapid in speech as Anderton—and frequent tea-meetings, for which even the humblest teetotaler tried to smarten himself, if only with a flower in the buttonhole.

The third description comes from another outsider, the engineer Thomas Wright, who firmly resisted teetotal attempts to convert him. The Garibaldian lifeboat crews of the 1860s lent the teetotal movement one of its last bursts of genuine working-class zeal: this meeting attracted about 200—some highly respectable in appearance, others whose faces denoted former 'slaves to drink'. One reformed drunkard 'after observing that for many years he had scarcely ever had a decent rag to his back, and was often without food, "all through drink", proceeded to dilate upon the fruits of teetotalism: the fruits in his case being, to use his own words, "this slap-up suit of black and this watch", pulling the latter article out of his pocket'. After giving the price of each article, he 'turned his back to the audience to enable them to obtain a back view of the coat, exclaiming at the same time, "There's the fruits of

8. RATTING AT A LONDON PUBLIC-HOUSE IN THE 1840s. Note that the spectators come from all social classes. From H. Mayhew, *London Labour & the London Poor*. [see p. 49]

9. THE PRESTON COCKPIT: FIRST MEETING-PLACE OF THE PRESTON TEETOTALERS, formerly the cockpit of the Stanley family until they abandoned Preston in 1830. From W. Livesey, *The Earliest Days of the Teetotal Movement* (private circulation, 1900), p. 137. [see p. 127]

10. Dicky Turner, the reformed plasterer, who first applied the word 'teetotal' to total abstinence from spirits, wines and beer. Enthusiastic but simple-minded. *Preston Temperance Advocate*, 1836. [see p. 125]

11. A teetotal meeting in Stepney in 1844. *Metropolitan Temperance Intelligencer & Journal*, 27 Apr. 1844, p. 129. [see p. 127]

teetotalism for you" '. He concluded by holding the watch above his head and shouting 'Who wouldn't be a teetotaler?' The watch was of course the sign of respectability among contemporary working men, but many artisans must have agreed with Wright that such exhibitions degraded their class.[1]

It is not surprising that outsiders, and even the leaders of the anti-spirits movement, found all this absurd or even disgusting. But what precisely was occurring at these meetings? Most obviously, recreation—at a social level and at a period when novel recreations were scarce and expensive. In the early days, teetotal meetings sponsored several short speeches from working men rather than one long lecture from a professional orator. The teetotal 'experience meeting' had to rival the public-house 'free-and-easy', and Harry Anderton resembles the modern pop-singer more closely than the subsequent respectability of teetotalism might lead us to expect. Other teetotal advocates sang and danced on the platform, or attracted attention by dressing eccentrically. Thomas Worsnop entered Sedbergh carrying a flag and waving a rattle, and seduced bystanders into hearing his teetotal message by first singing 'Drops of Crystal Water' to the tune of 'Oh! Susannah'. Robert Dransfield gained an audience by standing on his overcoat and posing as a lunatic.[2]

Lacking the time and education needed for preparing a polished, grammatical and reasoned argument, and sharing the puritan's belief in the significance of personal witness—teetotal working men embellished their personal histories with scraps of human anecdote, to ward off any lingering suspicion that their temperament was sour or morose. Growing self-confidence enabled them to adopt a music-hall style involving repartee between speaker and audience. John Hockings, Birmingham's 'teetotal blacksmith', was a master at this approach, as the following example of his oratory shows: 'he had often formed the subject of capital jokes, and it was stated on one occasion when he had to pass through a dreadful snow storm that he had been found dead at Woodstock with two pounds of ice on his stomach! (Great laughter.) They had to wage many a war: yes, and thank God they had achieved many a victory! (Loud applause.) One of the first cries against it was that it was only a tory trick, or a radical trick, or something of that sort. He had in his recollection a man who entertained that notion. He was a mechanic, earning between £2 and £3 per week, who used to be often singing

> Home, home, sweet home;
> There's no place like home!—

And sure enough there was "no place like home", for there was but one chair in it, and that had no bottom to it: and there was but one table, and that was the soap box. (Laughter.) And this was all the result of drunkenness [cf. Plate 24]. He was a fellow-workman, and a better disposed man, and a kinder husband, was not to be found when sober. I asked him to sign the pledge one night: he knew I had signed: but he refused. "Ah, Jack," he said, "I can see through it all: its all a tory trick, and I'd have my right arm cut off before I'd be led away to pledge myself. Ah, I'd expected better things of thee, Jack." At last I caught him on a Friday night. (Laughter and applause.) That's the time to catch 'em lads: that's the time to take 'em: when the pocket's empty; when its nothing but water and work.'[3] Refracted through the reporter's occasional wordiness, this teetotal speech has all the fluency, familiarity, shapelessness, colloquialism and humour of a professional working-class entertainer. With Hockings' dialect, gestures and inflexions, it possesses all the immediacy of the comic turn. To modern eyes, nineteenth-century popular religion seems a strange combination of high-mindedness and sheer good fun.

But the temperance meeting had a more serious function: it witnessed a peculiar form of secularized conversion experience. By no means all members of teetotal societies were 'reformed drunkards'. Many took the pledge for example's sake, and had no 'past' to atone for. Many teetotal societies allotted separate 'experience meetings' to the reformed drunkards, but always paraded them as trophies on their platforms and processions. No conversion seems to have occurred at the three meetings already described, but conversions were frequent. When Thomas Worsnop, woolcomber, made his début on the teetotal platform with the pronouncement 'I have begun to abstain; I will have no more *swill*', tears were rolling down his cheeks and falling at his feet. Audiences in the 1830s did not feel the modern need to avoid the public shedding of tears, and Carlyle noted that working men discussing temperance spoke 'evidently from the heart'.[4] The drunkard's misery was a theme suffused with drama and tragedy for working people who, if not themselves at that time in poverty, would probably be so at some stage in their lives—in the early years of parenthood and in old age.

Although teetotal meetings were often linked with religious recruiting-drives, they in fact mark a phase in the secularization of the conversion experience. As political attitudes came to be held with almost religious fervour, the political conversion-experience—the sudden recognition of social injustice or political error—became widespread: Oastler, Thomas Cooper, the many converts of T. H. Green and the early socialists spring to mind. The temperance conversion resembled the religious conversion, but substituted social aspiration for doctrinal belief. According to Leuba, J. B. Gough's conversion was 'practically the conversion of an atheist: neither God nor Jesus Christ is mentioned. The sense of his degradation and worthlessness does not involve in his mind responsibility for sin to others; he is absorbed in his own self.'[5] Accounts of Gough's conversion were circulated widely and were included among the *Ipswich Temperance Tracts*. Churchmen were naturally alarmed, and Bishop Wilberforce rightly warned his hearers against mistaking 'a seeming of moral recovery from natural or secondary causes, for the renewal of the soul by the influence of the Spirit of God'.[6]

Religious conversion begins with a consciousness of sin: teetotal conversion began with the drunkard's recognition of his misery. Uneducated listeners readily identified with the reformed drunkards who lectured on these occasions and who were now so demonstrably changed in outward appearance. Almost insensibly, therefore, the listener acquired a 'faith' in teetotalism which he recorded by signing the pledge at the end of the meeting. At first the teetotal society had no control over the convert beyond personal rebuke; sanctions were therefore built up by ensuring that 'works' rapidly followed 'faith', in the third stage of the conversion sequence—recantation. Almost as soon as they had taken the pledge, reformed drunkards mounted the temperance platform. Their addresses were too stereotyped to be spontaneous; clearly the pattern of conversion was learned. The personal testimony begins with a familiar list of sins, suitably bowdlerized; these inevitably bring misery, which vanishes only with the signing of the pledge. 'Here I stand one of the most notorious drunkards that ever stood before the public,' began 'J. R.' a Salford reformed drunkard, at a temperance meeting in 1835: 'I am sure that everybody in Salford must know me, for I frequently have been seen without shoes on my feet, and without a hat to my head; and many times I have pawned the coat off my back for that destructive drink: I would have done anything in order to obtain it'—and so on.[7] When safely rooted in the past, these sins—for audience and speaker—acquired all the excitement of the horror-film.

The origins of the repudiated drinking habits are never discussed, the pledge-signing always leads to happiness and prosperity: these were plainly fantasies produced for an occasion, not real-life narratives. The reformed drunkard was providing the teetotal society with a vulgarized *Grace Abounding*. But such addresses greatly helped the former drunkard—for by publicly discussing his past he could come to terms with it; his public stand committed him to his new life, and helped to distance past miseries from the present. Some teetotalers even competed in piling up imaginary and now-discarded sins which could be recounted with no sense of shame, as though they had been committed by somebody else. Taine regarded this production of living testimony to theological truth as a 'thoroughly English notion'; it was certainly effective with early teetotal audiences, however much it might disconcert the theologians.

The final stage in the conversion process—'justification'—was the sense of joy which many reformed drunkards undoubtedly experienced at the remarkable transformations teetotalism had produced in their lives: 'I soon experienced such an improvement in my sight', said William Smith, a clogger and self-confessed 'wild man of the woods' in appearance, 'that my spectacles were unnecessary, my rheumatism and other complaints disappeared, and I grew so much more bulky, that I had to make a loop of a rosin end to lengthen the waistband of my trowsers, that it might meet and button, and I was so increased in agility that I could frisk about like a lad of seventeen. Thus was I reclaimed. . . .' Richard Turner told a meeting in 1837 that 'his heart felt more than his tongue could express; his heart leaped for joy, and he had reason to feel thus elated. Think what I WAS and what I AM'.[8]

The third function of teetotal meetings cannot be discerned merely from studying the teetotal meeting itself: it can be discovered only after observing the contemporary environment. The teetotal conversion bridged the gulf between the respectable and the unrespectable poor. The pledge-signer was promising to change not only his complete circle of friends but also his whole mode of life [see Plates 12 and 13]. The temperance conversion often accompanied a separate religious conversion, for in those days Christians could still be distinguished by appearance and conduct as well as by belief. Converted in a Wellington Methodist revival of the 1830s, William Smith joined a friendly society, became a teetotaler and local preacher, married a young lady he met at a class-meeting, and took a better job all in a remarkably short space of time. In a society with few recreations beyond religion and drink, there was no middle way. Teetotal tracts correctly portrayed the individual as poised between dramatic alternatives, though they exaggerated the extent to which he was in command of his own fate. Drinking habits were becoming the businessman's yardstick for distinguishing the trustworthy from the unreliable, the minister's criterion for dividing the sheep from the goats. The teetotaler's journey through life resembled Pilgrim's progress: the terrible dangers and beguiling temptations which beset his path could be resisted only by relying on the support of one's friends, by drawing upon inner resources nurtured since childhood, and by shunning any occasion which might relax the will. It was a frightened, narrow and unfulfilled existence, for the terrible consequences of infidelity, immorality and drunkenness could be seen on every side; but it was a way of living which made for strong-mindedness and individual achievement.[9]

To help the new converts, the early teetotal societies monopolized much of their time: they were appointed to some petty office and encouraged to atone for past misdeeds by converting as many of their fellows as possible. Their changed life was emphasized by badges and regalia, and by the flags and banners of the teetotal procession [see Plate 14]. 'We live in an age of advertising,' wrote *The Templar of Wales* in 1875, 'and what more resplendent and dazzling advertisement could we have than our gaudy collars?'[10] Members of the teetotal society visited the convert in his home, inquired after his welfare, accompanied him to meetings and encouraged him at every stage to commit himself publicly to his new mode of life. Reformed drunkards often faced cruel ridicule from former drinking companions, who resented this implied criticism of their conduct. If only to compensate for lost friends, converts banded together and withdrew from a world rife with temptation. The number of joint activities was expanded until they became almost coextensive with the broad area for which the teetotal movement prescribed norms of conduct. Teetotalers provided each other with respectable company and patronized temperance counter-attractions to the public-house. The early teetotal societies, like so many nonconformist chapels of the day, were genuine communities, and teetotalism constituted a form of freemasonry among working men. In this way, respectability was recruited.

The fourth role of the teetotal meeting can be discerned only through studying the respectable middle-class members who were present. These were Quakers, individualists, dissenters and men of character—key-figures in the religious and philanthropic movements which cemented the early Victorian alliance between middle and working classes. Their support was vital to the prosperity even of a Chartist locality, and teetotal societies depended heavily upon them, especially in rural areas. Here were the Cadburys, the Carpenters, the Sturges, the Samuel Morleys, the Henry Sollys and the Hugh Masons—men who built their political hopes upon the radical alliance of dissenters with respectable working men. They were the equivalents in the early Victorian teetotal world of the intellectuals in the world of late Victorian Labour: respectable and high-minded individuals seeking to influence working people in favour of their cause by going to live among them.[11] Like so many contemporary philanthropists, these men were presiding over an extension of public concern to social outcasts formerly not deemed worthy of citizenship. Religion was recruiting itself from ever lower social levels, and in the process was gradually losing its other-worldly attributes. Even in its anti-spirits phase, the temperance movement made the democratic assumption that all classes should take the same pledge, because all classes suffered from the same temptations. The temperance movement's respectable supporters were gaining allies for the radical attack on privilege, deference, corruption and violence—grooming working men to add their numbers to the energy and righteous indignation of the radical middle class. For a middle class which lacked social concern for, and support from, the masses could never hope to overturn aristocratic government.

Many teetotal speakers, like John Cassell, overcame the working man's very real terrors of public speaking by learning addresses parrot-fashion; some, like Richard Turner, made serious blunders when venturing into abstruse aspects of teetotal advocacy like the Bible wine question—that 'radio three' of the teetotal recreational world. John Dunlop in 1840 noted how teetotalism had uncovered 'a large amount of native oratory among the humbler classes'; for such men the new profession of temperance agent was created, a useful stepping stone to higher things. For Thomas Whittaker the teetotal platform was 'one of the best schools for training any one ambitious of public life this country offered'.[12]

The anti-spirits leaders were alarmed. Teetotalism seemed to be moving in secular directions, and was giving too much power to uncultivated laymen; the clergymen who dominated the B.F.T.S. found themselves losing control of the movement they had helped to establish. Furthermore the elevating tone was being drained out of the movement by the vulgarity and purely recreational character of the teetotal meeting. Nor had the anti-spirits movement originally been designed to promote social mobility or to enable working men to set an example to their superiors; once these developments were joined to radical and dissenting views, schism in the temperance movement was inevitable. Moderationist complaints can broadly be described as cultural, psychological, religious and political.

Teetotal confessions seemed 'calculated rather to disgust than to persuade'.[13] With drunkenness as with prostitution, nineteenth-century lecturers often dwelt unduly upon the details of the vice they were combating. Leaving aside questions of taste, it was certainly wrong to lend fascination to the forbidden sin by harping upon it. Nor was the drunkard, by associating closely with other reformed drunkards in a highly emotional atmosphere, likely to become a balanced human being. To the more cultivated moderationists, whose religion was much less emotional and Corybantic, teetotal confessions seemed shameless. But three pleas can be made in defence of the teetotalers. Their crude methods at least converted former drunkards whom the B.F.T.S. had been unable to reach; without his broad dialect, Thomas Whittaker [see Plate 15] in the 1830s would have made little impact on the miners in the north-east. Again, like many successful evangelical movements, teetotal effort was unfairly discredited by many 'false Christs'—by the bogus Magnus Klein in the north, for instance, and by 'Father Moore' in the west; complaints against these adventurers were still being made in the 1870s. Finally, rational advocacy was not unknown in the teetotal movement. Dr. Grindrod in the 1830s and 1840s argued the physiological case with some sophistication. Dr. F. R. Lees engaged in public argument for thirteen hours with a pertinacious moderationist. Marathon but inconclusive public debating contests were as frequent in the temperance movement as they were among contemporary Owenites. During the early 1840s Dr. Lees engaged in several, and often published them as tracts—though not always with the concurrence of his sparring-partners.[14]

The moderationists' psychological objection centred on teetotal extremism. In their attitudes to convention, too many teetotalers moved from dissent to defiance. For instance they claimed that moderate drinkers were 'the chief promoters of drunkenness', because drunkards were more likely to follow their example. Some teetotalers made a virtue of their extremism:

'truth was always extreme', said the veteran Lees in 1895: 'a thing was either truth or falsehood, never in the middle. Virtue was virtue, not half vice.'[15] Yet some advocates of unpopular causes, notably G. J. Holyoake —and even some teetotalers, like Wilfrid Lawson and Samuel Bowly—managed to present their case without giving offence. Why were so many teetotalers unable to do likewise? Largely because of their social position. Bowly and Lawson were not reformed drunkards, and therefore felt no need to redeem a drunken past by impassioned attacks on their former sin. If energetic advocacy produced conversions, nineteenth-century religious organizations were shrewd to exploit the talents of former apostates like Thomas Cooper and Joseph Barker: for the reprobate burns to atone for his past misdeeds. A similar sense of haste also affected many who had no 'past' to live down, but who regretted the many religious opportunities which they had neglected: 'how many souls might have been saved, who are now lost, if I had but begun this blessed work earlier!' exclaimed Mrs. C. L. Wightman, the Shrewsbury temperance reformer, in 1858.[16] Again, unlike many early teetotal speakers, Bowly and Lawson had no need to earn their living by their tongue, and were therefore less tempted to court applause. And because they were not working men, they never experienced the excitement of the unaccustomed appearance on a public platform or the exhilaration of feeling that their class had discovered a cure for drunkenness which had eluded the educated and the wealthy. Extremist panaceas and austere religions attract the under-privileged, for the existing situation is too painful for them to contemplate anything but a sudden transformation.

Perhaps the most convincing excuse for teetotal extremism was the vulgarity and cruelty of the opposition which teetotalers often faced. Working-class neighbourhoods have always resented individual working men who 'give themselves airs', and many temperance reformers did just this. Nineteenth-century England witnessed a continuous guerrilla warfare between rough and respectable working men. At Leeds in June 1839, two women appeared in court for assaulting the wife of Mr. Judd, a teetotaler. The incident occurred during a fight which broke out after Judd had been burned in effigy outside his house in the working-class area named Pottery Field. Publicans did not shrink from the crudest expedients for retaining their customers. Just as opponents of the Salvation Army in the 1880s organized a parody in the form of the 'Skeleton Army', so publicans in the 1830s engineered 'anti-teetotal demonstrations' or parodies of the teetotal festival. At Huddersfield after a visit from Father Mathew in 1843, local brewers gave 360 gallons of beer for a demonstration which, according to a teetotal source, ended in 'filthy and disgusting scenes'. In summer 1841 a teetotal picnic in Wychwood Forest—largely composed of women—began well with an opening hymn and addresses. But during tea, 'drunkenness, ignorance, and brutality in the shape of bands of men from the surrounding village . . . surrounded the platform, and perhaps never did vice and ignorance appear in a more degraded and disgusting form'. Urged on by a carbuncled Charlbury doctor, the mob broke up the idyllic scene. A procession of 300 anti-teetotalers, three-quarters of them boys, broke up Father Mathew's visit to Bermondsey in 1843 and had to be chased off by the police. No doubt the London publicans were behind it—for some men were decorated from head to foot in hop-leaves, others were carrying five-gallon cans of beer, and all were holding pint pots. So disgraceful did opposition tactics sometimes become that teetotalism actually profited. On Whit Monday at Preston in 1833, the teetotal forces marched soberly with band and banner to their meeting and contrasted very favourably with the drunken procession of 'anti-hypocriticals' who preceded them.[17] The difficulties facing the teetotalers were great enough without opposition of this type, and it is not surprising that teetotalers drew together exclaiming 'he who is not with us is against us'. Bitterness was endemic in a debate between adversaries who, by their very conduct, could not avoid taking sides.

Religious objections were often raised to teetotal oratory: were they sincere? 'Never knew an objector to Teetotalism, who had *only* an objection professedly derived from the Bible' wrote John Dunlop: fear for pocket, friends, health, or reputation were, in his view, 'the real obstacles, not the pretended Bible objections'.[18] Each side industriously searched the Bible for support: 'every "creature of God" was good!' said the moderationist (illogically, if he already abstained from spirits); 'all things were lawful but not necessarily expedient!' the teetotaler replied. 'Look at the water-drinking animal creation!' urged the teetotalers (admitting a kinship between man and brute which, in Darwin, they vigorously repudiated). 'See how the Bible wines failed to intoxicate!' they persisted (elaborating forms of Higher Criticism which elsewhere they abhorred). Convinced that the Bible wines were non-intoxicating, teetotalers in Cornwall, Lincolnshire and elsewhere insisted on using Beardsall's or Wright's specially manufactured communion grape-juice. By the late 1830s, fortified by tales of reformed characters sent back to their vice by sips at the altar-rail, teetotalers provoked furious controversy within nonconformist congregations. These disputes nourished a second religious criticism. Teetotalers too readily assumed that abstinence automatically improved the character; they ignored the new and more insidious weaknesses which tended to replace the old sins. Despite Wilberforce's warnings, the notion that Christianity was a quality superadded to the life of the individual—rather than an influence suffusing the whole—was all too common among evangelical Christians. Charles Kingsley was one of many who opposed teetotalism for generating 'that subtlest of sins spiritual pride'.[19]

Finally the moderationists' political objections. They feared the dangers of 'enthusiasm' which in the 1830s readily took a political turn and, two centuries before, had provoked revolution. Teetotal addresses displayed many of the qualities listed by Coleridge as characteristic of the demagogue.[20] Working men on teetotal platforms were stepping out of their appointed station, and might one day leave teetotalism for less reputable causes. Worse, teetotal advocates were often wanderers by temperament, or drifted into itinerant speechifying when unemployed. Temperance work seemed actually to be spreading social indiscipline.

All these moderationist complaints had substance; yet many sceptics were captured by one seductive teetotal argument: wielding the scriptural exhortations 'that no man put a stumbling-block . . . in his brother's way' and that 'it is good neither to eat flesh, nor to drink wine, whereby thy brother stumbleth, or is offended, or is made weak' (*Romans* xiv, 13, 21), teetotalers argued that unless the respectable lent their support, adherence to a teetotal society would be a public confession that one had a shameful past, and the temperance movement would lose all its refining influence. Many high-minded teetotal leaders—Henry Solly, James Sherman, J. J. Gurney, Thomas Guthrie and Samuel Morley among them—were as afraid of causing others to sin as of sinning themselves, and in capitulating to this 'weaker brethren' argument, allowed vice to infringe the liberties of virtue.

Turning from the overall controversy to the particular schisms promoted by teetotalism, the history of the anti-spirits societies in the manufacturing towns of northern England reveals an affinity between extremism and low social status. The early Preston and Rochdale anti-spirits societies were supported by their local M.P.s and by local public figures. Moses Holden at Preston and Benjamin Barton at Blackburn linked the anti-spirits society with local adult education schemes; Livesey, James Harrison and T. B. Addison, besides supporting the anti-spirits society, were all prominent supporters of the Preston Institution for the Diffusion of Knowledge. The first committee of Preston Temperance Society consisted principally of 'ministers, doctors, and moneyed men'. Members of the local literary and philosophical societies and of the urban intelligentsia—such as John Bright and C. T. Thackrah in Rochdale and Leeds, respectively—were prominent. The meeting which created the Leeds Temperance Society was chaired by Newman Cash—railway promoter and merchant—in the presence of Marshall, the leading flax manufacturer.[21] These inventors and manufacturers were precisely the groups which sponsored the anti-slavery and franchise reform movements in the northern towns.

But when an anti-spirits society adopted the teetotal pledge, gentility usually departed in a hurry. The rise of teetotalism within the anti-spirits movement constitutes a *coup* by an élite of working men allied with radicals and nonconformists. 'I speak the sentiments of a large class of society,' said the moderationist Plint at the Leeds debate of 1836: 'NOT OURS' retorted his teetotal hecklers.[22] For as soon as emphasis switched from preserving the sober to reclaiming the intemperate, the temperance movement outgrew its original respectable basis of support. The drunkard needs constant attention if his cure is to prove permanent, and this the original anti-spirits leaders were not prepared to give; a similar conflict lay behind the Vice Society's supersession of the more respectable Proclamation Society at the beginning of the century. Moderationist respectability was accompanied by caution, lack of drive and insensitivity to the working man's needs. 'If they would work', said Livesey, 'there is no objection to men of rank or wealth, but *they will not.*'

To judge from the surviving private correspondence between Lord Stanhope, president of the British and Foreign Society for the Suppression of Intemperance from 1839, with his Society's secretary John Burtt, Livesey's assessment of aristocratic powers of work was correct. For Stanhope, though a courageous and enthusiastic defender of teetotalism, seems to have taken no part in the day-to-day activity of his organization. He merely presided from a distance—making a policy suggestion here, presiding over a meeting there, but doing little else. Observers of modern political parties have noticed a similar relation between activism and social class: the well-to-do take a small part in the daily running of political organizations because they have less need of the recreation they provide, they lack the lively spirits who make the meetings more interesting, and they have other opportunities for confirming their own social status. The contrast between the anti-spirits and teetotal society reflects the familiar distinction between the liberal and the radical organization: in contrast to the anti-spirits movement, teetotalism offered the attractions of a sudden and dramatic social transformation. The consequent gulf between aspiration and existing reality ensured not only that there was much more work to do, but also that the members would feel sufficiently inspired to accomplish it. Its strength lay in the personal commitment of its members, not in the social prestige of its leaders.[23]

The first schism occurred as early as 1830 at Warrington, where the anti-spirits vicar clashed with humble teetotal pioneers from the Independent Methodist chapel in Stockton Heath. At Preston, trouble resulted in 1832 from introducing teetotalism into the anti-spirits society; there were many complaints of teetotal open-air meetings on Sunday and of teetotal speeches tinged with radicalism. At Middlesbrough in 1835 James Maw, a future Chartist, joined with local Primitive Methodists in championing teetotalism against anti-spirits leaders, and walked through the streets advertising his cause by waving a rattle. At Kendal, religious and class divisions intertwined: Unitarians and working men championed teetotalism against the religious and anti-spirits orthodoxy of local respectability. But schism was most dramatic at Leeds, where the moderationists—much against their will—were forced into an open debate with their teetotal opponents and were defeated.[24] The decline in social status which accompanied the move towards teetotalism in Rochdale is strikingly reflected in the handwriting of its minute-book. Over forty years later John Bright told a meeting of Birmingham publicans why he had left the Rochdale society at this point: 'I absented myself a very long time ago, when I was quite young, from temperance meetings to a great extent . . . because I did not like to hear the language in which you were spoken of.' The meeting of the teetotal Thomas Whittaker, in his fustian trousers and check shirt, with the Penrith moderationist wearing a gold-chain and carrying a silver-topped cane epitomizes the social gulf between teetotalers and moderationists.

Only five lists of teetotalers' occupations have been found—for Derby (1836–), Aberystwyth (1836–8), Oswestry (1840), Middlesbrough (1851) and Manchester (1860); these cover 2,142 individuals of both sexes. Unfortunately teetotal registers were not compiled with the needs of twentieth-century historians in mind. A third of the signatories give no occupation: should one assume that they were gentlemen of leisure? or out of work? Even where occupations are given, who but the experienced local historian knows the social status of a 'shipbuilder', 'agent' or 'jeweller'? These defects in the material must be lived with. Revd. E. W. Edgell, visiting a temperance meeting at Westminster in 1838, found an audience of 'bricklayers' labourers, and people who sell things in the streets; not however without a mixture of respectable persons'. His analysis is confirmed by the five lists, which include some occupations unmistakably at the bottom end of society—72 labourers, 39 porters, 15 sweeps and 4 excavators. The vast majority are tradesmen: there are 47 weavers, 89 shoemakers, 47 tailors and 31 carpenters. At Oswestry there are 27 colliers and 6 rockmen, and at Middlesbrough 70 sailors. But there is also a leavening of decidedly respectable individuals—9 nonconformist ministers, 3 booksellers, several shopkeepers, a schoolmaster and a librarian. It is quite clear that these societies gathered recruits from all social levels below the aristocracy and gentry.[25]

From schism at the local level to schism between the national societies. The first national teetotal organization was the British Association for the Promotion of Temperance [see Figure 8]. Lancashire in 1833 contained about a third of the British anti-spirits movement's membership, and at Livesey's instigation a meeting of local temperance society representatives was held in September 1834. The meeting urged societies to raise an agency fund, to concentrate on personal visitation, and to supplement moderationism with a teetotal pledge. In 1835 the second conference, chaired by Rev. Joseph Barker, followed the advice of the Manchester delegates and formed itself against Livesey's wishes into a national society, the B.A.P.T. The Association tried to affiliate on a teetotal basis with the B.F.T.S. but the negotiations failed; by 1836 it had become militant enough in its teetotalism to adopt the 'long' pledge, which forbade the offering as well as the drinking of intoxicants. It despatched as teetotal missionaries Thomas Whittaker to the north and James Teare to the midlands and west. These two Lancashire working men were the first among many northern temperance lecturers seeking to stir up self-reliance among working men in the south. The teetotal movement showed none of the anti-slave trade movement's timidity about sending lecturers all over the country; nor did its lecturers always show Clarkson's concern for decorum on the platform. Early teetotal lecturers held forth at fairs, street corners—anywhere where crowds were gathered.

Teetotalism was slow in establishing itself among Londoners. A meeting held in August 1835 in the Regent Street rooms of a master-tailor named Grosjean led eventually, with the aid of lectures from Preston's teetotal zealots, to the formation of the New British and Foreign Society for the Suppression of Intemperance, the first London-based national teetotal society. Here again working men were enthusiasts for the new development; the Society's first South London teetotal auxiliary was founded by William Morris, a typefounder, with a few mechanics and labourers to aid him. Despite friendly professions, the new society aimed, through moderate teetotal advocacy, to absorb all the members of the B.F.T.S. Yet this could never be done unless the Society allowed the more moderate 'short' pledge: in 1836 it therefore bartered its exclusive long pledge for money and influence. By allowing its members to take either pledge, it attracted away from the B.F.T.S. prominent nonconformists and wealthy Quakers like Dr. Pye Smith and Richard Barrett.[26] While the B.F.T.S. now obtained most of its funds from the £1–£5 group, the N.B.F.S.S.I., which after 1838 changed its name to the New British and Foreign Temperance Society, obtained most from the £5–£99 group. Neither society raised much from gifts under £1; like other early Victorian reform movements they probably found that it was not profitable to depend on small working-class subscriptions, even if they could be obtained.[27]

London and the south provided funds for the N.B.F.S.S.I. and most of its leading donors were Quakers. At least half the Society's annual income came from donations over £5 and its total receipts from donations rose from £300 in 1836–7 to over £3,500 in 1840–1. Like the B.F.T.S. it spent half its funds on administrative expenses and salaries, half on propaganda. Lord Stanhope, an eccentric but progressive man of science, presided, and by 1840 the Society employed seven agents of whom at least four had learnt their teetotalism from Lancashire advocates. London teetotalism prospered at first: *The Times* in July 1839 watched teetotal excursionists embarking in the rain for Herne Bay and bearing the jeers of a London dockside crowd 'with perfect placidity'. Compared with the impressive teetotal procession through London in 1839, Hetherington's *Odd-Fellow* considered the coronation procession 'a mere bauble'.[28]

John Dunlop, who had by now become a teetotaler, was asked by a parliamentary committee where the temperance movement had so far made

FIG. 8

National temperance organizations: 1830–1873

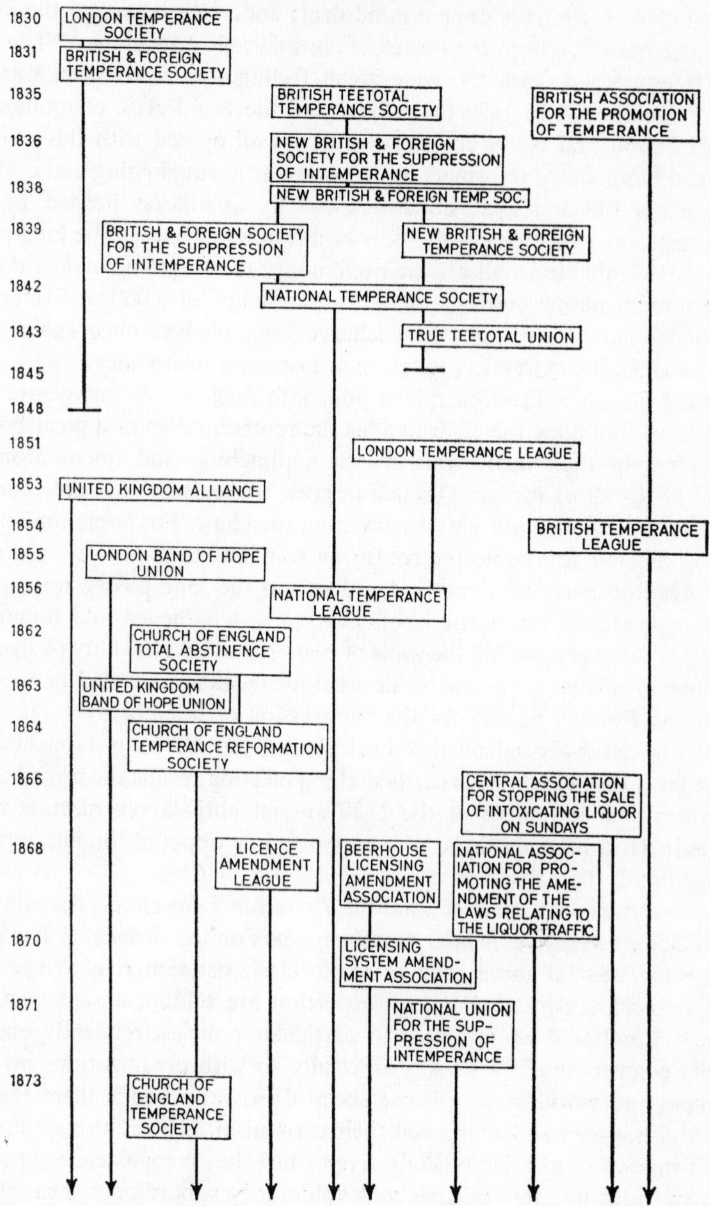
1830 LONDON TEMPERANCE SOCIETY
1831 BRITISH & FOREIGN TEMPERANCE SOCIETY
1835 BRITISH TEETOTAL TEMPERANCE SOCIETY
BRITISH ASSOCIATION FOR THE PROMOTION OF TEMPERANCE
1836 NEW BRITISH & FOREIGN SOCIETY FOR THE SUPPRESSION OF INTEMPERANCE
1838 NEW BRITISH & FOREIGN TEMP. SOC.
1839 BRITISH & FOREIGN SOCIETY FOR THE SUPPRESSION OF INTEMPERANCE
NEW BRITISH & FOREIGN TEMPERANCE SOCIETY
1842 NATIONAL TEMPERANCE SOCIETY
1843 TRUE TEETOTAL UNION
1845
1848
1851 LONDON TEMPERANCE LEAGUE
1853 UNITED KINGDOM ALLIANCE
1854 BRITISH TEMPERANCE LEAGUE
1855 LONDON BAND OF HOPE UNION
1856 NATIONAL TEMPERANCE LEAGUE
1862 CHURCH OF ENGLAND TOTAL ABSTINENCE SOCIETY
1863 UNITED KINGDOM BAND OF HOPE UNION
1864 CHURCH OF ENGLAND TEMPERANCE REFORMATION SOCIETY
1866 CENTRAL ASSOCIATION FOR STOPPING THE SALE OF INTOXICATING LIQUOR ON SUNDAYS
1868 LICENCE AMENDMENT LEAGUE
BEERHOUSE LICENSING AMENDMENT ASSOCIATION
NATIONAL ASSOCIATION FOR PROMOTING THE AMENDMENT OF THE LAWS RELATING TO THE LIQUOR TRAFFIC
1870 LICENSING SYSTEM AMENDMENT ASSOCIATION
1871 NATIONAL UNION FOR THE SUPPRESSION OF INTEMPERANCE
1873 CHURCH OF ENGLAND TEMPERANCE SOCIETY

the most impression: 'we have done little with respect to what may be regarded as the dregs of society', he replied: 'they probably drink even more than they did ten years ago; with regard to the respectable portion of the working classes, we have done a good deal; and, with regard to the middle classes, we have . . . been the means of considerable advantage.'[29] The long-pledge men gained from the widespread feeling that teetotalism was progressing too slowly. In 1839 the majority of the N.B.F.T.S. committee, the North London and many country auxiliaries all agreed with three visiting American temperance reformers in favouring a thoroughgoing and exclusive long pledge. But the East London and City auxiliaries headed by Earl Stanhope wanted the Society to allow both types of pledge. The long-pledge men were defeated in small private preliminary meetings and staked their all on the annual public meeting. Before an audience of 4,000 in Exeter Hall they demanded a return to the exclusive long pledge; once again, as at Leeds in 1836, the extremists rested their hopes on democracy.

Edward Grubb, a Preston-trained nonconformist teetotal advocate, stood before Lord Stanhope the chairman 'as the representative of a great body of tee-totallers in the North' and 'as the unflinching and uncompromising enemy' of the short pledge. Discussion grew so heated that Lord Stanhope could preserve his dignity only by vacating the chair. For some time pandemonium reigned, and amid the confusion someone began to play the grand organ. Dunlop eventually restored order, and the long pledge was upheld; thus ended, after seven hectic hours, 'the most lengthened and tumultuous meeting . . . ever held within the walls of Exeter Hall'.[30] The short-pledge men, including Lord Stanhope and some wealthy Quakers, seceded to form the British and Foreign Society for the Suppression of Intemperance—the 'Suppression Society'—based on the short pledge, but allowing its members to go further if they chose. This earth-shaking meeting recalls the clash between moderates and extremists at the 1830 annual anti-slavery meeting or the dispute in 1885 between those who supported or opposed linking organized feminism with the Liberal party.

'The real cause of a quarrel', said the *Temperance Spectator*, describing the 1839 incident twenty years later, 'rarely appears on the surface.'[31] The pledge controversy was far more than a simple clash between rival remedies for intemperance. Self-interest and self-assertion are seldom absent from such disputes. Emotional commitment to particular policies frequently obstructs sensible compromise.[32] This was especially so with organizations involving dissenters and working men whose social deprivation made them eager for office and honours and sharpened their extremism. Schism also results from the self-interest of salaried officials. Even when they recognize the superiority of a new principle, few officials will voluntarily subordinate themselves to newcomers. When creating the T.G.W.U. Ernest Bevin wisely ensured its success by retaining all officers of constituent unions at full pay.[33]

Apart from personal antagonisms, struggles for office—and the self-interest of liquor-selling lodging- and coffee-house keepers defending their livelihood—the controversy revealed antagonisms involving class, region, organizational structure and personality. Broadly speaking, short-pledge men were of a higher social standing than long-pledge men, and were therefore more hostile to American innovations. The short-pledge men did not wish to dismiss servants who refused to work without alcohol, or to deprive their guests of intoxicants. Only the long pledge could force wealthy teetotal City bankers and peers to cut themselves off from friends and relatives and form a self-contained abstaining sect, as working men had long been forced to do. 'Alas, for Lords Stanhope and Bexley, and their hospitable boards!' exclaimed the *British Critic* in 1839, 'what is a peer without wine on his table?'[34] Lord Stanhope was not in fact betraying the temperance movement's original objectives, for those objectives had always been ambiguous. The anti-spirits pioneers had not realized at first that the attack on drunkenness through personal abstinence would eventually involve so complete a break with normal social life. The correlation between extremist standpoint and lower social grade is repeated in all subsequent temperance schisms—between teetotalers and anti-spirits movement, long- and short-pledge men, prohibitionists and moral suasionists. It can also be seen in the feminist, anti-slavery and secularist movements. Several factors seem to be relevant: the activists' closer contact with the evil under attack leads them to lose the sense of proportion which the more remote leadership can maintain. Furthermore the well-to-do have more to lose by sudden change and extremist methods, and the humble delight in demonstrating their moral superiority to those in authority.

To say that the pledge controversy was also a contest between London and the provinces—especially between London temperance leaders and working men from the northern manufacturing towns—is virtually to repeat what has already been said; artisans from the north were among the most self-confident working men in the 1830s, and the most willing to flout upper-class leadership in London. In the 1839 pledge controversy, as in the American civil war controversy in the early 1860s, the 'democratic' cause was more popular in Lancashire than in London. The long-pledge men wanted to limit the number of Londoners on the executive committee; the executive committee of the short-pledge Suppression Society, formed after the schism, consisted of not more than 30 persons all 'resident in or near London'.[35] Northern long-pledge men regarded London as the modern Babylon, as a centre of vice and temporizing, whose inhabitants could not distinguish between sociability and mere gregariousness.[36] Whereas in the 1790s the anti-slave trade leaders in London had been able to exclude provincial supporters from policy making, by the 1830s provincial self-confidence had grown too strong; no doubt provincial criticism of the London short-pledge leadership was strengthened by the fact that many long-pledge men had recent experience of resisting a timid London leadership in the anti-slavery movement.

Thirdly, the pledge controversy was partly a disagreement over the management of the temperance campaign. Organizations formed to subvert authority incur the perpetual hazard that the anti-authoritarianism of their members will turn against their own leadership. This happened again and again in the Methodist, feminist and socialist worlds, and quite as frequently in the temperance movement. There are many parallels between the 1839 temperance schism and the 1908 schism between the W.S.P.U. and the Women's Freedom League. At the 1838 annual meeting Lord Stanhope brushed aside a working man's suggestion that members of his class should be voted on to the committee; only men of leisure could conveniently hold such posts, he said.[37] The long-pledge men of 1839 were enthusiastic democrats; and as their American ally E. C. Delavan declared at the annual meeting, 'there could be no aristocracy of principle in the temperance cause'.[38] Yet their success was only partial: even after 1839 working men were denied entry to N.B.F.T.S. committees, and the short-pledge men predictably took precautions which would prevent future *coups* through the Suppression Society's annual meeting.

Finally, the pledge controversy represented a schism between contrasting personality types. Like the moderationists of the early 1830s and the 'moral suasionists' after 1853, the short-pledge men in 1839 were tolerant gradualists who disliked transatlantic attempts to coerce rather than persuade. The short pledge attracted them because it would win over moderates who, once enlisted, could be educated into more consistent conduct. The long pledge, they said, was too exclusive. By contrast, the long-pledge men were the uncompromising and dedicated enthusiasts, fearless of alienating their friends and convinced that success could and should be quick. Pioneers are individualists whose spirit of inquiry can seldom be halted at any one point. Some anti-spirits men progressed to teetotalism, prohibitionism and vegetarianism as easily as some free traders moved on to pacifism, universal suffrage and attacks on primogeniture. Criminal law reformers who opposed the death penalty in some instances later came to oppose it in all. As Edward Grubb himself put it, this was 'not a difference of opinion merely, but, with a certain party . . . a compromise of truth'.[39]

Schism does not necessarily damage a movement in the short term, for the schismatic's need to prove himself generates increased energy. Though the pledge controversy must have confused and even antagonized many outside observers, it actually increased aggregate teetotal resources. The funds of the two London teetotal societies more than trebled in 1840; but although their total resources increased between 1838–9 and 1840–1 by £1,300, only £800 of the increase was spent on extending propaganda. Schism therefore greatly increased the funds spent on salaries and office expenses. The funds

THE BRITISH AND FOREIGN

Temperance Intelligencer.

[In consequence of an accident which happened to the wood-cut intended for this number, just as we were going to press, we have been compelled to substitute the cut now given. The fifth of the "Steps of Intemperance," will appear in our next.]

Vol. III No. 156] SATURDAY, NOVEMBER 2, 1839. [Published Weekly. Price One Penny.

"WHICH WAY SHALL I TURN ME?" or, Ruin and Salvation.

Old Fuddler.—Come along, Charley my boy; come along! Only just one glass! A short life and a merry one! that's my ticket.

Charles.—Well, you're a good natured fellow, tho' you've ruined yourself by drinking. I was thinking about abstaining; but surely one glass won't hurt me!

Tee-totaller.—Don't listen to him, my dear Charles. You see what drinking has done for him. If you take one glass you won't know when to stop. You promised to go to [illegible] meeting. Come, and learn the blessings of Total Abstinence.

12. 'Which way shall I turn me?' The temperance periodical stresses the dramatic choice between domestic peace and affluence—drink, disease and death. From *British & Foreign Temperance Intelligencer*, 2 Nov. 1839, p. 425. [see p. 132]

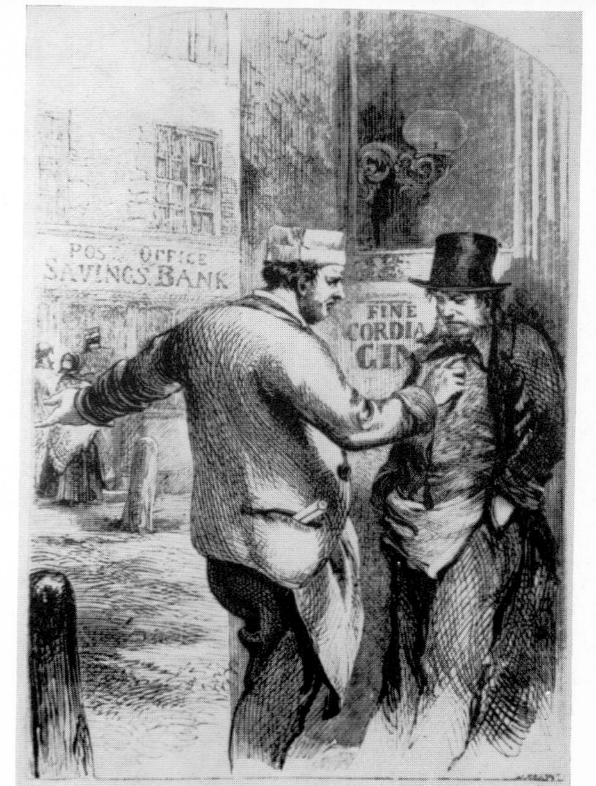

13. 'The Savings' Bank and the Losings' Bank'. From J. W. Kirton, *Four Pillars of Temperance* (1865). [see p. 132]

14. AN EARLY TEETOTAL PROCESSION passing through Lord Street, Liverpool, 20 July 1837. Note the prominence of banners, and the participation of Catholics and Welshmen in the procession. From *Preston Temperance Advocate*, Oct. 1837. [see p. 132]

15. TEETOTALISM AND SOCIAL MOBILITY. THOMAS WHITTAKER. Originally a Preston mill-hand, then pioneer teetotal lecturer in the 1830s, eventually mayor of Scarborough. From his *Life's Battles in Temperance Armour* (1884). [see p. 25]

of the two teetotal societies rose very fast for two or three years after their foundation, but by 1841 they were rapidly declining. With temperance as with feminism, the inefficiency resulting from schism eventually led to reunion.[40] Apart from their contrasting pledges, the two societies did not differ markedly, and in 1842 the Quakers, by threatening to cut off their donations, forced them to amalgamate in the pledgeless National Temperance Society. The easiest way to amalgamate competing organizations is to show sweet temper and ensure that they have a sizeable overdraft.[41]

The northern teetotalers were unimpressed: 'we have little faith in London societies, unless well watched, and founded upon correct principles,' said the B.A.P.T.'s *National Temperance Advocate.*[42] The National Temperance Society, dependent on a small number of wealthy donors, chiefly Quakers, remained somewhat timid and unimaginative until the 1860s. Earl Stanhope objected to its high membership fee and refused to join. According to John Dunlop it seriously hindered London teetotalism because it failed to work closely with surviving auxiliaries and with London working men's societies.[43] After the disturbing events of the 1830s therefore, London teetotalism settled down to a quiet decade punctuated only by Father Mathew's visit to London in 1843.* The movement was jolted out of its routine of tract distribution and public meetings only in the 1850s, with the arrival from America of a new personality, J. B. Gough.

Meanwhile the anti-spirits movement had entered into a sad decline. After its failure to unite with the teetotal organizations, its secretary Owen Clarke darted about the country trying to undo their work. The B.F.T.S. regularly attacked teetotalism and even tried to identify it in the public mind with socialism and infidelity. Though some teetotalers like Silk Buckingham tried to keep a foot in both camps, most of its supporters seceded, including several wealthy Quaker donors. In 1840 the B.F.T.S. emphasized its divergence from the teetotalers by abolishing pledge-signing as a qualification for membership; yet its funds declined throughout the 1840s. Some special factor operated on the B.F.T.S. which did not affect other evangelical charities at the time, for the annual receipts of the Church Missionary Society doubled during the 1830s; the Church Pastoral-Aid Society's income quadrupled between 1837 and 1849; and the London City Mission receipts increased fivefold during the 1840s. B.F.T.S. funds were always tiny when compared with these great charities. Whereas the British and Foreign Bible Society raised £100,000 a year throughout the 1830s and 1840s, the highest B.F.T.S. total was £1,912 in 1834. The funds of the Lord's Day Observance

* As this book is concerned only with the English temperance movement, it provides no sustained account of Father Mathew's activities. They are comprehensively if rather unimaginatively described in Rev. Father Augustine's *Footprints of Father Mathew* (Dublin, 1947).

Society were comparably low, but far from declining during the 1840s they were decidedly buoyant.

In 1842 the Bishop of Norwich regretted that the annual meeting had to be held in so small a room [cf. Plate 7].[44] Teetotalers began to interrupt B.F.T.S. annual meetings; in 1844 a teetotaler named Miller made 'signs of the most marked insult' while Bishop Stanley pleaded for a spirit of Christian conciliation. This was simply a more extreme version of the defiance which Edward Grubb had shown to Earl Stanhope in 1839. The newly self-conscious working class delighted in exposing the hypocrisies of contemporary philanthropy; the sabbatarian, anti-corn law and anti-slavery movements also suffered in this way during the 1840s.[45] Teetotalers like Dr. Pye Smith deplored such proceedings; but in 1845–6 the B.F.T.S. lacked the courage to hold any annual meeting at all. In 1845 gifts were received from Queens Adelaide and Victoria; yet the B.F.T.S. was now 'busily engaged in doing nothing at all'.[46] By 1847 income had sunk to just over £100, and the secretary Owen Clarke was forced by other duties and by 'very severe affliction, both personal and domestic' to resign. For some years the Society had been advertising in vain for a clerical secretary. Owen Clarke handed over his post to a Mr. Thomas Reynolds, 'earnestly recommending' him and the Society to the Divine blessing 'and the enlarged support of the Christian public'.[47] But the Christian public did not oblige, and in December 1848 Mr. Reynolds and his Society disappear from view.

7

The Teetotal Leadership: A Biographical Analysis: 1833–1872

What sort of people supported the teetotal movement in these years? It is unfortunately impossible to analyse the mass membership because few membership-registers have survived, and because the confessions of reclaimed drunkards are stereotyped and lack essential biographical details. Analysis has therefore been confined to the 382 teetotalers most prominent in the movement between 1833 and 1872—all of whom received memoirs or obituaries (however inadequate) in temperance periodicals or reference books.*

Leadership did not come from any particular age-group. The founders of the temperance movement in the 1830s were middle-aged. Buckingham, Collins, Dunlop, Finch, Livesey and Father Mathew were all in their forties when they embarked on the agitation, but some of the earliest teetotal lecturers—Lees, Teare and Whittaker—were much younger. In 1835 the average age of the 36 most prominent contemporary temperance reformers was forty-five. The predominance of the middle-aged is not sustained among the 196 teetotal leaders whose date of birth is known and who took the teetotal pledge before 1846: these came from all generations and included several youths, several old men. The prevalence of religious and class prejudice in the 1830s ensured that reforming zeal was not confined to the young; people of all ages were indignant against the *status quo*. The teetotal leadership for the whole period between 1828 and 1872 was also drawn from all age-groups, but of the 355 whose birth-years are known, 71% came from the

* I originally prepared a biographical appendix for this chapter, but considerations of space unfortunately force me to omit it. Anyone who wishes to consult it can do so by writing to me. This sample includes all British names listed in W. Logan, *Early Heroes of the Temperance Reformation*: T. Lythgoe, *Biographical Key*: J. Inwards, *Memorials of Temperance Workers*. A more subjective criterion for inclusion has also been adopted: the more prominent individuals in P. T. Winskill's vast *Temperance Standard Bearers*, together with those who received obituaries in temperance periodicals. Biographical information has been supplemented wherever possible from all available secondary and primary sources. Many of these temperance memoirs are of course uncritical or uninformative on biographical details which we would now consider essential.

generation born between 1795 and 1824. The attitudes of this generation were formed during years when evangelicalism spread throughout the country, moral reform at home accompanied fighting overseas, the attack on the slave trade showed what reforming agitations could achieve, the astonishing expansion of the dissenting denominations began, and a nation-wide radical working-class organization first developed.

There is a marked regional bias in the birthplaces of the 261 leading teetotalers for whom information is available. Lancashire (40) and Yorkshire (35) contributed far more than any other county, and each contributed more than London and the four home counties combined. The rural counties of the west and north contributed rather more than those of the south-east. While the combined total of Devon, Somerset and Gloucester was 21, and the combined total for Northumberland, Cumberland, Westmorland and Durham was 18—Kent, Sussex, Norfolk and Suffolk could raise only 10. Although 88 of the 261 were born south and east of a line from the Wash to the Severn, many of them moved out of their rural environment to the towns either as temperance workers or—like Passmore Edwards, Christopher Hodgson and George Howlett—to broaden their intellectual freedom and career opportunities. Teetotalism accentuated the temperance movement's predominantly urban flavour by destroying its original rural network of clergymen-supporters. Until the 1860s in country areas it depended on isolated individualists, often Quakers, who lacked sympathy with rural habits of mind. C. D. Faulkner of Deddington, Charles Jupe of Mere, Thomas Judge of Brackley, J. J. Faulkener of Oxford and R. D. Alexander of Ipswich struggled to promote an urban receptiveness to new ideas. Nineteenth-century teetotal lecturers resembled seventeenth-century sabbatarians in introducing progressive urban values to the backward rural areas. For whereas the seventeenth-century's 'dark corners of the land' lay in the north and west, two centuries later they lay primarily in the rural south and east. And whereas in the seventeenth century the literacy rate was lowest in the north, by the early nineteenth century it was lowest in the south.[1]

Thomas Whittaker's autobiography reveals the intensity of the rural opposition faced by some of the early teetotal lecturers. To conservative rustics teetotalers seemed simply out to make trouble: 'you are a Methodist, I thought your sort had had enough of coming here,' said one of J. C. Farn's opponents in a mining village during the 1830s.[2] Some teetotal lecturers reciprocated by developing a hearty contempt for backward-looking southern working men. William Gregson had experience of 'the independence, the self-reliance, the industry, and the honesty of the working-men of Lancashire' and, as his biographer points out, he formed a low opinion of the Brighton working men among whom he worked as a missionary. They fully justified the low estimate the gentry formed of the working man's character—for 'the amount of dissipation, trickery, deception, and wretched fawning that he came across among the poor of Brighton was, as he expresses it, something fearful'.[3] Yet Teare and Whittaker as they traversed the south on their teetotal tours of the late 1830s had allies whom they probably never recognized; for in many respects their efforts were complemented by the London Working Men's Association, whose missionaries might be more overtly political but whose audiences and ultimate objectives were similar. When the Chartists Lowery and Duncan visited Cornwall in 1839 they found James Teare's temperance societies outwardly hostile; yet Lowery found that there were many teetotalers among the individuals interested in learning more about Chartism.[4]

Whereas in America the temperance movement originated outside the industrial areas and stood for the assertion of rural and 'frontier' as opposed to urban values, this was not so in England, where the expanding frontier lay rather in the towns. Like Mark Rutherford's Brother Scotton, one of the first teetotalers in the country town of Cowfold, teetotalism in nineteenth-century England stood for 'urban intelligence as against agricultural rusticity'.[5] Temperance reformers were as eager as Karl Marx to eliminate the distinction between town and country, and to rescue country populations from what he called 'the idiocy of rural life'; they blamed contemporary drunkenness on feudal relics, not on industrial realities. Almost as frequently as the Chartist and anti-corn law movements, the teetotal movement denounced feudal revels and the late-night pranks of aristocratic hooligans [see Plate 17]. For teetotalers the middle ages constituted no arcadia of sobriety, but rather a drunken and servile era, to be contemplated with disgust. In the Isle of Man the Primitive Methodist teetotaler Robert Fargher epitomized—like many other teetotalers in their localities—the attack on feudal traditionalism and obscurantism: with his radical *Mona's Herald* he belaboured the local establishment and was imprisoned three times for libel. 'Feudalism has faded before civilization, and serfdom before liberty,' wrote the *National Temperance Chronicle* on 1 January 1846, 'but the drinking-customs, which should have perished with them, have survived.'[6]

Urban teetotal societies evangelized the surrounding rural areas: John Bright and the temperance reformers did this at Rochdale in the 1830s just as Thomas Cooper and the Chartists did it at Leicester in the 1840s; teetotalism could survive in rural areas only if continually regenerated by urban missionaries, for teetotal agricultural labourers could seldom persist in conduct disapproved by the village squire or clergyman.[7] The pillars of teetotalism in rural areas were therefore often eccentrics or Quakers who had little to lose by an additional eccentricity, and whose income could not be threatened by squires and parsons. Amid the long-continued hostility of an authoritarian rural hierarchy, rural temperance effort even at the end of the century lent an air of progressiveness to a Liberalism which in the towns was beginning to seem old hat.

The young man's move from country to town often signified a plumping for social mobility. The nineteenth-century temperance movement was the movement *par excellence* of the self-made man. Like so many of the movements with which it was allied—anti-slavery, feminism, liberationism and free trade—it was struggling to open up opportunities for talent, against a corrupt and antiquated paternalism. It advertised the existence of the self-made man and propagated his (often idealized) style of life, at the expense of the aristocratic ideal of leisured and unearned wealth. No less than 38 of the 382 in the sample pursued a 'self-help' career, and many took a pride in it. Several showed real enterprise, and were the first to see an opportunity and to exploit it. Thomas Cook's travel agency is the most striking example, but there are many others—John Horniman in tea, James Barlow in cotton, W. H. Darby in shipping: Cassell, Saunders, Chambers and Collins in press and publishing: Eskholme in brass manufacture: and Charles Watson in ventilation systems. Men like Horniman and Cassell had none of the aristocratic bias attaching to many tradesmen—they had no fear of boldly advertising their products; Richard Allen defied the exclusiveness of Dublin drapers by refusing to serve a seven years' apprenticeship before opening his own shop; he placed the signboard 'free trade hall' over his doorway. The temperance movement probably helped many more to success than would be apparent from studying its members at any one time, for membership of a temperance society was often only the first step on the upward ladder; temperance leaders often complained of self-made men who shook off any connexion with the movement which had helped to create their success.

What precisely was meant by 'self-help' in this context? The 'self-made man' was contrasted with the feckless and lounging working man and with the idle and incompetent aristocrat [see Plates 16 and 17]. The important criterion was that personal fortune should have been won largely through personal effort—through skill, intelligence, energy and self-denial. But while the story always concluded with riches, it seldom began with rags; many 'self-made' men had received from their parents a good educational or religious grounding, and had even been given that grain of capital which had launched them on their careers. The opportune legacy appears in the careers even of those two self-help paragons John Cassell and Henry Vincent. Still, in both cases the legacies were put to good use, and if in old age at least five temperance leaders accepted pensions or subscriptions—they could of course feel that the money had been given voluntarily, and that it had been earned by a lifetime's reforming effort: the same could not be said of the pensions filched from the taxes and rates by the indolent aristocrat and the improvident pauper.

The teetotal leadership included ideologists as well as practitioners of 'self-help'. Joseph Livesey publicized the ideas of Benjamin Franklin, his mentor. The teetotal publishers Cassell, Collins and Chambers produced guides, textbooks and exhortations for the aspiring working man. T. B. Smithies and John Cassell in the 1850s—with their *British Workman* and *Working Man's Friend*—pioneered the improving illustrated paper for working men: the first such papers to become really popular. They publicized self-made careers like that of George Stephenson. Although the Chartists R. K. Philp and Henry Vincent were never prominent in the teetotal movement, in their later years they often addressed temperance societies in their lecture-tours. Philp himself eventually moved from moral exhortation into more practical work for self-help when he published cheap handbooks: by 1888 the most popular of these, *Enquire Within Upon Everything* (1856), had sold over a million copies. The self-help ideology was spread through lectures as well as through books; this was Henry Vincent's speciality in later years, but it was also a field cultivated by the religious leader with the common touch—by Hugh Stowell Brown for example, with his eulogies of cleanliness, sobriety and integrity: his attacks on swearing, gambling and sporting. Samuel Smiles himself does not seem to have joined the teetotal movement, but he pleased temperance reformers in 1849 by contributing some articles on temperance to *Eliza Cook's Journal*. In *Self-Help* he upheld Joseph Brotherton as a model for imitation, and stressed the need for working men to free themselves from self-imposed taxation: 'of all great public questions, there is perhaps none more important than this'. It would of course be wrong to assume that all members of temperance societies took the world for their arena: many aimed no higher than a post in their local borough council or chapel. The vast officialdom in Methodist chapels 'created an interior social mobility, within the chapel community, far more important than that exterior mobility, from rags to riches, of which Methodist historiography is so proud'.[8]

Industry and commerce offered the greatest area of opportunity for a working man in this period, and the occupations of the leading teetotalers were predominantly urban. Taking the occupation held for the longest period after signing the pledge, information exists for 311 of the 382 in the sample. Over a third of the sample were 'professionals'—that is, either full-time temperance workers or religious leaders. Up till 1872 there were three types of temperance lecturer: the part-time gentleman-amateur, the full-time temperance agent and the freelance professional. In the earliest days of teetotalism, only the first category existed. The pioneer temperance reformers—Livesey, Collins, Father Mathew—themselves engaged in temperance lecturing; since Henry Forbes' return from Glasgow to found the first English anti-spirits society, the temperance movement had always included several amateur lecturers—businessmen who lectured in their spare time. John Finch the Liverpool iron-merchant combined business with temperance advocacy when visiting Ireland and Scotland in the 1830s. George Hastings and

TABLE 3

Occupational Analysis of Prominent Teetotalers: 1833–1872

Occupation	No.	Occupation	No.
Nonconformist/R.C. minister	49	Sugar merchant	1
Temperance agent/official	43	Messenger	1
Clergyman	23	Landscape gardener	1
Textile manufacturer	22	Bookbinder	1
Newspaper proprietor	10	Shoemaker	1
Doctor	9	Journalist	1
Draper	8	Carpenter	1
Publisher	7	Coffee-shop keeper	1
Landowner	7	Flour dealer	1
Banker	7	Lecturer	1
Corn merchant/miller	6	Cocoa manufacturer	1
Schoolteacher	5	Pin manufacturer	1
Commercial traveller	4	Butcher	1
Lawyer	4	Farmer and brickmaker	1
'Merchant'	4	Shoe manufacturer	1
Master brassfounder	3	Hatter	1
Surgeon	3	Coach trimmer	1
Iron merchant	3	Civil servant	1
Carpet manufacturer	3	Textile factory employee	1
Judge	3	'Shopkeeper'	1
Housebuilder	3	Refreshment-rooms proprietor	1
Insurance agent	3	Printer	1
Ironstone mineowner	3	Miner	1
Railway company employee	2	Bolt and screw maker	1
Author	2	Newsagent	1
Cheesefactor	2	Newspaper editor	1
Book-keeper	2	Travel agent	1
Professor	2	Dyeworks owner	1
Bank employee	2	Artist	1
Cabinetmaker	2	Beadle	1
Auctioneer	2	Coffee roaster	1
Biscuit manufacturer	2	Mechanic	1
Farmer	2	Timber merchant	1
Solicitor	2	Master silversmith	1
Shipowner	2	Shipbroker	1
Mineowner	2	Rollermaker	1
Factory manager	2	Superintendent, rate office	1
Tea merchant	2	Dentist	1
Wool merchant	2	Papermaker's employee	1
Leather manufacturer	1	Manager, gutta percha company	1
Wholesale grocer	1	Ironmonger	1
Silk mercer	1	Tailor	1
Land surveyor	1	Printer/stationer	1

Christopher Hodgson, commercial travellers, gave temperance lectures while waiting for a train; the practice was so common in the 1860s that the National Temperance League specially commended such lecturers in its annual report. The prominent temperance reformer H. J. Wilson returned from a deputation to America on the Contagious Diseases Acts, with Sheffield's first typewriter.[9]

Perhaps the most important of these amateur temperance lecturers in the 1850s and 1860s was the Quaker Samuel Bowly, who specialized in lecturing the well-to-do in a series of 'drawing-room meetings'; the many clergymen and ministers who occasionally agreed to preach a temperance sermon fall into the same category.

Once the temperance movement had been launched, the profession of full-time temperance agent was created. Wages were usually negotiated *ad hominem*, but in the 1860s the ceiling was about £100 a year plus travelling expenses. Agents were usually paid by the week or even by individual lectures, on a short-term engagement. There were no pension arrangements, and when a lecturer retired, an appeal was often launched on his behalf. By studying the previous occupations of the 15 in the sample for whom information is available, we can discover their social status. The profession at this period was exclusively male: three had been tailors, two shoemakers, two nonconformist ministers and one each of the following: carpenter, coachspring-maker, cap manufacturer, blacksmith, soldier, sailor, millhand and woolcomber. Judging by their income, they stood midway in status between the temperance movement's office-clerks (£50 a year) and its organizing secretaries (at least £200 a year). Robert Rae, the successful secretary of the National Temperance League appointed in 1861, began at £200 a year but by 1867 had almost doubled that figure. The secretary assigned routes and tasks to the agents and supervised them closely. He usually sent agents to the societies affiliated to his organization, but sometimes arranged to loan them to other temperance organizations or to share the cost with individual temperance societies or subscribers.

The agent's job could be depressing and sometimes dangerous. In June 1866 the British Temperance League's general purposes committee discussed a letter received from its lecturer Fred Atkin, who was about to lecture in the open air at Wirksworth: he asked 'if the Committee would support him against any opposition that might be raised'. Temperance lecturers who published their memoirs were either temperamentally cheerful or unusually discreet, for they discuss the hostility they faced without elaborating on the depression they must often have felt. J. S. Balmer's biography sympathizes with the teetotal lecturer John Clegg Booth, who frequently found no temperance friends to greet him at the place arranged for a meeting. Singing the popular song 'I'd be a butterfly', he would walk through the streets amid ridicule until he could attract an audience. 'All honour to the man who could thus become a fool in order to reach and lift up his fellow men. . . . No one can tell how his fine spirit was tried by this kind of work.' These men were separated from their families for long periods, and their job could be very exhausting. There was much travelling, and many of the duties were arduous or even embarrassing: temperance lecturers in the 1860s were expected to collect funds, promote the circulation of tracts and temperance newspapers, and report regularly to their employers on the work accomplished. Surviving minute-books show that these reports were scrutinized closely. Explanations were often asked for—when engagements had been missed, time was unused, expenses were excessive, or oratory too extreme; William Gregson often offended on the latter count. When the British Temperance League asked its agent Duxbury to explain the size of his travelling expenses in March 1868 he sent a reply which 'was in every respect unbecoming, manifesting a spirit altogether at variance with the work in which he is engaged'.[10] The minute-book does not reveal the rights and wrongs of this particular dispute, but agents were very vulnerable when criticized. They occasionally met in conferences, but they were never powerful enough to impose conditions on their employers. No doubt this was partly because, to judge from offers recorded in the minute-books, so many people wanted to enter the profession.

With such drawbacks, why were posts so much in demand? One reason must be that the relationship between agent and temperance society was never a mere cash nexus: both employer and employee were joint members of the same crusade; political enthusiasm and idealistic fervour gave impetus to many temperance agents. The chances were that the agent himself had been reclaimed from poverty by teetotal influences. Though supervision was close, the minute-books show several instances of benevolence to temperance lecturers: when the British Temperance League's agent J. D. Matthias became a widower, the League paid his £3 travelling expenses from Scarborough to Haverfordwest, where he wanted to bury his wife, and lent him £5 to meet the necessary expenses. The agents seem to have been granted occasional rest-periods and at least two weeks' holiday a year. On 21 January 1873 the League's secretary told the general purposes committee that he had visited the sick lecturer J. C. Booth and found him 'very weak, and depressed in spirits, because he could not do any work for the payment he was receiving from the League'. The secretary was instructed to write to Booth 'assuring him that he need not make himself uneasy in any way on this matter'.[11]

A second major attraction of the profession was the fact that it was one of the routes out of the working class. While some self-educated working men were content to remain in their trades as weaver-poets and popular philosophers, others were more ambitious: hence the attractions of schoolteaching, journalism, nonconformist preaching, teetotal lecturing or drinkselling. The possibilities in the profession itself were glittering—witness the 12 guineas a lecture earned in the 1850s by the American reformed drunkard and freelance professional J. B. Gough; even the less successful lecturer F. R. Lees received two guineas a time.[12] Short-term engagements had their drawbacks, but they did at least ease the transition from full-time agent to freelance professional. Even the humblest temperance agents spent part of their time lecturing freelance; several published short autobiographies as brochures, and advertised for commissions in the temperance press. Some even engaged in small-scale trading on their own account: John Hockings, 'The Birmingham Blacksmith', for instance, sold Brummagem temperance medals while on temperance tour. But J. B. Goughs were rare; it was more usual to progress from temperance agent to a post as commercial traveller, mission worker or insurance agent; many took lecturing posts with other reforming organizations. Professional lecturers were prominent among the many Victorians who had a direct personal interest in the promotion of reforming movements. When one cause dried up, lecturers hunted round for posts elsewhere. George Thompson was one of several anti-slavery advocates who became temperance speakers, and the National Temperance Society attracted an Anti-Corn Law League lecturer named Greig into its service. Of those who began as temperance lecturers, Robert Dransfield went to the Reform League: Samuel Insull to the Financial Reform Association: and Messrs. Stallwood, Millington, Cluer and W. C. Ellis to Chartist platforms.

Of the laymen in the sample, the 22 textile manufacturers constituted by far the largest occupational group. If retailers and clothing manufacturers are included, the number rises to 37—more than a tenth of the whole. Thirty-five others were in some way involved in producing or consuming reading-matter. Education always featured high among the other interests of leading teetotalers. Like the Anti-Corn Law League, the movement itself was seen by its members largely as an educational crusade, supplementing the more academic work of the schools with education in the practical business of life. Nineteen manufactured or sold food and non-intoxicating drink, to which the temperance movement hoped to divert funds formerly spent on alcohol; if housebuilders and furniture makers and distributors are included, the number in the sample who stood to gain directly from temperance work, whose interests were promoted in temperance tracts, and whose products were advertised in temperance periodicals, rises to 31. Others stood to gain in a less direct way—notably the industrialists, mineowners and shipowners who were opening up new areas of industrial prosperity: the Corys and Kenricks in South Wales, the Darbys in Denbighshire, the Pease family in Darlington—men whose railways, mines and factories demanded from the employee a self-discipline which had to be actively inculcated if serious accidents and hindrances to production were to be avoided.[13]

It might perhaps be argued that these industrialists were creating in the towns a degree of overcrowding, air-pollution, work monotony and recreational impoverishment which more than nullified their efforts for temperance—or even that their temperance work was a feeble attempt to atone for the ravages they were creating in working conditions and living standards. Some teetotal leaders may have been thoughtless employers, flourishing on the misfortunes of their employees—or, like James Barlow of Bolton, throwing respectable craftsmen out of work by their technological innovations.

But many, including twelve in the sample, were by contemporary standards enlightened (if by modern standards, authoritarian) employers, who denied that their own interest could ever conflict with the long-term interest of their employees. Several pioneered half-holidays, recreational and canteen facilities, improved housing and better factory conditions. Titus Salt, the Richardsons of Bessbrook, Thomas Bazley and the Cadburys were outstanding here. Many teetotal leaders attacked the evils of industrial society—bad sanitation, excessive factory hours, air pollution, lack of open space. Although *arrière pensée* may lie behind the zeal of several teetotal entrepreneurs, those who entered the food and non-intoxicating drink trades often did so precisely *because* these were harmless occupations.

The many examples of self-denial in the movement reduce one's suspicions of its other-worldly style of advocacy. The business integrity of these men is often stressed by their obituarists. The failure of Bath's 'Bank of Deposit', of which the teetotal pioneer J. H. Cotterell was chairman, caused him to realize all his property, including his house and furniture, and to distribute the proceeds among those whom his influence had led into the concern. Passmore Edwards' creditors gave him a banquet when, in the 1860s, he repaid the debts from which the law had released him many years before. Self-denial inspired by temperance principle is equally frequent. The abandonment of fine cellars by men like Lawson, Trevelyan and Hope may have been an extravagant gesture designed to catch the public eye, but it was no mean sacrifice to abandon the malting aspect of a corn dealer's trade—as did Joseph Sturge, G. W. Harrison, James Haughton, John Andrew and others. F. N. Charrington and Jesse Sessions cut themselves off from the sources of family wealth; Samuel Bowly and Richard Cadbury lost custom when they ceased to provide customers with wine; the doctors John Higginbottom and William Batchelor lost patients when they abandoned alcoholic prescription, and generous donors like William Hoyle sacrificed to the cause a large portion of their children's fortunes. Several teetotal leaders in industry—six in the sample—retired early from money-making to concentrate on philanthropy. Even where the teetotal leader could do nothing but gain from the movement, he could always argue—like the Anti-Corn Law Leaguers—that his own personal interest coincided with that of the community. With some reason, for how could the drunkenness, disorder and irregularity of eighteenth-century life ever have been tolerated in industrial England? If the need for industrialization is accepted, the historian of the temperance movement—unlike the historian of the Anti-Corn Law League—can hardly dispute the excellence of the cause: he will criticize only the means adopted in its name.

The scarcity of landowners, public servants and rural supporters among the leading teetotalers is noteworthy. Queen Adelaide and Queen Victoria subscribed to the B.F.T.S., and Queen Victoria later acted as patron to the

Church of England Temperance Society. But both these organizations were less concerned with reclaiming the drunkard than with banding together the sober; both were quite ready to admit moderate drinkers to membership. Teetotalism trenched so severely on social life that only the most exceptional situation could make it respectable enough for the British monarchy. Even when George V took the pledge during the first world war, his action was always something of an embarrassment. As for the aristocracy, J. S. Buckingham in 1845 said that he had sat at table with about 500 members of the middle and upper classes in the previous year and had found only two or three who were water-drinkers;[14] by 1872 the movement was only beginning to attract support from High Society. Supporters from these groups before 1872 usually diverged from their class not only in their teetotalism, but also in several other respects.

Of the seven landowners in the sample, Earl Stanhope was an eccentric, and even he repudiated those aspects of the temperance movement which attracted the most working class enthusiasm in the north of England—that is, the long pledge movement. Captain Trotter was distinguished by his fervent evangelical zeal [see Plate 26]; Lord Claud Hamilton's temperance sympathies were rare among Conservatives—though he held land in Northern Ireland where, as in Scotland, it was easier to combine temperance zeal with Conservatism. Sir W. C. Trevelyan and Sir Wilfrid Lawson, Sen., were both decidedly progressive individuals, untypical of their class. Hugh Owen, the one civil servant in the sample, was a Welsh nonconformist unusual for the scale of his rise in society. The three teetotal squires in the sample—Tucker, Shafto and Potto Brown—were all nonconformists, and two owed their fortunes to commerce. Potto Brown was one of those resolute, almost eccentric 'characters' without whom rural nonconformity and temperance could hardly have survived. Joseph Tucker did in Bedfordshire what Potto Brown did in Huntingdonshire; he acted as the champion of local temperance sentiment. In Pavenham he created a model temperance village which was often lauded in temperance periodicals. When visiting Brown, Tucker and Robert Shafto, the Primitive Methodist squire of Bavington Hall—teetotal lecturers found themselves moving at an unexpectedly elevated social level.

Many teetotal leaders from 1833 to 1872 were distinctive in personality. The mid-twentieth-century eye is struck by their immense energy, self-confidence and optimism. One recalls the octogenarian George Cruikshank dancing the hornpipe: the septuagenarian John Finch, still championing the co-operative schemes in the 1850s which had brought him a lifetime of failure: and old Potto Brown on his deathbed in 1871, sending the local clergyman away because he never was beparsonized in his life and was not going to be so then. A glance at their local government work at once reveals their drive. At least 76 of the sample were active here—and this is probably a serious under-estimate. Taking the highest office attained, the sample of 382 includes 20 J.P.s, 18 mayors, 17 councillors, 9 poor law guardians, 8 aldermen, 3 members of school boards and one member of a board of health. Many teetotalers were active in the movement for municipal reform, and local obituaries often stress the intensity of the temperance leaders' local pride—from Edward Vivian, who believed Torquay to be the most beautiful place in the world and helped to make it into a resort—to William McKerrow, whose personal career embodies the history of Manchester during his lifetime. Local pride led at least four in the sample to become local antiquarians, and temperance zeal led another four to campaign for an improved water supply. Intensity of feeling on political, social and religious matters sometimes made them controversial personalities—like Hugh Mason of Ashton, Hugh Stowell of Manchester, or G. W. Harrison of Wakefield—men who were loved or hated by opposed sections of the town, but who could never be regarded with indifference. During the 1840s and 1850s two individuals, the teetotaler Robert Fargher and his opponent G. W. Dumbell, acted as the Isle of Man's Cobden and Palmerston, its Gladstone and Disraeli: their personal antagonism dramatized the clash between two cultures, two philosophies of life.

Many teetotal leaders had what Bagehot called 'the first great essential of an agitator—the faculty of easy anger'. In their minute-books and private correspondence they may display a shrewd flair for publicity but they betray not a hint of cynicism or doubt as to the justice of their cause. They did not always succeed in sublimating the violent passions against which their whole movement constituted a protest. For they saw life as a battle, and their combativeness issued in vehemence of expression, in the uplifted finger, the earnest countenance and the thumping of the table so often noted by observers: in fractiousness within teetotal organizations, and even in physical violence. Speaking at Clitheroe during the 1847 general election, Edward Grubb was seen to inflict two black eyes on an opponent who was distributing beer to his audience, and then immediately to continue talking politics 'like an inspired man'. To an opponent who called him 'a bloody liar', the teetotal advocate Robert Dransfield retorted 'I am for God. You are for the worst devil in hell, and, if you pull me down while I am speaking, I'll give you what Paddy gave the big drum!'[15]

Several teetotal leaders were 'puritanical'—that is, serious-minded, afraid of laughter, hostile to horse-racing and theatres, thrifty in time, money or opportunity. At least seven of the sample championed the anti-smoking movement, many more were non-smokers, and temperance tracts often argue that smoking promotes drunkenness by fostering thirst while depriving natural drinks of their savour. Thomas Cook published several anti-smoking tracts and a periodical, the *Anti-Smoker*. But few temperance societies went as far as the Leeds Temperance Society which aimed in 1849 to eliminate 'a gross and glaring inconsistency' by incorporating a pledge against smoking into its teetotal pledge.[16] Without their strong sense of stewardship, these men might not have survived the bitter hostility they often faced, nor have sustained the ceaseless activity their wide interests demanded. Seldom suffering fools gladly, they often made enemies with their tactless ways and their preference for attack rather than defence. Flippant friends were cast aside early in life, and the obituaries of at least nine in the sample note that a somewhat grim exterior masked a golden heart within. Probably there were many more puritans in the sample than were actually recorded, if only because their fellow workers must have taken such a temperament for granted. Yet it is dangerous to generalize from these few isolated examples; the case of the Preston teetotaler Harry Anderton emphasizes the light-heartedness of some early teetotal advocates. There were always 'cheerful puritans' in temperance organizations whose lecturers were militantly gay. Eleven of the sample fall into this category. Again, if many teetotal leaders were aggressive by nature, milder temperaments than those of the mature Livesey, of Father Mathew or of Samuel Bowly could hardly be imagined. Without a comparative sample from the contemporary general public, one cannot say whether teetotal leaders were in general more puritanical or more aggressive in manner than other people; one might however expect the leaders in any reforming movement to possess more energy, single-mindedness and combativeness than their contemporaries.

It is but a short step from individualism to eccentricity. It would be rash to accept uncritically the many contemporary complaints of eccentricity in teetotal leaders, for today's eccentricity is often tomorrow's enlightenment. Nevertheless incidental biographical details make it clear that by any standard at least fourteen of the sample are strong candidates for the title; some, like F. W. Newman, almost gloried in their eccentricity. Indeed it is only to be expected that a protest movement should attract individuals already rebelling against convention. The temperance movement owed much to aristocratic eccentricity: to the Stanhopes, Lawsons, Trevelyans and—later in the century—to the Carlisles. And it thrived on the eccentricity which at that time was more broadly diffused throughout society than it is today. Widespread celibacy and chronic ill-health: formidable income-differentials: pronounced religious, regional, craft and class characteristics: the absence of mass media: less standardized child-rearing practices: a relative reluctance to travel: frequent inbreeding within the local community—these and other factors accentuated and diversified contrasts in personality. Hence even lunacy, let alone eccentricity, was far more readily tolerated in nineteenth-century society than it is today. 'No society in which eccentricity is a matter of reproach, can be in a wholesome state,' J. S. Mill pronounced in his *Political Economy*.[17] Liberalism was the ideology of the eccentrics, Mill's *Liberty* their charter; nineteenth-century society and politics were greatly enriched by their prominence.

Furthermore, until the removal of dissenters' disabilities, nonconformists were dissenters also in many of their daily habits. The sample includes at least thirteen 'men of principle' who—for reasons which often seemed footling to their contemporaries—refused office, honours or profits if by acceptance they felt they would compromise their ideals. Certain social groups like the Quakers deliberately cultivated what the wider society saw as eccentricity: by becoming water drinkers, such people had no conformity to lose. Yet in one respect even the temperance movement helped to promote conformity: for it was powered largely by the desire of hitherto excluded groups—nonconformists and (after Manning embraced the cause in the 1860s) Catholics —for the wider society to acknowledge their social needs and moral standards. A similar desire for recognition may have motivated the three individuals of foreign or Huguenot descent in the sample.

The link between temperance reformers and educational causes has already been stressed. The temperance movement was one of several contemporary reforming movements which flourished on the inequality of educational opportunity in Victorian England: which attracted working men whose poverty or social background denied them the schooling their intelligence merited, and dissenters whose beliefs excluded them from Oxford and Cambridge, where the literary culture of the governing classes could be acquired. At least 27 of the teetotal leaders qualify as 'intellectuals' in the broad sense that they had decidedly academic interests or were in some way connected with academic societies—though the clerical background of Oxford and Cambridge ensured that the movement gained few academic supporters there till the 1870s. Two individuals from contrasting social spheres typify the combination of intellectualism and eccentricity which nourished the teetotal leadership: Earl Stanhope of Chevening and J. J. Faulkener of Oxford. Earl Stanhope, like his half-sister Lady Hester Stanhope, inherited all his father's individuality. He was the first aristocrat to join the teetotal movement, and the diversity of his interests illustrates how richly Britain's public life was once endowed by the eccentric strain within her aristocracy. President of the Medico-Botanical Society, vice-president of the Society of Arts, Fellow of the Royal Society, translator of two German plays produced on the London stage and an early enthusiast for flying machines—he was a well-intentioned, progressive and unsectarian family-man who somehow managed also to be a militantly anti-Catholic, anti-Reform Bill Tory. But Stanhope was too solitary and too ingenuous to acquire political influence, though for years he wearied the House of Lords with pleas for factory legislation and assaults on the reformed poor law. By adopting the so-called 'wild boy' of Bavaria in 1832, he involved himself in a host of embarrassments; yet as president of the B.F.S.S.I., he displayed a better-developed political sense than many a teetotaler. He embraced total abstinence in 1831, 'when I suffered, as I had done occasionally, from a weakness of the stomack and a want of appetite': it was another of the many health-cures which preoccupied him throughout his life. Yet his temperance correspondence breathes a much-needed distaste for 'wild fanatics' and for puritanical attacks on the publican. Unfortunately his catholicity, his tolerance, and his eagerness to avoid entangling temperance in politics and sectarianism were not appreciated by teetotalers, and after 1842 he fades from the forefront of the temperance stage.

J. J. Faulkener, Oxford's leading teetotaler and Chartist,* shared Stanhope's courage and curiosity. He 'was one of those pleasant companions who always will have an opinion'; Joseph Taylor recalled that 'there was no unnecessary reserve about him, and being observant, he was never ashamed of asking questions from the fear of being thought ignorant. He was full of general knowledge, and it was always at the service of any who required it.' The son of a nonconformist schoolmaster, vigorously anti-Catholic, staunchly Liberal, hostile to capital punishment and nostalgic for the days when Oxford University catered for poor scholars—he closed his grocer's shop to visit the Great Exhibition in 1851. He opened Oxford's first reading-room on his premises and, as a pacifist, used his shop-window to advertise the number of Crimean War casualties during the victory celebrations of 1856. At one time in his life, Faulkener doubted the truth of eternal bliss after death, and he was known to have been somewhat depressed just before he was found drowned in the river.[18]

Teetotalism and Liberalism attracted men fascinated by science and convinced that rational inquiry must promote human progress; their enthusiasm even led them to experiment on their own bodies—for this is what teetotalism amounted to, until its compatibility with health became widely accepted. Experiment was often pushed further, for the teetotaler Isaac Pitman described meat as 'the brandy of diet'.[19] At least 12 of the sample were vegetarians, and teetotalers featured prominently in the vegetarian world. Vegetarianism was adopted partly on humanitarian grounds—at least 11 of the sample were active in movements combating animal cruelty; but health considerations were also influential. The teetotaler's belief in the virtues of 'natural' foods combined with his conviction that man is what he eats.

Teetotalers' physiological individualism readily extended to unorthodox medical allegiances; eight of the sample moved in this direction. Although nine doctors appear in the sample, several joined the movement only in the 1860s; in the medical as in the religious world, the early teetotalers challenged professional expertise. Homoeopathists, hydropathists and Morisonians were the dissenters of the medical world, threatening its established church—the College of Physicians. Both teetotalers and opponents of the

* I am most grateful to Raphael Samuel, of Ruskin College, Oxford, for generously providing me with several biographical details on Faulkener.

Contagious Diseases Acts campaigned against 'these terrible aristocratic doctors' as Mrs. Butler called them. Temperance reformers combined their libertarian and medically dissenting views when they took a prominent part in the movement against compulsory vaccination. F. W. Newman was a leading national figure, and anti-vaccination legislation was championed in parliament by two temperance reformers, Joseph Pease and Wilfrid Lawson. Teetotalers were often sarcastic about the doctor's skill; Canon Basil Wilberforce infuriated the profession by saying that some doctors 'if they went down inside you with a lighted candle, could not tell what was the matter with you'. His contempt for the medical profession was shared by Wilfrid Lawson, Cardinal Manning, F. W. Newman and many other temperance leaders.[20]

The desire for a common man's medicine, which would emancipate the individual from the conservative corporate medical authorities in London, naturally attracted many working men; dietary providence could perhaps banish sickness, just as thrift could banish bankruptcy. Free trading believers in the natural harmony of interests also inclined towards 'natural' remedies for disease. '*Laissez faire*', wrote Cobden in 1856, 'seems as applicable to the medical profession as to trade.' With Livesey, teetotalers plunged into their cold baths: with F. R. Lees, they shunned their steaks: and with Dunlop, they experimented with dry rubs and early morning runs. 'I have great faith in nature—in . . . the *vis medicatrix naturae*' wrote Livesey; medicine interfered with the beneficent course of nature.[21] The connexion between teetotalism and hydropathy is epitomized in the picture of Joseph Livesey, walking about Preston with his hydropathic bath; the links were still strong in that young temperance reformer and amateur hydropathist, Keir Hardie.[22]

Ill-health may have been more prevalent among leading teetotalers than in the general public. Unfortunately, with health as with eccentricity, one cannot generalize without a control sample from the general population. It must simply be recorded that at least six of the teetotal leaders suffered from chronic ill-health, and that such supporters made it difficult for teetotalers to convince the public that abstinence was compatible with health. A dietary reform advocated on valetudinarian grounds will naturally attract those who suffer from ill-health. Perhaps all reforming movements attract members of this sort: 'if anything ail a man, so that he does not perform his functions,' wrote Thoreau, 'if he have a pain in his bowels even . . . he forthwith sets about reforming—the world.'[23]

Political allegiance is known in 127 instances: of these, as many as 119 were Liberals. The late-Victorian temperance society was closely integrated with the Liberal party: one of a complex of organizations—chapels, trade unions, co-operatives, branches of national reform organizations—whose popular appeal made it unnecessary for the party to establish distinctive organizations for working men.[24] In the movement's early years, when quietism was more widespread among dissenters, when fewer teetotalers were enfranchised and when Gladstonian Liberalism was only beginning to take shape, the alignment was less pronounced, and teetotalism was more readily described as an *alternative* to political action. Nevertheless, at least eight teetotal leaders before 1872 were key figures in their local Liberal party structure. Teetotalers' importance in the Liberal party stems as much from the quality of their support as from their numbers; temperance reformers were particularly important in developing the Liberal press, not only through their teetotal periodicals, but also in at least 19 instances through Liberal, denominational and local newspapers.* Joseph Livesey himself established an important provincial Liberal paper; so also did one of his two pioneer teetotal lecturers—Thomas Whittaker. Temperance reformers of course brought headaches to the Liberal leaders; their cause was not universally popular in the party—least of all with the party leadership, which moved gracefully among London society's well-stocked dinner-tables.

Four of the eight Conservative teetotal leaders were Anglicans and of these, three were clergymen of strongly evangelical outlook. Two of the eight were active in Manchester, one in Ireland and one in Scotland—all localities where it was easier than elsewhere to combine teetotalism with Conservative sympathies. Religious allegiance is known in 273 instances, of whom only 38 were Anglicans. Many of these were probably Conservatives, though at least nine were Liberals. At least three of the Anglicans had a business background, at least three had pronounced scientific interests and many were eager to influence working men. They included a temperance reformer as prominent as Wilfrid Lawson, Jun.—though he turned to Anglicanism only after a dissenting upbringing, and never defended the political privileges of the established church. Many of the Anglican teetotal leaders had evangelical views—despite the suspicions of teetotalism rife in this wing of the Church between the late 1830s and the early 1860s. Obituarists note a willingness among Anglican teetotal leaders to join with nonconformists in public work. As prison-chaplains, William Caine and John Clay were prominent for investigating links between drink and crime. Thomas Spencer, whose progressive agencies transformed the village of Hinton Charterhouse, was deeply interested in poor law reform. Rev. Theodore Dury, Hugh Stowell, Canon Bardsley and Prebendary Grier were examples of teetotal clergymen whose sympathy with working men led them also into defending the men against their employers—in the factory hours movement or, in Grier's case, in the miners' strike of 1893.

Nonconformist predominance in the sample is overwhelming: all but 41 of

* I have developed this point in my article '"A World of Which We Had No Conception". Liberalism and the Temperance Press, 1830–1872', *Victorian Studies*, Dec. 1969.

the 273 were dissenters. Involvement in a crusade which required its supporters to endure personal self-sacrifice and even persecution naturally attracted religious groups with a recent tradition of suffering for their beliefs. Seventeenth-century religious conflicts, for many of these dissenters, were very much a matter of present-day politics. It was not simply that in at least six instances there were treasured family connexions with puritans and covenanters: Anglican persecution seemed still very much alive to nineteenth-century dissenters who refused to pay church rates and saw the established church carrying off their property. For these people, the Civil War had never really ended. Joseph Livesey, the founder of teetotalism, was among their number. Joseph Taylor stood in the grocer's shop of Oxford's teetotal leader J. J. Faulkener in the 1850s and saw an undergraduate throw in some tea, saying 'he had made a mistake, and bought tea at the shop of a Radical'. Such Anglican arrogance naturally inspired resentment, and William Gregson's biographer reveals how at least one temperance lecturer delighted in shocking local clergymen with his pert challenges to their authority.[25] The temperance and prohibitionist movements, while never in total accord with liberationism, had many common members and shared many common attitudes. Those dissenters who in the 1830s abandoned the Whig alliance for independent radical political action found many sympathizers among temperance reformers. Liberationist candidates at the 1847 general election—Joseph Sturge at Leeds, George Thompson at Tower Hamlets, G. W. Alexander at Wakefield—all tried to limit expenditure on drink during their election campaigns.[26] At least thirty-six (9% of the sample) supported the Liberation Society. Teetotal leaders participated in some or all the reforming movements which threatened aristocratic authority. Inequalities in nineteenth-century England were still dispersed rather than cumulative; individuals in quite different income-groups could share resentment at aristocratic oppression.

Eight English and Scottish teetotal leaders left the established church for dissent: sometimes, as with Gregson, because they found teetotalism opposed by the parson. Of the Scottish teetotal leaders, only one came from the Church of Scotland, whereas the Free Church provided six. The United Presbyterians, the Scottish denomination closest to England's militant dissent in outlook, contributed five influential teetotal leaders. By the late 1850s, a higher proportion of United Presbyterians was teetotal than in any other Scottish denomination.[27] The United Presbyterians resembled the Cowherdites in making a contribution to the temperance movement out of all proportion to their size. Cowherdite influence, though exercised through only three representatives, was the greater because these three individuals lived in Manchester, were to some extent interrelated and included Joseph Brotherton, one of the temperance movement's few early contacts at Westminster. They were to make an even larger contribution to the prohibitionist movement. Likewise the Scotch Baptists' one contribution was Joseph Livesey; the Swedenborgians' one contribution was Henry Sutton, the prominent temperance journalist; and though Lady Huntingdon's Connexion contributed only two to the sample, one of these was Benjamin Parsons, author of a major temperance textbook and rejuvenator of his locality—Ebley, in Gloucestershire.

Through the person of Father Mathew, the Catholics made a dramatic contribution to teetotalism; but he was a lone figure, with influence mainly in Ireland. Only two other Catholics appear in the sample—relatively minor figures, also active only in Ireland. The scarcity of Catholic priests in the movement before Manning, the proverbial drunkenness of Irish immigrants, the strength of teetotalism in Lancashire and the popularity of early temperance work among Irish protestants might lead one to expect that the early teetotal movement was anti-Irish or anti-Catholic in its aims. Admittedly at least nine teetotal leaders were militantly anti-Catholic, including the evangelical zealots Stowell and Maguire; but two of the teetotal leaders, Sturge and Haughton, opposed the anti-Catholic hysteria of 1850–1, as did the temperance sympathizers Henry Vincent and Richard Cobden. The teetotal movement did not attract support from all the leading anti-Catholics, and the movement was strong in many areas—Cornwall, for example—where Irish immigrants were lacking. Although the London teetotal societies associated only reluctantly with Irish teetotalers in 1841,[28] the leading Quaker teetotalers, especially Joseph Sturge, kept in the closest contact with Father Mathew, and the teetotal movement as a whole showed him the greatest cordiality. 'To my beloved Brethren, of the Society of Friends,' Father Mathew told Mrs. Carlisle, 'I owe a debt and obligation surpassing all calculation. O would to God that all who profess themselves followers of Jesus, were like the English Friends.'[29]

The most striking feature of the religious analysis is the prominence of the Quakers. As early as 1830 their yearly meeting was buzzing with zeal for the anti-spirits movement, and by 1839 Quakers were repeatedly hinting to William Lucas, the Quaker brewer of Hitchin, that he really should abandon his livelihood. Though a relatively small denomination, the Quakers produced far more teetotal leaders than any other—24% of those whose religious allegiance is known. Nor was their importance solely in numbers; Quakers were prominent in the small group of generous and pioneering subscribers to the teetotal cause, and Quakers converted temperance reformers as important as Father Mathew and George Cruikshank. The first anti-spirits society, at New Ross, was formed in a Quaker meeting-house. A Quaker was among the first three teetotal doctors; a Quaker, John Giles, was the first to get up a teetotal meeting in London, and the first to organize a temperance association for London Catholic temperance societies; and one of the three teetotal squires—Joseph Tucker—was a Quaker. The meeting to form the first Band of Hope in 1847 was held in the house of a Quaker, James Hotham of Leeds. Another Quaker, R. D. Alexander, published the movement's most successful series of tracts; Samuel Jarrold of Norwich also did valuable work in this line.[30]

The prominent role allotted to women by Quakers helped to get the temperance movement as a whole accustomed to the idea of employing women in reforming work. And at a time when most other denominations barred their doors, persecuted pioneer teetotal lecturers, like Clarkson in the early anti-slave trade movement, could usually rely on Quakers to provide refuge and a meeting place. When other members of their class shunned the vulgarity of the teetotal meeting, Quakers often provided the hard core of well-to-do attenders on whom the society's survival depended. Quaker independence of local opinion, especially in rural areas, made them particularly receptive to new ideas from the towns: they sometimes became invaluable supporters of teetotalism and a powerful educational influence on the whole surrounding countryside.[31] The death of a leading Quaker supporter like Joseph Eaton in 1858 could disrupt temperance activity in an entire locality. It is hardly surprising, then, that many teetotal leaders, including Livesey himself, greatly admired the Quakers; ten teetotal leaders actually themselves became Quakers.

Of the 273 teetotal leaders whose religion is known, Congregationalists came third, with 30; of the rest, Baptists and Wesleyans have 27 and 25 respectively, and Unitarians have 15. But if all 40 Methodists, excluding Wesleyans, are grouped together, they outnumber all but the Quakers. Although even by 1872 the leading dissenting denominations were not united in support of teetotalism, the movement attracted many of their most prominent members. James Sherman, Newman Hall, William Armitage, Samuel Morley and Frank Crossley (Congregationalists), Hugh Bourne and Dr. Antliff (Primitive Methodists); F. W. Newman, M. D. Hill and the Carpenters (Unitarians); Samuel Bowly, J. J. Gurney and the Cadburys (Quakers); Jabez Burns and Francis Beardsall (Baptists); J. R. Kay of Bury and Charles Garrett (Wesleyans). Several lay teetotal leaders gave generously to church- or chapel-building: Thomas Clegg, William Collins I and Hugh Birley to the established churches: Charles Jupe, Potto Brown, Samuel Jarrold and Richard Peek to dissenting chapels.

The importance of denominationalism among teetotal leaders should not be exaggerated, for teetotal leaders of all denominations shared common religious attitudes—the belief that religion must recruit itself more widely among working men, and that this would best be achieved through involvement in social reform: the belief in mission work: the reaction against absorption in liturgical and theological questions: and the conviction that Christians of all denominations should work together. Charles Booth in the 1890s was impressed by the similarity in the religious outlook of teetotal societies whatever their denominational label. The teetotal movement sometimes witnessed strikingly ecumenical moments, as Father Mathew's own account of his conversion to teetotal work reveals. 'It was the Quakers in Cork were always asking me to do something about the people's temperance societies, and one day Mr. Oldham—a member of the Established Church too, he is—at a Temperance meeting said to me "you are the man, Father Mathew—if you'll undertake it, it will succeed". ' Father Mathew's close co-operation with nonconformist teetotalers and his public handshaking with Bishop Stanley in 1843 must have moderated anti-Catholicism among English protestants at the time. Nonconformists in Shepton Mallet would co-operate with the Unitarian Henry Solly in temperance work at a time when in other spheres they would have nothing to do with him.[32] While the movement was at times turned to the purposes of interdenominational rivalry, and although in men like G. W. Harrison it had its bitterly sectarian aspect—the obituarists of 23 teetotal leaders particularly noted the unsectarian outlook of their subjects. National teetotal organizations disliked any attempt to limit the scope of the Christian mission. Six teetotal leaders strongly opposed Calvinism, and there were close connexions between teetotal and mission work. G. M. Murphy, G. W. McCree and William Logan were among the most prominent of many teetotal mission workers in the slums. At least 24 of the sample either were themselves missionaries or financed missions. The offices of teetotal lecturer and town missionary were interchangeable, and many teetotal leaders, especially the Quakers, engaged in personal mission work. Joseph Livesey throughout his life stressed the need for personal visitation, and practised what he preached.

Teetotal missionaries struggled to uphold rural standards of conduct in an urban environment. A double process seems to have been at work: while teetotal lecturers tried to implant in rural minds an urban independence of thought and conduct, teetotal missionaries tried to implant in urban minds a rural sense of community and of social discipline. The many teetotal leaders who had themselves moved from country to town recognized the urgency of this task. Thomas Guthrie was shocked at the contrast between his Edinburgh parish and the country parish of Arbirlot where he had worked till 1837; the contrast could be compared, he said, 'to nothing else than the change from the green fields and woods and the light of nature, to venturing into the darkness and blackness of a coal pit'.

Immigrants to English cities needed protection against the strangeness and uncertainty of urban life, and it is noteworthy that Celtic peoples who moved to large English cities tended to form distinct temperance organizations. These were seldom confessedly regional groupings: temperance societies which were in practice recruited from Welshmen, Irishmen and Scotsmen were usually attached to Calvinistic Methodist, Catholic or Presbyterian chapels, respectively—though temperance societies were founded specially for

Welshmen in October 1831 at Manchester and in February 1832 at Liverpool; several others were founded shortly after—according to Winskill 'in connexion with the various Welsh congregations in Liverpool and district'. The role of the nineteenth-century temperance society resembles that of the voluntary associations which modern social anthropologists have discovered in twentieth-century African towns. The early career of Sir Hugh Owen, founder of the Metropolitan Welsh Total Abstinence Society, shows how a strong-minded Welshman in early Victorian London centred his social life on his Calvinistic Methodist chapel and directed his teetotal effort towards London Welshmen.

Likewise with the Irish: Henry Mayhew records the prevalence of mutual help among London Catholics in the 1840s, and it was natural that the temperance society should frequently appear amongst them, often without affiliation to or even encouragement from the national temperance organizations. When the Rev. Sisk administered the pledge at the Chelsea Catholic Temperance Association's first meeting in November 1838, the 33 signatories were mostly 'persons in humble life, chiefly labourers, and natives of Ireland'; again, the 50 or 60 who took the pledge from Father Rigby at Barnsley in July 1840 were mainly Irishmen.[33] One objective of Father Mathew's temperance visit to Glasgow in 1842 and to several English towns in 1843 was to raise the reputation of Irishmen in Britain. During his 1843 visit, he sometimes administered the pledge in the Irish language: his best-attended meetings were held in the Irish quarter: and the bodyguard formed to defend him when in London consisted of Irishmen or—at Deptford—of Irishwomen, with shillelaghs inside their umbrellas. But English towns also received many *English* immigrants. The highly regionalized pattern of denominational loyalties in nineteenth-century England probably ensured that here too denominational temperance societies were really disguised regional associations, or at least encapsulated such associations. But such relationships—perhaps often consisting only of a few individuals within the society—are concealed from the religious historian unless he immerses himself in the details of the local temperance and chapel world; many will never be rediscovered at all.[34]

If one may guess at the temperance reformer's hopes, community sanctions would be preserved in towns through small religious groups and voluntary societies, and respect for law and order would be so internalized as to supersede the aristocratic regulation of movement and opinion still characteristic of rural life. Rich and poor in the towns would be brought into contact through a kindly, rather than authoritarian, paternalism: social discipline would be secured through example-setting, not through coercion: and the social gulf between rich and poor would be reduced by thrift and mutual help among the poor, not through direct attacks on the property of the rich. The ideas of teetotal leaders were formed in a predominantly agricultural society, and social and economic attitudes between the 1830s and the

1870s were only in the process of adapting themselves to industrial conditions. 'If the bleak Yorkshire fells are needed to account for the sombre genius of the Brontë sisters,' it has been argued, 'so it needs Fordhays Farm fully to account for Hugh Bourne.' Not all teetotalers spent their childhood thus, but like Samuel Smiles himself many of them undoubtedly took some aspects of rural conduct as models for urban behaviour.[35] Their ideology, like so many aspects of nineteenth-century Liberalism, was backward-looking—appropriate to a rural rather than industrial situation.

Temperance reformers unconsciously believed that an industrial population might one day resemble a society of rural smallholders and craftsmen freed from aristocratic supervision: that the structure of the community was potentially so simple that state intervention would rarely be required to reconcile its internal contradictions: that the economic relations of industrial society would not prevent individuals from building up, through their own efforts, the modicum of capital they needed for personal independence: and that respectability could be obtained simply through individual moral restraint, and was equally feasible for all members of the community. Temperance workers only slowly realized that industrialism was reimposing in a new form restraints on individual liberty which, to all appearances, had at last been thrown off: that the cramping social hierarchy which seemed to be breaking up was being replaced by a new and potentially less responsible hierarchy: and that sobriety and many other virtues might become more difficult for some sections of the population than for others.

The teetotal leaders' marked bias in favour of nonconformity requires us to see the teetotal society in relation to chapel life as a whole. With the social history of nineteenth-century nonconformity as yet unwritten,* this is very difficult. But some points can be made. The temperance society was, firstly, a unifying influence on the nonconformist community: temperance work conveniently united nonconformists from different social grades. The lower-class members were provided with an ideology which explained existing social evils without alienating them from their wealthier co-religionists. Through the pledge-signing, the latter could make a symbolic sacrifice which enhanced their acceptability with the humbler members, and distinguished them from the Anglicans whom they might otherwise have been tempted to join; the whole congregation was welded together by a distinctive dietary pattern which enabled it to present a united front to the world. To some extent their social peculiarity threw teetotalers into each others' society. In the words of a teetotaler and carpenter of the 1830s 'we were not only moved by the same opinions, but we were bound together in a common

* For imaginative and pioneering ways into the subject, see A. Allan Maclaren, 'Presbyterianism and the Working Class in a Mid-Nineteenth Century City', *Scottish Historical Review*, Oct. 1967; and Robert Currie, *Methodism Divided. A Study in the Sociology of Ecumenicalism* (1968).

brotherhood, we helped one another. When I shook hands with a teetotaler I felt towards him a kind of heart communion.'[36] Several of the teetotal leaders were personally related, though such connexions—particularly with Quakers—often *preceded* the adoption of teetotal sympathies. The movement as a whole owed much to the great teetotal families—the Lawsons, Cadburys, Carpenters, Sturges and Peases. There were some fruitful husband-and-wife partnerships—John and Mary Priestman of Bradford, James and Mrs. C. L. Balfour of Chelsea. Father–son partnerships were naturally less common in the early stages of the movement: but the Wilfrid Lawsons father and son, William and Thomas Cash, and Jabez and Dawson Burns did much for the cause.

Secondly, teetotal societies gave special opportunities to the laity. Like many nonconformist bodies, they provided laymen with opportunities for leadership. In any clash between laymen and ministers, the teetotal cause tended to be identified with the laymen. This seems to have lain at the root of the clash between teetotalism and the Wesleyan Conference in 1841. Methodist schismatics seeking to increase lay influence within the Wesleyan connexion were more enthusiastic for teetotalism, at least until the 1870s, than the Wesleyans. Thus in Rochdale in the 1830s Wesleyan Associationists steadfastly supported teetotalism, whereas Wesleyans steered clear. Likewise in the Catholic world the League of the Cross aroused considerable Catholic lay enthusiasm and much hostility from the priesthood. Clergymen and ministers apprehensive at laicizing tendencies within the temperance movement could point to the eagerness with which temperance advocates assumed the title 'Revd.' and appropriated religious hymns for secular purposes.[37] The prominence of laymen in the temperance movement may be one reason why evangelical clergymen were far more likely than high churchmen to support it. It certainly helps to explain why the temperance movement was so bedevilled with disputes, for these often arose—in the temperance movement as elsewhere in the nonconformist world—from the struggle for power within the congregation or denomination. The schisms within the pseudo-masonic temperance body the Good Templars, active in England from the 1870s, arose from just this cause. 'Good Templarism has always seemed to me a society set on foot to put little men into big places,' wrote Thomas Whittaker; 'and as there are so many little men, they cannot all be provided for, and hence the scramble. . . .'[38] A man could gain respect and honours in a nonconformist congregation or temperance society when he could get them nowhere else. At both national and local level, temperance organizations easily drifted from mutual help to mutual admiration: testimonials were frequently presented, long and uninformative eulogies of departed members were carefully entered up in national temperance minute-books, and much flattery was exchanged between speakers at annual meetings. In 1857 the National Temperance League had to mollify an aggrieved supporter named Beaumont who complained, according to its minutes for 3 April, of 'the want of due attention upon his attending former London Meetings': a soothing letter had to be sent, hoping for the pleasure of his attendance at future gatherings.

Thirdly, the teetotal society played a central part in recruitment. The nonconformist congregation seems to have been divided into 'members' and 'hearers'—the latter attending some services and sharing some attitudes, without being fully admitted into the congregation.[39] Full members were recruited from the 'hearers', and the congregation had every reason to increase their number; this was done through the host of voluntary activities taking place on the chapel premises during week-nights—mothers' meetings, sales of work, mutual improvement groups, Christian Endeavour, cottage meetings, missions, Bible readings, choirs, Dorcas Clubs, sports clubs, plays. Among these bodies, the teetotal society was prominent, and it pursued the same role (unfamiliar to modern eyes) of combining moral reform with recreation. As a Presbyterian mission minister put it, in Charles Booth's survey of the 1890s, teetotal societies constituted the churches' 'fishing-ground' for their more regular membership—from younger age-groups through the Band of Hope, and from lower social levels through the teetotal experience meeting.[40]

Teetotal work played an integral part in the revivals which enlisted many hearers as full members.[41] Pledge-signing often marked an important stage in the conversion process, and often itself sparked off a revival. Thomas Whittaker described how, when spreading teetotalism in the north-east in the 1830s, he took the largest chapel in a colliery village: 'the galleries . . . would be beaded with men round the front, who, resting their elbows on the ledge, with upturned faces looked and longed for what to them was a new life. The hymn commencing—"Pledged in a noble cause", when announced from the chair, would bring such shouts of "Hallelujah" from a dozen voices as made the chapel ring; and as the tales of experience were told, and the words of exhortation given for the leading of a better life, the mellowing influence pervading the place was such as in my experience I have never felt before nor since.'[42] Teetotalers gave much publicity to the religious revival they had induced at Wilsden in 1835, and similar effects were observed in early Welsh teetotalism: 'spiritual zeal at summer heat is destruction to the liquor traffic' said one of its leaders. The connexion between revivals and temperance work persisted through the 1859 revivals to the last great Welsh revival of 1905.[43]

The religious beliefs of teetotal leaders were more important for giving them their immense energy than for channelling it in any particular direction. It seems probable that the temperance movement—like the revival itself—succeeded primarily in preserving or restoring the morals of the religious, rather than in influencing the irreligious and the indifferent. Pious nonconformist mothers and Sunday school teachers often feature in the early background of leading teetotalers, but so little information survives on their childhood that much of what follows must be highly speculative. For 28 of the sample, a pious parentage is specifically mentioned by obituarists, and this omits parents who were clergymen, ministers or local preachers. In some cases—as in that of John Finch—the child would react against the parents' beliefs, but these instances are relatively rare, and the child often reverted to the parents' views later in life. In common with most contemporary dissenters, many teetotalers received an upbringing which implanted guilt-feelings; these were drawn upon later in life by the temperance movement and by other religious organizations. Dissenters did not believe in educating children differently from adults; no apprehension was felt at stimulating their lively imaginations, or at preparing them for the anticipated sudden conversion. Reared on Fox's *Martyrs* and Bunyan's *Pilgrim's Progress*, many teetotalers must in childhood have endured fears similar to those of Thomas Okey, terrified as a boy of having 'unwittingly committed that mysterious, undefined, unpardonable sin against the Holy Ghost, and that hell fire were my portion'.[44] Jabez Tunnicliff, founder of the Band of Hope, recalled his remorse as a child after telling a lie. He woke up at night while the family were talking below: 'I thought that Satan was hurrying to my bed to carry me away. I screamed for help, and urged my sister, who ran to my assistance, to make haste, lest I should be seized before she could prevent his doing so.'[45]

The recollections of three leading teetotalers—Charles Bent, Joseph Rowntree and Robert Gray Mason reveal possible influences on the minds of many teetotal leaders. During his unregenerate days as a prize-fighter, Bent often recalled the advice of his father, a Wesleyan shoemaker and local preacher: 'many a time, when I have been going into the ring to fight, my father's advice has flashed across my guilty mind, when he told me always to keep company with those that were better than myself, and these impressions have caused many feelings of anguish and bitterness to me, on account of my being what I then was'. Joseph Rowntree, the Scarborough temperance reformer—in the midst of a wine party held to celebrate his admission to the York Merchants' Company in 1824—suddenly asked himself 'what would my mother think to see me under such circumstances?' On went his hat and out he walked, never again to attend such parties. Robert Gray Mason's conversion took place when he was acting as doorkeeper at a Cambridgeshire ball: 'the more I gazed on that frightful picture before me at that ball, I felt it to be a sort of hell upon earth. So deep was the lesson on my mind, and the impression on my heart, that I was afraid that God, in his righteous vengeance, would swallow up the wicked multitude with an earthquake. Under this alarming conviction I rushed from the inn without the utterance of a single word to any one, and at an hour or two past midnight ran off as fast as if the Devil was intent to stop me. Indeed I made a physical effort, for hearing a tempting uproar behind me to allure me back, I gave a kick at the Enemy of souls, after the manner that one horse would kick at another—and away I ran till I became breathless, and the bond was broken, I trust for ever. To God alone be all the praise. . . .' The effect of child-rearing did not cease with the pledge-signing. Indeed, the early teetotal movement passionately held that lives could be transformed even into old age by the individual admonition. The memory of such warnings could be a constant spur to further moral exertion. Many years later Mason recalled his meeting at the age of 21 with Richard Tabraham the Wesleyan temperance reformer: 'I think I still hear him, in sweet, soothing strains, saying, "*Robert, don't forget that you are a sinner.*" He seemed anxious, above all things, to impress that important sentiment on my soul.'[46]

One final religious factor common to almost all the teetotal leaders before 1872 is their public profession of religious belief. Several unorthodox teetotal leaders—Joseph Barker, for example—were gradually extruded from the teetotal movement which they did so much to create. John Finch was expelled from the Liverpool temperance movement in 1837 after objecting to the singing of the doxology at the end of a temperance meeting. References to the Trinity, salvation by faith alone, the atoning blood of the Lamb and many other theological items were frequently crowded into the prayers with which temperance meetings opened in the 1840s.[47] Despite the alignment between unbelief and teetotal practice in the early Victorian period, the official teetotal movement carefully preserved its reputation with the religious public by repudiating all heretical connexions. When the teetotal shoemaker and infidel William Empson asked John Cadbury—secretary of the Birmingham temperance society—for a testimonial to his sobriety, Cadbury refused in no uncertain terms: 'William Empson, I want to hold no communion with thee, and I have ordered others to hold no communion with thee! Thou hold'st infidel principles William Empson!' Despite their debt to John Finch, teetotal leaders strongly opposed Owenism; two of them—F. R. Lees and Mrs. C. L. Balfour—wrote pamphlets against it. In his *Owenism Dissected* (1839) Lees, in his most arrogant controversial manner, firmly denied that man is a creature of circumstance; and at least two other teetotal leaders, Dr. Grindrod and Edward Morris, openly opposed Owenism. Socialists who distributed tracts at a teetotal festival near London in 1840 were expelled, 'and to show their detestation of their detestable principles the tee-totalers tore up their tracts and threw them to the winds'.[48]

Secularism was one of the few reforming causes from which the teetotal leaders abstained. Involvement in early Victorian teetotalism, like support for C.N.D. in the 1950s, was 'a capsule statement of a distinctive moral and political outlook'.[49] The attack on the drink trade rallied together groups and individuals who disliked many other aspects of British society, and teetotal leaders moved easily from one form of protest to another.

TABLE 4

Other Reforming Activities of Prominent Teetotalers: 1833–1872

Prohibition	100	Owenism	2
Anti-slavery	41	Home Mission Society	2
Anti-Corn Law League	40	Financial Reform	2
Peace movement	39	Religious Tract Society	2
Liberation Society	36	Anti-duelling	2
Mechanics' institutes	22	Church Missionary Society	2
Anti-C. D. Acts	15	S.D.U.K.	2
Sunday schools	15	Climbing boys	2
Bible Society	14	Governor Eyre committee	2
Chartism	12	Hospitals	2
Animal cruelty	12	Aborigines Protection Society	2
Educational voluntarism	12	Lifeboat Society	1
Sanitary reform	11	Soldier's Friend Society	1
Complete suffrage	10	Anti-air pollution	1
Ragged schools	10	Lancasterian schools	1
Sabbatarianism	9	Administrative reform	1
Co-operation	8	Early Closing Association	1
Support of north in American Civil War	8	Anti-flogging	1
Factory regulation	8	Anti-Gambling League	1
Anti-smoking	7	Penitentiary movement	1
Free press	6	Anti-birth control	1
London Missionary Society	6	Church Pastoral-Aid Society	1
Public libraries	6	London Society for Promoting Conversion of the Jews	1
Sunday opening of museums	5		
Penal reform	5	Phonetic Society	1
Freehold land movement	4	London City Mission	1
Volunteer movement	3	Baptist Missionary Society	1
Freedman's aid movement	3	Aged Female Society	1
Reform League	3	Society for Bettering the Condition of the Poor	1
Pro-Garibaldi	3		
Y.M.C.A.	3	National Thrift Association	1
Anti-opium trade	3		

Over a quarter of the teetotal leaders supported the prohibitionist movement, and a tenth were active in both anti-slavery and anti-corn law movements. The anti-slavery connexion persisted into the 1860s when temperance leaders were prominent advocates of the north in the American Civil War. The Peace movement and the Bible Society, with 39 and 14 supporters respectively—were especially attractive to Quaker teetotalers.

Temperance reformers were much concerned at the sufferings of women—not only through drink, but also through sexual exploitation. The movement encouraged a few women on to its platforms; and although the men took the limelight, nine of the sample were women. Helen Blackburn listed eight teetotal leaders among the pioneer feminists; she might have included many more, for feminism in its various forms attracted at least twenty of the sample. The very act of joining a teetotal society involved a modest form of feminism: the belief that resources should be diverted from purely male pleasures to expenditure which could benefit the whole family. At least fifteen of the sample campaigned against state regulation of prostitution; F. W. Newman and H. J. Wilson were as prominent in Josephine Butler's campaigns as they were in the temperance movement. Several other teetotal leaders stimulated public concern at the problem of prostitution in other ways. John Edgar, the anti-spirits pioneer, wrote *Female Virtue—its Enemies and Friends* in 1841 for the London Society for the Protection of Young Females. J. Miller, author of the important medical work *Alcohol, its Place & Power* (1857) two years later published *Prostitution, Considered in Relation to its Cause and Cure*. William Logan wrote a study of *The Great Social Evil*, and Mrs. Wightman, James Raper, A. B. Craigie and Benjamin Parsons were among the many temperance workers who were as interested in reclaiming prostitutes as in rescuing drunkards.[50] Temperance reformers often stressed the link between the two evils: prostitutes congregated in public-houses, and could endure such a life only by drugging their moral sense with alcohol. Teetotal tracts see the first glass as the respectable woman's first step towards the lowest brothels of London.[51] Yet the alignment between temperance and feminism was never complete; John Bright was a temperance reformer whose anti-feminist views could hardly have been stronger; and while drinksellers were usually hostile to feminism, the brewer Stansfeld appears among Helen Blackburn's pioneer feminists.

Apart from the many religious and missionary movements supported by teetotal leaders, their reforming interests can broadly be described as humanitarian, educational and counter-attractive. Humanitarian causes were particularly popular with the Quakers; the teetotal movement united with the movements which promoted peace and penal reform, and which opposed animal cruelty, capital punishment, duelling and slavery. It was one of several movements which attacked the prevailing level of violence in society. The many educational movements which teetotal leaders supported had similar aims; even where teetotal leaders did not join a national educational society, they often helped to manage the local British schools, public libraries and mechanics' institutes. Temperance reformers were eager to inculcate thrift, not only through the savings banks—which at least eight of them actively supported—but also through building societies and the freehold land movement. Democratization of property-ownership was decidedly a teetotal policy.

As for counter-attractive movements, 11 teetotal leaders campaigned for sanitary reform, 7 for public parks, 8 for factory regulation; and, at the local level, several agitated for improved water-supplies and for recreational counter-attractions to the public-house. Clearly these men knew that moral exhortation was not enough; by no means all temperance reformers concentrated on the more negative forms of counter-attraction—on depriving the public-house of its charms, or on banning the public-house altogether. Five of the teetotal leaders favoured the Sunday opening of museums and art galleries as counter-attractions to the public-house, whereas nine, as staunch sabbatarians, repudiated such a policy. Wherever the counter-attractive policy required increased taxation or state intervention though, teetotal leaders were divided. Here their timidity—understandable in the contemporary context—dimmed their progressiveness, and they eventually gave way to reformers whose ideology was better adapted to the realities of industrial life.

Teetotal leaders were also divided on political reform movements. The movement's dissenting supporters were always divided between militants and quietists: a division which eventually led to the creation of a separate prohibitionist movement. As good Liberals, many teetotal leaders supported franchise extension, where this seemed compatible with good administration; but the movement's bias at first lay away from Westminster and towards the domestic hearth. Where teetotal leaders did engage in politics, they tended to choose movements in which employers and employees could campaign together—complete suffrage, the freehold land movement, educational and moral crusades, and above all the Anti-Corn Law League.

Apart from Joseph Sturge, Joseph Livesey was the most prominent of the temperance reformers to champion the League. His zeal for cheap corn stemmed partly from disappointment with the teetotal movement's failure rapidly to eliminate poverty. Comparing the 1840s with the 1830s, he noted that drunkenness had declined and teetotal membership had advanced, yet poverty had become even more widespread, 'which is most convincing that OTHER CAUSES are at work producing this great difference'. Livesey concluded that 'the times regulate drinking more than drinking the times'. Full of ideas and enthusiasm for the League, he made his greatest contribution through publishing his illustrated four-page *Struggle*; this paper attacked the corn laws together with related evils, and was designed specially for working men. Livesey claimed that through the *Struggle*, which at its peak enjoyed a circulation three times that of *The League*, he could address 'the mass of the people in all our large towns'.[52] His contribution to the League agitation did not pass unnoticed by its leaders.

Other personalities linked the two movements. John Bright was only the most conspicuous of several League supporters who had previously lectured for temperance societies. Teetotalers often provided the hospitality and the audience which League lecturers in rural areas badly needed. The League reciprocated at its banquets by providing teetotal drinks for those who preferred them.[53] But the affinity between the two movements was never complete. The League employed Alexander Somerville, a notorious drinker, as journalist: and also a beerseller named Murray as lecturer, though with some misgivings. And if Anti-Corn Law Leaguers often publicly recommended teetotalism, they seldom did so for its own sake, because this might have fragmented their movement: they recommended it because, like the moral force Chartists, they felt that it would enhance the dignity of their supporters, and by implication discredit their opponents. Still, many of the Anti-Corn Law League leaders sympathized privately with the teetotal movement—as their personal abstinence after 1846 reveals. Prentice, Perronet Thompson, Villiers, Cobden and Bright all praised voluntary abstinence in later years, for they knew that free trade could bring prosperity only to a temperate people.[54] Both causes posited the existence of a natural harmony if human beings would only behave rationally within rationally designed institutions. Both were opposed by rural interests anxious to keep up the price of grain—sometimes even by the use of violence: many free traders recognized that reducing the demand for intoxicants would have the same effect on corn prices as extending overseas grain supply.[55]

Here, then, is a formidable range of public concern—even by nineteenth-century standards. J. H. Raper was not the only teetotal leader whose biographer could boast that he had been 'identified with every movement that has made for national righteousness and social improvement'.[56] So the ideal-typical teetotal leader between 1833 and 1872 is a remarkable personality: a self-made, Lancashire-born, urban manufacturer of uncertain age—he has a lively conscience and believes in speaking his mind. Plain-living, progressive and upstanding, he votes and acts Liberal in local and national politics. He is active in personal philanthropy and feels passionately about peace, prohibition, free trade and religious liberty.

How does he react to the Britain of the 1960s? He nods his approval at the retreat (from Britain) of poverty, at the emancipation of women, the spread of education and the continued extension of humanitarianism. But he is puzzled at the survival—in a society enjoying universal education—of nationalism, high taxation, gambling, mass recreation and the Conservative party. And why, he asks, are chapels and political meetings so ill-attended? Where are the active citizens, the campaigners and the dissenters? Ecumenical and socially concerned the dissenters of the 1960s may be, but how have they come to lose their influence on the national life? His response therefore combines pleasure with regret—and nowhere more than in his attitude to young people. The growth of drugtaking astonishes him—for he spent a lifetime in denouncing drunkenness in Europe, and did he not also promote a campaign against the opium trade in the Far East? And how can intelligent young people repudiate the obvious virtues of respectability in their conduct and clothing? On closer inspection, though, his initial doubts seem unimportant, for his attitudes to young people could never be those of his successors in the temperance movement of the 1960s. He sees in many of them the same unselfish concern for principle (now often labelled 'self-sabotage'), the same individualism, idealism, suspicion of the state and impatience with the *status quo* which he himself had displayed—and not only in his younger days either. And he finds that they too are attacking the two great monsters which filled his own horizon: war and poverty.

8

Temperance and Religion: 1828–1872

In 1870 the Rev. G. W. McCree contrasted the prosperity of the contemporary temperance movement with its insecurity in the 1830s. He recalled a time when only the pulpits of James Sherman and Jabez Burns were available for London teetotalers; since then, there had been a striking increase in the number of temperance organizations, periodicals, temperance hotels and religious supporters.[1] What does this signify for the history of religion and of temperance in the period? Teetotalism in the 1830s was opposed by many religious bodies. Many religious leaders feared that teetotalism was substituting a purely secular and ethical crusade for the reliance on divine grace. The progressive Stanley of Norwich was the only bishop prominent on teetotal platforms. Teetotalers could always rely on support from a small minority of clergymen; indeed in 1836 the Vicar of Keighley, Theodore Dury, chaired teetotal meetings which were denounced by Robert Heys, a local dissenting minister. Thomas Beaumont spoke of Anglican support for teetotalism in 1841 and claimed that 'for numbers and zeal in its support, they exceed every other class of ministers'. Yet this was not true in London: 'they thought it a sin to look at us', James McCurrey recalled of Anglican attitudes to the early London teetotalers.[2] Nor does it seem to have been true in the country as a whole: two lists of ministerial abstainers published in temperance periodicals in 1837 and 1848 show the overwhelming predominance of nonconformists over Anglicans within the early teetotal movement.

285 ministers were listed in 1837, and 566 in 1848: of these, only 5% and 4%, respectively, were Anglicans: the rest were nonconformists. In both lists, Congregationalists constituted about one-quarter: the largest number in 1848, and in 1837 second only to the Calvinistic Methodists. Baptists came third in both lists, with 21% in 1837 and 15% in 1848. Primitive Methodists contributed only 4% in 1837, but in 1848 came second with 19%. Calvinistic Methodists were the largest group (26%) in 1837, but in 1848 were fourth with only 12%. All other denominations contributed 10% or less—the Wesleyans only 10% in 1837 and 5% in 1848.[3]

Despite the indifference of nonconformist denominations to early teetotalism, most contributed individuals prominent in the new movement. The Congregationalists gave it James Sherman of the Surrey Chapel: John Angell James of Birmingham: and W. R. Baker, author of important teetotal textbooks. The Baptists provided Francis Beardsall, a leading teetotaler of the 1830s; even the Wesleyans produced Robert Gray Mason, a teetotal lecturer who at one time seemed almost as successful in Scotland as Father Mathew in Ireland. The official Wesleyan condemnation of teetotalism in 1841 was never unanimously accepted within the denomination, and many teetotalers fought battles in the 1840s for entry into their chapels: 'I have never met with anything of this kind before', wrote T. Padman from Thetford to Jabez Bunting: 'I know not how to act. I have not strength of nerve to contend with them. I want your advice.'[4] Teetotalism was stronger in the Methodist offshoots from Wesleyanism; they gave more freedom to the layman as against the minister: to the local chapel, as against the centralized hierarchy. So enthusiastic for teetotalism were many Cornish Wesleyans that they defied the conference in 1841 and formed a sect of their own. The Primitive Methodist Conference recommended temperance societies as early as 1832, and in 1841 ordered unfermented wine to be used at communion; their leader Hugh Bourne often defended teetotalism publicly. Teetotalism made rapid strides among Bible Christians in the west of England, under the leadership of the denomination's second-in-command James Thorne. The Calvinistic Methodists were also enthusiastic, for teetotalism was closely associated with successful Welsh revivals during the late 1830s.[5]

A mere counting of heads would neglect the importance of the Catholics, who do not feature in the two lists. A few Catholic temperance societies were formed in the late 1830s and received a great boost from Father Mathew's activities in the early 1840s. But his failure to evolve an efficient temperance organization for consolidating his gains and the tendency of Catholics to keep themselves to themselves, prevented Catholic teetotalism from making a wide impact until rather later.[6] The Unitarians, although they contributed only 2% of the teetotal ministers in 1848, were also more important than their numbers suggest. Their beliefs made it difficult for them to co-operate with Christian temperance reformers at the local level,[7] and their contribution was made largely through talented and energetic individuals. In John Finch they produced one of the most energetic teetotal pioneers; and in F. W. Newman and M. D. Hill, two of the movement's most intelligent and influential supporters. The Quakers are also absent from the lists, yet their crucial importance to the early temperance movement has already been stressed. In most denominations, at least until the 1870s, most ministers were hostile or indifferent to teetotalism. Only in small denominations like the Bible Christians, Cowherdites and Evangelical Union was teetotalism really popular.

By the 1860s the picture had changed substantially. A list of teetotal ministers published in 1866 included 2,760 names, as compared with the 566 of the 1848 list.[8] Once again the list was not exhaustive: too much must not be deduced from comparing it with previous lists. Still, the advance of the Anglicans between 1848 and 1866 from 4% to 22% of the total must be significant; by 1866 the Anglicans were the largest group. The Congregationalists, with 19%, came second on the list; their 532 names constituted nearly a quarter of their total ministry. The Wesleyans (7%) were still low down on the list; and in 1862 only one Wesleyan preached a temperance sermon—as against 16 Anglicans, 16 Baptists, 9 Congregationalists, 3 Presbyterians, 2 Primitive Methodists and one Wesleyan Reformer.[9] The proportion of the total contributed by the dissenting denominations in 1866 had fallen in almost every case. Yet among the petitioners for Sunday closing in 1863 the Wesleyans, with 48% of the signatories, reigned supreme; the Congregationalists with 10% were their nearest rivals, and Anglicans contributed only 3%. It was perhaps easier to attract Wesleyans into the temperance cause when it was allied with sabbatarianism.[10]

Despite the relative decline in nonconformist dominance, teetotal progress was being made in all denominations from the 1850s. In 1860 Dawson Burns estimated that a sixth of the 1,400 Baptist ministers in Britain were abstainers, and that another third were sympathetic to the temperance movement. In 1862 about half the intake of dissenting theological colleges had become teetotal.[11] In all the denominations, the men of the future were by now becoming teetotalers: H. J. Wilson and Newman Hall among the Congregationalists: John Clifford and C. H. Spurgeon among the Baptists: and the Wesleyan Charles Garrett, a founder of the *Methodist Temperance Magazine* launched in 1868. Among the Congregationalists the champion of teetotalism was Samuel Morley: among the Quakers, Samuel Bowly and Edward Smith. Through their close links with the National Temperance League, Quakers helped to promote teetotalism within the established church during the 1860s. As Edward Smith put it, when recommending the League to the annual meeting of the Friends' Temperance Union in 1864: 'they must seek to influence the most influential people. If they proceeded from the bottom, the upper classes were not easily brought under influence'.[12]

The change began in the late 1850s, and stems from a shift in the attitudes to teetotalism among a group of evangelicals, the church party which had turned against teetotalism in the late 1830s. Anglican evangelicals had never been united against the teetotal movement—witness the temperance zeal of W. W. Robinson and Rev. Spencer Thornton. But an acceleration in Anglican teetotalism did not occur till Rev. Stopford J. Ram, evangelical Vicar of Pavenham, mobilized the many isolated teetotal clergymen. During 1857 he tried to compile a list of Anglican abstainers, and was greatly helped by Mrs. Wightman, the evangelical wife of a Shrewsbury vicar.[13] Strongly influenced by a fellow-evangelical, Catherine Marsh, she found teetotalism extremely helpful in converting local working men in 1858, and wrote up her experience in her influential book *Haste to the Rescue!* The book became popular at just the time when the Ulster revival had demonstrated the links between teetotalism and religious recruiting. Ram advertised in the press during 1859, asking all abstaining clergy to contact him; he received 158 answers. A teetotal address was then published, signed by 112 teetotal clergymen from all parts of England.[14]

The address claimed that drinking customs frustrated all contemporary efforts for the social and religious improvement of the people. Clergymen might labour with tracts and sermons, but still their Sunday evening congregations were outnumbered by 'the hideous assemblages' in drinking places. Special instruments must therefore be used against special evils: teetotal association might remove impediments to salvation. The clergy—inspired by Christian charity rather than by Christian duty or Biblical injunction—must set a teetotal example, otherwise they would never influence working men. Dean Close developed the point in 1862: if clergymen would take up the temperance question 'they would draw the people around them'.[15] The address insisted that teetotalism was quite compatible with health. 'Is it not drink above all things which . . . keeps back numbers from the house of God?' it perorated: 'which degrades the masses of society, and mars almost every effort to win souls to Christ?' The list includes several clergymen who had long supported teetotalism—notably W. W. Robinson, Henry Gale and William Caine. Evangelicals were prominent among the signatories: headed by the arch-evangelical Dean Close and concluded by the evangelical Ram, six of its first nine signatories were evangelicals.* The list includes an Associate Secretary of the Society for Promoting Christianity among the Jews, an Associate Secretary of the C.M.S. and three Associate Secretaries of a church society much loved by evangelicals—the Church Pastoral-Aid Society. If the signatories who can be identified in the subscription-lists of the Church Pastoral-Aid Society's 1859 annual report are assumed to be evangelicals, 45 of the 112 clergymen in the 1859 teetotal list were certainly evangelicals, seven possibly; on 60 there is no information. But many leading evangelicals were not on the list—which included no bishops and few distinguished clergymen.

In 1860 the address was signed by the evangelical Robert Maguire, Vicar of Clerkenwell, and in 1861 by Canon Ellison, Vicar of Windsor. The drawing-room meetings of Samuel Bowly and Mrs. Fison organized by the National Temperance League—together with the League's distribution of over 10,000 copies of *Haste to the Rescue!* to every clergyman in the kingdom —helped to prepare the ground for founding the Church of England Total

* I am most grateful to Rev. J. S. Reynolds for providing me with this information; and to Dr. Walsh for help with this paragraph.

Abstinence Society (later Church of England Temperance Society) in 1862. Indeed, the National Temperance League claimed the credit for its foundation. Dean Close became president, Rev. H. J. Ellison chairman of committee, Maguire and Ram secretaries. In 1864, 433 abstaining clergymen were listed in England and Wales. By 1866 this figure had risen to 484, the leading dioceses being Lichfield with 9·9%, London with 8·9%, Chester with 7·2% and Manchester with 7·0% of the total. The familiar pattern of urban dominance, with London surrounded by relative apathy, was repeated here—though with more support from the west midlands and less from the south-west than was customary in other temperance organizations. The strength of teetotalism once more lay in the north of England, though here the leadership came from London. The relative predominance of support in the north would appear even more striking if related to the number of clergy in each diocese, because Anglican clergy were thickest on the ground in the south.[16] Clearly these figures include only a fraction of the teetotal clergy active at the time, for according to the *Temperance Spectator* on 1 June 1866, there were 1,600 abstaining clergy in that year, whereas the C.E.T.S. listed only 578. In the sphere of temperance, therefore, the 1860s saw an Anglican advance over dissent comparable to the Anglican incursion into penitentiary work in the 1850s: but with temperance the evangelicals pioneered the new development, whereas with penitentiaries the pioneers were high churchmen.

The monthly *Church of England Temperance Magazine* issued after 1862 contrasts markedly with the teetotal publications of the 1830s. It has none of the full-blooded radicalism of Livesey's publications: none of the crude woodcuts mirroring the prejudices rife among working people in the north. All is utterly out of touch with the realities of working class life. But these limitations did not preclude prosperity: by the late 1860s the bishops were once again beginning to join the temperance movement—partly, no doubt, in emulation of Archbishop Manning who in 1868 publicly committed himself to the prohibitionist movement and from 1872 combined this with active Catholic teetotal work in his 'League of the Cross'. The annual income of the C.E.T.S. rose rapidly—from £218 in 1863 to £790 in 1867; during the 1870s the Society went from strength to strength.* By 1877 its organization covered the country, and its annual income had risen to about £7,000 a year.[17] In 1875 the Queen became the Society's patron: 'our success is almost enough to turn our heads,' said a speaker at the annual meeting of 1876. In his thanksgiving sermon Canon Ellison spoke of 'the increase of our income to an extent beyond our most sanguine expectations'.[18]

How do we explain this success? Partly it stemmed from the Society's adoption of the 'dual basis' in 1872: from the combination in one organization

* I am most grateful to Mr. Gerry Olsen, King's College, University of Western Ontario, Canada, for guidance on C.E.T.S. revenue.

of reclamation work through teetotal association with more general temperance work through the association of non-abstainers.[19] In some ways this involved a return to the basis of the old British and Foreign Temperance Society—in that it once more attracted the wealthy into temperance work and repudiated any sectarian insistence on teetotalism. This gave it the funds to develop the counter-attractive policies pioneered in the 1860s by the National Temperance League: street-stalls to supply coffee to working men were sent out during the 1870s, and reclamation work in the police courts became important after a police court missionary was appointed in 1876.

From the late 1860s, therefore, it was becoming uncommon for religious leaders publicly to oppose temperance effort. Rev. J. R. Stephens surprised a Sunday closing meeting in 1867 when he said he was quite prepared to meet working men in public-houses. Bishop Fraser of Manchester provoked a storm in 1870 when he claimed that bitter beer was a good preparation for preaching a sermon. And in 1877 Canon Harper of Selby was a lone voice in pleading that clergymen should be sociable with their parishioners in the public-house;[20] the C.E.T.S. firmly put him in his place. By the 1870s the temperance movement had therefore acquired an almost exclusively Christian flavour. Differences of denominational structure, differences in theology—these seem to have had little effect on this uniform pattern. Charles Booth, discussing temperance societies in the 1890s, claimed that they were 'almost all connected with some Christian church or mission, and there are few churches or missions which do not interest themselves in work of this kind'.[21] What does this striking change signify? At first sight, increasing success for both religion and temperance. In reality, accelerated secularization of religion and accentuated élitism within the temperance movement. Each of these aspects must now be considered in turn.

Early Victorian atheists were often teetotalers: this is not surprising, given the freethinker's enthusiasm for rationality and self-improvement, and his desire to outdo the Christians in upholding the existing moral code. Rationalists like G. J. Holyoake, George Combe and Henry Hetherington were eager for Christians to abandon their squabbles over doctrine and liturgy, and to unite behind the crusade for moral reform.[22] The official temperance movement was always flanked by a fringe of societies largely composed of working men but not directly attached to any orthodox Christian or temperance body. In 1852 the *Westminster Review* described this new form of puritanism as 'physical puritanism'—puritanism of the body—and noted that cleanliness and temperance had become 'the very religion of the materialist'. Bradlaugh himself learnt his atheism at a temperance hall, and in 1858 a secularist noted the existence of 'a deep undercurrent . . . tending towards Free-thought' in the temperance movement.[23]

The orthodox temperance movement struggled to avoid the world-centredness of the atheist teetotaler. It made direct appeals to religious leaders, attached its societies to religious organizations wherever possible, conducted its propaganda in religious phraseology, and shunned all contact with atheists like John Finch and Joseph Barker. Yet if the movement was to gain working class support, and, indeed, to recruit itself at all—it often had to appeal to worldly motives. Viewed in historical perspective, the temperance movement unconsciously realized atheist objectives by emphasizing man's control over his own fate, his capacity to triumph over sin, and the irrelevance of many Biblical statements as guides to modern living.

Any belief that dietary choice could influence human health conflicted with the superstition that disease was divinely ordained and was even to be welcomed as a sign of divine favour. 'From the time I became a teetotaler', wrote Joseph Barker, 'I have never had one half-hour's toothache.' The belief that human health was governed by natural laws which every individual could perceive for himself was held by teetotalers, secularists and phrenologists alike—yet it was only beginning to find acceptance among orthodox Christians. If inanimate machines worked so well with constant attention, asked Robert Owen, 'what may not be expected if you devote equal attention to your vital machines, which are far more wonderfully constructed?'[24]

Notions of human powerlessness were attacked from other directions by teetotalers. Evangelicals traditionally regarded men as depraved creatures incapable of pleasing God with their paltry 'works', which were as 'filthy rags' in His sight. Man could be reclaimed only through accepting divine forgiveness, which involved subscribing to a set of precise beliefs. 'Christianity', wrote Wilberforce, 'calls on us . . . not merely in *general*, to be *religious* and *moral*, but *specially* to believe the doctrines, and imbibe the principles, and practise the precepts of Christ.' Many early Victorian evangelicals therefore looked on teetotalism—with its stress on purely secular motives, and its attempt to supersede doctrinal and liturgical controversy by a united crusade for moral reform—as 'a subtle form of "works", and tending to self-reliance and self-righteousness'.[25] Teetotalers challenged such fatalistic attitudes to sin. They fearlessly asserted that drunkards could be reclaimed; they went still further in their attack on individual moral responsibility by arguing that drunkenness resulted not from a man's own weakness but from the peculiar qualities of the drink, or even from an environment studded with drinkshops. By the 1880s R. W. Dale was commenting upon the rarity with which sermons now mentioned the doctrine of justification by faith in its original sense; far more frequently was it argued that we are justified through faith because through faith we become personally righteous. Such an emphasis on 'works' would have alarmed the earlier evangelicals.[26] Teetotalers contributed towards this change: for them the world was not a vale of tears but a place in which man, by his own efforts at improving himself and his environment, can attain genuine happiness.

This meliorism inevitably led teetotalers into an early form of Bible criticism, and even into challenging the Bible's authority as an infallible guide to modern life. Once again teetotalers were unconsciously doing the secularists' work for them.[27] The prohibitionist F. W. Newman even went so far as to reject the Bible and conventional Christian morality as a guide to present-day life; he wanted it superseded by public legislation founded on scientific investigation and inspired by belief in moral progress. Though few teetotalers went as far as he, most argued that the Bible at no point praised intoxicating drink, and some working men even taught themselves Hebrew so that they could defend their teetotalism against religious attack.[28] Elaborate glosses were provided on the real nature of the wine mentioned in the Bible, and abstruse written and oral discussions were conducted on what had really happened at Cana. Still more dangerous in the eyes of the orthodox was the teetotaler's tendency to argue that the Bible message was conceived in conditions quite different from those of the modern world, and that therefore its injunctions could not be followed literally in every case.

This attitude had been present in teetotalism from the start. Even if the wine at Cana was intoxicating, Livesey argued in his *Malt Lecture*, 'it does not follow that in another age, and under other circumstances, for the purpose of accomplishing a great reformation, abstinence may not be necessary'. During a long controversy in 1840–1 between the *Bristol Temperance Herald* and F. R. Lees in the *British Temperance Advocate*, Lees insisted that many Biblical statements conflicted with 'the facts of natural history, and the evident results of anatomical experiments'. Lees even maintained that if the Bible, properly interpreted, conflicted with teetotalism—he would reject the former and cleave to the latter. Only an academic hair's-breadth now separated him from the atheist who held that the Bible's failure to censure Noah for his drunkenness was 'only one of the numerous instances of the imperfect and perverted morality of the Bible'.[29]

There was an outcry from the orthodox, for these statements justified J. Angell James' fear that teetotalers were 'determined if the Bible stand in the way of their notions to shove it aside'.[30] In answer to teetotalers who claimed that Christ, if he did not recommend teetotalism, 'did not live in Shoreditch in the nineteenth century', the B.F.T.S. claimed that to Christ at Cana 'the actual circumstances of our country at this day, were as fully present as those by which he was surrounded'.[31] In 1841, 'cries of "shocking", and confusion' from moderationists greeted quotations from a teetotal hymn which spoke of the teetotal star coming 'like redeeming power': behind such protests lay a shrewd suspicion that the teetotal movement was turning religious techniques to secular purposes, and was overturning evangelical theology into the bargain.[32] One historian has argued that the loss of faith in the nineteenth century stemmed not from the effects of scientific discovery or from the higher criticism, but from 'a sensed incongruity between a vigorous and hopeful meliorism and the doctrinal legacy of the Christian tradition'.[33] Yet this is to separate the inseparable: in the 1840s teetotalers were pronounced meliorists who believed that their practice was soundly based in scientific truth, and who actively engaged in Bible criticism in order to defend it.[34]

The whole notion informing the 1859 Anglican teetotal manifesto—that moral reform must often precede religious conversion—flatly contradicted the message of William Wilberforce's *Practical View*: 'remove the Theology', said his son Samuel in 1861, 'and you take away the morality.'[35] However it might rationalize the change, late-Victorian religion concentrated increasingly on moral reform—as the early Victorian atheists had always hoped it would. In 1881 the Evangelical Alliance, so suspicious in the 1840s of the temperance movement, passed a resolution urging the importance of uniting Christians behind the legislative attack on intemperance. Edmund Gosse described such emphasis on the need for social and moral reform as 'quite recent as a leading feature of religion'.[36] Why, then, did it occur?

The pioneers of Anglican teetotalism in 1859–60 were perhaps deliberately vague about their real motives. The reasons provided in Dean Close's *Why I Have Taken the Pledge* (1860) certainly give no general explanation. The change was of course presented as part of the Christian campaign against heathendom. The notion that drink customs constituted a form of rival worship to Christianity had long been prevalent in religious circles. 'It is not in bowing the knee to idols that idolatry consists', wrote Wilberforce, 'so much as in the internal homage of the heart.'[37] Teetotalers capitalized on such ideas by writing books with titles like *The Idolatry of Britain* or by drawing pictures like Cruikshank's 'Worship of Bacchus'. The church and the tavern were each conceived as housing their congregations—the problem being to empty the taverns into the church. There had always been similarities between the atmosphere of church and tavern—the priest/publican: hymns/pub-songs: stained glass/frosted glass: the altar rail/the bar: the bar handles/the altar candles: the altar/the bar back. The competition between church and tavern was implicitly recognized even before the 1820s—when magistrates often closed taverns during the hours of Sunday morning church service. The church and tavern, whose recreational facilities had for so long been complementary, now began to turn against each other. In a desperate rear-guard action, some late-Victorian Christians bought up public-houses and converted them into coffee palaces [see Plate 22].

Thomas Whittaker thought that denominational temperance societies were created, not by universal charity, but by religious rivalry—'not by true religion, but by the want of it'. In the 1830s teetotalism flourished among some nonconformist groups partly because nonconformists, by joining the new movement, could publicly demonstrate their moral superiority to the established church. 'In those days', wrote a commentator fifty years later, 'it was expected of the Nonconformist . . . that he should exhibit a much higher type of moral and religious character than his Church of England brother aspired to, otherwise he lost his very *raison d'être*.' By the 1860s inter-denominational rivalry seems again to have been at work—but in the reverse direction: many mid-Victorian Anglicans hoped that disestablishment might be staved off by an established church which excelled nonconformity in its social and moral utility. Canon Wilberforce despised church defence organizations as a way of saving the Church of England: 'true Church Defence is not platform agitation', he wrote, 'but . . . Church Aggressiveness in the face of evil.' To some extent he and his like succeeded in their aim. Referring in 1879 to the C.E.T.S., Hugh Price Hughes urged nonconformists to 'look to their laurels,—the Church of England is taking the wind completely out of their sails'. The late-Victorian Anglican resurgence in the face of dissenting attack is fully reflected in temperance history.[38]

Once the seriousness of the threat from rationalism became clear, and once all denominations had established their temperance departments, the attack upon drunkenness became something which could unite Christians against the foe. Anglican evangelicals had long been co-operating with dissenters on reforming crusades. The temperance movement pushed the trend further: on late-Victorian temperance platforms Anglicans co-operated with Roman Catholics and even with Unitarians. 'He held that conversion was far above, and of greater importance than, any denominational differences of whatever kind,' wrote G. W. McCree's biographer: 'the same might be said of many temperance workers.'[39] Mission work and close contact with the poor encouraged such sentiments: ecumenicalism has always flourished on the fringes of the Christian community, whether it be in the mission field overseas or in the slum mission at home. For missionaries know how formidable is the Christian task, how feeble are Christian resources; unless all Christian assets are mobilized, the task seems impossible. Furthermore, mission work brings Christians into contact with people more easily influenced by a moral example than by theological argument. Just as seventeenth-century moral reform crusades united protestants more afraid of Catholicism than of each other, so nineteenth-century temperance reform united Christians who feared the rationalist more than any fellow Christian. 'Let the enemy appear at the gates . . .', wrote Canon Ellison in 1878, 'and . . . former animosities are at once perceived to be trivial and are forgotten under the sense of the common danger.'[40]

Christians and temperance reformers were often quite unabashed in announcing the unimportance of theological tenets. 'Argument never yet made a vital Christian, and never will,' wrote the prohibitionist H. S. Sutton.[41] Temperance reformers were staunch believers in 'practical religion'—the religion of daily conduct rather than of book-learning. The great advantage of the moral crusade was that it diverted attention away from the shaken intellectual foundations of the Christian faith. In a whirl of reforming activity Christians would have little time for doubt. Perhaps the most famous temperance reformer identified with this important religious transition was T. H. Green. Nowhere is it more true than in the mid-Victorian moral reform crusade that the full influence of evangelicalism becomes apparent only when one follows the sheep who stray from the fold.[42] Green's great influence stemmed from his capacity to substitute for shaken doctrinal belief a faith in the doctrine of citizenship and in the politics of reform. 'Though the failing heart cries out for evidence, at the worst live on as if there were God and duty, and they will prove themselves to you in your life.'[43]

It is doubtful whether, in the long term, religion profited by these developments. 'A good deal of what passes as religion nowadays', complained Bishop Fraser in 1875, 'seems fond of parading behind bands and flags through the streets, but is seldom found in a place of worship.' Christian willingness to preach the word in theatres, public-houses and temperance societies made greater concessions to irreligion than Christians imagined. By the 1880s religious organizations were even promoting cricket clubs—a policy which half a century before would have been unthinkable.[44] Like so many organizations attached to religious congregations, the temperance society constituted a half-way house between participation in and rejection of Christian association. In ultimate effect, if not in original intent, the temperance movement has been one of several agencies which in modern times have gradually deprived the churches of their social function. The moderationist critics of teetotalism were therefore correct in pinpointing its long-term secularizing tendency: yet what was the alternative for mid-Victorian Christians? If they shunned so attractive a crusade, they would in the short term condemn themselves to impotence. It is also doubtful whether in the long run the temperance movement gained by the partnership; for as soon as temperance societies came to be attached almost exclusively to religious organizations, they were bound to acquire some of the respectability of their hosts.

'Most organisations appear as bodies founded for the painless extinction of the ideas of their founders,' said Leonard Courtney, of Christians who supported the Boer War.[45] For two of the earliest temperance leaders—Joseph Livesey and John Dunlop—the extinction was decidedly painful; from the 1830s until their deaths they made periodic cries of protest at the directions their temperance movement was taking. Livesey's complaints were accentuated by his lifelong contempt for the ceremonial with which human beings like to surround themselves. On one occasion, when invited to give a sermon, he saw the Bible resting upon a tasselled cushion, removed it, and deliberately sat upon it before beginning to speak. By 1870 a distinctly nostalgic strain had crept into Livesey's comments on the early days of the movement: 'I know that the hearts of our teetotalers in primitive times were knit together far closer than they are at present,' he said. Far from rejoicing at the improved prosperity of the temperance movement, he merely contrasted its mood with the idealism and self-denial of early teetotalism, and deplored its relative lack of achievement. 'The success of our early efforts has fallen so much short of our expectations', he wrote in 1871, 'and so much remains yet to be done, that but for the encouragement I constantly receive from my friends, I fear I should lose much of that hope by which we are sustained.'[46] The contrast between the early and later movement did not exist merely in the mind of an old man sighing for the vigour of youth: a real change had occurred in the movement during his lifetime. In 1882 at the age of 88, Livesey visited the annual meeting of the British Temperance League at Preston; with the aid of his son and daughter-in-law he walked round the chapel where the delegates were assembled, shaking hands with a few he recognized, but too old and ill to speak. Many in the chapel were deeply moved; at Thomas Whittaker's suggestion, they struck up the verse beginning 'Praise God from whom all blessings flow'. The meeting then acted upon a delegate's suggestion that a minute be spent 'in asking God to carry on the work commenced by Mr. Livesey'.[47] It was the most ironic moment in Livesey's long and eventful career: for Livesey had opposed the foundation of the League in the 1830s, and rightly feared that formal temperance organization would damage the cause irreparably.

Livesey's basic complaint about the later temperance movement was that it had become almost exclusively religious; from this followed several ancillary objections. Livesey always intended that there should be a temperance *reformation*—he never intended that it should degenerate into a mere 'movement'. He wanted it to influence the whole population, not merely the church- and chapel-goers. He therefore aimed to set teetotalism on a foundation acceptable to all. Yet his hopes were not fulfilled: despite the scientific and medical basis of his *Malt Lecture*, teetotalism became, as he himself complained in 1868, 'a useful expedient only, for the furtherance of denominational religion'. Likewise John Dunlop, struggling in the 1840s to compile medical testimonials on teetotalism, frequently complained that temperance societies showed insufficient zeal. Despite their firm Christian faith, both men would have agreed on this point with the temperance movement's atheist critic, G. J. Holyoake: in the hands of the temperance movement, he complained, temperance was becoming 'the cause of a small number of people, when it ought to be the cause of the great majority of the population'.[48] The minute-books of the British and National Temperance Leagues in the 1860s show temperance evangelism taking the form solely of lecturers fulfilling 'engagements'; when no engagements could be arranged, temperance organizations did not respond by sending their agents to preach in the highways and byways, as the pioneer teetotalers had done—but by transferring them to collecting subscriptions or promoting newspaper circulations.

As soon as its societies attached themselves to nonconformist congregations, the temperance movement's advocates tended to become professionals. In the early days of teetotalism, no temperance lecturers had been paid, most were working men, and all gave their time free of charge. Livesey constantly urged a return to this practice in later years: 'let me assure you . . . that this work is not to be done by proxy . . .' he insisted in 1871. As early as 1837 he had expressed the hope that there would never be any distinction between 'clergy' and 'laity' in the movement. Temperance societies should rely on themselves for speakers and not depend on itinerant advocates from other places.[49] By the 1850s Livesey feared that the movement would soon be 'dwindling into a mere formal service; the work to be done merely speaking at the "hall", and that chiefly by a paid agent'.[50] His was a lost cause: in the temperance movement in the 1840s, as in the Primitive Methodist denomination, it was widely felt that advocacy should no longer be left to working men and amateurs. In this the temperance movement was merely partaking in the general professionalization of nonconformity in the early Victorian period.[51] The way was already being prepared for a temperance movement with no personal experience of the drunkard's miseries, and which merely passed the time listening to itinerant lecturers who spoke about them. The popularity of J. B. Gough's theatrical lectures in the 1850s is proof enough that this was occurring. If any contact with the poor was still retained, this was often through the paid missionary. 'I would rather have one good plain disinterested teetotaler,' said Livesey, 'who gives every week what time he has to spare to the cause, than fifty vice-presidents who do little or nothing.' Not surprisingly, it became common for old temperance workers to lament the trend of the times.[52]

In the 1850s the old 'experience meetings' were being replaced by 'drawing-room meetings'. By the 1870s the public procession of reformed drunkards had become a rarity, though Livesey saw it as 'a living, moving lecture in the face of all men; an appeal to the senses which cannot be misunderstood' [see Plate 14].[53] The temperance movement was, in short, once again becoming respectable. In 1881, the year of the London Temperance Jubilee, Gladstone publicly testified to this fact by conferring knighthoods on two prominent teetotalers—William Collins II and Hugh Owen; Edward Baines had already been knighted in the previous year. Not only had teetotalism brought prosperity to many of the old members: the successful movement was also attracting new adherents from a higher social grade. With success came funds, and hence the demand for the temperance hall. Bradford Temperance Society built the first of these in 1837, and many others followed—barely distinguishable from nonconformist chapels [see Plate 18]. This involved the temperance society in extensive fund-raising activities, which had little to do with the reclamation of drunkards. Livesey and Whittaker felt that temperance halls did more harm than good: yet they were powerless to arrest the tendency.[54] Livesey's sentiments are common among the founders of successful social movements, who loathe the formalism of organizations and resent the constraint which success imposes upon spontaneity and initiative. Yet Father Mathew's ultimate failure shows that organization, with all its disadvantages, is essential for ultimate success.

By the 1850s a further development had occurred to alarm Livesey—the tendency to concentrate on rearing the children in sobriety instead of reclaiming their parents. Without depreciating such efforts, Livesey insisted that work among adults must not be allowed to suffer: 'to retreat from the great world of grown drinkers in order to teach boys and girls merely, is, to my mind, an indication of weakness, and rather a symptom of despair'.[55] In the 1830s temperance work among children began in several places independently. During his temperance tours of the mid-1840s, Dr. Grindrod devoted special effort to educating children in temperance principles; many years later he claimed to have formed many juvenile temperance associations some time before the Band of Hope was founded in Leeds in 1847; he even claimed that the name was being used two years before then, though he never produced any evidence for this. Once again it is clear that an important temperance innovation was 'in the air' and should not be credited to any single individual. As Grindrod wrote during the controversy in 1883, 'the name is of little consequence. Who did the work?'[56] In 1847 Mrs. Anne Carlile, while visiting Leeds Sunday School children, first applied the term 'Band of Hope' to groups of children organized for temperance work. The widow of an Irish Presbyterian minister, she had for many years been active in prison visiting, temperance work and prostitute reclamation. The organizer of the meeting addressed by Mrs. Carlile was a Leeds Baptist minister and shoemaker's son, Rev. Jabez Tunnicliff, teetotaler, anti-Calvinist and energetic composer of temperance songs.[57] On 2 September 1847 a ladies' committee of the Leeds Temperance Society was appointed to visit local schools,[58] and the new movement was safely launched.*

By March 1849 the Leeds Band of Hope had pledged more than 4,000 young people between the ages of six and sixteen. Managed by twelve ladies and a president appointed by the parent committee, the Band of Hope took care that adults should not dominate the proceedings: children were encouraged to sing temperance songs and if possible to influence their parents.[59] From its very origins the Band of Hope was closely connected with Sunday school work. Many members were attracted by its annual outings, and it

* The history of the Band of Hope has yet to be written: the official history—R. Tayler, *The Hope of the Race* (1946)—is a mere brochure. Much valuable evidence on what occurred at meetings could still be gleaned from old people who were members in their childhood, and there is useful information in F. Smith (Ed.), *The Jubilee of the Band of Hope Movement* (1897). But an adequate history will not be written until we possess a full-scale study of the nineteenth-century Sunday school.

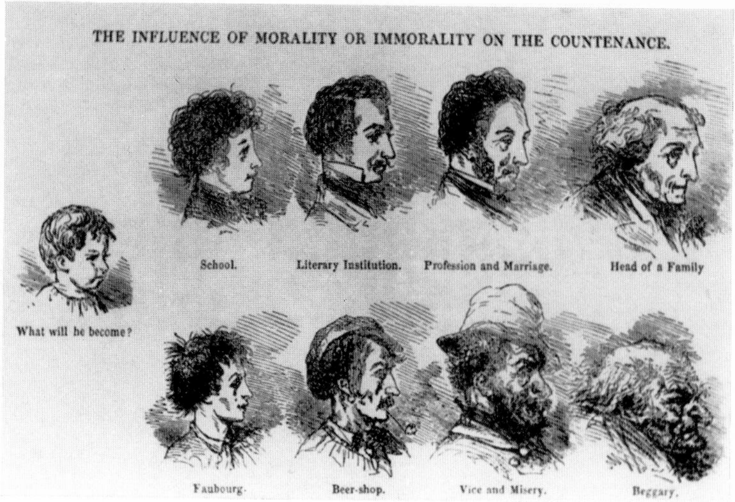

16. THE CHOICE BETWEEN ROUGH AND RESPECTABLE STYLES OF LIFE which faces every individual—portrayed by Cassell's *Popular Educator*, 1852. Here the professional man is contrasted with the man whose moral failings have assigned him a lower social position. From S. Nowell-Smith, *The House of Cassell, 1848–1958* (1958). [see p. 150]

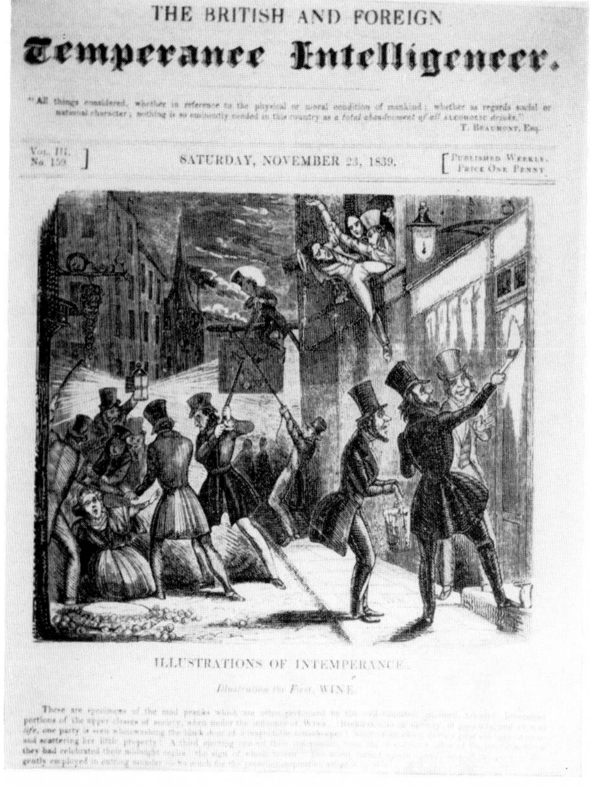

THE BRITISH AND FOREIGN

Temperance Intelligencer.

"All things considered, whether in reference to the physical or moral condition of mankind; whether as regards social or national character, nothing is so eminently needed in this country as a *total abandonment of all* ALCOHOLIC *drinks*."

T. BEAUMONT, Esq.

VOL. III. No. 159] SATURDAY, NOVEMBER 23, 1839. [PUBLISHED WEEKLY. PRICE ONE PENNY

ILLUSTRATIONS OF INTEMPERANCE.

Illustration the First, WINE.

17. A TEETOTAL VIEW OF ARISTOCRATIC DRUNKARDS. Teetotalers attacked drunkenness at both social extremes; here respectable citizens are being molested by idle wine-drinking young aristocrats. From *British & Foreign Temperance Intelligencer*, 23 Nov. 1839, p. 449. [see p. 149]

18. THE FIRST PERMANENT TEMPERANCE HALL, BRADFORD, 1837. Hardly distinguishable from a nonconformist chapel. From *Preston Temperance Advocate*, June 1837, p. 41. [see p. 191]

19. AN EARLY MASS MEETING OF THE BAND OF HOPE. Exeter Hall, London, 1852. 6,000 children were present; the Band of Hope had been in existence for only five years. From *Illustrated London News*, 21 Feb. 1852. [see p. 193]

never restricted itself exclusively to temperance work. The pledge was not very onerous to children, most of whom had not even experienced temptation. By 1851 the movement was strong enough in Bradford to allow the formation of the first Band of Hope 'Union' of societies; and at the mass children's demonstration in Exeter Hall in 1852, 6,000 children were present [cf. Plate 19].[60]

By January 1860 there were 120 Bands of Hope in London; the London Band of Hope Union employed three agents and divided London into districts, each with its own superintendent.[61] The Manchester and Salford District Band of Hope Union, founded in 1863, included ten societies at first, but during 1864 the first of several demonstrations in the Free Trade Hall was promoted. In 1865 a periodical *Onward* was begun; it was intended for children, and included music, stories and poetry but no pictures until 1872. The Union appointed its first agent in 1866, and grew so fast that by February 1871 it boasted 166 societies and had become the largest in the kingdom—with six affiliated local Unions, representing 100 societies.[62] *Onward*'s circulation increased sevenfold between 1865 and 1871. 'Our Band of Hope conductors should strive to form such an hatred to the drink in the minds of their members', said the chairman of the Lancashire and Cheshire Band of Hope Union in 1872, 'as will, in the next generation, at least, be irresistible and sweep the whole traffic away.'[63]

In 1870 *Onward* described what Band of Hope meetings should be like: they began with a temperance hymn and prayers, then came the chairman's address. Music, readings, recitations and speeches followed, and were concluded by the chairman's speech and appeal for pledge-signing; the meeting then ended with a prayer. The chairman of the Lancashire and Cheshire Band of Hope Union suggested in March 1872 that meetings should be held fortnightly with occasional picnics, tea-meetings, singing-classes and exhibitions of dissolving views.[64] Bands of Hope were respectable institutions from the start, as a writer in 1860 testified: 'without meaning any disparagement to the merits of the early temperance reformers, we must say that the juvenile cause has fallen into the hands of those who possess a much larger amount of discretion, tact, and intelligence than did the leaders of the adult societies'.[65] Strenuous efforts were being made by the 1870s to preserve this respectability. A writer in 1870 attacked dialect recitations, for Band of Hope meetings should educate the young in purity of language and manners. He was very particular about the recreations provided: 'nothing should be read that is absurd, or ridiculous, or questionable in its moral tone.'[66] The editor in 1870 endorsed this view—the movement was becoming a recognized institution of the country and its tone must be upheld: 'we are not now fighting for bare existence but for pre-eminence, and every step we advance requires one of equal preparation and fitness.'[67]

The growth of the Band of Hope between 1847 and 1872 seems to indicate a decline in the almost millennial enthusiasm of the early teetotal movement. It also represents the increased self-consciousness of temperance reformers as a community, as an élite whose children must be protected against the snares of a wider world. In October 1870 the British Temperance League's general purposes committee resolved that 'as the proper training of the Youth of both sexes in the principles of true temperance is believed to be the most effectual means by which our movement will be brought to a successful issue', the League's agents should address young people 'where the Society is willing to substitute such lecture for an ordinary one'. The blood relationship between so many leading temperance reformers both reflected and created a certain inward-looking mentality in the movement. Not only did it cater for parents and children: it also, in some cases, even tried to restrict marriages with outsiders. By inducing female supporters to vow that 'if he will not drink water he shall not have me', some temperance reformers were intruding into their movement that group endogamy which enables the sect to preserve itself from worldly taint.[68]

However ecumenical teetotal leaders might be in their public statements, their humbler followers found it difficult to shake off sectarian tendencies. Livesey fought off suggestions that an entrance-fee should be charged at temperance meetings, for this would exclude precisely those working men whom the movement most needed to influence. Evangelization was less and less the movement's objective, however, and the last burst of genuine working-class teetotal zeal came with the Garibaldian Life-Boat crews of the 1860s.[69] Far from initiating a national reformation, teetotalism from the 1840s gradually became a way of drawing the line between the righteous and the unrighteous. The pledge-signing became a means of attracting individuals out of 'the world' instead of a weapon for transforming it; too frequently it involved, not a dramatic transformation of the individual's life, but an expected change in his growth to maturity within a drink-free environment. The *Cornwall Teetotal Journal* of 1842 admitted that many teetotalers misinterpreted the text 'come out from among the ungodly, and be ye separate'.[70] The teetotal movement never completely lost its missionary fervour, as Livesey's protests against these developments show. But it was one of the tragedies of his later life that his protests were usually without effect.

The rules adopted by the Leeds Temperance Society in 1843 indicate the tendency. Half-yearly tickets were issued to members, price one penny, and no person was admitted to members' meetings except by showing the ticket.[71] This was a sad decline from the welcome which the early Preston teetotalers had given to all—friends and enemies alike. One teetotaler complained in 1842 that when he visited some temperance meetings 'the door has been opened very slowly and cautiously, and some person has peeped out rather suspiciously, as if the inmates were hatching treason'.[72] While teetotalers on the platform were zealously calling upon all to join their movement, the officials at the door were carefully excluding all who most needed to come in, and were thus ensuring that the speaker addressed only the converted. Once the temperance movement had become an exclusive community, it needed to be entertained by professional lecturers; what could be more natural than to charge for entrance to meetings? The old amateur lecturers were gradually superseded by men like John Ripley or J. B. Gough—who gave recreational speeches which did not in the least affect the daily conduct of their audiences. George Lomax, an old teetotaler, lamented the change in 1868: 'unfortunately for the cause . . . there is a craving for the "comic element". A comic song, a grotesque attitude, a ludicrous anecdote, a turbid stream of unmeaning nonsense, accompanied by "sound and fury signifying nothing", are frequently more popular than the highly instructive and soul-inspiring discourses of Dr. Lees . . . I . . . am wishful to see our platforms occupied by men who not only understand our principles, but are qualified to maintain the moral and intellectual dignity of our noble movement.'[73]

It was easy for nonconformists to make a virtue out of their exclusion from power, and to treasure the 'clanship and the satisfaction of belonging to a society marked off from the great world'.[74] The *Saturday Review*—organ of the fashionable intelligentsia of the 1850s and 1860s—found itself entering an entirely unfamiliar world when it glanced at some temperance periodicals on 25 December 1858. A world with its own servants, doctors, tradesmen, schools, insurance schemes and even with its own funeral directors—a small and comfortable world as reassuring for its members as the public-house for its customers. 'Born within this world', it commented, 'you need never travel out of it.' Yet political quietism and moral élitism represented only one of two tendencies within mid-Victorian nonconformity. Utterly dissimilar in appearance yet in reality displaying many similar responses, this second tendency lay in the demand that society as a whole pay homage to the moral standards of nonconformity by enacting prohibition. Yet prohibitionism was no more congenial to Livesey, for it sapped moral suasion from quite a different direction: although by concentrating attention on political agitation it abandoned the quietism and exclusiveness which he deplored, it encouraged teetotalers to think that all could be won through a political *coup*. The move from a psychology of persecution to a psychology of dominance shifted the temperance movement away from the crusade for individual reclamation towards the demand for group status. This shift began in 1853 with the foundation of the United Kingdom Alliance.

9

The Resort to Prohibition: 1853

In its overall pattern the temperance campaign resembles the campaign for female emancipation: it begins with an attempt to get parliamentary action, suffers from an early defeat, and then engages in long years of extra-parliamentary work before returning to Westminster in force. The temperance movement's initial political defeat occurred in 1834: only after 1853 did it turn again to Westminster through the energetic activities of the United Kingdom Alliance. By 1872 the prohibitionist movement had become a flourishing organization, and dominated the whole temperance movement. Its history has never been written,* yet its activities are full of interest and significance.

Like so many new moves in the nineteenth-century temperance movement, prohibitionism in the 1850s owes much to American influence. In vain did English temperance reformers before 1853 suggest a parliamentary or prohibitionist temperance movement:[1] without an American precedent, such proposals were doomed. In 1851 the state of Maine introduced prohibition, and just as the visit of the American Susan B. Anthony sparked off the W.S.P.U. in the early twentieth century, so the visits of F. W. Kellogg and the Beecher Stowes sparked off the United Kingdom Alliance in 1852–3. The American connexions of the Alliance were particularly evident between 1853 and 1857 when its aim was simply to introduce the 'Maine Law', or prohibition, into England. English Alliance supporters often spoke of American prohibitionists in what now seem exaggerated tones of adulation. But the American connexion persisted long after 1857, and prominent American puritans like Neal Dow were often invited to lecture in England.

Americanism attracted English radical and nonconformist support, but repelled English aristocrats and Anglicans, who asked themselves 'can there

* The official history by M. H. C. Hayler, *Vision of a Century* (1953) contains valuable information, but is uncritical and very uneven in quality. A. E. Dingle, of Monash University, Australia, is now working on its political connexions between 1872 and 1895. D. M. Fahey, of Miami University, U.S.A., is studying the temperance question, 1891–1908. David Wright of Waterloo University, Ontario, Canada, is writing on the Liberal party and the liquor licensing question, 1896–1910. This book covers most of the important aspects up to 1872. But the Alliance deserves a scholarly book in its own right.

any good thing come out of Nazareth?' F. W. Newman claimed in 1865 that the close balance between the English political parties prevented them from originating any reforming movement, and that American ideas therefore had to fill the gap. Hostile M.P.s in the 1870s found that the most effective way to discredit English prohibition was to visit America, and when they had returned, to dilate upon infringements of the liquor laws there. In 1872 H. A. Bruce felt that Plimsoll's revelations dealt the Permissive Bill 'a more deadly blow than it had ever before received'.[2]

The founder of the Alliance, Nathaniel Card, was a nephew of George Birkett—the Quaker who helped establish some of the earliest English anti-spirits societies. Born in Ireland in 1805 and connected with Irish philanthropic movements, Card moved to Manchester for business reasons in 1836. In the early 1850s after witnessing the squalor of Angel Meadow, a Manchester slum district, he is alleged to have returned home 'sorrowful and musing'. Then, 'falling down in his closet before the throne of grace, he earnestly besought the Lord to open a way of amelioration, and to change the habits of the morally and physically depraved people, of whom so large a portion of the population is composed'.[3] After preliminary soundings in the philanthropic world during 1852, he secured offices in Manchester. He was a shy man who disliked speaking in public; he exerted little influence on the development of the Alliance, because he died in 1856; but the founding of British prohibitionism owes much to his idealism and persistence.

In October 1853 the first aggregate meeting—chaired by the Gloucester Quaker Samuel Bowly, launched the Alliance on its long career. Explicitly condemning disputes on matters of opinion, and encouraging all to unite in a crusade for social reform, the initial declaration of the Alliance held that the state must not be expected to protect or to regulate harmful trades, that total and immediate prohibition of the liquor traffic was 'perfectly compatible with rationable liberty', and that it would foster 'a progressive civilization'.[4] All who approved Alliance objectives and who contributed to its funds were to be members. The General Council, consisting of several hundred members, was to meet each October and elect the president, the ornamental vice-presidents and the real organizers of the Alliance campaign—the Executive Committee. The Alliance admitted non-teetotalers to membership, and was therefore able to profit from the valuable services of a man like Professor F. W. Newman before he became an abstainer. Like the C.E.T.S. after 1873, the Alliance could always attract funds from several comparatively wealthy non-abstainers whose sympathy with the attack on drunkenness would never otherwise have been enlisted. Lord Brougham, for example, was a non-abstainer who refused to support teetotal societies but who gave invaluable aid to the Alliance. Wilfrid Lawson, Alliance parliamentary leader in the 1860s, though personally a teetotaler, was famed for the wines at his table—a fact which would have shocked the long-pledge men of 1839 and which some condemned as inconsistent and even hypocritical. But most Alliance supporters were former moral suasionists, hoping to recapture in prohibitionism the dynamism and idealism which teetotalism had possessed in the 1830s. Several Alliance leaders had been founder members of the Manchester and Salford Temperance Society, designed in 1851 to co-ordinate local temperance work.[5]

In its earliest years the Alliance followed Cobden's recipe for success. Until 1857 it concentrated on fixing its principle in the public mind, and thus evaded attack on minor issues of detailed application.[6] After 1857 it sought to channel the enthusiasm it had generated into support for a precise and apparently practicable objective—by adopting the 'Permissive Bill' or 'local veto'.* This Bill originated in an anonymous article by the brewer Charles Buxton,[7] which suggested that a five-sixths ratepayer-majority should be empowered to ban drink shops from any locality. In drafting the Permissive Bill, the Alliance simply reduced the required majority from five-sixths to two-thirds. The Alliance never felt strongly committed to the Bill's details, and always insisted that its adoption represented a tactical rather than a policy change. If the Alliance had been able to win complete and immediate prohibition, it would never have fallen back on Permissive Bill gradualism. But in the 1850s public opinion was so hostile to the Maine Law that the Alliance had to pursue its ultimate objective by instalments. It was convinced that prohibition, once locally enacted, would bring benefits so obvious that other areas would rapidly adopt it. Why should the indifference of the country at large be allowed to prevent areas which already wanted prohibition from introducing it locally?

The peculiar qualities of the Permissive Bill attracted many Liberals not influenced primarily by temperance considerations. Drafted by M. D. Hill and others two years after the demise of the Board of Health, the Bill was born into a world where localism was temporarily supreme. Many mid-Victorian voluntarists were inspired by hostility to London rather than by hostility to the state: when the decision to curtail individual liberties was taken locally rather than nationally, the most drastic interference with private freedom became tolerable. The origins of modern welfare legislation are to be found largely in permissive legislation, and the Alliance saw the Public Libraries Act as a precedent. Samuel Pope, its secretary, wanted to apply the permissive principle in other spheres.[8] The 'decentralizing' aspect of the Permissive Bill attracted several politicians—especially F. W. Newman, who was alarmed at the overworking of parliament and at the decline in local initiative. Many mid-Victorian decentralizers found their ideal of

* Because 'local veto' was, in the eyes of most of its supporters, only a means of obtaining complete prohibition, I describe its advocates throughout this book as 'prohibitionists'. The term 'local option', loosely used at the time, I employ only to denote a system of licensing reform which allows the ratepayers *several* choices of policy, rather than the Permissive Bill's 'all or nothing' choice.

government in the Anglo-Saxon folk-moot or, as admirers of the American system, in a paradise of local parliaments à la Tocqueville.[9] Decentralization also attracted those who realized the clumsiness of uniform national licensing legislation when local attitudes to the drink question varied so strikingly; and also those who favoured the general principle of introducing experimental legislation into limited areas before adopting it nationally.[10]

In 1870 the Alliance claimed that decentralization was the policy of the day; as M.P.s gradually came to resemble delegates of the electorate, they would find it increasingly difficult to overrule minority opinion with imperial legislation. Therefore 'we affirm the ever-increasing necessity of the "collective wisdom" at Westminster to cede its legislative power, in all difficult and important internal and non-political questions, to the distributive wisdom of the localities'.[11] In so far as the Alliance based its case on the need to adapt national licensing legislation to varying local conditions, it was—in an increasingly uniform society—relying on a wasting asset. Nor did parliament after 1867 become as powerless to overrule minority opinion as the Alliance envisaged. Furthermore, the very features of the Permissive Bill which attracted some, alienated others. The 'revolutionary simplicity' of a Bill which granted legislative power to the electorate seemed unconstitutional and even reactionary to radicals who loathed the plebiscitary regime of Louis Napoleon.[12]

Other politicians were attracted by the 'democratic' appearance of the Permissive Bill. One unfortunate consequence of class segregation in the Victorian city was that magistrates tended to live in areas where relatively few public drinking places were needed: yet they were responsible for licensing in a far wider locality. To respectable working men in the poorer districts, the magistrates' readiness to grant licences outside their own residential areas looked like an attempt to discriminate against the property and convenience of the respectable poor in favour of the property and amenities of the rich. Hence the popularity of a Bill which empowered all ratepayers to decide whether the existing licensing system could continue, or whether—in their locality—drinkshops should be entirely banned. For years J. H. Raper, the Alliance parliamentary agent, held up a sovereign and offered it to anyone who could name a magistrate who had voted to license a public-house next to his own home. Yet the Alliance was attributing to magistrates' selfishness what really stemmed from the social situation: Lord Bramwell rightly pointed out in 1885 that public-houses were not licensed in upper-class areas because in a locality of private cellars and private drinking there was no demand for them.[13]

Furthermore, the opponents of the Alliance thought the Permissive Bill undemocratic in three respects. It severely limited ratepayers' control over the licensing system: they could say only 'all or none', not 'less or more'. Again, the Alliance—unlike its American counterpart the Anti-Saloon League—

attacked the *trade* in vice, not the vice itself. This was in some ways perhaps the best course for the Alliance, as a political organization, to take. For if there had ever been any doubt whether it was within the province of the state to outlaw any commercial activity, the anti-slave trade movement had dispelled it; whereas to outlaw drinking itself would involve trespassing too far on individual liberty. Besides, public agitations need their scapegoats, and just as the nineteenth-century purity movement needed its evil brothel-keepers, so the temperance movement needed its villainous drinksellers. This policy had one unfortunate and undemocratic consequence, however: it would inconvenience the poor more than the rich. The lower the social grade of the drinker, the greater his dependence on public drinking facilities—for the rich man had the foresight, the capital and the cellar required to safeguard his private supply. Here was one reason for the *Morning Star*'s complaint that the Permissive Bill was 'monstrously aristocratic'. The paper would have been even more disgusted to know that so prominent an Alliance supporter as Dawson Burns did not oppose the sale of drink in hotels: 'the hotel system is one by itself,' he told a select committee in 1878: 'and it may be fairly contended that while a traveller is residing at a hotel, it is as though he were in his own house'. He later asked for permission to append a note to his evidence, emphasizing that this was his own opinion and not that of the Alliance.[14]

The Permissive Bill seemed undemocratic in a third respect: it proposed to enfranchise only the ratepayers, not the whole population. Yet only a small proportion of the population were ratepayers; still fewer tended to vote. One critic maintained that to empower a $\frac{2}{3}$ majority of ratepayers would be to enable $\frac{2}{15}$ of the population to dictate to the remaining $\frac{13}{15}$. For Chamberlain in 1893 the figures were $\frac{1}{15}$ dictating to $\frac{14}{15}$. Such a vote would maximize the power of a small but energetic minority.[15] The Alliance publicly admitted that it depended for support on an élite of working men.

Alliance policy can, however, be defended against all three criticisms. The Permissive Bill's insistence on an all-or-nothing choice sprang from the tactical requirements of the Alliance campaign, not from any distrust of the democracy: it needed a rallying-cry which would attract enthusiastic support from individuals anxious to keep their hands clean. Furthermore, it is probable that some Alliance supporters championed the local veto only in the hope of forcing governments into making concessions: prohibitionists seldom objected to modifying the Bill's details and many would probably have agreed ultimately to some form of local control. Secondly, the fact that it would inconvenience the poor more than the rich was a purely unintended consequence of the Permissive Bill, and cannot be used as evidence against the democratic faith of its advocates: indeed, Alliance supporters believed that their measure would itself help to equalize social conditions throughout the community.

Thirdly, the Alliance chose the ratepayer-franchise only because the migratory habits of many working people made it impossible to construct a register of all inhabitants. The enthusiasm of the Alliance for democracy can hardly be questioned. The wide franchise of America was their ideal. They were supported by several prominent Chartists, and their enthusiasm for franchise extension in the 1860s was backed by tangible aid to the Reform League. In the 1872 Permissive Bill debate, Lawson even offered to include a clause disfranchising from the local veto electorate any person paying more than a specified amount in rates. The Fabian Society in 1898 feared that the Permissive Bill, far from being undemocratic, placed an exaggerated faith in the moral aspirations of the democracy: Whitechapel and Soho *alone* would never produce a majority for prohibition: licences should be controlled by a representative body far more broadly based. 'Legislation on the principle of asking the blind to lead the blind,' the Society pronounced, 'is not up to the standard of modern political science.'[16] As for the complaint that the Permissive Bill gave undue influence to a small minority of activists—this constituted an *attack* on democratic theory, which assumes that non-voting signifies tacit consent to abide by majority decisions, that voters will take the trouble to vote against any policy which they strongly oppose, and that citizens will band together to campaign for measures which they enthusiastically support. The Alliance always supposed that the Permissive Bill—as a controversial measure which intimately concerned the personal welfare of every individual—would give citizens experience in making political choices and give them a real sense of participation in government.

Nevertheless the *Bee-Hive*, organ of the London trades societies in the 1860s, felt that the Bill deserved no mercy, and insisted that advocates of manhood suffrage could not consistently support it. Politicians need to consider the views of the whole population, and in their eyes the undemocratic aspects of the Permissive Bill were a serious drawback. The Sunday trading riots reminded parliament in 1855 that working people in large towns could take drastic action against what they called 'class legislation'; fear of riot played a most important part in discrediting the Permissive Bill, many of whose critics dwelt on the disorder which local veto polls would provoke. Mr. Ker Seymer in 1863 preferred 'a certain amount of drunkenness' to the existence of rankling discontent among the masses. The argument of 'the devil you know . . .' was often used against temperance legislation in the nineteenth century, and culminated in the much-quoted speech of Magee, the Whig Bishop of Peterborough for whom liberty was preferable to compulsory sobriety. Likewise *The Times* had argued against the Board of Health: 'we prefer to take our chance of cholera and the rest, than to be bullied into health.'[17] Again, politicians knew that the last places to adopt the Permissive Bill would in fact be those which most needed it: the large towns which, if they provided much of the support for the temperance movement, also furnished the publicans with their most formidable weapon—the urban mob.

At a time of widespread hostility to state intervention, the Alliance had to make out a case for the most drastic infringements of individual liberty. Furthermore Alliance arguments had to attract predominantly nonconformist supporters who were voluntarists in most other spheres; with its headquarters at Manchester, the Alliance lay in the centre of the free-trade camp. And if it were to influence sections of society hitherto untouched by the temperance movement, the Alliance had to intellectualize its apologia. How was this platform created? By the political theorists? The speeches of Samuel Pope, secretary of the Alliance, mentioned only one such authority—Guizot's statement in his *History of Civilization* that the progress of society 'not only allows, but absolutely depends, upon the subjection of individual wills to the public power'.[18] But at the start of that prohibitionist primer—Dr. F. R. Lees' *Alliance Prize Essay*, first published in 1856—Bentham features prominently; how far was he responsible for the resort to prohibition?

Lees admitted 'a strong leaning towards the great practical test or index of BENTHAM, one of the profoundest writers on Jurisprudence to whom this country has given birth'. Most of his first chapter was spent in proving that 'the general principles of law laid down by BENTHAM' were 'in perfect accordance with the views of the "Alliance" '.[19] Bentham's direct approval for prohibition could not be cited, but much play was made with his suggestions for regulating the trade in poisons and strong drinks, and it was implied that Bentham would have included beer and wine among them. Lees cited Bentham's *Principles of Penal Law* to the effect that in hot climates it would perhaps be more humane to prohibit than to permit the use of intoxicants. But the real hope of winning over the Benthamites lay in showing that prohibition followed logically from Bentham's basic principles. To cite in support of Alliance policy his view that government should pursue 'the greatest happiness of the greatest number'—as did Washington Wilks amid cheers at an Alliance meeting in 1864—was of course to beg many questions. 'I want to know how you reconcile with that principle', said Wilks, 'a system which ruins many for the advantage of only a very few, which makes more orphans and widows than the bloodiest campaign.'[20] Still more valuable to the Alliance was Bentham's reaction against extreme libertarianism in his *Principles of the Civil Code*: 'Liberty, which is one branch of security, ought to yield to *general security*, since it is not possible to make *any* laws but at the expense of liberty.'[21] Like the Alliance, Bentham resolutely attacked those who assumed that liberty consists solely in freedom to do anything which will not harm others. 'The very phrase, liberty of the subject,' said Dawson Burns in a famous debate of 1879, 'involves that we require, in granting individual liberty that there must be restriction and restraint.'[22]

Robinson Crusoe's liberty was unrestrained, he said, only before the arrival of Man Friday.

It is doubtful whether the Alliance quoted Bentham for any other reason than to give a respectable intellectual pedigree to policies already decided upon for other reasons. Bentham's ideas had been well known for decades, yet there were few signs of prohibitionism in England before the transatlantic influences of the early 1850s. Lees' quotations from Bentham were highly selective: for example, he omitted to mention Bentham's scorn for the notion that legislation could root out fornication and drunkenness.[23] It is probably significant that Lees gave only a very small proportion of his *Prize Essay* to philosophical justifications of prohibition; the vast bulk of the book consists of facts, testimonies and statistics. Pragmatic considerations and face-to-face contacts with other philanthropists were the real influences pushing temperance reformers towards state intervention: 'here *practice*, and not *theory*, is our best guide,' wrote Livesey in 1860 when justifying his attack on free trade. Until the Alliance began its quarterly *Meliora* in the 1850s it is doubtful whether the name of a single political theorist had been mentioned on a temperance platform. Dr. Lees was one of the few temperance leaders with a close knowledge of political theory, and he was therefore well equipped to spread temperance principles in new, and more refined, quarters.

To judge from the recruits attracted into prohibitionism in the late 1850s, he succeeded: men like the Earl of Harrington, Lord Brougham and M. D. Hill owed much to Benthamism. Utilitarians may have 'looked with disfavour on State intervention', as Dicey claimed, but their faith 'in the supreme value of individual liberty' clearly had its limits. For Dicey failed to point out that the puritanism from which utilitarianism inherited 'some of its most valuable ideas' also fostered communitarian and even socialistic attitudes, to which in his view utilitarians were thoroughly opposed; he also failed to stress that the humanitarianism, which he rightly saw as an accompaniment of individualism, conflicted with mere libertarianism in important respects. Slavery, animal cruelty, drunkenness and immorality could be eliminated only through drastic restraints on the freedom of the individual. Most prohibitionists were not, however, troubled by such problems: their movement had been created by a social situation, not by political theorists.[24]

The only other theoretical influences on Lees when writing his first chapter were negative in character: political theorists who minimized the role and dignity of the state, and against whom Lees reacted strongly. He approved Thomas Arnold's *Introductory Lectures on History* for denying that the state can ever be morally indifferent, and he ridiculed those for whom law was the logic of the stick. In its resolute challenge to *laissez-faire* notions, therefore, the Alliance owed little to theoretical justifications of state intervention: everything to the peculiar situation in which it found itself. The sheer necessities of temperance reform forced the Alliance leaders after 1853 to evolve for themselves a political theory which anticipates the ideas of many late-Victorian thinkers, notably T. H. Green. The only distinguished writer on politics who wrote for the Alliance was F. W. Newman, and he joined the crusade only after the apologia had been elaborated by lesser-known figures.

Prohibitionist political theory had three essential features: a belief that the state could never be morally indifferent, an organic conception of society and a positive definition of liberty. This complex of beliefs will now be outlined, using the Alliance's own words wherever possible. The temperance movement was founded partly to fill the gap created by the retreat of the state from the supervision of morality; but by the 1850s temperance reformers were demanding that the state should resume its former role. The Alliance leaders fully recognized the significance of their standpoint in the history of political theory. 'The Whigs and Radicals, since Bentham, have tried to throw away good principles which had been either neglected or perverted,' said Samuel Pope in 1865. F. W. Newman saw in prohibition 'the turning-point in the new view of the position of governments in the earth'. Since the Restoration the state had abandoned its role as moral guardian of its citizens; it was 'the cardinal heresy of the Liberal party in both continents' to accept such a situation. Alliance leaders believed that their efforts would rejuvenate politics in general: 'we cannot succeed in giving vitality to a great moral principle', said Pope, 'without effecting more than our immediate object.' Alliance efforts would 'infuse a new morality into state-action'. This enhanced view of the state gave a central place to the dignity of Law, which Lees described as 'the Logic of social life—the development of national experience. Law has a potency in moulding the plastic population, which is even more important than its penal function.'[25] It was a 'vulgar fallacy' to oppose law to liberty: utility must be the test of legislation.[26]

The Alliance made high demands of the state: it must teach, discipline and educate its citizens: feed and clothe its delinquents and orphans. Government '*must* not only resist wrong', said Lees, 'but do many things necessary to *prevent* wrong'.[27] Prohibitionists firmly denied that politicians 'could not make men moral by act of parliament'. The state could promote morality by making the environment more conducive to it. The 1830 Beer Act revealed the harm the state could do, and Alliance meetings responded with emotion when speakers cited the prayer 'lead us not into temptation'. Prohibitionists welcomed the dictum of Gladstone that the state 'ought to make it easy to do right and difficult to do wrong', hoping that his belief in a state conscience would lead him to embrace their cause. Like the factory reformers of the 1840s Alliance men in the 1850s countered *laissez-faire* clichés with the slogan 'what is morally wrong, cannot be politically right'. Just as the gaslamp had curbed theft, said Lees, so the local veto would curb drunkenness.[28]

This outlook led prohibitionists to evolve organic notions of the state. Lees vigorously attacked the policeman theory of government in his *Prize Essay*, arguing that the Social State was no mere artefact but 'supremely a true "natural State", deserving of all honor [*sic*] and obedience—*not* a mere "Police man" and "Contrivance", but a natural growth from the seed of Humanity, an *organism*'.[29] The organic metaphor reappears in the *Alliance Weekly News* of 7 November 1857, where the state is described as 'an individual organism; a *collective individual*'. The state, like the individual, must ensure that its moral powers regulate its immoral potentialities; just as the individual takes the pledge, so the state must enact prohibition. The Alliance believed that society's prime aim was 'not individuality, but socialism; that is, the maintenance implicitly of the guarantees which have been decided to be common rights'. The best form of society was 'that which secures the greatest amount of social advantage and protection with the least sacrifice of individual independence'.[30]

The Alliance was acutely conscious that urbanization made nonsense of traditional libertarianism: 'the liberty which a man may claim if he live alone so that no other man can be injured by his conduct, and the liberty to which he has a right when surrounded by thousands of his species, all of whom have the same natural rights as himself, are very different things.'[31] F. R. Lees' *Prize Essay* complained that the 'policeman theory' of the state created confusion by 'enunciating the rights and ethics of Perfect men and Paradise, instead of the practical duties incumbent upon us in this work-a-day world of imperfection and sin'.[32] Prohibitionists outlined for government a far more protective role than was fashionable at the time; they were as convinced as Robert Owen and T. H. Green that in modern society individual perfection was impossible in isolation. All members of the community must be raised up together. The Alliance apologia might almost be used to defend the modern welfare state. Need society be so arranged, it asked, that 'no feeble one shall stand, no defenceless person be protected, no ailing body supported'. Was there not 'a certain amount of care which society should collectively bestow on its weak, its unformed, and its misformed members, so that there shall be amongst them as little necessity of failure, as much freedom from temptation . . . as shall at any rate secure . . . to every one of them the possibility of standing?'[33]

Yet underlying this passage is a concept very different from that of the welfare state: namely, the idea that government must create an environment in which citizens are able to help themselves. The care which the Alliance wanted government to bestow on its citizens did not involve direct provision for their welfare: the aim was to give indirect aid by cultivating citizens' initiative, rationality and providence. It is important to realize the context in which the Alliance was evolving its new approach to social organization: the *Bradford Observer*, attacking the teetotal pledge in 1841, declared 'we really think that it is consistent with the economy of Providence to surround man with temptations to excess, and leave to his moral and religious feeling, the victory of triumph'. This view was not often so forcefully expressed, but it was widely held—among rationalists and Christians alike. The Alliance recognized that this attitude, if carried to its logical conclusion, would convert every religious institution into a bar-parlour. It denied that there was any simple choice between state intervention and individual liberty: the choice lay rather between drastic punitive intervention and preventive legislation. 'Social evils,' said F. W. Newman, 'if not prevented, have to be punished'; the prohibitionist Lord Harrington often cited Beccaria's dictum: 'preventive justice is far better than punishing justice'.[34] Prohibitionist arguments resembled those for the fencing of industrial machinery. True, the individual by taking care could avoid danger; but the fact remained that a certain proportion would not avoid it. The only remedy was to fence it off.

Such concepts inevitably led to a more positive notion of liberty. The Alliance fully realized that moral progress would demand infringements of individual liberty, negatively conceived. In the words of a supporter: 'nothing can be plainer than that, in a well-ordered and vigorous society, general welfare must *always* override individual interest'.[35] From its earliest years, the Alliance defined liberty in positive terms—as 'the state of a balanced and rational exercise of power, defined by the constitutional limits of the law'.[36] For F. R. Lees, the policeman theory of the state ignored some of the most important problems of politics. Liberty was only a means to a higher end: 'it is not mere exercise of faculties that we live for, but for such a development of them as harmonizes with the true hierarchy of human powers; not for the development of self-will, but the frequent denial of impulsive will for moral will. . . .'[37] Not that the Alliance wanted to make moral conduct compulsory: this would of course be self-defeating. Like sabbatarians anxious for laws against Sunday trading, prohibitionists wanted only to modify the environment in order to make moral conduct feasible. They knew well that, in the existing society, many citizens were incapable of enjoying real freedom. Few could deny that prohibition, if successful, would extend the drunkard's real freedom; and by curtailing the liberty of the husband it might promote the freedom of his wife and family. Prohibitionists closely in contact with the mid-Victorian slum realized that government had actually to *create* the rational citizen who makes his economic decisions after mature consideration of his long-term self-interest.

In contrast with so many of its contemporaries, the Alliance believed that advancing civilization demanded not less interference with individual liberty—but more. One prohibitionist in the 1860s claimed that while the state might retreat from restrictions on trade, it was advancing towards restrictions on factory hours and brutal sports: the 'cardinal virtue of State action' was 'freedom to do right, opposition and loss of liberty in doing wrong'.[38] If state intervention had been harmful in the past, wrote Lees, this was not because state intervention was in itself harmful, but simply because it had hitherto been ill-informed—'it is not necessarily *less* Legislation that we want, but *wiser*'. Like T. H. Green, Lees felt no presumption against state control: each case must be decided on its merits. After all, without the state even property itself could not exist.[39] In its early years the Alliance cited as precedents for liquor restriction the quarantine laws, protective legislation against poisons, adulteration, obscene literature, noxious fumes and explosives. These measures, which took away a liberty, were apter precedents than the Public Libraries Act, also often cited, which bestowed one. Alliance dependence on support from Lancashire cotton magnates and other industrialists probably explains why it rarely cited factory legislation as a precedent, but in the 1870s it felt safe in pointing to a host of humanitarian and moral regulations in justification of state interference. The decline in cock-fighting, duelling and betting and the spread of public education seemed to show how the state could civilize the population.[40]

The desire for moral progress was an essential feature of the nineteenth-century campaign to extend state intervention. Factory legislation owed much to the desire for self-improvement among an élite of working men; housing legislation flourished on the desire to prevent sexual promiscuity; public supervision of the water supply sprang largely from the desire to curb drunkenness. In the late-Victorian period the attack on immorality led almost imperceptibly into more direct attacks upon poverty; the train of thought was well expressed in a meeting called to discuss the protection of young girls in 1885, just after W. T. Stead's revelations.[41] 'One of the effects of these revelations', said Hugh Price Hughes, 'is that they have shown us . . . that we cannot touch any point of this hideous vice . . . without also touching a thousand points in our ordinary life in which lie concealed the evil which has produced these hideous fruits, but which evils we have never suspected. We have seen how the whole thing hangs together . . . and therefore we once more learn that it will be impossible to do anything in furthering morality by the law of the land without also touching the economical relations of society.' Both Hughes and a previous speaker, Dr. Pankhurst, who made a speech to the same effect, supported the Permissive Bill. All this helps to explain the close connexion between religion and social reform in the nineteenth century. It also lends support to the dictum that in the history of political thought 'to cull and admire the finest flowers alone does not tell us enough of the soil in which they are planted'.[42] The achievements of the great political theorists are placed in perspective, perhaps even scaled down, when they are juxtaposed with the attitudes and problems of their less articulate but more practical contemporaries. Practical problems forced on the Alliance theoretical questions which the academics elaborated only later.

The drink issue exposed the conflict within mid-Victorian Liberalism between the claims of individual liberty and of moral progress. It is hardly surprising that it inspired the Liberals J. S. Mill and T. H. Green to take up contradictory standpoints. Both wished to see drunkenness eliminated from society, but Green was more closely acquainted with the problem. A water-drinker in his Rugby schooldays, he tried unsuccessfully to reclaim his brother from intemperance in the 1860s, participated in Oxford licensing and coffee-house movements in the 1870s, and held posts in the Band of Hope and the Church of England Temperance Society. Mill always firmly resisted temperance pressure, and acted on the belief that alcohol was necessary to health. At the 1868 election he insisted that the use of alcohol was 'a subject on which every sane and grown-up person ought to judge for himself under his own responsibility'.[43] His only contact with the Alliance was therefore to attack the Maine Law in his book *Liberty*, whereas Green joined the Alliance in 1872 and became a vice-president in 1878, and championed local option in his famous lecture on 'Liberal Legislation and Freedom of Contract' in 1881.

Mill's attitude to the drink question was governed by his belief that the natural order, if only meddling humanity would leave it alone, was as self-acting in promoting morality as in creating wealth: the drunkard's humiliation was nature's warning against self-indulgence. Mill opposed the Maine Law for the same reasons that inspired his opposition to the Contagious Diseases Acts: the individual would progress morally only if the state left him entirely unfettered in his moral choices. In 1870 he told a parliamentary inquiry that the state should not try to wipe out venereal disease by regulating or inspecting prostitutes in garrison-towns, for it was not 'part of the business of Government to provide securities beforehand against the consequences of immoralities of any kind'.[44] While society might gain in the short term by prohibition or by Contagious Diseases Acts, in the long term such meddling short-cuts would deprive society of the self-reliant and morally mature citizens essential to progress. For Mill there *was* no conflict between the claims of individual liberty and of moral progress. In him, as in many mid-Victorian Liberals, there was an almost stoic acquiescence in suffering, as an essential concomitant of human progress: by thoughtlessly rushing in to relieve it, the state would unduly complicate the task of the moralist.

By contrast Green was far less patient with existing evils: like many prohibitionists he had personal experience of slum visiting and of the violence endemic there; he was also impressed by the prohibitionist zeal of the working class élite. Several prohibitionist critics of *Liberty* felt that in his 'applications', Mill betrayed an ignorance of practical affairs. Green would have agreed with the prohibitionist who exposed Mill's major error as 'that of regarding civilization not only as being in a much higher state than it actually is, but also of being much more widely spread'.[45] Many mid-Victorian Liberals half-feared the uneducated masses they were introducing to political power, but whereas Mill relied upon proportional representation to contain them, Green's fears, nourished by his bitter disappointment with the Liberal

20. Temperance oratory: J. B. Gough. Adept at the recreational temperance lecture for predominantly female, and partly well-to-do, audiences. From J. B. Gough, *Orations* (1878). [see p. 212]

21. Militant puritanism: F. R. Lees. A radical intellectual, and antagonist of Gough in the 1858 lawsuit. From F. Lees, *Life of F. R. Lees* (1904), aet. 45. [see p. 213]

22. INSIDE THE BAR AT THE 'EDINBURGH CASTLE', LIMEHOUSE: THE FIRST 'COFFEE PALACE'. The religious texts must have warned many working men off the premises. From E. H. Hall, *Coffee Taverns, Cocoa Houses & Coffee Palaces*, c. 1879, p. 56. [see p. 304]

HARVEST 1866.

PRIZES

OF THE VALUE OF

SEVENTEEN POUNDS

(To be spent at the option of the winners, in Coal, Food, Furniture, or wearing Apparel) will be given as below for

FARM LABOUR

PERFORMED BY ABSTAINERS FROM ALL INTOXICATING LIQUORS.

For the greatest number of acres of Meadow Grass cut the most expeditiously in a workmanlike manner by two or more mowers **THREE POUNDS.**

For the next quantity similarly cut by two or more Mowers **TWO POUNDS.**

For the largest number of Acres of Meadow Grass similarly cut in a workmanlike manner by one Mower **THIRTY-SHILLINGS.**

For the next largest number of acres similarly cut by one Mower **ONE POUND.**

For the largest number of acres of wheat reaped, tied, and shocked, without help, the most expeditiously in a husbandlike manner by two men **THREE POUNDS.**

For the next largest by two men **TWO POUNDS.**

For the largest number similarly reaped, tied, and shocked, by one person **TWO POUNDS.**

For the next largest by one person **1 POUND.**

For the largest number of Ricks made and thatched by one person in the most workmanlike manner **1 POUND.**

For the largest number of Acres of Swedes or Turnips well and expeditiously hoed by one person in the most husbandlike manner **1 POUND.**

These Prizes are open to all persons living in the Parish of Mere, who shall be Pledged Abstainers from the 1st of May to the 31st of October, and who shall enter their names as competitors before the 1st day of May, 1866.

In case there should not be two parties competing for a prize, it will not be awarded. Every effort will be made to secure perfect impartiality in awarding the Prizes.

All further information or particulars may be obtained of

Mr. C. JUPE, or
Mr. J. FARLEY RUTTER.

PRINTER, BOOKSELLER, AND STATIONER, MERE.

23. A TEETOTAL STRATEGY FOR ATTACKING HARVEST BEER. From Miss J. Rutter's temperance collection, Mere, Wilts. [see p. 309]

defeat at the 1874 general election, drove him into the same prohibitionist camp as that arch-enemy of democracy, Thomas Carlyle. Mill argued that 'the only part of the conduct of anyone, for which he is amenable to society, is that which concerns others';[46] he believed that drunkenness should be punished only when it caused obvious harm to the public, as when a policeman or soldier incapacitated himself for public duty. But Green had his eyes on the drunkard's wife and children, who might be harmed directly. Prohibitionists had their eyes on the acquaintances whom the drunkard might lead astray: and even, after late-nineteenth-century research on eugenics, on his unborn children. 'The excessive drinking of one man', said Green, 'means an injury to others in health, purse, and capability, to which no limits can be placed.' Prohibitionists might admit that the drunkard's miseries encouraged the world to remain sober: but they argued that, for the drunkard himself, 'wisdom to do [comes] *pari passu* with the departure of zest for doing'; it was important to prevent the man from ever becoming a drunkard. F. W. Newman's attack on Herbert Spencer applies equally to Mill: 'he denounces the vicious poor, seems to inculcate that we ought to let them die out, overlooks the fact that children reared to vice, or tempted to vice in early years, deserve pity and aid, not cold contempt'.[47]

Mill endows his normal citizen with 'too much of the psychology of a middle-aged man whose desires are relatively fixed, not liable to be artificially stimulated by external influences; who knows what he wants and what gives him satisfaction or happiness'.[48] He assumes that the adult individual always knows better than the state what is in his own best interest, but admits that *laissez-faire* principles cannot operate where children or lunatics are involved. Yet the prohibitionists claimed that many adults were 'very much in the condition of children', and that the drunkard was 'almost like a paralysed man; you may tell him to move his hands, and it is just what he wants to do, but he cannot do it'.[49] Green and the Alliance never underestimated the gulf between intention and action, and their short-term remedies, unlike Mill's, did not operate solely in the classroom. They regarded the law itself as a powerful educational influence. Education alone could never benefit the drunken family, said Green: drunkenness must first be checked by legislation which will produce 'a dead lift of the national conscience'. Moral suasion and education were remedies which acted slowly, whereas a drunken population 'naturally perpetuates and increases itself': Green was impressed by the fact that it was 'dangerous to wait'.[50]

Prohibitionists therefore advocated a far more positive role for the state than Mill, for whom liberty increased with every decrease in government control. His prohibitionist critics argued just the reverse—that civilization depends upon restraining individual liberty, whereas 'in the most barbarous and uncultivated nations, the more is liberty indulged'. Though the Alliance admitted that Liberals had in the past promoted progress by demolishing old institutions and customs, it believed that construction was also very necessary.[51] Green was first roused into public controversy on the temperance issue in 1873 by Harcourt's Oxford attack on a 'grand-maternal Government which ties nightcaps on a grown-up nation by act of Parliament'. Green argued that opponents of licensing legislation failed to distinguish between 'that liberty of the subject which is compatible with the real freedom of others, and that which merely means freedom to make oneself a social nuisance'.[52] Green's quest for moral progress led him further than mere prohibition: he also advocated housing inspection, provision of allotments and compulsory education. Prohibitionists' zeal for construction sometimes led them into an enthusiasm for state power which even the twentieth century would regard as dangerous: 'surely where there is any conflict of liberties', the Alliance pleaded, 'the individual should give way to the State, and not the State to the individual'.[53]

Lying behind Green's outlook was an admiration for the puritan commonwealth of the seventeenth century, a deep respect for the moral idealism of nonconformist culture and memories of an evangelical upbringing. By contrast, Mill's broad culture led him to fear any legislation which might foster a Calvinistic 'pinched and hidebound type of human character'; like Arnold he wished to encourage in his contemporaries a Hellenistic self-assertion and spontaneity which would complement the Christian emphasis on humility and self-denial.[54] Yet in their political and social outlook Mill and the Alliance had much in common, and many prohibitionists regretted that so distinguished a man should be quoted by publicans for their own selfish purposes. The Alliance helped to publicize the 'constructive' Liberalism of T. H. Green. When temperance legislation was described, in his 1881 lecture, as 'the next great conquest which our democracy, on behalf of its own true freedom, has to make',[55] the Alliance printed the lecture in full in its periodical, and later issued it as a tract especially recommended for distribution among intelligent politicians. It was advertised for sale at 3d. each, 1/– for six, or 12/6 for 100 on eight distinct occasions in the *Alliance News*, and was also advertised by the British Temperance League. Whereas when Mill died he received only the briefest attention in the *Alliance News*, and was accused of ideas 'in every point of view, defective and misleading', Green was honoured in 1882 with an enthusiastic full-column obituary.[56]

Alliance innovations in political theory did not go unquestioned in the temperance world. With this advance in temperance doctrine, as with every other, bitter feelings were aroused. How far was the Alliance campaign inspired by dissatisfaction with moral suasion—that is, with attempts to eliminate drunkenness through reclaiming individuals? The views of Nathaniel Card himself are obscure; he is a shadowy figure, and even the better-known prohibitionists had to be guarded in their criticisms, for their success depended largely on attracting support from existing temperance societies. Teetotalers from Livesey to Father Mathew were certainly disappointed that progress was so slow. Even in the heyday of teetotalism in the late 1830s, only 10% of temperance society membership consisted of reformed drunkards. An intelligent champion of moral suasion in the *National Temperance Chronicle* for 1846 was not at all confident in his opposition to legislative compulsion.[57] 'There is movement without any thing like corresponding progress' wrote the *Scottish Temperance Review* in July 1848: 'there is the play of machinery, but the produce is scanty. Societies, after a few months' active labour, cease to work, or only move by fits and starts.' There were complaints of poor attendance at temperance meetings in the late 1840s, and the foundation of the Band of Hope at that time owed much to the belief that adults could never be reclaimed in large numbers. Joseph Livesey's disappointment with temperance progress after the 1830s has already been noted, and by 1853 John Dunlop wrote of the 'prodigious amount of drunken *vis inertiæ* to be counteracted among the Millions; which cannot be effected by mere moral suasion'.[58] Dunlop and Livesey were pioneer moral suasionists who both at first supported prohibition in the hope that it would rejuvenate their movement. Samuel Bowly, Jabez Burns, F. R. Lees, Edward Grubb and James Teare were among the many prominent advocates who welcomed the new move.

The hopelessness of unassisted moral suasion seemed to be demonstrated by the collapse of Father Mathew's teetotal campaign. His early efforts marked the culmination of moral suasionist crusading and he was said to have enrolled nearly six million teetotalers during his campaigns in Ireland during the early 1840s. But the Famine seriously obstructed his efforts and by 1853 his movement had collapsed; he himself was stricken with paralysis, too poor to follow unaided the advice of doctors who urged him to move to a warmer climate.[59] Temperance reformers did not conclude from his failure that universal abstinence was impossible in the existing social system, but simply that the moral suasionist campaign had been too loosely organized and that the state had allowed hindrances to be placed in its path. Father Mathew himself encouraged such ideas: 'the efforts of individuals, however zealous, were not equal to the mighty task,' he claimed in 1853, whereas the Alliance struck '*at the very root of the evil*'. Once again, thwarted temperance reformers, instead of reconsidering the whole basis of their agitation, attributed their failure to unforeseen and removable hindrances. So with drink as with education, the failure of voluntarism led to the demand for state compulsion.[60]

Unlike its late-nineteenth-century American counterpart, the Alliance never campaigned directly for moral suasion; it sought rather to complement existing moral suasionist societies. Its inaugural declaration invited all temperance reformers to join 'in their individual capacity' but stressed that the

Alliance was completely distinct from existing moral suasionist societies. When Wakefield prohibitionists and moral suasionists amalgamated in 1857, T. H. Barker quoted against them the words of the executive's resolution: 'the work and basis of the Alliance and of the Temperance Society are essentially distinct.'[61] The Alliance regarded the prohibitionist and moral suasionist movements 'as the two poles of a galvanic battery, neither being powerful without the other'.[62] It attacked only the *trade* in intoxicants; if drunkenness were to be eliminated, moral suasionist societies would still be needed to discourage the home manufacture and consumption of drink. Nevertheless friction soon arose between prohibitionists and moral suasionists, and schism once again resulted.

Some prohibitionists, including Lees, claimed that moral suasion was insufficient for most individuals, that temperance reformers must adapt their course 'to the moral and sensient nature of man', [63] and must require the nation to deliver itself from temptation. By 1863 the Alliance was arguing that all the efforts of the moral suasionists had not substantially reduced the number of drinkshops or of drunkards, nor had they converted a large proportion of the public to total abstinence. What was needed was an environmental change; 'knowledge only invokes the intellect which is passive, while institutions and usages evoke the active feelings of our nature. The battle is unequal. . . .'[64] *The Times* in 1863 noted 'a curious dualism and inconsistency' between the moral suasionist and prohibitionist movements: the former paraded the numbers who had been reclaimed through exertion of willpower whereas the latter dwelt on the hopelessness of such a remedy.[65] Moral suasionists feared that the energetic Alliance might supersede their own societies; indeed prohibitionists in some areas assumed that this would eventually occur. In 1857 Joseph Livesey complained that the temperance movement suffered when its forces were divided in every community between distinct teetotal and prohibitionist organizations.[66] Disputes between the two wings of the movement became rife in the late 1850s, particularly in Scotland. But the dispute in England was sharpened by the Alliance's clash with two individual moral suasionists—J. B. Gough and Joseph Livesey.

The two protagonists in the Gough–Lees lawsuit contrast so strongly in personality that they might have been born for conflict. J. B. Gough [see Plate 20] was an American reformed drunkard commissioned by the National Temperance League during the 1850s to lecture throughout the British Isles. Though unimpressive in physique, he could play upon the emotions of his largely female audiences like a musician with an instrument, modulating the tone of his voice to suit the mood. His graphic accounts of *delirium tremens* thrilled Exeter Hall. He could work up an emotional tension which forced shouts of applause from his hearers, who 'wept, laughed, cheered, shivered alternately, sometimes the tears choking the laughter'. Shaftesbury in 1854 described him as 'a marvel—a real marvel', and George Howell half a century later had never heard his equal. Gough was extremely mobile on the platform—darting hither and thither with dramatic gestures.[67] The process was exhausting: Joseph Taylor, watching him closely from behind while he was performing in Exeter Hall, 'saw the perspiration in drops, and a sphere of vapour on the back of his coat'. Several temperance reformers recalled that Gough's informal conversation was surprisingly dull. He was no scholar, and could not speak successfully on subjects outside the temperance question. His appeal was solely to the emotions, not to the intellect.[68]

How different was F. R. Lees [see Plate 21]! Unlike Gough, he had no sordid past to capitalize upon. He made his name in the temperance world by an impromptu defence of teetotalism at the famous Leeds meeting of 1836, and obtained a doctorate from Geissen university for attacking Owenism. After engaging in teetotal journalism and public debate during the 1840s, sometimes to the alarm of the theologically orthodox, Lees became one of the leading Alliance spokesmen in the 1850s. Interested in many other radical causes, he stood for parliament several times. Like Gough he was physically unimpressive, 'a little thin-faced, thin-bodied man, volatile as water, and as easily agitated';[69] but his speeches were very different—they were uncompromisingly didactic, and therefore far less well-paid than those of J. B. Gough. Lees made no concessions to his hearers, and sometimes unintentionally caused his audience to sympathize with his opponents—so mercilessly did he wield his logical powers. He must have bored many an audience, and certainly stultified many a press controversy, by his zeal for semantic precision and by his refusal to concede the most footling point to his critics. To make matters worse, he lacked a sense of humour: during a visit to the Oxford Botanical Gardens, a local temperance reformer asked him the use of some well-developed thorns they were looking at: 'I know nothing of ultimate uses,' Lees replied.[70]

Still, Lees had his more sympathetic aspect: he was utterly dedicated and amassed vast quantities of temperance 'facts'—for which, like Gradgrind, he had an exaggerated respect. With his turgid, over-documented, unduly vehement and fractious writings on the physiological and Biblical aspects of temperance advocacy, he made himself the foremost temperance scholar for half a century. He hated pomposity, and his belief that he enjoyed personal access to Truth filled his life with bitter controversy; in 1897 his burial service was appropriately disrupted by noisy sectarian disputes. Truth, for him, was 'always extreme', and he displayed the philosopher's childlike simplicity in personal relationships. Absent-minded, unpractical, absorbed in his studies, he possessed the self-educated man's tendency to dogmatize. In his old age, with his long beard and experience, he became an impressively patriarchal figure.[71]

In 1857 these contrasting personalities were sucked into a public dispute much larger than themselves: between two organizations, the London-based moral suasionist National Temperance League and the Manchester-based prohibitionist United Kingdom Alliance; between two schools of temperance agitation, the political and the a-political; and between two styles of lecturing, the serious-minded and the recreational. Prohibitionists were exasperated when Gough claimed that in America the Maine Law was 'a dead letter'; moral suasionists were furious when Lees hinted that Gough had not entirely abandoned the use of stimulants. The Quaker network which ran the National Temperance League at once sprang into action, Gough sued Lees, and Lees had to apologize publicly. Many temperance reformers regretted the unnecessary expenditure, the bitterness and the discredit which resulted. The effects of the squabble lasted for years, and produced two separate national temperance congresses in London during the exhibition year of 1862—each of which refused to recognize the other. In July the National Temperance League executive declined the British Temperance League's invitation to its annual conference 'in consequence of Dr. Lees having been announced as one of the speakers'.[72] Moral suasionists were still assaulting prohibitionists in the *Temperance Star* as late as 1869.

Yet the dispute was not now between prohibition and exclusive reliance on moral suasion, for during the 1850s and 1860s the moral suasionist organizations became quite active in campaigning for piecemeal legislative restriction of the drink trade: *all* sections of the temperance movement contributed supporters to the movements for Sunday closing and beershop regulation. The National Temperance League worked quite closely with Gathorne-Hardy in his legislative attack on the beershops in 1857, and during 1858 it supported a scheme for opposing the issue of new drink licences in London; its deputation in 1858 told the Bishop of Oxford that though a moral suasionist organization 'they were disposed to avail themselves of any legal assistance which sound statesmanship might suggest'. Likewise the British Temperance League during the early 1860s took an active interest in proposals for Sunday closing. Many moral suasionists joined the Manchester-based Central Association for Stopping the Sale of Intoxicating Liquors on Sunday, founded in 1866 [see Figure 12]. The National Temperance League and the Alliance differed about means, not about ends. A League spokesman in 1863 said that in every town the people 'ought to have, by some board or otherwise, the power of licensing . . . houses according to the supposed requirements of the place';[73] it was not far from here to the local veto. Moral suasionist societies could still in theory accommodate doctrinaire free traders, but in practice their mood was increasingly favourable to legislative control; the dispute between the League and the Alliance was a dispute only about the degree and the timing of control.

Of more lasting significance was the dispute between Joseph Livesey and the prohibitionists, again a clash between contrasting personalities. Reforming pioneers often deplore the directions their movements eventually take; Caroline Norton and Florence Nightingale regretted developments within the feminist movement, just as John Edgar regretted teetotalism. Joseph Livesey did not at first oppose the Alliance, though as early as November 1854 he was attacking the view that the evil lay in the drink 'traffic' rather than in the drink itself.[74] The Hyde Park riots against sabbatarian restriction in 1855 seem to have reinforced his fears that prohibitionist agitation would be fruitless unless teetotalism first prepared the public for it. In 1857 Livesey complained that 'the infant Alliance . . . had not used the old teetotal societies well' and publicly questioned whether the complementary agitations for prohibition and teetotalism really required two separate organizations. He admired the Alliance for its stiff resistance to Gladstone's proposals for freeing the trade in wine during 1860, and gave £5 to Alliance funds in recognition of it. But in 1862 he voiced complaints at the Scottish Temperance League's annual meeting and published them as a pamphlet, to which the Alliance issued a rejoinder.

Livesey wanted to restore the primacy of moral suasion in the temperance movement: although the Alliance helped incidentally to propagate temperance principles, he saw it as diverting temperance reformers from their true course; many of his friends 'so soon as this Permissive Bill was launched, slid away from our meetings, and declared that their attendance was unnecessary, as everything would be done by a *coup d'état*, and that if we insisted on that law, the work would be done'.*[75] The main enemy, he insisted, was the drink, not the trade in drink; even if the Permissive Bill were enacted, it could never solve the problem of home brewing. To this the Alliance replied that with twenty years' work the moral suasionist movement had made only a small proportion of the population into abstainers, and had not appreciably reduced the number of drinkshops or of drunkards. While it had convinced many people that drink was an evil, environmental pressures prevented conduct from according with belief: hence the need to alter that environment. Livesey replied that the Permissive Bill could be obtained only with great delay and difficulty, if only because M.P.s had not themselves been dissuaded from drinking, and would only reluctantly enforce on others conduct which they did not themselves adopt. Livesey's experience of Preston elections led him to doubt whether temperance could ever prosper by political involvement: the drink interest was powerful at elections and bribery was rampant.[76] Even if passed, the measure—with its 'all or nothing' choice—would rarely be enforced; the temperance party was unlikely to win a two-thirds ratepayer majority, least of all in the large towns where temperance legislation was most needed. Besides, it would promote civic strife, and

* H. Carter, *The English Temperance Movement* (1933), pp. 103–11, discusses the whole controversy capably and at length.

would hardly create the right atmosphere for a reasonable settlement of the temperance question.

To this the Alliance replied that M.P.s were best influenced through electoral activity, that Alliance political activity could itself help to purify elections, and that the struggle with the drink interest helped to build up 'a righteous and godly people'. The Alliance displayed none of Livesey's distaste for conflict, but almost courted it. While admitting that prohibition was the ultimate ideal, Livesey said that the main aim should be to obtain legislation which would benefit the moral suasionist movement: 'only one hour cut off the Saturday and Sunday nights' drinking in all the 140,000 houses throughout the kingdom would far exceed, in lessening the evil, the closing of a few country public-houses'.[77] Earlier weekday closing, total closing on Sundays and closer control over the publican—these were practicable measures likely to win the support of politicians and the public. Livesey thought it dangerous for the temperance movement to alienate the public by setting up as a distinct group at elections, if only because this led to political disputes within the movement. He had never felt the Alliance's contempt for the existing licensing system, and as early as 1834 had recommended bringing beerhouses under magistrates' control, reducing opening-hours, increasing licence fees and appointment of public-house inspectors by the parish.[78] But the Alliance insisted that popular control was preferable to magistrates' control, and that Livesey would never obtain the prohibition he claimed to support merely by agitating for something else.

The Alliance ignored Livesey's concluding plea for unity within the movement, and his wish that Alliance resources should be spent on teetotal education rather than on a fruitless political agitation. Far from treating Livesey's criticisms as a moderate and constructive contribution towards discussing the temperance question, the Alliance rebutted them as a threat to its existence. The Alliance 'is the ordained outburst of time, not the crotchet of an individual . . . Providence, brooding over the ideas of the age, is its real author.'[79] In 1870 T. H. Barker the Alliance secretary returned to the attack, and urged Livesey to 'atone' for his remarks by giving the Alliance his blessing. Livesey in his reply regretted the dispute: 'all the leading spirits of the U.K. Alliance are my old friends, whom I highly respect . . . everything approaching to antagonism has given me pain.' 'If you knew all', he added, 'you would give me credit for having for the last number of years exercised a great amount of forbearance.' Nevertheless, he remained unalterably opposed to Alliance policy. As a prohibitionist, he regretted the adoption of the Permissive Bill in 1857, which had tied the Alliance to a democratic agitation: 'after mixing with the working classes all my life, and after observing their conduct both at municipal and parliamentary elections, I am sorry to say, I believe they are not to be trusted.' The Alliance would get far more by accepting more stringent parliamentary regulation of the trade than by insisting on prohibition. Livesey claimed to be '*a thorough prohibitionist*' and urged the Alliance to return to its policy of campaigning for a Maine Law: 'the Alliance changed its policy once, and it never made any such pretence to infallibility as not to be able to change again.'

By doubting the wisdom of relying on mass electoral support, Livesey struck at the root of Alliance doctrine, and Barker rejoined by resolutely voicing his faith in democracy: 'in order to lead and elevate the people to a great act of self-emancipation, you must let them see that you dare and do *trust them*; that you are earnestly seeking their true welfare, and not merely trying to climb to position and place through them.' In 1870 the Alliance, with its mounting parliamentary support, seemed about to grasp success: but Livesey shrewdly perceived that it was '*time*, not argument . . . that is to arbitrate betwixt us'. He continued to recommend a return to the old moral suasionist methods in temperance meetings and periodicals. 'Let a candidate come out as a *teetotaler* and *prohibitionist, the best man we can select*,' he said in 1872, 'and let an election turn solely upon our question, and I should like to know of a single borough or county in the United Kingdom where he could be carried.'[80] In 1873 he issued another pamphlet, which repeated his old arguments. Once again he ridiculed the prohibitionist tendency to assume that the real evil lay in the drink traffic rather than in the drink. 'Just go round to a few of the public-houses on a Saturday night, and you will soon see whether the buyers or the sellers are the most important personages in keeping up the drink traffic'; it was patently absurd for the Alliance to suggest that such people were longing for protection from the trade.[81] Livesey held to his views until his death.

It was a painful dispute, for Barker clearly admired the old teetotal pioneer, and Livesey hated opposing old fellow-workers. Once again it was a dispute over means, not ends. Livesey wanted the Alliance to imitate the Anti-Corn Law League, in which he himself had played a prominent part: to concentrate on educating the public before trying to coerce parliament. Livesey deplored the vast Alliance expenditure of money and energies which could have been better applied to teetotal propaganda. Whether such funds could ever have been raised for moral suasionist campaigning he did not stop to ask. Yet in view of the subsequent history of the temperance question, his distrust of the mass electorate was justified. Equally shrewd was his suspicion that temperance reform would never be obtained through large semi-political, semi-philanthropic organizations. He had always preferred personal visitation to their philanthropy by proxy, and his outlook on the temperance question was less distorted by political considerations than that of the Alliance. As Henry Carter wrote of the first round in the controversy 'to read the two pamphlets in succession is to pass from the work-a-day life of industrial England to the council-chamber of a political headquarters'.[82]

Livesey's criticisms were publicized by the enemies of prohibition in the

National and Scottish Temperance Leagues, and also in parliament.[83] 'You have perhaps done more to obstruct and discourage us', wrote Barker in 1870, 'than any dozen other temperance men could do.' To the end of his life Livesey found an audience for his complaints of the Alliance and its 'everlasting teasing of Parliament'.[84] Livesey's arguments were still influential in the 1930s; Henry Carter deployed them against current Alliance temperance policy while writing the first twentieth-century history of the temperance movement.

10

Prohibitionists and Their Tactics: 1853–1872

Who were the prohibitionists? Like the teetotalers they were drawn from all age-groups. Although in 1853 the founder was 48 and the first president 56, three young men—T. H. Barker, F. R. Lees and Samuel Pope—were active in the Alliance during the 1850s. Regionally, the predominance of the north persists. The Alliance headquarters till 1918 remained in Manchester, which contributed far more than London to Alliance funds in this period: prohibitionists constantly complained of London's apathy. In their total donation, however, both London and Manchester outpaced all other cities. In its regional pattern of strength, the Alliance resembles the National Education League in being firmly based north of the Boston–Gloucester line, with high concentrations of support in south Lancashire, the West Riding and the north-east coast. To lend particularity to the analysis, biographies have been compiled wherever possible of the 234 identifiable prohibitionists who gave £5 or more to the Alliance in the financial year 1868–9;* an additional nine such donations were anonymous. The birth-places of 96 are known, and of these 21 came from Lancashire, by far the largest total for any county. 19 came from Scotland, and the rest were scattered thinly throughout the country, with no county even approaching these two areas. 'Deep under the superficial controversies of English society', wrote Bagehot in 1864, 'there is a struggle between what we may call the Northern and business element of English society, and the Southern and aristocratic element.' That 'sea of political darkness' in the home counties of which Ernest Jones complained in 1852, and which separated London from the radicals in the provincial towns, can also be seen in Alliance subscription-lists. Had England possessed a peasantry,

* This biographical information is printed in full in my article 'The British Prohibitionists: 1853–72. A Biographical Analysis', *International Review of Social History*, 1970. This article provides a much fuller analysis of the individuals who embraced prohibition in the 1860s; only a brief summary of parts of this article has been included here. I am most grateful to several public libraries for help with this analysis—especially to those in Birmingham, Cardiff, Liverpool, Darlington, Hull, Glasgow, Manchester and Leeds.

radical movements like prohibitionism and the Manchester School's attack on feudalism might have attracted more rural support.[1]

The Alliance drew supporters from several social grades. Between 1853 and 1874, it gained about a quarter of its funds from donations under £5, and over a third from donors of more than £5 but less than £100. Up to 1869 donors of £100 or more accounted for another third, but by 1873–4 this proportion had risen to almost a half. In the year 1868–9, three people contributed one-fifth of the total Alliance income, and the average annual donation from 3,018 people was £2 19s. 5d. Still, the Alliance was never widely supported among the wealthy or the well-born. Sir W. C. Trevelyan, the first Alliance president, and a progressive but eccentric agriculturist, gave the Alliance £6,150 between 1853 and 1869. During the 1860s Sir Wilfrid Lawson, Sen., a progressive Cumberland Liberal landowner and a deeply religious nonconformist, was giving at the rate of £500 a year; his son, Wilfrid Lawson, Jun.,* became the Alliance's parliamentary spokesman in the 1860s. The only other prominent titled Alliance supporter in the 1850s was the Earl of Harrington, a Benthamite Liberal and brother of the teetotal Earl Stanhope. In the 1868–9 sample, the occupations of only 172 are known: of these only 13 were farmers or landowners, and even these were eccentrics, dissenters or men with manufacturing connexions. Other rural supporters tended to be outspoken dissenters like Thomas Judge, 'the *enfant terrible* of Northamptonshire politics'. He was a radical grocer of Brackley, who championed the Liberal cause against the local gentry.[2] From this, as from the teetotal sample, all the 'governing class' professions—landowning, law, church, the civil service, the armed services and brewing—are markedly under-represented. Alliance hostility to the political class at Westminster is therefore hardly surprising. The Alliance believed that a really representative parliament would have capitulated long ago to the temperance movement. Like Cobden's League, it therefore besieged the politicians, and tried to frighten them with its mass organization and pressure; as Wilfrid Lawson put it, 'parliament only does right through fear'.[3]

The Alliance drew most of its major donors from industrial manufacturers —particularly from north-eastern England, Manchester, Glasgow, Cardiff and Dublin. Of the 172 in the 1868–9 sample whose occupations are known, 39 were textile manufacturers—by far the largest group. Often with a self-help background, these men were well known in their trades, with a local reputation for initiative and business integrity. Several were progressive employers, if judged by the standards of their time. What were their motives? Any mid-Victorian charity could of course bestow social and political benefits on its subscribers. In 1871 for instance, the Alliance offered a vice-presidency to all

* Henceforward I will refer to him simply as 'Wilfrid Lawson'; his father, who died in 1867, was less prominent in Alliance history; when he features at all, he will be referred to as 'Sir Wilfrid Lawson, Sen.'.

who gave £1,000 a year or more to its guarantee fund. Ambitious men could thus buy their way into public life, and Liberal M.P.s could in this way gain status at Westminster with their party's radical tail. But there were also motives peculiar to Alliance supporters. These men were optimistic about the ultimate consequences of industrialization, but they were anxious to ensure that the wealth it would bring would be sensibly used by their employees. The Alliance attracted several prominent penal reformers; M. D. Hill, the Recorder of Birmingham, was a major figure in the Alliance during the 1850s, and eventually influenced his friend Henry Brougham to declare publicly his admiration for what he called the 'Grand Alliance'.

Mineowners like Handel Cossham and the Pease family were concerned at the irregular habits of drunken employees, and had everything to gain from supporting the temperance movement. In 1871 James Clark, the Somerset shoe manufacturer, told an Alliance meeting that 'he had the misfortune to have one of the very worst of the liquor-shops opposite his factory, and it was a perpetual source of nuisance. As he sat in his counting-house paying the money to the workmen, he saw them spending it in that noxious place, and had no power whatever to put it down.'[4] A sober work-force would also improve British competitiveness abroad, and would extend the home market for consumer-goods. In so far as the temperance movement encouraged working people to conserve their own resources, it could claim to give more relief per £ donation than other charities: as one prohibitionist wrote in 1869 'our workpeople, were they sober, would be able to put up with short time without inconvenience'. F. W. Newman took these arguments still further. Drink prevented working people, he said, from becoming 'little capitalists'. Strikes he regarded as superfluous because the difference between wages offered and wages demanded was always far less than the amount a teetotaler saved in a week. This bizarre interpretation assumed that strikes were fought purely over the level of wages, uncomplicated by questions of status: and that they were unconcerned with the ratio between wages and profits.[5] In a more class-conscious age, the Alliance could hardly have publicized such views without alienating the democracy: but in the mid-Victorian period, the concept of respectability deeply permeated the political outlook even of working men.

It would be wrong to assume that the donors of small sums were necessarily poor. During the financial year 1863–4 we can use the original census returns to investigate all the donors listed in four randomly selected small towns—Bridgwater, Lewes, Liskeard and Cirencester. This shows that even the smallest amounts were often given by citizens of consequence. To take but two examples: Whinfield Robinson of Liskeard, who gave only 10/6, was a grocer with 2 servants and 12 employees; Edward Sealy of Bridgwater, who gave only 5/–, was a bookseller/printer/stationer with a staff of six. Furthermore, to analyse only donors of £5 or more would be to ignore the prohibitionist leaders within the working class. The Alliance was probably correct in believing that its numerical strength lay with what the *Economist* called 'upper class workmen, the humblest of the middle classes, and, generally speaking, persons below the class of gentlemen': with men like George Howell, John Cassell, George Potter, Thomas Burt, William Lovett and several other old Chartists. 'Let there be any extension of the franchise', the Alliance claimed in 1859, 'that shall make the registration spoon dip low enough to take up the cream of the working classes, and we shall sweep all before us in the House of Commons.'[6]

Positioned midway between the two predatory social forces of aristocracy and pauperism, middle- and working-class respectability was strongly attracted to prohibitionism. The *Alliance News* publicized bad behaviour at both social extremes: from the after-dinner scrapes of the youthful Lord Randolph Churchill in 1870 [cf. Plate 17][7] to the squalid miseries of slum life noted in its weekly column 'Barrel and Bottle Work'. Prohibitionist social pathology was conducted in terms of aristocratic corruption and oppression; a different diagnosis, which attributed drunkenness to the less creditable aspects of industrialization, could hardly be expected from an organization so heavily dependent on wealthy industrialists and ambitious tradesmen. The Alliance saw the licensing system as the instrument of a gentry eager to avoid taxation by levying indirect taxes, keen to boost the value of its urban property together with the price of the barley grown on its estates, by spreading public-houses throughout the poorer districts. The system secured the ancillary advantage of holding the people in subjection, discouraging self-improvement, hindering political instruction and stifling religious liberty. The magistrates rejected Lovett's application for a music licence for his progressive National Hall school, Holborn, yet they granted it to the publican who succeeded him in the premises. 'Publicans can always have such licences,' he wrote bitterly, 'but not so those who would have music apart from the means of intoxication.'[8] But men like Lovett were equally hostile to working men at the bottom of society who acted as pawns of the aristocracy: to the 'lambs', the racegoers, the wifebeaters, the spongers off the rates. Richard Brazier, a stout Alliance man and a Banbury whitesmith, frequently pressed local poor law guardians to allow teetotalers and drinkers each to provide for their own poor—for he knew that the teetotalers would gain by the change.[9]

A brief glance at the prohibitionism of William Lovett clarifies the nature of the Alliance's popular appeal. Lovett had always been enthusiastic for temperance and respectability within the working class. He was a member of the Alliance from the first, and in 1870 wrote four anonymous articles in the *Alliance News*. In these he saw drink as the explanation for the failure of his radical panaceas to curb crime, pauperism and conservatism. National prosperity depended on the use working people made of their capital: 'if they spend it in drink, it is at once wasted and done with; but if they spend it in necessaries and comforts for themselves and families, they produce a continually increasing market for themselves and families'. He insisted that education could never benefit children reared in a drunken home. To talk of 'the liberty of the subject' when opposing temperance restriction was an absurdity.[10] Lovett's ideal was a society of thrifty citizens, who married late and outlawed all forms of waste—war, crime, political and religious sectarianism, extravagance and drunkenness. His demonology was filled largely by pleasure-loving aristocrats who encouraged working men into wrong courses—through the racecourse, the public-house, the election bribe and brutal sports. His autobiography explicitly repudiated socialism, and its message stands forth in its concluding exhortation: 'remember . . . I implore you, that all just and efficient government must depend *on the intelligence and virtues of the great mass of our people*.' Like the Alliance itself, Lovett was doomed to disappointment. For C. F. G. Masterman was right: the nineteenth-century English working man was 'much more allied in temperament and disposition to some of the occupants of the Conservative back benches, whose life, in its bodily exercises, enjoyment of eating and drinking, and excitement of "sport", he would himself undoubtedly pursue with extreme relish if similar opportunities were offered him'.[11]

Two factors convinced the Alliance that it enjoyed the support of an élite among working men: its Manchester Free Trade Hall meetings, always crowded with Lancashire artisans: and its canvasses, conducted in many parts of England in the early 1860s, which seemed to show more enthusiasm for temperance restriction the larger the town and the lower the descent in the social scale. Yet the Lancashire artisan was exceptional in his class; and the canvasses, apart from falling into most of the traps which sociologists are now trained to avoid, went no lower in the social scale than the householder, and ignored the views of drinkers in the 'dangerous classes'. Roebuck in 1864 denied that 13,165 Sheffield Sunday closing petitioners really represented local working-class opinion, and produced a counter-petition signed by 24,000 Sheffield adult manual labourers.[12] The Alliance always exaggerated the extent of its popular support. Even the most educated working men were not united behind prohibition—witness the hostility of the *Bee-Hive* and of G. J. Holyoake. As for the humbler grades of working man, the Alliance believed that in their hearts they favoured prohibition; if their environment warped their conduct, they were in fact 'really praying that . . . temptation may be removed from them'. A comforting but misleading illusion: for temperance propaganda from its earliest days faced persistent ridicule from the rival culture within the working class. The temperance tract was no match for the jaunty, rabelaisian sarcasm of the publicans' posters, ditties and ballad-sheets. That compendium of London low-life versification, *The Coal-Hole Companion*, contains several arrestingly obscene parodies of the temperance song. 'The opinion of the drunkard is with us,' said Pope in 1856, 'his habit is the reverse.' This was not an argument likely to convince the politicians: working men could always be found to riot against licensing restriction, and to break up Alliance meetings. Though the Alliance deprecated these as 'rather the unworking classes . . . a crowd of roughs—a congregation of scamps', and saw them as pawns of the publican, politicians could not afford to ignore such groups, as their response to the Sunday trading riots in 1855 showed.[13]

Support for the Alliance cannot be understood solely in terms of social class, for class loyalties cannot explain why prohibitionists chose this particular reforming interest and not others; why F. W. Newman supported the Alliance, but not his brother John; why George Howell supported it, but not Alexander Macdonald. Prohibitionists show the same ebullience of temperament which characterized the teetotalers: fast walkers, early risers, cramming their days with a host of miscellaneous activities, they could hardly fail to be influential in their localities. Some had retiring natures, some were puritanical, many were controversial. Conscientious refusals of office were common among them: J. R. Wigham twice refused a knighthood, Richard Hall refused to pay the additional income tax required by the Abyssinian War and Wilfrid Lawson refused Campbell-Bannerman's offer of a privy councillorship in 1906 because 'if a man did his duty, it brought its own reward with it'. Many were men of high intelligence, whose radicalism was drawn more from a scientific than from a literary culture. The links with hydropathy, anti-smoking and vegetarianism so common among teetotalers are again apparent. F. W. Newman was the only university figure in the 1868–9 sample, though by that time the Alliance was beginning to attract radical intellectuals in Oxford and Cambridge. Three individuals—R. S. Newall of Gateshead, Peter Spence of Manchester and J. R. Wigham of Dublin—patented inventions, and many promoted educational institutions.

Blatchford may have been right in 1902 when he branded temperance reformers as men of one idea, but he could not have done so in 1869. Teetotalism (85), disestablishment (63) and popular education (22) were the three interests most attractive to the 1868–9 sample; the anti-slavery connexions persisted in the prohibitionist support for the north during the American Civil War; the feminist connexion, in the 11 who supported Josephine Butler's crusade.[14] Sylvia Pankhurst's list of anti-feminists might almost be a list of those who opposed the Alliance: 'from first to last, its opponents were mainly the professional Party politicians who objected to the penetration of women into their particular sphere, the brewing interests, the wealthy unoccupied "men about town", and the naval and military officer class.' Prohibitionism flourished on that alliance between feminism and middle-class puritanism of which Bernard Shaw complained so bitterly.[15] Still, in 1868–9, the leading Alliance donors were almost entirely male—218 out of 234: and many of the women were widows or spinsters, perpetuating the generosity of departed husbands or imitating the generosity of male relatives. Women accounted for only 6% of all donors in 1859–60, and this proportion fell steadily to 2% in 1873–4. Women gave an even smaller proportion of the total receipts: 2% in 1859–60, 1% in 1873–4. Women rarely spoke at Alliance meetings, and the permanent organization at Manchester was entirely in male hands. Women were useful for their campaigning enthusiasm, for their organizing skills and for fund-raising, but no woman became prominent as a prohibitionist advocate in the period. There is a striking contrast here with the National Temperance League, which in the 1860s and 1870s entrusted three women—Mrs. Fison, Miss Robinson and Miss Weston—with the task of extending temperance principles to new social groups.

Many of the prohibitionists' pet causes were 'anti' causes: as the prohibitionist F. W. Newman himself once admitted to an amused dinner-party—'Oh! I am anti-slavery, anti-alcohol, anti-tobacco, anti-*everything*.' It was of course in a sense constructive to adopt such policies in the early Victorian period, but prohibitionists were also often constructive in a more positive way.[16] At least ten of the 1868–9 sample provided counter-attractions to the tavern, often at their own expense, in the form of coffee-houses, temperance hotels and 'British Workman' public-houses. J. T. Rice of Bentham, William Enfield of Nottingham and R. E. Farrant of London were keen housing reformers; Joel Cadbury was a pillar of Birmingham's medical charities; Alderman J. Barlow and Benjamin Whitworth improved their local water supplies. Two of the sample, Cardinal Manning and the Manchester Conservative W. R. Callender, were well known for opposing the Liberal school of political economists, though in this they went further than most temperance reformers. In fact two members of the sample, G. T. Livesey and Manning, clashed over the gasworkers' strike in 1889.

The prohibitionists were overwhelmingly Liberal in inclination. 72 of the 218 male donors in the sample held office in local government, and several were household names in their localities. The Corys in Glamorgan, the Peases in Durham and the Darbys in Denbighshire opened up new sources of local wealth through exploring mineral deposits. Of the 75 in the sample whose political views are known, no less than 67 were Liberals: furthermore these were often men 'who would have become keen party workers if there had been a constituency party'.[17] The Conservatives were invariably Anglicans, often vigorously evangelical. The closer the investigation of prohibitionist beliefs, the clearer it becomes that the most important single influence on these men was their religion. The Alliance in 1853 had wisely launched itself with hymns, prayers and a sermon, and its leadership was largely nonconformist. Quakers were prominent as donors and activists. In Nathaniel Card, they provided the Alliance with its founder: in John Hilton, with its second parliamentary agent. Several of the 1868–9 donors were related. The leading Alliance donors in Cardiff and Dublin were almost all relatives, and in its very origins the Alliance was largely a family concern. Its preliminary meetings were held in the house of the Cowherdite Alderman Harvey; among other prominent Alliance men present were his Cowherdite brother-in-law Joseph Brotherton and his son-in-law James Simpson. Harvey occupied a central position in the Alliance from 1853 till his death in 1870. Brotherton's friend James Gaskill, also a Cowherdite, was another pioneer prohibitionist, and left £1,000 to the Alliance when he died in 1870.

Of other denominations, Charles Jupe the Wiltshire silk manufacturer and Congregationalist was a major donor. The Unitarians were important especially for their intellectual contribution: M. D. Hill helped to draft the Permissive Bill and F. W. Newman was the most original and intelligent prohibitionist spokesman and pamphleteer of the 1860s. By the late 1860s, Anglican support for the Alliance was growing. Of those who attended the 1857 Alliance ministerial conference, the three most prominent English denominations, well ahead of the rest, were the Congregationalists (33%), the Anglicans (16%) and the Baptists (15%). No Catholic was prominent till Manning joined the Alliance in 1868, though even after that year Manning was a relatively isolated figure among his priesthood.[18] Among the 124 donors in 1868–9 whose religion is known, 53 were Quakers, 14 were Anglicans and 12 were Wesleyans. Nonconformity was as prominent in prohibitionism as in teetotalism, and personal philanthropy was the ideal: William Gregson in the late 1850s marvelled to see the quantity of food carried away from the Jupe family table for distribution to the poor;[19] Joseph Lingford the Quaker baking-powder manufacturer of Bishop Auckland and Thomas Emmott the Oldham cotton manufacturer gave a free tea to the aged poor of their towns every New Year's Day. Though it might be argued that these men could well afford their charity, many took great personal trouble to help their fellow-townsmen, and some sacrificed business profits on the altar of moral principle. It is difficult to deny that these men were doing their best to relieve the miseries which surrounded them in the only way that they knew.

The Alliance between 1853 and 1872 was attracting support, then, from three social groups of mounting political influence: from articulate working men, many of whom were enfranchised in 1867; from feminists, whose political agitation was beginning in the 1860s; and from nonconformists, who were at last shedding their quietist cocoon and with it their sense of social inferiority. In the perspective provided by the twentieth-century rise of the Labour party, these men might seem to constitute 'the conservative, right-wing front in relation to social problems',[20] but in their own day they were decidedly radical individuals—enthusiasts for scientific innovation and social progress, deeply concerned at the suffering they saw around them, passionately indignant against those in authority.

How did the local veto become a political issue in the early 1870s? Considering the political strength of the drink interest and the extent of parliament's hostility to temperance extremism, the position the Alliance had achieved by 1871–2 was remarkable, and by no means inevitable. It was attained largely through organization and energy which inspired admiration even from its opponents. Alliance efficiency was at once its glory and its weakness—because its leaders' skill in political agitation deceived both themselves and the public as to the real strength of public support for their policy. The Alliance, though now less well known than its predecessors the Catholic emancipation, parliamentary reform, anti-slavery and anti-corn law movements, represents the culmination—even the *reductio ad absurdum*—of the techniques elaborated by these campaigns. It saw itself as participating in this great tradition of reforming agitations: 'the Alliance movement would make the fifth great struggle in this century', said F. W. Newman in 1865, 'and it would be as successful and as triumphant as the others'.[21] If energy and resourcefulness alone could have brought political success in mid-Victorian England, the Alliance would certainly have succeeded.

Alliance strategies differed somewhat in emphasis from those of the Anti-Corn Law League. Both movements recognized the need to educate the public, but the Alliance concentrated far more on educating parliament. It felt that the obstacle to its success lay there, rather than in the population at large. Admittedly it covered the country with auxiliaries and agents and filled its timetable with public meetings. Yet the educational content of its agents' speeches is far smaller than that of teetotal lectures in the 1830s or of League speeches in the 1840s. Vague denunciations of the drink evil and assertions that prohibitionist success was inevitable replace the more precise physiological and moral debate which Livesey and the teetotalers initiated. The Alliance agitation was designed 'not so much to create public opinion, as to create an opinion about public opinion'.[22] Although governments require the aid of 'interest groups' in the day-to-day administration of existing policy, they rarely require the aid of 'cause' groups campaigning for a *change* of policy. The latter must therefore attract government attention by conspicuous displays of their power. The Alliance was skilful in conspicuously displaying four great facts, each of which must now be considered in turn: the strength and universality of support for its remedy, the urgency of its reform, its money power and the wealth of supporting argument for its policy.

In the 1850s conspicuous display of numerical strength was attained largely through the public meeting—favoured weapon of those with numbers on their side, and a political instrument far more important then than now. The Anti-Corn Law League used it against the Anti-League just as the teetotalers had used it against the moderationists. The Alliance recommended towns' meetings, chaired by the mayor, whose resolutions could convey the impression of local prohibitionist unanimity. The public meeting, like the public procession, had the ancillary advantage of assuring those present of the strength and righteousness of their cause. Ostensibly didactic in aim, temperance meetings were often in reality merely expressive: hence the exasperation which interruptors evoked. Champions of free speech outside the temperance hall, temperance reformers inside it were almost totalitarian in their zeal for unanimity. A publican recognized at such a meeting claimed that women rushed to scratch his face and that the lecturer said that there was blood on his head, on his house and on his children and that he would go to hell. The publican no doubt exaggerated, but there is no reason to doubt the witness who told the 1853–4 public-houses committee that there was 'no chance of a fair and free discussion at any meeting where religion comes into question', particularly when temperance periodicals—despite their tendency to censor embarrassing incidents—often record the firm repression of interruptions at their meetings.[23]

Public meetings could emphasize the universality of support for a cause by gathering enthusiasts from all classes, all countries and all parts of England. Exeter Hall specialized in parading supporters of all colours and classes on its platforms, and although the Alliance had fewer high-ranking supporters than many evangelical societies, it did its best. Samuel Pope was willing to encourage any 'great name' on to Alliance platforms, however obnoxious politically or personally. He told Brougham in 1859 that Canon Stowell 'is well known as a man of great energy and small discretion but he is, among a certain class *extremely* popular, and therefore a power which may sometimes be used with advantage. I have often rejoiced that he is not *identified* with our agitation, but have, as often, been glad to avail myself of his rough enthusiasm.' He went on to say that on most political questions Stowell was 'profoundly ignorant'. In the same letter Pope told Brougham that he 'would go great lengths' to get him into the chair at an Alliance meeting in Manchester's Free Trade Hall: 'while we are unwilling to appear intrusive or importunate', he wrote in 1860, 'we are convinced that *nothing* would give so great a stimulus to our year's agitation as your lordship's presence at a great public meeting prior to the assembly of Parliament'.[24] Alliance minute-books, which survive from the 1870s, show vigorous correspondence being conducted with notabilities before the annual meeting—beginning with attempts to get distinguished sympathizers to preside or to speak, ending with hurried arrangements with less eminent supporters after refusals from those originally invited.

The unanimity of different areas could best be displayed through the congress, bazaar or fête. The 1855 Alliance fête, probably modelled on that of the Anti-Corn Law League, enabled female supporters to display their organizing ability and raised £2,777 for the funds. More ambitious was the international convention held by the Alliance in 1862, whose proceedings were published. But here, as with the international temperance congress of 1846, the delegates were almost exclusively Anglo-American. This instrument reappears in the late-Victorian imperial temperance congresses which heartened English temperance workers by associating them with more successful temperance workers from the colonies.

Secondly, conspicuous display of urgency. Apart from the large-scale canvass, used to some effect in the early 1860s, the petition was the prime weapon here. Like the Anti-Corn Law League, the Alliance used this to inform parliament—not so much that distress existed—as that something must be done about it. It was a way in which groups as yet lacking in parliamentary support could gain access to M.P.s. Petitioning, like canvassing, had the incidental advantages of keeping local organization in trim, giving focus to a campaign and educating the public. Before the introduction of the Permissive Bill in 1869, 4,000 petitions carrying nearly 800,000 signatures reached the Commons. By 1872 the latter figure had reached 1,388,075.[25] The Alliance usually had the advantage in petitioning contests, because petition signatures are more easily collected for altering than for maintaining the *status quo*. Publicans when roused could normally beat the temperance party at petitioning, but they usually concentrated on depreciating the petitions of their opponents. Temperance reformers retaliated by parading the obscenities and forgeries to be found in anti-temperance petitions; the publicans' 1872 petitions fell into some discredit when they were found to include the names of Sir Wilfrid Lawson, 'Bob Lowe' and Gladstone (twice). M.P.s, when investigating the drink question in debates and public inquiries, often found themselves arguing less about the validity of remedies for the drink problem than about the likelihood that these remedies really enjoyed public support. Like Chartists attacking the Anti-Corn Law League, publicans attacking the Alliance conjured up visions of dragooned Sunday school children obediently signing the unintelligible petitions presented to them by Sunday school teachers. It is of course always difficult to refuse a request for a signature—it seems such a modest favour to perform—and publicans quite rightly doubted its validity as an index of public opinion. Before the 1872 Permissive Bill debate 'vast rolls of petitions, requiring in one case a sort of rude machinery for their elevation to the table, amused and astonished the House', yet the *Standard* on 9 May was unimpressed: 'with the means and appliances at the disposal of the society it would be possible to get up an agitation for colonising the moon.'[26]

Another way of demonstrating the urgency of reform was through the parliamentary question; this depended on access to a sympathetic M.P., but the Alliance had no parliamentary leader till 1862. The mass deputation was designed to obtain policy statements from ministers; through the status of its members and the weight of its argument, the deputation might influence government policy and gain space in the press. The apparently spontaneous constituent's letter to his M.P. was also useful. Temperance circulars and periodicals sometimes urge readers to impress their M.P.s by delivering 'a few simple, earnest words from their hearts'. Running through all these urgency techniques was the opportunist tactic of 'improving' the disaster. The Alliance kept its eye on the latest tragedies—railway accidents, riots, cholera outbreaks, the cotton famine or the greatd epression, and turned them to its own purposes. This was a secular adaptation of a most effective religious technique: 'when the mind is softened by calamity, and alarmed by danger, then may the functions of the Pulpit be exercised with the greatest hopes of success.'[27]

Thirdly, conspicuous display of money-power. Large funds were useful partly for their own sake but also to advertise the success of a campaign. Furthermore fund-raising, like petitioning, helped to spread the new gospel. Alliance money-power, like that of the evangelical charities, was displayed through the published subscription-list and also through the much-advertised 'guarantee fund'. The Alliance subscription-list for 1872–3 occupies 55 octavo pages, nearly half the annual report for the year. Initially arranged alphabetically but later by county, these huge lists publicized the donations of all. In the 1860s and 1870s, the Alliance paraded its wealth by grouping together its subscriptions for five years in its 'guarantee fund'. The first of these began in 1865 with a target of £30,000, later raised to £50,000; the second, aiming at £100,000, began in 1871. Both targets were reached; for the latter, £90,000 was given or promised within a year. The level of total Alliance receipts rose to a new plateau at the beginning of the two campaigns [see Figure 9]. Samuel Pope at the 1871 annual meeting stressed the propagandist

FIG. 9

United Kingdom Alliance: real and nominal income: 1853–1900

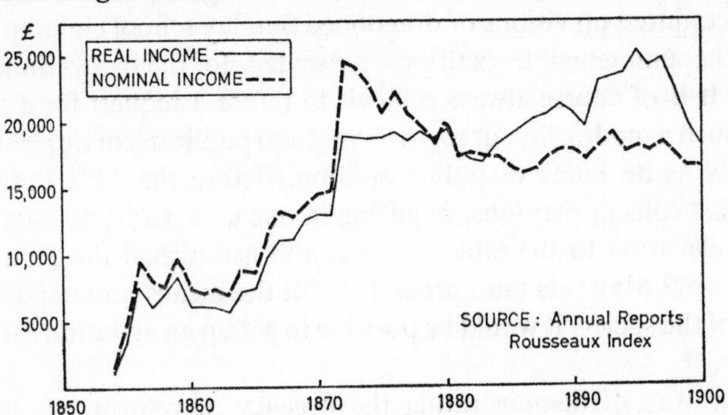

value of the guarantee fund: 'the raising of a hundred thousand pounds fund would do more to change hesitating opinion amongst politicians than any other resolution or argument we could possibly address to them'. The number as well as the size of the subscriptions was important: the fund 'must consist of large and small, must have a wide basis; as £100,000 from a hundred thousand subscribers would have more weight and representative value than the same sum contributed by a few'. Like Labour Party fund-raisers in the 1960s, the Alliance with its guarantee funds in the 1870s was busily mobilizing numbers against wealth and privilege.[28]

The income graph shows that the Alliance grew most rapidly at the time when the Liberation Society and the anti-vaccination movement were also making rapid strides.[29] Between 1853–4 and 1871–2 Alliance total receipts rose thirteenfold, whereas between 1857 and 1872–3 National Temperance League funds rose only fourfold [see Figure 1]. From 1872 Alliance nominal income fell sharply until 1886, and stagnated thereafter: whereas the fall in prices during the great depression ensured that it did not seriously feel the effects of this decline till the very end of the century. Between the two quinquennia 1855–9 and 1872–6, Alliance income rose by 185% whereas real national income *per capita* rose by only 44%; by the 1880s, however, this situation had been reversed. Alliance real income rose by only 15% between the quinquennia 1876–80 and 1896–1900 whereas real national income *per capita* in the same period rose by 55%. After 1872, therefore, the status of the Alliance in national life was being undermined. The Liberal party embraced the local veto only after prohibitionism had passed its prime, and even the 1908 Licensing Bill could not push the nominal receipts up to the level of the early 1870s.[30]

One historian sees 'the intensity of the [temperance] agitation after 1850 fluctuating with the *per capita* consumption of alcohol, which in turn fluctuated with good or bad times'.[31] The first of these two assertions is more questionable than the second. For the years 1820–50 it is probably untrue to say that the temperance movement prospered when *per capita* consumption increased. Admittedly the anti-spirits movement succeeded in the late 1820s because there were fears of an impending second gin age: likewise teetotalism attracted support partly because of the sudden appearance of the beershops. Yet it is by no means certain that *per capita* alcohol consumption was increasing in those years: evidence both statistical and literary for an increase is unreliable, and there is some weighty evidence that the temperance movement was founded at a time when the drink evil had already begun to diminish. From 1850, when the figures were more reliable, there certainly does seem at first sight to be some correlation between temperance prosperity and the increase in *per capita* drink consumption. United Kingdom *per capita* beer consumption rose markedly between 1859 and 1876—from 23·9 to 34·4 gallons; and between 1862 and 1875, United Kingdom *per capita* spirits consumption rose from 0·83 to 1·30 proof gallons;[32] within this period, temperance organizations saw great prosperity. Nevertheless, the fit is by no means perfect. From 1866 to 1871, the years when the Alliance agitation was mounting to its climax, the rise in *per capita* beer and spirits consumption had ceased, and after 1872 the Alliance began to decline, whereas beer and spirits consumption figures resumed their rise until 1876. National Temperance League receipts rose steadily during the 1860s, but not those of the British Temperance League. The fluctuation in temperance funds seems to centre on a political situation—on the 1871–2 licensing crisis—and not on the figures for drink consumption. Nor did the Alliance itself link its prosperity with the increasing level of drinking—drink statistics rarely feature in its propaganda. Although the prosperity of the temperance movement was related to the existence of a drink problem in the broadest sense, it would perhaps have been unusual among reform movements if its prosperity had fluctuated directly with changes in the intensity of the evil it attacked.

The mid-Victorian prosperity of the Alliance is better explained in terms of the political and religious situation in the period, which saw nonconformists militant and still unreconciled to the establishment, and religious leaders seeking ways of attracting the irreligious masses recently revealed by the 1851 census. The fluidity of the political situation in these years was accentuated in 1867 by franchise extension, which presented great opportunities to a militant reforming movement backed by nonconformist and middle and working class support. As for the National Temperance League, its prosperity during the 1860s probably owed more to the new policies and personalities introduced during that decade, than to changes in *per capita* drink consumption; for in these years it acquired new and far more imaginative leadership, and grew strong on the foundations laid by J. B. Gough, the successful lecturer of the 1850s. The lack of such leadership in the British Temperance League, whose minute-books show an unimaginative acceptance of accustomed routine, was probably responsible for its relatively poor showing.

The Alliance argued that the huge sums it raised—by financing immediate and vigorous agitation, would ultimately reduce the total cost of the prohibitionist campaign. But the absolute size of the Alliance annual income—by the early 1880s several times that of the National Liberal Federation and in 1882 twenty times that of the National Union of Conservative and Unionist Associations—inspired hostility in some quarters.[33] In the 1860s fear of large centralized bodies with access to large funds hindered the growth even of party organization. Intelligent observers like Joseph Livesey or W. S. Jevons asked whether the huge sums spent by the Alliance were really being effectively employed. Alliance fund-raising certainly provoked emulation from the drink interest. Lawson in his memoirs recalled Bass's statement that 'for every £1 we could put down, the Trade could put down 100. He might without exaggeration have said 1,000.'[34]

How did the Alliance attract new subscribers? Many Victorian charitable donations were not spontaneous, but solicited; rich philanthropists like Samuel Morley were besieged with begging letters. Although the Alliance did not obtain the £1,000 they requested from him in 1871 they induced many rich manufacturers and merchants from the northern industrial towns to contribute to their guarantee fund of that year—especially businessmen from Manchester, Bradford and Birmingham. Alliance representatives were often sent out to raise funds in the cotton exchanges of the north, and duplicated letters from its secretary seem to have been sent annually to leading subscribers, inquiring how much they intended to give during the coming year. After noting the recent death of two leading subscribers, Samuel Pope in one such letter dated 3 October 1859 emphasized that 'it is very important that we know . . . before the council commits itself to any scheme, how far our funds will be sustained'. Likewise T. H. Barker in August 1863 stressed the need for subscribers to step up their forthcoming contributions because the cotton famine prevented many customary subscribers from giving as much as usual.[35]

In its fund-raising the Alliance resembled other temperance organizations. When the National Temperance League was in trouble during 1863, it sent two of its leading supporters to beg special donations from several leading subscribers; when it was considering building a new headquarters in March 1865 it sounded out the atmosphere by circularizing its leading donors before launching a public fund; and when the British Temperance League contemplated expanding its newspaper in November 1859, it prepared a long list of individuals worth approaching for extra funds. Subscriptions were collected by the League's lecturers, by local treasurers, by special 'collectors' who were paid 10% commission on every new subscription they obtained, or—in the case of the Alliance—by the district superintendents. The leading donors in themselves constituted a small community, and were regularly consulted on policy. They were also invited to social functions; when the National Temperance League moved into its new Strand headquarters in December 1866, it invited its principal subscribers to an inaugural tea-meeting. A more elegant way of soliciting funds was the *conversazione*, at which speeches were delivered and discreet slips of paper distributed on which individuals would state the sum they intended to subscribe.[36]

Unless the organization was bold enough to use legacies as income—as did the R.S.P.C.A. towards the end of the nineteenth century—lump sums, especially legacies as large as Joseph Eaton's in 1858, were highly prized because they could be invested. This enabled the organization to emancipate itself from the tyranny of fluctuations in public opinion. Hence the survival of temperance and sabbatarian organizations into a twentieth-century world which provides them with a woefully inadequate current income. It is not clear how much fund-raising occurred at Alliance annual meetings, or how far it was done publicly. By the early twentieth century, however, the W.S.P.U. had developed fund-raising at the annual meeting to a fine art—so that its annual gatherings resembled bingo-halls, with one donor capping the promises of his predecessors. Fund-raising required considerable initiative and shrewdness from permanent Alliance officials; the most successful organizers of nineteenth-century charities could not afford to share the other-worldliness of some of their donors.

The pattern of Alliance expenditure is quite as important as its sources of income. *A priori* one would expect many conflicts of interest between subscribers and permanent staff on how the money should be spent: the latter, with a vested interest in gradual success and in accumulating a reserve, the former with an interest in rapid results. However this may be, such antagonisms were hardly likely to be documented. The general impression conveyed by Alliance minute-books in the early 1870s is one of efficiency, a close watch being kept on the expenses of Alliance agents. In his circular to subscribers in October 1859, Samuel Pope emphasized that 'no money is ever asked for by the Alliance to *pay old debts*. The secret of our success is the knowledge of our means beforehand, and our rigid rule *never* to anticipate our income.' From 1853 to 1873 at least half Alliance expenditure went on tracts, advertisements and written propaganda—a far larger proportion than was spent by the National Temperance League [see Figure 10].[37] The proportion absorbed by

FIG. 10

United Kingdom Alliance expenditure pattern: 1853–1875

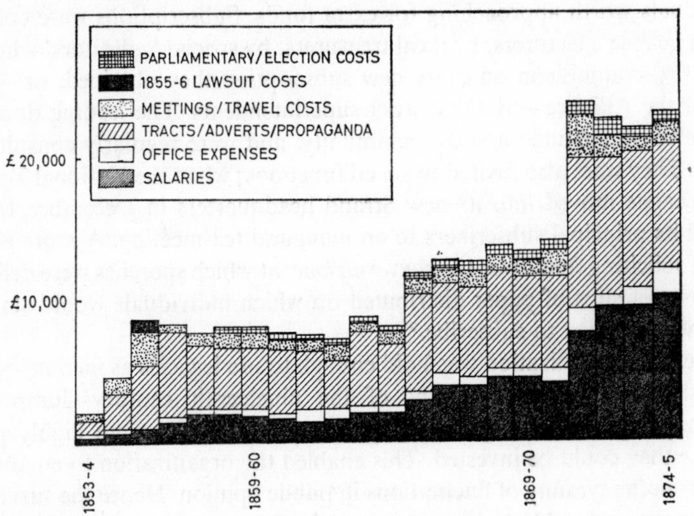

office expenses dwindled from 13% in 1853–4 to 5% in 1873–4; expenditure on meetings and travelling expenses also fell, from 12% in 1853–4 to 5% in 1873–4. Only a relatively small proportion of the total expenditure went on parliamentary and electoral expenses—never more than 5%. But proportionate expenditure on salaries steadily rose—from 15% in 1853–4 to 43% in 1873–4, reflecting the gradual extension of the Alliance agency network throughout the country.

Alliance expenditure patterns contrast with those of the National Temperance League, which spent proportionately less on salaries as the years went by—67% in 1858 and only 21% in 1873–4. The League greatly expanded its expenditure on meetings, and by 1873–4 was also devoting 9% of its expenditure to counter-attractive temperance work in the army and navy. Taking two fairly representative years, the Alliance in 1854–5 spent £539 on salaries, £494 on office expenses, £786 on meetings and travelling expenses and £2,490 on written propaganda. The corresponding figures for 1868–9 were £4,551, £685, £1,152 and £6,887 with a new source of expenditure—£611—on parliamentary and election expenses. Most expenditure on written propaganda went on the two periodicals *Alliance News* and *Meliora*, both of which made a small loss during the 1860s; far less was spent on tract distribution.

The fourth way in which the Alliance conspicuously displayed its strength was through exhaustive argument; it displayed energy and ingenuity not only in devising plausible arguments for prohibition, but also in bringing them to the notice of prominent individuals. When Charles Buxton the brewer in 1855 published an article deploring the effects of drunkenness, the Alliance lost no time in making capital out of it. F. R. Lees in 1856 created the *Alliance Prize Essay*, a large compendium of half-digested 'facts' which was to prohibitionists what the 'condensed library' was to Anti-Corn Law Leaguers. 'If every other book that has been written and printed on the question were destroyed', said T. H. Barker, in 1859, 'the cause would still have a noble literature, an ample vindication, and a complete argument.' The *Essay* may have helped bring Archbishop Manning into the Alliance, but was Queen Victoria able to keep awake while Florence Nightingale read it to her?[38] Lees never intended that it should entertain: it was an urgent and emphatic plea for immediate action, full of statistics and testimonies, and typical of its author: it 'was not penned to tickle the ear, but to convince . . . '.[39] It was typical also of Alliance argument—piling up testimony to the harm resulting from drunkenness, without considering the practicality of the remedy or fairly assessing its advantages against its demerits. Yet on the whole Alliance apologetics never reached a higher standard than in the late 1850s: with the Stanley–Pope discussion, published in *The Times* in 1856, the Alliance provoked J. S. Mill into a somewhat unsuccessful counter-attack. All this suggests that the quality of a reforming movement's argument varies inversely with the strength of public support for its policy. Until the movement has a sure footing, it has to defend itself by argument; when success approaches, it tries to bludgeon its remaining opponents by emphasizing the inevitability of its success.

The Alliance often obscured the most important issues in controversy by over-proving its case, and by pedantically pinpointing the most trivial errors —grammatical and otherwise—in the arguments of its opponents. In their periodical's weekly columns of 'barrel and bottle work' or 'fruits of the traffic', Alliance leaders tried to condition the public into accepting the local veto by listing the immense miseries resulting from drink, without supporting argument. Just as the Liberation Society saw State-Churchism as the root of all evil, so the Alliance saw everywhere the evil consequences of drink. It never approached controversy in a constructive frame of mind: it regarded opposing arguments, not as useful contributions towards solving a difficult problem, but as threats requiring to be 'dealt with'.

The press necessarily reflects existing public opinion; an association combating established social attitudes can often gain public attention only by founding a periodical of its own. 'Conspiracy of silence of the press', wrote Josephine Butler in similar circumstances, 'has done us this service—in that it has forced us to create a literature of our own.'[40] At first the Alliance paid for space in the weekly *Atlas*; finding this too cramping for its growing activity, in 1854 it founded the *Alliance*, whose first edition of 20,000 was exhausted in a matter of hours. The Alliance claimed that its periodical was the largest and cheapest penny weekly in the kingdom. The repeal of the stamp tax in 1855 and of the paper duty in 1861 enabled the Alliance to improve its size and quality; by 1859 it had attained a circulation (including free distribution) of 14,000–15,000.

Before 1855, temperance newspapers had been greatly hindered by the need to avoid printing 'news' if they were to remain exempt from the government stamp. During the 1850s the *Alliance News* devoted its front page to general news, the second to the 'liquor list' of miseries resulting from drink and to reports of prohibitionist meetings, the third to editorials and correspondence, the fourth to advertisements and news items. It was so successful that Cobden wanted the peace movement to imitate it.[41] Edited by the energetic Henry Sutton, the *Alliance News* enlarged the audience of speakers at its public meetings and ensured that heresy was extinguished. Press and parliamentary attacks were often printed in full, together with their refutation. The circulation of its periodical was as vital to the health of the Alliance as blood circulation to the health of the individual. It was 'the backbone of the entire organisation', although like the temperance meeting it was probably patronized largely by the converted.[42] Together with the National Temperance League's *Temperance Record* it took the lead in championing the restriction of the drink trade in the press during the 1860s.

The Alliance showed energy in making influential individuals aware of its arguments; like early twentieth-century American prohibitionists, it knew that if a small minority of 'opinion makers' could be won over, prohibition would be accepted by the nation as a whole.[43] In the late 1850s it made a special effort with this group. In 1859 an excellent but short-lived series of *Alliance Monthly Tracts* was begun, and in 1858 its quarterly review *Meliora* was founded for 'minds of a finer cast, a higher culture, and a more studious habit'. Owing to uninspired editorship,[44] the periodical was never a success and was discontinued in 1870. The Alliance made special efforts to attract three sections of 'opinion makers'—politicians, religious leaders and philanthropists. During the wine licence debates of 1860 all the peers were presented with copies of the *Alliance Prize Essay*. In 1864 Lord Robert Cecil sourly complained that the stationery distributed to M.P.s before the Permissive

Bill debate 'would alone have been sufficient to burn a hundred licensed victuallers alive'; and in 1873 another opponent of the Alliance objected to being 'saturated with literature'.[45] To this the Alliance after 1860 added the personal pressure of its parliamentary agent J. H. Raper, and held up for imitation the model of Dobson Collet, secretary of the newspaper stamp agitation, 'boring the members till they were obliged to promise him to support them, as their only chance of peace and quietness'. Where a politician was exceptionally influential—as in the case of John Bright—the Alliance organized a private deputation, partly to consult and partly to influence him. E. C. Delavan and T. H. Barker called on him in 1867, and in October 1878 he was interviewed by the whole Alliance executive, who wanted advice on parliamentary tactics.[46]

For winning the support of religious leaders the Alliance relied upon three techniques. Firstly, the personal deputation to individual religious dignitaries: this proved remarkably successful with Manning. Secondly, the appeal to the annual denominational conference: 'we claim the great Methodist families as ours by right of their founder's will,' declared the Alliance to the Wesleyan ministerial conference in 1859.[47] Thirdly, following Anti-Corn Law League precedents, there was the ministerial conference. The 1857 Alliance conference was attended by 353 ministers, and many dissenting ministers signed its declaration against the drink trade.

As for the philanthropists, the annual congresses of the National Association for the Promotion of Social Science presented the best opportunity. At the 1861 congress J. H. Raper was seen spreading the Alliance gospel to all who would listen: 'there was not a half-disclosed friend that he did not ply with argument, persuasion, and documents, until he won him over.'[48] In the 1850s the Alliance was hindered within the Association by aristocratic influence, by the Association's fear of connecting itself with cranks, and by the great philanthropic influence of publicans and brewers. Even the very limited temperance discussion at the 1858 Congress provoked rumblings of discontent from the publicans' organ, the *Era*.[49] The Alliance was brought prominently before the Social Science Association by its president Henry Brougham. During his lifetime there were many rumours that he was himself a habitual drunkard, but this was emphatically denied by his otherwise hostile biographer.[50] In the 1820s and 1830s Brougham championed free trade in beer, and in 1835 wanted licensing entrusted to a popularly elected local body.[51] But in the late 1830s he turned against the radicals, and advocated stricter control of the beersellers. He was probably influenced in favour of liquor restriction in the 1850s by John Cassell, with whom he had been corresponding, and by his friend and regular correspondent M. D. Hill. When Brougham referred at the 1859 Congress to the 'Grand Alliance', Samuel Pope delightedly claimed that his speech had given the cause 'a ten years impetus'.[52]

But Brougham was too old for his views to carry much weight; nor could he devote much energy to the Alliance cause. Even his limited connexion with the Alliance caused him personal embarrassment. After hearing that illness had prevented Brougham from attending a temperance meeting in 1860, Lord Lyndhurst wrote that he was 'exceedingly sorry for your illness, but not at all sorry that you do not attend that ridiculous meeting'.[53] Brougham again recommended the Permissive Bill at the 1860 Congress, and in 1861 even maintained that drunkenness inevitably results from moderate drinking. But the support from Brougham alone could not obtain easy access for the Alliance to the annual congresses. The Alliance complained that temperance was admitted for discussion to the 1861 congress only 'with ill-concealed reluctance'.[54] G. W. Hastings, the ambitious secretary of the Association, disliked temperance legislation and brusquely told Brougham in 1862 that 'we have had quite enough of the Permissive Bill and the Grand Alliance at our former meetings. Even teetotallers wish the subject to rest for the present'. Here, as elsewhere, there are parallels with the campaign against the Contagious Diseases Acts, for G. W. Hastings in the 1870s was equally obstructive to Josephine Butler's agitation.[55] Although Brougham never withdrew his support from the Alliance, he henceforth displayed less public zeal in its favour.

In 1863 Hastings used a technical objection to prevent the Alliance from obtaining a resolution from a Congress meeting on the drink traffic, and in 1864 the Alliance found the Congress situation 'worse this year than ever'. There were complaints in 1866 that Hanbury the brewer, who chaired a meeting on the causes of crime, prevented William Caine from discussing the link between drunkenness and infanticide in London. In the late 1860s however the tide seems to have turned, and at the Bristol congress of 1868 Hastings was publicly displaying moderate enthusiasm for the Permissive Bill which he had privately denounced only three years before. By the 1880s temperance legislation had become the Social Science Association's only remedy for the social evils of the day.[56]

From the first, the Alliance set its sights at Westminster. Parliament's power to help or hinder the temperance movement was particularly apparent in the mid-1850s. Sabbatarians and temperance reformers combined in 1853 to secure the Forbes–Mackenzie Act, which introduced complete Sunday closing into Scotland; in 1854 they secured the Wilson Patten Act, which curtailed Sunday opening hours in England. Yet in the same period, Parliament also showed its continuing power to make the task of temperance reformers more difficult. Denunciations of the Beer Act had become common in temperance circles by the 1850s, yet in 1853–4 an important parliamentary committee, sympathetic to free trade, was investigating the licensing system. Again in 1855 parliament, in complete defiance of temperance opinion, responded to riots in Hyde Park by extending public-house opening hours. On this occasion even the National Temperance Society complained that no M.P. had defended the temperance cause. After Buckingham's failure in 1834, no temperance voice was heard in parliament till the 1860s, and licensing debates centred entirely on the free trade issue. M.P.s in 1852 were so ignorant of temperance principles, that if Cobden had not championed the teetotal argument against cheap beer during the malt tax debates, their case would have been entirely ignored. A leading M.P. who sympathized with the Alliance said in 1854 that he could publicly express his support only 'when you have converted the constituencies'. The Alliance deplored the lack of public men ready to educate the public by taking a stand of their own accord, but equipped itself for the prolonged extra-parliamentary agitation which seemed to be the only way of getting them to move.[57]

Alliance auxiliaries were kept quite distinct from local temperance societies. They retained sole control over their own funds and were solely responsible for fighting local elections, but during general elections they had to concede far tighter control to the central organization; if they accepted subsidies from Manchester, they were rigorously supervised. The auxiliaries do not seem to have been prominent in the agitation; they were ephemeral bodies, contributing only 5% of the English subscriptions in the 1860s, and only 2% by the 1890s.[58] Unlike the teetotal societies they had no continuous recreational purpose; their duty was simply to agitate at strategic moments. To arouse any continuous local enthusiasm, the temperance movement needed drunkards to reclaim, just as Josephine Butler's campaign needed prostitutes to rehabilitate. The driving-force of the Alliance came from above rather than from below—from a handful of wealthy donors and from a few energetic Manchester-based organizers. The launching of prohibition in 1853 began a change in the character of local temperance activity quite as far-reaching as the changes brought about by teetotalism in the 1830s. Alliance auxiliaries were hardly more than foils for the permanent officials; at times, the prohibitionist 'movement' has the appearance of a mere stage-play.

From the first, the Alliance distributed propaganda at by-elections. Like Josephine Butler's supporters, Alliance men knew that a minority group could gain more publicity from intervening in a by-election than from large-scale intervention amid the distractions of a general election. Yet they never found their Colchester: unlike Josephine Butler's crusaders, they never succeeded—by timely and successful intervention in a crucial by-election—in pushing the Liberal leaders into concession. In 1855 the Alliance urged its supporters to intervene also in municipal elections, and from 1856 the country was divided into districts supervised by agents.[59] Here was an important contrast with the moral suasionist organizations, whose propagandist energies depended far more heavily on local initiative. Moral suasionist lecturers were usually sent to an area at the request, and often at the expense, of local subscribers. By contrast, the Alliance had its own agents on the spot, and could therefore react more independently and selectively in the face of local needs. During 1857 the Alliance, in drafting the Permissive Bill, equipped itself with a precise parliamentary policy and by 1866 England and Wales—except for parts of South Wales—were covered by an organized system of agents, controlled directly by the Alliance executive committee.[60] By 1868–9 there were three general deputational lecturers and agents, six occasional lecturers and eleven superintendents of the Alliance regional agencies. Agents were expected to organize local election committees, promote petitions, collect funds, hold meetings, question candidates, watch the local publicans and fully acquaint themselves with local politics. Occasionally, they were also required to lobby M.P.s at Westminster.

Alliance funds were used very sparingly at election time; part of Joseph Eaton's legacy was placed in an electoral reserve-fund in 1858 and used in the 1859 general election. But in 1868, Alliance funds were not used to support any candidate because in no constituency was the Permissive Bill the sole question at issue. When an election fund was at last established in 1873, it was kept 'altogether distinct from Alliance funds' and was formed on the private initiative of a few wealthy Alliance supporters.[61] Like their predecessors in the anti-corn law and complete suffrage movements, prohibitionists educated the public through submitting 'test questions' to candidates at the election hustings. The replies enabled the Alliance at each general election to assess its strength in the new parliament; the annual divisions on the Permissive Bill enabled it to keep these assessments up to date and indicated where pressure needed to be applied. The practice of extracting pledges from candidates on particular issues first became common in the anti-slavery campaign after 1826; the painful process was used by the Alliance to impress politicians with the importance of the prohibition question. Yet politicians found the weapon less painful when used by the Anti-Corn Law League because free trade fitted more easily than prohibition into the complex of attitudes held by the members of a leading political party.

In 1859 the Alliance formed 'Electoral Permissive Bill Associations' composed of electors willing to urge the local veto on local candidates and M.P.s. These associations were required to compile lists of sympathetic electors, invite them to a meeting, form a committee, canvass the constituency, prepare a revised list of supporters indexed by area and by surname, and then inform the candidates or members of their power. By 1872 there were eight Permissive Bill Associations in London alone and the Alliance contemplated establishing a central register to consolidate the information thus obtained. In the same year the Alliance parliamentary leader, Wilfrid Lawson, urged 'a more decided and definite' electoral policy. Spurred on by Kimberley's words to an Alliance deputation of 1872—'at present we think you are the weakest party'—the Alliance in 1873 appointed a full-time electoral organizing secretary J. W. Owen at £200 a year, to correspond with and to visit local committees.[62]

The Alliance promised to find a suitable candidate in any constituency whose existing candidates refused to support its Bill; when one candidate was already prepared to support the Permissive Bill the Alliance council pledged itself to give him 'every possible support, by deputations, lectures, and the distribution of publications'. At the 1872 annual meeting it was resolved to form committees in each constituency to analyse the voting register and to incorporate the results in a central Alliance national voting register. These efforts were strongly supported by the International Order of Good Templars, a pseudo-masonic organization of the most extreme temperance zealots. Benjamin Whitworth claimed that 'he would vote for the bluest Tory if he were only right on this question, rather than vote for a Liberal who was wrong'. Not all Alliance supporters felt so single-minded, and three years later Handel Cossham stressed that though an individual might stand on principle and refuse to drink, 'when he acted with a political party he must act with common sense and go with that party, otherwise he could not get from them that which he wanted to get'. There were cries of 'principle' from the audience, to which Cossham replied 'yes, he was talking of principle, and of the only way men could carry out principle'.[63] During the 1874 election the Alliance executive committee sat continuously to watch the results come in. The sequence of telegrams recorded in its minute-book conveys something of the excitement with which the Alliance leaders, now deeply involved in electoral activity, scrutinized the results.

How did the Alliance regard the existing political parties? Although in 1857 the prohibitionists feared ridicule if they insisted on returning parliamentary candidates on this one issue, their attitude hardened in the 1860s; in 1868 a leading parliamentary agent pronounced the Alliance test question 'the candidate's bugbear'.[64] Such tactics virtually forced dishonesty and broken promises on many parliamentary candidates, or extracted from them promises so vague as to be politically worthless. Some critics felt that it was unconstitutional and un-English to demand public pledges from candidates. *The Times* in 1863 described Alliance tactics as 'unscrupulous terrorism' and Gladstone in 1865 considered them 'deplorable fanaticism'.[65] The Alliance refused to support Samuel Morley at the 1868 Bristol by-election and Edward Baines at Leeds in 1874 because, though genuine temperance reformers, they had refused to support the Permissive Bill unreservedly. Through adopting this policy, the Alliance antagonized some of the leading temperance reformers. The history of the Liberation Society in the late 1870s shows how effectively Liberal support could have been won by adopting a more conciliatory attitude.[66]

Yet conciliation of the existing political parties was precisely the policy which the Alliance despised. Its self-chosen mission was to infuse 'principle' into politics. Nineteenth-century pressure groups like the Alliance closely resemble pressure groups in twentieth-century America: by initiating national debates on national issues of policy, by weakening the role of local issues, personalities and interests in political life, and by disciplining M.P.s in hustings and division-lobby, they helped to unify the nation and to create a national political community.[67] Like Cobden in the 1840s, the Alliance in the 1850s scorned the existing political parties. In the first Alliance hustings speech, Samuel Pope said that future political discussion must turn 'not on emasculated political dogmas which may be of real or of very doubtful utility, but on great questions of social ethics'. He divided M.P.s into Palmerstonians, Opposition and 'Outsiders', and said that if he became an M.P. he would join the Outsiders.[68] Pope's remarks during his Stoke campaigns in 1857 and 1859 closely resemble those made by the Chartist Henry Vincent during his eight contests between 1841 and 1852; they appealed to those who saw the existing party system as fraudulent and outmoded, and who longed for some sort of co-operation between good men of all parties in the task of genuine social reform. 'The great party of the future,' said the Alliance in 1856, '. . . will be devoted to the development of great problems of social ethics, to the exclusion of the exhausted questions of the past.'[69]

For the Alliance, the traditional and self-interested attitude to elections was symbolized by the bodies of publicans mobilized in every constituency, 'the most dangerous political combination of modern times'.[70] The Alliance claimed that not less than a fifth of the borough voters were directly engaged in the drink trade. Yet it sought to counter one evil merely by substituting another; it tried to beat the publicans at their own game by organizing ruthless bands of supporters in every constituency. With the Alliance, as with Josephine Butler's agitation, such tactics were extremely unpopular with the politicians. The Alliance had no qualms about the fact that its Devonport supporters in 1865 'hardly more than fifty . . . made up for their comparative paucity by their steadfast unanimity', and made Brassey's election possible;[71] for as long as the franchise remained so restricted, the Alliance could look on this little band as spokesmen for the unrepresented masses. Alliance men had no reason to respect the existing electoral machinery as long as it remained undemocratic.

In its early years then, the Alliance declined all party allegiance. A newly founded pressure group cannot afford to alienate potential support by identifying itself too closely with any one political party: it needs to appeal to national interests and to capitalize on every prevailing discontent. In the 1850s a sizeable minority of the politicians sympathetic to the Alliance were Conservatives, and as late as 1872 Lawson begged support from members of both political parties; in the same year, the Alliance was decidedly embarrassed by G. O. Trevelyan's attempt to identify prohibition as a Liberal policy. Political neutrality had other advantages; pressure groups which identified themselves with a particular party, like the late-Victorian temperance and

Home Rule movements, found that they were almost powerless when their party was in opposition. Similar non-party tactics have been adopted by many reforming agitations, including the feminist organizations of Mrs. Fawcett and Mrs. Pankhurst.

Yet in a cause which, by the 1860s, patently aroused more sympathy in one party than in the other, it is arguable that an explicit party connexion might have been more helpful. Tory supporters had always been a minority among prohibitionists, and as long as it remained a non-party organization, the Alliance could not officially threaten the Liberal party with the loss of political support. The arguments for a party alignment grew all the stronger in the late nineteenth century, with the dwindling of the private member's legislative influence. In 1869 a hostile critic with inside information revealed that it had been 'several times discussed' by the Alliance executive whether to coalesce with one political party.[72] Although in its alliance with Liberalism the prohibitionist movement never became as frankly partisan as the National Education League, in 1874 it officially expressed sympathy at last with the Liberal party. Lawson, impressed with the powerlessness of the private member, urged Sir William Harcourt in 1876 to become leader of the temperance party, and later consulted Bright privately on the best parliamentary tactics to adopt.[73]

If the Alliance eventually aligned itself behind a political party, it never adapted its parliamentary tactics accordingly. Even in the early twentieth century its effort was still centred on the private member, whereas the suffragettes, recognizing the changed power-situation at Westminster, brought all their influence to bear on cabinet ministers. Party influence and pressure of business had so limited the power of the private member by 1901 that the Alliance agent J. D. Hilton looked 'extremely doleful' when asked what he thought of present-day parliamentary procedure: 'it is almost impossible for a private member's Bill to get through,' he said.[74] While the Alliance may have gained in self-confidence by its frequent backward glances at previous reforming agitations, precedents were in some respects a real hindrance.

Officially the late-Victorian Liberal connexion of the Alliance represented a policy change, yet in reality it merely acknowledged publicly an alignment which had always existed. The Alliance candidates of the 1850s and 1860s—Lawson, Lees, Pope and Cossham—were all extreme radicals seeking, like Miall in the Liberation Society, to liven up the Liberal party. When the Alliance in 1859 supported the candidature of Ernest Jones, the *Weekly Record* indulged in a splendid outburst: 'when we see our movement dragged through an election at the heels of adventurers, and made the synonyme of Chartism, and put upon the lowest platform of politics, we should be recreant to the cause if we held our tongue.'[75] Of the Alliance supporters whose political views were known, said F. W. Newman in 1865, there were 'at least eight democrats for one Whig or Tory'. If the Liberal party had been more responsive, the Alliance would probably have allied with it much earlier. As it was, the Alliance until the 1860s 'had nothing but frowns and denunciations to contend against, from the most Radical section of the Liberal party, the leaders of which feared, and therefore hated anything that might divide and weaken their ranks'.[76]

When Samuel Pope contested Stoke in 1857, he was accused of 'dividing the Liberal interest'; he retorted that Stoke Liberals were so anaemic in their principles that they were hardly distinguishable from the local Conservatives. Like later American prohibitionists, the Alliance was trying to force its policy on a major political party by threatening to split its vote. What the Alliance was really doing was to pioneer the machinery and mentality of the mass party in an age when the party leadership was only beginning to adapt itself for its new role. Pressure groups like the Alliance were the self-appointed policy-makers and electoral organizers of the late-Victorian political parties. They forced on to the politicians most of the issues dominating late-Victorian Liberal party programmes—Home Rule, trade union legislation, disestablishment and temperance.

How did all this machinery function during the first phase of Alliance activity from 1853 to 1860? At first the Alliance was very successful in catching the public eye. By June 1854 it had issued 4,500 membership cards, sent Dr. F. R. Lees to report on the American situation, surveyed the customers of Manchester drinkshops and sent witnesses to the parliamentary committee on public-houses. In 1855 the publicans helped to publicize the existence of the Alliance by violently breaking up its meetings in Bristol, Birmingham and Dudley. Prohibitionists, like the liberationists, learned to expect violence from their opponents. George Howell recalled half a century later how Bristol prohibitionists in the 1850s had defended the lecturing platform against their menacing publican opponents.[77] 'I am just off to the Permissive Bill meeting,' wrote H. J. Wilson to his sister in 1871: 'very doubtful if I shall get home with my skin complete'; he had already been knocked on the head at a previous meeting. The violence of Alliance opponents culminated in the bursting of a flour bag on the chest of Frederick Temple, Bishop of Exeter, at an Alliance meeting held in Exeter during 1872. The whitened bishop remained surprisingly calm under the insult, and the Alliance may well have gained more than it lost by such incidents.[78]

Nevertheless the Hyde Park riots of 1855 represented a serious short-term setback. Though ostensibly in protest against Lord Robert Grosvenor's Sunday Trading Bill, these riots were really a protest against all evangelical restrictions on popular recreation. The Wilson–Patten Act [see Tables 8 and 9], which in 1854 closed drinking places for a large part of Sunday, was often mentioned as a grievance during the riots by the press, by the rioters and by Hyde Park orators.[79] The riots shocked parliament into severely modifying the Wilson–Patten Act after holding a hasty and biased parliamentary committee. The incident was used for decades by the opponents of licensing restriction as a warning against curtailing the liberties of working people in the great cities. R. A. Cross in 1880 said that if Sunday closing were introduced he would not be responsible for the peace of London. The riots were still being discussed before the royal commission on liquor licensing appointed in 1896.[80] A glance at the newspapers of 1855–6 shows that the Maine Law had already become a general topic of conversation, and in 1856 *The Times* published the important debate between Lord Stanley and Samuel Pope, the Alliance secretary. The Alliance began its electoral activities during a by-election at Marylebone in 1854 by placarding the constituency and urging voters to oppose any candidate who refused to pledge himself to independence of the publicans. It gave similar advice to Southampton electors, who in the 1856 by-election were urged to 'take no shuffling evasion'.[81]

The first general election faced by the Alliance in 1857 came a year too soon for them. Alliance supporters had not yet framed the Permissive Bill, and therefore had to content themselves with submitting a test question which asked candidates whether they would support a permissive measure to refer the prohibition question to the people. The only prominent Alliance supporter to contest a seat in 1857 was its secretary Samuel Pope, who intervened at Stoke-on-Trent as third contestant when the other two candidates failed to meet Alliance requirements. Cobden would have found Pope's programme highly acceptable—it included full commercial, civil and religious freedom, the ballot, open diplomacy and local control of education. Pope sternly denounced the Tories and echoed the moral force Chartists when he maintained that 'there was nothing which our present rulers so much dreaded as the sobriety of the people'.[82] Victorious on the show of hands, Pope withdrew from the contest before the poll. The Alliance claimed that at the 1857 election 65 successful candidates promised to support inquiry into the desirability of prohibition; of these only 33 promised to support the introduction of a Permissive Bill. The latter figure included members primarily from boroughs in Scotland, the north of England and the midlands, but even the Alliance admitted that many of these had given their assent under electoral pressure and might fall away in time of trial.[83] The *Weekly Record*—sympathetic to, though not officially the organ of, the National Temperance League—contrasted the triviality of the Alliance achievement with the pretentiousness of its claims, and was not convincingly refuted.[84]

The Alliance was hardly more successful at the 1859 election, despite spending £420 14s. 0d. on 'parliamentary election expenses'. Though Samuel Pope enjoyed much popular support and waged an exciting campaign at Stoke with the aid of George Thompson, he was defeated. He received 569 votes, but one of his rivals emphasized that many of these votes were cast for his radicalism rather than for his prohibitionism; one Stoke publican said that he knew several local publicans who were supporting Pope. But the Alliance claimed that Stoke's 296 drinksellers had increased the votes for Ricardo and Copeland—Pope's rivals—by 195 and 215, respectively. Many Whig and Tory voters combined against Pope, and the election result reinforced the Alliance in its belief that it could hardly lose by franchise extension.[85] At Bristol in 1859, 400–500 teetotalers held back their votes till late in the day, and by voting for Langton allegedly caused the defeat of Slade the Tory by 80 votes. Seymour, the Alliance candidate at Southampton, was returned; and though Alderman Heywood the Alliance candidate at Manchester was defeated, he did at least raise 5,448 votes.[86] In retrospect the Alliance's most important contest in 1859 occurred at Carlisle, where after an unsuccessful attempt in 1857 the young Wilfrid Lawson was returned with Sir James Graham. But Lawson had not yet publicly espoused prohibition, and his return resulted largely from local influence. The Alliance claimed that 78 of the successful candidates—almost all from English boroughs—favoured the Permissive Bill principle, or at least would not oppose the Bill's introduction; 57 of these were Liberal and 21 Conservative. Only 13 M.P.s however—11 of them Liberal and 2 Conservative—were ready to vote for the Bill's introduction. Once again the *Weekly Record* sprang to the attack, noting that nearly every teetotal M.P. was pledged against the Permissive Bill.[87]

Looking back over the organizational and electoral achievement of the Alliance by 1860, it can be said that the new organization had achieved little, but showed much energy and promise. It had already fulfilled four of the five preconditions which one historian considers necessary for the success of a political school.[88] Its leading spirits were bound together by a common social background, by ties of personal friendship and even by family connexion. Their principles constituted a valuable critique of political economy and of contemporary attitudes to the state, and were seen as such. If applied to other areas in nineteenth-century society they could well have fulfilled the second requirement—that the school's principles should be fruitful enough to supply and replenish legislative programmes. In 1881 T. H. Green's lecture on 'Liberal Legislation and Freedom of Contract' revealed the political possibilities inherent in the Alliance philosophy. Thirdly, by the end of the 1850s the Alliance certainly possessed the minimum organization needed to popularize its ideas; and, fourthly, it had also won the confidence of powerful and dissatisfied groups interested in political change. Within the next 25 years it was to gain access to the highest political circles, and to achieve the last necessary precondition—the permeation of existing political parties. The explanation of why, after meeting all these preconditions, the Alliance leaders eventually failed must be discussed by other historians. What must be considered here is the Alliance campaign between 1860 and 1872 to influence the political parties; for this, the reader's attention must at last return to Westminster.

11
Mounting Temperance Pressure: 1860–1870

During the 1860s the Alliance made rapid progress: it helped to ensure the final defeat of the free traders, acquired its greatest parliamentary leader, helped to broaden the franchise, and made the temperance question one of the most pressing political issues. The attack on free trade had three distinct aspects: the restoration of the beershops to the magistrates' control between 1830 and 1869: the opposition to Gladstone's attempt at opening up the wine trade in the early 1860s: and the successful campaign against the free licensing policy of the Liverpool magistrates.

The number of beershops rose quickly after 1830 [see Figure 4], but the Whig and Tory attack on them faced strong radical opposition. As early as 1834 there were signs of the mid-Victorian division between temperance and free trading radicals; for when Knatchbull proposed restrictions on the beershop, J. S. Buckingham the temperance pioneer argued that where the question lay, not between free trade and monopoly but 'between public convenience and public morality', a temperance reformer could choose only restriction.[1] Knatchbull's Bill passed easily; besides tightening up on the qualifications required of beersellers, it created a distinction between beerhouses with off- and on-licences. By the late 1830s, the anti-beershop movement had gained Brougham's support, and in 1840 beerhouse rating qualifications were raised further. During the 1840s the number of beersellers' on- and off-licences plunged dramatically. There was no further important change in beerhouse law till 1869, but the free traders had not yet succumbed; in the early 1850s the *Morning Chronicle* ran a vigorous campaign against the monopolistic brewers, and the full-scale inquiry into the licensing system conducted by the Villiers committee in 1853–4 was strongly influenced by free traders; it proposed to abolish the arbitrary distinction between public-houses and beershops, and to enable any person of good character to get a licence provided that he could pay high licence fees tied directly to the size of the local population.

Many years elapsed before a government steeled itself to attempt a full-scale licensing reform. But in 1860 Gladstone embarked on a limited but adventurous and imaginative scheme to open up the wine trade. Like *per capita* malt consumption before 1820, *per capita* wine consumption before 1860 was stagnating, and Gladstone in 1855 pronounced the wine duties 'the scandal of our tariff'.[2] His experiment in 1860 was not inspired by temperance sentiment: he was not himself a teetotaler, and his 1860 budget speech was delivered with the aid of 'a great stock of egg and wine'. Observation of continental habits convinced him that free trade and sobriety went hand in hand. His experiment was inspired primarily by a zeal for peace and free trade, and was a painstaking appendage to the Cobden–Chevalier treaty. It involved much intricate negotiation and research, and helped to make the sessions of 1860–1 into what Gladstone 37 years later described as 'the most trying part of my whole political life'.[3] The general burden of the detailed negotiations between Gladstone in London and Cobden in Paris was that Cobden tried to push Gladstone into conceding the lowest possible duty on *vins ordinaires* in order to compensate the French for reducing their duties on British manufactures. Cobden believed that there was a large and hitherto untapped British market for these cheaper wines, and that a bold reduction in duty would 'have a most important result in the revenue, and the social habits and the morals of the country'.[4] Gladstone had great difficulty in deciding on the extent of tax reduction, but eventually fixed upon a tax of 1/– a gallon for all wines under 26° proof; and 2/6 for wines between 26° and 42°, with 3d. for every degree above 42°.

Duty reduction was only one branch of his wine policy; he still had to open up the wine trade. 'All my wish,' he told Baines, 'is first to open some new, and cleaner channels for consumption, secondly not to create a new monopoly.'[5] His system steered midway between the public-house and beerhouse systems. He instituted virtual free trade in off-licence wine sales, and for on-licence wine sales he sought uniform application by giving the excise responsibility for granting wine licences, and by allowing magistrates' veto only on the specific grounds listed in the Bill. Gladstone tried to open the trade from two directions—first, by enabling any shopkeeper not expressly excluded by the statute to obtain an off-licence for selling wine: second, by enabling eating-houses to take out annually renewable on-licences for wine consumption.

The measure embarrassed temperance reformers in several ways. Temperance considerations clashed with the interests of the many northern manufacturers who stood to gain from increased trade with France; they also clashed with the popular gospel of free trade as expounded by Bright and Gladstone. Temperance reformers, normally free traders in most other spheres, had to explain why their principles did not apply here. Face-to-face with Gladstone in March 1860, an Alliance deputation could do little but quote formulae and testimonials: all the sophistication, subtlety, imagination and success lay with Gladstone.[6] Temperance reformers also lost face when forced to oppose gradualist proposals for reducing drunkenness; for the advocates of universal teetotalism or outright prohibition could never accept Gladstone's policy of championing the good drinking places against the bad, the weak intoxicants against the strong. But by resisting such a policy, the temperance reformer revealed his eagerness to acquit his conscience of responsibility for the drink evil and his ineffectiveness as a practical reformer. Gladstone felt little respect for the protests of the National Temperance League, for he knew that its members had it 'as much in view to acquit their consciences, to liberate their souls, and to wash their hands of all responsibility as to prosecute a real and earnest opposition to the Bill'.[7]

Still more embarrassing—temperance reformers were not uniformly hostile to Gladstone's measures. Several teetotal M.P.s argued, with John Bright, that 'health and temperance may be both gainers by the introduction of light wines into this country'.[8] The Alliance alone firmly resisted Gladstone's proposals, and spent £200 on its campaign: 'our organization has made itself felt in Parliament,' it wrote, 'its documents have been quoted, its doctrines propounded'.[9] There was one further reason for temperance embarrassment: the publicans were on the same side. Free trade principles were as vigorously contested by their spokesman Ayrton as by any temperance reformer, and the *Spectator* on 3 March found this 'one of the most suspicious alliances ever yet seen in political action'. The drink trade's hostility was of course far more influential with the government[10] but the publicans were divided amongst themselves, though united against the free-trading beersellers; the brewers were also divided on the question. Clearly there was no united 'drink interest' in 1860, though there were already portents of the alliance between publicans, property-owners and Conservatives. On 8 May the *Standard* claimed that 'if rights of this indefeasible character are to be abrogated there is no knowing where the spoliation will end. It is the publican to-day, but to-morrow it may be the grocer, the butcher, or the baker.' *The Times* on 21 February noted that the brewers 'usually so strong in their partisanship of Liberal metropolitan members', seemed 'all at once to have been converted to the principles of Conservatism'.

Still, Gladstone got his measures through almost undamaged, and as finally enacted, his reform had the following provisions: the excise, and not the J.P.s, were to grant on-licences, with the same conditions of tenure as for publicans and beersellers. Aspiring retailers had to serve notice of their application on the justices who, after hearing the applicant, could reject his application on specified grounds, subject to an appeal to quarter sessions. Any shopkeeper was enabled to take out an off-licence. The *Morning Star* on 12 April was delighted with a Bill which seemed 'a step in advance towards a more rational state of things, when a man will no more require a permission for the sale of wine or beer than he does for that of beef or bread'. Gladstone took his quest for free trade still further in 1861, when he enabled anyone licensed as a wholesale spirits dealer to take out a retail licence for selling small quantities to be consumed off the premises; in 1863 a smaller measure extended the same opportunity to beer-dealers. In 1861 Gladstone also enabled anyone to sell table-beer for off consumption, and enabled beershops to take out wine licences.

Gladstone's 1860 measures were not strikingly successful. They were of course sufficient to make the fortunes of Messrs. Gilbey. Founded in 1857, and determined to break down the exclusiveness of the wine trade, the firm responded to Gladstone's legislation by rapid reductions in price, and by creating a network of local agencies for selling wine throughout the country. But Gladstone never succeeded in making wine the regular drink of the

FIG. 11

Gladstone's drink retailing licences: 1861–1880

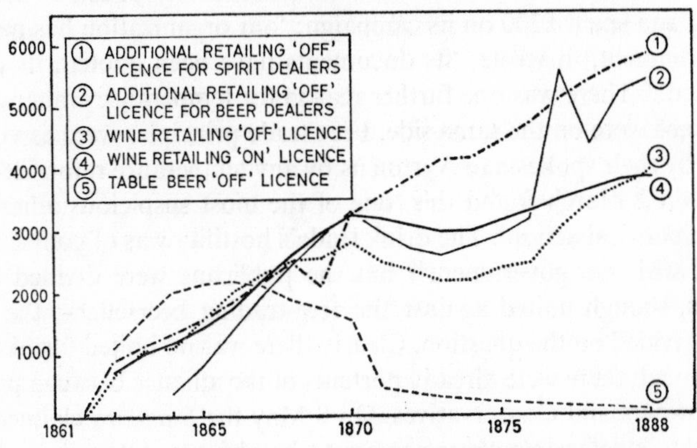

SOURCE: G. B. Wilson, *Alcohol and the Nation*, pp. 395–6

English working class, though he no doubt increased the popularity of expensive wines and of the 'little dinner' in mid-Victorian society. By 1866 the gross United Kingdom consumption of wine had doubled, and imports of French wine had overtaken Portuguese; yet even in that year France supplied only about a quarter of British wine imports. Nor did the total wine revenues collected after 1860 exceed those raised before; the annual average receipts for the wine duties in 1855–9 were £1,835,000; for 1865–9 this figure had fallen to £1,421,000. And though in the 1860s the gross and *per capita* consumption figures for wine rose more quickly than those for other intoxicants, by the 1870s wine was falling behind spirits and beer. What occurred after 1860 was not a general change in taste from gin and beer to wine, but a general increase in the gross consumption of *all* intoxicants—from which wine benefited more than other drinks only during the 1860s. To judge from the number of wine licences issued [see Figure 11] Gladstone's measures never made as great an impact as the 1830 Beer Act, despite the astuteness with which they were conceived and executed.

Some important developments in Liverpool during the 1860s prevented free licensing from being carried further. By 1853 many Liverpool magistrates felt that considerations of character should be the sole ground for refusing a licensing application, and that magistrates should not be required to estimate a neighbourhood's drinking needs. They felt that the law of supply and demand would indicate the number of drinkshops needed, and that only a single uniform licence for the sale of all types of drink was required. During the 1860s they conducted a two-pronged campaign: to force their principles on the Liverpool licensing magistrates, through altering their composition; and on the politicians, through pressure for a special Liverpool free licensing measure. From 1862 to 1866 their efforts ensured that free licensing prevailed in Liverpool; Gladstone and the Home Secretary watched developments closely for guidance on national policy. Free licensing measures for Liverpool were introduced into parliament in 1863 and 1865, but were defeated by a combination of prohibitionists and publicans; and in 1866 an accession of numbers to the restrictionists caused the Liverpool magistrates to reverse their free trade policy. Though parliament still had champions of free licensing long after the 1860s—Gladstone, William Rathbone, Robert Lowe and Auberon Herbert—the policy had ceased to be politically feasible.

The beersellers were now in a far weaker position. The magistrates were now more popular, and the radicals less enamoured of free licensing, than they had been in the 1820s; in 1869 therefore, Selwin-Ibbetson, a Tory private member, persuaded an unresisting parliament for the coming year to entrust the magistrates with licensing all new beerhouses and refreshment-houses. Henceforward the excise was to grant or renew the beerhouse on-licence only on production of a certificate from the justices assembled at the annual licensing meeting. The measure was renewed annually till embodied in Bruce's 1872 Licensing Act; it constitutes an important stage in the Webbs' process of 'legislative repentance' for the sins of 1830. In 1880 and 1882 the magistrates were given full control over beerhouse off-licences, and in 1880 Gladstone himself abrogated the other branch of Goulburn's policy of 1830 by reintroducing the beer duty. Here then was a striking retreat from free trade, at a time when in many other spheres it was being ever more widely applied. The Alliance only assisted at these important changes: it never felt happy working with the publicans, and although it always welcomed a reduction in the number of drinking places and an extension of restrictions on them—its platform was prohibition and nothing less.

During the 1860s Alliance influence at Westminster grew. In 1860 it appointed J. H. Raper as its first full-time parliamentary agent. A Liberal partisan, peace advocate and former Wesleyan Sunday school teacher, Raper had fainted in 1857 at the news of Bright's election defeat at Manchester. His appointment according to the *Alliance News* two years later was 'the best thing the Alliance ever did'.[11] Raper was well informed on the drink question and shrewd in anticipating the actions of politicians in particular situations. M.P.s during drink debates hurried into the lobbies to be primed by him. The agent had to coach M.P.s on his question, because they seldom concerned themselves with it until immediately before the subject came up in parliament. The agent reminded supporters when they should attend and scrutinized legislation as it passed through parliament. For some years the Alliance had been searching for an M.P. to act as its parliamentary spokesman: Sir Walter Trevelyan did not wish to enter parliament, and Samuel Pope could not get himself elected. The man who eventually undertook the task was at first a stop-gap, though he lived to defend the Alliance case in parliament for over forty years. He was Wilfrid Lawson, M.P. for Carlisle, and 'a Cobdenite of the Cobdenites'.[12]

Lawson was a most unusual combination of humanitarian and humorist. A really courageous opponent of war and imperialism and one of the few who dared to brand the Boer War as 'cowardly and infamous', he takes his place in the long line of independent squires who specialized in exposing the extravagance and immorality of those in authority. He was a late-Victorian Sibthorp, who never allowed party considerations to affect his conscience; in 1871, though he must have known that his political career would suffer thereby, he publicly declared in the debate on the civil list that 'the country did not get its money's worth for what it had given',[13] and voted in an absurdly small minority. The art of government, for Lawson, did not lie in adapting laws to human weaknesses, but in setting standards by which men should shape their conduct. Like the pioneer temperance politician J. S. Buckingham, he never lost his youthful incredulity that politicians should reject his rational suggestions for domestic reform. The careers of several temperance politicians recall to mind Pascal's maxim that 'if a man decided to follow reason, he would be reckoned a fool by the greater part of the world'.

Yet it was Lawson's exaggerated rationality which prevented him from becoming a rather sour and disillusioned preacher. For when his rationality brushed against the reality of politics, it inspired humour at the incongruity of it all: when Bernal Osborne left the House of Commons, Lawson became its chief jester. Somehow he managed to point up the contrast between belief and conduct without any note of bitterness, and therefore became a constant delight to an assembly far more worldly-wise than he. The one burst of laughter observed from Disraeli throughout his political career was evoked by one of Lawson's jokes, and it was he who later spoke of Lawson's 'spirit of gay wisdom'.[14] The purity of Lawson's ideals and the innocence with which he approached political situations frequently directed him to the contrast between the politician's profession and his practice, and made him more sensitive than his colleagues to the ironies of political life. His speeches, like Cobden's letters, frequently gasped at the contrast between Christian belief and Christian practice. With £10,000 a year from his Cumberland estates, he could well afford his good table, his hunting, his billiards and his career devoted to the pursuit of consistency at the expense of office. Popularity inevitably came to a man with so conciliatory a manner; no one can read his memoirs without capturing his zest for politics, which for him were filled with 'great fights', 'tremendous rows' and 'wonderfully exciting times'.

The rational man who laughed at the incongruities of politics could, however, take another course: he could insulate himself from reality by assuming that when the electorate failed to vote as he wished, a reform bill would put things right. If the reformed electorate of 1832 failed to give adequate support to Little Englandism and local option, then try the working men: if they disappointed, try the agricultural labourers: if they failed, then enfranchise the women! Lawson also protected his ideals by assuming that an ill-intentioned and covert interest-group was distorting man's natural rationality. He was much loved by children, perhaps because he never really lost his own childlike attitude to the world. Considering that the writer had sat almost continuously at Westminster for forty years, the banality of the political explanation in his memoirs is remarkable. How was it possible for the people to allow futile wars to divert them from the domestic reforms so desperately needed? Whereas J. A. Hobson blamed a conspiracy of capitalists, Lawson found a part-explanation in drink, which provided the necessary tax revenue, propped up the Conservative and imperialist party and drugged the people. Lawson did not allow the extension of public-house opening-hours during the Golden Jubilee to pass unnoticed: for him, the two English Gods 'the God of Battles and the God of Bottles' were allies. He suffered from the outsider's obsession with mythical political plots; '*who is it* that really gets up these schemes of Burglary and Murder?' he exploded to Bright on imperialist ventures during 1878. For him, as for Cobden, war scares were 'got up' by interested journalists 'sitting in a snug Editor's room and writing leading articles hounding on your countrymen to the slaughter'.[15]

Though he resembled Cobden in many respects, Lawson unfortunately lacked Cobden's political shrewdness. His wit caused amused Westminster audiences to doubt the seriousness of his intent, and his involvement in many reforming causes prevented him from becoming what Cobden had become by 1845—'the incarnation of a principle'.[16] Indeed, had Cobden written an autobiography, free trade would have been far more prominent there than temperance was in Lawson's memoir; for Lawson's narrative ignores many crucial moments in his temperance career, and sheds no light on his relations with the Alliance. The rigidity of Lawson's faith in local option obstructed the compromises essential for real achievement and discouraged the empirical researches necessary for temperance progress: the contrast with William

Tebb's management of the anti-vaccination movement after 1880, or with Stansfeld's management of the case against the Contagious Diseases Acts, is striking. Lawson's party leaders came to regard him as 'crotchety';[17] this did not worry him unduly, for he sought the good opinion, not of contemporary party leaders, but of God and posterity. From his lonely pill-box he sniped at every government of whose conduct he disapproved, and in his copious journal recorded the precise reasons for every parliamentary vote he gave. He was, in short, a protesting politician, anxious to keep his hands clean from the corruptions and responsibilities of power, and happier when his party was in opposition rather than in office. Like Cobden his master, he would have grown with experience of office if he could only have been induced to stay there for six months without resigning. Lawson took upon himself the task which G. P. Gooch attributes to W. L. Courtney: 'to challenge prejudice, to test tradition, to ventilate ideas, and above all to hold aloft the moral ideal in moments of national passion and national temptation'.[18] One's appraisal of Lawson must ultimately depend on the importance one attaches to this task.

Such was the man who introduced the Permissive Bill into parliament for the first time in 1864. Lawson was supported by 2,549 petitions bearing 482,413 signatures, but during the debate Bright said he favoured municipal control of licensing, and Roebuck, who depended on the Sheffield drink interest for electoral support, vigorously attacked the Bill.[19] Lord Robert Cecil was very hostile in the *Saturday Review* for 11 June, and Sir George Grey the home secretary remained unconvinced: the Bill was defeated by 292 votes to 35. Liberals were overwhelmingly dominant among the supporters, and constituted over half the opponents. Three-quarters of the majority came from English seats, whereas M.P.s from outside England constituted over half the minority.

Prohibitionist weakness in the English country areas was never paralleled in the countryside outside England—that is, in the 'Celtic Fringe'. Indeed the geographical pattern of late-Victorian Liberalism is foreshadowed in the regional patterns of several early Victorian radical reforming movements. John Vincent has recently spoken of the 'enormous expanding social frontier' enjoyed by the Gladstonian Liberal party throughout its life. The expansion of this frontier can be clearly seen in the subscription-lists of the United Kingdom Alliance. In its earliest years, the Alliance made rapid progress in Wales; no fewer than 42 of its 64 auxiliaries in 1856–7 were situated there. A strong identification existed between temperance and Welsh nationalist aspirations, and the passage of the Welsh Sunday Closing Act in 1881 was an important moment in the growth of Welsh national consciousness. Whereas English prohibitionism was stagnating by the late 1870s, the Alliance continued to expand in Wales until the late 1880s. The extension of the franchise to rural labourers in 1885 was accompanied by a marked leap in the number of Welsh subscribers, and Welsh donations when expressed as a percentage of British donations rose from the 1–2% level which they had occupied since the 1850s, to a new plateau of 4–5%.[20]

The Alliance case was now being more frequently heard on the hustings. At the 1865 election, Lawson at Carlisle was probably not helped by his prohibitionist activities, but the campaign was dominated by purely local concerns, especially by the traditional antagonism between the Lonsdales and their enemies. Though Lawson enjoyed Bright's written support, and increased his vote by seventy in comparison with 1859, he was defeated. Pope failed to get in at Bolton; and at the 1866 by-election, Handel Cossham, the Congregationalist colliery-proprietor from Bristol, failed to get in at Nottingham; Louisa Stanley's 'out and out vulgar Radical of low birth and a Dissenter'[21] could expect little from the unreformed electorate. These events convinced the Alliance that only franchise extension could improve the situation. For prohibitionists did not share Robert Lowe's belief that 'drunkenness, and facility for being intimidated' increased with every descent in the social scale: when the *Weekly Dispatch* tried to identify the Alliance with Lowe's unpopular views, the *Alliance News* insisted that 'in proportion to their number, the unworking classes are, at least, as guilty in this matter as the working'.[22]

The Reform Leaguers came from precisely the class which supported the Alliance. Several prominent prohibitionists attended the 1858 reform conference; George Howell himself had publicly defended the Permissive Bill in his Bristol days; and temperance reformers abound among the Reform League's vice-presidents and provincial connexions. Howell used temperance societies as one way of contacting the right type of working man; Reform League circulars encouraged London temperance reformers to attend Reform demonstrations and to bring along the flags and banners with which they had graced the Garibaldi meetings;[23] 3,000 temperance reformers participated in the League's procession of 11 February 1867. Howell was in close contact with both the Lawsons, and of the £621 raised at the start of the League's agitation £95 came from three leading Alliance men—Sir Wilfrid Lawson, Sen., Samuel Pope and William Hargreaves. Howell described Lawson as one of the 'few, *very few*, wealthy friends to whom we can appeal'; he produced a further £250 in November 1866. 'Had it not been for you, Sir Wilfrid and Mr. Morley,' Howell told him on 5 June 1867, 'and some ten others, our League could not have accomplished so great a work.'[24] Not all temperance reformers supported the Reform League: the National Temperance League opposed all such political connexions. But the identification was close enough for opponents of franchise extension like Robert Lowe to quote the Permissive Bill as one of the absurd measures which would gain ground if reform took place. 'It is clear', said the Alliance before the 1868 election, 'that the publican power is doomed.'[25]

Rash prophecy! For the 1868 election revealed how franchise extension was only one of the four changes necessary before authority could be dislodged. Morley's defeat at the Bristol by-election in May 1868 revealed that it was still necessary for temperance reformers to find ways of influencing the selection of candidates. Though a genuine temperance reformer, Morley was not sectarian enough in outlook to support either the Alliance or the Liberation Society. Admitting his good qualities but deploring his lukewarm temperance views, the Alliance used its influence against him; by helping to ensure his defeat, it reaped unpopularity with local Liberals and did nothing to improve the situation at Westminster. Temperance reformers also still needed to purge British elections of their drink bribes. In 1868 the Alliance asked supporters to report on the electoral conduct of the local drink interest; the reports of the election commission, it claimed, must evoke 'alarm and disgust'.[26] Thirdly, the election campaign stressed the importance of influencing the politicians who set the issues before the electorate; for despite T. H. Barker's reminder that the Irish Church 'does not kill off some tens of thousands of people every year, nor fill the workhouses, the lunatic asylums, and the gaols',[27] Gladstone brought disestablishment to the centre of the political stage. The Alliance therefore did not feel justified in establishing a central candidates' fund, though it encouraged local deputations and was willing to provide propaganda and lecturers.[28] The 1868 election occupied far more space than previous elections in the *Alliance News*, and detailed constituency reports were being printed some months before polling began.

The crucial constituencies were Bristol, Northampton, Bolton and Carlisle. At Bristol, F. W. Newman complained that the Liberal committee's control over the selection of candidates ensured that the new electors 'were accounted as nothing, and the contest went on precisely as if there had been no addition to the constituency'.[29] On this occasion the prohibitionists did not oppose Morley who, after warding off rotten oranges with his umbrella on the hustings, found himself returned. At Northampton F. R. Lees was disastrous as unofficial prohibitionist candidate; he merely succeeded in splitting the Liberal vote, incurring the enmity of Bradlaugh and getting himself placed at the bottom of the poll. At Bolton Samuel Pope's candidature embarrassed many Liberals, not least those who were members of the Bolton Beer and Wine Sellers' Association. Its ill-tempered disputes were shrewdly published in full by the *Alliance News*; most of the members voted Tory, despite the eloquence of William Morgan who 'intended to support the principles of Reform, if he never sold another gill of ale'.[30] Two Tories were returned for Bolton, and Pope had merely succeeded in swelling the Tory gains in urban Lancashire. Lawson's Carlisle was the only constituency to return a leading Alliance supporter—and here local family influence, perhaps assisted by Roman Catholic support, was responsible. At no election in these years did the Alliance succeed unaided in securing a seat for one of its leading members.

Despite these disappointments, the prohibitionists were still gaining influence. Analysis of donations in 1873–4 shows that in every area except Essex and Rutland the number of donors had risen much faster than population since 1861–2. Progress was most marked in the midlands, the northern border counties, Monmouth and Ireland, but the relative position of the south-east had fallen still further. As a machine for influencing public opinion, the Alliance was now formidable. Its public meetings—usually held in town-halls, chapels, schoolrooms, temperance halls, mechanics' institutes or in the open air—culminated in the annual meeting. 2,539 meetings were held in 1873 throughout England and Wales; the 238 meetings held in February were attended by 60,455 people. If no person attended more than one meeting, this would mean that more than 620,000 people attended prohibitionist meetings during the year—from a total adult population of more than 12,000,000. Of course many temperance reformers attended several meetings, and the total number therefore affected was much smaller. Furthermore these meetings were mostly held in areas where the Alliance was already strong: 37% of the meetings identified were held in the five northernmost counties, which also contained 42% of the total number of donors for the financial year 1873–4. If the Alliance had really aimed to convert the whole country, it should have imitated the Anti-Corn Law League and sent lecturers into the heart of enemy territory: that is, into the rural areas of the south-east. This was done only sporadically—in Dorset and Kent, for instance. All organizations founded on voluntary support have to show results to their subscribers, and are therefore forced to hold many of their meetings where support is already strong. Yet Alliance funds were by now so large that it could have broken out of this dilemma and ceased to be what it always remained, a decidedly *provincial* movement.

Five major temperance organizations now existed in England: were they in fighting trim for their impending battle with the drink interest? A convenient way of discovering the answer is to study the honorary or active officials whom these organizations possessed in common: for when two organizations disagree, their common members have to take sides and resign from one organization or the other. The strength of the links between the Alliance, the British Temperance League and the Central Association for Stopping the Sale of Intoxicating Liquor on Sundays [C.A.S.S.I.L.S.] is immediately apparent. This is not surprising, because all three were Lancashire-based organizations; the British Temperance League had always been far more thoroughgoing than the London-based National Temperance League, and total Sunday closing in itself constituted a form of prohibition. Some of the major figures in the Alliance—Pope, Harvey, Whitworth, Jupe, Steinthal—were also vice-presidents of the British Temperance League, and 25 of the 79 British Temperance League officials are known to have supported prohibition. Likewise key figures in the Alliance were also prominent Sunday closers: Sir Wilfrid

Lawson was a vice-president of both organizations, and C.A.S.S.I.L.S.' general council included T. H. Barker, the Alliance secretary, and J. H. Raper, its parliamentary agent. Officially the Alliance believed that moral suasion must be supplemented by prohibition, and until the late 1870s suspected gradualist measures like Sunday closing; yet 12 of its 81 leading figures—in their individual capacity—supported the moral suasionist British Temperance League, 6 the moral suasionist National Temperance League and 11 the Sunday closing movement. The Alliance may have treasured the purity of the prohibitionist gospel, but its members were free to support more gradual

FIG. 12

Links between major temperance organizations: 1864–1867

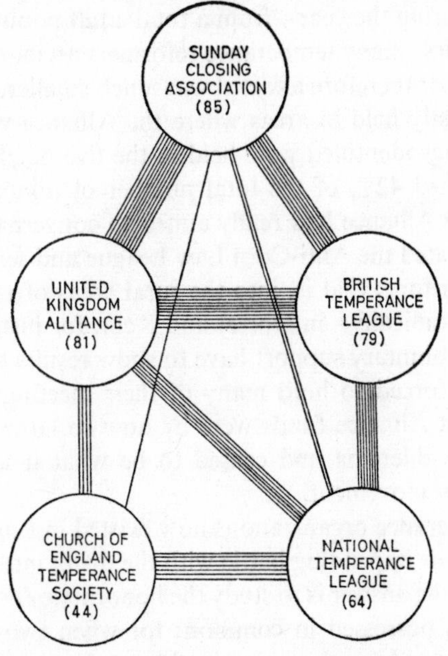

remedies by simultaneously supporting other temperance organizations; to some extent, then, criticisms of prohibitionist rigidity miss their mark.

Also noteworthy is the relative isolation of the Church of England Temperance Society. The Alliance and the British Temperance League were powered by militant provincial nonconformists, and one would hardly expect them to cultivate close links with a temperance organization whose 44 prominent officials included 31 clergymen and 6 members of the armed services. A few zealous evangelical clergymen managed to combine membership of both Alliance and C.E.T.S.—notably Dean Close and Rev. G. T. Fox—but C.E.T.S connexions were understandably closer with the National Temperance League; for the C.E.T.S. would hardly have been founded without National Temperance League help in the early 1860s. The type of dissenter active in the League —Smithies, Edward Baines, Charles Gilpin, Samuel Morley, Hugh Owen, William Tweedie—was far less hostile to the *status quo* than were the fiery zealots in the Lancashire-based temperance organizations; British Temperance League supporters like Drs. McKerrow and Lees could hardly have survived in the conciliatory and gradualist atmosphere of the London-based organization. Still, it would have been surprising if there had been *no* links between two Leagues whose ostensible purposes were identical, and they did in fact possess several common members. They were on cordial terms during the 1860s, and seem to have acted on a tacit regional division of labour. The National Temperance League minutes for 22 July 1859 report a letter from the Bacup temperance society 'declining the services of the League agents and suggesting they should be more confined to the South and East of England'; and when a ministerial temperance conference was proposed in June 1872, the League agreed to organize it if held in London, but left the matter to the British Temperance League if it were held in a northern town.

One further point: the analysis shows clearly that despite all the quarrels in the temperance world, there were many links between the major temperance organizations. Even the Alliance and the National Temperance League, which had quarrelled bitterly in the late 1850s, possessed six officials in common during 1865–6, though significantly their executive committees had no common members. Several busy individuals acted as connecting links: Joseph Thorp, president of the British Temperance League, should perhaps take the prize—for he was also a vice-president of the Alliance, the National Temperance League and C.A.S.S.I.L.S. Consolation prizes must go to Dean Close, a member of the Alliance, the National Temperance League and the C.E.T.S.; and to Lawrence Heyworth and Robert Charleton, who were both prominent in the Alliance as well as in the National and British Temperance Leagues. The United Temperance Council, formed in the early 1860s to coordinate temperance activities, had not eliminated the divisions between temperance organizations, and enjoyed very limited powers. But clearly there were in the 1860s potential sources of united temperance action, if the threat from without proved sufficiently serious.[31]

Franchise reform in 1867 made it much easier for parliament at last to face the licensing question squarely. The need for this had been recognized ever since the Villiers committee of 1853–4, and as far back as 1857 a Liberal government had promised to introduce a licensing measure. For some time a draft Licensing Bill had lain in the Home Office, and after 1867 many people outside the temperance movement realized that democracy must be made safe through educational and licensing reforms. As H. A. Bruce the new home secretary put it in the Permissive Bill debate of 12 May 1869, franchise extension had weakened the power of vested interests, and M.P.s could 'feel themselves at greater liberty to deal with such a question as the present according to their own inclinations, and with less fear of the influence of that portion of their constituents more immediately concerned than they have hitherto done'.

A reformed parliament, in 1868 as in 1833, would perhaps have the moral courage to pass measures unpopular with small but organized groups in the electorate and with the poorest sections of the community. In 1869 Thomas Hughes urged parliament to pass a Sunday Trading Bill because it 'now for the first time represented every class, and, therefore, had the whole country at its back'.[32] In 1868 Gladstone publicly announced that he was disposed 'to let in the principle of local option wherever it is likely to be found satisfactory', but told Manning privately in October that stringent legislation would end in sharp recoil, and that political considerations severely restricted his freedom of action. 'The effect of having to act for others', he characteristically wrote, 'in whatever degree, as to certain great matters, instead of enlarging tends to narrow my discretion in some other matters, about which they are much divided, and in which they would on the one side or the other much resent my taking a strong part against them. My duty therefore is to watch, and to strike in upon opportunity, which I have the more hope of doing in proportion as I can remain at present unpledged. I wish well to as much restraint in the liquor traffic as the public will bear without offensive distinction between classes.'[33]

Gladstone told a deputation in March 1869 that a licensing measure could be carried only 'by the ripeness of the public mind'.[34] The Alliance's role was to create that ripeness, and one way of doing so was the annual debate on the Permissive Bill. Before Lawson moved its second reading on 12 May 1869, 4,000 supporting petitions arrived, signed by nearly 800,000 people. The atmosphere was sympathetic; Bruce agreed that the number of drinking places should be related to the local population, but thought that a Permissive Bill would merely foster riots. Lawson resisted pressure to withdraw his Bill in view of the government's intention next session to bring in their own Licensing Bill, and attracted 87 supporters as against the 35 of 1864; opposition votes fell from 292 to 193. The regional pattern in the division was very similar to that of 1864; indeed, in none of the divisions before 1875 did county members from any of the home counties or East Anglia support the Bill. Liberals and Conservatives were almost equally represented among the Bill's opponents till 1873, but nonconformist radicals were prominent among its supporters. 'In the Tory party', said Lawson in 1880, 'the leaders educate the party, and in the Liberal party the party educate the leaders.'[35] It would be rash to assume that all the supporting votes reflected sincere enthusiasm for the Bill. Many were protests at the government's failure to introduce its own licensing measure; others were mere responses to a well organized constituency pressure group. Until the Commons, like Congress, instituted the ballot or evolved a formal procedure for preventing such issues from reaching the floor, many members would be forced to choose between committing political suicide or voting against their convictions. A secret ballot in parliament in the 1870s would have killed off the Permissive Bill just as it would have killed the eighteenth amendment in America half a century later.

A Licensing Bill was announced in the Queen's speech in February 1870, and there were many temperance protests when the government failed to introduce it later in the session. In Lawson's Permissive Bill division on 13 July, 90 supported him and only 121 opposed; but there was a high abstention rate, and many of the opponents were away watching the Prince of Wales opening the Thames Embankment. In October, Lawson noted how in Permissive Bill debates the sound of the division bell caused members to rush *out* of the House instead of rushing in; in a division where public feeling ran high both for and against, members wanted to save their consciences and their seats.[36] It was clearly becoming urgent for the government to act, and Bruce in September privately admitted to being 'absolutely pledged' to a licensing measure in the next session. 'No subject seems worthier the attention of a Government who w[oul]d earn the gratitude of a nation,'[37] wrote Bishop Fraser to Gladstone in November. Gladstone did not disagree; an attempt at legislation was to follow in a matter of months.

12

The Government Response: 1871–1872

For three reasons, the years 1871–2 mark a turning-point in temperance history. This was the first occasion on which politicians had to grapple directly with the popular pressure group whose influence had been mounting in the provinces since the 1830s. So far, this book has seen events largely through temperance eyes; we can now see how the movement appeared to the men who were moulding government policy. Secondly, these years saw an important shift in party attitudes to the drink question; in 1871–2 Gladstone's great administration was beginning to lose impetus, and enthusiasts for the alleged 'Conservative reaction' magnified the government's every mistake. Among those mistakes many critics included H. A. Bruce's administrative and political blunders on the licensing question. Many Liberals after 1872 went further, and blamed Bruce for their party's new and electorally burdensome identification with temperance restriction. Until 1872 both political parties opposed intemperance, both had recognized the need for temperance legislation; Knatchbull-Hugessen, for one, denied that the Liberal party need ever have offended the drink trade.[1] Finally, the licensing crisis of 1871–2 marks the culmination of the simple contest between regulationists and prohibitionists; it was the first occasion to reveal the full practical implications of the tactics prohibitionists had adopted since 1853. After 1872 public discussion on the temperance question was complicated by debates on municipalization and nationalization which continued well into the twentieth century.

Though he acquired a public reputation for ill-temper, Bruce was really a genial personality. A cultivated family man, freed from money worries by inheriting property in South Wales, he had been a successful local magistrate who had acquired a solid reputation as M.P. for Merthyr from 1852 to 1868. Unoriginal, somewhat indolent, unimpressive and perhaps unduly frank as an orator—he was unlikely to go far in politics. But as an expert on mining and educational questions, he seemed well qualified to succeed Sir George Grey in the difficult post of Home Secretary after Gladstone's great victory in 1868. Yet Bruce had become unpopular some time before introducing his ill-fated Licensing Bill of 1871; the press and the clubs disliked his leniency towards murderers and republicans, and he seemed incompetent in regulating London cabs, inactive in social reform. Some of these press attacks were unjust, and Bruce's task was made the more difficult because of an unfortunate and temporary lack of experienced senior civil servants at the Home Office. Furthermore the government machine had not yet adapted itself to the increase in public business: 'the confusion and duplication of work is really frightful,' wrote Robert Lowe, urging a reallocation of work between ministries in December 1870. Bruce was also burdened with Knatchbull-Hugessen as under-secretary of state; he had not wanted this jealous and ambitious man in the post, and felt that he had 'no personal weight' and very little information.[2]

Bruce's temperament and social background had kept him out of the temperance movement, and in 1868 he firmly resisted pressure from Permissive Bill zealots among his constituents. But he was an enthusiast for self-help, and earned Shaftesbury's repect for his social conscience. He rejected the Permissive Bill as unfair to the very poor, and had 'no faith in any remedy for intemperance but the improved intelligence and morality of the people'. But he was no doctrinaire opponent of state intervention, and in January 1871 found 'much that is alluring' in the schemes for municipal management;[3] he was anxious to reduce the number and improve the quality of public-houses. A draft licensing measure went through the cabinet in December 1869; Bruce's chief advisers were apparently Rutson, his secretary, and S. G. Rathbone, the Liverpool advocate of the Gothenburg scheme. Even at this stage Bruce found that the subject involved 'an enormous amount of detail, very puzzling to understand, and worse to carry in one's memory'. His task was complicated by the fact that influential Liberals disagreed on the licensing question. Gladstone still adhered to his free trade beliefs of 1860: 'unfortunately Gladstone cares for nothing but "Free Trade", which the House won't have', Bruce told his wife in December 1871: '. . . I cannot get him really to interest himself in the subject.'[4] Bright wanted licensing entrusted to the town councils; Fawcett, Lowe and others favoured free trade. Bruce himself does not seem to have been wholehearted in his enthusiasm for a licensing measure; while Home Secretary he tended to take up several projects simultaneously, and then drop them, instead of pressing fewer measures more firmly. In autumn 1870 he was contemplating a Corporation of London Bill (which came to nothing) because he felt that the Home Office 'ought to do something *great* in the coming session—beyond a Licensing Bill'.[5] He was soon to find even a Licensing Bill beyond his powers.

In the cabinet's January 1871 list of proposed legislation, the Licensing Bill occupied seventh place—second in Gladstone's category of 'second order' Bills. Bruce was still having difficulties with it as late as January 1871: he told parliament in April that the licensing question was 'a subject, the difficulties of which no one could rightly estimate who had not taken them into consideration'.[6] In cabinet discussions during the winter, the Bill was made harsher towards vested interests, and opening-hours were reduced. On 3 April 1871, Bruce introduced his Bill to a rather thin House whose galleries were crowded with representatives from the drink interest. His speech was tedious and ill-delivered, and his Bill was complicated; it occupies 90 foolscap printed pages.[7] Besides consolidating and simplifying existing law, it dealt with four major areas: responsibility for licensing, number of licences, opening-hours and police. The Bill confirmed the recent reaction against the free trade principles of 1830 and gave the magistrates responsibility for almost all drink retailing. It proposed four types of licence: 'publicans' general' (on and off) for all liquors, 'publicans' limited' (on and off) for all but spirits, 'innkeepers' ' (on) for houses accommodating travellers and providing meals, and 'eating-house' (on) for all drinks except spirits, but to be consumed only with meals. Where localities in the same licensing area had different needs, the licensing jurisdiction was to be divided into smaller units.

Bruce aroused most hostility with his proposals for reducing the number of licences. Premises would be required to meet a prescribed rating qualification which would increase with the density of the local population. The magistrates' power to refuse the renewal of a licence would be limited by outlining specified grounds for refusal. Still more controversial were Bruce's proposals for relating the number of licences to local needs and opinion. Bruce admitted that the Permissive Bill embodied the 'very valuable principle' of giving a say to the ratepayers.[8] He therefore proposed that at the general annual licensing meeting the justices should decide whether any fresh licences were required for their licensing districts, and if so how many. A three-fifths ratepayer majority would be empowered to reduce (but not increase) this figure—though only where the number of licences exceeded one per 1,000 inhabitants in towns, and one per 600 inhabitants in rural areas. Considering that throughout England and Wales in 1871 there was one on-licence per 201 persons, this provision could have produced a radical change.

Once the number of licences to be issued had been agreed upon, the first two categories of licence would be separately put up to tender in the form of an annual licence-rent, whose proceeds could be applied to the local rate. This would free the magistrates from suspicion of corruption, because they would no longer be making invidious comparisons between applicants. It would also gain some of the monopoly-value for the public—who paid for the police and had bestowed the monopoly in the first place. And by allowing free removals of licensees within the licensing district, Bruce's measure would prevent drink manufacturers from creating local monopolies. During the first ten years after the passage of the Bill, existing licensees, unlike their newly licensed competitors, would be confirmed in possession of their licence, would benefit from the monopoly situation and would be required to pay only a reduced licence-rent. This would compensate them for their eventual loss of monopoly, when they too had to tender for renewal at the end of the ten-year period. In his speech Bruce clearly asserted the claim of existing licensees to compensation if their licence was discontinued, though he admitted that parliament had never recognized a vested interest. Lawson might argue that licences had to be renewed annually, but 'the fact was that the justices nearly always renewed these licences unless the holders of them, by bad conduct, had rendered themselves unfit to hold a licence'.[9]

Thirdly, Bruce proposed a sharp reduction in opening-hours; weekday off-licence hours would be curtailed at both ends of the day, and standardized throughout the country; beerhouse and public-house on-licence hours would be assimilated and further curtailed; Sunday opening-hours would also be modestly reduced. Bruce admitted the principle of local control when he proposed to enable a three-fifths ratepayer majority to empower the magistrates to curtail weekday evening closing-hours to 9 p.m. and to close drinking places entirely on Sundays. Finally, there were Bruce's policing measures. Licences were henceforth to be taken out in the name of the owner rather than of the resident manager, and offences were to be automatically endorsed on the licence; the owner would therefore have a strong incentive to ensure good management. This was designed to produce what Bruce in April described as 'a system which should be self-acting', and which would minimize the disadvantages of restoring control to the magistrates. Bruce proposed to tighten up penalties for breach of closing regulations, for allowing bad characters to assemble, and for allowing adulteration and drunkenness on the premises. The penalty for drunkenness in the streets and in drinking places was raised to £1, with the alternative of imprisonment. Bruce insisted on the need for proper inspection of drinking places: 'an efficient inspection could . . . be conducted only by a body of men superior to the ordinary police, and not charged with ordinary police duties.' He calculated that the annual licence-rent paid by existing licence-holders would bring in £130,000 annually, which would finance an efficient body of public-house inspectors. He envisaged a substantial force of inspectors: there would be one inspector-in-chief, and one inspector would be assigned to each of the districts into which England and Wales were divided. Every large town and district would have 'a carefully-selected and well-paid body of men' under a superintendent. Bruce believed that the inspection and closing-hour provisions would cause 'a considerable decrease in the number of public-houses'.[10]

In the debate which followed, Lawson said he would still champion the Permissive Bill, but the Tory Selwin Ibbetson said Bruce's Bill contained 'many points which had his hearty and cordial support'.[11] On the whole, M.P.s' immediate response was not hostile, but this was the calm before the storm. The drink trade reacted far more rapidly than the temperance movement; its reactions were all hostile, though in varying degrees. 'Has anyone forgotten the storm of popular indignation which raged through the country like a hurricane . . . ?' asked the *Licensed Victuallers Guardian* on 6 January

1872: 'its like was never known before!' By 27 April 1871, the publicans' *Morning Advertiser* was vigorously denouncing the Bill as centralizing and despotic. Denunciations of Bruce's 'French spy system' were made,[12] but the main attack in the Trade press was directed against the 'confiscatory' proposals.

There were some moderating voices. Mr. Candelet urged the Manchester publicans not to meet Bruce's Bill with a direct negative: they must try to make it workable. The Yorkshire Brewers Association favoured an inspection system, and the *Brewers Guardian* adopted a most reasonable standpoint throughout the year.[13] The *Brewers Journal* and the *Wine Trade Review* on 15 April also welcomed the proposal for inspectors. Nor was the drink interest united at this time. The *Brewers Journal* frequently sniped at the Country Brewers' Society, and the free trade brewers of Burton, Edinburgh and Dublin emphasized the divergence between their interests and those of the brewers who owned public-house property; they felt they might specially suffer by licence limitation.[14] But as the hostile campaign mounted, moderating and discordant voices were drowned in the clamour; a formidable machine was being created which, like the contemporary Church Defence Institution, was to nourish the impending 'Conservative reaction'. The Country Brewers Society gained many new members and amassed a special fighting-fund of £21,000—far more than the total Alliance receipts for the year. While only 45 petitions with 3,601 signatures were presented for Bruce's Bill, 1,160 petitions with 822,965 signatures were sent against it.[15] 'It is scarcely too much to say that the whole country, from end to end, is placarded with deceptive appeals against the Bill,' wrote the hostile *Record* on 22 May. Liberal speakers at public meetings threatened to put Trade interest before party, and several M.P.s complained that such pressures infringed the dignity of the House.[16]

The drink trade felt that its deputations had been treated with scant courtesy, that it had been insulted by Bruce's parliamentary speech of 3 April, and that it should have been consulted during the drafting of the Bill. The Licensed Victuallers' Protection Society had in fact offered its help before the Bill was introduced, and the brewers had also been preparing their own scheme for licensing reform.[17] The tone of the *Morning Advertiser* became childishly offensive towards the Liberal leaders. An editorial on 22 September spoke of 'the everlasting gush of Mr. GLADSTONE', and on 30 June referred to Bruce's 'utter want of all governing capacity'. Particularly damaging was the argument that Bruce was initiating a general attack on property. For Bruce was extremely unlucky in the timing of his Bill; the Commune erupted at the precise moment when the Bill was being discussed in the country. 'Any political riot small or great in [Paris] is an event of the first importance for all Europe,' declared the *Spectator* (4,000) on 12 February 1870.* When the Commune burst forth in

* Circulation figures (1870) from Alvar Ellegård, 'The Readership of the Periodical Press in Mid-Victorian Britain', *Göteborgs Universitets Arsskrift* LIII (1957).

spring 1871, many English papers became almost hysterical in their attacks on it, and many parallels were drawn with the Terror. According to the *Pall Mall Gazette* (8,000) these events demonstrated 'the fragility of the basis on which the complex fabric of modern society rests'. The Queen was indignant in her journal at the 'most dreadful news from Paris' on 27 May, and at the activities of 'these horrid Communists'. John Bright, recuperating from his illness in the country, imagined his way into the minds of his cabinet colleagues in London: 'I fancy you always thinking of France and of Paris,' he wrote to Granville on 29 May.[18] Lord Salisbury in the *Quarterly Review* challenged the Liberal faith in progress and prophesied a clash between property and democracy. Contemporaries knew that London also had its republicans; in the match girls' procession in April, many observers doubtless detected *petroleuses*; and red sashes and caps of liberty were seen in mid-April among Hyde Park demonstrators. Property's shift towards Conservatism, already in progress for more long-term reasons, was accelerated by Bruce's Bill.[19]

In this situation Disraeli's speech at Manchester in April 1872—which firmly upheld Queen, Lords and Constitution as against Liberal 'cosmopolitanism'—was bound to pay political dividends; the drink interest had everything to gain from championing property against 'Bruce the Communist' as the *Licensed Victuallers Guardian* called him on 22 April 1871. His Bill was seen as one of several Liberal attacks on property; the publicans backed a Public Rights Defence Association, formed during winter 1871 'to maintain and defend the collective or individual social rights and liberties of the public, irrespective of party, whenever those rights and liberties may be unjustly attacked'. In the 1880s the drink interest was a power behind the Liberty and Property Defence League, which included the 1872 Licensing Act in its blacklist of socialistic measures.[20] Bruce's opponents were thus able to attract wealth and property; they could also attract numbers. For no cry was more popular than the complaint that the government was setting up a Frenchified spy-system. The aged J. R. Stephens could be relied upon to rouse working men with such accusations. In a 1½ hour speech to Stalybridge working men, reported in the *Licensed Victuallers Guardian*, Stephens stirred his audience with thrilling forecasts of a government spy system directed from London which would undermine the liberties of provincial communities. Bruce's spies were 'ready to pounce upon any man or any society that the government of the day chooses to think is in opposition to it'; similar sentiments were expressed by mass meetings at Sheffield. Working men were in fact divided on the issue. In London, Hartwell opposed the measure whereas Applegarth supported it.[21] In May a Liverpool Permissive Bill petition was signed by 10,170 mechanics and 7,023 labourers, yet in November 1872 the town was threatened by riots against the relatively mild Licensing Act of that year.[22] At Manchester there were meetings and counter-meetings, and whereas the *Bee-Hive* prudently kept silent on the measure, *Reynolds' Newspaper* (200,000) denounced it as class legislation. The popular weeklies were mixed in their immediate reactions but gradually climbed on to the hostile bandwagon. Their hostility was inspired by the traditional fear of monopoly, and by distaste for the wealth of the brewers; they did not normally raise the objection that Bruce's Bill was a feeble substitute for the social legislation which the government should be passing.

The Times (63,000) admitted correspondence from all viewpoints, and insisted on the need for some restraint on the Trade; indeed it felt that Bruce had been too lenient on existing licensees. Among the national papers, there was no clear political alignment on the issue. The Liberal *Daily News* (90,000) was quite favourable, the Liberal *Daily Telegraph* (190,000) hostile. The *Morning Post* (3,500), the *Standard* (140,000) and *John Bull* (3,000) were Tory papers whose initial reaction was not markedly hostile, but whose criticisms became more forthright when it became clear which way the wind was blowing. By 30 December the *Standard* felt it safe enough to describe Bruce's Bill as 'the most perfect *fiasco* of the year'. Several leading Liberal provincial papers showed more sympathy to Bruce than the metropolitan papers, and at Preston Thomas Walmsley, an old teetotaler, complained that 'government were a little too afraid of a London mob, who could in no way be said to represent public opinion'. In the religious press there was no clear-cut division between Anglican and nonconformist; the high church *Guardian* (6,000) and the evangelical *Record* (3,000) were both sympathetic to Bruce, as were the leading dissenting organs. Some dissenting papers, notably the *Methodist Recorder* (25,000), felt that Bruce had not gone far enough. Of the Catholic papers, the *Universe* and *Tablet* refrained from comment, but the *Weekly Register* and *Catholic Opinion* were both enthusiastic for the government measure. Manning at this time was whipping up Catholic temperance sentiment; he held several public meetings, and in July prompted a petition from 170 of the clergy in the Westminster archdiocese in favour of licensing restriction. The *Morning Advertiser* even accused the humbler London Catholics of being employed at Alliance meetings to throw out opponents. Certainly Manning evoked loud cheers from the audience of St. James's Hall when he arrived on the platform in May.[23]

Bruce needed a really enthusiastic temperance press if he was to overcome the drink trade. Manning pronounced his Bill 'the first honest and earnest grappling with this question', but few prohibitionists were so willing to accept instalments towards their utopia.[24] Instead, they accused Bruce of compromising; few followed the wise advice of the chairman of the National Temperance League's executive committee, who urged that 'teetotalers should . . . not strive so much for what they wished as for what there was just now a fair and reasonable chance of obtaining'.[25] Edward Baines and Samuel Morley might be prepared to accept the government's proposals, but few prohibitionists had their sense of proportion. James Haughton, for example, found the Bill 'a sham, and not even meant to strike a serious blow at the liquor traffic'—as though a Home Secretary could afford to do such a thing.[26] The Alliance praised some aspects of the Bill, but at a conference on 6 April 1871 helped to ensure its failure by expressing 'disappointment and profound regret' that Bruce 'has not dealt with this momentous question in a more sagacious and statesmanlike manner', and by declaring that his ten-year compensation proposal 'merits the prompt reprobation of the country'.[27]

Although the prohibitionists said they would not oppose the Bill's second reading, their obsession with their Permissive Bill ensured that Bruce had no really enthusiastic body of opinion behind him, for the moderate licensing reform organizations which sprang up at this time [see Figure 8] possessed neither power nor wealth. Bruce on 16 May showed justifiable irritation to an Alliance deputation at the 'lukewarm support' they had given his Bill, and in parliament on the same day he blamed the Alliance for diverting public feeling 'from plans which were efficacious to those which were delusive'.[28] He is alleged to have told Peter Rylands that he 'expected to be opposed by the brewers and the publicans; but it is not they who have defeated me, but the United Kingdom Alliance'. Several of Bruce's contemporaries agreed that he had been badly treated by the temperance movement.[29] Yet even if it had been prepared to support Bruce, the temperance movement was far too riddled with internal divisions and squabbles to give him the necessary impetus. Temperance reformers were either too extreme or too lukewarm in their attitudes to legislation. While the Alliance went further than Bruce in one direction, Livesey did not go as far. Licensing reform could never get to the root of the evil, he said in March 1871: liquor was responsible for drunkenness and 'not merely the external arrangements for its consumption'.[30] One might have expected the minute-books of the moral suasionist British and National Temperance Leagues to hum with activity in support of Bruce, yet this was not in fact the case. The government eventually decided to bring in a more modest licensing measure in the next session, and Bruce's 1871 Bill was never even given a second reading debate.

Throughout the 1871–2 licensing crisis there was no clear party polarization on the temperance issue; but in the months between the introduction of Bruce's first and second measures, there were signs of this impending development. Take first the parliamentary division on the Permissive Bill in 1871. Instead of mobilizing support for Bruce's Bill, the Alliance directed all its efforts towards the annual Permissive Bill debate in May. Influential in the debate was Justin McCarthy's article in the Liberal and rationalist *Fortnightly Review* (2,500), which argued that prohibition 'where it is least needed it is practicable; where it is much needed [i.e. in the towns] it is impracticable'. Bruce even accused Lawson of being 'the greatest obstructive in dealing with this question',[31] and tried to prevent M.P.s from abstaining, so as to reveal the Permissive Bill's real unpopularity at Westminster. The regional pattern of voting in the division was unchanged, but for the first time there were fewer Liberals than Conservatives among the Bill's opponents. This trend went further in later years, so that by 1875 party polarization was not far away.

TABLE 5

Party Votes on Permissive Bill Divisions: 1864–1875

DIVISION		SUPPORT					OPPOSITION			
		LIBERAL	CONS	LIB/CONS	HOME RULE	INDEPT	LIBERAL	CONS	LIB/CONS	HOME RULE
Leave	10 Mar 64	55	12	1	—	—	15	16	5	—
2R	8 June 64	33	1	1	—	—	151	111	30	—
2R	12 May 69	70	12	5	—	—	93	81	19	—
2R	13 July 70	74	13	3	—	—	56	54	11	—
2R	17 May 71	99	18	7	—	—	94	97	15	—
2R	7 May 73	69	10	2	—	—	137	155	28	1
2R	17 June 74	56	17	2	—	—	78	195	26	2
2R	16 June 75	71	11	2	1	1	94	255	22	—

Party allegiance from Dod's *Parliamentary Companion*.

There were other signs of party polarization on the issue during these months. Two young radical prohibitionists—Lawson and G. O. Trevelyan—went on a country-wide lecture-tour during the recess, in which Trevelyan declared that the Liberal party 'must ere long become a temperance party', and that 'the key-note of all Liberalism' was 'the paramount and unlimited authority of popular control'. Though Liberals had dominated the Alliance since its foundation, nobody had hitherto tried so publicly to link its cause with the Liberal party. An embarrassed Alliance vigorously protested its political neutrality when the prohibitionist but Tory Bishop of Gloucester (Disraeli's candidate for the see of Canterbury in 1868) objected to these developments.[32] From the Tory side too there were signs of change. Not only were there merciless Tory attacks on Bruce for his incompetence; there were signs that the drink issue was encouraging the London suburbs into the Tory embrace. At East Surrey, which had not sent a Conservative to parliament for thirty years, the Conservative brewer Watney was returned at a by-election held on the death of the Liberal brewer Charles Buxton. Watney was supported by the formerly Liberal *Morning Advertiser*, and Glyn told Gladstone that among the issues influencing the result ' "Beer" was *the* thing'. In his speech at Whitby in September, Gladstone foreshadowed the alignment of the Liberal party behind the provincial 'masses' as against the metropolitan 'classes'. London newspapers, he said, reflected 'the opinion of the clubs, rather than the opinion of this great nation'.[33]

More serious for the Liberals' long-term future were the signs of a Tory alternative to their social policy. During these months the Liberal gospel of self-help and philanthropy, temperance and education, was attacked by Ruskin: he strongly condemned philanthropists who specialized, not in improving the environment, but in reclaiming its victims once they had been corrupted by it. Whereas Bruce saw the government's Licensing Bill as 'a necessary supplement to the Education Bill', several Conservatives showed an implicit sympathy with Ruskin's viewpoint.[34] In a much-reported speech at Liverpool, Lord Derby stressed that before temperance reformers could hope to reform lower class habits 'they must begin by reforming their dwellings'; in January 1872 he supplemented this with a firm attack on puritanism. J. R. Stephens at a beersellers' dinner in March blamed popular sufferings on the factory system, and not on drunkenness.[35] And when several Tory aristocrats dallied in the autumn with Scott Russell's 'new social movement'—advocating shorter working hours, housing reform, provision of recreational facilities and several other social improvements—all the signposts pointed towards 'Tory Democracy'. Until the coming of Dutch William, said the *Church Times* on 20 October, the people had enjoyed fresh air, good beer and innocent recreation. Let England return to the old catholic ways and forsake the puritanism and political selfishness which had caused such suffering to the people. The time was ripe for Disraeli to make a memorable speech, and he responded. At Manchester in April 1872 he spoke up for popular recreations, briefly referred to the Liberal government's attack on the publicans, and emphasized that the people must be enabled to enjoy pure air, pure water, better homes and pure food, for 'the first consideration of a Minister should be the health of the people'.[36]

Yet if only out of self-respect, the Liberals had to persist with their modified temperance legislation. Bruce now had the additional handicap of his past failures, and his letters to his wife reveal clearly his unhappiness in office. He seems to have performed even his limited task badly, for some publicans felt strongly after their deputation of 9 April 1872 'that insult had been added to injury'; and when Kimberley took responsibility for the Bill in April, he found it an ill-prepared 'confused mass of absurdity'.[37] The Bill was introduced into the House of Lords on 16 April. It dealt with three main questions: responsibility for licensing, opening hours and policing measures. It retained the 1871 Bill's provision that magistrates should be the sole licensing authority, and its objective of preventing local monopolies; but it abandoned any attempt to relate the number of licences to local population through licence auctions and ratepayer control, though it did propose to secure uniformity by enabling the home secretary to veto the grant of new licences. Kimberley denied that licensees had any proprietary claim on their licences, but admitted that the publican 'has such a customary enjoyment of the licence that it should not be taken from him without fair and just reason being shown'.[38]

On opening-hours, the 1872 Bill originally proposed that all drinking places should not open till 7 a.m., and that they should close at midnight if within four miles of Charing Cross; at 11 p.m., if elsewhere in the metropolitan police district and in towns with 10,000 inhabitants or more; and at 10 p.m. elsewhere. On Sundays and other holidays, public-houses would open at 6 p.m., and in the evening would close one hour earlier than on weekdays. Thirdly, the policing proposals. A progressive penalty system culminating in automatic forfeiture of the licence was instituted for licensing offences; the fine for public drunkenness was raised from 5/– to 10/–; children under sixteen were excluded from public-house premises; and there were provisions for checking adulteration. A special system of police inspectors was proposed, with not less than one inspector per 100,000 inhabitants; but in contrast to the 1871 Bill, they were not to be appointed by the Home Office, but by the bodies which already appointed the rest of the police.

There was far less public comment than in the previous year. Most papers were mildly favourable, but even the nonconformist papers gave it little attention. Only the Wesleyan *Watchman* (1,000) on 7 August sounded a crusading note: 'the question now is, Who is to be master—the publican or the nation?' The Trade press detected in some of the police proposals a government suspicion that theirs was not a respectable and legitimate trade. Many regretted that the government had once again ignored the Trade's own reform proposals, as embodied in Sir Henry Selwin Ibbetson's licensing measure. Schemes for compensating dispossessed publicans from a rent levied on remaining licensees were particularly popular with the Trade. The drink interest was still somewhat fragmented: antagonism between London and provincial publicans, and between publicans and wine merchants opened out during the year.[39] There were also disputes between those who wanted to mould the government Bill through co-operation and those who wanted to mount a campaign for its rejection. During 1872 the *Morning Advertiser*, formerly a Liberal paper, adopted a hectoring tone towards the government and began to favour a Whig/Tory coalition; during the summer, it indicated its shifting allegiance by repeatedly trying to define its own peculiar brand of Liberalism. Its editor, Col. Richards, claimed in July that his paper would always remain Liberal 'in the sense which every honest Englishman gave to it': this meant that it would support the Constitutional party against Gladstone's government. The paper saw itself as consistent in its opinions: it was the Liberal party which had changed. There was some justice in this view, for in the past the Liberals had not been closely identified with restrictive temperance legislation. Yet in a rapidly changing society, political parties are often forced to seek new roads to old destinations.

The paper was by no means enthusiastic for Conservatism at this stage, and was not bowled over by Disraeli's two major speeches of the year.[40] But its tone towards the government was sarcastic, carping, unconstructive and somewhat vulgar. Its attacks on 'this un-English Minister', 'this "Liberal" curfew-monger' on 18 September were downright offensive. This change in the paper's mood pleased many publicans, but not the *Licensed Victuallers' Guardian*, which advocated co-operation with the government and condemned the *Advertiser*'s insulting style.[41] Towards the end of the year, however, the *Guardian* found itself threatened by the *Licensed Victuallers' Gazette*—a new paper of its own size and character, but with the *Advertiser*'s opinions. The *Guardian* soon came under new and more militant management, and joined the shrill chorus; on 23 November it described Bruce's new Act as 'at once revolutionary and despotic. It combines socialism with absolutism and the worst form of domestic tyranny.'

Once again the temperance movement gave the government little help, for it remained politically paralysed by its strange combination of non-political quietism and impractical political extremism. Joseph Livesey and the National Temperance League remained sceptical of all legislation, and there is no mention of the 1872 Bill in the League's minute-books; by contrast, the militants in the *Temperance Star* and *British Temperance Advocate* found the new measure mere 'tinkering of the most imbecile kind', and 'a wretched abortion'.[42] The prohibitionists had learned nothing from the events of the previous year. In a speech at Exeter Hall in April, Lawson admitted that the Bill would do some good despite its timidity; but like all Alliance leaders, he did not allow government offers of compromise to deter him from the course dictated by consistency and conscience.[43] In three editorials between 18 and 20 April *The Times*, while welcoming the stimulus which the Alliance had given to temperance opinion, deplored its rigid attitudes during the present crisis. On 19 April it stressed that it was 'a far greater triumph to reform, to improve, and to keep going in good order, than to abolish altogether'. To no avail: the eyes of the Alliance could not be deflected from the forthcoming Permissive Bill division. Lacking resolute support from any section of public opinion, Kimberley and Bruce had somehow to carry their Bill through parliament.

The Duke of Richmond led the opposition campaign to amend the Bill in the House of Lords; he did not oppose its second reading, which passed without a division. Before it had proceeded further, the Permissive Bill had to be given its annual airing in the Commons. There is no sign in the press that the Alliance had made much progress with public opinion. 1,332,287 individuals signed the petitions in its favour; Manchester (102,407), London (77,685) and Liverpool (73,119) headed the list, and as before most signatories came from industrial towns in the north of England or from areas outside England altogether. Though Lawson sought support from both parties, the Permissive Bill was badly damaged by Plimsoll's revelations about the failure of prohibition in America. The Alliance was deprived of its annual division by a supporter's mistaken adjournment at the end of the debate.[44] Meanwhile Kimberley was ably conducting the Bill through the House of Lords, making a few concessions but also resisting many demands for weakening it. There was much cross-voting: the Bill's critics included several Whig peers who were not too fond of the government—notably the Dukes of Cleveland and Somerset. Conversely, Kimberley could rely on the bishops. While the debate therefore revealed an incipient Tory alignment behind the drink interest, it also highlighted the existence within their party of a group which would always prevent that alignment from being complete.

In these years there were faint signs of the new directions the drink question was to take; on 4 March 1870 the Commons rejected Mr. Dalrymple's motion to create reformatories for forcibly confining habitual drunkards. Dalrymple's notion that habitual drunkenness is 'a disease, which . . . got possession of the nervous centres' became more popular in later years.[45] Likewise Lord Grey's proposal—rejected in the Lords' debate on 7 June 1872—for empowering local authorities to institute a local Gothenburg scheme. During its stay in the Lords, Bruce's Bill had become kinder to the publicans, who were now better protected against unfair prosecution; the magistrates were given some discretion about whether to remove a licence after a specified number of offences, fewer offences were to count towards such disqualification, opening-hours on weekdays and Sundays were extended, the proposal for public-house inspectors was rejected, and the home secretary's veto over new licences was abolished.

The rushed, and at times confused, atmosphere in which the Commons debated the Bill during the hot months of July and August support J. S. Mill's belief that legislative details are best entrusted to a Commission of Legislation rather than to a representative assembly. Bruce moved the second reading on 11 July, hoping that the Commons would debate the Bill 'with total abstinence from anything like party objects or party views'. Selwin Ibbetson praised the Bill, and in later debates helped Bruce to defend it against its more extreme opponents. Lawson's attitude was rather more positive than before; supporting the second reading, he urged Bruce to 'stick to the hours he has laid down in this Bill, and if he does so we will stick to him and will carry the Bill'. More might have been achieved if temperance reformers had adopted such a policy earlier.[46] Summing up, Bruce said that his Bill assumed that 'as long as public-houses were well managed, it was not the duty of Parliament to reduce the number of those establishments. The duty of the Government was to maintain order and not to restrict the supply of liquor to the public.'[47] There was much give-and-take in the debates, but they were conducted in a mood of increasing exasperation. There were many complaints at government indecision, and even at their 'sharp practice'—with debates so late in the night and so late in the session. Members had been 'pulled out of their beds and deprived of their holiday', Sir Henry Hoare complained.

Anyone who scrutinizes the divisions and amendments will see that this was a non-party measure; admittedly the critics were more numerous on the Tory side, but none was more vociferous than the Liberal W. V. Harcourt, who on 26 July pleaded for 'some protection against that form of legislation, which, in the name of liberty, put everybody into prison, and in the name of humanity treated everyone with cruelty'.[48] There was much cross-voting, and few Conservatives rejected *all* the government's proposals. Towards the end of the debates, Bruce lost control of the situation more than once; retreats were made, then retracted, and the publican press grumbled at the way in which the Bill was being pushed through. Gladstone especially irritated them by successfully defending his wine merchants against their assaults. As the Bill emerged from the Commons, drunkenness penalties had been increased, statutory opening-hours had been extended still further and an 'elastic' principle had been introduced, which enabled magistrates to increase or reduce evening closing-hours in a locality by one hour [see Tables 8 and 9]. The general mood at the end of the debates can be gauged from an M.P.'s remark which Bass recalled later in the year: 'at the close of the long and fruitless Saturday afternoon's debate' the M.P. had exclaimed 'for God's sake let us call a division'.[49]

Of all the responses to Bruce's measure, that of the working men was perhaps the most crucial to its success. The conflicting deputations of working men and their mutually contradictory letters to the press gave the government little guidance on whether riots would result. The popular weeklies disagreed amongst themselves, and their criticisms reflected the traditional radical loathing for 'class legislation'; both the *Weekly Dispatch* (140,000) and *Reynolds' Newspaper* urged protests in Hyde Park (as in 1855) against Bruce's Bill. Only *Lloyd's Weekly London Newspaper* (500,000) stressed the need to improve the environment before drunkenness could be eliminated.[50] Rare was the popular newspaper which squarely faced the real problems; few radicals showed themselves as progressive in outlook as those constructive Liberals who recognized the need for moral progress to supersede *laissez-faire* principle; few had the vision of those Tory and clerical newspapers which stressed the need for social legislation before sobriety could be expected. On the temperance question in 1871–2 the working men and those who catered for them showed no greater enlightenment than the government; many of them were governed by outworn prejudices and mistaken assessments. Public meetings in Sheffield addressed by J. W. Burns revealed some local hostility to the measure, which was whipped up by the *Sheffield Daily Telegraph*, one of the few major Conservative provincial newspapers. When the local temperance leader, John Taylor, tried to address a meeting in August 'a tremendous shout of derision arose from all parts of the square, which culminated in a general uproar'.[51]

In some areas during the autumn, working class hostility took a violent turn. In late August a Cheltenham mob, turned out of the public-houses at the new closing-hour, descended on two Cheltenham clubs and forced them to close too. When the publicans closed at the new hour in Maidstone on 17 August, 'numbers of men went about from place to place, shouting and demanding to be served'; the police kept them in control, but on the next day a military picquet was needed to round up soldiers fraternizing with the mob. At Exeter, popular hostility to the new closing-hours mingled with resentment at the price of bread. Many shop-windows were smashed, and a demonstration was held outside a local club: for a time the mob was in command of the town. At Wolverhampton crowds gathered outside the Tiger Inn with 'taunts, jeers, and satirical remarks', and groaned and hissed at the police when told to move on. Liverpool publicans deliberately fomented riots by distributing broadsides and talking of 'one law for the rich and another for the poor'. Libertarian sentiment was strong among working men in these years. At Coventry in August a local club was attacked by a mob singing 'Britons never shall be slaves'—the song which anti-sabbatarian Hyde Park rioters had sung in 1855. In Oxford, crowds assembled at Carfax in September to do the same, and at a meeting of 2,000 Ipswich working men in December, the audience—after hearing several libertarian speeches—concluded with Rule Britannia and the national anthem.[52] But the most serious riots were at Ashton; for two and three-quarter hours in October 1872 J. R. Stephens addressed a packed audience at Stalybridge Town Hall. His speech was filled as usual with colloquialisms, dialect-forms and bantering interchange with his audience, and displayed much knowledge of local customs and personalities. He denounced teetotal hypocrisy, and as in 1871 pronounced the public-house 'older than the monarchy itself'; he urged his audience to get up a public meeting on the subject. On 3 November, the first Sunday when local public-houses were closed at 9 p.m. instead of at 10, 10,000–15,000 people met together at Ashton and demonstrated outside the home of Hugh Mason, the local temperance leader. Soldiers had to disperse the crowd, which was singing 'Rule Britannia'.[53]

The temperance movement's conduct during 1871–2 provoked much controversy in later years. Though temperance reformers lacked influence at the top and bottom of society, they did help to force the temperance question to the political forefront in these years. Yet there is a tragic contradiction in their role, for once the government had steeled itself to the point of legislating, nobody gave it less help than the temperance reformers themselves. Either they adopted a quietist and moral suasionist stance, or their prohibitionist rigidity obstructed the compromises essential to successful legislation. The licensing question was difficult enough for home secretaries to solve without this extra hindrance: 'if an angel from heaven were to come down and bring in a Licensing Bill', said Lord George Cavendish in 1874, 'he would find it too much for him'.[54] Chamberlain had similar problems when introducing the Gothenburg scheme in 1876–7; his reflections might well have come from Bruce after 1871–2—'I had organization to the right of me, to left of me, and I was left in the middle to be supported indeed by a great body of impartial and intelligent opinion, of opinion which was not organized and which was consequently totally unable to compete with the two organizations to which I have referred.'[55] Support could be drummed up only for conflicting sectional interests. The crisis illustrates the defects of a political system which expects the public interest to emerge from the clash between opposed pressure groups.

Criticisms of prohibitionist policy during the crisis were often heard later: Handel Cossham voiced them on the Alliance platform as early as 1875. When Joseph Chamberlain later attacked the prohibitionists for their conduct in 1872, the Alliance claimed that it had 'positively helped to pass' the measure; even today the Alliance claims to have 'worked strenuously' to obtain it. As for the 1871 Bill, prohibitionists often tried to exculpate themselves by quoting Bruce's own words: 'it was not true that the bill was withdrawn in consequence of opposition of the publican interest . . . it was on account of want of time to carry the measure.' Admittedly Bruce's Bill was well down in the cabinet's January 1871 agenda: perhaps the Bill would not have passed even if the temperance reformers had been more helpful. But at least the Bill would have been discussed further in parliament, thereby enabling public opinion to be roused in its favour. The Alliance did its best to hinder the mobilization of support for both government measures. Wemyss Reid, editor of the *Leeds Mercury*, was one of the few editors to give vigorous support to Bruce; yet he was bitterly attacked for his pains by the local prohibitionists.[56] It was lack of enthusiastic support for the Bill which made Bruce feel that the Bill must be withdrawn; the complaint about lack of time was a device well known at Westminster—a mere excuse for a change of policy. In 1871–2, far from clarifying opinion, Alliance clamour had obscured it: and far from facilitating legislation, Alliance rigidity had obstructed it.

Higher up in society there was some sympathy with Bruce, whose political career was now in ruins: 'without doubt time and reflection will do you justice' Gladstone told him in 1874.[57] To some extent Gladstone was right: the subsequent progress of prohibitionist influence within the Liberal party made Bruce's 1871 Bill seem a moderate and reasonable solution to the temperance question. His 1872 Act did not lack supporters even at the start. 'To the general community', wrote *The Times* on 31 December, in its editorial summary of the year, 'it is no small advantage that the streets of towns are now quiet and almost deserted for an hour before midnight.' In February 1873

Bruce himself was delighted with the Act's results, and he strongly defended it against Conservative amendments in 1874. It is impossible to measure the Act's effects on the level of drunkenness. The number of publicans' spirit licences levelled off in the early 1870s and actually declined thereafter in relation to population. In England and Wales the absolute decline in the number of beerhouse on-licences which had begun in 1870 continued steadily thereafter, though in the mid-1870s a marked increase began in the number of beerhouse off-licences. United Kingdom *per capita* consumption figures for wine and beer did not begin to fall till 1877; those for spirits began to fall only in 1876 [see Figures 3 and 5]. The level of drunkenness proceedings continued to rise throughout the years 1862–77, though these figures are as much an index of temperance sentiment as of actual drunkenness.[58]

When explaining his temperance views to Dr. Acland in 1882, Bruce described his 1871 Bill as 'much the best & most comprehensive ever yet proposed'—a Bill which 'fell thro', more on account of its merits than defects'.[59] He had conveniently forgotten his own administrative and political ineptitude in 1871–2, yet several distinguished politicians came to share his view. On several occasions in the early 1880s T. H. Green publicly deplored Alliance attitudes towards the 1871 Bill. W. L. Courtney also felt that the Bill should have passed, and in 1890 Lord Randolph Churchill regretted that his party had modified the 1872 Act in 1874. In 1891 Ripon told Bruce that after recent Commons' temperance debates he must be looking back now 'with a grim pleasure to those much misunderstood proposals' of 1871.[60] Gladstone himself felt that Bruce had been badly treated by the public while Home Secretary: 'you suffered when in office intense injustice out of doors from causes some of which I was not able to understand and none of which I could appreciate.' In one of those dignified letters of consolation which only Gladstone could write, Bruce's recently bereaved widow was informed in 1895 that the 1871 Bill had been 'somewhat wantonly rejected'; like Campbell-Bannerman four years later, Gladstone believed that if it had been passed into law, Bruce's 1871 Bill 'would by this time have done much to mitigate intolerable evils'.[61]

13

Liberalism and the Drink Question*

For Henry Carter, the 1871–2 licensing crisis was 'a decisive moment in English Temperance history'; for R. C. K. Ensor, it was 'one of the source-points in the history of parties'. Ensor describes how Bruce's first Licensing Bill 'raised a storm of opposition from the publicans and the liquor trade generally', and how the Alliance 'refused . . . to give it any effective counter-support'. Bruce's second Bill was weaker, he says, but 'still very contentious'. Until 1871 'the liquor industry, like other industrial interests, was apt to be liberal' and until the early 1870s the Conservative party had been far less successful than the Liberals in attracting the support of 'permanent interests'. But thereafter the support of the liquor trade provided the Tory party with a substantial income—facts which 'provide no small part of the explanation why conservatism was so much more successful in the forty years after 1871 than in the forty years before that date'.[1] Research conducted only up to the year 1872 cannot prove or disprove Ensor's assertions about the link between drink and Toryism after that date; closer study of the 1871–2 crisis does however supplement Ensor's account. For Ensor's brevity, without actually fostering error, makes him liable to misinterpretation.

Four criticisms of his discussion can be made. Firstly, his brief account exaggerates the unanimity of the drink trade against Bruce's Bills. His interpretation is difficult to reconcile with the fact that on 16 July 1872 the *Brewers Guardian* was describing the 1872 Bill as 'with a few very trifling amendments . . . more just and equitable in several important respects to the Trade . . . than any of the schemes which have been previously introduced'. On 13 August the paper claimed that the Bill in some of its clauses was 'destined to materially benefit the brewing interest and the owners of property, in the future'. While the paper disliked some parts of the new Act, it was anxious to protect a measure which it had taken such trouble to mould. Nor was the drink trade's opposition indiscriminate, even to the 1871 Bill. A publican as prominent as Candelet, for instance, praised some aspects of it, and wanted

* This discussion has benefited considerably from correspondence with Professors H. J. Hanham and John Vincent, though neither is responsible for any of my assertions.

it modified rather than rejected. Many sections of the drink interest throughout the crisis period wanted licensing reform of some kind, and the framing of the 1872 Act as it passed through parliament owed much to their suggestions. It is important to stress once again that the 'drink interest' was still internally divided at this time. Still, this aspect of Ensor's interpretation is broadly correct: Bruce's Bills did arouse formidable and at times vigorous hostility to the Liberal party from some sections of the Trade. 'Beer was once a great Liberal power, as surely to be reckoned on the Liberal side as Land was to be reckoned on the Conservative side', wrote the *Economist* on 20 December 1873: 'it is only in our day that the Tories find their safest if not their ablest candidates among the scions of the great brewing and distilling firms.'

A second modification of Ensor's interpretation: he did not stress the non-party nature of Bruce's Bills. For many years Tories had championed temperance legislation. Lawson in 1872 sought support for the Permissive Bill not only from the Liberals 'as the advocates of local self-government', but also from the Tories as 'essentially the friends of order'.[2] Conservatives of course disliked the temperance movement, for the prosperity of the landed interest depended largely on barley; Tories ignored the teetotal case when agitating in the 1850s against the malt tax. Again, mid-Victorian Tories were less enthusiastic than Liberals for the concepts of self-help and local democratic self-government. But many Tories vigorously attacked intemperance by other means: the campaign against the beerhouses owes much to the Tories Pakington, Selwin Ibbetson, Gathorne-Hardy and Knatchbull; for the Conservative party was always anxious to preserve public order in the countryside. In the late 1850s, the National Temperance League co-operated quite closely with Gathorne-Hardy in its attempt to legislate against the beershops, and parted with him only after mutual expressions of respect. Among the other Conservative champions of temperance legislation were Forbes Mackenzie, M.P. for Liverpool, who secured Sunday closing for Scotland in 1853: Wilson Patten, M.P. for North Lancashire, who had English Sunday opening-hours curtailed in 1854: and Mr. Somes, M.P. for Hull, who championed English Sunday closing during the 1860s. 21 of the 78 M.P.s 'generally favourable' to the Permissive Bill at the 1859 election were Conservatives.[3] Opposing the third reading of the 1874 Licensing Bill, Lawson had good reason for appealing against it to the consciences of 'the Conservative Members . . . the country Gentlemen, the old traditional friends of order and good government'.[4]

Any government of the early 1870s, whether Liberal or Conservative, would have felt obliged to pass some sort of licensing measure. In 1868 the Conservative Home Secretary himself admitted that 'more extensive police arrangements' were needed. A Tory government would in fact have had less to lose than a Liberal government by opposition from predominantly Liberal brewers. The Tories' relatively pragmatic attitude to legislation would also have made temperance restriction easier for them.[5] The Conservative party had never been as enthusiastic for free trade as the Liberals: here was an area, as Tory opponents of the beerhouses often argued, where free trade principles did not apply. While Liberals might dislike state promotion of morality, Tory traditions saw the state as 'a partnership in every virtue and in all perfection';[6] furthermore by the 1870s the flourishing Church of England Temperance Society lent religious respectability to the temperance movement. Some Tories wanted temperance legislation if only to free magistrates from the discredit they incurred through their licensing role: hence the attraction of licensing boards for the Conservative Canon H. J. Ellison.[7]

The temperance legislation of 1871–2 therefore had a non-party flavour, like a great deal of social reform in the period.[8] Bruce saw his post as 'a non-political office'; 'whenever I propose a measure of national advantage', he said at Glasgow in 1873, 'I look forward as securely to the support of the Opposition as I do to the support of members of the Ministry.' He told a deputation in May 1871 that temperance legislation was 'not a party question'.[9] Even when moving the second reading of his 1872 Licensing Bill, he 'felt satisfied that . . . no party views or considerations would be allowed to enter into their treatment of this question'. Whatever happened afterwards, Bruce in 1871–2 owed much to Tory co-operation. When Bruce introduced his 1871 Licensing Bill, Selwin Ibbetson expressed 'great satisfaction' that he was at last dealing so boldly with the subject. When Bruce withdrew the Bill, R. A. Cross, the future Conservative home secretary, said that he hoped the government would not shrink from a complete measure next session. Viscount Sandon, another Conservative, expressed a similar regret—claiming that many Conservatives would have helped the government to pass 'a good sound measure'. The 1872 Licensing Act was in fact one of many measures which the Gladstone government passed with Conservative support against radical indifference or hostility. Selwin Ibbetson welcomed Bruce's second Bill 'with the greatest satisfaction', and Conservatives co-operated in improving it at every stage.[10]

During the debates on the 1872 Bill, disunity was rife within both parties; on 10 August 1872, the *Licensed Victuallers' Gazette* noted that the majorities which pushed through the Bill's most obnoxious clauses included both Conservatives and Liberals. Prominent in the debates were Liberals of many contrasting views: Harcourt disliked temperance legislation altogether, Auberon Herbert's first and last love was free trade, Anstruther wanted some degree of local control, Lawson wanted the local veto. Outside parliament, John Bright was advocating municipal control of licensing, and the free trade remedy was being canvassed privately by Gladstone and publicly by Fawcett. The Gothenburg scheme further complicated the picture, for it was shortly to attract Joseph Chamberlain and Bruce himself.

The Conservatives in 1871–2 were also divided. While Selwin Ibbetson, the Duke of Richmond and Lord Salisbury co-operated with Bruce and Kimberley in the hope of defending the Trade, some Tory newspapers were beginning to doubt the value of temperance legislation by itself; more urgent, they said, were housing reforms, sanitary reforms and increased and improved recreation. By contrast, the Anglican wing of the Tory party voted in House of Lords divisions to make licensing regulation more stringent. The *Church of England Temperance Magazine* on 1 April 1872 hoped that Conservatives would never ally with the publicans, and the *Record* on 15 November found it 'impossible to deprecate in too strong language even the semblance of a common cause between Conservatism and beershops'. Yet despite this Tory disunity, by autumn 1872 the Alliance could discern the beginnings of a Conservative alignment with the drink interest—an alignment which 'must end . . . in ultimate disaster to the party, since the progress of public opinion will infallibly be in the direction of public virtue'.[11]

In August 1872 the Conservative candidate at the Preston by-election claimed that Bruce's Licensing Bill was 'the silliest bill and the most tyrannical that ever found its way on the statute book'. He devoted a quarter of his speech to it, and claimed that the prohibitionists would do away with the foaming tankards and roast beef of merry England.[12] Although the Liberal party was united behind a good candidate, the Conservative won a decisive victory. 'Preston is a great disappointment', wrote Glyn to Gladstone on 14 September: '*I* hardly hoped to win, but did hope to make a closer fight'.[13] The Liberal attorney-general, speaking at Exeter in October, attacked local Tories for making political capital out of riots against the new Licensing Act: 'in no spirit of party . . . but with the assent of the whole Legislature . . . did Government endeavour to deal with this matter'.[14]

Nevertheless, by the early 1870s the attack on temperance legislation had certain attractions for the Conservative party. Its role after 1867 was to appeal for working-class support only by stressing the interests which they shared with the middle class.[15] Opposition to Bruce's Bills was a 'cry' which could unite traditionalist working men, who feared despots and spies, with nervous businessmen who feared any threat to their property—particularly if some hints could be dropped that Conservatives would tackle more fundamental social questions in a pragmatic spirit. This was not difficult with Disraeli as party leader and with Shaftesbury's factory legislation a recent memory. On the licensing question, political capital might be made from upholding individual liberty against the state—desirable anyway for Conservatives afraid that working men might one day gain control of the state machine.[16]

Throughout the 1871–2 licensing crisis, Disraeli kept his options open. It is curious that in a crisis so important to the history of parties neither Gladstone nor Disraeli spoke a word in parliament. Gladstone was silent partly because he lacked enthusiasm for the direction temperance reform was taking, partly from his belief in ministerial autonomy, partly from his preoccupation with foreign affairs and the monarchy, and partly from his general indifference to all legislation passed by his first ministry after 1870.[17] Disraeli probably acted from his policy at the time of preserving 'the utmost reserve and quietness' while the government discredited itself. Like Theodore Roosevelt, he was sensible enough to avoid making clear pronouncements on the drink question. After 1868, in this as in other spheres, he simply needed to keep quiet and wait for votes to fall into his lap.[18] According to Lawson, none of Disraeli's speeches and letters committed him to supporting even the publicans, let alone the temperance reformers. Several radicals and temperance reformers suspected that Disraeli, who in the 1850s had pronounced beer a necessity of life, himself used alcohol liberally before speaking in public. But in 1871–2 his sole statements on the question were to note, semi-humorously, in 1871, that 'the unfortunate licensed victuallers of England seem to me to be the class selected this Session to be baited by Her Majesty's Ministers': to make the briefest reference to the question in his Manchester speech of April 1872: and in 1873 to express a languid faith that popular habits would improve without the aid of legislation.[19] It was therefore very easy for the Conservative party later to champion the drink interest. By 1874 this alignment had become so pronounced that Gladstone felt it necessary to redress the balance. The 1872 Licensing Act, he said, 'was not one which was debated as between party and party, but one which was carried with the general assent of the House'.[20]

Thirdly, Ensor exaggerated the importance to the Tory party of the drink interest's shift in allegiance: the events of 1871–2 were significant only because they accentuated long-term trends working at a far deeper level. Money from the drink industry cannot explain the success of late-Victorian Toryism: the party was not short of money before the Trade moved towards a Tory alliance: the party continued to rely, after 1872 as before, on money from the landed interest: and no proof has ever been produced that the Trade did give generously to the party after 1872.[21] Far more important in explaining the change is the shifting allegiance of wealthy dissenters and of the propertied and educated classes in general. Reactions to the Commune and fears for the security of property were more important than the licensing question in weakening the Liberal party, and received proportionately more attention in Disraeli's two famous speeches of 1872. Attacks on Bruce's Bills were so effective only because they drew upon this underlying fear.

Finally, Ensor telescopes unduly the length of time it took for the drink interest to shift its allegiance. Even the most militant opponent of the Liberal government in 1872—Col. Richards—showed little enthusiasm for Conservatism. Some sections of the Trade supported the Conservatives long before 1871–2: the established wine-merchants, for instance, who resented the intrusions into their trade which resulted from Gladstone's free trade measures: also wealthy brewer-bankers from the south of England like Sir

Edmund Lacon of Great Yarmouth and the Cobbolds of Ipswich.[22] At several moments in the 1860s Liberal sections of the drink trade grumbled at Liberal free trade legislation, just as in 1871–2 they grumbled at excessively restrictive measures. Reactions to Gladstone's wine licence scheme during 1860 showed how easily brewers might be pushed into Tory arms. Gladstone gave further offence to the brewers in 1862 when he abolished the inconvenient hop duty; for he introduced a brewer's licence which M. T. Bass six years later still considered 'a blot, a special blemish' on his great financial schemes.[23] While there was no national swing among publicans towards the Tories even by 1868, in constituencies where the Liberal candidate was identified with temperance views a local swing could occur much earlier—as at Rochdale in 1857, at Leicester in 1859 and 1861, at Bolton in 1865 and 1868, and at Bristol in 1868; but the candidatures of Pope at Stoke in 1859 and at Bolton in 1868 show how rash it would be to assume that trade considerations invariably caused Liberal drinksellers and drink manufacturers to switch their allegiance when faced with a Liberal temperance candidate.[24]

Nor was the shift in allegiance at all complete, even after 1872. The Conservative party never felt entirely happy in its role as defender of the drink trade.[25] No prominent Conservative ever opposed the temperance movement as vigorously as Harcourt supported it in the late 1880s. Several Liberal Unionist and Tory M.P.s in Scotland and Lancashire in the 1880s tried to prevent the Conservative government from officially opposing temperance legislation, and when Salisbury failed to act on the report of the royal commission on liquor licensing, there was much Tory restiveness.[26] Likewise the Liberals after 1872 were never entirely happy with their temperance alliance. Professor Hanham argues that the Trade switched its allegiance to the Tories only in constituencies where Liberalism was identified with a temperance candidate .'It was not so much the Gladstone government as the temperance movement and the gradual identification of the Liberal party with the United Kingdom Alliance which finally drove the publicans into the Conservative camp.'

Gladstone's fiscal wizardry still had its charms for the brewers, and his abolition of the malt duty in 1880 greatly impressed them. Opposition was pointless, said Watney, the brewer chosen to fight Gladstone's proposals in detail: 'Gladstone knows more of my business than I do myself.' Samuel Whitbread well knew the difficulties of securing this reform, and often told Sir Algernon West that 'he marvelled how it had been possible'.[27] Gladstone was still bidding for brewer support in 1882 with his policy of a 'free mash tun'.[28] Secessions of drink manufacturers from the Liberal party occurred steadily over a period of forty years, not suddenly in 1871–2. Only by the 1890s was there any approach to a clear party division on the temperance question; even then, there were always powerful Liberal opponents of Harcourt's local option schemes. Ensor's exaggerations can best be seen from analysing the number of brewing and distilling interests in the two parties.

Although the Whig/Liberal party had 24 such interests in the parliaments from 1859 to 1873, the Conservative/Peelite groups had as many as 16 in the same period; indeed the parties in the 1868 parliament were evenly balanced, with seven such interests each. And although the Conservative party had 30 brewing and distilling interests in the parliaments from 1874 to 1885, the Liberal party had as many as 22. Even in the 1906 parliament seven Liberal M.P.s were partners or directors in liquor companies, though admittedly there were by then twice as many in the Tory camp.[29] For several reasons, then, Ensor's arresting interpretation of the 1871–2 crisis needs to be qualified.

Ensor's is not the only important interpretation of the crisis. Henry Carter's view is somewhat different. Instead of attributing the shift of political allegiance mainly to the publicans' dislike of Bruce, Carter blames the Alliance's 'direct action' policy adopted in 1872—the temperance policy of entering politics on its own account where necessary. This policy, he argues, 'gave a sudden jolt to a social reform movement in which Conservatives and Liberals had co-operated up to that time';[30] henceforward temperance became an increasingly Liberal policy. Carter goes too far, however, when he argues that in 1872 'it was possible . . . to regard the passage of the Permissive Bill as a non-party enterprise'.[31] For in that year the Alliance leaders were almost all ardent Liberals, as were the great majority of its sympathizers in parliament. Given the progress made by the temperance movement within the mid-Victorian nonconformist denominations, the influence of the temperance ideology over the type of mid-Victorian working man who voted Liberal, and the militant Liberalism of so many temperance leaders—it was inevitable that the Liberal party would eventually align itself behind a temperance programme. For after 1867 the party needed to broaden its base, and temperance reformers were eagerly clamouring to enlist. Bruce's clumsiness in 1871–2 may have hastened, but it did not initiate, that enlistment; nor did the Alliance policy of 'direct action' alter the situation significantly. The Alliance and its leaders had been politicizing the temperance movement since the 1850s; and though Lawson might still, in the early 1870s, appeal for support to both political parties—the division-lists on the Permissive Bill made it increasingly clear that only one of the two could respond.

Yet the temperance movement had been moulded since the 1830s by individuals socially far removed from the Liberal leadership; indeed, throughout the 1850s and 1860s the Alliance despised Whigs as heartily as Tories, and drew hardly any of its recruits from the high-minded élite which co-operated with the Whigs at Westminster. It would therefore have been surprising if friction had not resulted from the attempt to link up the temperance movement with the Liberal party. In analysing the reasons for such friction, it is necessary to discuss the relationship between the temperance movement and the Liberal party in more general terms. It is important to distinguish between three ways of tackling the drink problem: between the attempt by any means to reduce the evil of drunkenness, the attempt to achieve this end through total abstinence, and the attempt to achieve it through prohibition.

The connexion of the first of these three campaigns with the Liberal party seems to have been strong throughout the party's history. Perhaps the alignment was already present in the seventeenth century, for nonconformists were accusing Anglicans of intemperance at least as early as the 1680s, and in the mind of Judge Jeffreys—speaking of a generous host at Newcastle in 1684—Whiggery and drink were already opposed: 'they tell me such a man is a Whigg,' said Jeffreys, 'but I find it's no such thing, he is an honest drunken fellow.' In Manchester during the 1790s there was a clear antagonism between 'Church and King' publicans and dissenting reformers; the conservative mob was usually organized and fortified from the public-house before it sallied forth to break up reforming meetings.[32] Radicals under Cobbett and Hunt realized the political capital to be made by abstaining from intoxicants, as well as the need for sobriety among their followers. Many years before 1829, Political Protestants were refusing ale from a determination 'not to be diverted from their purpose'.[33]

There is a clear connexion between Liberalism and the nineteenth-century campaign for electoral purity. While in many constituencies Liberals were as corrupt as Conservatives, the early Victorian efforts at reform were championed most prominently by the Whig Lord John Russell, and opposed most persistently by the Tory Col. Sibthorp. The individual candidates who spurned aid from publicans were usually Liberals or radicals. Cobbett and Burdett paid much attention to popular sobriety at their elections during the Napoleonic Wars.[34] Three Whig philanthropists—two of them Quakers and the third strongly influenced by Quakerism—were among the pioneer advocates of electoral sobriety. J. J. Gurney began his assaults on drunkenness and corruption at Norwich elections in 1819. Before 1832, parliamentary reformers hoped that franchise extension would greatly reduce electoral corruption and at several places in 1832 the reformers' victory was celebrated with drink-free dinners for wives as well as husbands. Liberals were bitterly disappointed when the Blackburn by-election of 1832 registered no change in electoral habits.[35] When Joseph Pease stood for parliament in 1832 he refused to canvass and spent no money on the election; and during his elections of 1835 and 1837 T. F. Buxton repudiated the distribution of free beer. Liberal nonconformists —especially Quakers—were the most ardent upholders of electoral sobriety. Sometimes, like William Foster in 1834, they took individual action and opposed any candidate who distributed drink;[36] this was precisely the course recommended by the Alliance at Marylebone and Southampton by-elections in 1854 and 1856, respectively.

During the 1840s the anti-corn law and complete suffrage movements vehemently denounced electoral corruption: the League even described itself as 'at once the teacher, purifier, and emancipator of the constituencies'.[37] The radical Henry Vincent fought eight electoral campaigns between 1841 and 1852 largely from a desire to convert the election from a drink-soaked fight between local factions into a 'great battle-ground of principle'. He was supported by York Quakers in 1848 for the same reasons as Barkley, his predecessor there—because his Quaker admirers disliked electoral corruption.[38] Many Liberals thereafter tried to prevent drunkenness and corruption at their elections—George Thompson, G. W. Alexander and Joseph Sturge at Tower Hamlets, Wakefield and Leeds respectively, in 1847: Robert Lowe at Kidderminster in 1859: J. S. Mill at Westminster in 1865: W. V. Harcourt at Oxford in 1868. William Lovett in 1869 campaigned to exclude election meetings from public-houses and in the 1880s Joseph Arch refused even to canvass when standing for parliament.[39]

In these years, Conservatives were identified in the public mind with the resort to electoral corruption. *Some* Conservatives of course favoured electoral purity: evangelicals like Wilberforce and Henry Thornton bequeathed a tradition of electoral purity to the Conservative Lord Ashley, who expressed delight after his election at Bath in 1847 that 'not a penny during six months was expended on Beer'.[40] Dean Close continued this tradition with his suggestion in *The Times* of 29 July 1865 that public-houses should be closed during general elections. Yet such scruples were more common among Liberals; the contrast was accentuated when the temperance party became more clearly aligned with Liberalism in the 1880s. Ostrogorski noted that late-Victorian Tories were far more skilful than the puritanical Liberals at organizing social functions for their political supporters;[41] by that time Tories were holding their ward-meetings in public-houses far more frequently than their rivals.

The movement for voluntary abstinence—as distinct from the more generalized attack on drunkenness—was also taken up more frequently by Liberals than by Conservatives. Liberals were the first supporters won by the Preston teetotalers in the 1830s; indeed, this is an aspect of the 'formation of the Liberal party' which occurred long before the 1850s, and which owed nothing to the patronage of Mr. Gladstone. The Liberalism of the temperance reformer was important because he was one of the most energetic of party workers and was often an active Liberal journalist. 'The best fighting men in the ranks of the Liberal army', said Lloyd George in 1898, 'were the Temperance men, and from an electioneering point of view the Liberals could not afford to quarrel with these men.'[42] When the party democratized its structure in the 1870s, shopkeepers, clerks and the better class of workmen—just the class from which temperance societies were recruited—became the most active party workers. Temperance societies, like chapels and trade unions, constituted the equivalent of the Liberal party 'branch' in the late-Victorian period.[43]

Despite this undoubted affinity between the Liberal party and the temperance movement, there were many strong critics of teetotalism within the party.

For many Liberals, teetotalism was too readily turned to the purposes of popular religion, too eager to mobilize social pressures against the individual, too prone to oversimplify complicated social problems. Teetotalism had emerged too low down in society ever to attract more than a handful of radical M.P.s at Westminster. Many Liberal M.P.s argued that teetotalism was good enough for the ex-drunkard, but that the sober should not be deprived of their pleasures merely because their 'weaker brethren' abused them. There was a vulgarity and a rigidity about organized teetotalism which repelled many of the finer Liberal minds. These Liberals were still more alarmed when teetotalers moved forward from moral suasion to prohibition.

Cobden and Bright are examples of Liberals who could stomach the first but not the second. On several occasions in the 1840s and 1850s Cobden strongly praised water-drinking. His American travels impressed him with the utility of temperance societies; his European travels convinced him that English working men needed these societies more than most. Cobden believed that temperance, by civilizing working men and enabling them to store up their capital in the freehold land movement, would assimilate the English middle and working classes.[44] Bright's nonconformist origins ensured that his identification with the temperance movement was even closer. In his youth he had lectured for the Rochdale Temperance Society, and by 1842 he was president of the British Association for the Promotion of Temperance. He even composed a temperance tract, and always excluded decanters of wine and spirits from his house; throughout his life he retained a dislike of 'society, smart people, hot rooms, elaborate meals, ceremonious observances'.[45] Nevertheless Bright in his autobiographical memoir written in the 1880s did not even mention his early temperance connexions, and Cobden by 1864 could claim that he was 'not one . . . who attaches very much importance to the beverage which men may take'.[46] This change stemmed partly from their increasing impatience, as experienced politicians, with the sectarian attitudes of the temperance movement: partly from the alcoholic medical prescriptions which the illnesses of middle age were thought to demand: but primarily from their distaste for the mounting influence of extremism within the movement.

The Alliance admired Cobden as the man of principle, and convinced itself as early as 1857 that he was on the brink of supporting prohibition; on 8 April 1865 the *Alliance News* claimed that Cobden, if he had lived, would soon have supported the Permissive Bill.[47] Yet Cobden would never have done so from conviction, for like many good Liberals he believed that the population would never be civilized through sumptuary laws. Abstinence must proceed from the free choice of the citizen. W. L. Courtney neatly expressed the Liberal view some years later: 'the object of legislation should not be to take away from man the opportunity of sinning, but to take away from him the desire to err.' Cobden found the issue embarrassing only because he shared the Alliance outlook on so many other questions; before the 1864 Permissive Bill debate, therefore, he declared his dislike of such measures but 'decided *magnanimously* to run away' from the division.[48] Bright, surrounded with prohibitionist relatives, took a more courageous stand. He denounced the 'well intending but impracticable' proposal as unconstitutional and unfair to publicans. As an experienced politician, he was more concerned than the Alliance about the feasibility of enforcement. He told the Quaker yearly meeting in 1874 that 'parliament had no more power than the smallest vestry until public opinion had become convinced'. At his 1878 interview with the Alliance executive, and in his private contacts with Lawson, Bright helped to guide the prohibitionists into more practical courses, for like Cobden he shared many Alliance attitudes. He liked the decentralizing and democratic aspects of Alliance policy, and during the 1880s wanted the licensing power transferred from the magistrates to the municipal authorities.[49]

Prohibition was even less attractive to the Whigs, valuing as they did 'balance of mind, self-possession, moderation, a taste for or a habit of compromise': these were qualities which the Alliance never displayed.[50] Hartington, we have been told, 'looked on politics as a field of duty for his class, in which a man needed above all things the reasonable habits of mind that come from a life of leisure and ease. The problems of government had to be met as they arose. Those problems of government were not too difficult, if agitators like Chamberlain did not stir up trouble.' Yet 'a life of leisure and ease' was precisely what most Alliance leaders lacked; and although they were never in complete accord with Chamberlain, they came from a similar social background. Misunderstanding between Liberal temperance reformers and Whig politicians could hardly have been avoided.[51] For the evangelical pietism, the authoritarian collectivism and the struggle for respectability which characterized nonconformist communities were completely alien to the Whig aristocracy. In 1872 Lord Edmond Fitzmaurice ridiculed G. O. Trevelyan for 'going about the country in the character of the Rev. Mr. Stiggins and promising the good things *of the world to come* to those who agree with [him]. What an awful place heaven on Lawsonian principles w[oul]d be. Angels drinking toast and water and reading U.K.A. tracts.'[52]

By analysing the votes given on other significant issues by M.P.s who voted in the Permissive Bill divisions of 1864, 1870 and 1876, we can see why the Permissive Bill so embarrassed Cobden and Bright, and why it antagonized the Whigs. On each motion, two distinct questions have been asked: first, of the total prohibitionist vote in that year, what percentage support the motion? Second, of the total anti-prohibitionist vote in that year, what percentage support the motion? In party votes the prohibitionists are predictably more favourable than the anti-prohibitionists towards Liberal measures in all three years. More interesting is the prohibitionist and anti-prohibitionist response to non-party issues. The prohibitionists of 1864 were far readier than the anti-prohibitionists to support Sunday closing (51% of the prohibitionists, as against only 9% of the anti-prohibitionists), but were rather less enthusiastic for free licensing (16% as against 25%).

At first sight it is perhaps surprising that free licensing could attract any prohibitionists at all, for the Alliance during the 1860s was vigorously attacking the free licensing policy in Liverpool. The explanation is that many prohibitionists favoured limited regional experiments on licensing matters, and that many shared the free licensers' distaste for the magistrates' regulation of public morality through the licensing system. Many agreed with J. H. Raper when he said in 1862 that free licensing 'would lose its terrors' if the ratepayers could be enabled to veto the licensing of disorderly houses; many shared James Haughton's view that 'a trade which it is right for one man to follow ought to be free to all'.[53] While most prohibitionists preferred to wait for the enactment of the Permissive Bill before supporting free licensing, a few disliked magistrates' discretion even more than they disliked drunkenness. On franchise extension (57% as against 37%) and on the ballot (43% as against 19%) the prohibitionists showed themselves markedly more democratic than their opponents.

The prohibitionists of 1870 were again far more enthusiastic than their opponents for Sunday closing (58% as against 18%); and on the repeal of the Contagious Diseases Acts (35% as against 14%) and of the game laws (23% as against 4%), prohibitionists were far more eager than anti-prohibitionists to challenge the morality and authority of aristocracy. The motion of 24 June 1870 which opposed going into committee on the Education Bill was supported by 60 M.P.s and opposed by 421; as the high-point of nonconformist opposition to the Bill, it is particularly interesting. No less than 21 of the 60 were prohibitionists, and it is hardly necessary to say that prohibitionists were far more likely than anti-prohibitionists to support the motion (23% as against 5%). Unfortunately too few M.P.s voted in the two significant divisions of 30 March 1871 on trade unions for any firm contrasts to be drawn. The motion to make the persistent following of blacklegs a crime attracted only 7 of the 33 prohibitionists who voted, and only 3 of the 33 anti-prohibitionists who voted. The motion to make the individual liable to be charged with the crime of picketing attracted only 7 of the 32 prohibitionists who voted, but as many as 16 of the 29 anti-prohibitionists who voted. If any conclusion can be drawn from these figures, it is that parliamentary prohibitionists were less hostile to the trade unions than their opponents.

Three non-party divisions of 1876 illustrate prohibitionist sympathy with humanitarian measures. Whereas 24% of the prohibitionists opposed vivisection, only 10% of the anti-prohibitionists did so. The equivalent figures for abolishing the death penalty were 18% to 2%, and for removing women's disabilities 41% to 22%. On Sunday opening of museums, prohibitionists were less rigidly sabbatarian than their opponents: 19% supported Sunday opening as against only 9% of the anti-prohibitionists. But on the proposal to extend Lubbock's Bank Holiday Act, the equivalent figures were 8% and 17%. Temperance reformers knew how public holidays, under the existing licensing laws, tended to be drunken occasions. The relatively democratic views of the prohibitionists again become apparent from the division on extending the county franchise (59% as against 12%) and on licensing boards (64% as against 1%): on the latter measure, 87% of the prohibitionists who voted in the division supported the proposal. Both the Permissive Bill and licensing boards attracted M.P.s who wished to supersede the magistrates as sole licensing authority.[54]

If prohibitionist M.P.s differed in important respects from many of their fellow Liberals, it is clear that they were decidedly Liberal on many other issues. J. M. Robertson in 1912 claimed that many temperance reformers supported the Liberal party 'on the sole ground of their desire for a better control of the drink trade, caring for no other Liberal measure, and even disliking other Liberal tendencies'.[55] This may have been true for 1912, but it was certainly not true for the mid-Victorian period. The prohibitionist attachment to the Liberal party was far more than an incidental by-product of the nonconformist/Liberal alliance, far more than a mere marriage of convenience. The prohibitionist political outlook merely pushed to an extreme liberal tendencies shared throughout the party—even by the Whigs. What were these common tendencies?

Tories and Liberals contrasted markedly in their attitude to extra-parliamentary pressure groups. While Tories like Disraeli or Salisbury publicly explored the deceptions and distortions involved in mobilizing a public agitation, Liberal leaders deferred to, and even on occasion stimulated, such movements. This contrast sprang from two distinctive features of the Liberal outlook: the desire for moral progress and the belief in popular control. Tories responded languidly to reforming crusades because they believed that suffering in this world is not easily removed. It is difficult to imagine a Liberal in the 1870s showing the relaxed attitude to the drink problem which Disraeli displayed in 1873 when he remarked that popular habits were 'as likely to purify and refine as the tastes of any class I know'. Liberals were far more restive under the wrongs of the world, and readier to believe that outside criticism of governments could be justified. Indeed, they regarded responsible public criticism as a necessary counter-balance to the corrupting influences of power: in the words of Lord Grey, 'there never was an extensive discontent without great misgovernment'.[56] Liberal distrust of irresponsible power-wielders made their party always suspicious of monopolies; hence their continued dissatisfaction with the nineteenth-century licensing system. At first they tried to supersede the magistrates' authority through opening up the trade in wine and beer. By the 1860s this policy seemed to be conflicting with the Liberal objective of moral improvement; under inspiration from several directions, the party's enthusiasm therefore shifted towards popular control of the drink trade. As early as 1835 the Whigs drafted a municipal reform Bill with proposals for popular control of licensing; with the aid of the Alliance and of Joseph Chamberlain, this policy gradually made progress within the Liberal party.

This shift is reflected in Gladstone's changing views on the licensing question. While he always encouraged the moral suasionists, he puzzled the prohibitionists with his consistent opposition to their panacea. 'The Philistines have caught our Sampson,' wrote F. W. Newman in 1872, 'have blinded him, and make him grind in their own mill.' Gladstone's lifelong enthusiasm was for free trade; in 1881 he was still antagonizing the temperance reformers by trying to facilitate the sale of drink to railway passengers, and in his somewhat fulsome letter to Messrs. Gilbey as late as 1894 he reveals his enthusiasm for the firm as 'the openers of the wine trade'. So enthusiastic was he for free trade in wine that there were persistent rumours during his lifetime that he had some financial connexion with the firm.[57] By the 1880s, however, Gladstone was becoming more sympathetic towards public management. In 1888 he saw the principle of 'converting a licence into an estate' as 'quite intolerable' and rejoiced at the defeat of the Tory proposals for compensation in 1888 and 1890. He told Lord Thring in 1894 that 'for many years' he had been 'strongly of opinion' that the Gothenburg scheme 'offered the sole chance of escape from the present miserable and almost contemptible predicament, which is a disgrace to the country'.[58]

How can we explain this shift in Gladstone's emphasis? Certainly not by positing the existence of a conversion to Alliance ideas, for in 1894 Gladstone branded its policy of reducing the number of licences as 'little better than an imposture' if regarded as a complete solution to the temperance problem. The explanation lies in the changed character of the drink trade in the 1880s. The entrepreneur of classical economics was an individual; the increased size and impersonality of drink manufacturing firms in the 1880s made it much easier for Liberals to tolerate state control. The spread of the tied-house system and the democratization of ownership in the drink industry during the 1880s explains Gladstone's change of outlook: in 1895 he described 'the large introduction of the brewers as capitalists' as 'a most threatening circumstance'. The Liberal shift from reliance on free trade to reliance on public control therefore eventually captured the most convinced free trader of them all.[59]

In addition to their belief in accountability for power, prohibitionists and Liberals shared a common ideal of government: they believed that governments should bring impartiality and rationality to bear on the management of public affairs, and should encourage these qualities in the governed. The Liberal outlook, said Robert Lowe in 1877, consisted 'in a view of things undisturbed and undistorted by the promptings of interest or prejudice, in a complete independence of all class interests, and in relying for its success on the better feelings and higher intelligence of mankind'.[60] A sober people would be more likely to range freely and without bias over questions of policy, whereas for many Liberals, drinking and thinking were mutually exclusive. Liberals aimed at peacefully removing social disharmony and class prejudice. Temperance, prohibition and co-operative societies, by enabling working men peacefully to accumulate capital, seemed to be the route to the Liberal society: they could peacefully assimilate working- and middle-class styles of life.

Although a harmonious and classless society might be the long-term objective of many prohibitionists, they could seldom be described as men without bias or passion: the flagrancy of contemporary social evils oppressed them too deeply. It is clear that prohibition was the feature of temperance policy which many Liberals found it most difficult to stomach: for by relying on the votes of the majority to control the conduct of the minority, prohibition seemed to be actually opening the way to class legislation, at least in the short term. It is significant that the champions of proportional representation —J. S. Mill and W. L. Courtney—resolutely opposed the Permissive Bill. After 1867 many Liberals were concerned, like the Whig bishop Magee, 'to protect the liberty of the few against the power of the many'. Indeed Liberal attitudes to Ulster show that the party could never quite agree on how far the majority is entitled to curb the freedom of the minority. Magee memorably voiced Liberal doubts about the Permissive Bill in two striking and subtle sentences during the House of Lords debate on the Licensing Bill on 2 May 1872: 'if I must take my choice . . . whether England should be free or sober, I declare— strange as such a declaration may sound, coming from one of my profession— that I should say it would be better that England should be free than that England should be compulsorily sober. I would distinctly prefer freedom to sobriety, because with freedom we might in the end attain sobriety; but in the other alternative we should eventually lose both freedom and sobriety.'[61]

The immediate response of Lawson and some other temperance reformers was to misquote the bishop and accuse him of assuming that in some way the intemperate individual could be free, whereas the real antagonism which influenced Magee was that between 'freedom' and '*compulsory* sobriety'.[62] 'Genuine liberty cannot be put in opposition to sobriety—nor even to prohibition,' said the *Alliance News*, missing the point on 11 May 1872, 'for the prohibition of the wrong is one of the conditions of a free social government . . . government is restraint—the prohibition of the social bad.' Prohibitionists believed that the state must curb drinking: 'I am no believer in drunken freedom,' Manning told a London Alliance meeting in May 1872. 'I believe such freedom is not liberty. . . . Who loves true liberty must be both just and good . . . wheresoever there is sobriety there will be liberty by an inevitable moral law . . . where sobriety exists, that, by necessity, will generate liberty.'[63]

Only one contemporary philosopher could give memorable expression to such a sentiment in opposition to Magee, and the Alliance did not hesitate to quote him in September. 'Liberty? The true liberty of a man, you would say, consisted in his finding out, or being forced to find out the right path, and to walk thereon. To learn, or to be taught, what work he actually was able for, and then by permission, persuasion, and even compulsion, to set about doing of same! That is his true blessedness, honour, "liberty", and maximum of well-being; if liberty be not that, I for one have small care about liberty.' The quotation came, of course, from Carlyle's *Past and Present*. In his essay on 'Shooting Niagara', Carlyle ridiculed those who supposed that 'reform' consisted in removing restrictions on liberty rather than in securing moral improvement. When asked to attend a Permissive Bill meeting in Chelsea in April 1872, Carlyle in refusing declared: 'my complete conviction goes, and for long years has gone, with yours in regard to that matter; and it is one of my most earnest and urgent public wishes that such Bill do become law'.[64] Before Theodore Cuyler, an American prohibitionist visiting England about this time, Carlyle 'broke out into a terrible denunciation of dramshops and "whisky", which did my soul good to hear. Gough never surpassed the red-hot vehemence of the old man's philippic against "the horrible and detestable damnation of whisky and every kind of strong drink" .' As for the problem of compensating the drink interest, Carlyle said he would tell any publican who made such claims to 'go to your father the devil for compensation'.[65] Zeal for progress thus brought many Liberals into alliance with Carlyle—a man whose ideas in many other spheres they detested.

The prohibitionists' enthusiasm for state intervention should not be allowed to conceal their affinity with the mainstream of Liberalism in yet another respect. At the back of many a Liberal's mind lay visions of a society in which the citizens' self-directed and uncoerced rationality harmonized the conflicting demands of freedom and order. In the tradition of John Locke, Liberals believed that man enters society in order to escape arbitrary control by other human beings; they hoped that ultimately the state would wither away, and displayed what the hostile Sidney Webb called an 'administrative Nihilism'. Here is the vision in the words of two famous Victorian Liberals. After free trade had dissolved mighty empires and gigantic armaments, said Cobden in 1846, 'at a far distant period, the governing system of this world [would] revert to something like the municipal system'. 'We may still believe in the ultimate realisation of a perfect order without coercion,' said W. L. Courtney many years later, 'and of the service that shall be perfect freedom.'[66]

The Permissive Bill could hasten the arrival of such a social order in several ways; its decentralizing element would educate the citizens in political decision-making;[67] its puritanism would curb that urban extravagance and material self-indulgence which many Liberals feared were weakening the citizen's self-dependence and integrity. Although Liberalism originated in the urban revolt against aristocratic privilege, Liberals were never quite at home in the big cities of the nineteenth century. 'Depend upon it,' wrote Bright to Cobden in

1861, '*suffering* and *suffering only* will teach wisdom. Riches,—success in life —great prosperity, beget a self-confidence and puff up the mind, until truth becomes hateful, and flattery is the only welcome food you can administer.'[68] The improvement of living standards was never the central concern of nineteenth-century Liberalism. Material progress was worth pursuing only when compatible with the people's independence, moral development and capacity for self-support. In 1901 Sidney Webb complained that nineteenth-century Liberalism ' "thinks in individuals". It visualizes the world as a world of independent Roundheads, with separate ends, and abstract rights to pursue those ends.'[69]

Liberalism aimed to reduce the power of the state by reducing the citizen's claims upon it—a policy which, when pushed to its extreme, fostered an asceticism scarcely distinguishable from the semi-anarchism of Edward Carpenter or of the Owenite socialist who argued in 1841 that 'freedom must commence with a denial to the stomach'. Liberals wanted the citizen to be thrifty and abstinent. Fresh air, plain food, natural medicines—these would enable citizens to be independent of each other: 'it is only by reducing our Want-nature', wrote the prohibitionist journalist H. S. Sutton, in 1847, 'that we become partakers of that full liberty wherewith Christ makes free.'[70] Most Liberals, however, did not take their belief in internalizing social discipline to these extremes; it was sufficient for them that prohibition would supersede government's order-keeping role. 'I'm worth more than ten policemen,' said the temperance reformer Revd. J. Broadbent;[71] the more Broadbents there were, the cheaper and the less powerful government would be. It was in the spheres of education and temperance that Liberals first abandoned their hostility to state intervention, for if the state could promote these virtues in the citizen, it might eventually retire from the field altogether.

At first sight the prohibitionists advocated a dramatic *increase* in the power of the state over the individual, an increase which even today would not be acceptable; but in reality, their state intervention took a peculiar form. The Alliance never wanted centralized and continuous regulation of drinking habits. Rather the reverse: for prohibition would deprive politicians of a licensing system which was used as a way of distributing rewards to those who had served their class and creed. The Alliance was concerned above all to register a protest at the prevailing level of drunkenness; it was not unduly bothered about the details of enforcement. It was not very enthusiastic about Bruce's proposals for inspecting public-houses, for these implied the continuing existence of the evil, whereas prohibitionists wanted it swept away entirely. By simultaneously depriving the government of drink revenues, by reducing the need for police and by nourishing local self-government—the Permissive Bill would actually minimize the contact between the state and the citizen. 'It is a most dishonouring and dangerous tendency of our age to increase the extension of Government agency,' wrote the *Alliance News* on

7 January 1871, after discussing the decentralizing character of the Permissive Bill. Prohibitionists were often the most convinced opponents of state intervention elsewhere,[72] but their experience of the slums convinced them that alcohol was a pernicious and untouchable article. The community should not sully itself even by raising taxes from it: cheaper drink would be more widely consumed: hence the simplicity of the choice—free trade or prohibition. Many Alliance supporters did not see prohibition as a permanent necessity: as M. D. Hill put it, 'a break in the custom might, in our present state of civilisation, be all that the case requires'.[73]

The contradiction, then, between prohibitionism and the Liberal suspicion of the state was not as great as appears at first sight. Yet there was a collectivist vein in some Alliance leaders which fitted very awkwardly with Liberal ideas. Prohibitionists often insisted that society had the right to protect itself from the drunken and the ignorant. William McKerrow, when defending compulsory education in 1875, scornfully dismissed any notion of liberty as 'the right of every one or any one to do what he pleases, irrespective of the rights and interests of others',[74] and nonconformists sometimes showed an almost irresponsible contempt for 'property in vice'.[75] The Alliance applied to the community at large the 'socialism' of chapel life. 'The religious socialism of the dissenting communities is very remarkable,' wrote Beatrice Webb in 1886: 'each circle forming a "law unto itself" to which the individual must submit or be an outcast.'[76] The more politically experienced Liberals never really understood the millennial communitarianism of the prohibitionist world, for 'hidden in every Dissenter is a Fifth Monarchy man, struggling to get out'.[77] Mid-Victorian nonconformist temperance reformers, like seventeenth-century Calvinists, displayed two largely contradictory tendencies: a militant individualism, which the Liberal party found acceptable: but also an authoritarian collectivism which was, for many Liberals, impossible.

14

Drink and English Society in the 1870s

The second chapter of this book outlined the role of drink, drinksellers and the drink interest in the 1820s. Before assessments can be made of the various campaigns against drunkenness, some picture must be drawn of the situation as it existed in the 1870s, after half-a-century of temperance agitation. This involves discussing the attempts made since the 1820s, both inside and outside the temperance movement, at making sobriety more feasible in English society; for many of nineteenth-century England's most effective campaigners against drunkenness never joined temperance societies or Alliance auxiliaries. These individuals can be broadly described as 'counter-attractionists'—that is, men who believed in attacking the drink problem by directly modifying the environment. They differed in several respects from other campaigners against drunkenness. In their gradualism and lack of sectarianism, they resembled and often included the free traders: but in their concern with modifying the drunkard's environment they resembled the prohibitionists. Counter-attractionists were never a cohesive group with a distinctly formulated policy, a formal association or an official parliamentary spokesman. Symbolic of their diversity is the fact that two of the most prominent counter-attractionists were the atheist G. J. Holyoake and the devout evangelical Lord Shaftesbury. Instead of focusing on a single vice like temperance reformers, counter-attractionists attacked several social evils simultaneously. Nor were counter-attractionist motives always purely philanthropic, for they included railway promoters, coffee-house proprietors, soft-drink manufacturers and even publicans and brewers among their number.

In retrospect the counter-attractionists seem the most practical of all nineteenth-century opponents of drunkenness, in that their campaign's demands of working men were less impossible than those of free traders, moral suasionists or prohibitionists. With their relatively modest aims, the counter-attractionists produced a gradual but real improvement in the working man's environment. Too sharp a distinction should not be drawn between temperance reformers and counter-attractionists, for temperance reformers of all types recognized the effectiveness of a counter-attractive policy: they differed only about how counter-attractions could be financed. Temperance reformers usually argued that abstinence alone would furnish working people with the money to provide enough counter-attractions to the public-house. The counter-attractive campaign will therefore be considered in its broadest aspect; *all* attempts between the 1820s and the 1870s at making the environment more favourable to sobriety will be discussed. This will make it possible also to consider how the role of drink, of drinksellers and of the drink interest altered during those years.

Marked advances were made in increasing the safety, availability and attractiveness of the less intoxicating thirst-quenchers. Technological change improved both the quality and the supply of water. The New River Company first began generally substituting iron pipes for timber in 1810. These could sustain greater pressure and therefore, despite the discontinuity of the mains supply, cistern-storage and a continuous water supply at last became possible. In 1808 and 1809, respectively, the East London and West Middlesex water companies adopted the reservoir as a means of depositing sediment, and in 1829 James Simpson constructed the first effective sand filter-bed in London—improvements which spread only slowly to other companies. During the 1840s, storage reservoirs to provide against drought appeared; but early Victorian London water companies still supplied only well-to-do customers who could afford the plumbing necessary to connect their houses to the mains supply.[1] In 1845 water companies supplied only a small section of town populations—only 5,000 of Bristol's 130,000 inhabitants, only 8,000 of Birmingham's 40,000 houses and only a quarter of the houses in Norwich. 23% of Manchester's houses in 1847 enjoyed a direct supply; 28% were supplied by taps in the street and 49% were not supplied at all. The poorer citizens depended on rain-water and the local pump; by the 1840s little had been done to adapt nature's intermittent water supply to the continuous needs of the poor.[2]

Even where the poor enjoyed access to a communal tap, they lacked the time to get all the water they needed, and unlike the rich they had no cisterns for storing up a day's supply. Londoners who depended on the water company's communal taps were little better off, in the 1850s, than their contemporaries at Merthyr—who at times of drought had to queue at the local springs for half the night before getting their supply. A coalwhipper told Mayhew in 1849 that porter was as cheap a drink as any other except water, and easier to get.[3] In 1850 Ashley found it heartbreaking to think that thousands of Londoners were deprived of this 'essential prop and hand-maid to morality'. The first Metropolitan Water Act of 1852 instituted stringent government supervision of water supplies, and ensured that Thames water intakes were sited above the highest tidal points, that reservoirs were covered, and that water was filtered before supply. Many M.P.s had already come to believe, like Chamberlain in the 1870s, that private management of the water supply was incompatible with public morality: that the supply of water to the poor was 'not a legitimate source of profit'.[4]

The rapid growth of great cities and Dr. Snow's discovery in 1854 that cholera spread through the drinking of water-borne sewage increased the urgency of improving water supplies. Several mid-Victorian provincial cities overcame the formidable political obstacles to public management in this sphere. Liverpool corporation obtained authority for its Rivington scheme in 1847 but local opposition held up the beginning of work till 1852, and water did not flow till 1857. Meanwhile Manchester corporation, by launching its Longdendale scheme in 1851, took over complete responsibility for providing local water; by 1862 its water service was paying its own way. Merthyr launched its system of reservoirs and filter-beds in 1859, but in Birmingham local opposition was so strong that similar improvements there did not occur till the 1870s. There were technological as well as political obstacles—as revealed by Manchester's difficulties with its comparatively modest Longdendale scheme. Rusting conduit-pipes, leaking tunnels, flood damage and landslips held back a scheme which turned out to be far more costly and far less adequate than was at first anticipated. In the words of the superintending engineer 'everything had to be designed anew, with special reference to the work to be performed'. By the 1870s water supplies had considerably improved. Daily *per capita* water consumption in Liverpool rose from 8·24 gallons in 1846 to 28·7 gallons in 1861. And although in 1869 150,000 inhabitants of Birmingham still depended on wells for their water, the situation was shortly to improve. By 1876 only 14,000 out of Manchester's 70,366 houses lacked a piped water supply.[5]

Much remained to be done. 'There was scarcely a pint of water in London', said Shaftesbury in 1871, 'which was not distinctly unhealthy, and . . . a great deal was positively unsafe.' Furthermore in rural areas, though sewage pollution was less serious, the cost of improvement was for many years prohibitive. In many institutions in the 1870s, beer was still preferred to water as the staple drink. Eton College continued to brew its own beer till 1875 and Winchester boys were still drinking beer with their meals in 1872.[6] Clearly the 'water reformer' was attacking the drink problem at its root. Could he rely on temperance reformers for aid? Edwin Chadwick, a convinced counter-attractionist, received little help from them at the Social Science Congresses, and received something close to a rebuff when in 1877 he urged Lawson to help him in improving the water supply.[7]

Lady Buxton, the brewer's wife, and Robert Stafford of Seager, Evans & Co., the distillers, were quite as active as the teetotalers in promoting drinking fountains after 1859; the secretary of the Metropolitan Free Drinking Fountain Association complained that teetotalers were 'somewhat negligent' in subscribing. The National Temperance League in the 1860s pressed the managers of the Crystal Palace and the London Zoo to provide more drinking fountains, but its relations with the organized movement for drinking fountains were not entirely harmonious. The latter movement was launched by Mr. C. Melly of Liverpool, working through the Social Science Congress. It owed more to the sanitary reformers—to Lord John Russell, and the Earls of Carlisle and Shaftesbury—than to the temperance movement. 'W[h]ere the working man was given a chance of improvement he always availed himself of it,' said Shaftesbury at a drinking fountains meeting of 1859.[8] In 1860 Shaftesbury declared that if drinking fountains were established in the East End, 'water would carry the day over gin, beer, or any thing else of an intoxicating character'; yet the Alliance in the same year sneered at Hanbury's donations towards a Strand fountain as 'a slight attempt at atoning' for his connexion with fountains of another order. By 1872 the London association, with funds far smaller than those of the Alliance, had 300 drinking fountains to its credit.[9]

Important steps were taken to improve the quality and availability of milk in towns. 'Railway milk' began to oust the unsatisfactory milk provided in many urban dairies, and about 1870 Lawrence's cooler was widely adopted. The cattle plagues of the 1860s produced an improvement in London's delivery supplies from country areas, and by 1870 London's milk trade was organized almost as Charles Booth found it in the 1890s. Adulteration of milk was first made an offence in 1860, but responsibility for the offence was difficult to prove until compulsory medical inspection of wholesale and retail milk firms began in 1875. Although by 1870 London had eight private milk companies, the dietary value of milk was not yet widely recognized, and townsmen bought it less as a beverage in its own right than for making tea, coffee and milk puddings. *Per capita* consumption in Liverpool in the 1880s was still only a pint of milk per week, and in 1886 Londoners consumed only one-fifth of a pint per day. Real progress in getting milk accepted as a beverage was not made till the 1930s—with the spread of milk bars, the advertising campaigns of the Milk Marketing Board and state provision of cheap milk in schools. The government consolidated this change with its nutritional propaganda during the second world war.[10]

More important in promoting sobriety was the gradual development of non-intoxicating cordials. In 1847 the chemist Dr. Hooper of Hooper Struve established his London branch to develop the non-medicinal aspect of his soft drinks business. In the north of England during the 1840s ginger-beer and nettle-beer were very popular among working men, and by 1852 every public-house in the Staffordshire iron districts was selling cordials. In the late 1840s Mayhew estimated that London supported 1,200 street sellers of ginger-beer, sold at 1d. or ½d. a glass. Intoxicants were excluded from the Crystal Palace in 1851—1,092,337 bottles of Schweppes' soda-water, lemonade and ginger-beer being sold instead. The teetotalers deserve some credit for these developments: while Father Mathew was speaking in London in 1843, ginger-beer was being sold to his audiences at 1d. a bottle. Publicans found that they had to provide cordials if they were to retain their teetotal customers. Joseph Barker noted in 1861 how the teetotaler asking a publican for a non-intoxicating drink was now received quite courteously whereas 20 years before he would have been insulted.[11]

Yet G. J. Holyoake felt that temperance reformers had not done enough to encourage the cordial trade: 'where is the Temperance Allsopp', he asked, 'who has made the pale ale of Adam an object of desire to distant lands?'[12] John Perry, a Yeovil reformed drunkard, blacksmith and temperance hotel keeper in the 1860s, fixed an automatic temperance bar in front of his hotel: passers-by could insert a penny for the non-intoxicating drinks automatically supplied. But Perry's conduct was rare enough to gain special mention in a book of temperance reminiscences. Holyoake's complaints were echoed by Robert Seager, who established several cordial shops in Ipswich but found his fellow temperance reformers disappointingly apathetic. Teetotalers were not inventive in developing palatable cordials: William Beckett experimented with them without much success, and Francis Beardsall's attempts to make unfermented wine from grapes and other fruits came to naught. Teetotal periodicals advertised 'temperance beverages', which usually took the form of fruit essences to be diluted in water, but no temperance reformer manufactured cordials on a large scale.[13] The temperance movement never showed the anti-slave trade movement's inventiveness in discovering alternative ways of satisfying the needs which fostered the abuse under attack.

In the 1890s Charles Booth noted that many London publicans sold ginger-beer, though admittedly their customers usually wanted it mixed with spirits.[14] Teetotalers usually suspected such enterprise: they wanted to keep their members out of the public-house altogether. They therefore accused the publicans of adulterating their cordials with alcohol, and once more lost sight of their main objective—the eradication of drunkenness—in their sectarian pursuit of consistency.[15] There was a large market for cordials, if only some temperance reformer with initiative had taken Holyoake's advice. In the hot summer of 1868, the *Standard* pined for the cheap cordials obtainable in continental cities: the only cordials available in London were the highly priced drinks sold without ice in the crowded public-houses. By the 1870s, however, the number of cordial manufacturers had begun to rise very quickly in relation to other occupations [see table 6]. Thus while Dorset county and Norwich city had only one and three ginger-beer and cordial manufacturers respectively in 1841, they had 28 and 24 respectively in 1881—an increase far greater than the expansion in the number of drinksellers.[16]

Temperance reformers were more active in popularizing hot non-intoxicating drinks. While the switch from beer to tea may have stemmed partly from the lack of resources in the early nineteenth century, its continued popularity in the 1860s can be explained only by a change in taste. 'Every poor family is becoming a tea drinker two or three times a day,' wrote Cobden in 1864; chancellors of the exchequer were beginning to welcome the development in their budget speeches.[17] Three factors prompted the striking increase in *per capita* tea consumption after the 1840s [see Figure 2]: firstly, a steady tax reduction after the Napoleonic Wars. By the 1840s the temperance motive for reducing the tea duties was beginning to carry weight.[18] Together with an increased spirit duty, reduction of the tea duty was a leading fiscal objective of that vigorous counter-attractionist W. E. Gladstone, who completed the process with his reductions during the 1860s. From 1815 to 1900 there was an even sharper reduction in the selling-price of tea. John Horniman began the sale of packet teas in 1826 and John Cassell, the pioneer teetotal advocate, vigorously promoted cheap teas in the 1840s. Eighteenth-century Quakers—notably the Barclays, Whitbreads and Lucases—were prominent for manufacturing beer, the eighteenth-century temperance drink; likewise nineteenth-century Quakers—Tuke, Mennell and Horniman—were prominent in distributing tea, the nineteenth-century temperance drink. The first tea samples were sent home from India in 1838 and the Assam Tea Company was founded in the following year: thereafter, a gradual switch in taste took place from Chinese to Indian tea. By the 1840s, there was little difference in price between a cup of tea at 2d. and a pot of beer at 3d.[19]

One further encouragement to tea consumption was teetotal propaganda, which helped to discredit the belief that tea harmed the nerves and digestion—or at least helped to neutralize such fears by emphasizing alcohol's disruptive effects on the digestion. The religious tea-meeting seems to have been held in Warminster at least as early as 1815, but the daily Quaker 'tea-drinking' was still unfamiliar to J. J. Gurney in 1832, and teetotalers undoubtedly helped to popularize the use of tea at social gatherings in the 1830s. The Tradestown Temperance Society, anxious to supersede the drunken dinner-party, claimed to have invented the *soirée* in 1830. The word had in fact been used at least since 1820, but teetotalers certainly popularized such gatherings.[20] The idea of associating tea-drinking with these events at first seemed absurd; it was greatly popularized by the Preston teetotalers, whose periodicals enthused about the steaming urns to be seen on such occasions.[21] The idea of 'tea' as an afternoon social occasion gradually spread through English society during the 1840s, but the tea-drinking was a predominantly dissenting social function; Anglicans continued to entertain mainly through dinners.[22]

Until the late 1840s the *per capita* coffee consumption continued to rise. By 1841, London boasted 1,600–1,800 coffee-shops for all classes including the poorest working men. These provided coffee at 1d. to 3d. a cup; Mr. Pamphilon in 1840 was selling coffee at 1½d. a cup to 1,500–1,600 working men a day in St. Giles. The nineteenth-century coffee-house appealed to a much lower social class than its eighteenth-century predecessor, whose customers had now migrated to the club. In 1849 Lovett attributed the great reduction in drunkenness he had observed in the previous 28 years primarily to the increase in the number of coffee-houses and reading rooms.[23] By the 1850s, however, coffee was rapidly succumbing in popularity to tea. *Per capita* cocoa consumption, on the other hand, was rapidly increasing by 1842, though it usually cost 4d. a cup and was consumed only in the best class of coffee-house. It was much advertised in teetotal periodicals and was manufactured by several Quaker temperance reformers—notably by the Cadburys, Frys and Rowntrees. After the Cadbury innovations of the 1860s, its consumption increased even more quickly than that of tea.[24]

In establishing eating- and drinking-places outside the public-house, temperance enthusiasm combined with commercial enterprise. Temperance societies, in order to preserve their membership, had from the first promoted temperance hotels. But Holyoake complained of their bad management and called them 'penal settlements of teetotalism'; genuine temperance reformers, he said, would surely have formed an association of such hotels, with recognized standards and an annual conference.[25] His complaints were echoed within the temperance movement itself, yet they cannot be uncritically accepted. Many temperance hotels were speculative ventures unconnected with local temperance societies; indeed, their gambling and disorderly practices often caused teetotal societies to boycott them.[26] Some brothels called themselves 'temperance hotels' in order to calm suspicions. Again, temperance hotels were handicapped in competing with the public-house; their philanthropic origins hindered them from offering many public-house political and recreational attractions. Innkeepers could rely on the substantial profits made from selling intoxicants, whereas temperance hotelkeepers had no such resource and depended on a limited clientèle. Hence the drabness of many temperance hotels. A few succeeded, especially in Scotland. Thomas Lamb, a Dundee grocer and teetotaler, ran refreshment rooms which eventually grew into a successful commercial temperance hotel built in 1851. This was one of the first in Scotland—the previous temperance hotels in Edinburgh being intended mainly for tourists. Lamb was so successful that further extensions were made in 1868 and 1872.[27]

Temperance reformers were more successful in providing eating-houses outside the public-house, and were soon able to abandon the field to commercial firms. Pamphilon was supplying cold meats and coffee to about a hundred mid-day customers in 1840, and other London coffee-house keepers provided bread and small snacks. But the idea of providing 'public houses' to sell coffee and snacks to working men originated with philanthropists in Dundee in 1853. This movement soon spread to Glasgow and Manchester, and by 1863 was spreading to London [cf. Plate 22]. By the 1860s the growth of working-class suburbs had created an urgent need in towns for working men's restaurants. Instead of carrying their lunch to work and eating it in a public-house, working men began to buy hot meals at mid-day. The first

'British Workman Public House' was launched at Leeds in 1867, and similar establishments had begun to supply cheap meals in Liverpool and Manchester. In Liverpool in 1875, after the visit of Sankey and Moody, it was decided to run these companies on commercial lines. The publicans did not always welcome such changes. Layard, as commissioner of works in the 1860s, tried to start up a dining place in Victoria Park; he aimed to imitate continental parks by providing beer and a cheap meal for working men, but the publicans would have none of it.

Coffee- and eating-houses sprang up everywhere at this time [see table 6]. Whereas in 1841 only two coffee- and eating-houses are recorded in Norwich and two in County Durham, by 1881 these figures had leapt to 25 and 104. This new demand elevated John Pearce from his costermonger's barrow—the 'Gutter Hotel'—to management of Pearce's Dining and Refreshment Rooms, 52 of which by 1898 were supplying 70,000 meals a day and drawing an average of seven farthings from each customer. Commerce and philanthropy also combined in the coffee-house movement of the 1870s.[28] The early temperance movement wanted working men to spend their leisure-time at home. Coffee shops were therefore discouraged almost as firmly as liquor shops.[29] Temperance reformers cannot therefore take credit for the spread of the coffee shop until they began to patronize the coffee-house movement in the 1870s. The first coffee palace—the Limehouse 'Edinburgh Castle' [see Plate 22]—was opened in London in 1873 by Dr. Barnardo. Coffee-houses were established all over the country, sometimes under aristocratic patronage and often in connexion with the two teetotal organizations most sympathetic towards counter-attractions after the 1860s—the Church of England Temperance Society and the National Temperance League. Philanthropic coffee-stalls were provided by the Church of England Temperance Society in the 1870s and the temperance movement also gave negative assistance in the 1860s by getting public-houses closed at night: for this created a need filled by a host of all-night coffee-stalls.[30] Much still remained to be done. The *Weekly Times* on 23 April 1871 complained that England had no first-rate café with music on the continental model; these have become common only since the second world war.

By the 1870s the restorative functions of alcohol had also been challenged—from two directions: partly by the improvement in working conditions which made restoratives less necessary, and partly by medical opinion which was turning against alcoholic prescription. Of the two great provocations to drunkenness—excessive work-strain and involuntary idleness—only the first had been resolutely tackled by the 1870s. Not only did the factory, in which an increasing proportion of the population was employed, make smaller demands on the physique and provide some shelter from the weather: it also eventually reduced working hours. Factory reformers saw their Ten Hours Bill as a temperance measure; for O'Connor, the Bill was 'if not a total abstinence, at least a national temperance enactment'. Without time for education, morality could hardly be fostered in the employee: 'can we teach the grounds or uses of the moral law without time?' asked Parson Bull. Several temperance reformers were active in the factory movement, which drew its most ardent supporters from the more educated working men eager to elevate their class. The Preston teetotalers Thomas Swindlehurst and Joseph Livesey both spoke at the factory hours meeting at Preston in 1835.[31] A similar desire to promote moral and intellectual self-improvement helped to create the early closing movement of the 1840s, which attacked the long hours worked by shop-assistants. By this time banks and merchants were beginning to close earlier in the day.

Little had been done by the 1870s to curb involuntary leisure. It was one of the tragedies of nineteenth-century England's looking-glass world that while some working men were grossly overworked, others were over-supplied with leisure. The under-employed included the poor who could not get work and the rich who did not seek it, and drink had its attractions for both. Even today the under-employed middle-class housewife is more likely than fully employed members of society to become an alcoholic; frequent were the nineteenth-century tales of concealed intemperance above stairs. Nor had any means been found of curbing those 'fatal fluctuations' in the economy which Ernest Jones considered 'ruinous to the moral character of a man'.[32] These continued to foster drunkenness till well into the twentieth century.

Irregular living accompanies irregular wages and irregular holidays; but if little had been achieved for the unemployed, the habits of the employed were becoming more regular with the standardization of holidays. Temperance reformers encouraged the general contemporary trend towards substituting the Saturday half-holiday for 'Saint Monday'. The factory economy required the simultaneous presence of large numbers of employees; it was worth granting a Saturday half-holiday if Monday's working hours could thereby be preserved. The Saturday half-holiday gradually spread southwards after the 1840s. In one Birmingham brassfounding factory in 1851, where there were many teetotalers, drunkenness was confined to the older hands, and Monday's absentee returned on Tuesday 'amidst the ridicule and hootings of his comrades'. In 1877 J. W. Pease still found that the largest percentage of accidents in his mines occurred on Mondays and Tuesdays, when many employees were recovering from their weekend drinking-bouts. St. Monday persisted longest among the craft trades: 'in many of our working communities. . . . men rarely go back to work until Tuesday morning', said one M.P. in 1883. The progress made by the 1870s should not therefore be exaggerated: St. Monday was still being observed in 1912.[33]

As for seasonal holidays, the temperance movement attacked the random spree which served as a substitute for a holiday in the lives of many working men. And by curbing drunkenness at Easter and Whitsun, it helped to prevent voluntary extension of recognized holidays. The nineteenth century also saw the gradual extension of the official holiday. Lord John Manners in 1842 claimed that men working sixty hours a week needed better relaxation than courses in astronomy or geology; if Englishmen misused their leisure, this was because overwork incapacitated them for it. Manners cast a wistful eye at continental habits and attacked English puritanism. Yet although praised by Ashley, his plea had no legislative result. Furthermore factory legislation, though it reduced continuous labour in one direction, increased it in another by standardizing the hours of work, and thus curtailing the customary holidays of certain privileged industrial groups.[34]

In the late-Victorian period the introduction of the summer holiday improved the situation. Parliament in 1871 launched the August bank holiday —an instant success: 'how much such a day of relaxation was needed, its universal acceptance proves', wrote the *Daily News* on the holiday's second birthday.[35] Like the Saturday half-holiday, the paid summer holiday seems to have originated in the north of England. Henry Ashworth the Bolton cotton-spinner allowed his workers holidays of this kind in the 1840s, but they did not become widespread till the 1880s. In the short run there were many complaints that such holidays promoted drunkenness, but in the long run they could only promote sobriety.[36] Temperance reformers played little part in these developments; but in altering attitudes to leisure, in accentuating the distinction between work and play, and in upholding Wilberforce's notion that recreation is 'intended . . . to restore us, with renewed vigour, to the more serious occupations of life',[37] they were more prominent. Significantly, one of the articles most often purchased by reformed drunkards and most often presented as a testimonial to the temperance orator was a watch: the contest between the temperance reformer and the publican was a contest between two attitudes to time.

Teetotalers helped to discredit the use of alcohol as a restorative; the ancient belief in the strengthening qualities of intoxicants helped to align many statesmen against their movement. Bright, Bradlaugh and Thomas Cooper all broke their teetotal pledges for medical reasons. Doctors—still regarded by the well-to-do as servants rather than as consultants—found it difficult to curb their patients' desire for alcoholic prescriptions. Individualism at this time extended even to medical diagnosis; it was widely held that each patient had his own peculiar constitution with which the doctor must acquaint himself. Remedies which might cure some might not suit others. 'Each man should be governed by the needs of his own health and the dictates of his own conscience,' said Harcourt, rebutting temperance arguments at Oxford in 1868.[38] So unscientific an approach provided many openings for alcoholic prescription, which was a central feature in the medical system evolved by an Edinburgh teacher John Brown, and replaced bloodletting as a cure-all in the

1830s. Influenced by Baron Liebig's theory that alcohol produced heat, Dr. Todd revived the system in the 1850s to a degree which justifies Dr. B. W. Richardson's belief that Todd was a man who 'having once made up his mind to a course, was most determined in that which he set his hand to': for Charles Hindley, M.P. for Ashton, Todd prescribed six pints of brandy in 72 hours. F. W. Newman even hinted that the Prince Consort might well have survived, had he not been subjected to similar treatment.[39]

Teetotalers actively combated such notions: 'many people complain of their stomachs', wrote the pioneer teetotaler Robert Kettle: 'but if the truth were known, their stomachs have more reason to complain of them.' Teetotalism undoubtedly relieved many individuals who had mistakenly resorted to large doses of alcohol in the hope that it would cure them.[40] But doctors resented amateur interference from teetotalers as much as they resented it from the Board of Health.[41] Their suspicion is understandable, for they were still fighting a running battle with folk-medicine. Temperance doctors were severely persecuted in their profession; Higginbottom of Nottingham and Batchelor of Luton were early martyrs in this cause.[42] Nevertheless a few doctors were prominent in the temperance movement. Dr. Beaumont was an early supporter in Bradford; Dr. Fothergill helped to found Darlington's moderation society; Dr. Mudge long remained a pillar of Cornish teetotalism; Dr. Syder was important for his medical lectures on alcohol in the 1840s, and in 1844 Grindrod began his successful 6½-year medical temperance mission—complete with lurid coloured slides portraying the effects of alcohol on the stomach. Teetotalers recognized the importance of attracting medical support, and as early as 1830 were collecting signatures for a medical temperance declaration. Further declarations—sponsored in 1836, 1839 and 1847—owed much to John Dunlop's energy. But these testimonies had little influence over M.P.s, if only because signatories did not always adopt teetotalism in their personal lives.[43]

By the 1870s alcoholic prescription had been effectively challenged. This was partly owing to experiments made outside the temperance movement but publicized by temperance reformers. In 1860 two Frenchmen—Messrs. Lallemand and Perrin—published research showing that alcohol was not broken down by the body to produce heat. In 1869 the National Temperance League founded the *Medical Temperance Journal*, edited by its secretary the young Baptist Scotsman Robert Rae. The National Temperance League also promoted conferences between temperance reformers and doctors in the 1860s; through Samuel Bowly the League taught Dr. B. W. Richardson, the leading opponent of alcoholic prescription in the 1870s, how best to win converts. F. R. Lees also contributed towards the change in medical fashion. Richardson later praised his writings, which used against alcoholic prescription arguments later taken up by doctors: 'the foundations of this particular question', said Richardson in 1881, 'were laid before I began to teach.'[44] The change was only gradual: Josephine Butler in the 1870s still depended on alcohol as a medicine, and in 1876 Sir William Gull was still prescribing port-wine for Disraeli's bronchitis, asthma and gout.[45] Though no important medical advance was pioneered directly by the temperance reformers, their failure to finance medical research stemmed as much from lack of resources as from lack of inclination. As soon as the movement gained support among the affluent in the 1870s, a temperance hospital was built in the Hampstead Road—the permanent buildings being complete by 1879.[46] The general public were very slow to accept attacks on alcohol from the doctors, let alone from teetotalers. A lively faith in the strengthening qualities of beer still persisted in rural areas at the end of the nineteenth century.[47]

Temperance reformers also challenged the widely-held belief that the fatness of the beer-drinker indicated his physical strength. Early nineteenth-century working people idealized the plump body and rubicund complexion of John Bull, tankard in hand. O'Connor's career showed that a public speaker of impressive physique carried weight with the masses. Although some seventeenth-century temperance tracts stressed that fatness signified physical weakness, the early teetotalers—several of whom happened to be physically unimpressive—found that their cause was greatly hindered by the 'fatness fallacy'. 'Show us a specimen like this with your water drinking' shouted a rowdy Lancaster audience, pushing a fat brewer before Joseph Livesey, lecturing on teetotalism there in 1834.[48] Teetotalers tackled this difficulty in two ways: as a concession to popular prejudice they paraded on their platforms robust teetotalers like John Hockings the teetotal blacksmith, Josiah Hunt the Almondsbury farmer and the obese 'Slender Billy' Howarth of Preston. But they argued elsewhere that while working men needed muscle, mere fatness was 'really troublesome, and far from being conducive to activity'. The lissom F. R. Lees even claimed that fatness was 'an indication of disease', and teetotalers later enlarged upon the slimness of teetotal athletes like W. G. Grace and Blondin.[49] Teetotalers correctly argued that alcohol fattens drinkers who do not cut down their food consumption. But alcohol actually emaciates the heavy drinker who 'drinks his meals', and who thus consumes insufficient minerals, proteins and vitamins.[50]

Teetotal attempts to alter the popular concept of the desirable physique coincided with the growth of athletic sports, which demanded exertion from human beings rather than from animals; they also coincided with industrialization, which often required quickness and alertness from its employees, rather than sheer physical strength, let alone fatness. The human economy, like the national economy, must now function with machine-like smoothness and rapidity. Joseph Barker noted in 1862 that teetotalism helped to standardize the human frame—adding weight to the thin and subtracting weight from the fat. By the 1860s corpulence seems to have markedly declined: Elihu Burritt in 1864 complained that the 'old-fashioned English farmer, of the great, round, purply-red face' was fast disappearing; the fat man, who had entered the nineteenth century as the embodiment of health, was rapidly approaching the figure of fun he has now become.[51]

The agricultural community was particularly slow to abandon its faith in the strengthening qualities of alcohol; nor did it welcome the gradual segregation, promoted by teetotalers, between recreational and economic activity. Part-payment in beer therefore remained prominent in the agricultural economy in the 1870s. The progressive Royston farmer Samuel Jonas was paying his men cash in lieu of beer in 1863 and Lord Shaftesbury forbade all truck payment to labourers on his estates in 1872;[52] but the many harvesting contests organized between teetotalers and drinkers [see Plate 23] had still not discredited harvest-beer as the best way to obtain hard work. An M.P. in 1862 could still defend it as the equivalent of the coal used to stoke up the engine; it was still being vigorously defended in parliament in the 1880s.[53]

By the 1870s politicians were less likely to fortify their oratory with alcohol. The change owed less to teetotal propaganda than to changes in the character of parliament. During the early nineteenth century, high-flown oratory went out of fashion and parliament became a far more businesslike, less histrionic body; M.P.s by the 1870s had become exponents of 'ginger beer and soda water oratory'. The association between drink and sociability persisted, though somewhat less obtrusively. By 1849 Lovett could claim that fines and footings in London workshops were 'now almost done away with'.[54] During the late 1830s at a shop meeting in one of the largest London printing offices, Robert Hartwell carried a resolution to place all proceeds from fines and footings in the Printers' Pension Society; most other London printing offices did likewise. Teetotal influence in trade union and religious circles certainly helped to produce this change. The unpretentious John Dunlop had difficulty in getting temperance orators to support his campaign against drinking customs: 'of constipated speech, he did not excel on the platform', wrote one of his colleagues, 'but in executive work, how wise and effective he was!' His relative lack of success highlights the dilemma inherent in nineteenth-century temperance agitation: effective reform could be achieved only through tedious and unexciting labour, whereas support for a reforming movement could be attracted only by extravagant claims and spectacular methods. A teetotal convert of Joseph Livesey who had more success in this sphere was Joseph Leicester, later radical M.P. for West Ham; he induced the Glassblowers' Union to abolish drink fines in 1859. The teetotal George Howell, however—working on a London building-site in 1855—still found that his stock rose markedly when he agreed to treat his fellow workmen.[55]

In the early 1860s, commercial travellers were abandoning their drinking usages, and by 1854 the abstinent Dunlop was no longer regarded as 'a teetotal Monster' at London dinner parties.[56] Although the efforts of individual teetotalers established a freedom to dissent from social customs, they were not directly responsible for the broader change, which merely substituted a smaller quantity of alcohol for a larger, a weaker drink for a stronger. With the growth of 'lunch' in the early nineteenth century and the postponement of dinner from 5 or 6 p.m. to 7 p.m. or later, white wine tended to be drunk with the meal and port was no longer consumed afterwards.[57] The change was promoted by Prince Albert in the 1840s, when he left the dining room fifteen minutes before the rest of the men and immediately joined the ladies. Disraeli detested after-dinner port-drinking, and the Prince of Wales continued his father's new custom. The change was also encouraged by the new habit, which few teetotalers approved, of after-dinner smoking. In 1851 G. R. Porter maintained that the revolution in upper class drinking habits since the late eighteenth century was 'one of the greatest, if indeed it be not the greatest, reformation that society has witnessed'. By the late nineteenth century, gout-rests had begun to disappear from the London clubs.[58]

By the 1870s alcohol was less freely used at religious festivals. It had not been banned from that most conservative of festivals—the funeral, for the teetotal funeral made very slow headway; but the related attack on funeral extravagance had begun by the 1870s. Burial clubs were discredited by Chadwick's revelations of the 1840s and by several murder cases; *The Times* and *Morning Chronicle* in 1849–50 attacked undertakers for extortion. But the conservatism of the poor was not easily overcome. Sunday mourners who stopped the returning funeral cortège at roadside public-houses were still arousing sabbatarian wrath in 1874; at the end of the century, Mrs. Bosanquet could still complain of widows who provided four horses and a carriage and pair for their husband's funeral, yet within a fortnight were begging the poor law guardians to feed their children.[59] But confirmations, communions and harvest-homes were celebrated far more soberly in the 1870s. Except among Primitive Methodists and some smaller sects, teetotal attempts to ban intoxicating wine from the communion service during the 1830s and 1840s usually failed; but Christians by the 1870s recognized the incongruity of drunkenness at religious festivals. During the 1850s Samuel Wilberforce reformed confirmation celebrations in his Oxford diocese, and several country parsons unconnected with the temperance movement reformed the harvest-home. Although after the 1830s temperance reformers promoted the teetotal harvest-home, their suggestions were not widely adopted until supplemented in the 1850s by the efforts of Lord Albemarle and R. S. Hawker. These changes sought to associate in recreation several groups who often took their enjoyments separately—employers and employees, upper and lower classes, wives and husbands. Though there was opposition from publicans and conservative labourers, the reformed harvest-home gradually became popular.[60]

Between the 1820s and the 1870s bishops tried to promote sobriety among their clergy; like the police constable, the clergyman was increasingly expected to shun the drinking place. Bishop Stanley in the 1840s tried in vain to alter the port-drinking habits of his clerical guests, and Bishop Blomfield reaped unpopularity for trying to eliminate clerical intemperance. But after 1845 Samuel Wilberforce succeeded in keeping his ordination candidates from lodging in Oxford inns. Many nonconformist ministers, like Joseph Barker in the 1830s, tried to put themselves 'above the reach of suspicion' by taking the teetotal pledge.[61] Through the League of the Cross, Manning later struggled to create a Catholic '*clero colto e civile*'. By the 1850s the easy-going familiarity between the parson and the casual drinker was disappearing everywhere except in the remoter parts—a situation wholly unprecedented in England and not paralleled on the continent. Although as late as 1869 clergy in the Carlisle diocese were still eking out their slender income by selling ale on Sundays, rare was the clergyman who—like Edward Monro—acquired popularity among local navvies by drinking beer with them.[62] Like the Northamptonshire vicar who defended hunting parsons against Samuel Wilberforce's onslaughts, opponents of the change argued that these reforms nourished 'that most mischievous and deadly error, that there are two sorts of Christianity, one for the clergy, and another for the laity'.[63]

One denomination resisted teetotal pressures: the Wesleyans. Teetotalers in 1846 tried to embarrass the denomination by noting that its centenary hall was built over a wine-vault. In Banbury in 1855 the Wesleyan circuit-steward was a brewer-founder of Hunt and Edmunds brewery; in Castle Donington in the 1860s, the Wesleyan Sunday school superintendent and circuit-steward was an ale and porter merchant; and in Newcastle-Under-Lyme in the 1870s the champion of the drink interest on the local council was Samuel Hyslop, the Wesleyan Liberal. The Wesleyans were among the last to form their own denominational temperance society. Nor were other nonconformist denominations ever united in support of teetotalism; the early Victorian Baptists in Banbury, for instance, depended heavily on the generosity of Austin's brewery. Most nonconformist ministers at this time inevitably deferred to their wealthier laymen, who were frequently publicans or brewers.[64]

In the spheres of thirst-quenching, relief of work-strain, medical diagnosis, sociability and religious festivity therefore—the role of alcoholic drink in English society had been challenged by the 1870s; how far had all these changes affected the level of drink consumption and drunkenness? Several sets of figures deserve investigation. Table 6 shows that the gross increase between 1841 and 1891 in the numbers manufacturing or retailing intoxicating drinks is not very much smaller than for other types of retailer or for the population as a whole. But the increase in the number of drink retailers and manufacturers occurs only between 1841 and 1871; thereafter numbers stagnate or even decline, whereas the figures for total population, for tailors and for the three food-retailing occupations (rivals for the working man's resources) steadily rise throughout the period. It is perhaps worth stressing that in a period when the *per capita* food intake rises more rapidly than the *per capita* consumption of intoxicants, drunkenness may well decline at the same time as drink consumption increases. In the temperance movement's first forty years therefore, the drink interest's supremacy had been challenged but by no means overthrown; indeed, these years saw the creation of a new type of drinkshop—the beerhouse—of which there were 50,000 by the 1860s. Yet the threat to the drink trade was mounting steadily: throughout the period the increase in the number of mineral-water manufacturers and coffee- and eating-house keepers proceeded continuously and far more rapidly than with any of the other occupations analysed.

A similar picture emerges from comparing occupations listed in local trade

TABLE 6

Numbers Occupied in the Drink Trade as Compared with Numbers Engaged in Other Occupations: 1841–1891. Both Sexes, All Ages, England and Wales

	1841	1851	1861	1871	1881	1891
TOTAL POPULATION (thousands)	15,914	17,928	20,066	22,712	25,974	29,003
Bakers	37,143	51,738	54,140	59,066	71,032	84,158
Butchers	44,938	62,185	68,114	75,847	81,702	98,921
Greengrocers/Fruiterers	7,908	13,418	18,045	25,819	29,614	40,963
Tailors	108,945	132,715	136,390	149,864	160,648	208,720
Shoemakers	187,943	240,252	250,581	223,365	216,556	248,789
Eating-house keepers & coffee-house keepers	1,542	?	3,955	5,452	8,173	11,535
Mineral-water manufacturers	541	?	1,360	2,555	4,662	6,691
Innkeepers/Publicans & hotelkeepers	53,246	?	66,260	77,049	70,106	78,013
Beersellers	5,629	?	15,767	16,361	16,583	17,606
Wine/spirit merchants	3,494	6,905	7,810	10,969	7,889	7,883
Brewers	9,357	?	20,352	25,831	24,567	26,312
Maltsters	7,965	?	10,677	10,356	9,531	9,088

NOTE: These census figures probably understate the extent of the relative decline in the drink trade. G. B. Wilson, basing his figures on licence-returns, records 38,799 beer-houses in 1841: 45,749 in 1871: and 43,976 in 1891; 44,218 brewers in 1841: 31,562 in 1871: and 10,477 in 1891; 9,243 maltsters in 1841 and 4,738 in 1871. According to his figures, the number of brewers was stagnating after the 1830s and by the 1850s was sharply declining; his figures also place the beginning of the decline in the number of maltsters at the late 1830s. See his *Alcohol & the Nation* (1940), pp. 386–8, 395–6. The decline in the number of brewers of course masks an increase in the scale and efficiency of remaining breweries.

SOURCE: *Parliamentary Papers* 1844 (587) XXVII, pp. 356ff.; 1852–3 (1691–I) LXXXVIII Part I, pp. ccxxiiff.; 1863 (3221) LIII Part I, pp. 295ff.; 1873 (872–I) LXXI Part II, pp. 81ff.; 1883 (C. 3722) LXXX pp. xviiiff.; 1893–4 (C. 7058) CVI, pp. xxviff.

directories at the beginning and end of the period; the percentage of local traders occupied in distributing intoxicating drink fell markedly in only three of five selected towns—Northampton, Whitby, Preston, Ripon and Banbury—between the 1820s and the 1870s: in Northampton from 18·1% to 13·8%, in Whitby from 12·3% to 8·0% and in Preston from 18·9% to 16·0%. In England and Wales the number of persons per on-licence rose slightly between the 1820s and the 1870s, but here too the really rapid decline came after 1871.*

TABLE 7

Persons per On-licence in England and Wales: 1831–1966

YEAR	TOTAL LICENCES	PERSONS PER ON-LICENCE
1831	82,484	168
1841	91,612	174
1851	95,484	188
1861	107,696	186
1871	112,884	201
1881	106,910	243
1891	105,006	276
1901	102,848	316
1911	90,586	398
1921	82,411	458
1931	77,049	517
1941	73,210	571
1951	73,421	595
1961	68,936	668
1966	75,544	636

SOURCE: G. B. Wilson, *op. cit.* p. 236; *Annual Abstract of Statistics.*

What do the consumption figures reveal? Joseph Livesey himself recognized that these were embarrassing to the temperance movement: 'when we apply to the true test', he wrote, '—the quantity of liquor consumed and the number of places that sell it—we find the facts are against us'.[65] Comparing the two five-year periods 1825–9 and 1865–9 for wine and spirits, and the years 1830–4 and 1865–9 for beer, it can be seen that *per capita* wine and beer consumption rose, and *per capita* spirits consumption fell [see Figures 3 and 5]. The mid-Victorian *per capita* rise in alcohol consumption, which for beer began in the

* Because so much liquor flowed through illicit channels in the early nineteenth century, the figures for the first half of the century considerably understate the number of drink facilities which actually existed. These statistics do not take account of the clubs so important in later years; nor can they allow for changes in the average accommodation offered by drinking places. Yet despite these imperfections, the figures are impressive enough as an indication of the contrast between the mid-Victorian and the modern situation.

1850s, for wine in the early 1860s and for spirits in the late 1860s, did not tail off till the late 1870s. *Per capita* consumption of spirits, beer and wine was still fluctuating with the business-cycle in the early twentieth century—the peak of consumption usually coming a year after the peak in business prosperity. As Sir William Beveridge put it in 1912, 'prosperity leads to riotous living'. A really striking and permanent decline in the level of drunkenness and of consumption set in only between the two world wars.[66]

All these figures must be interpreted cautiously. Fluctuations in the number of on-licences per head in these years indicate licensing policy rather than the

FIG. 13

Number of detections concerned with illicit distillation in England, Scotland and Wales: 1830–1880

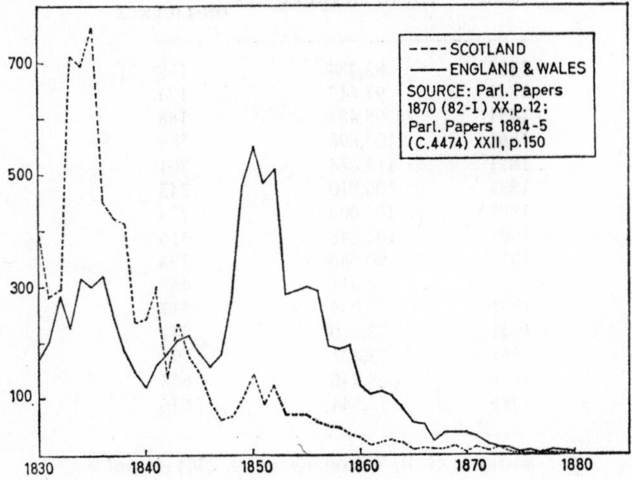

level of drunkenness; nor do *per capita* consumption figures necessarily indicate the incidence of drunkenness. Official consumption figures are marred by the decline in home-brewing, illicit distilling and smuggling during the period [see Figure 13]. To complicate matters still further, tastes were changing in the strength of the drinks consumed. Bass's brewery increased production sixfold between 1831 and 1847—an index of the swing from porter to light Burton beers.[67] The *Bee-Hive* on 10 June 1871 felt that M. T. Bass had 'probably done as much to promote a genuine temperance as the societies called by that name have done'. Among London working men by the 1890s porter had been replaced by the weaker 'fourpenny ale'.[68]

One might at first expect that figures for drunkenness arrests would indicate the relative prevalence of drunkenness. These figures certainly indicate the scale of the drink problem in the mid-Victorian period. The annual absolute total of such arrests in London during the 1860s never fell below 17,000 and during the early 1870s this total crept up to 30,000. The total number of summarily determined cases of drunkenness and of drunken and disorderly behaviour in England and Wales increased threefold between 1857 and 1876—from 75,859 to 205,567; the total of such offences was increasing much faster than the total for all other offences determined summarily, which rose in the same period from 293,374 to only 456,046. Taking four sample years—1860, 1864, 1870, 1876—we find that in each year the number of 'drunkenness/drunk and disorderly' offences determined summarily is far larger than the total number of indictable offences and far larger than any other category of offence determined summarily—even excluding the common assaults, for which drunkenness must often have been responsible. In 1870, for example, there were 51,972 indictable offences and 526,869 offences determined summarily; of the latter, no less than 131,870 were drunkenness or 'drunk and disorderly' offences, as compared with 74,985 common assaults, 12,704 game law offences, 44,757 cases of theft or attempted theft, and 35,681 offences against local acts and bye-laws.

Although arrest statistics strikingly reveal the scale of the mid-Victorian drink problem, two considerations make it doubtful whether they reliably indicate changing levels of drunkenness, still less of drink consumption. In the London arrest figures, there are sharp fluctuations from year to year, reflecting changes in administrative areas and in enforcement policy. And if drunkenness proceedings are related to total population in several localities, striking contrasts will be found from area to area. When the counties of England and Wales are grouped into twelve areas, the number of proceedings per 10,000 population in 1871 varies strikingly—from 17 in non-metropolitan Kent/Hertfordshire/Essex/Surrey, to 154 in Cheshire/Lancashire. Could the drinking habits of the two areas really have contrasted as markedly as this? In all twelve areas, the ratio of proceedings to population increased between 1861 and 1871—in some areas the increase was striking, from 50 to 88 in Cumberland/Durham/Northumberland/Westmorland, for instance, and from 93 to 154 in Cheshire/Lancashire.[69] Variations were equally striking as between different towns; in 1870 for instance, there were 21,113 drunkenness/drunk and disorderly offences determined summarily in Liverpool and 11,083 in Manchester, but only 2,244 in Birmingham.[70] An investigation of the figures for 1891 shows that the rate of proceedings per 10,000 population varied between different categories of town; the rate was far higher in seaports and mining counties than in London or manufacturing counties, whereas agricultural counties, the home counties and pleasure towns registered the lowest rate of all.[71] The impressive rise in the number of drunkenness proceedings between 1857 and 1876 is at least as likely to stem from increasing concern at the seriousness of the drink problem in those years as from any actual increase in consumption. But in so far as the statistical evidence proves anything, it casts doubt on the notion that the temperance movement by the

1870s had made any appreciable impact on drink consumption and drunkenness.

Literary evidence and statistics for the consumption of non-intoxicating drinks show that by the 1870s there were at least signs of change. H. A. Bruce in 1872 was convinced that improvement was taking place, even though a glance at the statistics was 'by no means reassuring'. There were many testimonies to the increased sobriety of the well-to-do. 'It is a mark now that a man is not a gentleman if he gets drunk,' said Roebuck in 1856; similar assertions were often made about the increased sobriety at lower social levels. How far this general change was due to the temperance movement is a matter for argument, and is not susceptible to statistical proof; the influence of the temperance movement on pledged teetotalers must, however, have been considerable. Statistics for the number of teetotalers between the 1830s and the 1870s are unfortunately almost as difficult to obtain as statistics for the incidence of drunkenness. The number of reformed drunkards who can be credited to the movement is very small. Even at the peak of the campaign for personal reclamation in the 1840s, and relying on temperance sources which, if anything, exaggerate the movement's achievements—the largest proportion of reformed drunkards to ordinary members seems to have been no more than one in ten.[72]

As for the total number of teetotalers in the country, several estimates were made in the 1840s. The National Temperance Society, one of the three leading English temperance organizations, listed a membership of 52,241 in 1849. In 1856 it found that the 80 societies responding to its questionnaire claimed 33,357 pledged members.[73] The Society was based on the south of England, and its membership was far smaller than the total number of teetotalers in England and Wales. The *British Temperance Advocate* on 15 August 1841 claimed, without supporting evidence, that there were four million teetotalers in the United Kingdom. Certainly Father Mathew was making Irish recruits in hundreds of thousands at the time; but many of these recruits soon lapsed, and the National Temperance Society in 1844 mentioned a figure of only 1,000,000. Peter Burne's *Teetotaler's Companion* in 1847 and Cook's *National Temperance Magazine* in 1844 hazarded 1,200,000. This estimate was based on the fact that returns of teetotal membership from places with a population of 1,830,877 produced 96,034 teetotalers. Assuming that this proportion typified the national situation, an estimate could thus be made of national strength.[74] In some areas the proportion of teetotalers to total population was quite high. In Preston in 1835 there were 2,000 teetotalers in a population of over 40,000; in Middlesbrough in 1851 there were 1,214 teetotalers of all sexes and ages in a population of 7,000; and teetotalers accounted for one in five of Frome's population in the 1860s.[75]

What of the hard core of active and comparatively wealthy teetotalers—who contributed to temperance society funds or who read teetotal periodicals? In the financial year 1861–2 only 979 individuals in England and Wales contributed to National Temperance League funds. In the financial year 1859–60 the United Kingdom Alliance, whose subscribers were not necessarily teetotalers, counted 1,100 donors in England and Wales; by 1873–4 this figure had risen to 4,796. Many teetotalers contributed only locally, and do not feature at all in these national lists; many did not make any contribution. The Alliance in 1861 claimed to have issued 58,000 membership enrolment cards to individual members, and to be linked with over 1,000 temperance societies and auxiliaries. The Temperance Permanent Provident Institution at this time enjoyed an annual income of £114,000 and the Temperance Permanent Building Society £77,000; but as late as 1870 the Rechabite teetotal friendly society had an adult membership of only 15,402.[76]

Another way of assessing teetotal numbers is through the circulation of teetotal periodicals. On 15 November 1843 the monthly *National Temperance Advocate*, one of the leading temperance periodicals, claimed a circulation of 9,500 per number, of which about 4,000 copies were distributed free. By 1858 the temperance movement was producing two quarterly reviews, four weeklies and about six monthly papers, though some of these enjoyed only a small circulation.[77] The *Alliance Weekly News* in 1859 enjoyed a circulation of 14,000–15,000, but much of this—as with most teetotal periodicals—was absorbed by free distribution. In 1861 William Tweedie the temperance publisher told Baines that in 1860–1 there were 13 large temperance associations in the kingdom, employing 40 paid lecturers, and enjoying a united income of £22,000 annually; there were three weekly newspapers with a united circulation of 25,000, six monthly magazines with a united circulation of over 20,000 and two quarterly reviews with a joint circulation of about 10,000; and in addition there were two periodicals for young abstainers—the Scottish *Adviser* (over 50,000) and the *Band of Hope Review* (over 250,000). On this basis, Tweedie estimated that in the United Kingdom there were 3,000,000 teetotalers of all ages, three-quarters of whom did not belong to teetotal societies. Newman Hall thought this an exaggeration: 2,000,000 was his estimate. T. H. Barker's 1861 estimate was also more cautious. Excluding child teetotalers in the Band of Hope, he felt that England and Wales could hardly contain less than 900,000 adult abstainers. Many of these were influential—they included the 3,000 clergy who signed the ministerial declaration and at least some of the 2,000 doctors who signed the medical certificate.[78]

The general impression conveyed is that by the 1860s there existed an influential and literate minority in the country of 'opinion makers', numbering well under 100,000 teetotalers. The efforts of this minority affected the personal habits of at least a million adult teetotalers; they probably influenced the conduct of many others who did not join teetotal organizations. The turnover rate of temperance societies, as of the British Communist Party between the wars, was very high: it would be unwise to estimate the influence of either organization simply from its membership at any one moment in time.[79] Many

Englishmen were influenced by the cult of respectability even though they never joined the formal organizations of the respectable. There were, in addition, several hundred thousand child teetotalers in the Band of Hope. Yet drunkenness was still rampant after thirty years of teetotal advocacy, still a flagrant social evil; teetotal membership was geographically patchy and was more common among dissenters than among other religious groups, more common among religious groups than among those who were apathetic towards religion. The movement had insulated an élite from temptation: it had produced no nation-wide temperance 'reformation'.

15

The Drink Trade and English Society in the 1870s

Any attempt to assess the power of drink in English society must consider not only attitudes to drink itself but also the social influence of drinksellers and drink manufacturers. For the drinkseller's social roles might well multiply and the drink manufacturer's social influence might well grow—at a time when drink consumption was actually declining. Bearing in mind once again the importance of the counter-attractionists, changes in the drinkseller's social role will first be considered: in his roles as recreation-provider and as provider of the community meeting-place. Then changes in the social, political and economic power of the organized 'drink interest' will be analysed.

Between the 1820s and the 1870s the drinkseller's recreational role was strongly affected by changes in his clientèle. Class segregation in drinking habits continued apace in this period; respectable individuals tended increasingly to drink in private. 'In this country', said G. R. Porter in 1852, 'no person, above the rank of a labouring man or artisan, would venture to go into a public-house to purchase anything to drink.' This change in manners is reflected in the public schools' battle against drunkenness: in Hawtrey's battle against 'the Christopher' at Eton, in Vaughan's speech-room oration against drunkenness at Harrow—the first blow against drunkenness there, and in Kennedy's insistence that his boys should preserve their social status by wearing mortar-boards and by shunning local taverns. Within the public school, education aimed increasingly at inculcating sobriety. Though Lord Salisbury might argue as late as 1886 that beer had done him no harm after a day's rowing at Eton, few public schools at that time still favoured beer as a beverage; for the athletic exercise increasingly popular in late-Victorian public schools was not compatible with drinking. But if the drink-seller was losing his more respectable customers he retained, and with the decline of home-brewing even extended, his lower class custom.[1]

Two influences which had fostered drunkenness in the 1820s were under attack by the 1870s: bad housing and traditional leisure patterns. The home could never become a recreational centre without improving its quality and altering popular attitudes to it. Middle-class homes had already begun to improve spontaneously. In 1851 G. R. Porter recalled that fifty years before, even prosperous shopkeepers in the leading London streets lacked carpets in their sitting rooms.[2] The early Victorian campaign to improve working-class housing went through three phases: it began in the 1840s with voluntary effort. The Society for Improving the Condition of the Labouring Classes carried out the first modest scheme for improved dwellings at Pentonville in 1844. The first block of working-class flats was built at Birkenhead in 1845. The same year saw the incorporation of the profit-making Metropolitan Association for Improving the Dwellings of the Industrious Classes, founded in 1842; it built the first block of working-class flats in London in 1848. Some artisans' model dwellings featured in the 1851 exhibition and several landowners built model cottages for their agricultural labourers.

During the 1850s voluntary effort languished, and legislation came to the fore. Shaftesbury's permissive Labouring Classes Lodging-Houses Act (1851) enabled districts with not less than 10,000 inhabitants to supply working people with better lodgings either by building new houses or by adapting old ones. This Act seems to have been applied only in Huddersfield, but more successful was Shaftesbury's compulsory Act for regulating common lodging-houses (1851): it insisted on minimum standards of cleanliness and ventilation. The repeal of the taxes on bricks and windows helped to cheapen homebuilding, and the Labourers' Dwellings Act of 1855 made it easier for local joint-stock associations to build working-class housing. The Torrens Act of 1855 and other sanitary reforms gave the authorities power over owners of insanitary houses. The third phase of working-class housing reform was once more dominated by voluntary effort. It was in 1864 that Octavia Hill held her crucially important conversation with John Ruskin. Before 1869 she had demonstrated the feasibility of good landlordism in Paradise Place and Freshwater Place. Alderman Sir Sydney Waterlow built his first working-class flats at Finsbury in 1863, and became chairman of the Improved Industrial Dwellings Company; by 1875 it had housed 1,433 families. The Peabody Trust Estates built their first block in Whitechapel in 1864 and by 1874 had housed 3,815 people. In 1867 the Artisans', Labourers' and General Dwellings Company was founded; it built its first estate, Shaftesbury Park, in the early 1870s. But all these schemes were modest. And because they were profit-making, they could never cater for those working men who most needed help. The only answer was municipal housing. The City of London built its Corporation Buildings in Farringdon Street in 1863, the first example of municipal working-class flats in London. But this was for a special purpose, and was not followed up on a large scale till the L.C.C. began building council houses in the 1890s.[3]

How much did temperance reformers contribute towards these develop-

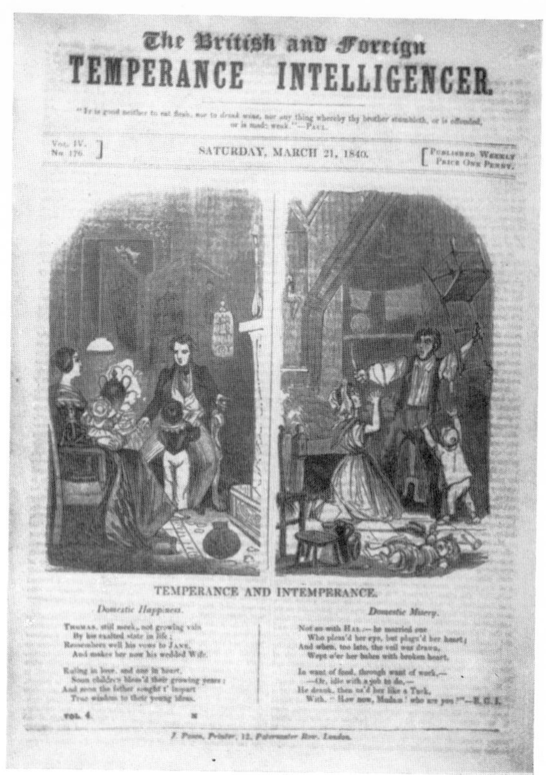

The British and Foreign
TEMPERANCE INTELLIGENCER.

"It is good neither to eat flesh, nor to drink wine, nor any thing whereby thy brother stumbleth, or is offended, or is made weak."—Paul.

Vol. IV. No 176. | SATURDAY, MARCH 21, 1840. | Published Weekly Price One Penny.

TEMPERANCE AND INTEMPERANCE.

Domestic Happiness.

Thomas, still meek, not growing vain
By his exalted state in life;
Remembers well his vows to Jane,
And makes her now his wedded Wife.

Ruling in love, and one in heart,
Soon children bless'd their growing years;
And soon the father sought t' impart
True wisdom to their young ideas.

Domestic Misery.

Not so with Hal,—he married one
Who pleas'd her eye, but plagu'd her heart;
And when, too late, the veil was drawn,
Wept o'er her babes with broken heart.

In want of food, through want of work,—
—Or, idle with a job to do,—
He drank, then us'd her like a Turk,
With, "How now, Madam! who are you?"—E.C.I.

VOL. 4. N

J. Pasco, Printer, 12, Paternoster Row, London.

24. Temperance and intemperance at home. *British & Foreign Temperance Intelligencer*, 12 Mar. 1840, p. 89. [see p. 321]

25. Canterbury Hall, Lambeth: a pioneer London music-hall. Note the drinkers at long tables in front of the stage. From *Paul Pry* No. 4 in the London Museum's volume 'Pleasure Gardens of South London, No. 2', p. 95. [see p. 324]

26. A TEMPERANCE FESTIVAL AT DYRHAM PARK, 10 AUG. 1840, where men, women and children join together in common enjoyment. Note the presence of the Union Jack; socialists who tried to distribute literature at this festival were indignantly expelled. The picture illustrates well the curious mixture of light-heartedness and seriousness which can be found in the nineteenth-century temperance movement. From the *London Tee-Total Magazine*, Sept. 1840, p. 260. [see p. 330]

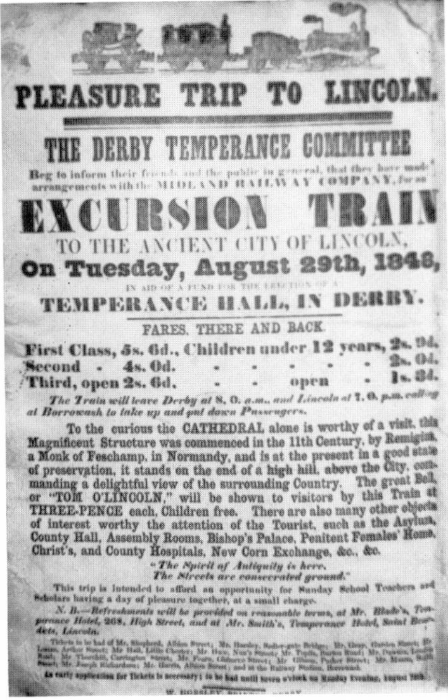

27. TEMPERANCE SOCIETIES IN THE 1840s OFTEN SPONSORED RAILWAY EXCURSIONS as counter-attractions to recreational drinking. Poster from Derby Temperance Society's collection. [see p. 330]

ments? The Shaftesbury Park estate excluded public-houses from the locality, and was managed in the 1880s by the prohibitionist R. E. Farrant. Several other temperance reformers, including F. R. Lees and John Dunlop, helped to promote schemes for sanitary and housing reform: but Thomas Beggs, active in both temperance and sanitary reform movements, advocated 'a more catholic spirit' among temperance workers—for 'if all the world were teetotalers, the sanitary movement would still be required'.[4] The *Bee-Hive* on 13 June 1863 argued that if Sunday closers devoted as much energy to building model dwellings as to agitation for licensing restriction they would achieve more for sobriety. Yet temperance reformers did make a modest contribution towards solving the problem. The two temperance utopias Saltaire and Bessbrook set a model for the factory village, and teetotalers were closely connected with the early building societies and model suburban estates. Teetotal orators constantly drew attention to the 'temperance villas' built by abstainers like John Hockings and James McCurrey; and the temperance movement's connexion with the freehold land movement has already been noted.

Furthermore the problem of building up the home as a recreational centre was partly an educational problem. Here the teetotalers were very active, for their aim was always to assimilate middle- and working-class styles of life. Drawing on his own experience, Thomas Whittaker expressed the temperance viewpoint: 'the home that had satisfied my wants as a drinker was not in harmony with my self-respect as a teetotaller, and I soon put myself in possession of a house rented at twelve pounds a year.'[5] In temperance meetings and through tracts and periodicals, teetotalers contrasted the squalid home of the drunkard with the genteel home of the sober [see Plate 24]. They strove to keep the husband by his domestic fireside, so that he would take his recreation in the company of his wife and children, and not with other men in the public-house. Yet even with abstinence, many nineteenth-century working men would have lacked the resources to create a pleasant home; besides, the warm community life of the urban slum encouraged them to prefer the informal collective life of the street, pub and market. These considerations did not prevent the temperance movement, by exhortation or—in the case of Father Nugent's Liverpool temperance meetings—by practical demonstration,[6] from teaching wives domestic economy so as to tempt their husbands to stay at home. The temperance reformer tried to harness the competitiveness which had hitherto led to physical violence or to drinking contests, for the competitive acquisition of property. He promoted the notion of the home as the place for recreation, even as the purpose of life itself: he popularized the cult of the 'private life', and fostered in working women that reticence about family matters—that abstinence from gossip—which characterized the respectable housewife.

Although in its legislation modern England pays greater lip-service to collectivism, its day-to-day life is in many ways *less* public, *less* communal, than it was in early Victorian times. With our private recreations and our private transport, we abandon once-popular communal leisure pursuits for the individualism and privacy of family life. By encouraging working people to retreat into domestic bliss, temperance reformers hindered them from articulating their grievances against social conditions. The only type of public life known to working people was the public-house debate, and from this the temperance reformer sought to draw them into the comparatively narrowing influences of the domestic fireside. Still, the temperance crusade challenged many flagrant evils when it campaigned for a new attitude to the home. Wife-beating in particular flourished on a combination of late-night drinking, squalid domestic surroundings and guilt in the husband at neglecting his family. Reformed drunkards often publicly apologized in exaggerated terms for their former neglect of their wives. 'We never has no angry words *now*,' said a teetotal coalporter to Henry Mayhew.[7] There was *some* connexion between the prosperity of the public-house and the squalor of the private house: 'I saw the misery that intemperate habits had occasioned in many homes,' wrote a former teetotal working man of his experiences in the 1830s, 'and that decided me as to the course I should adopt. I joined the movement. . . .'[8]

Temperance reformers also helped to modify working-class leisure patterns. The positive aspect of this policy lay in the provision of new recreations —of open spaces, libraries and music-halls; the negative aspect lay in the attack on the old recreations—on unlimited drinking hours, fairs and cruel sports. These several changes were not always promoted self-consciously, nor were they advocated by any one social group or political organization. The positive aspect of the campaign had made only limited progress by the 1870s, and Ruskin in 1877 could still write to working men that 'if I were in your place, I should drink myself to death in six months, because I had nothing to amuse me'.[9] Nothing could be done about the English weather, but some progress was made in providing towns with open spaces. The appointment of a parliamentary committee on public walks in 1833 shows that some M.P.s already recognized the existence of the problem; its intimate connexion with the drink problem was acknowledged in the parliamentary inquiries of 1834 and 1853–4. The first moves for improvement were made outside parliament. The earliest park was laid out on Preston Moor in 1833–5; Joseph Strutt gave Derby its Arboretum in 1840; but the most important event was the opening of Manchester's Peel Park in 1846. This was followed by the creation of parks in several other industrial towns in the 1850s. London secured Primrose Hill in 1842, Victoria Park in 1849, Battersea Park and the Victoria Embankment in the 1850s. The General Enclosure Act of 1845 restrained the enclosure of common land round London, and Slaney's Recreation Grounds Act of 1852 facilitated bequests of recreational land. Demand for the protection of commons from encroachment crystallized in the Metropolitan Commons Act of 1866. The Commons Preservation Society was formed in the previous year, but Octavia Hill did not embark on agitation for a large open space until the campaign for Swiss Cottage Fields in 1873.

With parks as with improved housing, temperance reformers were alive to the need. The teetotal J. S. Buckingham was one of the most energetic and imaginative of M.P.s who advocated public parks in the 1830s. The teetotal Joseph Sturge believed that exclusion from green fields 'contributed not a little to the demoralization of many of the working classes'; he battled in vain for public parks in Birmingham, whose corporation rejected his offer of a rent-free field in Edgbaston. Among other temperance reformers, Titus Salt offered £1,000 towards the cost of Bradford's first public park; John Guest was one of the leading campaigners for open spaces in Rotherham; Halifax's People's Park was a gift from the teetotal M.P. Frank Crossley in 1857; and Joseph Livesey was personally responsible for creating Preston's Avenham Park in 1847. Many drinksellers opposed public parks as damaging to their trade.[10] Some drinksellers also disliked another counter-attraction pioneered by temperance reformers—the public library. Ewart's Act of 1845 enabled several towns in the north of England to establish libraries; and where two-thirds of the ratepayers agreed, his Act of 1850 enabled towns to support libraries and museums from the rates. The adoption of this Act was opposed in Hull and Westminster in the late 1850s, in Colchester in 1871, and elsewhere by mobs which included 'friends of the beer-house interests'. Temperance societies, on the other hand, encouraged reading among their members and formed their own libraries. In Oxford they took the lead in campaigning for a local public library. Social reform has recently been credited to 'successive generations of predominantly middle-class reformers', who often faced bitter hostility from the working men, its prime beneficiaries. Birmingham and Newcastle-Under-Lyme progressives in the 1870s, eager for sanitary reform and for extending public facilities, faced hostility from local drink traders who allied themselves with some of the poorest local working people. Among these progressives, temperance reformers could usually be found.[11]

The mere provision of parks and libraries could not alter existing recreational patterns unless joined to a change in popular attitudes to leisure. Nineteenth-century England made little progress towards a more active encouragement of 'rational' recreation. Sabbatarian campaigns, by closing the Crystal Palace and preventing the playing of military bands in Hyde Park, did considerable harm. Some London publicans—the owners of the White Conduit Tavern or the Highbury Barn, for instance—showed great ingenuity and inventiveness in catering for new recreational tastes and in outwitting hostile magistrates. Yet Francis Place in old age rejoiced at the decline of London's tea-gardens, and by the 1860s the Covent Garden area had lost its night cellars. Several prominent Victorians regretted the English suspicion of popular enjoyment: Jevons looked wistfully at Denmark's Tivoli Gardens in the 1870s and wished that England could enjoy a similar freedom from puritanism. Prince Albert and other foreign observers deplored England's suspicion of public recreation and Frederic Harrison in 1867 maintained that the Sundays and holidays of foreigners 'make an Englishman blush for his own land'.[12]

In providing working people with relaxations which would divert them from drink, the publican was prominent. Nobody was more inventive between the 1820s and the 1870s in catering for popular recreational needs. His importance in providing upper class recreations diminished. By the 1840s the increased respectability of the stage, signalized by the Queen's command performance at Windsor in 1848, gradually weaned actors away from the inn. Modern theatre-drinking reverses the situation of the 1820s: drink profits now merely supplement income primarily derived from the dramatic performance. Similarly, the public concert gradually abandoned the tavern where it had originated, though the Crown and Anchor was still giving full-scale promenade concerts in the 1840s. For the poor, however, publicans provided the music-hall, whose emergence in the 1850s may well be a direct response to the increased respectability of the theatre. The London 'halls' conventionally originate in 1852, four years after the Queen's command performance, when Charles Morton the future impresario opened his 'Canterbury Hall' beside his Lambeth public-house. His originality should not be exaggerated: as urbanization increased the demand for mass entertainment and gradually created a distinction between spectator and performer, the music-hall evolved as a gradual formalization of the 'free-and-easy' [see Plate 25]. The music-hall developed naturally out of tendencies in the old London supper-rooms, the tavern concert-rooms and the variety saloons.

By 1843 concerts were often being held in London taverns; Liverpool beersellers were providing customers with music and ventriloquists in the same year, and 37 Liverpool drinksellers in 1849 employed 218 musicians and entertainers. Morton in 1852 was simply acknowledging the contemporary trend by moving some of his public-house recreations into a separate room. By extending to millhands the apparent bargain of admittance to floor-shows, tableaux, clog-dancing and acrobatics in return for the mere price of a drink, Liverpool and Manchester drinksellers in the 1850s gained at the expense of local theatres. In 1853 three large Manchester beerhouse music-saloons were attracting 25,000 customers a week, to what was virtually the sole public entertainment of local working people. Music-halls moved into the West End of London when Edward Weston opened his hall at Holborn in 1857, and Morton followed suit in 1861 by opening his first Oxford Music Hall in Tottenham Court Road. By 1868 there were 28 music-halls and 10 small tavern-halls in London, and 300 music-halls in the rest of Britain. The publican's capacity for exploiting new recreational needs has persisted into the twentieth century: public-houses were often the first places to put on a film-show and to instal television—before these recreations drifted into competition with their own.[13]

At least half the takings of London music-halls in the 1860s consisted of payment for drink: their tavern connexions prevented Shaftesbury from hiring them for religious services. Public-house customers, who earned their free drinks by entertaining the company, were the music-hall impresario's source of talent. The storm aroused by Charrington's late-Victorian efforts to exclude drink from London music-halls stems largely from the fact that drinking place and music-hall stood in the relation of parent to child.[14] Yet the music-hall can surely be included among the counter-attractive influences which fostered sobriety during the nineteenth century. The 'orders' called for between performances often prompted the consumption of drinks no stronger than ginger-beer; and as the profitability of drink-free entertainment became apparent, publican-managers replaced the drinking tables with stalls, pushed the drink to the back of the auditorium and eventually—with encouragement from the magistrates—hid it behind a screen. Music-halls achieved the temperance reformer's aim of inducing men to share their recreation with their families, and their drink profits fell whenever women were present. They also killed off the supper-rooms, those male preserves and haunts of the obscene song. Public-house entertainments had a warmth, immediacy and conviviality which mass entertainment can never provide; far from condemning the nineteenth-century music-hall, the historian can only lament its passing. Unfortunately temperance reformers—too keen to eliminate all vices at once—condemned the music-hall's low morality; but they failed to attract most working people to anything less spiced with the *double entendre*.

Nineteenth-century religious organizations were to some extent recreational bodies, and it is hardly surprising that they feared the publican's competition—particularly when he appropriated their star-turn, the hymn-singing. Temperance reformers could hardly contain their indignation at 'sacrilegious' tavern hymn-singing in the 1850s.[15] The recreational rivalry between chapel and tavern was exposed for all to see when the late-Victorian Salvation Army tried to prevent the Devil from appropriating all the best tunes. In the earlier period, Christians retaliated a little less crudely by sponsoring drink-free concerts. Liverpool Saturday evening concerts were organized by Mr. Caine, a Liverpool merchant, in 1844; they were soon attracting an average audience of 1,200, with the cheapest seats selling at threepence. Monday night concerts began in Birmingham town hall at about the same time. Bradford planned to build a concert-hall in 1849 and in the 1850s the Leeds 'rational recreation society' sponsored band-playing on the moor on several days a week. But these concerts probably attracted few people out of the public-house even on

Saturday nights, let alone on weekdays. They merely supplied entertainment to a different section of society.[16] The temperance society was itself a form of counter-attraction to the public-house and tried to appropriate many of its charms: to note only one example—the Trial of John Barleycorn, often performed by early Victorian temperance reformers, mirrors the less elevating 'Judge and Jury Clubs' which some publicans still sponsored.

Like the attempt to tackle bad housing, the attempt to alter traditional recreational patterns was partly a matter of education. New leisure patterns had to be advertised and 'opinion formers' encouraged to follow them; the temperance movement was important here, for it gave coherence and confidence to those who were adopting the new ways. Its task was made easier by the fact that urbanization uprooted many people from their traditional *milieu*, and therefore disturbed them in their traditional recreations. Here too counter-attractionism had its positive and negative aspects. Drinking was prominent in traditional recreational patterns, and between the 1820s and the 1870s the auxiliary attractions of the public-house were attacked through attempts at removing music-licences, excluding children, restricting opening hours and forbidding certain types of conduct. A late-Victorian publican would never have dared to organize the fight among his customers which the youthful Lord George Sanger witnessed.[17] Nor was the drinking place any longer a centre of family recreation at the end of the century: the 1839 Metropolitan Police Act forbade London drinksellers to provide spirits for consumption on the premises by children under sixteen; in 1872 this provision was extended to the whole country; in 1886 the drinkseller was forbidden to sell beer to children under thirteen. In the same period the homeliness of the public-house was reduced by an interior reorganization which increased the prominence of the bar.

The most important of these negative policies was the progressive restriction of opening hours. For temperance reformers this policy was very much a second-best; their prime objective was to close the door of the drinking place altogether, or at least to persuade the drinker voluntarily to shun it. Of doubtful value now, these closing regulations were beneficial in the early Victorian social situation. The idea of statutorily restricting drinking hours was a nineteenth-century innovation. Estcourt's 1828 Licensing Act made no provision about licensing hours except to recommend that magistrates close drinking places during Sunday morning service. After 1830 however, restriction steadily mounted, with only two small setbacks—in 1855 and 1874. Beerhouse closing legislation innovated in two respects: the 1830 Beer Act introduced the principle of statutorily restricting hours, and the Beer Act of 1840 introduced the principle of varying statutory closing hours in areas of differing population density. Both these innovations were extended to public-house opening hours during the period. The first statutory regulation of public-house hours was not introduced till 1839, and the idea of variable regulation was not extended to public-houses till 1872. Public-house hours were first restricted on Sundays and only in 1864 were weekday opening hours curtailed. A brief experiment was conducted between 1872 and 1874 in fixing minimum and maximum opening hours, and allowing local magistrates to vary actual hours within these limits at their discretion.

As with so much police legislation at the time, innovations in closing regulations were made first in London and were only later extended throughout the country. The first curtailment of Sunday opening hours, in 1839, initially applied only to London public-houses; but it was made permissive for other large towns, several of which adopted it in the 1840s. Similarly London public-houses were the first to incur weekday closing regulations, in 1864; these regulations were again made permissive for other parts of the country. Until the 1872 Licensing Act, therefore, weekday beerhouse and public-house closing hours were regulated on contrasting principles: beerhouse hours were most severely restricted in the countryside, whereas public-house hours were most severely restricted in the towns. But although London was the first to adopt statutory restrictions, its opening hours were always longer than those elsewhere. Its theatre public justified its late-night closing: its markets justified its early morning opening. We have seen how the 1872 Licensing Act tightened up the regulation of opening hours still further—yet statutory reduction of weekday drinking hours in the morning and afternoon was not introduced till the first world war, and the '*bona fide* traveller' was entitled to drink at any time. The special legislation against Sunday drinking stemmed partly from sabbatarianism and from desire to give drinksellers a Sunday rest, but it was also a way of preventing the conjunction of drinking time with the possession of leisure and money. If the views of magistrates and police and the statistics for drunkenness arrests are any guide to their effects, these Sunday restrictions succeeded. By 1874 therefore, substantial inroads had been made both on the drinking weekend and on the drinking weekday.

A more drastic way of attacking recreational drinking was to impose fines for drunkenness. The 1839 Metropolitan Police Act imposed a penalty of 40/– for public drunkenness in London, with extra penalties for the drunken and disorderly. The 1872 Licensing Act imposed a fine of 10/– for public drunkenness, 20/– on the second conviction within twelve months, and 40/– for the third; it also imposed more stringent penalties on individuals found drunk in charge of potentially dangerous articles, such as vehicles or firearms. Unlike moderate drinkers, temperance reformers had too much sympathy with the drunkard to favour such legislation. In their view, the man's reason was destroyed by the drink; prohibitionists even argued that the authorities must take the blame for granting him access to it. Punishments for drunkenness probably did little to reduce drunkenness: the police at this time aimed rather at preventing the drunkard from harming himself or the public—not at reforming him.

TABLE 8

Changes in Beerhouse Opening Hours: 1830–1874

LEGISLATION	AREA*	WEEKDAY HOURS	SUNDAY HOURS
1830 Beerhouse Act	All	4 a.m.–10 p.m.	1 p.m.–3 p.m., 5 p.m.–10 p.m.
1834 Beerhouse Act	All	5 a.m.–11 p.m.	1 p.m.–3 p.m., 5 p.m.–10 p.m.
1840 Beerhouse Act	London	5 a.m.–12 p.m.	1 p.m.–3 p.m., 5 p.m.–10 p.m.
	over 2500	5 a.m.–11 p.m.	1 p.m.–3 p.m., 5 p.m.–10 p.m.
	under 2500	5 a.m.–10 p.m.	1 p.m.–3 p.m., 5 p.m.–10 p.m.
1848 Alehouses & Beerhouses Act	London	5 a.m.–12 p.m.	12.30 p.m.–3 p.m., 5 p.m.–10 p.m.
	over 2500	5 a.m.–11 p.m.	12.30 p.m.–3 p.m., 5 p.m.–10 p.m.
	under 2500	5 a.m.–10 p.m.	12.30 p.m.–3 p.m., 5 p.m.–10 p.m.
1854 Sunday Beer (Wilson Patten) Act	London	5 a.m.–12 p.m.	12.30 p.m.–2.30 p.m., 6 p.m.–10 p.m.
	over 2500	5 a.m.–11 p.m.	12.30 p.m.–2.30 p.m., 6 p.m.–10 p.m.
	under 2500	5 a.m.–10 p.m.	12.30 p.m.–2.30 p.m., 6 p.m.–10 p.m.
1855 Sunday Beer Act	London	5 a.m.–12 p.m.	12.30 p.m.–3 p.m., 5 p.m.–11 p.m.
	over 2500	5 a.m.–11 p.m.	12.30 p.m.–3 p.m., 5 p.m.–11 p.m.
	under 2500	5 a.m.–10 p.m.	12.30 p.m.–3 p.m., 5 p.m.–11 p.m.
1872 Licensing Act	London	5 a.m.–12 p.m.	1 p.m.–3 p.m., 6 p.m.–11 p.m.
	over 2500	6 (or 5 or 7) a.m.–11 (or 10 or 12) p.m.	12.30 (or 1) p.m.–2.30 (or 3) p.m., 6 p.m.–10 (or 9 or 11) p.m.
	under 2500	6 (or 5 or 7) a.m.–10 p.m.	12.30 (or 1) p.m.–2.30 (or 3) p.m., 6 p.m.–10 (or 9) p.m.
1874 Licensing Act	London	5 a.m.–12.30 a.m.	1 p.m.–3 p.m., 6 p.m.–11 p.m.
	Towns or populous places	6 a.m.–11 p.m.	12.30 p.m.–2.30 p.m., 6 p.m.–10 p.m.
	Rural districts	6 a.m.–10 p.m.	12.30 p.m.–2.30 p.m., 6 p.m.–10 p.m.

* Figures in this column are for population in the area concerned.

A third branch of the negative attack on traditional recreational habits was the attack on the fair. Here too temperance reformers were active. Methodists had long been attacking the seasonal wake, to which their camp meetings were largely designed as a counter-attraction. Evangelicals detested violent popular sports and popish festivals; industrialists found them inconvenient. Several fairs were discontinued during the eighteenth century but the attack on the London fairs reached a peak in the 1820s; there were also several mid-Victorian casualties. In the north of England, wakes experienced a similar decline. Temperance reformers were prominent in ending Bradford's septennial Bishop Blaize festival, which had caused much drunkenness and industrial unrest in 1825, and in abolishing the Whitsun Derby football and the Shrewsbury show. In 1858 and 1861 there were rumblings in the National Temperance League's minute-book against London's Argyle Rooms, Coal Hole and Cyder Cellars.[18]

Temperance reformers argued that the expansion in retail trades, from which many of them drew their livelihood, had superseded the commercial role of the fair; these occasions were now 'not for the transacting of business of any kind, but merely for what is called *pleasure*, alias *drinking* . . . gam-

TABLE 9

Changes in Public-house Opening Hours: 1828–1874

LEGISLATION	AREA	WEEKDAY HOURS	SUNDAY HOURS
1828 Estcourt's Alehouse Act	All	No statutory restriction	No statutory restriction, but must be closed during morning service
1839 Metropolitan Police Act	London (& adopted by some other towns in the 1840s)	No statutory restriction, except closing midnight Saturday	Closed till 1 p.m.
	Elsewhere	,,	Closed during morning service
1848 Alehouses & Beer-houses Act	All	,,	Closed till 12.30 p.m.
1854 Sunday Beer (Wilson Patten) Act	All	No statutory restriction, except opening 4 a.m. Monday, closing midnight Saturday	12.30 p.m.–2.30 p.m., 6 p.m.–10 p.m.
1855 Sunday Beer Act	All	,,	12.30 p.m.–3 p.m., 5 p.m.–11 p.m.
1864 Public-house Closing Act	London & permissive in boroughs. From 1865, permissive everywhere.	4 a.m.–1 a.m., closing midnight Saturday	,,
	Elsewhere	No statutory restriction, except opening 4 a.m. Monday, closing midnight Saturday	,,
1872 Licensing Act	London	5 a.m.–12 p.m.	1 p.m.–3 p.m., 6 p.m.–11 p.m.
	over 2500	6 (or 5 or 7) a.m.–11 (or 10 or 12) p.m.	12.30 (or 1) p.m.–2.30 (or 3) p.m., 6 p.m.–10 (or 9 or 11) p.m.
	under 2500	6 (or 5 or 7) a.m.–10 p.m.	12.30 (or 1) p.m.–2.30 (or 3) p.m., 6 p.m.–10 (or 9) p.m.
1874 Licensing Act	London	5 a.m.–12.30 a.m., closing midnight Saturday	1 p.m.–3 p.m., 6 p.m.–11 p.m.
	Towns/populous places	6 a.m.–11 p.m.	12.30 p.m.–2.30 p.m., 6 p.m.–10 p.m.
	Rural districts	6 a.m.–10 p.m.	12.30 p.m.–2.30 p.m., 6 p.m.–10 p.m.

SOURCE: Tables 8 and 9 are based on *Granville Papers*, P.R.O. 30/29/68 ff. 48–72; *Parl. Papers* 1871 (104), II, pp. 489 ff.; *Parl. Papers* 1872 (288), II, pp. 303 ff. G. B. Wilson, *Alcohol & the Nation* (1940), p. 156.

bling and fighting'; they were feudal relics, or 'fossil memorials of obsolete degeneracy'. They had declined, said Dunlop in 1840, into 'mere assemblages chiefly for the purposes of amusement'.[19] The same arguments applied to the statute-hirings which were also declining in the mid-Victorian period. There was much to be said for the temperance viewpoint. Temperance societies were, as they themselves claimed, 'societies for promoting the civilization of England':[20] they well knew the violence and brutality which accompanied traditional recreations, some of which were deliberately promoted by self-interested publicans.[21] Derby football was a violent game, quite different in character from the modern sport of the same name. At the Yorkshire feasts, pugilists from each village attended the feasts of neighbouring villages: it was 'quite common to see several rings formed', recalled Joseph Lawson, 'in which men stripped to their bare skin would fight sometimes by the hour together, till the combatants were not recognisable, being so deformed by wounds and besmeared with blood and dirt'.[22]

The temperance reformer's attack on the fair had its positive as well as its negative aspect, for wise temperance reformers realized that if the fair were abolished, its recreational functions would have to be replaced. They helped to evolve two sober alternatives—the fête and the excursion. Frequently held at the same time as the local sports or fairs, temperance fêtes—particularly those in early Victorian Leeds—often showed inventiveness [see Plate 26], and the Crystal Palace fêtes held by the National Temperance League in the 1860s were grandiose occasions. Temperance reformers were increasingly successful in getting local clergymen to organize modest local fêtes as counter-attractions to the traditional but more drunken festival.

A more drastic remedy was to remove the members bodily from temptation through the railway excursion [see Plate 27]. Mechanics' institutes and temperance societies requisitioned steamers and trains for this purpose. It was through organizing a temperance excursion in July 1841 that Thomas Cook, the Leicester teetotaler, obtained inspiration for his travel agency. Though his was not the first railway excursion—Leeds Temperance Society was planning one in September 1840—it was certainly among the earliest. Temperance reformers readily patronized such events, just as respectable working men before the railway age had walked into London's rural suburbs at weekends, rather than remain drinking in the slums of St. Giles's.[23] Excursions were also organized by publicans; even where excursions were not drink-free, they helped to broaden the outlook of working people who had never previously travelled far from their locality. 'With change of place', wrote Hazlitt, 'we change our ideas; nay, our opinions and feelings.' The excursion also helped to bring husband and wife together in their recreation; it was among the agencies which enabled J. S. Mill in 1867 to claim that men and women had become 'for the first time in history, really each other's companions'. The railway excursion and the consequent rise of the holiday resort killed the Lancashire wake and civilized the local fair. G. J. Holyoake, when complaining that every Glasgow steamer did more than all the local temperance societies to promote sobriety, failed to note that, on weekdays at least, the steamers were as likely as not full of teetotalers.[24] By the 1880s the annual excursion of an energetic rural temperance society, like that of Mere in Wiltshire, could become an event eagerly anticipated throughout the year and an important influence in the cultural life of the whole area.

Accompanying the decline of wakes and fairs, and both assisting and assisted by the temperance movement, was the 'mighty revolution' in the character of popular sport which Howitt in 1838 claimed had taken place within the previous thirty years[25]—the gradual advance of intellectual over animal recreations. The temperance reformer vigorously attacked the rural sports—greasy poles, sack races and crude enjoyments patronized by the aristocracy; for him, as also for many Chartists, such occasions symbolized a bygone age of ignorant rusticity. He also attacked brutal sports, all of which had strong links with the drinking place and were often patronized by high society [see Plate 8]. The aristocracy could be attacked through their leisure patterns as well as through their taxation system, through attacking game laws as well as corn laws. Requiring unrestricted space, unspecified periods of time and a taste for animal cruelty, these sports were inconvenient in industrial society. At the same time, by depriving many of its employees of physical exercise, industrial society helped to create the demand for sports which required exertion from human beings rather than from animals. While Sheffield operatives in the 1860s still kept a pack of hounds, in most areas the factory system had transformed towns which had hitherto been merely 'the country a little thickened and congested' into urban centres with a culture of their own;[26] it extirpated the ancient sporting spirit except in those transitional phenomena, the circus and the racecourse.

What was to replace the traditional sports in industrial society? The temperance movement appeared at precisely the time when old working-class leisure patterns were dying out and before reduced working hours had created the new; it can perhaps be excused for its failure to foresee the recreational future. Like many Chartists and working-class radicals, the temperance movement saw the mechanics' institute and the public library, rather than the sports stadium and the yellow press, as the growth-points of the new leisure. If the earliest temperance reformers had survived like W. E. Adams into the Edwardian period, they too would have lamented the decline in popular concern with politics and self-education, the boom in 'pastimes . . . absolutely unknown to the general populace forty years ago'.[27] For although the new leisure patterns were more compatible with sobriety, they did no more than the old ones to develop intellectual culture and self-reliance.

The problem of leisure in an industrial society was solved through codifying sporting rules, which saved both time and space: and through catering for spectator sports, which facilitated vicarious athleticism. After the 1850s Christian Socialists helped to develop the cult of athletic sports. 1863 saw the foundation of the Football Association, 1869 the abolition of public executions, 1870 the first admission charge to a football game. The years 1870 to 1886 saw the zenith of W. G. Grace and the growth of tennis and rugby football. These changes brought both gains and losses to the temperance movement. Though drinking places remained centres of traditional sports, drinksellers showed their customary resilience in the face of social change: they organized or subsidized spectator sports, and annexed cricket grounds and sports clubs to their new premises. Thus the ten-mile race between Jem Pudney and Jem Rowan at Hackney Wick in spring 1860 was organized from the White Lion, which drove a flourishing trade throughout the day.[28]

Yet in the long run these sports, by diversifying popular leisure, damaged the publican's trade.

The traditional leisure-patterns were perhaps most deeply entrenched in the army—witness the frequency with which the R.S.P.C.A. found army officers patronizing clandestine cruel sports in nineteenth-century drinking places. It was widely assumed by army officers during the Crimean War that drunkenness and immorality in the lower ranks were inevitable. A soldier in the 1870s discussed the problem with Josephine Butler: the authorities, he said, 'expect us to be bad, and of course we are bad'.[29] But here, as elsewhere in the period, temperance influences helped to initiate changes. Like the governing classes as a whole, army officers were beginning to see that discipline was better promoted through sobriety than through drunkenness—an attitudinal change essential to the professionalism among servicemen which has developed so much further in our own day. Furthermore, in the services as in industry, the employer was only beginning to assume responsibility for the total welfare of the employee, instead of merely giving him a wage. Sidney Herbert, an enlightened secretary for war between 1859 and 1861, accelerated these changes, and took a particular interest in diversifying servicemen's recreation. Nevertheless at all stages in his mid-Victorian career, the serviceman depended on the publican. Even military recruiting in the 1860s still took place in the beerhouse: 'with the volunteer system you must get the men where you can find them' said the Duke of Cambridge in 1867.[30]

It is impossible to say whether the publican's role as the provider of prostitutes for civilians had declined by the 1870s; the puritans certainly won a striking success in 1864 when London's refreshment-houses were closed between 1 and 4 at night—because this severely weakened the position of Haymarket drinking saloons as the headquarters of prostitution in the West End. In garrison-towns, however, publicans in the 1860s were still active in catering for soldiers' needs. Even before inspection was enforced by the C. D. Acts, Aldershot publicans anxious for a good name were employing surgeons to ensure that women in their houses were clean.[31] Better-class prostitutes usually rented adjacent or nearby cottages from publicans on the understanding that customers would be collected only in his taproom; lower-grade prostitutes merely rented a room on his premises. A witness before a parliamentary inquiry in 1868 described a 'notorious house' in Aldershot: 'we at length reached a long room, furnished with chairs, forms, and narrow tables, and where, among some 200 soldiers, there were probably about 35 or 40 women. At our end a fiddler was playing on his instrument a lively tune, to which a few couples were dancing a merry accompaniment. Three or four persons, acting as waiters, were briskly engaged in seeking and attending to orders, bringing in beer, &c., which was shared by the soldiers with their female companions, who either sat by their sides, or, as was more frequently the case, on their knees. But, amidst all the loud talking, drinking, and singing, I heard no quarrelsome language used . . . everyone appeared in good humour.'[32]

Until 1825 all sailors were entitled to half a pint of 50–50 rum-and-water per day, and in addition a gallon of beer if required. The rum ration was halved in 1825 and halved again in 1850. The period also saw an improved supply of non-intoxicating drink: by 1815, ways had been found of keeping water sweet so that it could be drunk throughout the voyage. From the 1830s M.P.s connected with the temperance movement tried to get special concessions for teetotal servicemen. Several ships experimented successfully with alternatives to liquor money in the 1830s, and an optional food ration was introduced in 1847; by 1861 sailors could have cocoa, tea, coffee or lime-juice instead of beer, but W. S. Caine the temperance reformer was still agitating against the spirit ration in the 1880s. The earliest efforts at reforming the canteen system were made in the late 1850s, and in the 1860s the banding together of teetotalers on H.M.S. Reindeer originated the Royal Naval Temperance Society.[33] But real progress could not be made until the temperance movement adopted a more positive approach. The National Temperance League from the 1860s—working in the army through Miss Robinson, and in the navy through Miss Agnes Weston—tried to provide voluntarily what J. S. Buckingham had urged the government to supply as early as 1837: a 'marine asylum' for sailors in every port.[34] But even here the temperance movement's religious connexions made it difficult to provide really effective counter-attractions. The task was in fact formidable, for as a naval doctor put it in 1867 'a man who has no friends in port has nowhere to go to spend his evening except the public-house or the brothel'.[35]

Accompanying these direct improvements in service conditions were important indirect influences, especially in the navy. From the mid-Victorian period, by encouraging savings schemes and family responsibilities in the lower ranks, the authorities fostered a more rational expenditure pattern; for when sailors allotted half-pay for their families, they had less money and less inclination for extravagance when they set foot on shore.[36] And at the same time as violent fluctuations in the availability of money were being smoothed out, the replacement of sail by steam reduced dependence on weather conditions. This curtailed the sailor's unexpected leisure at the same time as railway transport was reducing the soldier's dependence on the publican. Despite all these changes, improvement was only beginning by the 1870s, and the publican continued to dominate servicemen's recreations for longer than in most other sections of British society.

How valid were Holyoake's complaints at temperance reformers' attitudes to recreation? Many temperance reformers—especially nonconformists—suspected theatres, dancing and Sunday secular enjoyments: 'we presume that nearly all our readers are opposed to the theatre', wrote the *Weekly Record*, a leading temperance paper, on 8 November 1862. Any attempt to popularize teetotalism through recreational activity was suspected by some temperance reformers, who denied that there was any need for light entertainment of any kind. 'No people', said Lees, epitomizing this view, 'were ever yet theatred into sobriety, danced into morality, or fiddled into practical philosophy.'[37] Many teetotalers in the 1860s protested when recreational interludes were introduced into the temperance meeting and when 'trashy tales' appeared in temperance periodicals. Some temperance reformers were more eager to deprive drinking places of their incidental attractions, on the ground that 'it was advisable to render vice repulsive', than to provide positive counter-attractions.[38] The vigour of their attacks on public-house entertainment stemmed from the fact that a conflict between cultures was involved. Many temperance reformers contested the belief of men like Owen that the removal of Sunday gloom would also remove Sunday drunkenness; they were often too ready to denounce all pleasures which they themselves did not happen to enjoy—too ready to assume that real joys and lasting pleasures none but Sion's children know.

In justice to them one must remember that the modern notion that one owes oneself leisure was then comparatively rare. Besides, in this movement as in any other, there was no unanimity. Earthly happiness was quite clearly the concern of temperance reformers as prominent as J. S. Buckingham, with his desire in the 1830s to promote the happy family-life: of Father Mathew in the 1840s, with his brass bands: and of Joseph Livesey in the 1850s, with his Saturday evening singing-meetings. Indeed, one of the main reasons for the friction between evangelicals and teetotalers in the 1840s was the teetotal impatience with suffering in this world. If temperance reformers often adopted a negative rather than a positive policy, this stemmed largely from their lack of funds, and from their belief that abstinence was itself the best way to finance improved recreation. Furthermore, as the century wore on, temperance reformers became more reconciled to light recreation. Samuel Morley's temperance zeal, which in youth had led him to oppose light entertainment, led him in old age to campaign for Emma Cons and the Old Vic. Reforming organizations tend to approximate in character to the institutions they are attacking. Much to the disgust of older teetotalers, their mid-Victorian successors appropriated for their societies more and more of the publican's attractions.

A combination of social forces and temperance pressure severely curtailed the drinkseller's importance as provider of local meeting places during the early Victorian period. The greatest blow came, not from the temperance reformers, but from the railway. Although some early railways used inns as stopping places, their role was soon taken over by railway stations.[39] As the railway prospered after the 1840s, so the drinking place declined; as the railway declined in the twentieth century, so the drinking place partially revived.

There was almost as close a kinship between the railway and the temperance reformer as between horse-drawn travel and the publican. In no place was the teetotal orator made less welcome than in the coaching village. Both the railway and the temperance society constituted a threat to the agricultural interest; temperance reformers invested in early railways, regarded them as a beneficent social and political influence, were employed on them, were encouraged by the railway companies, and travelled conspicuously on their trains.

English and French publicans were understandably hostile to the railway, but they had to come to terms with it; several London coaching inns became railway booking-offices. The last stage-coach from London to Birmingham ran in 1839 and from London to Bristol in 1843. By the 1850s drinking places were closing down all along the old stage-routes, and publicans were turning to farming. The Duke of Wellington told Miss Burdett-Coutts in 1847 that 'before the steam Invention' he had stopped six or eight times every summer at the Fountain in Canterbury, but since using the railway he never went there.[40] The coming of the railway to many rural spots was soon followed by the closing of local public-houses; temperance reformers like Charles Jupe or the Countess of Carlisle—who campaigned against redundant public-houses in old coaching villages like Endon in Wiltshire and Brampton in Cumberland—were only completing the work which the railways had begun. Short-distance road traffic, however, actually increased in volume during the railway age, and when the Leeds Tramways Order of 1871 introduced five pioneer tram routes leading out of the city centre, all five terminated at suburban public-houses.[41]

By cheapening and speeding up travel, the railway increased the number of travellers but reduced the number of stopping points and the requirement for lodgings. Hence travellers were lodged in fewer but larger establishments. The large 'resort' hotel originated in Switzerland. The word 'hotel' as used in the 1830s bore genteel connotations, but it soon came to denote mere size. Victorian station hotels began to appear in the 1840s; Derby station hotel was the first to be built into the station complex; York and Hull soon followed suit. Though these hotels continued to supply intoxicants, their lodging function was relatively more important. The great Victorian hotels began to appear in London in the 1860s, with the Grosvenor, Westminster Palace, Langham and the many station hotels: the provinces acquired similar public 'palaces'—notably Scarborough, with Brodrick's magnificent Grand Hotel, completed in 1867.

Early railway promoters did not always recognize the likely effects of the new form of transport on public sobriety, or that the reduced exhaustion of travel would also reduce the need for intoxicants. Their stations therefore provided drink facilities at least as lavish as those to which road travellers had been accustomed. Most early railway stations had sections assigned to the sale of intoxicants, or at least had their 'Railway Arms' nearby. Early railway travellers set off well fortified with bottles of spirits, and even in the 1870s they frequently treated railwaymen with drink.[42] Yet with all these qualifications, the railway probably did more for temperance in the nineteenth century—the gaslamp more for morality—than either the temperance movement or the Vice Society. Temperance reformers can hardly claim credit for these important changes, but they were more directly connected with the attack on the news-providing function of the drinking place, for in the 1850s they were prominent among the campaigners against the 'taxes on knowledge'. They also tried to dissuade working men's organizations from meeting in drinking places. With trade unions they had little success. Nothing came of Lovett's and Farren's schemes for district and trades halls, and in 1840 few London trade societies were meeting in coffee-houses except in the East End. In the 1860s Henry Solly, who tried to get trade unionists to meet outside the public-house, achieved little.[43] Nevertheless temperance reformers did strongly influence the habits of the classes from which trade union leaders were recruited. By the 1850s members of the ironmoulders' trade society were drinking so little that many publicans refused them access to club-rooms. Robert Hartwell, probably in the 1840s, induced the London Society of Compositors to move its house-of-call to private premises, though in the 1860s he was less successful in persuading London teetotalers to help him establish a London Trades Hall. Even where trade unions continued to meet in drinking places, their members may well have been influenced by temperance opinion; J. R. Stephens testified to the good behaviour of Lancashire trades delegates meeting in public-houses in the 1860s.[44]

Temperance reformers were rather more successful with the friendly society. Rural philanthropists often promoted teetotal friendly societies to rival those which met at the local public-house. In 1835 the temperance movement itself founded a teetotal friendly society—the Rechabites. By 1868 they boasted 13,000 adult members, though only in the 1860s did they begin to expand rapidly. In their early years they possessed little actuarial expertise. More important in reforming the friendly society was the gradual advance of the impersonal, actuarially sound and large-scale insurance organization. Once more temperance reformers helped to segregate economic from recreational activity. Those who had joined friendly societies for the entertainment were required increasingly to go elsewhere. Yet in the Edwardian period, the smaller Middlesbrough friendly societies were still meeting in public-houses. Co-operative societies usually kept themselves free from any drink connexions, and a proposal of 1866 that Bolton co-operative society should allow the use of a bar on their premises seemed 'an unnatural union' and provoked a storm. When Gladstone visited an Oldham co-operative spinning mill in 1867, he was told that 'temperance men were generally co-operators, and that many of the board of directors were such'. Parlia-

28. THE ENGLISH JUGGERNAUT. A temperance engraving portrays the enemy in all its frightfulness. Waste, violence, disease and death all spring from drink; but temperance forces are hastening to the rescue. From *The Struggle* (Ed. J. Livesey), No. 22 (1840s). [see p. 361]

29. Margaret Wilson, frequently arrested for drunkenness. Aged 23, widow, Primitive Methodist, calico weaver, born Manchester, can read. Offences: breaking windows at Luton. Previous convictions: 1856, vagrancy; 1857, drunkenness; 1857, assault; 1857, drunkenness; 1857, vagrancy (3 times); 1858, vagrancy; 1859, assault; 1860, wilful damage; 1864, drunkenness; 1865, drunkenness (3 times); 1866, stealing a jacket. 'Has been in several penitentiaries.' From *Register of Prisoners in Bedford County Gaol*, p. 124. [see p. 398] Mr. K. V. Thomas referred me to this source.

mentary supporters of the Permissive Bill used this alignment as evidence for popular sympathy with prohibition.[45]

Francis Place in the 1830s urged the establishment of working men's clubs which would allow beer-drinking. The mechanics' institutes were working men's clubs of a kind, but they were too closely tied to mutual improvement and upper-class patronage to attract customers from the public-house. As late as 1863 the *Bee-Hive* complained that while other classes had their clubs, working men were denied them.[46] The club movement of the 1860s shows that many temperance reformers were quite ready to give generously towards counter-attractions. Temperance societies had themselves been working men's clubs of a sort, but the first prominent teetotal working men's clubs formed separately from public-houses and from the temperance movement were in Salford in 1858, in Westminster under Miss Adeline Cooper in 1860 and in Notting Hill in 1861 under the prominent temperance reformer Mrs. Bayly. Henry Solly—Unitarian minister, former Chartist and temperance lecturer—founded the Working Men's Club and Institute Union in 1862, but lacked funds until he followed up Hugh Owen's suggestion of sending the prospectus to every temperance society in the kingdom. The result, he said, was remarkable: the Union was launched. 'It was generous-hearted Temperance Reformers', he later wrote, 'who at first welcomed, worked, and spent for the establishment of clubs.'[47]

But the teetotal and counter-attractive campaigns clashed frontally in the Union's subsequent history. For Solly found that teetotalers rarely visited the clubs, and that the exclusion of beer also excluded the publican's customers. Lord Lyttelton, an invaluable supporter of the Union, opposed the teetotal policy from the start. Against much opposition from the Union's original teetotal promoters, therefore, Solly eventually had beer admitted to the clubs. Drunkenness did not result, the clubs became self-supporting and temperance was promoted. Here, as elsewhere, teetotal innovations were taken up commercially and exploited even by the drink interest itself. By the late 1860s working men's clubs were spreading all over the country—including organizations for Conservative working men modelled on the public-house club. The continued importance of publicans in the political education of the working class is well illustrated, however, in the minute-books of Birmingham's Sunday Evening Debating Society. From the 1850s till 1886, Robert Edmonds of the Hope and Anchor, Navigation Street, opened his premises to weekly debates of a very high standard on cultural and political topics. There were usually about 30 members present, and sometimes as many as 100 spectators. Taking a few months at random, there were from July 1863 to November 1864, 14 debates on international affairs, 13 on domestic politics, 8 on criminology and social questions, 6 on literary and cultural topics, 5 on religion, 4 on labour questions, and 1 on local affairs. A publican who could house a working men's society which held 32 consecutive weekly debates in

1870–1 on the Franco-Prussian War, and eight consecutive weekly debates on 'miracles' in autumn 1874, was clearly helping to educate working men. When London deputations from the Reform League arrived in Birmingham, they readily participated in the Society's debates, and the Society formally sent its condolences to the families of Ernest Jones and George Dawson when they died. 'The Society was not only instructive,' said one of its leading members George Bill in 1882, '. . . many political and social movements had originated from this room.'[48]

The public-house's role as a trading centre was also firmly challenged in this period. Facilities for saving at interest outside the public-house proliferated during the early nineteenth century, and were deliberately promoted by the upper classes as a means of preventing intemperance. Duncan and others established the savings bank movement in Scotland after the Napoleonic Wars, and henceforth the savings bank movement grew quickly. Clergymen promoted village thrift, pig and clothing clubs and in 1861 the Post Office Savings Bank was founded; by 1870 it held £15,000,000 on deposit. Temperance tracts made much of the simple act of willpower which sent the individual to the 'savings bank' on one side of the street, or to the 'losings bank' on the other [see Plate 13]. But they exaggerated the advantages of saving from the working man's viewpoint; his life was precarious, and he was unlikely to live till the age of 61 when, according to one temperance tract,[49] he could receive £1,300 if he had invested 4/– a week continuously from the age of 21. At a time of distress his savings might deprive him, though not his thriftless neighbours, of poor relief. Abstinence alone could never preserve working men against poverty—witness the numerous appeals on behalf of aged and impecunious teetotal pioneers like James Teare and Thomas Swindlehurst.

The campaign against public-house wage-payment provoked two related attempts at reform: to separate wage-payment geographically from drinking places, and chronologically from leisure time. In the 1830s London temperance reformers established a registry to emancipate the London coalwhippers from depending on publicans for employment and pay. But publican competition was too powerful and, with the aid of the Quaker City bankers, teetotalers and others induced Gladstone in 1843 to set up an official registry. 'The stern principles of political economy must sometimes yield to the cry of misery and to considerations of humanity,' said one M.P. during the debate. Three coalwhippers leading the agitation abstained from intoxicants for long periods to prove to their fellows that their work could be done without the publican's aid. The official scheme succeeded, and at the time of Mayhew's inquiry there were 200–250 teetotal coalwhippers in London. This legislation was cited as a precedent for aiding the ballast heavers in 1852. On this occasion Mr. Wakley even suggested that if official registries were so successful in particular cases, they could surely be set up for *all* trades—a reform which did not materialize for over half a century.[50] It was difficult to enforce a legislative ban on these economic functions of the drinking place. Lord Ashley's prohibition of wage-payment by drinksellers in mining areas, obtained in 1842, was often evaded if only because the public-house still remained a convenient source of small change on payday. Shaftesbury was still campaigning against public-house wage-payment in the 1880s.[51] The second branch of the temperance policy was to recommend wage-payment in the morning and preferably not on a Saturday. 'It is the concurrence of money and time', said the *Temperance Society Record* in July 1832, 'which renders the payment of wages on Saturday evening an unfavourable circumstance to the dissipated and worthless.' The paper recommended wage-payment on Tuesday, but employers feared that this would simply spread intemperance over still more of the week. By 1868 however, the institution of the Saturday half-holiday enabled even Londoners to do their shopping before the Saturday evening drinking-bout.[52]

Between the 1820s and the 1870s the role of the drinking place in English society had therefore diminished as transport centre, news centre, meeting place and centre for economic transactions. The drinking place continued to act as the refuge for outlawed social groups like the secularists, but for more respectable gatherings many alternative meeting places had opened up. The lack of public buildings for communal activity, serious in the 1820s, was gradually being rectified. The lack of public lavatories in the 1890s was still forcing Hull citizens to buy drinks at public-houses in order to use their facilities, but in most places by the 1870s the number of public buildings, libraries and institutions had greatly increased. In the 1890s the Bell and Mackerel in the Mile End Road exhibited 20,000 stuffed creatures in cases, and in the 1920s Charlie Brown's Railway Tavern in Limehouse was still collecting curios from all parts of the world; but by that time there were many museums outside the public-house.[53] An incidental consequence of extending state activity since the 1820s has been the proliferation of so many types of 'public house' that the original public house has acquired a specialized meaning and a hyphen. There were now public-houses all over the country, said Lord Avebury in 1903, 'not for the sale of beer, but for the free use of books.'

Town halls, museums, picture galleries, public libraries, public lavatories, cinemas, public assembly-halls and trading centres have all become accessible to the general public since the 1820s. In addition the National Sunday League from the 1850s placed the temperance argument firmly in the forefront of its campaign to get drink-free Sunday recreations opened to the public; it succeeded in opening an increasing number of public and private museums and art galleries to the public on Sundays. The gradual alignment of religion behind temperance opened many more religious buildings to temperance societies, friendly societies and savings banks. The government's reliance on the public-house also declined during the period. To take only one example, the building of barracks in the north of England during the Napoleonic Wars and in the 1840s, together with the arrival of the railway, greatly diminished the publican's billeting role. By 1860 Gladstone could describe the old methods as 'a peculiar and antiquated system'.[54]

The economic, social and political power of the drink interest remained formidable in the 1870s despite 40 years of temperance agitation. In some directions its economic power had increased. The new speed of transport enabled brewers to supply a larger area, and thus made the economic and political fortunes of the firm of Bass. Important scientific developments cheapened brewing processes and made them less susceptible to seasonal fluctuation; the common brewer greatly increased his share of the market outside London. Improvements in policing greatly reduced the competition from illicit stills and retailers.[55] Figures for the number of detections connected with illicit distillation between 1830 and 1880 show that in England and Wales the total number of detections declined in this period—even in Ireland [see Figure 13]. This was a dramatic change; not only did it strengthen the revenue and the position of the official distillers: it also helped to make the official figures for drink consumption more accurate as a guide to actual consumption. The social and local political influence of the drink interest remained substantial in the 1870s. For Beatrice Webb, the banking and brewing families were 'easily first in social precedence' on the London social scene of the 1870s and 1880s. By the 1880s comments were being made on the frequency with which brewers received titles. There are in fact only six examples of peerages being granted to prominent brewers between 1868 and 1910, nor does the Trade seem to have been more greedy for honours than other businesses. But the wealth of late-Victorian brewers and distillers was prodigious; between 1892 and 1912 nine brewers, two distillers, one maltster and one wine-merchant died leaving more than a million pounds.[56]

By the 1870s the philanthropic power of the drink interest had been challenged, but not upset. As soon as charity became more scientific—as soon as attention came to be more closely fixed on the worldly welfare of the recipient than on the spiritual welfare of the philanthropist—attempts to prevent paupers from drinking became more insistent. After the 1830s this caused friction between publicans and poor law officials, and poor law reform was recommended largely as a temperance measure. From 1834 there was a tendency towards giving outdoor relief in kind rather than in cash.[57] In 1846 Queen Victoria ceased to give tickets for ale among her new year's gifts to the Windsor poor. Applicants to the cotton famine relief committees had to face rigorous scrutiny, and the Charity Organization Society emphasized that indiscriminate charity, by providing funds for drink, often deepened poverty. 'Alas!' wrote M. D. Hill to Brougham in 1861, 'we have learnt that to give without doing more harm than good is a difficult achievement.' Sir Charles Trevelyan and the Charity Organization Society came out publicly for temperance legislation in 1871.[58]

Three dramatic incidents show temperance reformers in this period struggling to expose the contradictions between the brewer's livelihood and his philanthropic role. At Birmingham in 1852 the temperance zealot Henry Gale provoked great indignation when he ventured to point out, at a meeting of the Church Missionary Society, that missionaries would be more effective if their drinking habits did not set a bad example to the natives. During the subsequent *mêlée*, Gale's glasses were trampled on and he was expelled from the meeting without being given a chance to defend himself.[59] The second incident occurred at the 1857 annual meeting of the Macclesfield auxiliary of the British and Foreign Bible Society. Several teetotalers tried to block the election of drinksellers and manufacturers as officers of the society; they broke up the meeting by creating what the local paper called 'one of the most disgraceful scenes ever witnessed in Macclesfield'. Such disturbances would be avoided, commented the *Alliance Weekly News* on 12 December, if religious societies had the sense to exclude from their committees 'persons whose presence is an outrage against the moral sense of a religious public'.

Perhaps most dramatic of all were the activities of the young F. N. Charrington. Walking to his ragged school one evening in 1873 from the family brewery in Mile End, he saw a man come out of a public-house and knock down his wife, who was pleading for money, into the gutter. Charrington at once looked up to see his own name in huge gilt letters above the public-house and realized in a moment the hypocrisy involved in his family's good works. Thenceforward he abandoned all income from the family brewery and worked for the poor in the East End. At a meeting for supporters of school board candidates he created a *furore* which rivals the incidents of 1852 and 1857. When the brewer William Hoare referred to ragged children wandering the streets without education, Charrington declared: 'why, it is you, Mr. Hoare, with your beer, and you, Mr. Buxton, and you, Sir Edmund Hay-Currie, with your gin, who are causing these wretched, ragged children to be roaming about our streets.' Great excitement followed, and amid the unprintable language of his opponents, Charrington sprang on to the platform and urged the meeting to support temperance candidates.[60]

Thomas Binney claimed that by 1850, the brewer T. F. Buxton could never have wielded such unchallenged influence in the anti-slavery movement. Teetotalers publicized the futility of a London City Mission which departed from the teetotal principles of its founder David Nasmith and accepted patronage from the Buxtons. During the 1850s the contradiction between the brewers' Sunday brewing and sabbatarian activities was similarly exposed. By the 1860s, temperance reformers had begun to influence a few conscientious brewers. R. J. Fremlin, the evangelical brewer-philanthropist of Maidstone, confined himself to the 'family trade' for this reason. W. E. Forster was one of many whose Quaker conscience made them reject any involvement in brewing profits; by the 1870s some politicians, including Hartington, feared that temperance attacks on publicans' respectability might lower the quality of entrants into the trade.[61] Nevertheless the Buxtons in the 1860s could still take a leading part in the agitation against Governor Eyre, and teetotal attacks on the respectability of drink manufacturers and sellers were sometimes so bitter that they achieved the reverse of their objective.

The representation of the drink interest on municipal authorities varied markedly from town to town, but municipal reform in the 1830s shook the drink interest's influence in at least some local authorities. In Banbury, Preston and some other towns the election of reformers to local councils in 1835–6 was celebrated by selling off the old silver tankards and wine cellars; with these developments, temperance reformers—including the Preston teetotalers—were sometimes associated.[62] John Cadbury took the lead in abolishing feasting among the Birmingham poor law guardians, and Banbury reformers sang:

> *'No more they'll enjoy*
> *Their old corporate dinners,*
> *And guttle, and guzzle,*
> *And quarrel, poor sinners!'*

Still, Joseph Chamberlain in Birmingham did not supplant the local Woodman regime till the 1870s, and the continued fear of the drinksellers' local political influence obstructed his schemes for municipalizing the drink trade. Furthermore Birmingham seems to have been exceptional in curbing the local power of drink at this time. Mid-Victorian brewers were powerful enough on local councils to obstruct many attempts at merging borough and county police forces. In 1872 the Licensing Act, with its local control provisions in regard to drinking hours, caused a marked rise in drink representation at Newcastle-Under-Lyme—from 9·4% of all successful candidates in 1835–71 to 19·8% in 1872–1914. In Leeds, drink representation rose rapidly in the town council up to its high-point, 16·9% of the whole, in 1902.[63]

At a national level throughout the period the drink interest was mobilizing itself—usually in response to outside attack.[64] The Licensed Victuallers' Protection Society was founded in London in 1833 to guard publicans against malicious prosecution by informers. Similarly the threat to the Trade represented by the Wilson Patten Act of 1854 inspired the formation in that year of the Licensed Victuallers' Defence League at Birmingham, in protest at the timidity of the local United Towns' Association. The crisis of 1869–72 stimulated a further mobilization: the Manchester Brewers' Association and the Brewers' Union date from 1870, the Liverpool and District Brewers'

Association from 1871; as for the Country Brewers' Society, its expansion after 1871 has already been noted. In 1872 the London Licensed Victuallers' Protection Society formed a London and Home Counties League which competed to some extent with the two Birmingham publicans' organizations. The latter amalgamated in the same year to form the Licensed Victuallers' National Defence League.

Although this reorganization was substantial, the influence of these bodies should not be exaggerated. Brewers and publicans in the north of England found it difficult to co-operate with the drink interest in the country towns of the south, and there were jealousies between provincials and Londoners—not to mention the conflicts of interest between wine merchants, publicans, beersellers, distillers and brewers. With all these qualifications, the political influence of drink was formidable: 'I know of nothing equal to the power you possess of managing and marshalling your forces,' said Bright to a Birmingham publicans' deputation of 1868. In 1880 Bright looked back somewhat wistfully to 1835, when there had been no organized publican hostility to the municipal reform Bill's licensing proposals: this could never have occurred in 1880.[65]

If anything, the brewers probably gained from the 1832 Reform Act. Whereas with the old constituency, Oxford, Shrewsbury and Newcastle had 35, 12 and 9 publicans respectively—in the new constituency the equivalent figures were 123, 83 and 174. And of five constituencies whose poll-books enable a comparison with previous elections, four—York, Leicester, Oxford and Shrewsbury—show the publicans in 1832 as a larger proportion of the total electorate than previously. During the 1830s several M.P.s testified to the electoral power of the drink interest.[66] The institution of beersellers' rating qualifications in 1840 brought yet another category of drinkseller on to the electoral roll. Temperance reformers often stressed the high proportion of drinksellers in particular constituencies before 1867, 70 publicans and 39 beersellers in a total constituency of 494 at Kidderminster in 1857, for example.[67] The magistrates in the 1860s were still using their licensing power as a way of distributing rewards for political service, and the democratization of share-capital in the late nineteenth century greatly increased the numbers financially interested in the Trade.[68]

Drink bribes at election time were another source of influence. Franchise extension in 1867 was less effective in promoting electoral sobriety than many radicals hoped; the 1868 election cost £600,000 more than its predecessor in election expenses. Indeed, treating was a convenient way of controlling large constituencies; it had long been more common in municipal elections, with their relatively wide franchise, than in national elections.[69] As long as drinksellers remained divided, and as long as drink was distributed indiscriminately and by supporters of both political parties, electoral corruption did not necessarily lend political influence to the drink interest. The candidates' distribution of drink was as much a bribe to the publicans as to the voters. Nevertheless such largesse helped to reinforce the role of the public-house as the centre of local political activity. Before this could be successfully challenged, many changes were required in political attitudes and social conditions. Only a start had been made towards this before the 1870s.

As long as voters had to travel long distances at election time, they could hardly be denied 'refreshment'. Before railways had taken much of the arduousness out of travel, and before the increase in the number of polling places—the withdrawal of such refreshment seemed equivalent to disfranchising the poorer electors. Improvement in both these respects between the 1820s and the 1870s made it possible to curtail the duration of polling. As early as 1840 Baines suggested that voting should take place on only one day.[70] As for committee rooms in public-houses—as late as the 1868 election for the City of London, 17 of the 23 Liberal and 7 of the 19 Conservative committee rooms were in licensed premises.[71] It was not till the 1860s that agitation for removing committee rooms from public-houses even began; in the 1880s M.P.s were still arguing that political parties would have nowhere to meet if they were excluded from public-houses. Dean Close's suggestion of 1865, that public-houses should be closed during the election, was not tried out till 1880; an M.P. in 1882 still considered it 'mere hypocrisy' to regard treating and bribery as equally blameworthy.[72]

Though change was slow, there was some progress during the period towards a more businesslike concept of the election, instead of regarding it as a sporting contest. Traditional attitudes were being attacked directly at the same time from another direction—by the radicals, Chartists, Anti-Corn Law Leaguers and others who wished to transform elections into nationwide contests of principle. Until the link between property-ownership and the holding of a parliamentary seat had been destroyed, elections were hardly likely to change in character. As one M.P. rightly pointed out in 1852, corruption among the electors accompanied corruption at Westminster.[73] Before the expenses of elections could be borne by the rates, said Gladstone in 1868, it must be decided 'whether sitting and voting in the House was a privilege to be enjoyed by the individual or a duty to be performed towards the community'.[74] If elections could be transformed into debates on how to improve social conditions, voters would have less reason to accept bribes. From being a saturnalia in which voters were given free drink and allowed to riot for a day in exchange for empowering their masters to rule them for seven years—the election could be transformed into a sober declaration of opinion. 'The spread of political *convictions* is the only efficient remedy for political corruption,' wrote the *Economist* on 1 August 1868. Active in this cause was the United Kingdom Alliance; several prohibitionist candidates between 1857 and 1868—Lees, Cossham, Pope and others—denounced local factions. The Alliance aimed to transcend local interests and corrupt practices by launching a national debate on matters of principle. Samuel Pope in 1872 considered that one of the tasks of the Alliance was to teach the political parties that they could only suffer by encouraging violence at elections. Its initial address claimed that the use of drink at elections was 'a public evil of fearful magnitude, which greatly counteracts the benefits of our representative system of government'.[75]

A further prerequisite for electoral purity was a changed attitude towards drunkenness and corruption; unless a widespread sense of shame accompanied conviction for bribery, anti-corruption legislation would ensnare only the poor or the conscientious candidate. Again, it was difficult to distinguish bribery from the gift-exchange which symbolized the continuance of long-standing social relations; as long as voting was still influenced by the bond between landlord and tenant or by the community sentiment of a locality, it was difficult to distinguish refusal to bribe from sheer meanness or stand-offishness. This was the standpoint taken by Col. Sibthorp when opposing early Victorian anti-corruption legislation; the problem still arises in modern Africa.[76]

How effective were temperance societies in combating this foe? They certainly suffered in the north of England by electoral corruption at the 1832 and 1837 elections. Only widespread educational campaigns could make treating seem as serious an offence as bribery. The effect of direct exhortation to electoral sobriety was probably very limited. Some individual candidates connected with the temperance movement—J. J. Gurney and Joseph Pease, for instance—repudiated corruption, though in both these cases the repudiation occurred before the temperance movement could have influenced them at all strongly. In some areas—as at Bath in 1832, at Bury St. Edmunds in 1841, and at Bath, Bristol and Manchester in 1852—the local temperance society's appeals secured from all candidates a promise not to open public-houses during the campaign. In 1841 Bradford Temperance Society canvassed 709 electors and induced 532 of them, together with over a hundred influential non-electors, to petition all committees against using public-houses during the campaign. The petition succeeded and one national teetotal organization urged all temperance societies to do likewise. At the 1868 election W. S. Caine and the Liverpool Permissive Bill Canvassing Association induced Liberals in all sixteen wards of the town to hold committee rooms and meetings away from public-houses, but the Association failed with the Conservatives in fifteen out of sixteen instances.[77]

The national temperance societies during election time usually issued a general appeal for sobriety; but these appeals displayed much of that desire to avoid complicity in evil which so often characterized temperance activity. The language of the National Temperance League's 1868 appeal was ridiculed by *The Times* on 31 October: it was impractical and far too pious in tone to influence the beer-drinker. How influential, then, were the temperance movement's efforts? Baines felt in 1861 that they had not been in vain;[78] though their direct influence was limited, temperance reformers were powerful in radical bodies like the Anti-Corn Law League and the Complete Suffrage Union. Temperance reformers could not single-handedly transform the character of British politics, especially when they lacked parliamentary influence. But they did help to create the climate of opinion which eventually made legislation effective after the 1880s. When Ostrogorski was investigating British political parties in the 1880s he still found election-time very reminiscent of Derby Day; to the women and children it brought 'all the excitement of a fair'. Nevertheless, elections were slowly losing their festive air and assuming their modern austerity. The turning-point seems to have come in the 1880s and not before.[79]

Surveying briefly then, from the temperance viewpoint, the changes between the 1820s and the 1870s in the influence of drink, of drinksellers and of the drink interest—there had been a marked change. Alternative thirst-quenchers had become cheaper and more accessible. Seasonal and religious festivals had become more sober, and the link between drinksellers and long-distance public transport had been severely weakened. In other spheres, only

TABLE 10

National Tax Revenue Raised from Alcoholic Liquors: 1819–1967

YEAR	TOTAL LIQUOR TAXATION (£1000s)	TOTAL TAXES FROM ALL SOURCES (£1000s)	PERCENTAGE OF TOTAL
1819	17,014	54,460	31·2
1829	16,932	52,523	32·2
1839	16,208	49,033	33·0
1849	16,356	54,325	30·1
1859–60	21,750	65,372	33·3
1869–70	24,899	66,727	37·3
1879–80	28,980	66,682	43·4
1889–90	31,162	78,678	39·6
1899–1900	41,686	108,496	38·4
1909–10	38,834	140,679	27·6
1919–20	133,873	998,960	13·4
1929–30	129,634	676,576	19·1
1939–40	130,806	1,049,189	12·5
1949–50	400,761	3,924,031	10·2
1959–60	390,728	5,630,529	6·9
1966–67	688,700	10,278,900	6·7

SOURCE: G. B. Wilson, *Alcohol & the Nation* (1940), p. 197; *Brewers' Almanack* (official handbook of the Brewers' Society, 1962); *Annual Abstract of Statistics* No. 104 (1967), pp. 269–70.

the basis for change had been laid. A start was made towards supplanting the drinking place as a trading centre and meeting place and as a 'home from home' for working men. The medical arguments in favour of alcoholic prescription had been challenged, together with the philanthropic prestige of the drink interest. But in some areas the influence of drink had probably increased—in the development of the music-hall for instance, and in the mobilization of political power. The association between drink and patriotism had hardly been shaken, and the proportion of the total national revenue raised from intoxicants had actually increased [see Table 10]. Robert Lowe in 1873 described the habitual drunkard as 'the sheet anchor of the British Constitution', and in the same year a friend of Lord Derby declared that 'we have drunk ourselves out of the American difficulty'—that increases in the liquor revenue had enabled the nation to pay off the Alabama Claims painlessly.[80]

So while on balance temperance reformers might claim a partial victory over their enemy by 1872, they had received powerful aid from without, and their victory was by no means as complete as the early teetotalers had hoped. The anti-spirits agitation had collapsed; the teetotalers had insulated only a small proportion of the population from temptation; prohibition, after nineteen years' agitation, had not yet been enacted; and the free trade campaign had been largely abandoned, after greatly expanding the number of licences for selling wine and beer. Only the counter-attractive and municipalization campaigns continued to gather force after 1872. With these conclusions in mind, we can now assess the achievement and character of the four anti-drink campaigns so far discussed.

16

Assessments

It is difficult to see how the counter-attractionist attack on the drink problem could fail to extend sobriety; can the same be said about the other four campaigns against drunkenness? Free licensing, total abstinence from spirits, teetotalism and prohibitionism were all remedies advocated by intelligent men, and which attracted extensive or influential support: only two of them, teetotalism and prohibitionism, have been studied by historians. Unfortunately nobody has yet analysed the campaign for free licensing, partly because its remedy was ultimately discredited; unlike the temperance movement, it left behind no champions to record its history with sympathy. Furthermore free licensing was never a campaign which aimed only at sobriety. It attacked, among other things, administrative corruption, extravagant government expenditure, class and religious oppression, war smuggling, illicit distilling and artificial tariff barriers between nations. And although the rational self-directed citizen was essential to its social ideal, it sought temperance through education rather than through restrictive legislation. The promotion of temperance was in reality no more than an incidental advantage of its licensing policy—though temperance received a rather higher priority in its public statements.

The free licenser was dominated by a wholly inappropriate model of the drink trade—and indeed of human nature. His ideal customer was a self-directed rational citizen who never made unpremeditated entries into a drinking place. When he entered, he knew precisely how much drink he intended to consume. His surroundings never caused him to modify his original intentions, and if he found the product unsatisfactory he immediately took his custom elsewhere. The number of drinksellers never exceeded the demand because only those who provided a good article remained in business: it never fell below the demand because competent men were always available and willing to enter the trade. This model had little contact with reality. Dawson Burns emphasized that in deciding whether to apply free trade principles in a particular area, one must first investigate the nature of the article concerned. 'Everything that looked like trade, and every bargain, was not trade,' said Samuel Pope in 1861. Livesey claimed that to defend free trade in intoxicants was as absurd as to require druggists to leave poison bottles unlabelled.[1]

Temperance reformers tried to draw back political economists from a doctrinaire insistence on free trade which was, after all, only a *means* to their end: the maximization of wealth. The prosperity of so disruptive a trade could never be compatible with national prosperity. 'I wish true political economy had long since been applied to this subject', wrote Livesey of the licensing question in 1855: '. . . for its verdict must have been to close every distillery, brewery, and drinkshop in the land'. Drinksellers and their victims burdened the sober with unnecessary police and other expenses; society had a right, said M. D. Hill, 'to stop mere indulgences which have a clear and practical tendency to create burdens on its funds'. The consumption of intoxicants did not create fresh wealth—it destroyed it.[2] For this reason, chancellors of the exchequer, once temperance sentiment had begun to influence attitudes at Westminster, actually welcomed a reduction of revenue here, whereas in other taxed articles such a reduction would have caused alarm. For the same reason, temperance legislation became one of the few spheres in which mid-Victorian nonconformists abandoned much of their hostility to monopoly: 'monopoly is very bad when the article is good, and monopoly is very good, when the article is bad,' said Samuel Bowly in 1863.[3] Such an apology for temperance legislation left temperance reformers quite free to defend *laissez-faire* principles elsewhere, and they often in fact did so.

There were three major flaws in the free licensers' attitude towards the drink trade: they exaggerated the rigidity of demand, over-estimated the mobility and rationality of custom, and exaggerated the ease and rapidity with which supply would approximate to demand. As early as 1798 Arthur Young admitted the importance of the first of these factors when he insisted that 'multiplied ale-houses are multiplied temptations'. Intoxicants, by promoting their own consumption, frustrated the laws of supply and demand. Free licensers claimed that an excess of bakers, butchers or grocers did not tempt the public to overeat: to which temperance reformers replied that the eating of bread and meat moderated hunger, whereas the alcohol drinking could actually stimulate thirst. 'Excess of supply', said Bruce in 1871, 'was not self-corrective to the same extent as it was in other trades.' Furthermore demand was pushed up by the auxiliary social functions of the drinking place. In opposition to the 'less licence' policy, Lord Salisbury claimed that he slept no better at Hatfield for the knowledge that his house contained a hundred beds: he forgot that drinking places, unlike beds, could manufacture the needs which they supplied. At an Alliance public meeting in October 1872 Professor Rolleston produced the familiar temperance rejoinder to arguments of this type by referring to the poor woman who said 'I can get my husband, sir, past two public-houses, but I cannot get him past twenty.'[4]

Whereas the grocer did not encourage the drinking of the relatively harmless tea on his premises, the drinkseller accommodated both sale and consumption of alcoholic drinks. It was easy for the customer to forget his original intentions and to consume more than was good either for himself or for his family.

The free licensers were mistaken when they assumed that in a free trade system the suppliers of bad beer would always suffer; for the highly rational and mobile customer was rare among pubgoers. Drinkers were often members of clubs which met regularly at one place for years; or else they shirked the emotional effort involved in changing their circle of acquaintances merely for the sake of getting a slightly better article elsewhere. Furthermore intoxicants like all liquids were easily adulterated, and adulteration actually becomes more prevalent with increased competition. This happened even with bread after the Assize of Bread was abolished in 1815—let alone after the Beer Act of 1830. In the sphere of drink, the rational and discriminating customer essential to free trade theory did not always exist, even where adulteration had not taken place. The individual could be the best judge of his own interest only where he had access to special knowledge; urban conditions made this knowledge more difficult for the layman to acquire. 'When we say that free competition must ultimately rid the market of inferior goods', wrote Robert Williams in 1870, 'we forget that life is often too short for fraud to be properly exposed. Honesty would be the best policy, and the interests of buyer and of seller would be identical, if we all lived for some two or three hundreds of years.'[5] Keynes put the argument more succinctly: 'in the long run', he wrote, 'we are all dead'.

Free licensers assumed that in a free trade system supply would rapidly adjust itself to demand; yet in towns the drinkseller's subsidiary social functions enabled him to respond to a declining demand for intoxicants—not by going out of business, as would necessarily occur in more specialized trades—but by installing dances, prostitutes, music and floor-shows. And if eventually he failed, his failure would be attributed not to insufficient demand but to unenterprising supply; his fate would not therefore prevent others from trying where he had failed. The bankruptcy of many early beersellers after 1830 did not prevent the number of beershops from rising till 1836: numbers did not drop until after the restrictive legislation of 1840.[6] In some areas, however, the free trade argument was falsified in the reverse direction: free licensers too readily assumed that anybody could sell beer—whereas capital, house-room and expertise were needed to handle so perishable an article. These handicaps could be overcome by obtaining capital from a brewer, but this was merely to restore the monopoly which the free licensers opposed.

Free licensers assumed that if the rational customer did not already exist, he would eventually be created by extending elementary education. As Robert

Lowe, a staunch free licenser, wrote in 1879 'in my opinion the causes of intemperance are to be sought in the ill-regulated minds and unbridled appetites of its votaries rather than in the lawful and useful trade whose legitimate uses they abuse'. Yet for many working men, mere intellectual counter-attractions were hardly likely to suffice. Mark Rutherford's education certainly enabled him to overcome drink temptations, yet even for him the struggle was intense: any man, he wrote, who has rescued himself from craving half a bottle of claret daily 'may assure himself that there is nothing more in life to be done which he need dread'. The educated classes produced many alcoholics; to name only a few well-known victims, there were Bradlaugh's wife, T. H. Green's brother, Henry Ashworth's son, George Cruikshank's father, Robert Owen's cousin Richard Williams and Sir John Simon's adopted daughter. Temperance reformers pointed to the many famous but drunken literary men: something more than mere book-learning, they said, was needed. 'People often talked about education', said Lawson, 'when they meant . . . merely instruction.'[7] It was not that temperance reformers lacked faith in education: it was simply that their concept of education was broader, and involved not only the classroom but also the domestic environment. Lord Shaftesbury would be far more effective in the ragged school movement if he became a teetotaler, said Samuel Bowly.[8] Temperance reformers argued that abstinence and prohibition were the best means of preparing the ground for the educationist—even of providing him with the necessary funds. 'Let the friends of education become the patrons and consistent members of teetotal societies,' wrote one teetotaler in 1843, 'and WE SHALL HAVE NATIONAL EDUCATION CARRIED ON BY THE PEOPLE THEMSELVES.'[9]

With drink as with prostitution, nineteenth-century England saw a singular reversal of public policy: but whereas with prostitution, the government moved from regulation to free trade, with drunkenness it moved in the reverse direction. For while free licensing may not have endangered sobriety as seriously as temperance reformers believed, it certainly did not relieve intemperance to the degree that free licensers anticipated. Too many of the social preconditions for the success of free licensing were lacking in nineteenth-century England. The advocates of free licensing expected too much of human nature, and like so many political economists, showed a marked ignorance of the capacity, situation and mentality of those whom their measures were primarily designed to benefit. By the 1880s, the free licensing policy had fallen into eclipse and has never been revived.

Yet in comparison with the other three remedies, free licensing had its virtues: its advocates were relatively unsectarian in outlook. They always admitted that the removal of drunkenness would require many concurrent improvements in society: they never posed as guardians of the sole possible remedy for the drink problem. Indeed, many of them supported the voluntary abstinence movement as a complementary remedy. In a coalwhippers' debate of 1843, Bowring argued that 'the state of intemperance of these men was occasioned by the interference of Parliament. Instead of an act of Parliament, they should send the Apostle of Temperance [i.e. Father Mathew] among them.' He was sorry, he went on, to see Gladstone 'departing from the sound principles of political economy'.[10] Free licensers never expected any dramatic and sudden change as a result of their policy; they were quite willing to try gradual solutions and, in particular, to encourage the consumption of weaker intoxicants at the expense of the stronger. However mistaken they may have been, their good sense in these respects contrasts refreshingly with the mentality of the three types of temperance reformer who must now be considered.

The history of the anti-spirits movement has been neglected because it was almost too successful; for its basic principle, total abstinence, was taken up by reformers and pushed so much further that the disciples turned against the pioneers. When teetotalers wrote the history of the temperance movement, they regarded the anti-spirits movement patronizingly as a movement which failed to follow truth to its fountainhead. Dr. Grindrod, a pioneer teetotaler, still alive in the 1880s when temperance jubilees were being held, argued that the temperance movement began with teetotalism and not with the anti-spirits agitation; he therefore opposed the holding of the jubilee in 1880, fifty years after the founding of the British and Foreign Temperance Society, and wanted it held two or three years later.[11] The history of the B.F.T.S. was interpreted by temperance historians entirely from the teetotal viewpoint; teetotalers regarded abstinence from spirits as illogical without abstinence also from beer. Yet it is now arguable that even the teetotal rationale was unsoundly based. The B.F.T.S. had in fact several virtues which teetotal historians failed to notice.

It introduced the temperance movement into Britain, distributed large quantities of propaganda and helped to make Britain aware that the drink problem existed. It did not confine itself to the relatively narrow task of reclaiming drunkards: it sought also to preserve the sobriety of the sober. Perhaps most important of all it tried to mobilize all sections of the community, including important sections of the drink trade itself, behind the campaign for sobriety. While the B.F.T.S. cut itself off from many opportunities by failing to encourage the spontaneous working-class moral enthusiasm which lay behind teetotalism, it did at least avoid the accompanying danger: the possibility that the temperance crusade might become a movement merely for extremists, who would alienate the most influential members of society. Teetotal historians write as though the loss of the respectable 'moderationists' in the 1830s constituted pure gain for temperance. This ignores the importance for nineteenth-century reforming movements of retaining the support of religion and aristocracy. The B.F.T.S. unlike the teetotalers was able to do this, whereas it rightly predicted that teetotalism would ally temperance with extreme political causes: indeed teetotalism killed off all chance of close co-operation between rich and poor in the temperance movement for a generation.

The loss of the moderationists also meant the final rupture between the temperance movement and all branches of the trade in intoxicating liquors; no longer would it be possible for temperance reformers to promote consumption of the weaker intoxicating drinks at the expense of the stronger. The triumph of teetotalism also meant the growth of a sectarian outlook which would deprive the movement of mid-Victorian philanthropic resources. So unfashionable had the temperance movement become by 1843 that Jane Welsh Carlyle shrank from taking the pledge in that year for fear that her action would appear in the newspapers.[12] The temperance movement acquired for twenty years the image of being 'an amiable fanaticism'[13]—however catholic in outlook some of its promoters might be. Teetotal historians tended to assume that when the B.F.T.S. died in 1848, its principles died with it. Yet these principles were revived with the Church of England Temperance Society's adoption in the early 1870s of the 'dual basis'—of moderation and teetotal pledges. Only on this basis could the temperance movement regain the width of social concern and the financial strength which would make really practicable temperance policies again feasible.

It would be wrong to over-react in favour of the B.F.T.S. Many of the teetotal movement's faults were already present in the anti-spirits movement: its close alignment with evangelical religion, its failure to realize the precise nature of the problems posed by an industrial and urban society, its principle of total abstinence as the core of the temperance campaign, and its lack of a genuine spirit of inquiry in dealing with social problems. Furthermore, the very fact that the anti-spirits movement was relatively fashionable brought with it the dangers of losing touch with the working man, and of failing to enlist him directly into the temperance movement. The teetotal movement never suffered from this danger, nor did it devote such disproportionate attention to intemperance overseas.

The most recent historian of the British temperance movement, Henry Carter, argues that the pioneer teetotaler Joseph Livesey 'judged by the standard of service rendered to the commonweal' was 'one of the really great Englishmen of the nineteenth century'. According to F. R. Lees, the teetotal movement 'arrested the progress of vice and the decay of the race'. How accurate are these claims? When a social evil declines, as drunkenness has undoubtedly declined in Britain during the last 150 years, it would be rash to assume that the movement aiming to promote that decline necessarily deserves the credit.[14] The temperance movement itself felt the need to counter what Dawson Burns called 'the pitiful accusation' that the temperance movement had failed because it had influenced only a limited proportion of the public. For F. R. Lees it was sufficient to retort that '*truth*, like physic, must be tried before it *can* fail'. He did not inquire whether public reluctance to try his movement's remedy could be attributed to some flaw in its character. Temperance historians made further claims: the pioneer teetotalers had not been motivated by self-interest: they were 'moved by motives perfectly correlated to their Divine mission, amongst which stand out pre-eminent a burning zeal, a devoted benevolence, and an unconquerable will'. Fifty years of temperance work enabled Dawson Burns to 'unhesitatingly affirm, that [apart from reclaimed drunkards] the men and women who, in all places, began the Temperance propaganda, were known to be animated by a desire, not so much to benefit themselves, as to do good to others'.[15] Although these late-Victorian assertions were unsupported by evidence or argument, the subsequent decline of the temperance movement has discouraged the twentieth century from testing them.

Yet if the opponents of nineteenth-century reform movements are regarded as sinners against the light, a distorted picture of nineteenth-century society results. There were always vigorous opponents of teetotalism and their criticisms deserve attention. G. J. Holyoake complained that temperance reformers were promoting 'comparatively the tardiest and most inefficient advocacy that the nineteenth century has seen'. It is impossible to prove conclusively that the level of drunkenness did decline during the first forty years of the temperance agitation, but even if we do assume that a decline occurred, there is no evidence for attributing this to the temperance movement. The more forthright teetotalers themselves admitted their disappointment with their limited success: 'in the early days', wrote Livesey in the 1860s, 'we felt that we were really engaged in a "*Temperance Reformation*". We gave heart and soul to it. . . . We seemed as if we would turn the world upside down. We scarcely feel in this mode now.'[16] It has already been shown that if the temperance agitation had any effect on drinking habits, it was only one among several influences.

There are further embarrassments for the eulogists of the temperance movement. There seems to be no direct relation between the intensity of temperance agitation and the decline of the evil. If the literary evidence can be accepted, the level of drunkenness was markedly declining in the late eighteenth century, before teetotalism appeared. And during the first forty years of temperance agitation the statistics for *per capita* consumption—increasingly accurate by the 1860s—show an actual increase; nor was this accompanied by any appreciable decline in the ratio of drinking places to population or to other trades. Again, the temperance movement was in marked decline at the time when the most striking, and statistically verifiable, reduction in the level of drinking occurred: that is, after the D.O.R.A.

regulations of the first world war. Temperance reformers cannot claim credit for the mid-Victorian trend towards milder intoxicants, for their movement firmly attacked the consumption of *all* intoxicants. Only two routes of escape are available to the defenders of the temperance movement: they can argue that, but for their movement, the figures for *per capita* consumption would have been even larger; and also that it is unfair to cut off the story at 1872, because the subsequent reduction in the *per capita* consumption figures owed much to the temperance movement's work *before* 1872. Both claims are unverifiable.

The teetotal movement in fact made two serious errors before 1872: it gave inadequate attention to the environmental factors creating drunkenness, and it was too sectarian for maximum effectiveness. In making the first of these errors the temperance movement deliberately rejected the analyses of the drink problem put forward by several prominent contemporaries; for even if Robert Owen's stress on environmental factors is ignored, Charles Dickens and Edwin Chadwick were preaching the same message. Dickens referred indignantly in 1844 to 'that monstrous doctrine which sets down as the *consequences* of Drunkenness, fifty thousand miseries which are, as all reflective persons know, and daily see, the wretched *causes* of it'. And in his sanitary report Chadwick emphasized that 'when intemperance is mentioned as the cause of disease . . . on carrying investigation a little further back, discomfort is found to be the immediate antecedent to the intemperance'. In attributing so many contemporary social ills—even the miseries resulting from the cotton famine—to drunkenness, temperance reformers sometimes completely lost their sense of proportion. Like the opponents of state-regulated prostitution the temperance reformers insisted, in John Morley's words, on 'treating prematurely brutalised natures as if they still retained infinite capabilities for virtue'.[17]

Most drunkenness in nineteenth-century England resulted from a social situation; teetotalers, by treating it as though it were compulsive or addictive, were usually on the wrong track. The hordes of prostitutes and drunkards in Victorian England were not psychological aberrations but the products of a particular socio-economic structure. To denounce the drunkenness of the nineteenth-century slum-dweller surrounded by warm and cheerful drink-shops and by a culture which justified their use—is as unreasonable as to condemn his mid-twentieth-century successors for race prejudice, or modern teenagers for sexual promiscuity: the environment acted as a constant incentive to the behaviour under condemnation. Without wider social changes, attempts to solve the problem by forming associations of abstainers could never hope to succeed.* Both the temperance and penitentiary movements in the nineteenth century acted on the assumption that sudden character

* The *Observer*, 4 Sept. 1966, announced that Reading Temperance Society was tackling the problem of premarital intercourse by forming associations of pledged virgins.

transformations could be produced merely by the sinner's exertion of will-power. Both movements claimed credit for rescuing isolated individuals from among the countless victims of an unjust social system which they did little to rectify. Teetotalers frequently broke their pledges because a mere pledge-signing did not modify the social conditions which had fostered the drinking. One of the most sensitive commentators on the nineteenth-century temperance movement noticed that 'most of our reformed drunkards were *spiritless* . . . men that did not seem to enjoy life'.[18] Like so many pioneer reformers the founders of teetotalism were in some respects behind the times in their attitude to their problem. The Good Samaritan model, involving individual compassion and reclamation, could never tackle the huge social problems thrown up by industrialization; nor could self-reliance and thrift effectively tackle poverty in a society whose peasants and craftsmen were in full retreat before agricultural and industrial capitalism.

The teetotaler's personal appeal for sobriety sprang from his ignorance of economic relationships. Teetotalers assumed that the working man's purchase of drink instead of property was voluntary—a valid assumption, perhaps, in a predominantly agricultural society, but far less valid in an industrializing society whose insufficient demand stems more from cyclical unemployment, low wages and social disruption. Inevitably the teetotal movement's expenditure on written and oral propaganda was largely wasted. Mayhew saw a man who had vigorously praised Cruikshank's *Bottle* drunk three hours afterwards, and Kohl observed that a quarter of the audience watching a temperance drama were drunk; while such spectacles might have been popular, they probably had little effect on daily conduct.[19] A more damaging indictment of the teetotal movement however, is the fact that many of its periodicals and even its tracts were calculated to appeal only to the sober; some outsiders accused the movement of aiming only to confirm the respectable in their respectability.

This is only the first of five brands of hypocrisy which have been detected in the movement by its critics; all of them have a grain of truth. The second is a development by Francis Place of the first: he thought he detected in the movement a machiavellian intention to demoralize the unsober by denouncing their vice, and thus to prevent them from rising out of their social sphere. For given that self-respect is the essence of sobriety, the drunkard's sense of shame makes his recovery even less likely.[20] Thirdly, it was convenient to focus attention on this vice not only to reinforce one's own respectability, but also perhaps because other vices at the time could not be discussed. Vaughan as headmaster of Harrow could lecture his boys on their drunkenness and Thomas Hughes could write of boys expelled from Rugby for 'smoking' but neither could discuss their sexual conduct. Drunkenness, which was widely supposed to lie at the root of all other sins was a convenient outlet for moral indignation. Another persistent criticism, nourished by the ubiquity of lapsed teetotalers, lay in the suspicion which Dickens often voiced: that temperance reformers themselves were often prepared to drink in private.[21] When the Alliance admitted drinkers to membership, its hypocrisy seemed flagrant. J. R. Stephens made full capital out of it in his speech at Stalybridge town hall in 1872. The popularity of the expression 'methody drinking' in the north of England shows how common such accusations were. Other critics, particularly Stephens, suspected a fifth and less excusable type of hypocrisy: the attempt of individuals themselves responsible for the miseries of industrial society to blame those miseries on their employees' weakness of will: the attempt of society to ease its conscience at the prevalence of drunkenness by providing a movement to denounce it, without embarking on the radical reforms necessary to remove the evil.

Two consequences—which seem more serious to posterity than they did to contemporaries—flowed from the teetotalers' belief that they could explain social ills in terms of individual moral failure: they failed to investigate the drink problem systematically and without bias, and they were—at least in the movement's earlier stages—relatively uninterested in financing counter-attractions to the drinking place. After forty years of temperance agitation, prominent observers were still lamenting the lack of precise information on central aspects of the drink problem. The absence of public inspectors in this sphere made research peculiarly necessary, for it is clear that 'one of the main limits on effective intervention by a government was its ignorance'. Yet teetotalers held to their panacea and collected only evidence that would support it. Their frame of mind was that of Wilberforce, who began reading a book after deciding on the propositions requiring to be proved, and then underlined the evidence in support. Such an approach was perhaps justified in exposing an evil, but not in prescribing the remedy.

This criticism does not make twentieth-century demands of nineteenth-century reformers because several of their contemporaries conducted detailed social investigations before championing reforms—Place investigating London morals and manners for instance, Edwin Chadwick and even Henry Mayhew. Even some temperance societies occasionally conducted intelligent inquiries. The Leeds Temperance Society in 1848 surveyed the temperance views of local religious leaders with remarkable impartiality, and the National Temperance League twice compiled maps of London's drink facilities—in 1860 and 1887. But these are exceptional instances: opponents' arguments were usually merely 'dealt with' or shouted down, seldom considered on their merits; too few temperance reformers shared Elizabeth Garrett's realization that 'degradation cannot be taken by storm and the animal side of nature will outlive crusades'.[22]

One reason for the wilful blindness of the teetotalers lies in their contempt for popular culture. So direct was its threat to their way of life that—unlike modern sociologists of the slums, safely removed from their subjects by several social degrees—teetotalers could not afford to risk the close contact involved in genuine investigation, or the objectivity which must accompany empirical research. Those who knew the poor well—Henry Mayhew in the 1850s for instance, or those two sensitive social commentators of the 1900s Stephen Reynolds and Miss Loane—knew that the complexities of the working-class situation must be studied closely before their conduct could safely be criticized. Parliamentary committees might have helped towards this if they had given less time to formal questionings of volunteer witnesses and more time to informal but penetrating research; but in practice they never interviewed pubgoers and therefore never discovered the pattern of life which moulded working-class drinking habits. 'If we would solve even the simplest of problems,' wrote Miss Loane in 1910, 'we must be willing to learn from the working classes, as well as to teach.' Sustained temperance research might have found—as did Miss Loane—that the 'vices' of the poor perhaps stemmed from a different set of ethical priorities, rather than from any moral inferiority to their social superiors.[23] The teetotal mentality makes G. D. H. Cole's verdict on Joseph Sturge applicable to many other teetotal leaders: 'his weakness was that, with all his ready sympathy, he looked much less at causes than at effects, and never penetrated below the surface ills of the society which he so ardently desired to reform'.[24] The politicians often legislated in complete ignorance of how their legislation would affect those who would feel it most. Temperance and other reformers frequently confused the issue by advertising irrelevant remedies. The riots which often followed gave ammunition to those who argued that parliament—in this and other spheres—should leave well alone.

William Acton's complaint against the penitentiary movement—that it failed to help the prostitute 'in the days of her prostitution'—applies also to the teetotalers who failed to sponsor counter-attractions.[25] Indeed, by throwing doubt on the publican's respectability and by depriving the public-house of its auxiliary attractions, teetotalers made it more of a mere 'drinkshop' than it need have been. They resisted both municipalization and the policy of increasing drink taxes because both would lend public recognition to a wicked trade.[26] And while individual temperance reformers might often support sanitary, housing and other environmental reforms, their movement's official attitude towards other social reform schemes was usually sectarian. Admittedly it provided temperance halls, temperance hotels, excursions and other counter-attractions—but only for those who had already abandoned the drink.

Sectarianism was in fact the second major defect of the teetotal movement. Fractious controversies over teetotal doctrine were endemic. Temperance periodicals sometimes unveil the bitter rivalries for power within the movement: the outspoken and independent *Temperance Spectator*, for instance, campaigned in 1859 against the British Temperance League's unenterprising leadership: 'we protest against the exclusive policy which these self-willed officials adopt. They claim the sole right to labor [*sic*] in the cause, and to decide what is and what is not to be done. They form around them a narrow circle of workers, and discountenance all others; they intrigue to secure office for their own friends, and exclude those who exercise an independent judgment.' Harsh language was used against compromisers and palliators; the reformed drunkard's onslaught against the moderate drinker perhaps aroused more indignation than any other teetotal characteristic.[27] But there were many other ways in which the teetotal movement was its own worst enemy: when John Dunlop, for instance, tried to work up a constructive agitation against drink usages and in favour of medical declarations, he was obstructed by temperance reformers with an interest in dazzling forms of advocacy and in spectacular legislative triumphs, rather than in steady and quiet forms of work.[28]

The teetotal movement's whole attitude to its task was narrowed by a sectarian outlook. Recruited primarily from nonconformists and working men, teetotalers were remote from experience of political power, and so their movement was circumscribed in its outlook by the immediate needs and experiences of its supporters. The most active teetotalers of the 1830s and 1840s fitted their teetotalism into a complex of beliefs which repudiated corrupt and aristocratic rule from London. They underestimated the need for physical coercion in society, and repudiated the customary methods of keeping public order—that is, the licensing system. In this they resembled the free licensers, but their experience of the Beer Act led them also to reject free trade. 'You are against both the magistracy and the excise?' asked Sir George Lewis, at a National Temperance League deputation during 1860: 'we think they both fail to a very great extent,' Tweedie replied, '—the excise thoroughly and the magistracy considerably.' Organized teetotalism provided another way of preserving public order which would weaken the authority of the ruling class and strengthen the social and political prestige of the ruled.

Very few magistrates supported teetotalism, and although Livesey concluded his *Malt Lecture* with an appeal for their aid, teetotal platforms more frequently rang with attacks on the magistrates than with appeals to them. The brewers and publicans whom the teetotalers attacked were often in some way dependent upon the support of a magistrate; brewers and magistrates moved at the same social level. The magistrates were at this period often well-to-do Tory squires or clergymen; nobody in 'trade' in Buckinghamshire, for instance, could become a magistrate in the 1850s.[29] This was precisely the social group whose power constituted an offence to many self-respecting nonconformists and working men. Rev. G. W. McCree in 1860 claimed that, though there were exceptions, 'fools, knaves, and profligates often climb to places of honour. Their riches, family influence, territorial possessions, political principles, or pushing impudence enables them to ascend to the seat of judgment. Such men are an eye-sore—a scandal—a nuisance.'[30]

Many reforming campaigns enjoy criticizing those in authority: often when power has been won, their underlying bankruptcy of ideas is exposed. For not only do the reformers lack experience in running the existing system of authority: they also lack blueprints for altering it. Guy Aldred found some reformers of this type in the early Labour party. These men, he wrote, 'were completely satisfied with preaching socialism. They had no real desire to accomplish any change, even though they thought they had. All they wanted was to gain artistic expression. For this they were prepared to endure hunger, to face hardship, provided always that they could interpose between themselves and that hardship a barrier of beautiful words.'[31] This legacy was to prove embarrassing once the Labour party gained office in the 1920s.

Many nineteenth-century reforming movements contented themselves with the setting of standards without seriously asking why so many people failed to live up to them. Instead, they indulged in the pious exculpatory protest at the wickedness of their generation.[32] Teetotalism was only one branch of a general policy, widespread among nonconformists, of trying to avoid contamination from evil by shunning all contact with it. One could avoid responsibility for war by abstaining from fighting, escape from sexual temptation through shunning the theatre and the novel, and avoid compromising one's principles by refusing ever to take office; if enough individuals displayed this attitude, the evils in question would wither away. In practice, however, such an outlook merely created an élite whose behaviour was distinct from that of the community at large. Drugs are prominent in both nineteenth- and twentieth-century attacks on the establishment: but whereas nineteenth-century dissenters ostentatiously abstained from them, their twentieth-century teenage successors conspicuously consume them. Like the modern French Communists, nineteenth-century teetotalers evolved their own bureaucracy, press, parliamentary machine, clubs, ritual, rewards and punishments: they constituted a distinct community within the state, protesting continually against 'the system' but unable—perhaps even unwilling—to overturn it. Was this wise? Joseph Livesey once recalled his refusal for many years to attend gatherings where wine was consumed: 'I am not sure but I have carried this feeling too far; it has tended to separate me so much from the influential classes that the temperance cause may have gained less than it would have done by my mixing more with them.' It was here that the B.F.T.S., and the Church of England Temperance Society, with its 'dual basis', gained over the rigid teetotaler in ultimate effectiveness. The teetotal movement between the 1830s and 1870s always remained, in Kate Courtney's words, 'too narrow to take the whole world in'.[33]

When applied at the national level, this policy required the state to turn away from evils like prostitution, betting, drunkenness or the drug traffic—to ban them, not to regulate them. A Congregational minister told the 1881 inquiry that Congregationalists—who seldom held public positions—usually opposed the Contagious Diseases Acts because, unlike the local authorities, they had little continuous contact with the evil in question.[34] 'How long shall this Traffic continue to be licensed by a *Christian* government?' asked the *British and Foreign Temperance Intelligencer* on 31 August 1839. A natural corollary of this policy was of course to blacken the evil to be shunned: to divide the community into sheep and goats. The English Peace Congress committee of the 1850s, anxious to emphasize the miseries of war, refused to help relieve Crimean War widows:[35] likewise the temperance movement, anxious to advertise the miseries of drunkenness, resisted publicans' attempts to patronize other recreations besides drinking [see Plate 28].

It is sometimes easier to understand a historical sequence if one imagines an alternative sequence and asks why it did not occur. Assuming the existence in the nineteenth century of a serious drink problem, the ideal temperance campaign might have run as follows. The campaign would not be associated with religious recruiting: propaganda would be centred on the medical and practical arguments for sobriety. For it was never clear in the nineteenth century whether teetotal principles were compatible with Christian belief, and apart from fostering endless disputes the religious connexion severely limited the movement's appeal. The idea of any sudden and complete abolition of drunkenness would be abandoned, and the association of abstainers would exist as only one branch of the temperance campaign. Any *a priori* approach to the complex problems of drunkenness would be rejected and research would be sponsored in many directions, together with detailed survey-work on conditions overseas and pilot-schemes in limited areas to test the various remedies suggested. A purely negative approach would be abandoned: taxes on non-intoxicating drinks would be removed, and commercial experiments would be promoted to develop new and more palatable types of non-intoxicating drink. Taxes on alcoholic drinks would be raised on a graduated scale according to their strength, and public-houses would be encouraged to sell food and non-intoxicating drinks; a few model public-houses would be established to show the feasibility of such a policy, and at every stage efforts would be made to work in co-operation with the most enlightened sections of the drink trade. Counter-attractions would be provided, including alternative places for wage-payment, an improved and more accessible water supply, parks, libraries, decent working-class housing and improved recreations, particularly at times when leisure was most abundant—above all on Sundays. In the existing state of education and public opinion, temperance legislation would still be needed, and total abstinence would survive—if only as the practice of alcoholics in sanatoria. Written and oral propaganda against outworn drink customs and unfounded medical theories, together with education in domestic economy, would still be required.

The individual items in this programme were by no means always impracticable at the time—indeed several were acted upon by contemporaries. When judged against this programme, Shaftesbury and Gladstone might be regarded as more effective temperance reformers than Gough or Lees, Pope or Lawson. Much of this programme was advocated by William Lovett, J. S. Buckingham, Joseph Livesey and G. J. Holyoake. Earl Stanhope soon faded out of temperance history, yet his strategy was wise—opposition to extremist attacks on the publican, and to any kind of religious or political entanglement. The extrusion of drinksellers and drink manufacturers from the temperance movement was never inevitable. Brewers had been active in the anti-spirits movement, Charles Buxton's article in the *North British Review* had influenced the origins of the Permissive Bill, and at several moments publicans co-operated with temperance reformers in opposing free licensing. If temperance reformers had followed Canon Harper's advice and encouraged parsons to enter rather than to shun public-houses, more might have been achieved for sobriety.

If the temperance movement had worked through the 'godly publican'—through men like the prominent Methodist New Connexion publican and choirmaster in early Victorian Dawley, William Tranter, who refused to serve drinks on Sundays, refused to serve customers who had drunk enough, and refused to allow bad language in his house: if the movement had fully exploited the strong connexions between religion and the drink interest—it might have kept more closely in touch with reality. A man like T. F. Buxton or a family like the Charringtons could certainly have been mobilized behind so reasonable a campaign. Indeed the evangelical vicar of Wendover in the 1840s promoted voluntary Sunday closing throughout his parish by forming a publicans' association, and Archbishop Manning in the 1860s made direct approaches to Catholic publicans in his diocese.[36] Late-Victorian Welsh drinksellers included many sympathizers with the temperance movement: of 1,173 Welsh publicans canvassed in 1878–80, 792 favoured total Sunday closing. As late as the 1880s Barclay and Perkins' Southwark brewery was paying six shillings more per week to its many teetotal employees who did not take their beer allowance, and supported special missionary work in the area. Charles Booth noted the many respectable drinksellers in the East End of London: 'go into any of these houses—the ordinary public-house at the corner of any ordinary East End street. . . . Behind the bar will be a decent middle-aged woman, something above her customers in class, very neatly dressed, respecting herself and respected by them. The whole scene comfortable, quiet, and orderly.'[37]

Nevertheless it is hardly necessary to say that so reasonable a temperance programme would have been totally impracticable in nineteenth-century conditions. For it presupposes a world in which drunkenness is no longer so serious an evil that observers are driven to extreme courses in trying to combat it. Nineteenth-century teetotalers detested the lighter forms of recreation because they saw daily the disastrous effects it seemed to produce. According to modern social surveys, teetotalers and drunkards congregate in the same regions. There is some evidence that this dietary polarization also existed in nineteenth-century England, though we lack the regional consumption statistics which could prove it. There is a high correlation between the number of drunkenness proceedings per 100,000 population in English counties during 1875 and the number of Alliance donors for the financial year 1873–4. This may merely reflect the police tendency to pursue a temperance policy only where local opinion demands it. But literary evidence also points towards polarization. Several temperance reformers noted that drunkards were less obtrusive in London—where drinking places were relatively few: where the relatively mild drinks, beer and tea, were notoriously popular: and where the temperance movement was always weak. Conversely, Bishop Fraser, when he moved from the south of England to Lancashire, the home of teetotalism, was shocked at the prevalence of drunkenness there: 'I had no idea of the extent of the ravages caused by intemperance till I came into Lancashire,' he told Gladstone in 1870. 'Here I see the demon in the fulness of his power—demoralizing, corrupting, criminalizing a noble people.' Extreme temperance policies were, and are, a natural response to excessive drinking. In a barbarous society needing to be civilized, there are some arguments for teetotal hypocrisy—often 'the result of the attempt to lay claim to new standards of conduct which proved to be too hard to maintain consistently'.[38] Furthermore the ideal temperance programme assumes the existence of temperance reformers not socially conditioned to use reforming agitations as a way of releasing their resentments against those in authority. In 1850 J. S. Mill spoke of temperance societies 'which *prima facie* have the air of an absurdity, being associations not for the purpose of doing, but of not doing something'.[39] Closer investigation shows that, whatever their ostensible role, the societies performed quite positive functions for their members.

All reforming movements have to work through citizens already predisposed for other reasons towards attacking the *status quo*: in the nineteenth century these happened to be predominantly nonconformists, women and articulate working men. If the teetotal movement underestimated the importance of directly tackling the environmental inducements to drunkenness, this was partly because working men were themselves enthusiasts for the cult of respectability. They themselves often blamed the publican for their poverty: one recalls the constant and pitiful repetition of the words 'twenty years of misery through drink' by the drunken coalporter's wife whom Mayhew interviewed.[40] Finally, if temperance organizations were riddled with disputes, this was largely because their members came from a social class not yet experienced in transacting business; and because any reforming movement whose members dissent from prevailing social habits is likely to be staffed by uncompromising individualists and even eccentrics. Politically experienced individuals were never sufficiently indignant with the *status quo* to take the lead in crusading against it. Gladstone would never have done so, and the campaigners against the Contagious Diseases Acts were lucky even to attract the support of a Stansfeld.

Reforming campaigns must also operate with accepted contemporary methods of agitation. The ideal nineteenth-century temperance programme could have been carried only by individuals not drawn from religious communities and oppressed social groups, and through organizations very different in character from the nineteenth-century reforming movement. It could never have been led successfully by a man with ideas as enlightened as those of the atheist G. J. Holyoake, for at that time all reforming movements required support from the religious public. Even with religious support there were not the funds, let alone the inclination, to adopt a counter-attractive policy. The temperance movement's limitations, said F. W. Newman, stemmed largely from 'the position, culture, and means of those by whom it was chiefly carried on'.[41] When the temperance movement attracted wealthy support for the first time in the 1870s, it immediately began investing more extensively in counter-attractions.

Eleanor Rathbone once formulated an excellent series of warnings on how best to win feminist objectives. She stressed the importance of 'concentrating effort on the maximum achievable rather than on the ideal, while never forgetting to keep that in mind as the ultimate objective'; the need, at the earliest possible stage in the drafting of a Bill, to influence the minister or the civil servants responsible for framing legislation; the importance of 'meeting your opponent's case as it looks to him, not as it looks to you'; the need to know when to release and when to restrain the use of emotion.[42] Excellent as this advice is, it assumes that reforming movements can be guided by individuals who can rationally deploy their weapons with almost machiavellian cunning. Admittedly the success of the Anti-Corn Law League and the R.S.P.C.A. in the nineteenth century owed much to their possession of leaders with these qualities: but Cobdens and Colams are very rare. The reformer's zeal and idealism is seldom compatible with the politician's concern for tactics and strategy. Reforming campaigns need to import drama and excitement into their agitation; few recruits would be won by a gradualist programme. With reform as with religion 'sensitiveness and narrowness, when they occur together, as they often do, require above all things a simplified world to dwell in. Variety and confusion are too much for their powers of comfortable adaptation.'[43] If temperance reformers tended to denounce all alternative remedies for their problem, so also did the Charity Organization Society and Josephine Butler.

Assessments

Many of the attacks on teetotalism so far listed are therefore unhistorical and even unfair. Besides, the teetotal movement achieved much—even though many of its achievements were incidental to its main purpose. Perhaps its greatest achievement was simply to express concern at the prevailing level of drunkenness, and to make society realize that this was intolerable. The teetotal leaders could well have written, with Ruskin: 'I simply cannot paint, nor read, nor look at minerals, nor do anything else that I like . . . because of the misery that I know of, and see signs of, where I know it not, which no imagination can interpret too bitterly.' Built into their philosophy was an impatience with poverty and an enthusiasm for a new society which their easy-going opponents never felt. Their impatience was salutary, for the evil was serious: 'I have seldom gone home', wrote Engels in 1844 of his Saturday evenings in Manchester, 'without seeing many drunkards staggering in the road or lying helpless in the gutter.'[44]

Teetotalers were certainly correct in thinking that English society could exist on a greatly reduced consumption of alcohol. The very recognition that drunkenness was a problem to be tackled by social reformers, however inadequate the remedy proposed, helped to solve that problem. For the teetotal movement's mistakes could all be eliminated by subsequent workers in the field. Furthermore, the pioneer teetotalers, walking arm-in-arm with the drunkard and convinced that society itself was largely responsible for his sins, helped to substitute compassion for condemnation. Traditionally, countrymen had treated the occasional drunkard as a figure of fun, but they had no pity for the habitual drunkard: the opponents of teetotalism often wanted him to be punished harshly.[45] Contrast Livesey's *Malt Lecture*: 'drunkards! We are your best friends. Your own companions despise you, the landlords despise you, and you are even shunned by many religious people as worthless characters. *We are your friends*: we pity your case, and are trying to save you.'[46] Teetotalers were extending the area of human compassion to the drunkard at the same time as Shaftesbury and Josephine Butler were extending it to the lunatic and prostitute: they were unconsciously paving the way for a society which would treat even its humblest citizens as worthy of consideration.

Teetotalers helped to create such a society in a second way, for at a time and in political circles where *laissez-faire* sentiment was extremely powerful, they set up a continuing criticism and limitation of it: they insisted, like the sabbatarians and the opponents of slavery, that morality demanded some limitation upon the doctrine. Thomas Clarkson, summing up the achievements of the anti-slave trade movement, declared triumphantly 'we have lived . . . to see the day, when it has been recorded as a principle in our legislation, that commerce itself shall have its moral boundaries'. Teetotal attacks on the Beer Bill and on Gladstone's wine licensing scheme carried forward this critique into a new generation. It must be admitted, though, that the style of argument used by temperance critics of free trade hardened their opponents' determination to resist state intervention in other spheres where it was even more necessary. For example, it is doubtful whether Lord Salisbury would have been so persistent an opponent of intervention on behalf of inebriates unless his libertarianism had been sharpened by conflict with advocates of the Permissive Bill: for the arguments he used against state intervention in the two cases were identical.[47]

One's attitude to the teetotal movement's third achievement will depend on one's assessment of the political possibilities open to the working class in nineteenth-century England; but if the relative social stability of the period was, from the working-class viewpoint, worth the heavy price which was paid for it, then the teetotal movement deserves some credit. The experience of Soviet Russia in the inter-war years makes us more sympathetic towards what Marx condemned as 'those small petty-bourgeois patching-up reforms which by providing the old order of society with new props may perhaps transform the ultimate catastrophe into a gradual, piecemeal and, so far as is possible, peaceful process of dissolution'.[48] By mobilizing in a common reforming movement members of both working and middle classes and by creating 'small-scale success systems' which enabled the under-privileged to adapt to their situation, the teetotal movement helped to prevent English society from splitting apart. Wealthy but generous teetotalers like William Hoyle who, according to his architect, 'seemed specially afraid of seeming pretentious in any way' and who told an Alliance meeting in 1876 that he would spend his fortune on eliminating the drink traffic before setting money aside for his children—helped to ensure that the injustices of social inequality never seemed too flagrant. William Wilson, the wealthy Bradford teetotaler and philanthropist, kept a house which 'like his person, was a pattern of plainness and simplicity'; such a man was more likely to inspire affection than resentment among fellow citizens who could never hope to retire at fifty with £20,000 as he had done.

The temperance and prohibitionist movements were two of several nineteenth-century campaigns helping to ensure that a more equitable social order would be realized through guilt in a minority of the wealthy, not through anger in the majority of the oppressed: campaigns which averted what Marx described as 'historically necessary conflicts' by ensuring that the well-to-do would retain a sense of social responsibility.[49] A German miner who visited Newcastle in the 1890s found two aspects of British society unfamiliar: he noted that 'the middle and the working classes are on very friendly terms . . . because they are brought together in clubs and religious organisations', and that 'the sects strive to outdo one another in the exercise of practical Christianity'. Both these aspects of British society had been actively promoted by the temperance movement; a social investigator in 1912 regarded it as 'the great strength' of Oxford's temperance movement 'that, unlike other forms of social amelioration, it attracts all classes to work for it'.[50]

It is not really helpful to regard such working-class co-operation as an example of 'false consciousness', for teetotalism actually marks an important stage in the *growth* of working-class consciousness: it fostered recognition that rapid social change was possible, encouraged the joining of reforming associations, promoted articulateness among working-class leaders. The new gospel was not forced on working men from above; on the contrary, it was *opposed* by many respectable people. Although by the early twentieth century, working men could regard the teetotal movement simply as an attack by the rich on the pleasures of the poor, or as an attempt to divert the poor from a more radical reordering of society, it bore quite another complexion between the 1830s and the 1870s; it flourished on the genuine desire for respectability and self-reliance which prevailed within the working class. The pioneer teetotalers show far more of the characteristics which Macaulay attributes to the reforming than to the conservative temperament: they were 'sanguine in hope, bold in speculation, always pressing forward, quick to discern the imperfections of whatever exists, disposed to think lightly of the risks and inconveniences which attend improvements, and disposed to give every change credit for being an improvement'.[51]

These were broad social developments for which the teetotal movement was not solely responsible, but in extending the area of dietary freedom its achievement was unique. J. S. Mill was not the only mid-Victorian Liberal to stress the importance of resisting social, as opposed to political, tyranny. Dietary freedom may now seem a footling liberty, yet the early teetotalers secured it at the cost of great personal suffering. When Sir Walter Trevelyan attacked toast-drinking in his after-dinner speech at the Alnwick reform gathering on Easter Monday 1853, he was greeted by hisses as well as by applause. Teetotal pioneers, even after attaining high positions in local government, refused to conform to traditional drinking customs; they rightly branded them as 'a disgrace to a free country'. Nor was this a liberty which could be appreciated only by the well-to-do. The London coal- and ballast-heavers, struggling in the 1840s to shake off the publican's control over their livelihood, owed much to Henry Mayhew: but teetotal working men were prominent in the campaign, and were supported by the temperance movement as a whole.[52] Teetotalers thus made an important contribution towards the flexibility in personal habits required by a rapidly changing society. Many mid-Victorian working men consumed a remarkable amount of alcohol in a day. Thomas Okey's father, a respectable Spitalfields weaver, regularly drank a tumbler of gin-and-water at lunch, a pint and a half of old ale at 1 p.m., another tumbler of gin-and-water at 7 p.m., and a pint and a half or a quart of old ale at 9 p.m. Okey's father was no drunkard, yet his health and that of many other working men must have profited considerably when the teetotal movement promoted new dietary patterns. The teetotal movement was, as Benjamin Parsons claimed, 'the first application of science to diet on a large and popular scale'.[53]

Teetotalism made less measurable but none the less real contributions towards diffusing many novel attitudes which were to prove salutary in future years. Teetotalers constantly stressed, for instance, the importance of socializing home demand. If teetotalism became universal, argued Benjamin Parsons, 'then a sum of money equal to *twice* the value of our foreign trade will be spent on the produce of our agriculture and manufactories'. From the 1750s Vanderlint and Bishop Berkeley led the challenge to the traditional belief that low wages and highly priced necessities were the only possible incentives to work. Teetotalers buttressed this campaign by educating working men in adjusting their patterns of consumption to the new situation created by affluence.[54] Teetotalers also emphasized the need to raise the dignity of women, though the drink trade also contributed here by providing many women with a career: women accounted for a fifth of the beersellers and publicans listed in the 1871 census.[55] Teetotalers stressed the importance of reconciling religion with the belief in material progress and the need to tackle the cultural problems posed by the extension of leisure in an urban setting. Though it later became backward-looking, teetotalism in this period was espoused by many imaginative, talented and progressive individuals. John Morley's assessment of the role of phrenology in the 1830s applies equally to the teetotal movement before 1872: 'to accept phrenology to-day would stamp a man as unscientific', he wrote, 'but to accept it in 1835 was a good sign of mental activity'.[56]

Temperance historians have formulated two contradictory interpretations of prohibition, the fourth campaign launched against drunkenness before 1872. Prohibitionists are described in the official history as 'men and women who . . . wrought a revolution in our social habits'; at the end of the book, published in 1953, there is no hint of modifying the original objective laid down a century before. For a moment, a note of doubt creeps in: 'we do not see all we are doing. But it is there.' But this mood is rapidly dispelled, and amid a flourish of Biblical echoes and quotations from temperance zealots enjoining courage, the official history assures its readers that whether they see their objective—their 'Vision Splendid'—accomplished 'here or hereafter', they will never have cause to regret that they pursued it.[57] Very different was Henry Carter's interpretation in 1933: it was inspired by the 'extraordinary attitude' of the Alliance in condemning the report of the 1931 royal commission for not suggesting ways of abolishing the drink trade altogether. Carter was encouraged in his criticisms by the contemporary reversal of prohibition in the United States and by the example of the

Alliance's leading nineteenth-century opponent Joseph Livesey, to whom his book was dedicated.

Carter attacked the claims of prohibitionists in 1932 that prohibition was 'the main objective to which the [temperance] Movement has been steadily marching for a century'. On the contrary, he said, the temperance movement began with moral suasion, and the pioneer of teetotalism eventually repudiated Alliance policy. Moral suasion made 'the greatest measure of progress . . . towards the solution of the national drink problem', for it educated the public in temperance principles, created a group of total abstainers and helped to get the environment gradually modified through inspiring moderate temperance legislation. By contrast, Carter continued, the Alliance agitation entangled the temperance question in party politics, diverted effort away from the fruitful moral suasionist movement and discouraged gradualist but practicable temperance legislation; its 'disastrous influence' actually wrecked Bruce's 1871 Licensing Bill. Carter's historical investigation had a pronounced present purpose, for he looked to the nineteenth century for guidance on what policies the temperance movement should pursue in the 1930s. He concluded that real temperance reform could be secured only through directly educating public opinion; effective legislation could come only later, and to reverse the order must lead to disappointment.[58]

From the perspective of the 1960s Carter's interpretation has three major defects: his criticisms of the Alliance seem justified, but his praise for the moral suasionists seems less justified. Carter was himself a member of the temperance movement and had not shaken off its undue emphasis on the need for moral exertion to precede environmental transformation. Secondly, as a Methodist minister he failed to ask himself whether even the moral suasionist branch of the temperance movement should have been so firmly tied to religious objectives. Finally, as Carter's purpose was not primarily historical, he never tried to *explain* the peculiar policy pursued by the Alliance.

If T. H. Barker, Samuel Pope or J. H. Raper had been told that after more than a century the aim of prohibition was as far as ever from being realized, they would not have been perturbed: as the *Saturday Review* wrote on 19 October 1872 'it never seems to occur to the energetic authors of the [United Kingdom Alliance annual] Report that there must be some weakness in a cause which needs perpetual agitation'. They would have replied that none the less the Alliance had helped to purify the political world, and had greatly accelerated the enactment of temperance legislation. They might also have argued that their efforts had revived the moral suasionist movement. It is true that the early prohibitionist movement owed much to moral suasionists' private disillusion at their relative lack of success, but the moral suasionist movement itself seems to have been reviving just before the Alliance was founded. Indeed prohibitionism seems to have originated partly in *consequence* of this revival. Although temperance activity was at a low ebb in the years 1844–7, thereafter the press gave it increasing attention.[59] The Exeter Hall meetings patronized by John Cassell in 1849, the temperance demonstrations accompanying the 1851 exhibition, the foundation of the London Temperance League—these events all show that there were signs of life before 1853. J. B. Gough, who was largely responsible for reviving the National Temperance League during the 1850s, first visited England in 1853—before the Alliance was founded. Articles on temperance appeared in the quarterlies before the Alliance machinery got under way—in the *Westminster Review* for April 1852, in *Blackwood's* for April 1853 and in the *Edinburgh Review* for July 1854. As early as 1853 the demand for licensing reform was strong enough to obtain total Sunday closing for Scotland, and partial Sunday closing for England was obtained in the following year.

Prohibitionists might argue that the Alliance was the pacesetter for temperance organizations in the late 1850s. But this does not allow for the beneficial effects of newspaper tax repeal and of the more favourable economic climate. Nor can it be reconciled with the timing of the renewed temperance growth. The British Temperance League's short-lived revival began almost simultaneously with the foundation of the Alliance. Its new name dates from 1854, the year when it began to issue its *Annual Register and Yearbook;* and it is from the mid-1850s—before the Alliance had really got under way—that we can date the League's more aggressive and extroverted mood. As for the National Temperance Society, its prosperity stemmed from its union with the London Temperance League in 1856, and from J. B. Gough's visits. The annual receipts of the two Leagues began to rise markedly in the mid-1850s, some time before the Alliance made any real impact. Even in the 1860s when the Alliance was making great strides, the National Temperance League's prosperity probably owed more to the terms of Joseph Eaton's legacy, which was framed to spur on the three leading temperance organizations: and to its shrewd policies of influencing the influential and (from about 1866) of selling out its stock in order to make a more immediate impact—than to any prohibitionist impetus.

Can the Alliance fairly claim to have inspired gradualist temperance legislation after the 1860s? Admittedly some Alliance supporters like Manning were prepared also to support more moderate reforms—and even regarded the Alliance agitation as a way of preparing the public for them; and we have seen that many prohibitionists, as individuals, backed gradualist temperance organizations. But once parliament had been got to the point of legislating, the Alliance was far more of a hindrance than a help. Like the suffragettes, prohibitionists obstructed at a later stage the campaign for legislation which, at an earlier stage, they had helped to create. The Alliance infuriated those who had imposed restrictions on the beershops in 1869; for it showed marked apathy towards the change while it was going through parliament, but later claimed the credit for it.[60] Alliance conduct in 1871–2 in fact hindered Bruce from resisting the publicans and helped to confuse parliament as to the real state of public opinion. While publicans in 1873 ordered M.P.s to vote with the minimum of discussion—so as to prevent the Permissive Bill from being talked out, as had occurred in 1872—Muntz's Alliance constituents brought a subtler form of coercion to bear; they urged him 'as he valued his immortal soul' to support their Bill.[61] M.P.s began to regard Alliance pressure as 'not right or constitutional', and Bruce claimed that it prejudiced the dignity and independence of the House.[62] With pressures such as these, parliament's votes bore little relation to its opinions. 'What —— nonsense it is,' exclaimed one M.P. to M. T. Bass on the 1863 Sunday Closing Bill, for which the M.P. promptly proceeded to vote. What was worse, parliament's time in the early 1870s was being wasted by conflicting demands from a host of reforming movements; John Bright likened the situation to the attempt of several omnibuses to get through Temple Bar at the same time.[63]

Failure to promote research into the drink question is a complaint which can be raised against prohibitionists as well as against teetotalers. The rich resources of the Alliance were spent on propagating ideal solutions, not on investigating existing reality. Opponents of the Permissive Bill often complained that 'if one-half the money and energy spent by the United Kingdom Alliance in an impracticable agitation had been devoted to rational purposes, a much greater unity of opinion would have existed at the present time'. Alliance leaders saw their problem as pressing, its remedy as self-evident; further inquiry was therefore, for them, superfluous. The Alliance sponsored only the type of research which seemed likely to confirm its preconceptions, and which would produce statistics to shock politicians and the public into following its advice. It industriously compiled huge 'national drink bills', and conducted large-scale canvasses designed to reveal the strength of support for temperance restriction. It also fostered a climate unconducive to research within the temperance movement. When Alliance supporters—Joseph Livesey in the 1860s, T. P. Whittaker and Lady Henry Somerset later—used their critical faculties to advocate a more practicable policy, the Alliance branded them as apostates. All this helps to explain why it was not an Englishman but a Swede, Magnus Huss, who made the greatest contribution to the nineteenth century's understanding of alcoholism. For in England the temperance and prohibitionist movements had so advertised the *moral* dimensions of the problem that its scientific aspects could only be effectively studied on the continent.[64]

The Alliance erected its inflexibility into a positive virtue, and allowed irrelevant considerations of loyalty to stifle the intellectual inquiry which the seriousness of the drink problem demanded. Like Josephine Butler and Richard Cobden, the prohibitionists regarded their movement as a school of principle—but whereas Cobden held to the demand for total repeal only in the hope of a government compromise offer, the Alliance spurned all such offers.[65] Like the Lord's Day Observance Society, the Alliance frequently looked reverently back to its founding principles of association, and its appeals to 'conscience and consistency' served an increasingly conservative purpose.[66] Frequently likening itself to the Anti-Corn Law League, the Alliance always imagined that a comparable success could be produced by similar energy and persistence; when challenged, it declared that its founders 'knew what they were about when they laid down the principles on which they would proceed'. One of the first objections raised by prohibitionists to drink nationalization in 1915 was that it would require the Alliance to abandon on grounds of expediency 'those foundation principles on which the great structure of Temperance Truth rests'. The Alliance policy of keeping to the 'straight road', its Hebraizing tendency to 'hold to the law', alienated many philanthropists and temperance reformers, and did nothing to illuminate the problem in question.[67] It is not surprising that one critic of the Alliance during the first world war complained of 'the danger of vested interests growing up in moral and philanthropic questions as in other things'. Principles too easily become tools for imposing simplicity on to complex situations—ways of avoiding the need for thought. 'They have each one swallowed a Pope', wrote Manning of the prohibitionists in 1874, 'and I have no chance with legions of Infallibilists.'[68]

In this and in other respects, the Alliance showed a remarkable lack of political sense. Nor did it present its case in ways likely to attract experienced politicians. It erected drink trading into an all-embracing, all-explaining evil which must be removed before progress could be made in any other sphere of social reform. The Alliance claimed to solve the problem of destitution for society as a whole, whereas the moral suasionists solved it only for their members. It brought forward its Permissive Bill as a certain cure for a remarkable assortment of evils: for unemployment, poverty, strikes, prostitution, political corruption, racial degeneration, religious and political apathy. In its concept of government and in its criticism of free trade, the Alliance had a fruitful basis for a wider policy, but it never grasped the opportunity for broadening its programme to include other necessary reforms. Prohibitionists were in a dilemma: a platform as broad as T. H. Green's could not be taken up by a campaign whose supporters entrusted it only with tackling the drink problem; yet the Alliance could attract politicians only by shaking off narrowness.

The Alliance was strengthened against contemporary criticism by the conviction that it enjoyed divine support. For T. H. Barker in 1871, the prohibitionist struggle was quite literally 'part—and oh, how large a part!—of the great war between Heaven and Hell'. Despite a century of divine delay, the author of the centenary history retained his predecessors' certainty 'that God is for us and for our work'.[69] Such beliefs made it easy to divide the world into vicious and virtuous, opponents and supporters. Righteous indignation might stir a public meeting, but it was not the emotion with which to make things 'go down' with parliament. Before condemning the temperance reformer's opponents, it is always important to remember that the official temperance organizations in the nineteenth century (like professional bodies within the contemporary medical world) were containing with difficulty an exuberant, ignorant and indiscreet popular absorption in their subject. The historian should not be deceived by the respectability of the official temperance propaganda which loads the shelves of modern libraries, for at the time it was published the purity of its message was sullied by the recently published but ephemeral crudities of popular temperance culture. Clergymen were hardly likely to be won over by *The Drunkard's Catechism*, for instance: 'I believe in the existence of one Mr. Alcohol the great head and chief of all manner of vice, the source of nine-tenths of all diseases . . .'. Similar gaffes helped to discredit temperance pressure during the 1871–2 licensing crisis. Politicians were disgusted in 1871 when told that Bradford temperance reformers were circulating a placard entitled 'The Publican's Prayer' and beginning 'Our father which art in hell'. In the heat of battle the Alliance campaign, particularly in its lower echelons, tended to become a mere contest against 'the dragon-trade of our land', and prohibitionist vehemence merely frightened the drink trade into organizing its political influence still more efficiently.[70]

Politicians accustomed to mediating between conflicting interests could have little common ground with such an organization. Experienced in dealing with men as they are, they found it difficult to make contact with an organization whose whole political conduct was governed by a notion of what men ought to be. In the eyes of men like T. H. Green, Joseph Chamberlain and G. J. Holyoake, the Alliance lost several opportunities for substantially reducing drinking hours, reducing the number of licences and removing private interest in promoting drink consumption. Any concession to government demands for compromise would of course have made the Alliance leadership unpopular with its extremist supporters; but wise reformers—William Wilberforce, or Shaftesbury with his ten hours compromise of 1850—brave the hostility of extremists and accept government concessions whenever they can get them.

The clumsiness of Alliance political tactics extended even to its treatment of individual politicians. Its rough treatment of Samuel Morley and Edward Baines at the 1868 and 1874 elections, respectively, has already been noted. 'Public men must make their choice,' said the Alliance in 1868, casting a sour glance in Morley's direction, 'and either go in with the liquor traffic, or go on with the temperance movement for its annihilation.'[71] It showed a certain hardness, a certain delight in forcing the individual M.P. to make an unpleasant choice. It also made no allowance for the many issues with which

M.P.s had to deal, and acted as though M.P.s could concentrate single-mindedly on the attainment of a single reform. 'A few hundred letters, each bearing the signature of a voter, laid upon the breakfast table of a member of Parliament,' said an Alliance supporter in 1870, 'would give him something to digest which might do him more good than his morning's meal.'[72] The logical development of such an approach was the horse-whipping of prominent public statesmen by early twentieth-century suffragettes.

From the politician's viewpoint, perhaps the most serious crime of the Alliance was its abdication of responsibility for working existing political machinery, and even for producing any immediate remedy for the drink problem. Alliance critics might well have used G. M. Trevelyan's words, when criticizing Clifford Allen's I.L.P. work in 1931: 'it seems to me that you . . . are shirking responsibility for the actual world we live in by proclaiming the advent of another in the distance which you cannot at the moment realize. It seems to me you refuse to help to save the ship when it is sinking, because you say you wish you were in another ship (yet unbuilt).' Although teetotalers and prohibitionists differed on many things, they shared the tendency to concentrate on protests rather than on more constructive action. In the words of the Alliance initial address: 'we . . . call upon our fellow countrymen, one and all, to enlist themselves . . . for the primary purpose of evoking a solemn National Protest against the entire traffic in strong drink.'[73] Although the Alliance knew well that it would take some years to get its Permissive Bill enacted, and still longer to get it applied throughout the country—it had no policy for immediately palliating the drink evil. It never used its ample funds to pay for drinking fountains, coffee-stalls and counter-attractions. It wanted a clean sweep: 'so long as the temptations remain', Wilfrid Lawson argued, 'your work is never done . . . sweep away the temptation itself, and the work is done once and for ever.' How different was the outlook of the Church of England Temperance Society in the 1870s: 'placed as we are in a world like this, and in a state of society that has grown up under this abnormal state of things, we must be politic and wise.'[74]

The Alliance abdicated all responsibility for working the existing licensing system, for in the words of George Thompson the former anti-slavery agitator, it believed that the drink trade was 'not an evil to be regulated, but a gigantic crime to be abolished'.[75] Its methods contrast completely with those of an organization like the Royal Society for the Prevention of Cruelty to Animals which, during the same period, pursued a steady campaign to build up legislation and evolved efficient machinery to ensure its enforcement. The Alliance never saw itself as 'a kind of auxiliary to the legislature'.[76] It refused to have anything to do with the existing licensing laws, for in the words of its founder 'our object is not to procure the enforcement of the present system, but to secure a better'.[77] The Alliance even regarded the failure of attempts to extend licensing regulation as 'absolute gain' for the prohibitionist cause, because such failures discredited the moderate alternative to its policy.[78]

'Shall LAW! its sanction give,
And license *men to live,*
By dealing death?'

went its inaugural hymn.[79]

Alliance leaders showed a marked indifference to practical problems aroused by their Bill. During a much-publicized debate with the prohibitionists in 1876, W. S. Jevons the economist was surprised that the Alliance secretary T. H. Barker should be so indifferent to attacks on the details of the Permissive Bill. But Barker replied that only the Bill's preamble would be passed at the second reading: 'it is not our bill', he emphasized: 'it is Sir Wilfrid Lawson's'. The Alliance was never much worried by complaints that prohibition could never be enforced: the law must condemn harmful practices even if it could not prohibit them. A law, for the Alliance, was good or bad in an absolute sense, not in relation to the changing character of society and the individual. 'The necessity for such a law does not arise from nor depend upon our competency to carry it out to the suppression of evil, but from considerations of public policy, which require that the law should condemn every practice which has a tendency to affect injuriously the interests of the community'; these words of Thomas Beggs indicate the prohibitionists' educational concept of Law as a standard to be lived up to, like the Ten Commandments, rather than as a regulation grappling with reality. 'If a law is salutary, when in operation,' said the Alliance, 'the want of enforcement is not an argument against the law, but a ground of complaint against those who should attend to its execution.'[80]

Politicians had to ensure the continuance of respect for the law, and knew well the limits of their powers. They also had to ensure the sufficiency of taxation for the purposes of government. The Alliance never clearly stated how the national revenue would be recouped once drink supplies had been officially cut off. Prohibitionists disliked indirect taxes, yet politicians knew well the bitter hostility which direct taxes encountered. The Alliance argued that national prosperity would increase so markedly after prohibition that no special provision would be necessary. This was no more than a pious hope.

The Alliance had an oversimplified conception of political decision-making: statesmen could not lightly lay aside 'this little difficulty' and 'the other little difficulty' as Samuel Pope urged Sir Charles Trevelyan to do when exhorting him at an Alliance meeting in 1870 to opt for the simplicity of the Permissive Bill.[81] The Alliance was in fact essentially a protesting body, and like its greatest parliamentary leader Sir Wilfrid Lawson, preferred the simplicity and liberty of opposition to the minutiae and compromise of office. The contrasting positions taken up by Sir George Grey, the Home Secretary, and the Alliance during the deputation of 1863 reveal the prohibitionists' relative indifference to questions of practicality. Sir George repeatedly tried to divert the deputation away from giving assurances of their power and from denouncing the evils of drunkenness—into explaining how their scheme could ever succeed in practice. 'We do not differ as to drinking being the cause of crime,' he said, 'but we differ as to the best mode of checking the evil.' And again: 'the only question really is, what is practicable?'[82]

Sir George might well ask: for there is every reason to believe that the Permissive Bill could never have been enforced. In the year the Alliance was founded, an M.P. in parliament described the unpaid rural constable—chosen from local tradesmen and afraid of antagonizing local opinion—as 'particularly unqualified to control public-houses and beershops'. Even among the professional police force in the towns, drunkenness was widespread; the 1829 Metropolitan Police Act forbade drinksellers to entertain or trade with a policeman, under penalty of up to £5; but police constables in the 1870s were still accepting free drinks from the publicans and bottles of drink offered them in the streets by the public. Manning was not alone among temperance reformers in complaining of police inability to enforce even the existing licensing laws; this laxity was the chief obstacle to F. N. Charrington's temperance efforts in the late-Victorian East End.[83] There were in fact good reasons for this apparent laxness. The police were powerless without a favourable public opinion, and in many slum districts this favourable opinion did not exist.

Furthermore the police relied on publicans for information about the criminal world: their responsibilities for enforcing the licensing laws and for controlling crime were to some extent contradictory. And the police knew that publicans and brewers were often powerful on local watch-committees. One of the symbols of Chamberlain's 'new broom' at Birmingham in the 1870s was the appointment of five special inspectors to enforce better observance of the licensing laws. A police official as distinguished as Sir Richard Mayne in 1868 could still speak of licensing offences as 'only an incidental and a police sort of crime'.[84] Occasionally temperance reformers tried to assist the police by forming 'vigilance committees' to enforce the licensing laws; but in this sphere, as with the self-appointed upholders of chimney sweeping regulations, voluntary action succeeded only in exasperating the public.[85] Admittedly these years saw a striking decline in illicit distillation in Scotland and England [see Figure 13]; but its persistence in Ireland shows how success in law enforcement could be obtained only with the support of local landowners and farmers. If the Victorian police force failed completely to enforce the laws against betting, and failed partially to enforce the laws on liquor licensing, they would hardly be able to enforce prohibition. Police attempts to suppress gambling in the 1850s merely lent a certain glamour to the practice.[86]

Given the level of public drinking in this period and the importance attached by many working men to their recreational freedom, the Permissive Bill if enacted would have been bitterly opposed, for drink regulation 'is a matter which depends almost more than any other form of social legislation for its effective administration upon almost the unanimous support of those subject to it'.[87] The wearisome disputes and problems of 'border smuggling' which followed the Forbes Mackenzie Act of 1853 and the Welsh Sunday Closing Act in the 1880s give a hint of the disputes with which the Permissive Bill would have covered the country. If enacted, the Permissive Bill would probably have been adopted—not in the industrial areas, where drunkenness caused most problems—but in a very few remote localities where it was least needed. This happened when the 'no licence' policy was adopted in twentieth-century Scotland; Lord Salisbury rightly condemned the 'rather Utopian view' that every ratepayer was eager to look after the morality of his neighbour.[88] Prohibition in America enhanced the social prestige of alcohol-drinking; it also fostered disrespect for the law and promoted corruption.

The Alliance airily brushed aside suggestions that the Bill would provoke dissension: nonconformist culture glorified conflict—against the snares of sin, and sometimes also against worldly oppression. Nonconformists found it difficult to be 'at ease in Zion': they must, like Pilgrim, spend their lives fighting—indeed, they felt that conflict positively developed the character. 'I wonder what man was born for,' Lawson retorted to one such objection, 'excepting to struggle. We live in a world full of sin, of wrong, and of injustice, and if we are not to struggle, the sooner we are out of this world the better.'[89] But although the Alliance did not shrink from conflict, it did not anticipate much opposition to prohibition once enacted: for it did not regard the conduct of drinkers under existing social conditions as any guide to their likely conduct under the new prohibitionist dispensation. Like members of the early Labour party, the prohibitionists criticized the existing social order by comparing it with an ideal social order, where human beings would behave in quite a different manner.

Alliance devotees conceived of prohibition in millennial terms: like drink for the drinker, the Permissive Bill for prohibitionists brought perfection into a disordered world. Their glowing accounts of the innocence and affluence of Bessbrook and Saltaire, the drink-free villages, show how deep is the debt owed by many nineteenth-century moral reform movements to the gradual transference of the Christian utopia from heaven to earth.[90] 'If only drink could be excluded from the surrounding areas', said J. G. Richardson, owner of Bessbrook in 1877, 'we might make a little Paradise of the place.' Just as the prohibitionist heaven had become the temperance village, so the prohibitionist hell had become the public-house, with all its associations. The energies which had once been directed at portraying the horrors of hell were unconsciously being directed towards removing the earthly temptations which smoothed the path towards it. Free licensing, said Lawson in 1863, had made Liverpool 'next door to a very hell upon earth'; for Manning, public-houses were 'the gates of hell'. Hell had almost become synonymous with the economic, social and physiological miseries associated with drunkenness—listed every week in the Alliance weekly periodical. And the enactment of the Permissive Bill, like Marx's final revolution, had become the Golgotha between the two eternities: before it, all might be misery: but after it, human nature would assuredly be transformed, and the former state would pass away.[91]

Many damaging criticisms can therefore be made of Alliance tactics. Yet it would be wrong to leave the matter there. Alliance attitudes require some explanation. If attention is directed more closely at its relationship with its supporters, it will be clear that the Alliance was in its way a highly successful body, and was performing functions which no moderate or non-political agitation could provide. Mid-Victorian Liberals liked to stress how readily the beliefs of an educated person would triumph over his personal interest: 'one person with a belief', wrote J. S. Mill, 'is a social power equal to ninety-nine who have only interests.' Slavery was terminated, said Mill, 'not by any change in the distribution of material interests, but by the spread of moral convictions'.[92] The Alliance certainly saw itself as selflessly working for a cause whose humanity and progressiveness must attract any man of sensibility. Yet it attracted quite precise groups in British society—groups hitherto largely excluded from political power—and the recruitment of an organization inevitably affects its policy. Rather than seek explanations for Alliance irrationality in the psychological maladjustment of its supporters, it is more profitable to explore sociological explanations.

The relevance of this approach is suggested by the fact that very similar policies were followed by the campaign against the Contagious Diseases Acts, which drew supporters from identical social groups. 'I do not want to make the working of the system more and more perfect,' William Krause a Woolwich missionary protested to the 1881 inquiry on state-regulated prostitution: 'I want to show its inherent viciousness.' His words might have been uttered by Nathaniel Card. 'I have no interest in the operation of the Acts,' Mrs. Butler told the 1871 royal commission on the Acts: 'it is nothing to me whether they operate well or ill, but I will tell you what you wish to know as to my view of the principle of the Acts'; the wording might have been Wilfrid Lawson's. 'Rulers require from time to time to be re-baptised in first principles,' Mrs. Butler announced at Manchester in 1870, 'and in that renewal to get rid of their theories of expediency, and state necessities, their slavery to precedent, and to deadly routine,—sometimes of their pride of race, lust of conquest, and forgetfulness of the claims of the humblest and poorest.' Her words might have been drawn from an Alliance manifesto.[93]

It therefore seems profitable to see the criticisms so far made of Alliance policy in the light of its supporters' social background. The failure of the Alliance to promote sustained research into the drink question can be explained from two directions: firstly, research was discouraged by the situation of the Alliance as a 'democratic' reforming movement. As long as a reforming movement—the Howard League, for example—maintains a dialogue with government, and values its close connexion with the civil service—it enjoys access to government information and concentrates on the type of argument likely to convince those in positions of power;[94] but as soon as it feels the need to coerce government through working up a mass agitation, it must adopt very different tactics. Instead of steadily accumulating expertise on the problem in question, it must diffuse its efforts in small spectacular campaigns designed to convince subscribers that they are getting their money's worth. The reforming leader becomes overwhelmed with the pressure of day-to-day business, is constantly pressed for short-term decisions, and is incessantly involved in intellectually emasculating and ultimately irrelevant fund-raising campaigns. The minute-books of the British and National Temperance Leagues, which survive for the 1860s, show organizations engulfed by the details of organizing demonstrations, publishing propaganda and periodicals, negotiating short-term loans, and racking their brains for ways of raising funds. Surrounded as he is by individuals who agree with him, faced by the constant need for publicly 'refuting' arguments raised by opponents—the reforming leader finds it difficult to preserve his contact with the real world and to prevent his cause from becoming an obsession. Calm and sustained research is possible only with an assured income. 'Facts and figures, serious investigation . . . these are all foreign to the atmosphere of hurry,' wrote the former suffragette Mrs. Billington-Greig—who abandoned the W.S.P.U. for this reason. 'In such heat of struggle', she wrote, 'one cannot see straight. Outside this atmosphere we may begin again and build the foundations of our future work.'[95]

Research was also discouraged by the social and intellectual situation of nonconformity, whence so many Alliance leaders were drawn. To Alliance leaders, the modern association between systematic investigation and social reform would have seemed unfamiliar. For Christians, whose faith attached such importance to retaining a firm religious belief, naturally carried over into their reforming activity many of the attitudes they acquired in their religious life. Devout Christians saw the world as deeply corrupted by sin and cynicism: it could be purified only through dramatic reclamation of the individual, or through catastrophic divine intervention. Likewise teetotalers and prohibitionists saw social reform entirely in terms of sudden 'conversion' —whether of the individual or of society as a whole. With prohibitionism as with religious belief, one was inspired by the knowledge of absolute principles which, once revealed, could not be shaken by new evidence.

How then can we explain the apparent political ineptitude displayed by the Alliance? The Old Testament fostered the belief that individual or national infringements of the moral law would meet with divine vengeance. Just as in primitive tribes incest can cause the crops to fail, so intemperance or sabbath-breaking could in nineteenth-century England cause national decay, industrial depression or some even more catastrophic sign of divine displeasure. Moral reformers scanned the horizon for signs of sin, as part of a campaign for national and individual self-defence against divine retribution. In mid-Victorian England, individual and national sins were plain for all to see; yet the authorities seemed to be doing nothing to tackle them. The social situation in the areas which supported the Alliance was closely paralleled in America; both situations evoked a similar response. Both English prohibitionists and American abolitionists found themselves in a rapidly changing society, with uprooted immigrants and new townships lacking in long-established and traditional institutions, with a traditional hierarchy lacking in authority and a traditional church unable to adapt itself in the face of rapid social change. In America the 'frontier' could be seen on the map; in England, it existed in the minds of the conscience-bound inhabitants of the new industrial towns. The 'narrowness, one-sidedness, and incompleteness' of nonconformist culture ensured that the abolitionists' 'gnawing sense of responsibility for the ills of society at large' was also felt by many English Christians. Wilfrid Lawson acknowledged the happiness of his own personal life, but confessed that whenever he made a speech he 'saw in the background the myriads of men and women who were not in those pleasant circumstances, and felt that all one said should more or less bear upon what is called the "Condition of the People" '.[96]

Yet the nonconformists and others who supported the Alliance, like the intellectuals who supported the American abolitionist movement, had not yet gained access to real political power. The law was administered by magistrates who, according to Joseph Cowen, were 'drawn from a class not acquainted with the social requirements of the people'. Alliance platforms rang with attacks on their inefficiency and corruption, on their self-interested manipulation of the licensing system, and on their drink connexions. 'Who is the brewer in the county?' asked Thorold Rogers at the Alliance annual meeting in 1874: 'he is the man who keeps the hounds, who serves the office of sheriff, finds subscriptions for county purposes, and in nine cases out of ten he is the most wealthy capitalist.'[97] Parliament was no better. The first Quaker M.P. was elected to parliament only in 1832, and though the Whigs traditionally sympathized with nonconformist grievances, they still retained their control over the Liberal Party. Prohibitionists were never strongly supported among the aristocracy which still, in the 1870s, dominated Westminster. Temperance reformers had been laughed out of parliament in 1834 and their views remained unrepresented there till the 1860s. For many prohibitionists the typical M.P. was not a well-meaning and conscientious representative, but a member of an alien class who had severely restricted religious liberty in the past and might well be related to the parsons and magistrates who were still selling up nonconformist property to pay church rates. M.P.s had to be forced by popular pressure to 'do right', for they would seldom do right of their own accord.

The Alliance deeply suspected parliament: 'if you go there', said Washington Wilks to an Alliance meeting in 1862, 'you scarce see around you a man animated by his own moral sense and feelings'.[98] Honest men left their provincial constituencies for Westminster and were corrupted by designing politicians, enervated by the lax moral atmosphere of the metropolis. These suspicions of parliament have influenced many 'outsiders' in English history —from country gentry to nonconformist industrialists, from intellectuals to humanitarians, from feminists to socialists. Cowen once described the long tradition of M.P.s 'who have stood steadily and strictly on principle, who did not seek emoluments, and did not care for glitter and gold lace—men who kept the lamp of freedom burning when its more pretentious friends were sunning themselves amidst the seductive and somnolent pleasures of official life'. The Alliance liked to see itself in this tradition. Josephine Butler in 1872 described the conduct of F. W. Newman in a deputation to the Home Secretary on the Contagious Diseases Acts: 'it was a wonderful sight to see that man and Bruce confronted. Mr. Newman, slight, old, nervous, and oh so spiritual looking, with a countenance, perfectly *awful* in its purity and intensity, and in its noble firmness, he reminded me of some ancient confessor, or holy martyr speaking the truth of Christ before Caesar . . . Mr. Bruce looked all flesh and blood and official haughtiness. . . .'[99]

So persistent a myth must have had substance. It was true that M.P.s lost much of their radicalism on arrival at Westminster; Lord Robert Cecil claimed that the House of Commons disliked 'anything approaching to abstract reasoning' and was indifferent to 'any considerations which do not promise a distinct practical advantage'. He went on to say that 'no one who has seen much of that assembly is likely to form an exaggerated estimate of human perfectibility, or to entertain any doubt of the enduring power of the law of selfishness'. The provincial radicals were also correct in assuming that the members of the House of Commons constituted an élite of wealthy individuals who differed markedly in their situation and outlook from the population as a whole.[100] But they were not entirely correct in their explanation of parliament's effects on its members: a conspiracy theory which assumed that moral corruption had occurred did not allow for the many other factors which might moderate the radicalism of a new M.P. Among these factors were the realization that all social change is opposed by good men, often for good reasons: that pressing matters have to be settled quickly before attention can be paid to long-term objectives or enduring philosophies: and that a government must, as far as possible, take into consideration the interest of the nation as a whole. 'It is quite a mistake to suppose that real dishonesty is at all common,' wrote Cornford: 'the number of rogues is about equal to the number of men who act honestly; and it is very small. The great majority would sooner behave honestly than not. The reason why they do not give way to this natural preference of humanity is that they are afraid that others will not; and the others do not because they are afraid that *they* will not. Thus it comes about that, while behaviour which looks dishonest is fairly common, sincere dishonesty is about as rare as the courage to evoke good faith in your neighbours by showing that you trust them.'[101]

How then could prohibitionists excluded from power discharge their pressing feelings of guilt? Only through the liberating protest. The apparent political ineptitude of the prohibitionists was really something more like conscious *defiance* of the aristocracy's customary political methods; a defiance whose stridency stemmed from lack of political self-confidence. The clinging to principle sprang from the belief that fixed guiding-lines were needed in so murky a world. Prohibitionist Liberals in the 1860s, like unilateralist supporters of the Labour party in the 1950s, supported a major political party only *faute de mieux*; they never ceased to deplore its timidity and lack of idealism. Their exhilaration in protesting against the licensing system reflects the frustrations of nonconformist life which made public agitation 'stimulating and refreshing to them in the highest degree'.[102] To expect the prohibitionists to advocate moderate policies was to deprive them of the exhilaration of destruction, to steal from them the conspicuous victory over the authorities that they craved.

It is now clear why 'failure' is hardly an apt way of describing the Alliance's inability to get the Permissive Bill enacted. For as far as its supporters were concerned, it was succeeding—as long as it continued to defy publicly the beliefs and methods pursued by those in authority. Prohibitionists themselves often claimed that their agitation would have achieved much, even if no legislation resulted from it. Joseph Chamberlain in 1893 spoke of the Alliance's 'great army of paid officers, who may almost be said to have an interest in the continuance of the agitation', and *The Times* referred to temperance reformers 'who draw either cash or notoriety' from the sport of publican-hunting. In so far as they imputed conscious self-interest to Alliance leaders, these two critics were wrong; but they were quite correct in recognizing that the Alliance, by the very process of agitating, was paying dividends. The Alliance provided the perpetual spectacle of an exhilarating challenge to the compromising morality of the powers that be; it was one of several groups within late-Victorian Liberalism which, in Sidney Webb's words, 'will reform nothing unless it can be done at the expense of their enemies'.[103] The Permissive Bill was a symbol, rather than a serious proposal for solving the drink problem: it publicly asserted the worth of a distinct culture and eased the consciences of those who felt alarmed at the extent to which the surrounding society either ignored or despised that culture. The prohibitionist campaign was indeed, as the Alliance argued in 1862, well calculated to 'build up a righteous and godly people'. English prohibitionism between 1853 and 1873, like American abolitionism in the 1830s, was 'the anguished protest of an aggrieved class against a world they never made'.[104]

The social and religious grievances of the prohibitionists also help to explain the peculiar attitude towards drink taxes and public management which they adopted. One might have expected prohibitionists to welcome increased taxation of drink as a way of promoting sobriety, yet in fact the Alliance despised such a policy. For not only would drink taxes and municipalization provide a grasping and untrustworthy government with immense wealth: they would also give the government an interest in fostering the vices of its subjects; the Alliance claimed that it would rejoice to find a government willing to abandon revenue from so tainted a source.[105] But there is a deeper reason for prohibitionist attitudes. Christians deeply sensitive to the sufferings caused by drunkenness were anxious to ensure that, at the final reckoning, they would not be held responsible for them. The more they allowed the state to become implicated in this evil trade, the more they themselves could be blamed at the last day. A temperance movement which declared for public management would be self-defeating, for like the anti-slavery movement it was designed to free its members 'from a load of guilt, which has long hung like a mill-stone about our necks, ready to sink us to perdition'.[106]

In 1901 Sidney Webb contested the assumption that any corporate action is unfair to the citizen who dissents from it: such an outlook makes government impossible, for 'we are all dissenters from some part or another of the action of the communities of which we are members'. Prohibitionists could never shake off the notion that their tax contribution represented 'a bill paid by a private man for certain specific commodities which he has ordered and purchased for his own use'.[107] Drink taxes seemed to them 'the price of blood' falling into the exchequer 'heavy with the curse of God'—regardless of their effect upon drinking habits. Similarly the Gothenburg and nationalization schemes must be strenuously resisted because they would implicate all citizens in a wicked trade.[108] While such an attitude has produced some of the finest examples of self-denial and heroism, it can also encourage a mere passing-by on the other side. In the anti-slavery, peace and temperance movements, it could foster—not the elimination of slavery, war and drunkenness—but the mere purging of one's own complicity in those evils. This objective was sometimes openly avowed by Alliance leaders: why had Sir Wilfrid Lawson reintroduced his Permissive Bill, asked Samuel Pope of an Alliance meeting in 1870: 'to discharge himself and us from the responsibility of remaining quiet pending the solution of this question'. 'Better, a thousand times better, that we struggle against a giant evil, even though we fail,' wrote T. H. Barker in the following year: 'than that we learn to look on in apathy and make no brave and heroic effort to save our fellow creatures from destruction. By this very effort we at least save ourselves from sinful complicity.'[109]

Such an attitude can be explained in historical terms, but statesmen cannot allow it to mould national policy. When Miall, in opposing the 1870 Education Bill, seemed to be influenced too exclusively by nonconformist objections, Gladstone emphasized the trouble the government had to take to allay passions, to smooth away difficulties, to induce co-operation and to show consideration for existing educational institutions. While Miall gave the government his support, said Gladstone, the government would co-operate with him in common objectives: 'but . . . when we think he looks too much to the section of the community he adorns, and too little to the interests of the people at large, we must then recollect that we are the Government of the Queen, and that those who have assumed the high responsibility of administering the affairs of this Empire, must endeavour to forget the parts in the whole, and must, in the great measures they introduce into the House, propose to themselves no meaner or narrower object—no other object than the welfare of the Empire at large'.[110]

The mood in which to regard the energy and idealism of the prohibitionists therefore seems to be one of sympathetic regret. Their resolute independence and consistency might in some circumstances deserve high praise; but the seriousness of the nineteenth-century drink problem and the prohibitionists' failure to tackle it effectively makes it regrettable, to say the least, that they never possessed Sir Thomas Moore's awareness that 'what I called conscience was just my own bloody conceit'.[111] Yet with prohibitionism, as with teetotalism, some benefits resulted: temperance legislation of some sort was needed at the time, and in so far as the Alliance helped to make temperance a 'burning question' it performed a useful function. Furthermore, the very act of focusing nonconformist resentments on attaining a purely symbolic measure channelled off potential sources of social disharmony into a relatively harmless contest. It is also important to distinguish between the attitudes of organized prohibitionism and of individual prohibitionists, for the latter often combined membership of the Alliance with support for a remarkable range of other philanthropic interests.

Furthermore if the Alliance's destructive attitude to the existing political system was in some ways misguided, that system *was* becoming inappropriate in the changed political and social situation created by industrialization and franchise extension. The strains to which prohibitionists and publicans exposed M.P.s in the early 1870s owed less to prohibitionist irresponsibility than to this new situation. If the Alliance tried to discipline M.P.s in parliamentary divisions and on the hustings, this was because no tightly organized party machine had yet appeared to take over the task. If reforming movements clashed during the early 1870s in their demands for parliamentary time, this was largely because the political parties had not yet assumed complete responsibility for setting an order of priority on extra-parliamentary demands, and for carrying them forward into legislation. Many of the criticisms made of Alliance parliamentary activity at this time apply equally to any modern system of party discipline.

Finally, if the Alliance took up some strange postures between 1853 and 1872, it did not differ in this from many reforming organizations catering in all generations for the resentments of oppressed social groups: working men, subject races, women, religious minorities, university students. The stranger their antics, the more the observer is forced to realize the long years of social deprivation which the reformers have endured. It is perhaps the great virtue of the Alliance that it lifted many nonconformists out of their quietism and encouraged them to participate both locally and nationally in political life. The experience thereby acquired of co-operating in constructive work with men of diverse views ensured that they—like all newcomers to the political life—learned much. It is perhaps significant that the Alliance never attracted the active support of nonconformists as experienced in public life as John Bright, Edward Baines, Joseph Cowen, Charles Gilpin or Samuel Morley. Nor did it always retain the support of men who entered political life as sympathizers with the local veto. Joseph Chamberlain was one of these, but by the late 1880s he was decidedly on the attack; by 1893 the Alliance was counter-attacking with accusations of political inconsistency.[112] In 1875 another active nonconformist politician, Handel Cossham, attacked the rigidity of Alliance political tactics. Cossham remained faithful to the Alliance, but another nonconformist supporter from the early 1870s—George Cadbury—later turned to municipalization and the public-house trust, claiming that the drink problem would never be solved 'by denouncing either intoxicating liquor or those who deal in it'.[113]

In accounting for these individual shifts in opinion, it is difficult to know how much to attribute to the declining ardour of old age, and to the alcoholic prescriptions which tended to accompany it. Nevertheless it is likely that the increased political involvement of Chamberlain, Cossham and Cadbury—and perhaps also the shifting political outlook of their class—gave them broader perspectives on the drink question: this change was sometimes accompanied by a move out of the dissenting community altogether. Even where views on the temperance question did not change, the dissenting connexion was sometimes abandoned in later life or in the second generation: Benjamin Townson, for instance, became an Anglican in his old age, and Wilfrid Lawson did not persist in his father's dissenting loyalties. At least three of the teetotal and six of the prohibitionist leadership samples followed Chamberlain into Liberal Unionism; so also did the prominent Liberal temperance reformer, W. S. Caine. Individuals like these had been shepherded by the Alliance and similar pressure groups on to the political stage, but soon learned to walk without guidance. Voluntary associations helped British democrats to shed that anti-government tendency which continues to bedevil French democratic parties.[114] Alliance agitation enabled all prohibitionists, whatever their subsequent course, to shed their sense of inferiority: in this way, it helped to heal the wound which had been festering in English society since 1662.

17

The End

Temperance ceased to be a live political issue after the first world war; temperance societies have dwindled in strength and influence, and their literature has become increasingly out of sympathy with modern life. This striking change is of course partly due to a decline in drunkenness; it is also partly due to the decline of nonconformity, for temperance organizations—like all political organizations staffed by militant dissenters—were preparing the way for their own demise. But one other influence has also helped to produce this change: the propaganda of the labour movement. If the nineteenth-century campaigns for sobriety are to be placed in perspective, some attention must be given to the arguments which discredited them with the thinking public.

One might have expected Chartism to pioneer some of these arguments. Yet many Chartist leaders, like their radical ancestors, showed considerable enthusiasm for abstinence: for this could not fail to increase the resources, single-mindedness and moral stature of their movement. The L.W.M.A.'s aim was 'to draw into one bond of UNITY the *intelligent* and *influential* portion of the working classes in town and country', and it therefore excluded 'the drunken and immoral' from its ranks.[1] After the setbacks of 1839, the importance of sobriety and education seemed greatly increased, for Chartism needed to consolidate its strength and attract middle-class sympathy. The need for sobriety therefore featured prominently in the booklet *Chartism* (1840) which Lovett and Collins wrote while in prison, and also in the 'knowledge Chartism' which Lovett tried to promote thereafter. Prison also reinforced the charms of teetotalism for Henry Vincent. At Francis Place's direction he read William Godwin's exhortations to rationality, and was also stirred by the news of Father Mathew's contemporary successes in Ireland: during 1840 he therefore became an enthusiast even for the pledge-signing brand of teetotalism, and in spring 1841 left London for a teetotal lecture-tour through the midlands and west of England. Several Teetotal Chartist societies had already been formed, and the pledge which Vincent administered to his audiences combined the moral and political motives for sobriety.

Vincent's efforts were soon scotched by O'Connor's denunciation of church, teetotal, knowledge and household suffrage Chartism in the *Northern Star* for 13 March and 3 April 1841. Though O'Connor himself championed Father Mathew, he feared, with some justification, that Teetotal Chartism was being used in 1841 to subvert his own leadership in the Chartist movement and deprive Chartism of the 'fustian jackets and unshorn chins' who always flocked to his meetings. In 1842 Vincent joined Sturge's Complete Suffrage Union, and Teetotal Chartism was dead. Though O'Connor was careful to exclude distillers, brewers and drinksellers from his Chartist estates, and though Ernest Jones in the 1850s renewed Vincent's attempt to unite the temperance and Chartist movements, Teetotal Chartism never revived.

The temperance and Chartist movements had much in common: a suspicion of Anglicanism and aristocracy, a belief in the moral elevation of the people, an admiration for the puritan heroes of the seventeenth century, a distaste for socialism, state intervention and restraints on individual liberty. It is not therefore surprising that the Chartists never became uniformly hostile to the temperance movement. Of the teetotal leadership sample, at least 12 sympathized with or were active in the Chartist movement, and F. R. Lees in 1842 pronounced the Charter 'the only remedy for national poverty and national impending ruin'.[2] Teetotal Chartism in fact represents an attempt to amalgamate two of the three contemporary movements which were competing in the 1840s to improve the condition of the people: Owenism, Chartism and teetotalism. Chartism and teetotalism were competing for the support of the same type of self-improving, serious-minded working man. In some areas, of course, there was friction between the two movements. Many teetotalers disliked the secular motives and political orientation of Chartism, and were alarmed when several teetotal advocates deserted temperance for Chartist platforms;[3] many Chartists felt that teetotalers were too eager to subordinate working men to middle-class leadership. Yet though the Chartist leaders were conscious of themselves as leaders of a newly emancipated working class, their attitudes had not yet separated from the old pan-class radical tradition. And when the mid-Victorian economic situation promoted harmony between working-class leaders and the radical middle class, the fundamental affinity between the ideas of the two movements became more obvious.

Both Lovett and Vincent had always believed in telling working men their faults: both despised O'Connor for encouraging their worst side with his flattery. Both became forthright in their attacks on the unrespectable poor. Vincent in 1843 announced that 'no one was more opposed than he was, to affording assistance to the idle and worthless'; widows and orphans, old people and the infirm had claims on the rates, but no others. 'There are two classes of hereditary paupers in this country, one at the top and the other at the bottom of the social scale,' he declared in 1871.[4] Several Chartists supported prohibition in the 1850s, and the United Kingdom Alliance had no more fervent supporter in the 1870s than the aged William Lovett. 'The lower strata of the working classes' enfranchised in 1867, Vincent complained in 1876, '. . . is indifferent to, or ignorant of politics—and is reached easily by money, flattery, and drink'. In the last speech of his life, Vincent urged his audience in 1878 to spurn Beaconsfieldism and hold to the Liberal standard.[5] The last surviving Chartist—W. H. Chadwick—appeared at the 1906 election on a *Liberal* party platform, with many years' temperance lecturing behind him.

Chartist leaders tended to couch their diagnosis solely in terms of conspiracy theories. 'Our enemies have besotted us,' said the Chartist Robert Lowery in 1838, 'and call us the swinish multitude.' The L.W.M.A. in its opening address attacked working men who 'drown their intellect' in the pothouse, and spoke of 'unprincipled governors, who connive at their folly, and smile while they forge for themselves the fetters of liberty by their love of drink'.[6] Among Liberals there is a long tradition of such assertions—a belief that the authorities are 'more afraid of the working classes when they think than when they drink'. The accusation reappears even in the early twentieth century when J. A. Hobson drew a parallel between the 'circenses' of ancient Rome and the 'cheap booze and Mafficking' of late-Victorian England.[7]

At first sight, there was much in Victorian England to support such a view. In the 1820s and 1830s governments reduced the price of beer and gin, rejected radical demands for the Sunday opening of museums as counter-attractions to the drinking place, and covered the country with beershops. It almost seemed as though there was a deliberate plot to make virtue difficult for the poor: illegitimacy was socially unacceptable, yet they were denied contraceptives; temperance was demanded of them, yet they were surrounded with drinkshops. Far more drinking places were licensed per head of population in working-class districts than elsewhere; some well-to-do commentators even defended this situation by claiming that it enabled willpower to be cultivated. 'The mental and moral, like the muscular powers,' said J. S. Mill, 'are improved only by being used.'[8] Barrels of beer were trundled up beside Anti-Corn Law, Complete Suffrage, Chartist and temperance open-air meetings of working people, and in the free distribution of their contents, all thought of political and moral reform vanished away.[9] Drink was used by wealthy candidates to control parliamentary elections, and to prevent their radical rivals from getting into parliament. Licensed drinking places—often run by retired minions of the governing class—provided such a wealth of drink revenue that the propertied classes could escape heavy direct taxation; they helped to create a society which founded 'the wealth, luxuries, and pleasures of the few, upon the poverty, crime, and misery of the many'.[10] A fiction of superior upper-class morality was preserved by a police force which publicized the intemperance of the poor, while quietly conducting upper-class drunkards to their homes without taking them to court.[11] When initiative came from below to tackle the drink problem through the temperance movement, the respectable classes were loath to join it, reluctant to allow public meetings and nervous about it in the House of Lords.[12] Parliament actually proliferated drink facilities for the poor, yet as soon as the sons of the rich were likely to be tempted into vice —by gaming houses and public-houses in upper-class districts—the authorities speedily took action.[13]

It was a formidable case, yet in the long run it was an unprofitable diagnosis, for it was backward-looking and ignored important changes in the structure of industry and in the pattern of working-class life. It was also inaccurate; for it exaggerated the unity and ill-intent of the authorities. While there *were* traditionalists—particularly in rural areas—who believed that popular recreations helped to keep the poor in their place, the urban authorities were becoming more aware that drunkenness hindered rather than helped social control; the spread of complex capital equipment and the increasing concentration of the population in crowded towns made sober citizens less dangerous than drunken slaves. Vice was, as Ashley pointed out in 1843, 'expensive to the public'.[14] Sobriety in their employees was readily encouraged, indeed enforced, by many early industrialists. And if the authorities failed to join the temperance movement or to promote stringent temperance legislation, this was primarily because they knew that the nation at large was less enthusiastic for such extreme remedies than many Chartists supposed. The government knew well that the temperance movement promoted sectarian purposes; the Tories, with their 'unintellectual support of familiar standards and habits of life'[15] were in closer contact with working-class opinion than were the energetic and idealistic Chartist leaders. It was fear of riot rather than fear of sobriety which restrained parliament's zeal for temperance legislation, and events in 1855 justified those fears. If the authorities cheapened gin and beer in the 1820s and 1830s, their enemy was not sobriety, but the smuggler and the illicit still. As soon as police efficiency improved, Gladstone pushed up spirit duties to the highest level they could safely bear.

If the government sometimes discouraged meetings of working men for self-improvement, this was because the authorities feared all popular meetings attended by Irish nationalists and revolutionaries. Drinksellers who allowed suspect working men's groups to meet on their premises were readily deprived of their licences; but whenever it was clear that the temperance movement was not in subversive or sectarian hands, the authorities gave it generous support. Father Mathew was fêted by London society, defended by the London police, championed by Irish peers, and in 1847 awarded a government pension; Lord Stanhope and the Earl of Arundel publicly took the pledge from him before London crowds in 1843, and Lord John Russell addressed a meeting designed to raise money for him.[16] The Whig *Morning Chronicle* welcomed Lovett's 'new move' and Vincent's temperance address. Peel spoke of Ireland's 'surprising and most laudable constancy' when Father Mathew's temperance campaign reduced the spirits revenue in the early 1840s. Gladstone in 1863 felt 'no surprise and no disappointment' at the fall in drink revenues as a result of the cotton famine, and by the 1880s M.P.s were cheering the news of their decline.[17]

Two Chartists penetrated more deeply into the drink problem: J. R. Stephens and Ernest Jones. Stephens was an enthusiast for sobriety, but denounced the temperance movement vigorously on at least five occasions: 1847, 1848, 1867, 1871 and 1872. He was one of several Chartists who believed that temperance reformers were—in the L.W.M.A.'s words—'nibbling at the effects and seldom speaking of the cause' of drunkenness.[18] He also suspected them of hypocrisy, and denounced their distortions of Bible teaching. Above all, their attack on that ancient institution the public-house offended against his deeply felt conservatism: 'will you tell me that when men, women, and children are 12½ hours in the mill—will you tell me that they are not liable to the temptation of wanting something to sup?'[19] Stephens' speeches in 1871–2 contrast markedly with those of Henry Vincent, who happened to be lecturing in the locality at the time. Stephens was of course very untypical among Chartist leaders. But many Chartists shared his suspicion that the temperance movement, by stressing the need for moral effort on the part of the poor, was not in fact promoting the interests of their class. When the *Leeds Mercury* attacked the working class in 1850 for its self-imposed taxation, Harney delivered a sharp reprimand at 'the insolence of those who dare to lecture the working classes on their "immorality" while they themselves live by the most immoral system that ever this earth was afflicted with'.[20]

Both Harney and Ernest Jones took Stephens' criticism further: they had all his forthrightness, without his backward-looking social analysis. Jones was too good a politician ever to repudiate the temperance remedy entirely, but he did anticipate the socialist critique of the temperance movement. While always urging abstinence upon the Chartists, he regretted the temperance movement's efforts to link teetotalism with religious bigotry, and in the *People's Paper* for 30 September 1854 published an analysis of the causes of drunkenness whose sophistication was seldom seen in either temperance or Chartist movements. Attacking the theory that education alone could prevent prosperity from automatically increasing the crime rate, Jones pointed out that the working man buys drink during prosperous times only because 'extreme privation breeds extreme indulgence. Had he not been cast so low yesterday he would not cast *himself* so low to-day. Had you not denied him *bread* last week, he would have denied *himself gin* in this. But those FATAL FLUCTUATIONS are ruinous to the moral character of a man. They make his very existence precarious, and endue his heart with a desperate, callous recklessness—a sort of "devil-may-care" disposition.' Men would be thrifty only if well paid and if given a stake in the produce of their labour. In June 1855 Jones denied that abstinence would enable the working class to own farms and factories: 'as though the people would not be plundered out of their savings,' he exploded: '—as though the system of competition and monopoly would not prevent those hopes—and as though the money saved would be more than a drop in the golden ocean of the competing capitalist.'[21] Such remarks set the temperance movement in a wholly unfamiliar light, but they were too far ahead of their time, and made little impact. Ernest Jones himself, no doubt largely for tactical reasons, supported local option at the Manchester election in 1868.[22]

Jones' ideas were soon forgotten, but not so those of his contemporary Frederick Engels, who discussed the drink problem quite fully in his *Condition of the Working Class in England* (1844). Admitting that the temperance societies had 'done a great deal', Engels observed that many of their pledged members lapsed within a few weeks; nor had the temperance movement's methods produced any noticeable decline in the general level of drunkenness.[23] He believed that the problem was too deeply rooted to be successfully tackled in this way. Before the introduction of machinery into the textile industry, the workers 'were "respectable" people and good family men. In the absence of temptations to immorality they lived God-fearing decent lives. There were no low public houses or brothels in the neighbourhood. The innkeepers whose houses they did occasionally patronise were also respectable men, generally substantial tenant farmers, providing good beer and insisting on orderly behaviour and early closing.' With industrialization, however, the working classes are crowded into great towns and deprived of good housing, good food, clean air and pure water: 'their mental state is threatened by being subjected alternately to extremes of hope and fear. They are goaded like wild beasts and never have a chance of enjoying a quiet life. They are deprived of all pleasures except sexual indulgence and intoxicating liquors. Every day they have to work until they are physically and mentally exhausted. This forces them to excessive indulgence in the only two pleasures remaining to them.' The immigrant Irishman, living in one filthy crowded room 'must get some pleasure out of life and so he goes and drinks spirits'.

Engels therefore condemned temperance reformers for failing to recognize the dramatic recent changes in the workers' environment: these made it unrealistic to ascribe their drinking habits to any failure of moral responsibility. Society treats the Irish immigrant 'in such a way that it is virtually impossible for him to avoid becoming a drunkard'. Spirits are readily accessible, the public-house the only source of friendship and company; the worker desperately needs to forget 'the hard and miserable life' that he leads. 'These and a hundred other influences are so powerful that no one could really blame the workers for their excessive addiction to spirits.' To make matters worse, the Beer Act of 1830 had 'encouraged drunkenness by increasing the opportunities for beer-drinking', and the consumption of spirits in England had risen from 1,976,000 gallons in 1823 to 7,875,000 gallons in 1837. The consequences of this striking increase in consumption were apparent to Engels in Manchester as he walked home every Saturday evening. As a result of those and accompanying changes, 'the working classes have become a race apart from the English bourgeoisie. The middle classes have more in common with every other nation in the world than with the proletariat which lives on their own doorsteps. The workers differ from the middle classes in speech, in thoughts and ideas, in customs, morals, politics and religion. They are two quite different nations, as unlike as if they were differentiated by race.'[24]

This interpretation strikes at the roots of the temperance movement. Yet despite the prominence of the temperance movement in Manchester, no temperance reformer commented on it; probably no temperance reformer even read it. If he had done so, he could perhaps have made two criticisms of Engels' argument. Firstly, Engels was seriously misled by uncritically accepting Alison's statistics for spirits consumption: this startling increase merely reflected the diversion of spirits from illegal to legal channels—owing to the drastic reduction of the spirits duty in the 1820s. Similar mistakes were made by the Webbs and the Hammonds when they uncritically accepted the conclusions of the 1834 drunkenness report.[25] This argument does not of course disprove Engels' contention that the level of drunkenness was extremely high. But Engels must face a second line of criticism. It is important to ask how far an absolute increase in the level of drunkenness really had occurred, and how far an already existing level of drunkenness was—in these new industrial conditions—becoming intolerable. No statistical proof can be offered either way, but it is unlikely that many historians would now accept Engels' rosy analysis of the eighteenth-century situation.

A glance at twelfth-century homilies and seventeenth-century temperance tracts suggests that complaints about the drunkenness of working men are as perennial as complaints about their idleness. Many social anthropologists and historians have emphasized that the prevalence of drunkenness depends as much on cultural tradition as on social organization.[26] Industrialization by no means created the problem of urban intemperance; recreational drinking sometimes results directly from squalor, overwork and underpay, but sometimes also from the possession of funds without an accompanying tradition which ensures their constructive application, and from the possession of leisure whose incidence is insufficiently predictable to ensure its rational use. Prosperity so automatically promoted beer-drinking in the eighteenth century that its consumption statistics are a good guide to wage-levels.[27] Furthermore, we now know that drunkenness persists even in the most equitable of social orders; though many of the social conditions fostering it have now disappeared, enough strains remain to prompt in a minority the desire for escapist drinking. Modern Russians are still taught to follow Engels in blaming alcoholism on a faulty social structure, yet the evil still survives in their own reformed society.[28] The mid-Victorian social structure was so unsatisfactory that Engels was tempted to blame it for every human discontent.

A third criticism of Engels' argument could hardly have occurred to a contemporary. Engels assumed that the social classes in England were drifting ever more widely apart, and his future collaborator Karl Marx was at the same time describing the ginshops as '*symbolical embodiments* of private property' promoted by capitalists who speculated on the refinement of crude artificially produced needs. Marx predicted in the *Communist Manifesto* that, owing to mechanization and the concentration of capital, an increasing number of craftsmen, shopkeepers and artisans would be 'hurled down into the proletariat'. The habits and attitudes of bourgeoisie and proletariat would inevitably diverge: indeed, Marx believed that, to the class-conscious working man, law, morality and religion had already become 'so many bourgeois prejudices, behind which lurk in ambush just as many bourgeois interests'.

Temperance history shows how Marx and Engels exaggerated the seriousness of the contradictions within contemporary capitalist society: how they exaggerated the incompatibility between capitalism and virtue in the citizen. Marx went on to argue that because ginshops epitomized the essentials of capitalist economic relations, they were 'therefore rightly the only Sunday pleasures of the people, dealt with at least mildly by the English police'.[29] At the very time when he and Engels were writing, industrial employers were struggling—in the temperance movement—to find a remedy for the evil; they were among the most eager critics of wakes, fairs and Sunday drinking. The capitalist employer Richard Cobden knew well that drunkenness lowered wages by lowering employees' requirements of life, but his immediate response was not to sit back contented at the situation—on the contrary, Cobden was one of the few public figures to defend the temperance movement in parliament.[30] As late as 1864 Marx still believed that 'everywhere the great mass of the working classes were sinking down to a lower depth' and that 'every fresh development of the productive powers of labour must tend to deepen social contrasts and point social antagonisms'. Yet still British society failed to split apart. Engels at the end of his life was reduced to sarcastic asides about 'British respectability' and 'the religious bigotry and stupidity of the English respectable middle class' which so frustrated the efforts of himself and Marx; 'the English proletariat is becoming more and more bourgeois' he complained in 1858, 'so that this most bourgeois of all nations is apparently aiming ultimately at the possession of a bourgeois aristocracy and a bourgeois proletariat *as well as* a bourgeoisie'.[31]

The panacea at that time being peddled by the temperance movement was of course utterly inadequate. But its appeal to the concept of respectability was powerful enough to attract an important section of the working class and to bind them together with employers, nonconformists and others to form a pan-class reforming movement. Central to the understanding of this movement is a social gulf which Engels ignored, but which helps to explain why English society did not split apart as he envisaged: the gulf between Anglican and nonconformist. In his *Communist Manifesto* Marx contemptuously dismissed 'economists, philanthropists, humanitarians, improvers of the condition of the working class, organizers of charity, members of societies for the prevention of cruelty to animals, temperance fanatics, hole-and-corner reformers of every imaginable kind' as sections of the bourgeoisie 'desirous of redressing social grievances in order to secure the continued existence of bourgeois society'. The continued prosperity of these organizations perhaps entitles them to more attention than he gave them.

Not that their remedies in themselves did much to stave off Marx's revolution: it is the co-operation between working and middle classes which these movements inspired which is significant—their perpetuation of 'bourgeois' attitudes within the working class for so much longer than Marx had anticipated. For fifty years Marx and Engels incapacitated themselves politically by branding such tendencies as 'repulsive' and by thinking of them as a 'bourgeois infection'.[32] The temperance movement was one of several mid-Victorian agencies delaying the emergence of any distinctive and lasting working-class ideology. But by the end of the nineteenth century the concept of 'respectability' was wearing thin, and Engels' point of view became fashionable among pioneer socialists. For Engels' basic objection to the temperance movement had never been refuted: it was neglected only because a temporary economic situation enabled many articulate mid-Victorian working men to convince themselves that they had falsified it in their own lives.

The conflict between temperance reformers and early socialists was far from total. After all, both were trying to tackle the problem of poverty, and Robert Owen himself had pronounced spirit-shops and small pothouses 'a scandal to the Government that permits their continuance'. He wanted drink taxes greatly increased and spirit licences progressively withdrawn; he banned drinkshops from New Lanark and welcomed Buckingham's 1834 inquiry into drunkenness; his disciple John Finch contributed much to early teetotalism. Though there was room for argument about the salience of drinkshops among the causes of poverty, few socialists would have disagreed with Sidney Webb's reaction, in a letter to Beatrice Potter: 'What I see in the Deptford slums does make me feel that drink is one great enemy'; Beatrice had herself written something similar in her diary only six years before. Local option and teetotal policies attracted many Labour pioneers—even in the Social Democratic Federation. Tom Mann, Will Thorne, George

Lansbury, Keir Hardie, Will Crooks and Richard Pankhurst were all temperance reformers before joining the labour movement.[33] John Burns in June 1890 protested at a Hyde Park anti-compensation meeting against 'the still further degradation of his class'; Ben Tillett late in 1891 urged workers to be sober if they were to stand up to their employers, and at Bradford in January 1892 found in drink the explanation for working-class apathy in the face of exploitation: 'the drink killed their ambition and their self-respect'. At a Deptford political meeting in the same month Sidney Webb produced a map of London on which all the public-houses had been marked with red dots, and delighted local temperance zealots by describing it as 'London's scarlet fever'.[34]

Even if early Labour leaders had disagreed with temperance attitudes, they would have been unwise to alienate so powerful a group by saying so publicly. Indeed Philip Snowden in the autumn of 1901 was trying to weld together the socialist and temperance movements behind a policy of municipalization and the local veto. The Alliance in 1901 claimed credit for training many people—including 'the *élite* of the working classes'—to think seriously about economic, legal and political problems.[35] Many early Labour M.P.s were abstainers;[36] temperance legislation attracted them in 1908 as in 1893. Take Arthur Henderson, for example, on the 1908 Bill: 'I do not know that during the time I have been associated with the House I ever heard a scheme unfolded which gave me such general satisfaction.' Keir Hardie did not think the Bill had gone far enough, and Will Crooks, in a long passionate speech, welcomed the Bill as one way of tackling slum conditions: 'because you can chloroform men day by day with drink they care not for the conditions under which they live.'[37] Writing in 1929, the German journalist Egon Wertheimer discovered that British Labour leaders, unlike their German counterparts, had never repudiated capitalist culture: they were, he wrote, 'essentially Puritan'.[38]

J. H. Roberts, the socialist and temperance reformer, even argued that 'there is nothing in Socialism, of itself, to justify the antagonism of any Temperance Reformer as such'.[39] As long as the need for 'personal effort' and 'the development of individual character' featured prominently in Labour party propaganda—as in Philip Snowden's writings—there would always be close links between the two movements.[40] As long as the party continued to stress the corrupting influence of the drink trade on British society and politics, there would always be common ground with the temperance campaign. In the 1920s V. W. Garratt was still, with Snowden's approval, blaming the drink trade for corrupting the press, and for aiming 'to dope the worker's mind and . . . make him less capable of understanding his condition'. The 1923 report of the Labour party inquiry into the drink question described the political influence of 'the Trade' as 'now a standing menace to promoters of reforms of any kind in Parliament'.[41]

The belief that an abstainer would be less corruptible in any contest between capital and labour had strong roots in the labour movement. Temperance reformers and trade unionists agreed that the man with savings and a character was more likely to prevail with the employers, less likely to be a blackleg.[42] Co-operative societies and trade union leaders took care to ensure that their officials were sober, and did all they could to promote sobriety among their members.[43] Abstainers constituted 'the backbone of the democratic political movement in this country', said Snowden in 1936.[44] The wide acceptance which such beliefs gained in the Labour party can be seen in Keir Hardie's determination to avoid social engagements promoted by members of other political parties, and in the suspicion which attached to J. H. Thomas as soon as he began drinking and attending banquets. As late as the 1950s, while beer-drinking was widespread among the rank-and-file in Yorkshire miners' unions, a union official who drank more than moderately was unlikely to retain his post.[45]

Ideological considerations apart, the Labour party had everything to gain by promoting sobriety in its members. But as socialist influences gathered force within the party it became clear that much depended on what *priority* was given to abstinence and temperance legislation. By 1914 the influence of temperance principles within the labour movement was being seriously challenged.[46] Five basic arguments affected the debate, and the semi-hysterical tone in which temperance reformers often rebutted them reveals how damaging they were seen to be. The five arguments were not all voiced at the same time or by the same individual: they have been gathered from many scattered socialist speeches and writings. The first argument revived the environmentalist critique wielded so effectively by Engels and used long before 1844; it was already being formulated by Robert Owen before the 1830s. Once the evil conditions existing among the people had been discovered at New Lanark, he was faced with two possible courses of action. He could of course penalize his employees for succumbing to the environment with which society surrounded them; but such methods had the great disadvantage of alienating them. The alternative was 'to change these evil conditions for good ones, and thus . . . supersede the inferior and bad characters, created by inferior and bad conditions, by superior and good characters to be created by superior and good conditions'.[47]

In the case of drunkenness, English society followed the first of Owen's two policies throughout the nineteenth century. The vast majority of those arrested for drunkenness were working men; the Sheffield police analysed the educational background of individuals arrested for drunkenness in the 1860s, and of a sample of 515 arrested during 1863–4, 228 had 'none', 276 were 'imperfect' and only 11 had an education described as 'good'. Only one of those whose occupations were listed was described as a 'gentleman', and 77 of the sample were unemployed.[48] If Engels was right to attribute drunkenness to environmental influences rather than to individual weakness of will, working men were being punished in thousands throughout the period for offences really committed by society. The judicial statistics reveal the scale on which these punishments were being administered to working people in the mid-Victorian period [see also Plates 1 and 29].

The second of Owen's two remedies was voiced long before the early twentieth-century Labour party embraced it. The *Poor Man's Guardian* on 16 July 1831 urged the British & Foreign Temperance Society to 'make the poor man's home comfortable' so that he would not need to patronize the ginshop. 'Change a man's conditions and you change your man,' wrote Joseph Arch, making the same point many years later in his autobiography.

TABLE 11

Punishments Inflicted for Drunkenness and 'Drunk and Disorderly' Behaviour in England and Wales: Four Sample Years

YEAR	PROCEEDINGS (determined summarily)	DISCHARGE	FINE	PRISON	OTHER
1860	88,361	31,110	49,697	3,993	3,561
1864	100,067	31,186	57,219	8,085	3,577
1870	131,870	22,514	92,060	13,713	3,583
1876	205,567	19,730	158,987	23,665	3,185

SOURCES: Judicial statistics for 1860, *Parl. Papers* 1861 (2860), LX, p. 32; for 1864, *Parl. Papers* 1865 (3534), LII, pp. 32ff.; for 1870, *Parl. Papers* 1871 (C. 442), LXIV, p. 32; for 1876 *Parl. Papers* 1877 (C. 1871), LXXXVI, p. 32.

The temperance movement rejoined that every working man could alter his own environment by altering his drinking habits and, if necessary, by moving to a better house. John Burns was still voicing this argument in 1904: 'it is not always the pigstye, it is too often the pig.'[49]

In 1894 Robert Blatchford roundly asserted that 'men instinctively prefer light to darkness, love to hate, and good to evil'; if this was not apparent in their actual conduct in a competitive society, this was because capitalist society distorted their natural virtue. If working people had good homes, sufficient leisure and good food, their drunkenness would disappear. Attacking the temperance movement, Blatchford argued that working men at least had a choice whether they were robbed by the publican, whereas the grasping capitalist employer gave them a choice only between exploitation and starvation. 'The real culprits, the people actually responsible for nearly all the drunkenness of the poor, are the grasping employers, the polluters of the rivers and the air, the jerry-builders, the slum-lords, and the detestable knaves who grow rich by the sale of poisoned and adulterated liquor.'[50] The contest between willpower and environment was so unequal, that temperance reformers were allegedly wasting their time by concentrating on moral exhortation. The socialist challenge was complete when temperance reformers were themselves accused of fostering the evil which they spent their lives publicly attacking. Harry Quelch pointed out in 1908 that those most anxious to 'protect' the working man from the drinkseller were precisely those who wanted to preserve him against housing reform and factory legislation. Sir Wilfrid Lawson, said Russell Smart, 'by the extortion he is enabled to exact from royalty and mining rents, grinds the Cumberland workers into that monotonous round of penurious toil whose only solace is alcohol'.[51]

Secondly, socialists insisted that universal abstinence could not improve the situation of the working class as a whole because 'the better economic condition of the abstainer is only possible by reason of the continued degradation of his fellows'.[52] In a free market, it was argued, wages fall to the smallest amount capable of providing employees with a living wage; where the majority act as though drink is a necessity, the sober minority can retain their drink-money for buying luxuries; but where *all* abstain, it becomes apparent to the employer that all can be induced to live on a smaller income; therefore the minimum wage falls, the employer's profits rise still higher, and the last state is worse than the first. One important effect of this analysis was to kill off one of the teetotaler's best arguments: that one could judge the blessings of universal teetotalism by observing the prosperity of temperance utopias. This was made brutally clear during the debate between the young Philip Snowden and the temperance reformer David Pickles in the correspondence columns of the *Keighley News* for January 1895. Pickles was trying to refute the arguments of a socialist lecturer Miss Enid Stacey. She had claimed that the workers would not gain by universal teetotalism, and Pickles rejoined by pointing to the prosperity of his native village, Cowling, which recently had severely reduced its drinking facilities: Cowling's inhabitants, he emphasized, now had £10 per head in the Yorkshire Penny Bank. In a long and eloquent letter, Philip Snowden, also a native of Cowling, pointed out that 'Mr. Pickles's whole energy has been spent in supporting his opponent's case', for it was integral to Miss Stacey's argument that the sober minority profits by its teetotalism only because the majority drink.[53]

The contradiction between class loyalty and the pursuit of respectability was at last exposed. The conflict was perhaps most neatly expressed by the Liberal J. A. Hobson, when he argued that 'we must learn to discriminate the two questions: "Drink as a cause of Poverty", and "Drink as determining who shall be poor" '.[54] Socialists saw it as one of the most flagrant evils of capitalist society that working men could not *en masse* profit from their own virtue.[55] Some socialists even contested the temperance reformer's assumption that the working man who abstained would necessarily profit even in society as at present organized—for in a competitive and classbound world, there were still a thousand ways of depriving a thrifty working man of his savings; it might be convenient for those who believed in self-help to assume that the unsuccessful lacked the worthy qualities of the successful—but it was not true.[56]

Perhaps the most striking section of Snowden's letter to the *Keighley News* was his insistence on the meanness of this teetotal utopia which temperance reformers were advertising. The inhabitants of Cowling might have savings of £10 per head, but this represented 'the moral, physical, and intellectual degradation of a community of the best brain and muscle to be found in "Merrie" England', for it was won by a scrimping and saving which diverted into a petty, hopeless and humiliating struggle all the self-respect which socialists wanted to mobilize behind the grandeur of their crusade for social regeneration. That £10 'represents, in short, every charge ever brought against established order by every agitator, from the maddest street corner orator to the arch-agitator Christ Himself; it represents injustice doubly damned, because inflicted on those whose virtues are made instruments to scourge them'. The socialist movement, Snowden emphasized, was 'fundamentally ethical' in character: 'it values results by a moral, not a money standard, and this is why my valuation of the poor man's savings differs so widely from Mr. Pickles's'.[57] Keighley's *I.L.P. Journal* was at this time busily exposing the inadequacy of Liberalism and quoting Russell Smart on the environmental causes of drunkenness. Its editorial on 6 January 1895 roundly announced the supersession of the temperance movement by socialism: 'by seeking to make the slum, the alley, the court and the sweating den a thing of the past, the Labour party claim to be the true Temperance Reformers.'

Philip Snowden's brush with an obscure temperance reformer helped to launch him on to his political career: but it is important to get his temperance viewpoint clear. Although he denied in 1895 that abstinence could ever be a panacea, he did not deny that abstinence would enable working men to strengthen their political position. In his attitudes to the 1908 Licensing Bill, Snowden reveals that unlike more thoroughgoing socialists his repudiation of the temperance movement was never complete. While still repeating the message of 1895 that 'the roots of the drink evil were deep down in our social system, and only by reform of that system could the remedy be found': while insisting that a reduction in working hours 'would be one of the greatest temperance measures'—Snowden in 1908 was very willing to go along with the Liberals in their purely restrictive temperance measure, for in his view it did at least contribute towards solving the drink problem.[58] Editorials in his weekly, the *Labour Leader*, show him diverging in emphasis from men like Quelch, Grayson and Russell Smart: for he insisted that drunkenness was a problem in all societies, and that though it might be intensified by 'landlordism or capitalism', it was not created by it.[59]

Temperance reformers could hardly remain quiet in the face of the socialist attack on their central creed: the cult of respectability. John Burns, a labour leader who remained convinced by the temperance case, denounced such arguments in his lecture on *Labour and Drink* in 1904; it was 'an absurd and vicious doctrine, and places a premium on dissipation', he said.[60] R. A. Jameson cited Ricardo in support of the view that the wages of labour tend to 'the lowest on which it is physically possible to keep up the population, or the lowest with which they will choose to do so'. Teetotalers, Jameson argued—far from being content with lower wages than their drinking compatriots—set themselves higher standards than their fellows. If workers could keep up wages for expenditure on drink, there was no reason why they should not do the same for expenditure on other commodities. Jameson's argument had been used sixty years before by Lovett in defence of trade unions.[61] Its weakness lay in the fact that seventy years of temperance effort had produced only a minority of teetotalers: socialists rightly argued that something must be done for the majority. Prohibition—even if secured—would not of itself ensure in former drinkers the changed pattern of consumption which, on Jameson's argument, would keep wages up.

Temperance reformers used other arguments: they claimed, for instance, that in a technological society requiring speed and accuracy of work, excessive drinking after a few years rendered men unemployable; and by depriving families of sufficient income, drinkers forced their womenfolk on to the labour market in competition with the men. Temperance reformers also claimed that a diversion of expenditure from drink to clothing, furniture, housing and other goods would relieve unemployment by enlarging the home market, particularly as the drink industry employed an unusually small labour force in relation to the amount of capital invested. They also argued that the increased efficiency of manufacture resulting from sobriety in the employee would make British goods more competitive in foreign markets.[62] None of these temperance arguments could effectively counter the socialists' *exposée* of the injustice of society as at present constituted. For Quelch, the inefficiency of the competitive system far outweighed the waste involved in the drunkenness of the employee: wastefulness was, for him, endemic in the capitalist social system.[63]

A third argument—frequently used by Edward Carpenter, but which influenced many members of the labour movement as they drifted away from radical nonconformity—was to depreciate the Victorian virtues: to dethrone, in short, the type of personality which the temperance movement for two generations had been trying to create. There had always been a conflict in the labour movement between the puritans and the pleasure-lovers, between those whose reformism stemmed largely from distaste at the extravagance of the rich and those who wanted affluence for the poor. The barrenness of the abstainer's life was forcibly expressed in the characterization of 'Holy Joe' in Richard Whiteing's popular slum-novel *No. 5 John Street*, published in 1899.

Thrift, said Stephen Reynolds in 1911, 'can easily be over-valued. Extreme thrift . . . has often a singularly dehumanising effect. It hardens the nature of its votaries. . . . It is all right as a means of living, but lamentable as an end of life.' Belfort Bax was making a complementary point when he argued that 'most men of strong character have been possessed of some vice'. What Tillett was describing by 1909 as 'nonconformist conscience and tea' seemed at least to some critics of the temperance movement less colourful, less vigorous, than 'socialism and beer'. It was not simply that the Victorian virtues were falling out of fashion: it was now suspected that they were being hypocritically inculcated by self-interested capitalists. Harcourt's temperance zeal was listed by Sydney Olivier in *Fabian Essays* as one of the frauds of capitalist society; for 'as the existence of the propertied class in modern societies does depend ultimately upon the observance by the bulk of the people of this conventional morality, the propertied class professes publicly to venerate and observe conventions which in its private practice it has long admitted to be obsolete'.[64]

The attack on the ascetic ideal was conducted most daringly by Edward Carpenter, who argued in 1896 that total abstinence often impoverished human nature, or even prompted revolutionary excesses; primitive religions, he said, catered for man's hedonistic as well as for his ascetic impulses.[65] Carpenter's focus of interest here was on the sexual impulse, but in an article published in 1907 he conducted a full-scale onslaught on all the Victorian virtues. Morality, he argued, is not a code of rules; men must cease to fear their passions, and cast aside the narrow concept of 'duty'; the new morality promoted by the socialist society would cast aside the hypocrisy and selfishness of the capitalist society, so that 'the motives of greed and the mean pursuit of money, which now weigh upon the world, will be like an evil nightmare of the Past from which the dawn delivers us'. In the *Socialist Review* for June 1909, Mary Pendered's attack on the temperance movement was more direct: she contested the temperance reformers' assumption that civilization would reduce man's desire for light recreation, and firmly repudiated puritanism. Man's craving for excitement was 'no more evil than his craving for bread'; indeed, the working man who entered the public-house sought the same pleasures which his betters sought at the opera—'stimulus and excitement'. Far from excluding working men from the public-house, society should sponsor recreation halls and gardens and 'recognize the psychological aspect of amusement'. She was in effect urging a return to the suburban tea-gardens which eighteenth-century Londoners had enjoyed [see Plate 2], but which puritanism had killed off after the 1820s.[66]

Carpenter's distaste for 'principle' was only one instance of the way in which socialists were repudiating the narrowness of traditional radical attitudes. The fourth socialist criticism of the temperance movement concentrated on its sectarian outlook. The rigid positions taken up by rival temperance reformers had often hindered the cause of true temperance reform, and even the friendly Labour party report of 1923 emphasized the need for a fresh outlook on the problem: 'the Labour Party, in the interests of temperance itself, deplores not so much the difference of proposals as the exclusiveness by which they are held'. When a reform has long been controversial, the report added, 'the champions tend to wear out ruts for themselves'.[67] This fresh socialist outlook involved a firm repudiation of attacks on the publican: for once it had become clear that social ills stemmed from the objective forms of production and not from the wickedness of individuals, bitterness in reform crusades became superfluous. Many socialists would have agreed with the plea of the *Brewers Journal* on 15 April 1871, that 'so long as the sins of society are created by the arrangements of society itself, they should not punish a shopkeeper for results which he cannot control'. The drink trade had indeed been unfairly singled out by the nineteenth-century temperance movement as a scapegoat for evils far more deeply rooted; socialists differed from temperance reformers in preferring to improve the management of drinking places instead of abolishing them outright. Not for Harry Quelch the policy of making drinking places more gloomy: he wanted 'popular restaurants under municipal ownership and control'.[68]

Here again the party clashed with the temperance movement, for as has been shown the latter would have nothing to do with the municipalization and nationalization so widely advocated in the party after the first world war. When a Fabian tract advocated such policies the Alliance denounced it hysterically as 'this treacherous and delusive publication'.[69] Although the 1918 Labour party programme included 'local option', this policy was placed alongside 'State control' and 'reduction of licences'.[70] Furthermore the Labour party conference in 1920 rejected prohibition and interpreted 'local option' as meaning 'full and unfettered power for dealing with the licensing question'. This definition was far broader than the Alliance version, for it involved conceding to the democracy not only the right to prohibit, but also the right to regulate and control the Trade. The relatively eclectic and unsectarian attitude adopted by the Labour party towards the temperance question is epitomized in the 1923 report's emphasis that no attempt should be made to commit the party to any one panacea if this excluded other remedies: for 'it may well be that they will all be required, to a greater or lesser degree, before the problem can be solved'.[71] So broad an outlook was seldom seen in the temperance movement.

The cumulative effect of the four leading socialist arguments against the temperance case lent support to a fifth and final shift in opinion—the removal of 'the drink problem' from its central position in the poverty debate. Some socialists felt that temperance reformers kept it there largely in order to advertise working-class vices. Fresh from an encounter with a drunken Westmorland carrier, Mrs. Thornburgh the vicar's wife in *Robert Elsmere* quotes approvingly her husband's view that 'it is our special business . . . who are in authority, to bring their low vices home to these people'. As long ago as 1874 Alexander MacDonald, one of the first two working men in the House of Commons, emphasized in a licensing debate that 'the working classes in this country were not addicted to early drinking, and he thought it his duty to vindicate them from the imputations that such was the case'.[72] The suspicion kept cropping up among working men, and especially among socialist critics of the temperance movement, that working people suffered by the centrality of the drink problem in political debate. In *Merrie England* Blatchford emphasized that 'many a highly-respectable middle-class gentleman spends more money on drink in one day than a labourer earns in a week', and according to Quelch the temperance movement was 'based on the assumption that the working man is a vile, incorrigible, drunken beast, incapable of self-control'. The trade unions were still being irritated by accusations of working-class drunkenness during the first world war. As late as 20 March 1923 during the debate on the capitalist system, human sinfulness was being pertly used to discredit the Labour party's utopia. 'Will the hon. Member tell me that under a Socialist system there would be no syphilitic children in the world?' Sir A. Mond asked Philip Snowden; 'will he tell me that, under a Socialist system, there would be no drunkards in the world and no off-spring of drunkards?'[73]

In these circumstances, the dethroning of the drink question was a development to be welcomed. Charles Booth accelerated the process by exploding the temperance reformers' exaggerated claims on the relation between drink and poverty. His investigators found that only 13% of the poor and 14% of the very poor in his sample owed their misfortunes directly to drink. Questions of illness, employment and family size were, he concluded, far more relevant to the problem.[74] While drink might operate as a cause of poverty at a remoter level, 'how distinguish between degrees of folly more or less recent or remote?' He wisely concluded that it was better 'to view and consider these unfortunates only as they actually exist'.[75] Booth's ideas influenced reformers of many types: Joseph Chamberlain at Birmingham in 1894 quoted his figures on the causes of pauperism in old age and vigorously attacked those who accused aged paupers of thriftlessness, insobriety or drunkenness. Such allegations were 'a libel upon the working classes of this country'—the 'easy excuses of men who strive thereby to serve their consciences and harden their hearts'. The argument was turned more explicitly against capitalism by a Keighley socialist named Horner in 1894: teetotalers who made such criticisms of old people receiving poor relief were, he said, 'egged on and supported by cunning capitalistic subscribers'.[76]

It was the temperance movement's exaggerated claims for its panacea which so irritated Ernest Jones in the 1850s.[77] By the 1900s, for all their energy and idealism, their radicalism and their faith in the future, temperance reformers of all kinds were no longer *avant garde* among social reformers. While the one-eyed fanatical teetotaler who rejected all other remedies might be, as the Alliance claimed, 'simply a man-of-straw set up by clever writers [e.g. Blatchford] for the purpose of being skilfully knocked down again',[78] the temperance movement by the 1890s was beginning to divert the working man from his proper concerns. Critics began to suspect the whole notion of isolating 'the drink problem' from other social questions with which it should be connected. 'There is no . . . separate Drink Problem', wrote J. A. Hobson in 1896. The temperance movement was diverting working men, in Quelch's words, 'from the real causes of social evils to some of its minor effects'. During the licensing debate on 15 October 1908, Victor Grayson stood up to move that the House adjourn to consider the question of the unemployed. Forced to leave the House on this occasion, he returned to the fray on the next day: 'there are thousands of people dying in the streets,' he insisted, 'while you are trifling with this Bill.'[79] It was a symbolic event, for it indicated that the long and unquestioned alliance between the temperance movement and the spokesmen of the working class had come to an end.

Bibliographical Note

I have published an extensive annotated bibliography in my 'Drink and Sobriety in England 1815–1872. A Critical Bibliography', *International Review of Social History*, XII (1967), Part 2; the specialist will not therefore need a full bibliography here. But the general reader may appreciate some guidance to the major sources; the footnotes will refer him to many others.

Although for this period the statistics are very unreliable, they constitute an essential starting-point, and are usefully collated and discussed in G. B. Wilson's *Alcohol and the Nation* (1940). Facts, and attitudes to the facts, are gathered in many parliamentary reports and papers. The most outstanding are the Select Committee of the House of Commons on Drunkenness, *Parl. Papers* 1834, VIII (559); the Select Committee on Public Houses, *Parl. Papers* 1852–3, XXXVII (855); 1854, XIV (367); the Select Committee of the House of Lords on Intemperance, *Parl. Papers* 1877, XI (171); 1877, XI (271); 1877, XI (418); 1878, XIV (338); 1878–9, X (113); and the Royal Commission on Liquor Licensing Laws, *Parl. Papers* 1897, XXXIV (8356); 1897, XXXV (8523–I); 1898, XXXVI (8694); 1898, XXXVII (8696); 1898, XXXVIII (8822, 8980); 1899, XXXIV (9075); 1899, XXXV (9379, 9076, 9379–I).

Hansard's *Parliamentary Debates* are of course invaluable for upper-class opinion about the facts; until the 1860s politicians were more concerned with free traders than with temperance reformers, who began to set their sights at Westminster only after 1853. Very few manuscript sources survive. The governing classes were not interested in the drink question before 1872, and nobody thought the private correspondence of humbler men worth preserving. Temperance society minute-books are invaluable where they survive; there are British and National Temperance League minute-books at Livesey-Clegg House, Sheffield. An interesting collection of correspondence between John Burtt and Earl Stanhope in 1839–40 is kept in the Bodleian Library, Oxford.

There are many serious gaps in the secondary literature. There is no published secondary work on the drink question as a whole in the nineteenth century, though Peter Mathias' 'Brewing Industry, Temperance and Politics', *Historical Journal*, 1958, and B. L. Crapster ' "Our Trade, Our Politics". A Study of the Political Activity of the British Liquor Industry, 1868–1910' (Harvard unpublished Ph.D. thesis, 1949) are both valuable. There is no good book on popular recreation, or on drink manufacturing and retailing—

though mindless antiquarian literature abounds. The London Guildhall Library's *Norman Collection* has several boxes of illustrations on drinking places in London. M. Gorham and H. McG. Dunnett, *Inside the Pub* (1950) and Mass Observation's *The Pub and the People* (1943) are the only really worthwhile studies of the public-house. On drinking customs, John Dunlop's *Philosophy of Artificial and Compulsory Drinking Usage* (1839) is encyclopaedic. Nobody has ever written about developments in the free licensing movement after 1830, but the Webbs' *History of Liquor Licensing in England, Principally from 1700–1830* (U.K.A. edn., 1903) is invaluable.

The temperance movement is better covered, though the secondary literature is partisan and strongly biased against the anti-spirits movement. Dawson Burns' superbly indexed *Temperance History* (2 Vols., 1889) is the best starting-point, but it should be supplemented with P. T. Winskill's less accurate and more biographical *Temperance Movement and its Workers* (4 Vols., 1892), and also with his *Temperance Standard-Bearers of the Nineteenth-Century* (2 Vols., 1897). These books were written too soon after the event to be fair and well-proportioned, but Henry Carter's *The English Temperance Movement. A Study in Objectives* (1933) is better in these respects. Admittedly it is partisan, but it is well-documented, particularly on the controversy between 'moral suasionists' and 'legislative compulsionists'. Roy Macleod's ' "The Edge of Hope" Social Policy and Chronic Alcoholism 1870–1900', *Journal of the History of Medicine and Allied Sciences*, Vol. 22, No. 3 (July 1967), and W. F. Bynum's 'Chronic Alcoholism in the first half of the Nineteenth Century', *Bulletin of the History of Medicine*, Vol. 42, (1968), illuminate a neglected aspect of the temperance question. Norman Longmate's *The Waterdrinkers* (1968) is readable, but it is superficial in interpretation and adds nothing new. To get the flavour of the temperance movement, the reader can do nothing better than read two books—Thomas Whittaker's exhilarating *Life's Battles in Temperance Armour* (1884) and Mrs. C. L. Wightman's *Haste to the Rescue!* (1862). The reader with an appetite for more must plunge into the wealth of annual reports and periodicals issued by the temperance societies, both local and national. There are excellent temperance libraries at London University Library, in the James Turner Temperance Collection: at the headquarters of the United Kingdom Alliance, Alliance House, Westminster: and at the headquarters of the British National Temperance League, Livesey-Clegg House, Sheffield.

The prohibitionist movement has been less well covered. Mark Hayler's *The Vision of a Century. 1853–1953. The United Kingdom Alliance in Historical Retrospect* (1953) collects much valuable material, but is an uncritical and somewhat disorganized exhortation to further effort, not an objective or complete history. The Alliance issued excellent annual reports and an informative periodical the *Alliance News*, but these have never been properly used; its manuscript minute-books from 1871 survive at Alliance House. There is no adequate history of any British temperance organization, local or national. There is a good biography of the most prominent early prohibitionist—Sir Wilfrid Lawson—by G. W. E. Russell, but his papers have not survived.

Nobody has ever written on Teetotal Chartism, or on its leader Henry Vincent; and until ecclesiastical history concerns itself more with the sociology of religion, it can offer little to the temperance historian. As for the conflict between temperance and socialism, this splendid subject awaits its historian. Several students are now helping to fill the gaps in the secondary literature; when their work is complete, it may at last be possible to write an adequate history of the drink question in the nineteenth century, and to engage fruitfully in cross-cultural comparisons. Particularly urgently needed are scholarly studies of the drink question at the local level. I have suggested some possible approaches in my 'Temperance Societies', *Local Historian*, VIII, No. 4 (1968), and VIII, No. 5 (1969). Mr. B. S. Trinder and I have written one local study—'Drink and Sobriety in an Early Victorian Country Town: Banbury 1830–1860', *English Historical Review* supplement, 1969. W. R. Lambert, 'Drink and Sobriety in Wales 1835–1895' (University of Wales Ph.D. thesis, 1969), is a valuable regional study.

I should perhaps briefly explain the relation between this book and my unpublished Oxford D.Phil. thesis (1966) on 'The Temperance Question in England. 1829–1869'. All the material has been entirely re-written and re-arranged since it was submitted in thesis form. Some sections have been published separately as articles and so have been entirely omitted here, or have been briefly summarized. New chapters have been added, and the time-span has been extended at both ends. My 'Drunkards and Reformers. Early Victorian Temperance Tracts', *History Today*, Mar. 1963, explores, rather superficially, a neglected and important field. Two climactic moments in early temperance history are analysed in (perhaps excessive) detail in my 'Two Roads to Social Reform: Francis Place and the "Drunken Committee" of 1834', *Historical Journal*, 1968, and in my 'The Sunday Trading Riots of 1855', *Historical Journal*, 1965. The temperance press up to 1872 is discussed in my article, ' "A World of Which We had No Conception": Liberalism and the Temperance Press, 1830–1872', *Victorian Studies*, 1969. Some comparisons are made between attitudes to drink and attitudes to sexuality in my 'Underneath the Victorians', *Victorian Studies*, 1968; and the motives of an individual temperance zealot are scrutinized in A. E. Dingle and B. Harrison's 'Cardinal Manning as Temperance Reformer', *Historical Journal*, 1969. For a biographical study of the prohibitionists, see my 'The British Prohibitionists, 1853–72. A Biographical Analysis', *International Review of Social History*, 1970. P. Hollis and B. Harrison, 'Chartism, Liberalism and the Life of Robert Lowery', *English Historical Review*, July 1967, explores the relation between social class and mid-Victorian politics, with reference to the autobiography of a Chartist and temperance reformer.

Bibliographical Note

General problems which arise in investigating reforming and philanthropic movements are discussed in my 'Philanthropy and the Victorians', *Victorian Studies*, 1966. My 'Religion and Recreation in Nineteenth-Century England', *Past and Present*, Dec. 1967, discusses some of the major themes in the history of nineteenth-century recreation. This article will shortly be supplemented by my 'Pubs in Victorian Towns' in H. J. Dyos and M. Wolff (Eds.), *The Victorian City* (Routledge, forthcoming). The above-mentioned items merely initiate discussion; much painstaking research must be completed, and much co-operation between scholars must be fostered, before justice can really be done to the subject.

Reference Notes

All books in the reference notes below were published in London unless otherwise stated. Full details of each item are included only at the first citation. These notes have been used entirely for references and acknowledgements, and do not amplify material in the text.

Chapter 1. Perspectives [pp. 19–36].

[1] (p. 20) Hansard's *Parliamentary Debates*, Third Series, Vol. 251 [future citations will take the form *3 Hansard 251*], cc. 470–1 (5 Mar. 1880).

[2] (p. 20) For real national income, see B. R. Mitchell & P. Deane, *Abstract of British Historical Statistics* (Cambridge, 1962), p. 367.

[3] (p. 21) R. G. McCarthy, *Drinking and Intoxication* (New Haven, 1959), pp. 104, 263. Arrest statistics from S[elect] C[ommittee] of the H[ouse] of L[ords] on Intemperance, third report, *Parl*[iamentary] *Papers* 1877 (418), XI, p. 315.

[4] (p. 22) J. A. H. Murray *et al.* (Eds.), *The Oxford English Dictionary*, I, p. 210; III, p. 692; Chamberlain is in S[elect] C[ommittee] of the H[ouse] of L[ords] on Intemperance, *Parl. Papers* 1877 (171), XI, Q. 2294. See also F. Bynum's excellent 'Chronic Alcoholism in the first half of the 19th century', *Bulletin of the History of Medicine*, Vol. 42 (1968).

[5] (p. 22) B[ritish] M[useum] *Add*[itional] *MSS.* 35142 (Place Papers), f. 40; cf. *A New Survey of London Life & Labour*, IX (1935), p. 243. I have discussed difficulties in the statistical evidence in my 'Drink & Sobriety in England 1815–1872. A Critical Bibliography', *International Review of Social History*, 1967, II, pp. 207–10.

[6] (p. 22) Some topics suitable for research are outlined in my bibliography, *loc. cit.*, p. 205.

[7] (p. 23) H. Butterfield, *The Whig Interpretation of History* (1931), p. 10; R. C. K. Ensor, *England 1870–1914* (1936), p. 409.

[8] (p. 23) British Council of Churches, *Sex & Morality. A Report . . . October 1966* (1966), p. 13; cf. B. R. Wilson, *Religion in Secular Society* (1966), pp. 37, 63.

[9] (p. 23) Roy Jenkins, in *Sunday Times*, 20 July 1969, p. 2.

[10] (p. 24) For Pain, see T. W. Rammell, *Report to the General Board of Health on . . . Banbury* (1850), p. 12. Mr. B. S. Trinder, area tutor organizer for adult education, Shropshire, referred me to this source. I am much indebted to him for help in this and many other ways. See also W. R. Fremantle, *Memoir of Rev. Spencer Thornton* (1850), p. 102. Michael Hennell of Ripon Hall, Cambridge, kindly referred me to this source.

[11] (p. 24) C. W. McCree, *George Wilson McCree. His Life & Work* (1893), p. 104.

[12] (p. 25) T. Whittaker, *Life's Battles* in Temperance Armour] (3rd edn, 1888), p. 234.

[13] (p. 25) R. C. K. Ensor, *op. cit.*, p. 555; for voting, see J. Vincent, *Pollbooks. How Victorians Voted* (Cambridge, 1967), p. 16.

[14] (p. 26) Samuel Pope, *Alliance News*, 29 Oct. 1870, p. 349.

[15] (p. 26) R[oyal] C[ommission] on . . . the Contagious Diseases Act, *Parl. Papers* 1871 (C. 408, 408–I), XIX, Q. 12,921. For estimates of the labour aristocracy's size, see E. J. Hobsbawm, *Labouring Men* (1964), p. 279; cf. H. J. Dyos (Ed.), *The Study of Urban History* (1968), pp. 146, 148.

[16] (p. 26) Cf. D. Riesman, *Abundance for What?* (1964), p. 154.

[17] (p. 26) See, for example, B. Webb, *My Apprenticeship* (2nd edn, n.d.), p. 143, writing in 1886.

[18] (p. 27) J. A. Hobson, *Work & Wealth* (1914), pp. 155–6.

[19] (p. 27) J. Vincent, *The Formation of the Liberal Party. 1857–1868* (1966), p. 79.

[20] (p. 27) Mr. Marks, quo. in *The Times*, 2 Dec. 1967.

[21] (p. 27) *New Statesman*, 29 Sept. 1967.

[22] (p. 28) O. MacDonagh, 'The Nineteenth-century Revolution in Government: A Re-appraisal', *Historical Journal*, 1958, p. 58.

[23] (p. 29) G. Orwell, *The Road to Wigan Pier* (Penguin edn, 1962), p. 57; cf. Oastler & Cooper, in G. D. H. Cole, *Chartist Portraits* (1941), pp. 84, 192. See also A. V. Dicey, *Lectures on the Relation between Law and Public Opinion in England during the Nineteenth-Century* (1905), pp. 63–4, 309, 399–400.

[24] (p. 29) Quo. in R. R. James, *Rosebery* (1963), p. 58; I owe this reference to Mr. M. C. Hurst; cf. E. J. Hobsbawm, *op. cit.*, p. 375.

[25] (p. 31) W. H. Beveridge, *Full Employment in a Free Society* (1944), p. 281. For the cotton famine's impact, see Bodleian Library, Oxford: *James Johnson Collection* (Temperance, 2), duplicated U[nited] K[ingdom] A[lliance] appeal for funds dated Aug. 1863. For Bradford, see Peggy Rastrick, 'The Bradford Temperance Movement' (Margaret MacMillan Training College unpublished essay, 1970), p. 40. I am most grateful to Miss Rastrick for allowing me to read her essay.

[26] (p. 31) On the founding of temperance newspapers, see my ' "A World of Which We Had No Conception": Liberalism and the Temperance Press, 1833–1872', *Victorian Studies*, Dec. 1969.

[27] (p. 31) M. Duverger, *Political Parties* (Tr. B. & R. North, 3rd edn, 1959), pp. 81, 85.

[28] (p. 31) H. J. Hanham, *Elections & Party Management. Politics in the Time of Disraeli & Gladstone* (1959), pp. 281–3.

[29] (p. 31) E. Halévy, *Victorian Years* (1961 paperback edn), p. 390.

[30] (p. 32) *Alliance News*, 24 Oct. 1890, p. 697.

[31] (p. 32) Quotations from M. Banton, 'Social Alignment & Identity in a West African City', in H. Kuper (Ed.), *Urbanisation & Migration in West Africa* (University of California Press, 1965), pp. 143–4; W. B. Schwab, 'Oshogbo—an Urban Community?' in *ibid.*, p. 103. See also G. Breese, *Urbanization in Newly Developing Countries* (New Jersey, 1966), pp. 92, 98; M. Banton, *West African City* (1957), pp. 180–1; P. Marris, *Family & Social Change in an African City* (1961), pp. 39, 42; K. Little, 'The Urban Role of Tribal Associations in West Africa', *African Studies*, 1962, p. 5; I am most grateful to Dr. Alan MacFarlane, for guiding me towards some of this literature.

[32] (p. 32) J. Arch, *Joseph Arch. The Story of his Life* (Ed. Countess of Warwick, 2nd edn, 1898), p. 34.

[33] (p. 33) T. C. Barker, writing in T. C. Barker *et al.*, *Our Changing Fare* (1966), p. 23; cf. John Burnett, *Plenty & Want* (1966), p. ix.

[34] (p. 33) J. C. MacKenzie, 'The Composition & Nutritional Value of Diets in Manchester & Dukinfield. 1841', *Transactions of the Lancashire & Cheshire Antiquarian Society*, 1962, p. 130; A. I. Richards, *Land, Labour & Diet in Northern Rhodesia* (1939), p. 400; cf. her *Hunger & Work in a Savage Tribe* (1932), p. 99; see also *Anti Bread Tax Circular*, 11 Apr. 1843, p. 116.

[35] (p. 33) Sir William Crawford & H. Broadley, *The People's Food* (1938), p. 2; J. Livesey, 'The Malt Lecture', *Ipswich Temperance Tract, No. 133* [henceforth cited as *Malt Lecture*], p. 17.

[36] (p. 33) W. J. Shrewsbury, *Alcohol against the Bible, & the Bible against Alcohol: A Lecture . . . 29 Sept. 1840* (1840), p. 34.

[37] (p. 34) *Times Literary Supplement*, 31 Dec. 1964, p. 1180.

[38] (p. 34) S. E. Finer, *Listener*, 7 June 1956, p. 751.

[39] (p. 34) Quo. in P. Fraser, 'Public Petitioning and Parliament before 1832', *History*, 1961, p. 210.

[40] (p. 34) H. Taine, *Notes on England* (Tr. & Ed. E. Hyams, 1957), p. 172.

[41] (p. 34) Cobden to Bright, 3 Oct. 1859, B.M. *Add. MSS.* 43651 (Cobden Papers), f. 21; Cowen, *3 Hansard 229*, c. 863 (17 May 1876).

[42] (p. 35) A. V. Dicey, *Law & Public Opinion*, p. 16; *3 Hansard 84*, c. 173 (26 Feb. 1846); Cecil, quo. in Lady G. Cecil, *Life of Robert, Marquis of Salisbury*, I (1921), p. 320—I owe this reference to Philip Williams. See also W. S. Jevons, *Methods of Social Reform* (2nd edn, 1904), p. 238.

[43] (p. 35) N. C. Hunt, 'Pressure Groups in the U.S.A.', *Occidente*, XII, No. 2, p. 123; cf. *Spectator*, 17 Dec. 1965, p. 802.

[44] (p. 35) D. Donald, 'Towards a Reconsideration of Abolitionists', in his *Lincoln Reconsidered* (Vintage Books, 1961), p. 20; cf. S. M. Elkins, *Slavery* (Chicago, 1959), p. 158.

[45] (p. 36) Pease, in his 'Liquor Licensing at Home & Abroad', *Fabian Tract No. 85* (2nd edn, 1899), p. 2; cf. A. J. P. Taylor, in *New Statesman*, 29 Sept. 1967.

[46] (p. 36) H. Marcuse, *One Dimensional Man* (Sphere Books edn, 1968), p. 25.

Chapter 2. Drink and Society in the 1820s [pp. 37–63].

[1] (p. 37) G. B. Wilson, *Alcohol & the Nation* (1940), pp. 236, 335.

[2] (p. 37) Cf. G. Kitson Clark, *The Making of Victorian England* (1962), p. 64.

[3] (p. 37) For the Dolphin scandal, see W. M. Stern, 'J. Wright, Pamphleteer on the London Water Supply', *Guildhall Miscellany*, Feb. 1953, *passim*; Chadwick to Sir W. Lawson, *Chadwick MSS*, University College London (draft letter 17 Apr. 1875); for London hospitals, R. C. Supply of Water in the Metropolis, Report: *Parl. Papers* 1828 (267), IX, p. 53; for Londoners in the 1870s, S.C.H.L. Intemperance, fourth report, *Parl. Papers* 1878 (338), XIV, Q. 559.

[4] (p. 38) T. F. Reddaway, 'London in the Nineteenth Century. III: The Fight for a Water Supply', *Twentieth Century*, 1950, p. 119; R. A. Lewis, *Edwin Chadwick & the Public Health Movement, 1832–1854* (1952), p. 51. For the brewers, see S[elect] C[ommittee] of the H[ouse] of C[ommons] on the State of the Police of the Metropolis, first report, *Parl. Papers* 1817 (233), VII, p. 68; cf. *3 Hansard 120*, c. 1292 (29 Apr. 1852); for pumps, see *Examiner*, 24 Sept. 1826, 8. Oct. 1826, & K. Clark, *The Gothic Revival* (3rd edn, 1962), p. 147.

[5] (p. 38) For milk quality, see *Temperance Penny Magazine*, Nov. 1842, p. 165; for Lancing, see B. W. T. Handford, *Lancing 1848–1930* (Oxford, 1933), p. 24; I owe the latter reference to Cormac Rigby. See also E. J. Hobsbawm, *Labouring Men*, p. 86.

[6] (p. 38) Quotation from P. Gaskell, *The Manufacturing Population of England* (1833), p. 109; cf. A. Ure, *The Philosophy of Manufactures* (1835), p. 387.

[7] (p. 38) For cordials, see J. C. Drummond & A. Wilbraham, *The Englishman's Food* (1957 edn) pp. 194, 339; H. Mayhew, *London Labour & the London Poor* (1861), I, p. 186; *Spectator*, 11 Jan. 1834, p. 37.

[8] (p. 38) *3 Hansard 22*, cc. 370, 377 (18 Mar. 1834).

[9] (p. 39) Quotation from W. Lovett, *Life & Struggles* (1876), p. 32; cf. S.C.H.C. on Import Duties, *Parl. Papers* 1840 (601), V, Q. 2742; J. C. Drummond & A. Wilbraham, *op. cit.*, p. 205. For 'saloop' see Charles Knight, *London*, IV (1843), p. 317.

[10] (p. 39) For coffee-house expansion, see S.C.H.C. on Drunkenness, *Parl. Papers* 1834 (559), VIII, Q. 2069; S.C.H.C. on Education, *Parl. Papers* 1835 (465), VII, Q. 810. For relative prices, see S.C.H.C. on Sale of Beer, *Parl. Papers* 1830 (253), X, p. 13.

[11] (p. 39) For 'theobroma', see *Poor Man's Guardian*, 10 Nov. 1832, p. 608; I owe this reference to Dr. Patricia Hollis; cf. I. A. Williams, *The Firm of Cadbury. 1831–1931* (1931), pp. 6, 39.

[12] (p. 39) S.C.H.C. State of the Police of the Metropolis, second report: *Parl. Papers* 1817 (484), VII, pp. 484–8; cf. *Poor Man's Guardian*, 4 Feb. 1832. S.C.H.C. on Sale of Beer, *Parl. Papers* 1830 (253), X, p. 37. S.C.H.C. on Import Duties, *Parl. Papers* 1840 (601), V, QQ. 2787, 2806, 2810.

[13] (p. 39) For 'rearings', see Rev. J. Clay, *25th Chaplain's Report of the Preston House of Correction . . .* (1848), p. 67; cf. 'Mass Observation', *The Pub & the People* (1943), p. 46.

[14] (p. 39) J. B. Braithwaite, *Memorials of Joseph John Gurney* (1854), II, p. 313.

[15] (p. 39) For revivalists, see J. Barker, *Life of Joseph Barker* (1880), p. 188; Place's comment is in S.C.H.C. Drunkenness, *Parl. Papers* 1834 (559), VIII, Q. 2052. For early teetotal martyrs, see P. T. Winskill, *The Temperance Movement & its Workers* (1892), I, pp. 211, 213.

[16] (p. 40) For drunken craftsmen, see J. Lawson, *Letters to the Young on Progress in Pudsey during the last Sixty Years* [henceforth cited as *Pudsey*] (Stanninglen, 1887), p. 93; W. Howitt, *The Rural Life of England* (1838), II, p. 294; Sheffield Town Council Committee on Drunkenness, *Report* (Sheffield, 1853), *passim*. For a drunken entomologist, see J. M.

Ludlow & Lloyd Jones, *The Progress of the Working Class 1832–1867* (1867), p. 19; [T. Carter], *Memoirs of a Working Man* (1845), p. 74.

[17] (p. 40) S.C.H.C. on Public-Houses, *Parl. Papers* 1854 (367), XIV, Q. 4700.

[18] (p. 40) On work-discipline see S. Pollard, *The Genesis of Modern Management* (1965), pp. 187, 193–4; cf. D. Bell, *Work & its Discontents* (Boston, U.S.A., 1956), pp. 21–9.

[19] (p. 40) Quotation from H. Mayhew, *London Labour*, II, p. 298; for 'climatic' spirit drinking, see *1 Hansard 35*, c. 887 (3 Mar. 1817), *3 Hansard 313*, c. 1422 (21 Apr. 1887); for Londoners in the 1890s, see C. Booth, *Life & Labour in London, Second Series*, III, p. 120.

[20] (p. 41) For prostitution, L. Faucher, *Manchester in 1844* (1844), p. 43; cf. (for drunkenness) R. C. Liquor Licensing Laws, *Parl. Papers* 1897 (8523), XXXV, Q. 11,777, referring to a much earlier period.

[21] (p. 41) N. Smelser, *Social Change in the Industrial Revolution* (1959), p. 278; D. J. Pittman & C. R. Snyder (Eds.), *Society, Culture & Drinking Patterns* (New York, 1962), pp. 49, 58; R. G. McCarthy, *op. cit.*, p. 108.

[22] (p. 41) M. E. Loane, *An Englishman's Castle* (1909), p. 249.

[23] (p. 41) For alcohol as anaesthetic, see A. Somerville, *Autobiography of a Working Man* (Ed. J. Carswell, 1951), p. 185; S.C.H.L. on Intemperance, *Parl. Papers* 1877 (418), XI, QQ, 9977–86. For Mrs. Cobden, see B.M. *Add. MSS.* 43656 (Cobden Papers), f. 234: Cobden to Joseph Sturge, 20 Nov. 1851.

[24] (p. 41) Quotation from K. Marx, *Economic Manuscripts of 1844* (Moscow, 1959), p. 117; cf. *Report . . . from the Poor Law Commissioners, on . . . the Sanitary Condition of the Labouring Population* (H.M.S.O., 1842), p. 130; M. Laski, in S. Nowell-Smith (Ed.) *Edwardian England 1901–1914* (1964), p. 152.

[25] (p. 41) For temperance societies & doctors' alcoholic prescriptions, see e.g. Mere Temperance Society, *M.S. Minutes* (in the care of Miss Joyce Rutter, Mere, Wilts.), 7 Dec. 1881. M. Rutherford, *Autobiography* (2nd edn, n.d.), p. 78.

[26] (p. 41) T. Carlyle, 'Chartism', in *Works* (Ashburton edn, 1888), XVII, p. 276. For Newport, see Lord G. Sanger, *Seventy Years a Showman* (1927 edn), p. 68.

[27] (p. 41) H. Jones, *Alcoholic Addiction* (1963), p. 11.

[28] (p. 42) On temperance tales, see my 'Drunkards & Reformers. Early Victorian Temperance Tracts', *History Today*, Mar. 1963.

[29] (p. 42) E. Hodder, [Life and Work of the Seventh Earl of] *Shaftesbury* (1886), III, p. 324.

[30] (p. 42) Drink-exchange, R. Finnegan, 'The Limba of Sierra Leone' (Oxford D.Phil. thesis, 1963), pp. 324–44; quotation from A. I. Richards, *Land, Labour & Diet in Northern Rhodesia* (1939), p. 45.

[31] (p. 42) Cock-and-hen clubs, B.M. *Add. MSS.* 35142 (Place Papers), f. 140.

[32] (p. 42) J. Lawson, *Pudsey*, pp. 13–14.

[33] (p. 42) For 'drinkings', see M. D. George, *London Life in the Eighteenth Century* (2nd edn, 1930), p. 292; W. Lovett, *Life & Struggles*, p. 31. For teetotal martyrs, see J. Dunlop, *Philosophy of Artificial & Compulsory Drinking Usage* (1839), pp. 86–7.

[34] (p. 43) Quotation from B.M. *Add. MSS.* 35150 (Place Papers), f. 86: Place to W. J. Fox, 5 Nov. 1835; for '*preoccupazione*' see E. C. Banfield, *The Moral Basis of a Backward Society* (Illinois, 1958), p. 111—the phrase is used by South Italian peasants.

[35] (p. 43) J. Clay, *op. cit.*, p. 34; Lady Bell, *At the Works. A Study of a Manufacturing Town* (1911 edn), p. 347. For whips-round, see J. B. Leno, *The Aftermath* (1892), p. 75.

[36] (p. 43) For Irish funerals, see S.C.H.C. on the State of the Police of the Metropolis, second report: *Parl. Papers* 1817 (484), VII, p. 355; *Moral Reformer* (Preston), 1 Aug. 1833, p. 234. For sensitive observers, see E. Hodder, *Shaftesbury*, I, pp. 47–8; E. D. & G. H. Rendall, *Recollections & Impressions of Rev. John Smith* (1913), pp. 18–19. I owe the latter reference to Cormac Rigby.

[37] (p. 43) On Oxford communion, G. Battiscombe, *John Keble* (1963), p. 18; cf. R. G. Wilberforce, *Samuel Wilberforce* (1881), II, p. 5. J. Pearce, *Joseph Livesey as Reformer & Teacher* (1885) [henceforth cited as *Livesey*], p. lxxv. G. O. Trevelyan, *Life . . . of Lord Macaulay* (2nd edn, 1883), p. 31.

[38] (p. 44) J. Dunlop, *op. cit.*, p. 80; D. Williams, *The Rebecca Riots* (Cardiff, 1955), p. 94; K. H. Connell, 'Peasant Marriage in Ireland', *Econ*[omic] *Hist*[ory] *Rev*[iew], Apr. 1962, p. 509.

[39] (p. 44) R. E. Leader, 'Places, Parsons, Publicans & People', *Trans*[actions] *of the Hunter Archaeological Society*, 1918, p. 7; cf. University College London, *Brougham MSS.*: W. Clarkson to Henry Brougham, 15 Feb. 1828.

[40] (p. 44) A. R. Ashwell, *Life of . . . Samuel Wilberforce*, I (1880), p. 62, n. 5.

[41] (p. 44) On church meetings in public-houses, see W. B. Johnson, 'The Inn as a Community Centre', *Amateur Historian*, II, No. 5, p. 135; on drunken clergymen, D. Newsome, *The Parting of Friends* (1966), p. 279; O. Chadwick, *The Victorian Church. Part One* (1966), p. 275. For Catholics in public-houses, see R. Samuel, 'The Catholic Church & the Irish Poor' (cyclostyled typescript, included among the papers submitted to the July 1966 'Past & Present' conference on popular religion), p. 46.

[42] (p. 44) O. Chadwick, *The Victorian Church*, p. 62; cf. T. Cocking, *History of Wesleyan Methodism in Grantham* (1836), p. 363; I owe this reference to Dr. Walsh.

[43] (p. 45) Joseph Barker, *Autobiography*, p. 205; cf. J. G. Shaw, *Life of William Gregson* (Blackburn, 1891), p. 72.

[44] (p. 45) P. T. Winskill, *Temperance Movement & its Workers*, I, p. 129.

[45] (p. 45) *3 Hansard 213* c. 335 (2 Aug. 1872).

[46] (p. 45) Rev. A. Wallace, *The Gloaming of Life. Memoir of James Stirling* (Glasgow, 1876), p. 27; cf. S. & B. Webb, *History of Liquor Licensing in England* (1903) [henceforth cited as *Liquor Licensing*], p. 102.

[47] (p. 45) For tradesmen meeting in public-houses, see A. Prentice, *Historical Sketches & Personal Recollections of Manchester* (Manchester, 1851), p. 18; B.M. *Add. MSS.* 35142 (Place Papers), ff. 57–8; *Drunkenness Committee* [of 1834], Q. 3007; B.M. *Add. MSS.* 27829 (Place Papers), f. 30; S.C.H.L. on Intemperance, second report, *Parl. Papers* 1877 (271), XI, Q. 4455; E. D. & G. H. Rendall, *op cit.*, pp. 52–3.

[48] (p. 46) S.C.H.C. on Wine Duties, *Parl. Papers* 1852 (495), XVII, Q. 3817.

[49] (p. 46) W. Howitt, *op. cit.*, II, pp. 234–5.

[50] (p. 46) G. M. Young, *Victorian Essays* (Ed. W. D. Handcock, 1962), p. 43.

[51] (p. 46) M. Young, 'The Distribution of Income within the Family', *British Journal of Sociology*, 1952, p. 311; cf. B.M. *Add. MSS.* 35143 (Place Papers), f. 7.

[52] (p. 46) Quotation from *The Labourer*, 1848, p. 245; cf. I. Pinchbeck, *Women Workers and the Industrial Revolution, 1750–1850* (1930), p. 307.

[53] (p. 46) Cf. P. Willmott & M. Young, *Family & Class in a London Suburb* (1960), pp. 20–1.

[54] (p. 46) cf. H. Jones, *Alcoholic Addiction*, pp. 48ff.

[55] (p. 47) Quo. from H. W. J. Edwards, *The Good Patch* (1938), p. 158, referring to Rhondda valley pubs of the 1930s; I owe this reference to Dr. W. R. Lambert. For women in the home, E. E. Evans-Pritchard, *The Position of Women in Primitive Societies & in Our Own* (Fawcett Lecture, 1955), *passim.*

[56] (p. 47) For drunken wives, see Lady Bell, *op. cit.* p. 344; E. Dückershoff, *How The English Workman Lives* (1899), pp. 68ff.

[57] (p. 47) *Quarterly Review*, Apr. 1818, p. 84; inns of course continued to provide food for longer.

[58] (p. 47) S.C.H.C. on the State of the Police of the Metropolis, first report: *Parl. Papers* 1817 (233), VII, p. 205; *The Times*, 10 Apr. 1827, p. 3.

[59] (p. 48) For state management, see E. Selley, *The English Public-House As It Is* (1927), p. 79.

[60] (p. 48) H. Taine, *Notes on England*, p. 10; cf. H. T. Buckle, *Miscellaneous and Posthumous Works* (Ed. H. Taylor, 1872), III, p. 441; L. Faucher, *op. cit.*, p. 28. Chamberlain, in S.C.H.L. on Intemperance, first report, *Parl. Papers* 1877 (171), XI, Q. 2364.

[61] (p. 48) G. F. Mandley, in B.M. *Add. MSS.* 27829 (Place Papers), f. 212; for foreigners' comments, see J. L. Hammond, *The Growth of Common Enjoyment* (1933), pp. 4–5.

[62] (p. 48) B.M. *Add. MSS.* 27825 (Place Papers), ff. 19–20.

[63] (p. 48) L. Faucher, *op. cit.*, p. 56.

[64] (p. 48) S.C.H.C. Public-houses, *Parl. Papers* 1854 (367), XIV, Q. 1172; S. Couling, *History of the Temperance Movement* (1862), p. 208; *3 Hansard 286*, c. 443 (21 Mar. 1884).

[65] (p. 49) For cricket, see H. S. Altham, *A History of Cricket* (1962 edn), p. 39; Sir P. Warner, *Lord's 1787–1945* (1946), p. 19; for Tom Spring, see Guildhall Library, London,

Norman Collection (Inns & Taverns, Vol. 2), G.R.I. 1. 5. For Combe, see his *Constitution of Man* (8th edn, 1847), p. 116.

[66] (p. 49) For 'play', see J. Huizinga, *Homo Ludens. A Study of the Play-Element in Culture* (1944), pp. 7–13.

[67] (p. 49) 'Lord' G. Sanger, *op. cit.*, pp. 128, 139; W. B. Johnson, *art. cit.*, p. 137; 'Mass Observation', *The Pub & the People* (1943), pp. 312–13; H. Mayhew, *op. cit.* III, p. 9.

[68] (p. 49) For Epsom, see *Saturday Review*, 27 May 1871, p. 655.

[69] (p. 50) Especially beersellers, see J. Clay, *26th Chaplain's Report* (for 1849), p. 49; S.C.H.C. on Public-houses, *Parl. Papers* 1854 (367), XIV, QQ. 1270–5.

[70] (p. 50) Anon, *My Secret Life* (Amsterdam, n.d., British Museum copy), V, p. 89.

[71] (p. 50) W. James, *Varieties of Religious Experience* (1960 paperback edn), p. 373; Gladstone quo. in *Devon & Cornwall Temperance Journal* (Plymouth), Jan. 1868, p. 3, speech at Werneth, 18 Dec. 1867.

[72] (p. 50) Rev. J. M. J. Fletcher, *Mrs. Wightman of Shrewsbury* (1906), p. 66.

[73] (p. 51) A Turberville (Ed.), *Johnson's England* (1933), I, pp. 147–8; N. C. Selway, *The Regency Road. The Coaching Prints of James Pollard* (1957), p. 21.

[74] (p. 51) For toll-houses, see *3 Hansard 99*, c. 501 (8 June 1848); *3 Hansard 78*, c. 632 (11 Mar. 1845); for trade union lodges, see E. J. Hobsbawm's excellent 'The Tramping Artisan', in his *Labouring Men* (1964). For pedestrians' drinking obligations, see *Preston Temperance Advocate* (Preston), Jan. 1836, p. 7 (for carters); F. Atkin, *Temperance Shots at Random* (Manchester, 1887), p. 208; J. Dunlop, *op. cit.*, p. 306; R. C. Liquor Licensing Laws, *Parl. Papers* 1898 (8694) XXXVI, Q. 26,312.

[75] (p. 51) e.g. T. Whittaker, *Life's Battles*, p. 263.

[76] (p. 51) A. E. Richardson & H. D. Eberlein, *The English Inn Past & Present* (1925), p. 177; H. Robinson, *Britain's Post Office* (1953), pp. 106, 116.

[77] (p. 52) For working men lodging in drinking places, see W. Lovett, *Life and Struggles*, p. 25; W. E. Adams, *Memoirs of a Social Atom* (1903), I, pp. 294–6; for the miners, see *Morning Chronicle*, 31 Dec. 1849, p. 5. For temperance hotels, J. Pearce, *Livesey*, p. cxliv; P. T. Winskill, *Temperance Movement & its Workers*, I, pp. 60, 119, 175.

[78] (p. 52) For 'old news' see *Teetotaler* (Ed. G. W. M. Reynolds), 7 Nov. 1840, p. 158; E. J Hobsbawm, *The Age of Revolution* (1962), p. 276; W. Howitt, *op. cit.*, II, p. 236. For co-ops, see O. Balmforth, *Huddersfield Industrial Society Ltd. A History of Fifty Years' Progress. 1860–1910* (Manchester, 1910), p. 32; W. H. Brown, *Heywood's Co-operative Centenary. 1850–1950* (1950), pp. 18–19; F. W. Peaples, *History of the . . . Bolton Co-operative Society, Ltd. . . . 1859–1909* (1909), pp. 29–30, 35–6, 443.

[79] (p. 52) L. Faucher, *op. cit.*, p. 52.

[80] (p. 52) H. Robinson, *op. cit.*, p. 116.

[81] (p. 52) R. K. Webb, *The British Working Class Reader 1790–1848* (1955), p. 33; D. Read, *Press & People. 1790–1850* (1961), p. 202.

[82] (p. 52) For Newcastle, *Weekly Record* [of the Temperance Movement], 21 June 1856, p. 107; see also S.C.H.C. on the Sale of Liquors on Sunday Bill, *Parl. Papers* 1867–8 (402), XIV, Q. 5452; *Northern Star*, 23 Apr. 1842, p. 6.

[83] (p. 53) The factory movement sometimes held public-house meetings—see J. T. Ward, *The Factory Movement 1830–1855* (1962), pp. 41–2, 167. For temperance meetings in public-houses, see *London Temperance Intelligencer*, 28 Jan. 1837, p. 81, & T. Whittaker, *Life's Battles*, p. 122; also W. R. Lambert, 'Drink & Sobriety in Wales. 1835–1895' (Univ. of Wales unpublished Ph.D. thesis 1969), pp. 79, 221. For Owen, see J. F. C. Harrison, *Robert Owen and the Owenites in Britain and America* (1969), p. 92. For the Reform League, Bishopsgate Institute, *Howell Collection*, No. 4052, Reform League Minutes, 25 Aug. 1865.

[84] (p. 53) *People's Paper*, 28 Aug. 1858.

[85] (p. 53) W. E. Adams, *op. cit.*, II, pp. 316–17. For the German Democratic Society, see A. R. Schoyen, *Chartist Challenge* (1958), p. 135. For women & radical politics, see *Poor Man's Guardian*, 14 Sept. 1833, p. 293.

[86] (p. 53) For Middlesex friendly societies, see *Bristol Temperance Herald* (Bristol), Apr. 1845, p. 27.

[87] (p. 53) Bentham, quo. in H. O. Horne, *History of Savings Banks* (1947), p. 28.

[88] (p. 53) G. Wallas, *Life of Francis Place* (4th edn, 1951), p. 6.

[89] (p. 53) S. & B. Webb, *History of Trade Unionism* (1920 edn), pp. 75, 150–1; F. Singleton, 'The Saddleworth Union 1827–1830', *Bulletin of the Society for the Study of Labour History*, Autumn 1962, p. 34; H. Ashworth, *The Preston Strike* (1854), pp. 45–9.

[90] (p. 54) E. P. Thompson, *The Making of the English Working Class* (1963), p. 418; for Owen, see *The Crisis*, 7 Dec. 1833, p. 115; 15 June 1834, p. 83. See also A. Briggs, 'Industry and Politics in Early Nineteenth-Century Keighley', *Bradford Antiquary*, 1952, p. 317.

[91] (p. 54) For the problem of meeting-places, see T. Frost, *Forty Years' Recollections* (1880), p. 132; [Scottish] *Chartist Circular* (Glasgow), 6 Feb. 1841, p. 301. For the N.U.W.C., see *Poor Man's Guardian*, 6 July 1833, p. 217; I owe this latter reference to Dr. Hollis.

[92] (p. 54) For trades parasitic on the drinkseller, see H. Mayhew, *London Labour*, I, pp. 78, 380; J. M. Weylland, *These Fifty Years* (1884), p. 231. For public-house commercial activities, see J. Dunlop, *op. cit.*, p. 22; Mrs. C. L. Wightman, *Haste to the Rescue!* (1862), p. 51. For Banbury, see *Banbury Guardian*, 9 Jan. 1851, p. 3; 3 Oct. 1850.

[93] (p. 54) For auctions, see F. Atkin, *op. cit.*, p. 196; for Holderness, see Sir G. Head, *A Home Tour through the Manufacturing Districts* (1836), pp. 255–6. For the army canteen, see N[ational] T[emperance] L[eague], *Annual Report 1888–9*, p. 15.

[94] (p. 55) E. T. Davies, *Religion in the Industrial Revolution in South Wales* (Cardiff, 1965), p. 49; this is an excellent book which deserves to be better known.

[95] (p. 55) M. Rutherford, *The Revolution in Tanner's Lane* (1887), p. 9.

[96] (p. 55) W. B. Johnson, *art. cit.*, *passim*; I. P. Collis, 'The Struggle for Constabulary Reform in Somerset', *Somerset Archaeological & Natural History Society Proceedings*, 1954–5, p. 83; L. Radzinowicz, *History of English Criminal Law*, II (1956), p. 305.

[97] (p. 55) H. Mayhew, *London Labour*, IV, p. 230.

[98] (p. 55) For fairs & feasts, see J. Lawson, *Pudsey*, p. 57; S. Bamford, *Early Days* (1849), p. 145. For the attack upon them, see *Quarterly Review*, Oct. 1820, p. 258; B.M. *Add. MSS.* 27827 (Place Papers), f. 221 (July 1836).

[99] (p. 55) Quo. in D. Newsome, *Parting of Friends*, p. 126.

[100] (p. 56) Quotations from E. J. & J. D. Krige, *The Realm of a Rain-Queen* (1943), p. 288; C. M. Arensberg, *The Irish Countryman* (1937), p. 155. See also C. M. Arensberg & S. T. Kimball, *Family & Community in Ireland* (Harvard, 1940), pp. 71, 260, 302–3.

[101] (p. 56) Quotation from J. Livesey, *Malt Lecture*, p. 4, cf. p. 7; for embarrassed teetotal tradesmen, see M. Taylor, *Memorials of Samuel Bowly* (1884), p. 14; H. C. Alexander, *Richard Cadbury of Birmingham* (1906), p. 21.

[102] (p. 56) For the Duke of Buccleuch, see R. V. French, *History of Toasting* (1881), pp. 86–7. *Banbury Guardian* (Banbury), 23, 30 Sept. 1858, 14 Dec. 1858.

[103] (p. 56) W. Cobbett, *Advice to Young Men* (1829 unpaginated edn), chapter on 'Advice to a Young Man'; cf. 'Mass Observation', *The Pub & the People*, pp. 176–7; W. R. Lambert, *op. cit.*, p. 37.

[104] (p. 56) *3 Hansard 22*, c. 290 (17 Mar. 1834); cf. G. W. Hilton, *The Truck System* (Cambridge, 1960), p. 30.

[105] (p. 56) Anon, *Essay on the Repeal of the Malt-Tax* (Total Repeal Malt Tax Association, 1846), p. 11.

[106] (p. 56) G. J. Holyoake, *Sixty Years of an Agitator's Life* (3rd edn, 1903), I, p. 73.

[107] (p. 57) H. Mayhew, *London Labour*, I, p. 31; S.C.H.L. to Consider the Bill . . . to prevent unnecessary Trading on Sunday in the Metropolis . . . , *Parl. Papers* 1850 (441), XIX, Q. 399; P. Mathias, *The Brewing Industry in England 1700–1830* (Cambridge, 1959), p. 101; P. Mathias, *English Trade Tokens* (1962), pp. 24, 28–9.

[108] (p. 57) R.C. on Poor Laws, *Parl. Papers* 1834 (44), XXVIII, p. 122A; *Drunkenness Committee*, QQ. 2223–6.

[109] (p. 57) S.C.H.C. on Public-houses, *Parl. Papers* 1852–3 (855), XXXVII, Q. 6360; *Drunkenness Committee*, pp. 53–9; H. Mayhew, *London Labour*, III, pp. 239–57; M. D. George, *op. cit.*, p. 298; Midland Mining Commission, first report, South Staffordshire, *Parl. Papers* 1843 (508), XIII, pp. xliii–1. Doherty, in *Parliamentary Review* (Ed. J. S. Buckingham), 1834, I, p. 878.

[110] (p. 57) Barley quotation from N. Seager, *A Practical Treatise on the Manufacture of Cheap Non-Alcoholic Beverages* (1888), p. 21.

[111] (p. 58) For barley's importance to farmers, see *Letter on the Repeal of the Malt-Duty;*

Addressed to a Member of the House of Commons. By a Country Gentleman (1835), p. 5; cf. *Edinburgh Review*, June 1829, p. 363; P. Mathias, *Brewing Industry*, pp. 387ff. For cattle-feed see *3 Hansard 26*, cc. 742, 750 (10 Mar. 1835). Some breweries refused to supply teetotalers with grains—see *London Temperance Intelligencer*, 4 Mar. 1837, p. 131; teetotalers were also sometimes refused supplies of yeast—see T. Hudson, *Temperance Pioneers of the West* (1887), pp. 55, 217; J. Boyes, *Early History of the Temperance Movement in Pudsey* (Pudsey, 1893), p. 11.

[112] (p. 58) For brewers, bankers and corn-dealers, see P. Mathias, 'The Entrepreneur in Brewing, 1700–1830', in *The Entrepreneur. Papers presented at the Annual Conference of the Economic History Society* (1957), p. 33; for the financing of industralization, see C. Erickson, *British Industrialists. Steel & Hosiery. 1850–1950* (Cambridge, 1959), pp. 15–17, 92, 95, 101. For bankers as sleeping partners, see Anon, *A Dispassionate Appeal to the Legislature, Magistrates & Clergy . . . against Mr. Calcraft's Proposed Bill . . . by a County Magistrate* (1830), p. 28. For savings deposits, see P. Mathias, *Brewing Industry*, pp. 278–9.

[113] (p. 58) Quo. from Thomas Roberts, *Drunkenness Committee*, Q. 4586.

[114] (p. 58) J. Livesey, in *Preston Temperance Advocate*, Apr. 1836 (supplement), p. 2; cf. W. West, *History & Topography of Warwickshire* (Birmingham, 1830), pp. 409ff. J. Finch, Jun. *Statistics of Vauxhall Ward, Liverpool* (Liverpool, 1842), pp. 28–9. For London, see R. W. Vanderkiste, *Notes & Narratives of a Six Years' Mission* (1854), p. 140.

[115] (p. 59) P. Mathias, *Brewing Industry*, pp. 265ff.

[116] (p. 59) For wine-merchants, see J. A. Hobson, *John Ruskin Social Reformer* (3rd edn, 1904), p. 2; cf. B. L. Crapster, ' "Our Trade, Our Politics". A Study of the Political Activity of the British Liquor Industry, 1868–1910' (Harvard unpublished Ph.D. thesis, 1949) [henceforth cited as *British Liquor Industry*], p. 242; for the impressiveness of London breweries, see A. Wynter, *Our Social Bees* (3rd edn, 1861), pp. 209–10; for brewers' philanthropy, see S.C.H.C. on State of the Police of the Metropolis, *Parl. Papers* 1816 (510), V, p. 162; for the lying-in charity, see *New British & Foreign Temperance Intelligencer*, 1 Sept. 1838, p. 283.

[117] (p. 59) F. K. Brown, *Fathers of the Victorians* (Cambridge, 1961), p. 405; for the London City Mission, see J. M. Weylland, *op. cit.*, p. 25. See also E. T. Cook, *Life of John Ruskin* (1911), I, pp. 10–14; G. Thorne, *The Great Acceptance* (1913), pp. 11–12.

[118] (p. 59) E. M. Sigsworth, 'Science & the Brewing Industry, 1850–1900'. *Econ. Hist. Rev.*, Apr. 1965, p. 540.

[119] (p. 59) *The Times*, 10 Apr. 1827, p. 3; cf. P. Mathias, *Brewing Industry*, pp. 320, 330–1.

[120] (p. 59) Adam Smith, *The Wealth of Nations* (Ed. Cannan, 1950), I, p. 103.

[121] (p. 60) S.C.H.C. on Public-houses, *Parl. Papers* 1854 (367), XIV, Q. 3759.

[122] (p. 60) Quotation from S.C.H.C. on Public-houses, *Parl. Papers* 1852-3 (855), XXXVII, Q. 4106. See also S.C.H.C. on Public-houses, *Parl. Papers* 1854 (367), XIV, Q. 3988; S.C.H.L. . . . Sale of Beer, *Parl. Papers* 1850 (398), X, Q. 92; *Edinburgh Review*, Sept. 1826, p. 446.

[123] (p. 60) P. Mathias, 'The Brewing Industry, Temperance & Politics', *Historical Journal*, 1958, pp. 101–3.

[124] (p. 60) For influence in local government, see J. Hart, 'The Reform of the Borough Police, 1835–1856', *Eng*[lish] *Hist*[orical] *Rev*[iew], 1955, p. 424; J. Hart, 'The County & the Borough Police Act, 1856', *Public Administration*, Winter 1956, pp. 405–6; cf. *3 Hansard 29*, c. 210 (2 July 1835). The percentages are from E. P. Hennock, 'The Social Compositions of Borough Councils in Two Large Cities, 1835–1914', in H. J. Dyos (Ed.), *op. cit.*, p. 323, and from F. Bealey, 'Municipal Politics in Newcastle-Under-Lyme 1835–72', *North Staffordshire Journal of Field Studies*, III (1963), p. 72.

[125] (p. 60) Anon, *Hints on Licensing Publicans* (1830), pp. 23–4; B. L. Crapster, 'The London *Sunday Advertiser* & its Immediate Successors', *Business History*, June 1963, pp. 109, 117; cf. D. Read, *Press & People*, p. 96; *London Teetotal Magazine*, Oct. 1840, p. 324.

[126] (p. 61) B. L. Crapster, *British Liquor Industry*, pp. 177–208; this section leans heavily on Crapster's thesis.

[127] (p. 61) For the political implications of licensing policy, see *3 Hansard 39*, c. 979 (12 Dec. 1837); *3 Hansard 145*, c. 1515 (10 June 1857); *3 Hansard 284*, c. 983 (14 Feb. 1884); *3 Hansard 289*, c. 1021 (20 June 1884).

[128] (p. 61) Transport House, *Henry Vincent Collection*, 1/1/10: Vincent to Miniken, 26 Aug. 1838; for beersellers, see H. P. Maskell, *Taverns of Old England* (1927), p. 191; the London–Leicester road is discussed in T. E. Kebbel, *Lord Beaconsfield & other Tory Memories* (1891), pp. 313–17—a reference I owe to Dr. John Vincent. For Shaftesbury, see A. Somerville, *Whistler at the Plough* (Manchester, 1852), No. IX, p. 55.

[129] (p. 61) G. P. Judd, *Members of Parliament 1734–1832* (Yale, 1955), p. 59; P. Mathias, 'Brewing Industry, Temperance & Politics', *Historical Journal*, 1958, p. 114.

[130] (p. 61) *Northern Star* (Leeds), 23 Sept. 1843, p. 2.

[131] (p. 62) Gladstone, *3 Hansard 252*, c. 1649 (10 June 1880); J. Morley, *Life of Gladstone* (1905), I, p. 513; Brougham quotation, *2 Hansard 6*, c. 403 (15 Feb. 1822).

[132] (p. 62) Brougham, *1 Hansard 40*, c. 1030 (9 June 1819).

[133] (p. 62) Quo. in P. Mathias, *Brewing Industry*, p. xi; cf. P. Mathias, 'Brewing Industry, Temperance & Politics', p. 106.

Chapter 3. Free Trade and the Beer Act: 1815–1830 [pp. 64–86].

[1] (p. 64) S.C.H.C. on the State of the Police of the Metropolis, first report, *Parl. Papers* 1817 (233), VII, p. 21; cf. *The Times*, 24 Nov. 1815.

[2] (p. 65) *1 Hansard 37*, cc. 938–9 (10 Mar. 1818).

[3] (p. 65) J. T. B. Beaumont, *A Letter to the Right Hon. Lord Sidmouth* (1817), p. 19; cf. *Brougham Papers:* T. Edwards to Brougham, n.d.; P. Mathias, *Brewing Industry*, p. 237.

[4] (p. 65) *2 Hansard 10*, c. 362 (23 Feb. 1824); *2 Hansard 13*, c. 136 (22 Apr. 1825).

[5] (p. 65) Anon. *Hints on Licensing Publicans* (1830), p. 28; cf. Sydney Smith, in *Edinburgh Review*, Sept. 1826, p. 448.

[6] (p. 66) *2 Hansard 10*, c. 951 (12 Mar. 1824).

[7] (p. 66) Licence figures in G. B. Wilson, *Alcohol & the Nation*, p. 394; for adaptations in 1815, see J. Bowles, *A Letter to Robert Wissett, Esq.* (1815), p. 48; *Oxford English Dictionary* (Ed. Murray), IV, Part 2, p. 172. For the retail revolution, see H. B. Fearon, *Suggestions & Correspondence relative to Magistrates' Licences* (1830), p. 39; cf. B.M. *Francis Place Newspaper Collection*, Set 42, f. 223.

[8] (p. 69) L. Chevalier, *Classes Laborieuses et Classes Dangereuses à Paris pendant la Première Moitié du XIXe Siècle* (Paris, 1958), p. v.

[9] (p. 70) On crime and drink figures, see *Drunkenness Committee*, QQ. 4065, 4063; C. Reith, *British Police & the Democratic Ideal* (1943), pp. 59, 127–8; S.C.H.L. on Intemperance, first report: *Parl. Papers* 1877 (171), XI, QQ. 1191–2; *Morning Advertiser*, 22 Jan. 1830; G. B. Wilson, *Alcohol & the Nation*, pp. 281ff.

[10] (p. 70) See O'Connor's complaints, in *Northern Star*, 21 Apr. 1838, p. 6.

[11] (p. 70) Brougham, *2 Hansard 24*, c. 420 (4 May 1830); cf. Mr. Bennett, *2 Hansard 25*, c. 867 (1 July 1830). For second 'gin age' fears, see *2 Hansard 22*, c. 847 (23 Feb. 1830), for example. McCulloch, *Edinburgh Review*, Jan. 1830, pp. 486, 493–4.

[12] (p. 70) e.g. by John Poynder, in S.C.H.C. Police of the Metropolis, second report, *Parl. Papers* 1817 (484), VII, p. 338.

[13] (p. 70) Quotation from *Examiner*, 8 Nov. 1829, p. 709; cf. *ibid.*, 17 May 1829, p. 307. See also T. Paine, *The Rights of Man* (Ed. H. B. Bonner, 1937), pp. 202, 233–4; McCulloch, *Edinburgh Review*, June 1829, p. 383.

[14] (p. 70) Gladstone, *3 Hansard 182*, cc. 1568–9 (17 Apr. 1866); cf. Ellenborough *Mirror of Parliament*, 1830, III, p. 2815 (8 July 1830). For beer prices, see S.C.H.C. on Sale of Beer: *Parl. Papers* 1830 (253), X, pp. 41, 43–4, 49, 123.

[15] (p. 71) *The Times*, 17 Nov., 24 Nov. 1815; cf. editorial in *The Times*, 20 Dec. 1815, p. 3. For Golden Lane, see P. Mathias, *Brewing Industry*, pp. 243ff.

[16] (p. 71) S.C.H.C. on State of the Police of the Metropolis, first report: *Parl. Papers* 1817 (233), VII, p. 21.

[17] (p. 71) Barclay, *1 Hansard 37*, c. 944 (10 Mar. 1818); for Beaumont's agitation, see *1 Hansard 37*, cc. 937–8 (10 Mar. 1818).

[18] (p. 71) *2 Hansard 6*, c. 1188 (18 Mar. 1822); *2 Hansard 7*, c. 328 (6 May 1822).

[19] (p. 72) Buxton, *2 Hansard 7*, c. 1695 (18 July 1822); Brougham, in S.C.H.C. on Sale of Beer, *Parl. Papers* 1830 (253), X, p. 55.

[20] (p. 72) *2 Hansard 8*, cc. 646–9 (21 Mar. 1823).

[21] (p. 72) S.C.H.C. on Sale of Beer, *Parl. Papers* 1830 (253), X, pp. 9–11.

[22] (p. 73) Robinson, *2 Hansard 11*, c. 229 (6 Apr. 1824).

[23] (p. 73) S.C.H.C. on Sale of Beer, *Parl. Papers* 1830 (253), X, p. 12.

[24] (p. 73) *Ibid.*, p. 71.

[25] (p. 73) Quotations from S. & B. Webb, *Liquor Licensing*, p. 110, n. 2; Lady Holland, *Memoir of Revd. Sydney Smith* (1855), II, p. 272; cf. *ibid.*, p. 267.

[26] (p. 73) *The Times*, 2 Oct. 1827, p. 3; quotation from *Brougham MSS.*, Univ. Coll. London, Sydney Smith to Brougham, 9 Mar. 1828.

[27] (p. 73) Barclay, in S.C.H.C. on Sale of Beer, *Parl. Papers* 1830 (253), X, p. 16; Hume, *2 Hansard 19*, c. 858 (21 May 1828).

[28] (p. 74) Peel quotations from Surrey County Record Office, *Goulburn Papers*, II/17: Peel to Goulburn, 6 June 1828; *Morning Herald*, 25 June 1830; cf. S. & B. Webb, *Liquor Licensing*, p. 113.

[29] (p. 74) *Morning Advertiser*, 22 May 1830; cf. Duke of Richmond, *2 Hansard 25*, c. 1094 (8 July 1830).

[30] (p. 74) Maberly, *Mirror of Parliament*, 1830, III, p. 2667; Vyvyan, *ibid.*, p. 2669 (1 July 1830).

[31] (p. 74) Gladstone, speech at Oldham, reported in *Oldham Chronicle*, 21 Dec. 1867; cf. *Hertfordshire Mercury*, 20 Mar. 1830; *Globe*, 13 July 1830.

[32] (p. 74) *Chartist*, 31 Mar. 1839; cf. *Manchester Guardian*, 17 July 1830.

[33] (p. 74) Sir H. Parnell, *On Financial Reform* (1830), p. 7; B.M. *Add. MSS.* 27789 (Place Papers), f. 231; *Hertfordshire Mercury*, 20 Feb. 1830.

[34] (p. 74) B.M. *Add. MSS.* 43649 (Cobden Papers), f. 202: Cobden to Bright, 29 Sept. 1851; for the previous history of the beershop plan, see *Mirror of Parliament*, 1830, III, p. 2659 (1 July 1830).

[35] (p. 74) Sir R. Heron, *Notes* (2nd edn, Grantham, 1851), pp. 182–3.

[36] (p. 75) *Bristol Mercury*, 2 Feb. 1830, p. 4; for the divided cabinet, see L. Brown, *The Board of Trade & the Free-Trade Movement 1830–1842* (Oxford, 1958), p. 9. For Lincolnshire, see Sir R. Heron, *op. cit.*, pp. 182–3. In Lincolnshire & Bristol, therefore, the statements of D. C. Moore, 'The Other Face of Reform', *Victorian Studies*, Sept. 1961, pp. 17, 22, do not seem to apply.

[37] (p. 75) Cornwall County Record Office, *Vyvyan Papers*, Political Correspondence 48/55: Eldon to Vyvyan, 18 Dec. 1829 (photostat copies).

[38] (p. 75) D. C. Moore, *art. cit.* p. 17.

[39] (p. 75) B.M. *Add. MSS.* 40340 (Peel Papers), f. 218.

[40] (p. 75) *Mirror of Parliament*, 1830, III, p. 2109 (3 June 1830).

[41] (p. 75) T. Hughes, *Tom Brown's Schooldays* (6th edn, n.d.), p. 115; Cobbett, *Political Register*, 27 Mar. 1830, p. 398; Peel, *3 Hansard 4*, c. 885 (6 July 1831). I owe this latter reference to Mr. M. G. Brock; cf. *Examiner*, 21 Aug. 1831, p. 531.

[42] (p. 75) Quo. from Ayrton, *3 Hansard 158*, c. 1245 (14 May 1860).

[43] (p. 75) *Vyvyan Papers*, 48/11 (photostat copy): Duke of Newcastle to Vyvyan, 15 Aug. 1829.

[44] (p. 76) Falmouth, *2 Hansard 25*, c. 1096 (8 July 1830); see also *2 Hansard 23*, c. 312 (15 Mar. 1830); *ibid.*, c. 697 (22 Mar. 1830).

[45] (p. 76) Waithman, *Mirror of Parliament*, 1830, III, p. 2660 (1 July 1830); Calcraft, *2 Hansard 24*, c. 15ff. (8 Apr. 1830).

[46] (p. 76) Lord Stanley's comment in *2 Hansard 24*, c. 324 (3 May 1830); cf. *Goulburn Papers*, II/17: Peel to Goulburn, 14 Oct. 1828.

[47] (p. 76) For these fears, see S.C.H.C. Sale of Beer, *Parl. Papers* 1833 (416), XV, Q. 3939; P. Mathias, *Brewing Industry*, p. xxii; Anon, *A Few Words on the Licensing System* (1830), pp. 20–1.

[48] (p. 76) *Political Register*, 27 Mar. 1830, p. 398.

[49] (p. 76) *Spectator*, 23 Jan. 1830, p. 51; for home brewing, see *Mirror of Parliament*, 1830, III, p. 2659 (1 July 1830).

[50] (p. 77) *Devonshire Chronicle*, 30 Oct. 1830, p. 4; London School of Economics, *Webb Local Government Collection*, Vol. 350, notes on the municipal corporations inquiry of 1834.

[51] (p. 77) Parnell, *Mirror of Parliament*, 1830, III, p. 2721 (3 July 1830); for urban interests, see *Newcastle Chronicle*, 20 Mar. 1830, *Bristol Mercury*, 23 Mar. 1830.

[52] (p. 77) Sibthorp, *2 Hansard 24*, c. 418 (4 May 1830). *Dyott's Diary, 1781–1845* (Ed. R. W. Jeffery, 1907), II, p. 89; I owe this reference to Mr. Brock.

[53] (p. 77) First quotation (Vyvyan) from *Mirror of Parliament*, 1830, III, p. 2669 (1 July 1830); Gooch, *Mirror of Parliament*, 1830, II, p. 1887 (21 May 1830).

[54] (p. 77) S.C.H.C. on Sale of Beer, *Parl. Papers* 1830 (253), X, p. 16.

[55] (p. 77) Quotation from *2 Hansard 23*, c. 342 (15 Mar. 1830); see also S.C.H.C. on Sale of Beer, *Parl. Papers* 1830 (253), X, p. 15; *Mirror of Parliament*, 1830, I, p. 561 (4 Mar. 1830); *ibid.*, 1830, III, p. 2662 (1 July 1830); *2 Hansard 25*, c. 865 (1 July 1830).

[56] (p. 78) C. Buxton, *Memorials of Sir T. F. Buxton* (1848), p. 234; S.C.H.C. on Sale of Beer, *Parl. Papers* 1830 (253), X, p. 19; *2 Hansard 23*, c. 175 (11 Mar. 1830); *Mirror of Parliament*, 1830, II, p. 1535 (4 May 1830); *2 Hansard 24*, c. 962 (21 May 1830); *Mirror of Parliament*, 1830, III, p. 2110 (3 June 1830).

[57] (p. 78) Quo. from *2 Hansard 25*, c. 866 (1 July 1830); for Calvert's investments, see *Morning Advertiser*, 16 Apr., 19 Mar. 1830. For other speeches by Calvert, see *2 Hansard 23*, c. 621 (19 Mar. 1830); *2 Hansard 24*, c. 19 (8 Apr. 1830); *ibid.*, c. 415 (4 May 1830).

[58] (p. 78) *Brighton Gazette*, 20 May 1830, p. 2; S.C.H.C. on Sale of Beer, *Parl. Papers* 1830 (253), X, pp. 15, 60; *Morning Advertiser*, 16 Mar. 1830; *2 Hansard 24*, c. 411 (4 May 1830); *2 Hansard 25*, c. 1094 (8 July 1830); *Mirror of Parliament*, 1830, II, p. 1886 (21 May 1830).

[59] (p. 78) For subsequent mobilization, see *Era*, 3 Feb. 1839, p. 221; 10 Mar. 1839 (supplement), p. 1.

[60] (p. 78) *Mirror of Parliament*, 1830, I, p. 1309 (8 Apr. 1830); *2 Hansard 24*, cc. 403 (4 May 1830), 956 (21 May 1830), 405 (4 May 1830); *2 Hansard 25*, c. 997 (6 July 1830).

[61] (p. 78) *Howick's Diary*, 3 May 1830; I am most grateful to Mr. Brock for lending me photostats of this diary, which is in Durham University Library. For the petitions, see *Mirror of Parliament*, 1830, III, p. 2668 (1 July 1830); cf. *Mirror of Parliament*, 1830, II, p. 1535 (4 May 1830); *Mirror of Parliament*, 1830, III, p. 2508 (21 June 1830).

[62] (p. 79) Vyvyan's list is in B. T. Bradfield, 'Sir Richard Vyvyan and the Fall of Wellington's Government', *University of Birmingham Historical Journal*, XI (1968), pp. 153–154; G. I. T. Machin, *The Catholic Question in English Politics 1820 to 1830* (Oxford, 1964), p. 188. See also *Vyvyan Papers*, 48/15: Vyvyan to the Duke of Cumberland, 22 Aug. 1829 (photostat copies); Sir Hughe Knatchbull-Hugessen, *A Kentish Family* (1960), pp. 177ff.; Sir Hughe kindly gave me much painstaking assistance on this topic.

[63] (p. 79) *Mirror of Parliament*, 1830, III, p. 2108 (3 June 1830).

[64] (p. 79) For complaints of late-night debates, see *Morning Advertiser*, 7 June 1830; *Howick's Diary*, 21 June 1830; for Sibthorp, *Mirror of Parliament*, 1830, III, pp. 2672–3 (1 July 1830). *Morning Herald*, 25 June 1830. Huskisson, *Mirror of Parliament*, 1830, II, p. 1892 (21 May 1830); *2 Hansard 25*, c. 877 (1 July 1830).

[65] (p. 79) *Morning Herald*, 25 June 1830; Sir E. Sugden, *3 Hansard 6*, c. 697 (27 Aug. 1831).

[66] (p. 80) Brougham quotations from *3 Hansard 43*, c. 1255 (5 July 1838); *The Times*, 30 July 1830, p. 2 (Yorkshire speech). For Peel's list, see B.M. *Add. MSS.* 40401 (Peel Papers), ff. 182–95: I owe the latter two references to Mr. Brock. See also Brougham, *Mirror of Parliament*, 1830, III, p. 2670 (1 July 1830); *2 Hansard 24*, cc. 420–1 (4 May 1830).

[67] (p. 80) Sir R. Heron, *Notes*, p. 183; *Vyvyan Papers*, 48/59: Vyvyan to Eldon, 30 Nov. 1829 (photostat copy).

[68] (p. 80) Vyvyan, quo. *Cornwall Standard*, 9 Aug. 1830; Mr. Brock provided me with this reference. Yarmouth quotation from *Great Yarmouth Pollbook* (1830), p. iv; cf. *ibid.*, pp. xxviii, xxxi. For Maberly, see *Abingdon Pollbook* (Abingdon, 1830), p. 33.

[69] (p. 80) Quotation from *Morning Advertiser*, 15 Apr., 20 Aug. 1831; see also *ibid.*, 20 Aug. 1831.

[70] (p. 80) *Ibid.*, 23 Apr. 1831; cf. *ibid.*, 14 Mar. 1832.

[71] (p. 81) Quo. from *Morning Advertiser*, 12 May 1831; cf. *ibid.*, 28 Apr., 4 May 1831; the 1834 writer was W. J. Fox, *Monthly Repository*, N.S. VIII (1834), p. 447. For the impact of parliamentary reform, see p. 343.

[72] (p. 81) S. & B. Webb, *Liquor Licensing*, p. 114.

[73] (p. 81) McCulloch, *Edinburgh Review*, Apr. 1835, p. 176.

[74] (p. 81) Robinson, *2 Hansard 12*, c. 737 (28 Feb. 1825); Goulburn, *Mirror of Parliament*, 1830, III, p. 2509 (21 June 1830); Sir H. Parnell, *op. cit.*, p. 60. For Oldham beershops, see *British Temperance Advocate* (Leeds, &c.), 15 June 1840, p. 77; cf. S.C.H.C. on Public-houses, *Parl. Papers* 1854 (367), XIV, Q.3676.

[75] (p. 81) S. & B. Webb, *Liquor Licensing*, p. 119.

[76] (p. 81) J. L. & B. Hammond, *The Age of the Chartists*, p. 149; W. L. Burn, *The Age of Equipoise* (1964), p. 281; cf. G. B. Wilson, *Alcohol & the Nation*, p. 101.

[77] (p. 82) Smith, quo. in Lady Holland, *op. cit.*, II, p. 310; cf. S. & B. Webb, *Liquor Licensing*, p. 116; R. G. Gammage, *Beershops: England's Felon Manufactories* (1864), p. 3; for contemporary comment, see *Leeds Mercury* (Leeds), 23 Oct. 1830; *Sheffield Iris* (Sheffield), 12 Oct. 1830; *3 Hansard 6*, c. 156 (17 Aug. 1831).

[78] (p. 82) Adam Smith, *op. cit.*, I, p. 457; cf. Slaney, *Mirror of Parliament*, 1830, II, p. 1888 (21 May 1830). Bruce, *Alliance News*, 12 Aug. 1865, p. 251.

[79] (p. 82) Quo. from G. B. Wilson, *Alcohol & the Nation*, p. 62; for figures, see *ibid.*, p. 331.

[80] (p. 82) *3 Hansard 123*, cc. 1676–7 (16 Dec. 1852).

[81] (p. 83) G. B. Wilson, *Alcohol & the Nation*, pp. 48–64.

[82] (p. 83) For the London witness, see *Drunkenness Committee*, Q. 49; for beer prices elsewhere, see *Preston Chronicle*, 20 Aug. 1831; D. M. Knox, 'The Development of the London Brewing Industry, 1830–1914' (Oxford Univ. unpublished B.Litt. thesis, 1956), p. 49; S.C.H.C. on Sale of Beer, *Parl. Papers* 1833 (416), XV, QQ. 2311ff., 3434–5, 3486ff., 3656, 4100ff. For Kendal see C. Nicholson, *Annals of Kendal* (2nd edn, 1861), p. 297.

[83] (p. 83) S. & B. Webb, *Liquor Licensing*, p. 120; for spirits consumption, see G. B. Wilson, *op. cit.*, pp. 336–7.

[84] (p. 83) For the Beer Act's effects on the brewers, see S.C.H.C. on Sale of Beer, *Parl. Papers* 1833 (416), XV, QQ. 3449ff.; *Brougham MSS.*, John Steed to Brougham, 20 May 1834; D. M. Knox, *op. cit.*, p. 2; *The League*, 9 Dec. 1843, p. 170. For beershop customers, see E. A. Pratt, *The Policy of Licensing Justices* (1909), p. 21; S.C.H.C. on Sale of Beer, *Parl. Papers* 1833 (416), XV, Q. 2887.

[85] (p. 83) S.C.H.C. on Public-houses, *Parl. Papers* 1852–3 (855), XXXVII, Q. 3759.

[86] (p. 84) D. M. Knox, *op. cit.*, p. 46; *Leeds Mercury*, 31 May 1834; S.C.H.C. Public-houses, *Parl. Papers* 1852–3 (855), XXXVII, Q. 665.

[87] (p. 84) Wallace, *3 Hansard 44*, c. 126 (10 July 1838); cf. *3 Hansard 4*, c. 504 (30 June 1834); S.C.H.C. on Sale of Beer, *Parl. Papers* 1833 (416), XV, Q. 3311.

[88] (p. 84) *Record*, 14 June 1830; *Brougham MSS.*, Zachary Macaulay to Brougham, 19 Apr. 1834; W. Wilberforce to Brougham, 15 Aug. 1831. Brougham, *3 Hansard 7*, c. 50 (15 Sept. 1831).

[89] (p. 84) Quotation from their petition, printed in *3 Hansard 3*, c. 843 (24 Mar. 1831).

[90] (p. 85) Villiers, *3 Hansard 158*, c. 806 (7 May 1860). For contrasting attitudes to the beershop, see R. Jefferies, *Hodge & his Masters* (1890 edn), chapter XXIII; G. Bourne, *Change in the Village* (1912 edn), chapter V. Petitions analysed from *House of Commons Journals*.

[91] (p. 85) Quo. from P.R.O. H.O. 73/8, returns from poor law guardians: reply from D. Smart (Westbourne Union, Sussex); for a radical M.P., see Warburton, *3 Hansard 44*, c. 123 (10 July 1838).

[92] (p. 85) S.C.H.L. . . . Sale of Beer, *Parl. Papers* 1850 (398), X, QQ. 29, 63, 323, 505.

[93] (p. 85) R. C. Poor Laws, *Parl. Papers* 1834 (44), XXXIV, appendix B.1, part V.

[94] (p. 85) Trevor, *3 Hansard 13*, cc. 259–61 (31 May 1832).

[95] (p. 85) N. Gash, 'The Rural Unrest in England in 1830' (Oxford Univ. unpublished B. Litt. thesis, 1934), p. 65; I am most grateful to Professor Gash for allowing me to consult his thesis.

[96] (p. 85) J. Clay, *26th Chaplain's Report 1849*, pp. 48–9; *24th Chaplain's Report 1847*, p. 17; *Chartist*, 31 Mar. 1839, p. 2.

[97] (p. 86) As contemporaries argued—see N. Gash, *op. cit.*, p. 67; S.C.H.C. Sale of Beer, *Parl. Papers* 1833 (416), XV, QQ. 119–22. For drunken rioters, see B.M. *Add. MSS.* 40401 (Peel Papers), f. 285; N. Gash, *op. cit.*, pp. 53–4. See also G. Rudé & E. J. Hobsbawm, *Captain Swing* (1969), p. 88.

[98] (p. 86) Quotations from *Morning Chronicle*, 24 June 1850, p. 4; cf. *ibid.*, 21 Nov. 1851, p. 4; 26 Nov. 1851, p. 2; 9 Dec. 1851, p. 4. For the competition fostered by the Beer Act, see *3 Hansard 16*, c. 338 (7 Mar. 1833); *3 Hansard 17*, c. 686 (26 Apr. 1833).

[99] (p. 86) *Brougham MSS.*, William Cartwright to Brougham, 20 Apr. 1831; cf. Ann Horner to Brougham, 24 Aug. 1838.

[100] (p. 86) *Ashton Reporter*, 9 Mar. 1872, p. 3.

[101] (p. 86) Solly, *Alliance News*, 17 June 1865, pp. 190–1; Lovett, *ibid.*, 9 July 1870, p. 221.

[102] (p. 86) Quotation from an unpublished paper on 'Middle Class Moral Reform & Working Class Leisure' presented at the Edinburgh Univ. symposium on 'Class and Class Conflict in 19th Century Britain' (1967) by Robert Storch, Wisconsin University; I am most grateful to Mr. Storch for allowing me to use this quotation. For more on recreation and state intervention, see my 'Religion and Recreation in Nineteenth-Century England', *Past & Present*, Dec. 1967, pp. 98, 111, 115, 123.

[103] (p. 86) B. Webb, *My Apprenticeship*, p. 238.

[104] (p. 86) S. &. B. Webb, *Liquor Licensing*, pp. vi–vii.

Chapter 4. The Origins of the Anti-Spirits Movement [pp. 87–106].

[1] (p. 87) e.g. William Collins, *Temperance Society Record* (Glasgow), I (1830), p. 120.

[2] (p. 87) J. Teare, *History of the Origin & Success of the Advocacy of the Principle of Total Abstinence* (1847), p. 13; brewers were active in anti-spirits societies in Cork & Penrith, see Father Stanislaus, 'Father Mathew & Temperance', *Capuchin Annual*, 1930, p. 166; T. Whittaker, *Life's Battles*, p. 98.

[3] (p. 87) R. I. & S. Wilberforce, *The Life of William Wilberforce* (1838), I, p. 131.

[4] (p. 87) R. V. French, *Nineteen Centuries of Drink in England* (2nd edn, n.d.), pp. 57, 36, 61.

[5] (p. 87) G. R. Owst, *Literature & Pulpit in Medieval England* (2nd edn, Oxford, 1961) pp. 426, 428, 435; Rev. R. Morris (Ed.), *Old English Homilies of the Twelfth Century* (Early English Text Society No. 53, 1873), p. 212. See also G. R. Owst, *Preaching in Medieval England* (Cambridge, 1926), pp. 32, 94.

[6] (p. 88) For Shene, see C. P. Matthews, 'The Laye Bretherns Statutes (Shene)', *Surrey Archaeological Collections*, XXXIX, p. 117; cf. L. Lessius, *Hygiasticon* (Cambridge, 1634), preface. For More, see Erasmus' comments in *Retrospective Review*, V, p. 253.

[7] (p. 88) Calvin, *Commentaries* (Tr. J. Harontunian & L. P. Smith, 1958 edn), p. 349; see also J. Hooper, *Early Writings* (Cambridge, 1843), p. 349; J. Jewel, *Works II* (Parker Society, Cambridge, 1847), sermon on *Romans*, XIII, 12; Archbishop Sandys, *Sermons* (Parker Society, Cambridge, 1841), p. 137.

[8] (p. 88) For radical sects, J. Horsch, *The Hutterian Brethren. 1528–1931* (Goshen, 1931), p. 139; cf. G. H. Williams, *The Radical Reformation* (Philadelphia, 1962), pp. 183, 191, 265; Christopher Hill, *Puritanism and Revolution* (1962 paperback edn), p. 141.

[9] (p. 88) R. V. French, *op. cit.*, pp. 150–1; H. G. Hudson, *A Study of Social Regulations in England under James I and Charles I: Drink & Tobacco* (Chicago, 1933), pp. 3–4; W. P. M. Kennedy, *Elizabethan Episcopal Administration* (Alcuin Club, 1925), II, p. 73; III, p. 151.

[10] (p. 88) Jeremy Taylor, *The Whole Works* (Ed. R. Heber & C. P. Eden, 1847–1852), III, p. 54; cf. *ibid.*, IV, pp. 205–6. See also James I, *Works* (1616), pp. 181, 218–20; J. B. H. Jones, 'Puritanism and Moral Legislation before the Civil War' (Univ. of Wales unpublished M.A. thesis, 1954), pp. 68–9; H. G. Hudson, *op. cit.*, p. 16.

[11] (p. 88) e.g. *British Temperance Advocate*, 15 Feb. 1841, p. 16; see also my article in *History Today*, Mar. 1963, pp. 178ff.

[12] (p. 88) U.K.A. *Lord Derby & the U.K.A.* (1872), p. 6.

[13] (p. 88) S. Harris, *The Drunkard's Cup* (1619), p. 21; for arguments resembling those used by the nineteenth-century temperance movement, see Anon, *The Way to Make all People Rich* (1685), p. 20; W. Assheton, *Discourse against Drunkenness* (1692), p. 33.

[14](p. 88) J. Geree, *Divine Potion to Preserve Spirituall Health, by the Cure of Unnaturall Health Drinking* (1648), p. 4; cf. M. Scrivener, *A Treatise Against Drunkennesse* (1680), pp. 126–7.

[15] (p. 88) D. Defoe, *The Poor Man's Plea* (2nd edn, 1698), p. 9; cf. T. Reeve, *God's Plea for Nineveh* (1657), p. 121.

[16] (p. 89) Milton in R. V. French, *op. cit.*, p. 204; his remarks were often quoted in 19th-century temperance tracts. For the Interregnum, see R. F. Bretherton, 'Country Inns & Alehouses', in R. Lennard (Ed.), *Englishmen at Rest and Play* (Oxford, 1931), pp. 160–1, 172; C. H. Firth & R. S. Rait, *Acts & Ordinances of the Interregnum 1642–1660* (H.M.S.O. 1911), I, pp. 913–14, 1023, 1133–6; II, pp. 393–5; G. Davies, *The Early Stuarts* (1937), pp. 302–3.

[17] (p. 89) *4 Hansard 30*, c. 1357 (17 June 1895); for Cromwell, see Christopher Hill, *op. cit.*, p. 319.

[18] (p. 89) Quo. from J. Downame, 'Disswasion from the Sin of Drunkennes', in his *Foure Treatises* (1613), p. 82; Milton, quo. in E. Legouis, 'The Bacchic Element in Shakespeare's Plays', *Proceedings of the British Academy*, 1926. See also D. Dent, *Sermon against Drunkennes* (1628), p. 5; R. B. Schlatter, *Social Ideas of Religious Leaders 1660–1688* (1940), p. 192.

[19] (p. 89) There are many references to foreign drinks in H. T. Buckle, *Miscellaneous & Posthumous Works* (Ed. H. Taylor, 1872), II, p. 363; cf. A. à Wood, *Life & Times* (Ed. A. Clark, 1892), II, p. 96. For beverages, see C. H. Denyer, 'The Consumption of Tea, & other Staple Drinks', *Economic Journal*, III (1893), p. 33; J. Crawford, 'History of Coffee', *Journal of the Royal Statistical Society*, Apr. 1852, p. 51.

[20] (p. 89) e.g. in *Temperance Spectator*, June 1859, p. 85.

[21] (p. 90) D. Defoe, *op. cit.*, p. 6. This paragraph is based on G. V. Portus, *Caritas Anglicana* (1912), p. 14; J. Woodward, *A Disswasive from the Sin of Drunkenness* (1769 edn), pp. 9–11; D. W. R. Bahlman, *The Moral Revolution of 1688* (Yale, 1957), pp. 67–83, 107.

[22] (p. 90) S. Hales, *Friendly Admonition to the Drinkers of Gin . . .* (1754 edn), p. 28; Anon, *Earnest & Affectionate Address to the Poor . . . in a Letter from a Minister to his Parishioners* (1770), p. 25. For the gin riots, see M. D. George, *op. cit.*, pp. 27ff.

[23] (p. 90) For temperance controversies of this type, see *Alliance Weekly News*, 22 June 1861, p. 1224; *Weekly Record*, 5 Sept. 1857, p. 317; *British Temperance Advocate*, 15 Dec. 1840, p. 145. The most monumental biographical temperance dictionary is P. T. Winskill, *Temperance Standard Bearers of the Nineteenth Century* (Liverpool, 1897, 2 Vols.).

[24] (p. 90) Quo. in Lady B. Balfour (Ed.), *Letters of Lady Constance Lytton* (1925), p. 129.

[25] (p. 91) *Monthly Review*, N.S., 1830, XV, p. 188. For sex propaganda, see J. A. Banks, *Prosperity and Parenthood* (1954), p. 29.

[26] (p. 91) Huskisson, *2 Hansard 7*, c. 1696 (18 July 1822); *Eclectic Review*, Oct. 1835, p. 283; for assertions that drunkenness had declined, see *Drunkenness Committee*, QQ. 36–7, 330; J. Bowles, *Letter to Robert Wissett Esq.*, p. 54; Buckingham, *3 Hansard 24*, c. 97 (3 June 1834); *The Times* 12 July 1831. There are figures for wine consumption in G. B. Wilson, *Alcohol & the Nation*, pp. 364–5; cf. J. G. D. (Ed.), *The Dunlop Papers, I: Autobiography of John Dunlop* (1932) [henceforth cited as J. Dunlop, *Autobiography*], p. 27; *3 Hansard 143*, c. 915ff. (15 July 1856).

[27] (p. 91) This historian is P. T. Cominos, 'Late-Victorian Sexual Respectability & the Social System', *International Review of Social History*, 1963, p. 225; M. J. Quinlan, *Victorian Prelude. A History of English Manners, 1700–1830* (New York, 1941), pp. 59–60; A. Smith, *Wealth of Nations*, I, p. 457.

[28] (p. 91) E. P. Thompson, *The Making of the English Working Class* (2nd edn, 1968), pp. 467, 813. For Bentham, see J. R. Poynter, *Society & Pauperism* (1969), pp. 121, 133; for the gin mania, see M. D. George, *op. cit.*, pp. 36, 41. For Place, see my 'Two Roads to Social Reform: Francis Place and the "Drunken Committee" of 1834', *Historical Journal*, 1968.

[29] (p. 92) R. Hunter & I. McAlpine, *Three Hundred Years of Psychiatry, 1535–1860* (1963), p. 589; cf. T. Trotter, *Essay, Medical, Philosophical, & Chemical, on Drunkenness, and its Effects on the Human Body* (2nd edn, 1804), pp. 2, 179.

[30] (p. 92) E. Darwin, *Zoonomia* (3rd edn, 1801), I, p. 367; D. King-Hele, *Erasmus Darwin* (1963), p. 33.

[31] (p. 92) Quotation from S.C.H.C. Import Duties, *Parl. Papers* 1840 (601), V, Q.2815. For coffee-houses, see *New Parley Library*, 1, No. 19 (13 July 1844), pp. 293–4. For textile exports, see Lawrence Heyworth in *Birmingham Journal*, 17 Sept. 1842, p. 3.

[32] (p. 93) T. Scott, *Essays on the Most Important Subjects in Religion* (9th edn, 1822), p. 213. For evangelical attitudes, see W. Jerdan, *Autobiography* (1853), III, p. 304; I owe this reference to Dr. Walsh; cf. J. H. Overton, *The English Church in the Nineteenth Century (1800–1833)* (1894), p. 94; H. Venn, *The Complete Duty of Man* (1841 edn), pp. 250–2.

[33] (p. 93) J. Bowles, *Reflections on the Political and Moral State of Society* (1800), p. 161; for Wilberforce, see D. Newsome, *The Parting of Friends*, p. 49.

[34] (p. 93) R. Tabraham, in *Temperance News & Weekly Journal*, 30 May 1846, p. 39, argued that a 19th-century Wesley would have been a temperance reformer; cf. E. C. Urwin, *Methodism & Sobriety* (1943), pp. 11–19. For Wesley's own attitudes to drink, see his letter to an unknown Bristol correspondent, 21 Jan. 1746, in the *Aberdare Family Collection*, Hammersmith. The present Lord Aberdare very kindly gave me access to this collection.

[35] (p. 93) For Quakers, see P. Mathias, *Brewing Industry*, p. 299; cf. James Grant, *Lights and Shadows of London Life* (1842), II, p. 207.

[36] (p. 93) J. Benson, *Life of the Rev. John William de la Flechere* (1835 edn), pp. 67, 78; Rev. J. W. Fletcher, *A Dreadful Phenomenum Described and Improved. A Sermon . . .* (Shrewsbury, 1773), pp. 41, 294: I owe both these references to Mr. Barrie Trinder.

[37] (p. 93) S. & B. Webb, *Liquor Licensing*, p. 84; for a general discussion of magistrates' restrictions in the 1780s, see *ibid.*, chapter III. See also the Vice Society's *Address to the Public, Part II* (1803).

[38] (p. 94) e.g. William Allen, *Christian Advocate*, 4 July 1831, p. 3; cf. F. K. Brown, *op. cit.*, pp. 404–5; M. Jaeger, *Before Victoria. Changing Standards & Behaviour. 1787–1837* (1956), p. 18; evangelicals expressed surprise, however, at the late appearance of other good causes. For an example, see R. I. & S. Wilberforce, *Life of William Wilberforce*, II, p. 463.

[39] (p. 94) W. Lovett, *Life and Struggles* (1876), p. 24; for the temperance reformer's enemies, see *Temperance Society Record*, Sept. 1830, p. 54; *Moral Reformer* (Preston), 1 July 1833, p. 205.

[40] (p. 94) *Edinburgh Review*, Oct. 1840, p. 41.

[41] (p. 94) *Ibid.*, June 1829, pp. 442–3; cf. E. J. Hobsbawm, *The Age of Revolution*, p. 127; A. de Tocqueville, *Journeys to England & Ireland* (Ed. J. P. Mayer, 1958), pp. 87–8.

[42] (p. 94) For temperance reformers modelling their work on the anti-slave trade movement, see *Parliamentary Review*, 1834, I, p. 385; *Sheffield Mercury*, 9 Aug. 1834; Canon Stowell, *Speeches . . . in Behalf of the Permissive Prohibitory Liquor Bill* (U.K.A. 1865), p. 31. For Buckingham, see R. E. Turner, *James Silk Buckingham. A Social Biography. 1786–1855* (1934), p. 112; see also *Preston Temperance Advocate*, Jan. 1835, p. 6.

[43] (p. 95) For the factory hours movement, N. J. Smelser, *Social Change in the Industrial Revolution*, pp. 277–8.

[44] (p. 95) For teetotal employees, see H. Mayhew, *London Labour*, III, p. 257.

[45] (p. 95) *Preston Temperance Advocate*, Aug. 1835, p. 62; *British Temperance Advocate*, 15 July 1840, p. 89; Dawson Burns, *Temperance History*, I, pp. 42–3.

[46] (p. 96) J. Livesey, *Malt Lecture*, p. 31; Spencer, *British & Foreign Temperance Intelligencer*, 1 Jan. 1843, p. 515.

[47] (p. 96) For pauperism, see Baines, *Mirror of Parliament*, 1834, III, p. 1989 (3 June 1834); *Drunkenness Committee*, p. xi; *Preston Temperance Advocate*, July 1834, p. 49. For Chadwick, *British & Foreign Temperance Intelligencer*, 7 Aug. 1841, p. 252; cf. J. Dunlop, *Autobiography*, p. 210.

[48] (p. 96) For accusations that the slave trade shed discredit on commerce, see M. G. James, 'The Clapham Sect: its Historical Influence' (Oxford unpublished D. Phil. thesis, 1950), p. 39. For the financing of industrialization, see C. Erickson, *British Industrialists. Steel and Hosiery 1850–1950*, pp. 15–17, 91–95, 101; Eric Williams, *Capitalism & Slavery* (Chapel Hill, 1944), p. 136.

[49] (p. 96) Christopher Hill, *Society & Puritanism* (1964), p. 427.

[50] (p. 96) A. Ure, *The Philosophy of Manufactures* (1835), p. 417.

[51] (p. 96) A. D. Gayer, W. W. Rostow & A. J. Schwartz, *Growth & Fluctuation of the*

British Economy, 1790–1850 (1953), I, pp. 222, 225–6; R. C. O. Matthews, *A Study in Trade-Cycle History: Economic Fluctuations in Great Britain, 1833–1842* (Cambridge, 1954), pp. 130–1.

[52] (p. 97) R. Jefferies, *Hodge & his Masters*, p. 345.

[53] (p. 97) J. Morley, *The Life of Richard Cobden* (11th edn, 1903), p. 16.

[54] (p. 97) R. Owen, *The Life of Robert Owen* (1857), I, p. 27; cf .the very similar incident in T. Lythgoe, *Biographical Key to the Picture Containing One Hundred and Twenty Portraits of Temperance Reformers* (Manchester, 1860), p. 65. Franklin, quo. in M. Weber, *The Protestant Ethic* (1958 edn, paperback), p. 49; cf. D. V. Glass (Ed.), *Social Mobility in Britain* (1954), p. 352.

[55] (p. 97) T. Carlyle, 'Past & Present', in *Works* (Ashburton edn, 1891), II, p. 155; cf. J. Finch, in *Drunkenness Committee*, Q. 3830; R. E. Turner, *Buckingham*, p. 311; S. Checkland, *The Rise of Industrial Society in England 1815–1885* (1964), p. 48.

[56] (p. 97) e.g. *Ipswich Temperance Tract No. 64;* there are several examples in the *London Temperance Tracts* (1839).

[57] (p. 97) J. Livesey, quo. in N[ew] B[ritish] & F[oreign] S[ociety] for the S[uppression] of I[ntemperance], *2nd Annual Report 1838*, p. 46.

[58] (p. 97) Gayer, Rostow & Schwartz, *op. cit.*, I, p. 222. For the home market, see W. Hoyle, *Our National Resources & How They are Wasted* (cheap edn, 1871); S. Fothergill, *The Threatening Element in England's Prosperity* (1871).

[59] (p. 97) For example, B.M. *Add. MSS.* 43656 (Cobden Papers), f. 380: Cobden to Joseph Sturge, 15 June 1857.

[60] (p. 97) J. Clay, *24th. Chaplain's Report 1847*, p. 70.

[61] (p. 98) J. Livesey (Ed.), *The Struggle*, No. 41, p. 4.

[62] (p. 98) Parsons, quo. in *Bristol Temperance Herald*, Apr. 1851, p. 58; cf. R. S. Fitton & A. P. Wadsworth, *The Strutts and the Arkwrights* (Manchester, 1958), p. 198.

[63] (p. 98) Buckingham, *3 Hansard 23*, c. 1362 (27 May 1834).

[64] (p. 98) A. de Tocqueville, *Democracy in America* (ed. P. Bradley, New York, 1960), I, p. 198; II, p. 117–18.

[65] (p. 98) N.T.L. *Annual Report, 1856*, p. 16.

[66] (p. 98) J. Ruskin, 'Crown of Wild Olive', in his *Works* (Ed. Cook & Wedderburn, 1905), XVIII, p. 506; cf. *ibid.*, p. 169 (unpublished fragment of 'Sesame & Lilies').

[67] (p. 99) J. Morley, *Gladstone*, I, p. 692.

[68] (p. 99) Dunlop, quo. in *Weekly Record*, 22 Mar. 1862, p. 98; cf. T. Clarkson, *History of the Rise, Progress, and Accomplishment of the Abolition of the African Slave Trade* (1839 edn), pp. 138, 333.

[69] (p. 99) Livesey, quo. in W. Logan, *The Early Heroes of the Temperance Reformation* (Glasgow, 1873), pp. 94–5.

[70] (p. 99) e.g. Roger Crab, in Christopher Hill, *Puritanism & Revolution*, p. 319; Henry Welbey in D[ictionary] of N[ational] B[iography], XIX, p. 1201.

[71] (p. 99) B. Franklin, *Autobiography* (New York paperback edn, 1962), p. 52; for Quakers, see P. Mathias, *Brewing Industry*, p. 299.

[72] (p. 100) J. Thornton, *Memoirs of Rev. John Thornton* (1843), p. 207; W. Tallack, *Thomas Shillitoe* (1867), p. 126.

[73] (p. 100) Christopher Hill, *Puritanism and Revolution*, p. 322.

[74] (p. 100) Dawson Burns, *Temperance History*, I, p. 413; P. T. Winskill, *Temperance Movement & its Workers*, II, p. 155. W. E. A. Axon (Ed.), *Joseph Brotherton. The First Teetotal Tract* (Manchester, 1890; first published 1821); *D.N.B.*, IV, p. 1304.

[75] (p. 100) S. Bamford, *Passages in the Life of a Radical* (2nd edn, Heywood, n.d.), p. 275; A. Prentice, *Historical Sketches & Personal Recollections of Manchester* (Manchester, 1851), p. 151; D. Read, *Peterloo* (Manchester, 1958), p. 159.

[76] (p. 100) Quotations from *Political Register*, 22 Jan. 1820, p. 697; 24 Nov. 1832.

[77] (p. 101) A. Fothergill, *Essay on the Abuse of Spirituous Liquors* (Bath, 1796), p. 29; Rev. R. Polwhele, *History of Cornwall*, VII (1816), p. 108; J. Yates, *Effects of Drinking Spirituous & Other Intoxicating Liquors, described in Four Sermons* (Glasgow, 1818).

[78] (p. 101) Dawson Burns, *Temperance History*, I, pp. 14–30; cf. A. C. F. Beales, *The History of Peace* (1931), pp. 45–54.

[79] (p. 101) *Christian Observer*, July 1826, p. 441; Aug. 1827, p. 497; Sept. 1827, p. 567;

May 1828, p. 340; Nov. 1828, p. 719; June 1829, p. 387. *Evangelical Magazine*, Jan. 1830, p. 24; Feb. 1830, p. 66; May 1830, p. 194; Nov. 1830, p. 477.

[80] (p. 101) Anon, *Autobiography of a Dissenting Minister* (5th edn, 1835), p. 38; Dr. Walsh referred me to this source. On American influence in general, see F. Thistlethwaite's two articles—'Atlantic Partnership', *Econ. Hist. Rev.*, 1954, p. 12, & 'America & Two Nations of Englishmen', *Virginia Quarterly Review*, Autumn 1955, p. 510; see also his book *The Anglo-American Connexion in the Early 19th Century* (Philadelphia, 1959), p. 79.

[81] (p. 101) Christopher Hill, *A Century of Revolution 1603–1714* (Edinburgh, 1961), p. 84; New British & Foreign Temperance Society [henceforth N.B.F.T.S.], *Third Annual Report, 1839*, p. 58. See also Vivian Vale, 'English Settlers in Early Wisconsin: the British Temperance Emigration Society', *Bulletin of the British Association for American Studies*, Dec. 1964.

[82] (p. 101) F. J. Klingberg, 'Harriet Beecher Stowe & Social Reform in England', *American Historical Review*, Apr. 1938, *passim*; cf. *British & Foreign Temperance Herald*, Dec. 1832, p. 145.

[83] (p. 101) F. Thistlethwaite, 'Atlantic Partnership', p. 3; cf. Gayer, Rostow & Schwartz, *op. cit.*, I, pp. 145–6, 181–2, 213, 215, 250–1.

[84] (p. 101) Quo. in *Rechabite Magazine* (Manchester), July 1850, p. 298.

[85] (p. 102) For the origins of the British temperance movement, see P. T. Winskill, *Temperance Movement & its Workers*, I, pp. 47–53; J. Dearden, *A Brief History of the Commencement & Success of Teetotalism* (Preston, n.d.), p. 17; *Church of England Temperance Magazine*, 1865, p. 20; *Temperance Penny Magazine*, Jan. 1836, p. 14; W. E. Moss, *1831–1931. Blackburn's First Temperance Society Centenary* (Blackburn, 1931), p. 5; G. C. Smith, *Intemperance . . .* (1829); Dawson Burns, *Temperance History*, I, p. 40; *Temperance Society Record*, Apr. 1831, p. 75; J. Pearce, *Livesey*, pp. cxi, cxii, cxv. For American influence in the B.F.T.S. see P. T. Winskill, *Temperance Movement & its Workers*, I, p. 73.

[86] (p. 102) *3 Hansard 24*, c. 109 (3 June 1834), for upper class anti-Americanism.

[87] (p. 102) J. Dunlop, *Autobiography*, p. 59; cf. *Drunkenness Committee*, Q. 4614.

[88] (p. 102) Hume, *Mirror of Parliament*, 1834, III, p. 1988 (3 June 1834); cf. Huskisson, *2 Hansard 10*, c. 362 (23 Feb. 1824).

[89] (p. 102) H. Jones, 'Alcoholism & Society', *New Society*, 21 Mar. 1963, discusses contrasts between French & English drinking habits. The teetotaler quoted is F. Beardsall, *British Temperance Advocate*, 15 Mar. 1839, p. 27.

[90] (p. 103) *Church of England Temperance Magazine*, Feb. 1863, pp. 133ff.

[91] (p. 103) For foreign speakers at temperance meetings, see Dawson Burns, *Temperance History*, I, p. 121; *London Temperance Tract No. 42*. For Buckingham, see R[oyal] S[ociety] for the P[revention] of C[ruelty] to A[nimals], *16th. Annual Report, 1842*, pp. 22–4.

[92] (p. 103) P. Burne, *The Teetotaler's Companion* (1847), p. 311.

[93] (p. 103) W. D. Killen, *Memoir of John Edgar* (Belfast, 1867), pp. 28, 32, 40, 48.

[94] (p. 103) For the movement in Northern Ireland, see Dawson Burns, *Temperance History*, I, p. 32; *Drunkenness Committee*, QQ. 3007–9. For the tracts, see especially the Hibernian Temperance Society's *Second Letter on the Effects of Wine & Spirits, by a Physician* (2nd edn), *A Letter to a Member of the Dublin Temperance Society, on the Supposed Value of Ardent Spirits in Relation to National Wealth, & The Address of the Hibernian Temperance Society to their Countrymen.* All these tracts were published in Dublin in 1830; I am most grateful to Mr. K. V. Thomas for drawing my attention to these tracts in his possession.

[95] (p. 104) Dunlop quotation in W. Logan, *Early Heroes*, p. 44; for feminist & anti-slavery parallels, see T. Clarkson, *op. cit.*, p. 180; Ray Strachey, '*The* [Feminist] *Cause*' (1928), pp. 32, 117–18. This account of the early Scottish movement is based on Dunlop's vivid description in *Scottish Temperance Review*, 1848, pp. 372–3; see also *Temperance Society Record*, Jan. 1831, pp. 8–9; J. Dunlop, *Autobiography*, pp. 59–62. For Chalmers' influence, see *ibid.*, pp. 303, 429. Chalmers also influenced Collins—see N.T.L., *Temperance Congress of 1862* (1862), p. 171.

[96] (p. 104) J. D. Walsh, 'Origins of the Evangelical Revival', in G. V. Bennett & J. D. Walsh (Eds.), *Essays in Modern English Church History in Memory of Norman Sykes* (1966), p. 157.

[97] (p. 105) Forbes' obituary is in *Bradford Observer*, 18 Oct. 1870; see also B.M. *Add. MSS.* 43383 (Bright Papers), f. 285: Bright to Cobden, 28 Nov. 1853. For Beaumont, see *Temperance Spectator*, Nov. 1859, p. 164. For Rand, see *Bradford Observer*, 28 June 1873, p. 8. For early developments in Bradford, see Bradford Temperance Society, *2nd Annual Report 1832*, p. 9; Dawson Burns, *Temperance History*, I, pp. 41–3; *Temperance Society Record*, June 1830, p. 6; July 1830, pp. 26–7.

[98] (p. 105) For early developments in England but outside Bradford, see A. Mounfield, *The Beginnings of Total Abstinence. The Warrington Societies of 1830* (Warrington, 1902), pp. 7–21; Dawson Burns, *Temperance History*, I, p. 42; P. T. Winskill & J. Thomas, *History of the Temperance Movement in Liverpool & District* (Liverpool, 1887), pp. 5–6.

[99] (p. 105) Bradford Temperance Society, *2nd Annual Report 1832*, p. 9; see the earliest entries in Leeds Temperance Society's *M.S. Minute Book 1830–45*, in Leeds Central Library's *Crosfield Collection.*

[100] (p. 105) M. Metford-Sewell (Ed.), 'Reform in the West of England. Extracts from the Journal of William Metford (1803–1832)', *Journal of the Friends' Historical Society*, XLV (1953), p. 26.

[101] (p. 105) Dawson Burns, *Temperance History*, I, pp. 43–4; cf. B.M. *Add. MSS.* 43667 (Cobden Papers), f. 53: Place to Cobden, 4 Mar. 1840.

[102] (p. 105) For Welshmen, see P. T. Winskill, *Temperance Movement & its Workers*, I, p. 75, IV, p. 99; for American influences, *ibid.*, I, p. 73.

[103] (p. 106) *Monthly Review*, N.S., XV (1830), p. 187.

Chapter 5. The Origins of Teetotalism: 1830–1834 [pp. 107–126].

[1] (p. 107) For Quakers, see B[ritish] & F[oreign] T[emperance] S[ociety], *First Annual Report*, *1832*, p. 59; *The Record*, 7 July 1831, p. 4; for women, *The Times*, 10 May 1837, p. 6; B.F.T.S. *Third Annual Report*, *1834*, p. 45. For Blackburn, see W. E. Moss, *op. cit.*, p. 8.

[2] (p. 107) Quotation from B.F.T.S., *1st Annual Report*, *1832*, p. 5; see also *The Record*, 7 July 1831, p. 4.

[3] (p. 108) B.F.T.S. *3rd Annual Report*, *1834*, pp. 8–9. For Caine, *Alliance News*, 6 Feb. 1902, p. 91.

[4] (p. 108) *British & Foreign Temperance Herald*, Feb. 1834, p. 22.

[5] (p. 110) Stanhope, in *British & Foreign Temperance Intelligencer*, 21 Sept. 1839, p. 378.

[6] (p. 110) *Parliamentary Review*, 1834, I, p. 37.

[7] (p. 111) *Drunkenness Committee*, p. vi–vii.

[8] (p. 112) Quo. from J. S. Buckingham, *History & Progress of the Temperance Reformation* (1854) p. 562; cf. p. 559.

[9] (p. 112) Ashley, *3 Hansard 67*, c. 62 (28 Feb. 1843).

[10] (p. 112) J. Harris, *The Christian Citizen* (1837), pp. 71–2.

[11] (p. 112) J. W. Green, *Metropolitan Temperance Intelligencer*, 25 Feb. 1843, p. 60.

[12] (p. 112) Quo. from *British & Foreign Temperance Herald*, Apr. 1834, p. 39; see also *ibid.*, May 1834, p. 52; *The Record*, 22 May 1834.

[13] (p. 113) B.F.T.S. *11th Annual Report*, *1842*, p. 20; for the Society's early disappointments see B.F.T.S. *2nd Annual Report*, *1833*, pp. 8–9.

[14] (p. 113) For criticisms of the B.F.T.S., see *Temperance Magazine and Review*, Dec. 1832, p. 296; Feb. 1833, p. 365; May 1833, p. 87. For Cruikshanks, see *ibid.*, Aug. 1832, p. 188; Dec. 1832, p. 296.

[15] (p. 113) *Moral Reformer*, 1 Aug. 1833, p. 257 (at Bolton).

[16] (p. 113) *Preston Temperance Advocate*, Sept. 1835, p. 66.

[17] (p. 113) W. Wilberforce, *Practical View* [of the Prevailing System of Professed Christians] (3rd edn, 1797), p. 290; Brougham, *3 Hansard 47*, c. 1236 (3 June 1839).

[18] (p. 114) R. Macnish, *The Anatomy of Drunkenness* (5th edn, Glasgow, 1834), p. 285.

[19] (p. 114) Swindlehurst, *Star of Temperance* (Manchester), 19 Nov. 1836, p. 369; R. Young's *Drunkard's Character* quo. in R. Hunter & I. McAlpine, *op. cit.*, p. 117.

[20] (p. 114) Anon, *Life & Poems of Henry Anderton* (1867), p. 78.

[21] (p. 115) *Report of the Public Meeting of the Leeds Temperance Society . . . 21st June*

1836 to Consider the Propriety of Adopting the Total Abstinence Pledge as the Exclusive Principle of the Society (Leeds, 1836), p. 18.

[22] (p. 115) *Address of the Hibernian Temperance Society to their Countrymen* (Dublin, 1830), p. 4; cf. Plint, in Leeds Temperance Society, *First Annual Report, 1831*, pp. 15–16; B.F.T.S. *First Annual Report, 1832*, p. 15; J. R. Gusfield, *Symbolic Crusade. Status Politics and the American Temperance Movement* (Urbana, 1963), pp. 40–1.

[23] (p. 115) C. H. Firth & R. S. Rait, *op. cit.*, II, p. 1050; for excommunication, see H. Davies, *The Worship of the English Puritans* (1948), p. 235. I owe the latter reference to Dr. Walsh; see also L. B. Wright, *Middle-Class Culture in Elizabethan England* (1958 edn), p. 194.

[24] (p. 115) For Livesey & Whittaker, see J. Pearce, *Livesey*, pp. cxxxv, cxlvii–cxlix; T. Whittaker, *Life's Battles*, p. 102; for Gough, see his autobiography, printed as *Ipswich Temperance Tract No. 132*, p. 24; for processions, see *Star of Temperance* (Manchester), 26 Sept. 1835, p. 22; *Journal of the N.B.F.T.S.*, 27 June 1840, p. 211; *The Times*, 9 June 1840, p. 4.

[25] (p. 116) For obesity, see *The Way to Make All People Rich*, p. 26; T. Tryon, *The Way to Health, Long Life & Happiness* (1683), pp. 54, 532.

[26] (p. 117) W. A. Pallister, *Essays, Chiefly on the Temperance Question* (1849), p. 8; Dawson Burns, *Temperance History*, I, p. 63.

[27] (p. 117) J. Pearce, *Livesey*, pp. 27–8; Bury Public Library, *Hewitson Scrapbooks*, III, p. 497.

[28] (p. 117) For early Preston teetotalism, see W. Pilkington, *The Makers of Wesleyan Methodism in Preston* (1890), pp. 182–3; T. Walmsley, *Reminiscences of the Preston Cockpit & the Old Teetotalers* (Preston, 1892), p. 17; *Temperance Spectator*, Jan. 1859, pp. 7–10; E. Grubb, *The Temperance & Other Poems of the late Henry Anderton* (Preston, 1863), *passim*; F. R. Lees, 'Memoir of James Teare', prefaced to F. Powell, *Bacchus Dethroned* (n.d.), p. iii; T. Whittaker, *Life's Battles*, p. 16; W. Pilkington, *Facts about the Origin of the Teetotal Principle and Pledge* (Preston, 1894), pp. 25ff.

[29] (p. 117) *Preston Chronicle*, 2 Apr., 1 Oct. 1831.

[30] (p. 118) T. Whittaker, *Life's Battles*, pp. 35–6.

[31] (p. 118) Livesey quotation in *Preston Chronicle*, 29 Sept. 1832. For Livesey's religious views, see F. Coupe, *Walton-le-Dale. A History of the Village* (Preston, 1954), pp. 155–6; J. Pearce, *Livesey*, pp. xiff.; *Moral Reformer*, 1 Mar. 1831, p. 88.

[32] (p. 118) J. Pearce, *Livesey*, p. xx.

[33] (p. 118) Quotations from J. Pearce, *Livesey*, p. 31; *Livesey's Moral Reformer*, 24 Feb. 1838, p. 60. For Livesey on personal visitation, see *Livesey's Moral Reformer*, 6 Jan. 1838, p. 3; 27 Jan. 1838, p. 29.

[34] (p. 118) Quo. from the offprint of Livesey's published letter dated 2 Feb. 1830 in P.R.O., H.O. 44/119; see also Anon, *Life & Poems of Henry Anderton*, p. 63; cf. *Livesey's Moral Reformer*, May 1838, p .106; *Preston Chronicle*, 18 Jan. 1834; *Preston Guardian*, 10 Feb. 1844.

[35] (p. 119) Quotations from *Preston Chronicle*, 21 June 1834; *Preston Pilot*, 5 Dec. 1835; cf. Pigot & Co, *National Commercial Directory, 1834*, p. 512. For teetotal claims, see *Preston Chronicle*, 12 Dec. 1835.

[36] (p. 119) R. C. O. Matthews, *op. cit.*, pp. 134–6; *Preston Guardian*, 30 Nov. 1844, p. 2; H. Ashworth, *The Preston Strike* (1854), p. 66.

[37] (p. 119) H. Carter, *The English Temperance Movement: A Study in Objectives. Vol. 1., The Formative Period* (1933), [henceforth cited as *English Temperance Movement*—no more volumes were published], p. 24.

[38] (p. 119) Livesey, *Drunkenness Committee*, Q. 1055; cf., *ibid.*, QQ. 1002, 1123; for the statistics, see Pigot & Co, *National Commercial Directory, 1834*, pp. 512–20.

[39] (p. 119) Quo. from *Moral Reformer*, 1 Jan. 1831, p. 26; cf. *ibid.*, 1 Apr. 1831, p. 117; 1 May 1831, p. 149. See also P.R.O., H.O. 44/119 (offprint of Livesey's letter, dated 2 Feb. 1830).

[40] (p. 119) *Preston Pilot*, 2 July 1831; *Preston Chronicle*, 2 & 9 July, 20 Aug. 1831.

[41] (p. 119) J. Pearce, *Livesey*, p. lxxv, and his letter in P.R.O., H.O. 44/119.

[42] (p. 119) *Moral Reformer*, 1 July 1831, p. 207; *Weekly Record*, 24 May 1862, p. 193.

[43] (p. 120) This account is based on J. Pearce, *Livesey*, p. lxxix; *The Youthful Teetotaler*

(Preston), June 1836, p. 43; *Moral Reformer*, 1 Jan. 1832. p. 25; 1 Feb. 1832, p. 58; J. Finch *Teetotalism* (Liverpool, 1836), pp. 4–6; J. Teare, *History of the Origin & Success of the Advocacy of . . . Total Abstinence* (1847), p. 9; J. Livesey, *Reminiscences of Early Teetotalism* (Preston, n.d.), p. 4.

[44] (p. 120) For Jackson, *Moral Reformer*, 1 Apr. 1832, p. 110; for Blackburn, *Temperance Society Record*, June 1831, p. 126; J. Livesey, *Reminiscences*, p. 4; for Pollard, *Moral Reformer*, 1 Apr. 1832, p. 123.

[45] (p. 120) For Brodbelt, see J. Pearce, *Livesey*, p. lxxix; for Swindlehurst, *Preston Chronicle*, 26 & 29 Jan. 1883; J. Finch, *Teetotalism*, p. 6; for Teare, *Alliance Weekly News*, 22 June 1861, p. 1224; J. Teare, *Origin & Success*, pp. 16, 19; J. Stephenson, J. Dearden & G. Toulmin, *The Origin & Success of Teetotalism* (Preston, 1864), p. 20; see also the heated controversy in *Alliance News*, 1863, pp. 277, 293, 301, 309, 317, 325, 334, 341 & *Preston Temperance Advocate*, Dec. 1837, p. 92.

[46] (p. 120) J. Pearce, *Livesey*, p. 81.

[47] (p. 121) T. Lythgoe, *Biographical Key*, p. 84; J. Teare, *Origin & Success*, p. 21; *Moral Reformer*, 1 Apr. 1833, p. 124; J. Pearce, *Livesey*, p. lxxxix. Unless otherwise stated, all quotations from the lecture are from the edition published as No. 133 of the *Ipswich Temperance Tracts;* this edition differs in some important respects from the version appended to J. Pearce's *Livesey*. Important divergences between these two versions have been noted in the text.

[48] (p. 122) Whiskey quotation from p. 10 of the Pearce edn of Livesey's *Malt Lecture*. For the lecturer in Wales, see *Star of Temperance*, 10 Dec. 1836, p. 398.

[49] (p. 124) N. Longmate, *King Cholera. The Biography of a Disease* (1966), pp. 165, 206–7, 235.

[50] (p. 125) King is quo. in T. Lythgoe, *Biographical Key*, p. 84; cf. *Alliance News*, 10 Oct. 1863, p. 325. For the gradual spread of Livesey's ideas, see *Preston Temperance Advocate*, Apr. 1836, p. 6 (supplement); W. Livesey, *The Earliest Days of the Teetotal Movement* (privately printed, 1900, unpaginated); J. Livesey, *Malt, Malt Liquor, Malt Tax, Beer, & Barley* (n.d.), p. 12; U.K.A. *23rd Annual Report, 1874–5*, p. 24.

[51] (p. 125) J. Teare, *Origin & Success*, p. 19; J. Dearden, *A Brief History of the Commencement & Success of Teetotalism* (Preston, n.d.), p. 20; W. Pilkington, *Facts about the Origin of the Teetotal Principle and Pledge* (Preston, 1894), p. 28; T. Lythgoe, *Biographical Key*, p. 84.

[52] (p. 126) Dawson Burns, *Temperance History*, I, p. 73. There was much controversy about the origins of the term: see *Notes & Queries*, 1853, 1858, 1876 etc. *Meliora*, June 1864, pp. 2–3; J. Pearce, *Livesey*, p. 65; J. Teare, *Origin & Success*, p. 26.

[53] (p. 126) *Moral Reformer*, 1 Aug. 1833, pp. 254–8; cf. N. McCord, *The Anti-Corn Law League 1838–1846* (1958), p. 37.

[54] (p. 126) H. Freeman, *History of the Total Abstinence Pledge Question*, pp. 6ff.

[55] (p. 126) *Preston Temperance Advocate*, July 1834, p. 53; W. Logan, *Early Heroes*, pp. 94–5; W. Pilkington, *Facts about the Origin of the Teetotal Principle & Pledge*, pp. 37ff.; J. Pearce, *Livesey*, p. 70; cf. *Northern Star*, 21 Dec. 1850, p. 4.

[56] (p. 126) *Preston Chronicle*, 12 Dec. 1835; *Record*, 23 May 1839, p. 3; for membership figures, see *Preston Temperance Advocate*, supplement for Apr. 1835, p. 5.

[57] (p. 126) Cf. H. D. Lasswell, *Psychopathology & Politics* (Chicago, 1930), p. 125.

[58] (p. 126) J. Livesey, *Malt Lecture*, p. 29; *Preston Temperance Advocate*, Sept. 1835, p. 65; cf. C.N.D., discussed in *New Statesman*, 1 Jan. 1965, p. 14.

Chapter 6. Moderationists Versus Teetotalers: 1834–1848 [pp. 127–146].

[1] (p. 129) Sir G. Head, *A Home Tour through the Manufacturing Districts of England* (1836), pp. 411–15; Joseph Taylor, in *Temperance Star*, 22 July 1870, p. 3; [T. Wright], *Some Habits & Customs of the Working Classes* (1867), pp. 138–48.

[2] (p. 129) F. Butterfield, *The Life and Sayings of Thomas Worsnop* (Bingley, 1870), p. 72; J. A. Hammerton, *Trial & Triumph: A Life & its Lessons; being a Biographical Sketch of Robert Dransfield* (2nd edn, Glasgow, 1892), p. 48; cf. B.M. *Add. MSS.* 43658 (Cobden Papers), f. 169: Cobden to Henry Richard, n.d. (c. 22 Oct. 1856).

[3] (p. 130) *Rechabite Magazine*, Oct. 1843, p. 154.

[4] (p. 130) F. Butterfield, *Thomas Worsnop*, p. 15; Carlyle's comment comes from a letter printed in an unidentifiable periodical in Mr. Henry Turney's collection of material on Chelsea Temperance Society.

[5] (p. 130) J. H. Leuba, 'A Study in the Psychology of Religious Phenomena', *American Journal of Psychology*, VII, No. 3 (Apr. 1896) p. 343; cf. W. James, *The Varieties of Religious Experience*, p. 207.

[6] (p. 131) *Banbury Guardian*, 15 Mar. 1849.

[7] (p. 131) *Star of Temperance*, 12 Sept. 1835, p. 7; for other examples of temperance confessions, see T. Hudson, *Temperance Pioneers of the West* (1887), pp. 49ff.; *Weekly Record*, 17 Nov. 1860, pp. 486–8.

[8] (p. 132) William Smith, in *Report of the Speeches Delivered at the Temperance Festival, held in the Cloth-Hall, Colne . . . 1836* (Leeds, 1836), p. 23; Turner, *Leeds Temperance Herald* (Leeds), 1 Apr. 1837, p. 54. For a fine example of the frightened teetotal mentality, see W. R. Lambert, *op. cit.*, p. 441.

[9] (p. 132) *Memoir of William Smith* (1904); this MS. was brought to my attention by Mr. Barrie Trinder. This is not of course the same 'William Smith' who spoke at the Colne temperance festival.

[10] (p. 132) *The Templar of Wales*, I, No. 9 (6 Sept. 1873), quo. in W. R. Lambert, *op. cit.*, p. 134.

[11] (p. 133) For Chartism, see B.M. *Add. MSS.* 34,245A: General Convention of the Industrial Classes 1839, I, f. 108: T. C. Salt to W. Lovett, postmarked 8 & 9 Mar. 1839; cf. P. Thompson, *Socialists, Liberals & Labour. The Struggle for London 1885–1914* (1967), p. 232.

[12] (p. 134) J. Dunlop, *Autobiography*, p. 139 (under Jan. 1840); T. Whittaker, *Life's Battles*, p. 373. For Cassell, see H. Vizetelly, *Glances Back Through Seventy Years* (1893), II, p. 51; for Turner, *Preston Temperance Advocate*, Oct. 1837, p. 79.

[13] (p. 134) B.F.T.S. *6th Annual Report, 1837*, p. 40; cf. *Preston Pilot*, 4 & 11 Oct. 1834.

[14] (p. 134) T. Whittaker, *Life's Battles*, p. 130. For false Christs, see *Star of Temperance*, 23 Apr. 1836, p. 135; T. Hudson, *Temperance Pioneers of the West*, p. 243; M. Klein, *A Brief Outline of the Life of Magnus Klein* (1837), p. 23; *British Temperance Advocate*, 1 Mar. 1871, p. 815. For Lees, see his discussion with Rev. J. Bromley, *British Temperance Advocate*, Dec. 1840 (advertisement sheet).

[15] (p. 135) Quotations from *London Temperance Tracts*, 1839 (unpaginated tract entitled 'Temperate Drinking the Chief Cause of Drunkenness'); cf. B.F.T.S. *10th Annual Report, 1841*, p. 62; & from F. Lees, *Dr. Frederic Richard Lees* (1904), p. 236.

[16] (p. 135) Mrs. C. L. Wightman, *Haste to the Rescue!* (1862), p. 46.

[17] (p. 136) The Leeds incident is reported in *Leeds Times* (Leeds), 15 June 1839: I am most grateful to Robert Storch of Wisconsin for referring me to it. For Huddersfield, see *National Temperance Advocate*, 16 Oct. 1843, p. 129; for Wychwood Forest, see *British & Foreign Temperance Intelligencer*, 26 June 1841; for Bermondsey, see J. F. Maguire, *Father Mathew: A Biography* (2nd edn, 1864), pp. 283–4. Fulham publicans also tried to rouse opposition to Father Mathew—see Rev. Father Augustine, *Footprints of Father Theobald Mathew* (Dublin, 1947), p. 294. For Preston, see *Preston Pilot*, 1 June 1833.

[18] (p. 136) J. Dunlop, *Autobiography*, p. 288.

[19] (p. 136) Quo. in Judge Parry, *Drink & Industrial Unrest* (1919), p. 5.

[20] (p. 137) R. J. White (Ed.), *Political Tracts of Wordsworth, Coleridge & Shelley* (Cambridge, 1953), pp. 70ff.

[21] (p. 137) Quotation from J. Finch, *Teetotalism* (1836), p. 6; cf. *Preston Pilot*, 30 Mar. 1833; for Leeds, see Leeds Temperance Society *MS Minute Book*, and information in *Biographia Leodiensis* (1865), with supplement, Ed. R. V. Taylor, 1867. For Blackburn, see W. E. Moss, *op. cit.*, pp. 8–11.

[22] (p. 138) *Report of the Public Meeting of the Leeds Temperance Society . . .* (1836), p. 37; cf. *ibid.*, p. 17.

[23] (p. 138) Livesey, *Moral Reformer*, 1 Aug. 1833, p. 253; cf. *London Temperance Intelligencer*, 3 June 1837, p. 232. For Stanhope, see the Bodleian Library's *Stanhope-Burtt Correspondence*, a valuable volume of MS. letters, 1839–40, to which Mr. Porter of Duke

Humphrey's Library kindly referred me. See also M. Duverger, *Political Parties*, p. 26; Kornhauser, 'Social Bases of Political Commitment: A Study of Liberals & Radicals', in A. M. Rose (Ed.), *Human Behaviour and Social Processes* (1962), pp. 332, 338.

[24] (p. 138) For Warrington, see A. Mounfield, *op. cit.*, pp. 23–7; for Preston, *Preston Pilot*, 18 May 1833; *Preston Chronicle*, 17 Jan. 1835. For Middlesbrough Temperance Society, *Souvenir 1836–1936* (Middlesbrough, 1936), p. 10. For Kendal, see Kendal District Society for the Suppression of Intemperance, *Full Report of the Proceedings . . . 1836* (n.d). For Leeds, see *Report of the Public Meeting of the Leeds Temperance Society . . .* (1836), p. 37.

[25] (p. 139) Quotations from J. Bright, *Alliance News*, 27 Mar. 1880, p. 195; E. W. Edgell, 'Moral Statistics of Parishes in Westminster', *Transactions of the Royal Statistical Society*, I (1838), p. 482. For Whittaker, see his *Life's Battles*, p. 97. The lists are as follows:

(*a*) the 82 of the first 100 signatories in Derby Temperance Society *MS. Register* (*in situ*) from 1836 whose occupations are listed.

(*b*) the 242 of the first 1,000 signatories in Aberystwyth Temperance Society *Register 1836–38* whose occupations are listed (National Library of Wales, MS. 8324D—microfilm copy).

(*c*) 131 teetotalers at Oswestry, *Journal of the N.B.F.T.S.*, 9 Mar. 1840, pp. 145–6.

(*d*) 486 male teetotalers in Middlesbrough, 1851, in *Bristol Temperance Herald*, Apr. 1851, p. 59; in addition, there were 368 female and 378 child teetotalers. Middlesbrough's total population at this time is listed as 7,000–8,000.

(*e*) 343 reformed drunkards attending a tea at Manchester in 1860, *Temperance Spectator*, 1 Dec. 1860, p. 181.

More of these registers are analysed, and similar conclusions are drawn, in W. R. Lambert, *op. cit.*, pp. 123ff.

[26] (p. 140) For Morris, see *Weekly Record*, 3 Oct. 1857, p. 347; for developments in London in 1836, see *Journal of the N.B.F.T.S.*, 1 June 1839, p. 198.

[27] (p. 140) Cf. B.M. *Add. MSS.* 43677 (Cobden Papers), f. 31, Cobden to C. D. Collet, 28 Aug. 1853.

[28] (p. 140) *The Times*, 24 July 1839, p. 5; Hetherington, *Odd-Fellow*, 25 May 1839, p. 82.

[29] (p. 142) S.C.H.C. on Postage, second report, *Parl. Papers* 1837–8 (658), XX, Part 2, Q. 8056.

[30] (p. 142) *Journal of the N.B.F.T.S.*, 25 May 1839, pp. 182–4.

[31] (p. 142) *Temperance Spectator*, Dec. 1859, p. 181; see also C. Buxton, *Life of T. F. Buxton*, p. 247; R. Strachey, '*The Cause*', pp. 281–2.

[32] (p. 142) L. Coser, *The Functions of Social Conflict* (1956), p. 68.

[33] (p. 143) W. Lovett, *Life & Struggles*, p. 68–9; A. Bullock, *The Life and Times of Ernest Bevin*, I (1960), p. 160; cf. B. G. M. Sundkler, *Bantu Prophets in South Africa* (2nd edn, 1961), p. 100.

[34] (p. 143) Quo. in *The Times*, 3 Oct. 1839.

[35] (p. 143) *British & Foreign Temperance Intelligencer*, 18 May 1839, p. 186 discusses the manœuvres before the annual meeting; quotation from *ibid.*, 15th June 1839, p. 226.

[36] (p. 143) J. Dunlop, *The Universal Tendency to Association in Mankind Analyzed and Illustrated* (1840), pp. 188–93, 225–7; cf. *Nonconformist*, 15 Nov. 1843, p. 777.

[37] (p. 144) Stanhope, *New British & Foreign Temperance Intelligencer*, 26 May 1838, p. 171.

[38] (p. 144) Delavan, *Journal of the N.B.F.T.S.*, 1 June 1839, p. 198.

[39] (p. 144) *British & Foreign Temperance Intelligencer*, 1 June 1839, p. 214; cf. E. O. Tuttle, *The Crusade Against Capital Punishment in Great Britain* (1961), p. 14.

[40] (p. 145) Cf. R. Strachey, '*The Cause*', pp. 277, 282.

[41] (p. 145) Cf. A. Bullock, *Ernest Bevin*, I, p. 189.

[42] (p. 145) *National Temperance Advocate*, 16 Jan. 1843, pp. 7–8.

[43] (p. 145) J. Dunlop, *Autobiography*, pp. 320, 325.

[44] (p. 146) Bishop of Norwich, B.F.T.S. *11th Annual Report*, *1842*, pp. 14, 18. For other evangelical charities, see G. M. Ellis, 'The Evangelicals and the Sunday Question, 1830–1860. Organized Sabbatarianism as an Aspect of the Evangelical Movement' (Harvard unpublished Ph.D. thesis, 1951), appendix A.

[45] (p. 146) B.F.T.S. *13th Annual Report, 1844*, p. 22; cf. *10th Annual Report, 1841*, p. 11; *14th Annual Report, 1845*, p. 3; *16th Annual Report*, p. 11; cf. *Carlisle Journal* (Carlisle), 21 Dec. 1839, p. 3; *Northern Star*, 28 Nov. 1840, p. 6.

[46] (p. 146) Quotation from Herzen's discussion of British philanthropic bodies, in M. Richter, *The Politics of Conscience* (1964), pp. 299–300; cf. *Star of Temperance*, 5 Nov. 1836, p. 355.

[47] (p. 146) Quotations from *Temperance Penny Magazine*, Dec. 1848, pp. 177, 179. For Owen Clarke's troublesome last years as Baptist minister of a small Kensington chapel, see *Temperance Spectator*, 1859, p. 24.

Chapter 7. The Teetotal Leadership: A Biographical Analysis: 1833–1872 [pp. 147–178]

[1] (p. 148) Christopher Hill, 'Puritans & the Dark Corners of the Land', *Trans. Royal Historical Society*, 1963, *passim*; L. Stone, 'Literacy & Education in England 1640–1900', *Past & Present*, No. 42 (Feb. 1969), p. 120.

[2] (p. 148) J. C. Farn, *Reasoner*, 21 Oct. 1857, p. 236.

[3] (p. 149) J. G. Shaw, *William Gregson*, p. 41.

[4] (p. 149) Lowery, *Weekly Record*, 25 Oct. 1856, p. 250; cf. *National Temperance Advocate*, 1846, p. 93.

[5] (p. 149) M. Rutherford, *The Revolution in Tanner's Lane*, p. 366, cf. p. 370; for America, see A. Sinclair, *Prohibition* (1962), pp. 38ff.

[6] (p. 149) Marx & Engels, *Selected Works* (2 Vol. edn, Moscow, 1962), I, p. 38; cf. *ibid.*, p. 54. For anti-feudalism in the temperance movement, see *Weekly Record*, 14 Dec. 1861, p. 467; *Temperance Penny Magazine* (Manchester), 8 Aug. 1835, p. 14; *British & Foreign Temperance Intelligencer*, 10 Apr. 1841, p. 113.

[7] (p. 149) G. W. Knighton, in *Temperance Weekly Journal*, 28 July 1843, p. 244.

[8] (p. 151) Quotations from S. Smiles, *Self-Help* (1884 edn), p. 292; R. Currie, *Methodism Divided. A Study in the Sociology of Ecumenicalism* (1968), p. 46. See also T. Mackay (Ed.), *Autobiography of Samuel Smiles* (1905), pp. 161, 164.

[9] (p. 152) N.T.L. *Annual Report 1859*, p. 23; for Wilson, see W. S. Fowler, *A Study in Radicalism & Dissent. The Life & Times of Henry Joseph Wilson 1833–1914* (1961), p. 54.

[10] (p. 154) For Atkin, see Livesey-Clegg House, Sheffield, *British Temperance League General Purposes Committee MS. Minutes*, 26 June 1866; J. S. Balmer, *Biographical Sketch of John Clegg Booth, Late Temperance Advocate* (York, 1874), p. 43. For rebukes, see *B.T.L. General Purposes Committee MS. Minutes*, 10 May 1860, 18 Sept. 1871. For Duxbury, see *ibid.*, 10 & 24 Mar. 1868.

[11] (p. 154) For Matthias, see *ibid.*, 26 Feb., 12 Mar. 1861; but see *ibid.*, 11 June, 16 July 1861. For Booth, see *ibid.*, 21 Jan. 1873.

[12] (p. 154) J. F. C. Harrison, in Asa Briggs (Ed.), *Chartist Studies* (1959), p. 142. For Gough, see *Banbury Guardian*, 15 July 1858; for Lees, see Livesey-Clegg House, Sheffield, N.T.L. *MS. Minutes*, 10 Oct. 1856.

[13] (p. 155) See the remarks of J. W. Pease, in S.C.H.L. on Intemperance, third report, *Parl. Papers* 1877 (418), XI, Q. 8490.

[14] (p. 157) *National Temperance Chronicle*, June 1845, p. 382.

[15] (p. 158) W. Bagehot, 'The Death of Lord Brougham', in *Collected Works* (Ed. N. St. J. Stevas), III (1968), p. 196; for Grubb, see J. G. Shaw, *op. cit.*, p. 19. For Dransfield, see J. A. Hammerton, *Trial & Triumph*, p. 71; cf. T. Whittaker, *Life's Battles*, p. 231.

[16] (p. 159) Quo. from Leeds Temperance Society, *MS. Minute Book No. 2: 1845–1851*, minutes for 5 Apr. 1849; cf. Joseph Barker, *Life*, p. 234; for Cook, see *Truth Tester, Temperance Advocate & Healthian Journal*, I, p. 43 (20 Aug. 1846); P. T. Winskill, *Temperance Movement*, I, pp. 188, 199; II, p. 107. For anti-smoking in temperance tracts, see e.g., Scottish Temperance League, *Pictorial Tracts*, No. 24, p. 2; No. 76, p. 3; *Ipswich Temperance Tract*, No. 91; *London Temperance Tract*, No. 15, p. 3; No. 35, p. 1.

[17] (p. 159) J. S. Mill quo. in J. M. Robson, *The Improvement of Mankind* (1968), p. 269; cf. Ray Strachey, *Millicent Garrett Fawcett* (1931), p. 161.

[18] (p. 161) Stanhope quotation from the Bodleian Library's *Stanhope-Burtt Correspondence*: Stanhope to Burtt, 9 July, 24 Nov. 1839; see also Aubrey Newman, *The Stanhopes of Chevening* (1969). Faulkener quotation from *Temperance Star*, 12 Aug. 1870, p. 3.

[19] (p. 161) A. A. Reade, *Study & Stimulants* (Manchester, 1883), p. 115.

[20] (p. 162) Quotations from Fawcett Library, Westminster, *Josephine Butler Collection*: Josephine Butler to Mr. Edmondson, 30 Jan. 1872; G. W. E. Russell, *Basil Wilberforce. A Memoir* (1917), p. 55; for Newman, see A. A. Reade, *Study & Stimulants*, p. 111; for Lawson—W. Lawson, *Wit & Wisdom* (2nd edn, 1886), p. 98; for Manning, A. W. Hutton, *Cardinal Manning* (1892), p. 248. See also 'Theories of Parliamentary Reform', in *Oxford Essays, Contributed by Members of the University* (1858), p. 55. The anti-vaccination movement is excellently analysed in R. M. McLeod, 'Law, Medicine and Public Opinion: the Resistance to Compulsory Health Legislation 1870–1907', *Public Law*, 1967.

[21] (p. 162) B.M. *Add. MSS.* 43650 (Cobden Papers), f. 197: Cobden to Bright, 21 Mar. 1856; J. Pearce, *Livesey*, pp. 54, 91.

[22] (p. 162) J. Pearce, *Livesey*, p. cxlvii; cf. J. F. Rutter, *1890: Jubilee of the Mere Temperance Society* (Mere, n.d.), p. 24.

[23] (p. 162) H. D. Thoreau, *Walden* (London, 1906 edn), p. 91.

[24] (p. 163) See H. J. Hanham's excellent 'Liberal Organisations for Working Men. 1860–1914', *Bulletin of the Society for the Study of Labour History*, No. 7 (Autumn 1963), pp. 5–7.

[25] (p. 164) Faulkener, *Temperance Star*, 12 Aug. 1870, p. 3; for Gregson, see J. G. Shaw, *op. cit.*, pp. 31–8.

[26] (p. 164) *National Temperance Advocate*, 1847, p. 95.

[27] (p. 164) *Meliora. A Quarterly Review of Social Science* (Manchester), II, No. 7, p. 257.

[28] (p. 165) G. W. M. Reynolds' complaint, in *The Teetotaler*, 12 June 1841, p. 60.

[29] (p. 165) Draft letter, n.d., in *Capuchin Archives*, Raheny, Dublin.

[30] (p. 166) *British Temperance Advocate*, 1 Feb. 1870, p. 707; for William Lucas, see G. E. Bryant & G. P. Baker (Eds.), *A Quaker Journal* (1933), I, p. 160 (17 Mar. 1839).

[31] (p. 166) G. P. Gooch, *Life of Lord Courtney* (1920), pp. 6, 10, 13, for the influence of the Fox family in Cornwall.

[32] (p. 167) Father Mathew quoted in a letter from Harriet Edgeworth to her brother M. Pakenham Edgeworth (in India) 27 Mar. 1841 (punctuation inserted): I owe this reference to Mrs. Christina Colvin. See also H. Solly, *'These Eighty Years', or The Story of an Unfinished Life* (1893), II, p. 2; C. Booth, *Life & Labour in London, Third Series*, VII (1902 edn), pp. 20–1; W. R. Lambert, *op. cit.*, pp. 203ff.

[33] (p. 168) Quotations from J. L. Watson, *Life of Thomas Guthrie* (Edinburgh, 1880), p. 31; *New British & Foreign Temperance Intelligencer*, 10 Nov. 1838, p. 364 (for Chelsea). On the general question of religious sects and urban immigrants, see J. B. Holt, 'Holiness Religion', *American Sociological Review*, 1940, p. 746; I. G. Jones, in G. Williams (Ed.), *Merthyr Politics* (Cardiff, 1966), p. 52. For Welsh temperance societies, see P. T. Winskill, *Temperance Movement & its Workers*, I, p. 75.

[34] (p. 168) For Catholics, see H. Mayhew, *London Labour*, I, p. 21; *Preston Temperance Advocate*, Aug. 1834, p. 64; *Teetotaler*, 12 June 1841, p. 60; for Barnsley, see Eli Hoyle, *History of Barnsley* (Barnsley, 1924), article 161; for Father Mathew, J. F. Maguire, *Father Mathew*, pp. 129–30; P. Rogers, *Father Theobald Mathew* (Dublin, 1944), p. 86. For a full account of Father Mathew's visits, see Father Augustine, *Footprints of Father Theobald Mathew*, Chs. 23, 27, 28.

[35] (p. 169) Quotation from H. B. Kendall, *The Origin & History of the Primitive Methodist Church* (n.d.), I, p. 7. For Smiles, see K. Fielden, 'Samuel Smiles and Self-Help', *Victorian Studies*, Dec. 1968, p. 166.

[36] (p. 170) J. C. Buckmaster (Ed.), *A Village Politician. The Life-Story of John Buckley* (1897), p. 85.

[37] (p. 170) For Rochdale, see D. A. Gowland, 'Rochdale Politics & Methodist Schism', *Wesley Historical Society, Lancashire and Cheshire Branch, Occasional Publication No. 1* (1965), p. 2; I owe this reference to Mr. Barrie Trinder. For the title 'revd.' see E. Grubb, *Henry Anderton*, p. xxxi.

[38] (p. 170) T. Whittaker, *Life's Battles*, p. 312.

[39] (p. 171) E. T. Davies, *Religion in the Industrial Revolution in South Wales*, p. 40.

[40] (p. 171) C. Booth, *Life & Labour in London, Third Series*, V (1902 edn), p. 155.

[41] (p. 171) E. T. Davies, *op. cit.*, p. 62.

[42] (p. 171) T. Whittaker, *Life's Battles*, p. 131; cf. *Preston Temperance Advocate*, June 1836, p. 50; N.B.F.T.S. *3rd Annual Report, 1839*, p. 64.

[43] (p. 171) Quotation from *Meliora*, II, no. 7, p. 257; for Wilsden, *Preston Temperance Advocate*, Mar. 1835, p. 20. For 1859 revivals, see N.T.L. *Annual Report, 1860–1*, p. 7; cf. C. R. Williams, 'The Welsh Religious Revival, 1904–5', *British Journal of Sociology*, 1952, *passim;* W. R. Lambert, *op cit.*, p. 194.

[44] (p. 172) T. Okey, *A Basketful of Memories* (1930), p. 7; cf. S. Fleming, *Children & Puritanism* (Yale, 1933), pp. 60, 160–1; cf. T. Whittaker, *op. cit.*, p. 16.

[45] (p. 172) Rev. H. Marles, *Life & Labours of Jabez Tunnicliff* (1865), p. 8.

[46] (p. 173) Bent, in T. Lythgoe, *Biographical Key*, p. 213; Rowntree in *Annual Monitor*, 1860, p. 213; Mason, in W. Logan, *Early Heroes of the Temperance Reformation* (Glasgow, 1873), p. 106. For Tabraham, see *ibid.*, p. 106. For conversion-experiences in other important temperance reformers, see G. W. E. Russell, *Sir Wilfrid Lawson* (1909), p. 3; E. Baines, *Life of Edward Baines* (1851), chapter 20.

[47] (p. 173) For Finch, see P. T. Winskill & J. Thomas, *History of the Temperance Movement in Liverpool & District*, p. 39; cf. *New Moral World & Manual of Science*, 2 Dec. 1837, pp. 47–8. For temperance attitudes to infidelity, see *Northern Star*, 24 Feb. 1844, p. 3; J. Lawson, *Pudsey*, pp. 111–12.

[48] (p. 173) For Empson, see *New Moral World*, IV (1838), p. 189; I owe this reference to Mrs. Eileen Yeo of Sussex University. Festival quotation from *London Teetotal Magazine*, Sept. 1840, p. 286.

[49] (p. 173) F. Parkin, *Middle Class Radicalism* (Manchester, 1968), p. 3, cf. pp. 5, 39, 41.

[50] (p. 175) Helen Blackburn, *Women's Suffrage* (1902), pp. 96ff.; P. T. Winskill, *Temperance Movement & its Workers*, II, pp. 80, 262; Rev. J. M. J. Fletcher, *Mrs. Wightman of Shrewsbury*, pp. 105–7; J. D. Hilton, *A Brief Memoir of James Hayes Raper* (1898), p. 150.

[51] (p. 175) e.g. *Ipswich Temperance Tract, No. 43*, p. 4; *No. 78*, p. 12; cf. Benjamin Parsons, in J. S. Buckingham (Ed.), *The Temperance Offering* (1852), p. 31.

[52] (p. 176) Quotations from Livesey, in *The Struggle* (Preston), No. 63 (undated); & Sussex County Record Office, *Cobden Papers No. 1*; letter to Cobden, 14 Feb. 1842. For circulation figures, see J. Pearce, *op. cit.*, p. lxii. For praise of Livesey by League leaders, see *Preston Guardian* (Preston), 9 Mar. 1844, p. 2; *The League*, No. 68 (11 Jan. 1845), p. 246.

[53] (p. 176) For rural lectures, see *Anti-Corn Law League Circular*, 5 Nov. 1840, p. 7; for banquets, see *ibid.*, 16 Jan. 1840, p. 2; Rev. W. Reid, *Temperance Memorials of the late Robert Kettle Esq.* (Glasgow, 1853), p. xlii.

[54] (p. 177) N. McCord, *Anti-Corn Law League*, p. 205; *The Struggle*, No. 235; *National Temperance Chronicle*, Apr. 1849, p. 446.

[55] (p. 177) *Anti-Corn Law Circular*, 3 Dec. 1840; cf. *Livesey's Moral Reformer*, Sept. 1838, p. 162.

[56] (p. 177) J. D. Hilton, *James Hayes Raper*, pp. 149–50.

Chapter 8. Temperance and Religion: 1828–1872 [pp. 179–195].

[1] (p. 179) *British Temperance Advocate*, 1 Jan. 1870, p. 701.

[2] (p. 179) Beaumont, *British Temperance Advocate*, 15 July 1841, p. 81; J. McCurrey, *Life of James McCurrey* (n.d.), p. 67; for Dury, see *Star of Temperance*, 14 May 1836, pp. 157–8; cf. J. G. Shaw, *William Gregson*, p. 10.

[3] (p. 179) Teetotal ministers in 1837 are listed in *London Temperance Intelligencer*, 1837, pp. 302, 343, 353, 359, 407, 458, 467; the *Bristol Temperance Herald*, Mar. 1848, p. 71, lists the ministers attending the 1848 ministerial temperance conference at Manchester. The *British Temperance Advocate*, July 1848, extra number, pp. 39ff., prints the teetotal ministers who signed the 1848 ministerial temperance certificate. See also Dawson Burns, *Temperance History*, I, p. 303.

[4] (p. 180) Quo. in W. D. Cooper, 'The Teetotal Movement, with particular reference to the North-East of England: 1835–1860' (Durham Univ. unpublished undergraduate thesis,

1968), p. 26. I am most grateful to Mr. Cooper for allowing me to read his thesis. For Congregationalism, see A. Peel, *These Hundred Years* (1931), p. 106; for Baptists, see J. McCurrey, *op. cit.*, p. 67; *London Temperance Intelligencer*, 1837, pp. 15, 55, 92.

[5] (p. 180) For the Methodist New Connexion, see S. Hulme, *Memoir of the Rev. William Cooke D.D.* (1886), p. 44; I owe this reference to Mr. Barrie Trinder. For Methodists, see W. J. Townsend, H. B. Workman & G. Eayrs, *A New History of Methodism* (1909), I, p. 465; J. McCurrey, *op. cit.*, p. 67; J. Boyes, *The Early History of the Temperance Movement in Pudsey*, p. 8; P. T. Winskill, *Temperance Movement & its Workers*, II, p. 156. For Bourne, see *Star of Temperance*, 8 Oct. 1836, p. 324; cf. P. T. Winskill, *Temperance Movement & its Workers*, III, p. 7. For Calvinistic Methodists, see W. R. Lambert, *op. cit.*, p. 212.

[6] (p. 180) *New British & Foreign Temperance Intelligencer*, 10 Nov. 1838 (Chelsea); *Northern Star*, 22 Aug. 1840, p. 2 (Bradford); Eli Hoyle, *History of Barnsley*, article 161; Dawson Burns, *Temperance History*, I, pp. 177–8 (London); cf. *Teetotaler*, 12 June 1841, p. 60.

[7] (p. 180) Kendal District Society for the Suppression of Intemperance, *Full Report of the Proceedings . . . February 8, 1836*, pp. 6, 11.

[8] (p. 181) For teetotal ministers, see *Temperance Spectator*, 1 June 1866, p. 88.

[9] (p. 181) For sermons, *Weekly Record*, 7 Feb. 1863, p. 58.

[10] (p. 181) For petitions, *Weekly Record*, 1863, *passim.*

[11] (p. 181) Dawson Burns, quo. in N.T.L. *MS. Minutes*, 13 Jan. 1860; see also R. Rae, 'Temperance in the English Dissenting Colleges', in N.T.L. *Temperance Congress of 1862* (1862), pp. 55–6.

[12] (p. 181) *The Friend*, 2 June 1864, p. 141.

[13] (p. 181) W. R. Fremantle, *Memoir of the Rev. Spencer Thornton*, p. 149; cf. *ibid.*, p. 101; I owe this reference to Rev. Michael Hennell. For Ram, see *Weekly Record*, 9 May 1857, p. 157.

[14] (p. 182) *Weekly Record*, 8 Oct. 1859, p. 380.

[15] (p. 182) Dean Close, *Alliance News*, 10 May 1862, p. 147.

[16] (p. 183) For the N.T.L. contribution, see N.T.L. *Annual Report, 1862–3*, p. 38; *Weekly Record*, 25 Jan. 1862, p. 29; N.T.L. *Annual Report, 1861–2*, p. 17. For the statistics, see C[hurch] of E[ngland] T[emperance] S[ociety] *2nd Annual Report, 1864, & 4th Annual Report, 1866.*

[17] (p. 183) S.C.H.L. on Intemperance, third report, *Parl. Papers* 1877 (418), XI, QQ. 9056–7.

[18] (p. 183) *Church of England Temperance Chronicle*, 1 June 1876, p. 108; 1 July 1876, p. 124.

[19] (p. 184) The constitution was printed in *ibid.*, 1 Jan. 1873, p. 10.

[20] (p. 184) F. W. Harper, *The Parson & the Publican* (1877), p. 21; cf. *Church of England Temperance Chronicle*, 1877, pp. 126, 155. For Stephens, see *Ashton Reporter*, 13 Apr. 1867, pp. 6–7; for Fraser, see Thomas Hughes, *James Fraser* (1888 edn), p. 207.

[21] (p. 184) C. Booth, *Life & Labour in London, Third Series*, VII (1902 edn), p. 20.

[22] (p. 184) C. Gibbon, *Life of George Combe* (1878), II, p. 233; Hetherington, in M. Hovell, *The Chartist Movement*, p. 57; Holyoake, *Reasoner*, VI, No. 145, p. 145; R. Owen, *A New View of Society*, p. 32.

[23] (p. 184) *Westminster Review*, Apr. 1852, pp. 409, 419; H. B. Bonner, *Life of Charles Bradlaugh* (1902 edn), I, pp. 12, 30; G. G. Gilham, in *Reasoner*, 24 Feb. 1858, p. 63.

[24] (p. 185) Joseph Barker, *Life*, p. 207; R. Owen, *A New View of Society*, pp. 8–9; cf. E. Gosse, *Father & Son* (Penguin edn, 1949), pp. 39, 47, 50; J. Lawson, *Pudsey*, p. 53; *National Reformer*, 7 July 1860, p. 1.

[25] (p. 185) Quotations from G. W. E. Russell, *The Household of Faith* (1906), p. 234; W. Wilberforce, *Practical View*, p. 16; cf. R. W. Dale, *The Old Evangelicalism & the New* (1889), p. 29.

[26] (p. 185) *Ibid.*, p. 52; cf. R. Harrison, 'Some Aspects of Theological Thought in Nonconformity', *Primitive Methodist Quarterly Review*, VII (1885), pp. 55, 59.

[27] (p. 186) G. Osborn, *Letter to Rev. W. J. Shrewsbury* (1841), p. 14; cf. Bird, in G. Bird & P. W. Perfitt, *Public Discussion . . . Whitehaven* (3rd edn, 1847), p. 11; B. Parsons, *Anti-Bacchus* (1840), p. 1.

[28] (p. 186) F. W. Newman, *Miscellanies* (3 Vols. 1869–1889), II, p. 171; for Hebrew, see J. Dunlop, *Autobiography*, p. 120; cf. G. Clarke, *Clarke Versus Osborn* (1841), p. 17.

[29] (p. 186) Quotation from *British Temperance Advocate*, 15 Feb. 1841, p. 21; the atheist is quo. in the *Reasoner*, 17 Sept. 1854, p. 182.

[30] (p. 186) James, quo. in S. Hulme, *Memoir of Rev. William Cooke*, p. 48.

[31] (p. 186) *Temperance Penny Magazine*, Jan. 1839, pp. 3–4.

[32] (p. 186) B.F.T.S. *10th Annual Report, 1841*, p. 62.

[33] (p. 187) H. R. Murphy, 'The Ethical Revolt against Christian Orthodoxy in Early Victorian England', *American Historical Review*, July 1955, p. 801.

[34] (p. 187) On the 'scientific basis' of teetotalism, see *Rechabite Magazine*, 1845–6 (preface). See also W. J. Shrewsbury, *Alcohol against the Bible, and the Bible against Alcohol* (1840), p. 34.

[35] (p. 187) Samuel Wilberforce quo. in S. Meacham, 'The Evangelical Inheritance', *Journal of British Studies*, Nov. 1963, p. 99; cf. W. Wilberforce, *Practical View*, p. 16.

[36] (p. 187) E. Gosse, *Father & Son*, p. 237; for the Evangelical Alliance, see N.T.L. *Annual Report*, *1881–2*, p. 9.

[37] (p. 187) W. Wilberforce, *Practical View*, p. 158.

[38] (p. 188) Quotations from T. Whittaker, *Life's Battles*, p. 340; *Northamptonshire Nonconformist*, 1889–1890, II, p. 18; I owe this reference to Raphael Samuel; Canon Wilberforce, *The Established Church & the Liquor Traffic* (Manchester, 1882), p. 3; Hugh Price Hughes in R. V. French (Ed.), *United Temperance Mission . . . Newport, Monmouthshire, 1879*, pp. 47–9.

[39] (p. 188) C. W. McCree, *George Wilson McCree*, p. 20.

[40] (p. 188) Quotations from H. J. Ellison, *The Temperance Reformation Movement in the Church of England* (1878 edn, first published 1869), p. 27; cf. D. W. R. Bahlman, *The Moral Revolution of 1688*, pp. 79–80.

[41] (p. 188) H. S. Sutton, *Evangel of Love*, p. 83; cf. Jabez Burns, *A Retrospect of Forty-Five Years' Christian Ministry* (1875), p. 42; F. R. Lees, 'The Life of William Hoyle', in W. Hoyle, *Wealth & Social Progress* (Manchester, 1887), p. 247.

[42] (p. 189) Noel Annan, *Leslie Stephen. His Thought & Character in Relation to his Time* (1951), p. 110.

[43] (p. 189) T. H. Green, *Works* (Ed. Nettleship, 1886), III, p. 273; see also *ibid.*, pp. 238, 261; cf. M. Richter, 'T. H. Green & his Audience: Liberalism as a Surrogate Faith', *Review of Politics*, 1956, pp. 448, 467; B. Webb, *My Apprenticeship*, p. 123.

[44] (p. 189) T. Hughes, *James Fraser*, p. 239; cf. J. Lawson, *Pudsey*, p. 73; B. Wilson, *Religion in Secular Society*, pp. 22, 158.

[45] (p. 189) G. P. Gooch, *The Life of Lord Courtney*, p. 416.

[46] (p. 190) Livesey, *Temperance Record*, 1 Oct. 1870, p. 472; 18 Mar. 1871, p. 123; cf. *Preston Guardian*, 20 Apr. 1872, p. 10. For the Bible cushion, see J. Pearce, *Livesey*, p. xxvi.

[47] (p. 190) *British Temperance Advocate*, Aug. 1882 (supplement), p. 16.

[48] (p. 190) Livesey, quo. in *Western Temperance Herald*, 1 July 1868, p. 101. Holyoake, quo. from G. J. Holyoake & G. E. Lomax, *Report of a Discussion on the Maine Law* (2nd edn, Blackburn, 1858), II, p. 20.

[49] (p. 191) Livesey quotation from *Temperance Record*, 5 Aug. 1871, p. 363; cf. J. Pearce, *Livesey*, p. cxxxvii.

[50] (p. 191) Quo. from *Livesey's Progressionist*, I, No. 15, p. 222.

[51] (p. 191) J. S. Buckingham in *Metropolitan Temperance Intelligencer & Journal*, 25 Feb. 1843, p. 59; N.T.L. *Annual Report*, *1856*, p. 22; J. Dunlop, *Autobiography*, p. 288.

[52] (p. 191) Livesey, quo. in J. Pearce, *Livesey*, p. cxxxix. Edward Grubb laments the trend of the times in *ibid.*, p. xcvi.

[53] (p. 191) Livesey, quo. in *Temperance Star*, 14 Apr. 1870, p. 7.

[54] (p. 192) *Livesey's Moral Reformer*, Feb. 1839, p. 213; T. Whittaker, *Life's Battles*, p. 336. For the knighthoods, see P. T. Winskill, *Temperance Movement*, IV, p. 42; cf. Josephine Butler, *Personal Reminiscences of a Great Crusade* (1896), pp. 394–5.

[55] (p. 192) J. Pearce, *Livesey*, p. cxlvi.

[56] (p. 192) The controversy is in *Alliance News*, 31 Mar. 1883, p. 199; 7 Apr. 1883, p. 220; 14 Apr. 1883, p. 228; 28 Apr. 1883, p. 267.

[57] (p. 192) R. H. Crofton, *Anne Jane Carlile & her Descendants* (St. Leonard's-on-Sea, 1950), pp. 22–4; Rev. H. Marles, *Jabez Tunnicliff*, gives more prominence to Tunnicliff in devising the new name.

[58] (p. 192) Leeds Temperance Society, *MS. Minute Book 1845–51*, entries for 5, 6, 26 Aug.; 2 Sept; 7, 29 Oct.; 18, 26 Nov. 1847.

[59] (p. 192) Rev. H. Marles, *op. cit*., pp. 243–6.

[60] (p. 193) R. Tayler, *The Hope of the Race* (1946), pp. 28–9, 32ff.

[61] (p. 193) *Band of Hope Record*, 1 Jan. 1860, p. 5.

[62] (p. 193) For Manchester, see *Temperance Star*, 17 Feb. 1871, p. 5.

[63] (p. 193) *Onward* (Manchester), Mar. 1872, p. 43.

[64] (p. 193) *Ibid*., Aug. 1870, p. 123; Mar. 1872, p. 42.

[65] (p. 193) *Band of Hope Record*, 1 Aug. 1860, p. 105.

[66] (p. 193) *Onward*, Aug. 1870, p. 124.

[67] (p. 193) *Onward*, Aug. 1870, p. 127; cf. *ibid*., Mar. 1872, p. 44.

[68] (p. 194) Quotations from B.T.L. *General Purposes Committee MS. Minutes*, 25 Oct. 1870; P. T. Winskill, *The Temperance Movement & its Workers*, II, p. 17; cf. the Anti-Corn Law League, in W. J. Conybeare, *Essays Ecclesiastical & Social*, p. 94.

[69] (p. 194) See the *MS. Minute Book 1865–7* of the First Cambridge (Excelsior) Life Boat Crew, in the care of Mr. David Moore, Lumen, Cambridge Road, Histon, Cambridge.

[70] (p. 194) *Cornwall Teetotal Journal*, Nov. 1842, p. 166.

[71] (p. 194) Leeds Temperance Society, *MS. Minute Book 1830–1845*, entry for 18 July 1843.

[72] (p. 194) *British & Foreign Temperance Intelligencer*, 16 Apr. 1842, p. 124.

[73] (p. 195) *Devon & Cornwall Temperance Journal & Permissive Bill Advocate*, May 1868, p. 73.

[74] (p. 195) M. Rutherford, *Autobiography*, p. 31.

Chapter 9. The Resort to Prohibition: 1853 [pp. 196–218].

[1] (p. 196) e.g. *New British & Foreign Temperance Magazine & Monthly Chronicle*, June 1841, pp. 161–4; cf. *Alliance* (Manchester), 11 Nov. 1854, p. 149; *National Temperance Chronicle*, Oct.–Dec. 1846 (three leading articles).

[2] (p. 197) H. A. Bruce, *3 Hansard 212*, c. 958 (11 July 1872). F. W. Newman, in U.K.A. *13th Annual Report, 1864–5*, p. 39; for exaggerated adulation, see M. H. C. Hayler, *Vision of a Century* (1953), p. 58; Plimsoll, *3 Hansard 211*, c. 477 (8 May 1872).

[3] (p. 197) T. Lythgoe, *Biographical Key*, p. 22.

[4] (p. 197) U.K.A. *Public Inauguration Proceedings* (1853), *passim*; see also U.K.A. *First Annual Report, 1853*, pp. 1–3.

[5] (p. 198) Brougham, *Weekly Record*, 30 Nov. 1861, p. 450; for Lawson's hospitality, see *3 Hansard 232*, c. 1926 (14 Mar. 1877); for Manchester & Salford Temperance Society, see its first three annual reports, 1851–4, in Manchester Central Library.

[6] (p. 198) Mrs. S. Schwabe, *Reminiscences of Richard Cobden* (1895), p. 279.

[7] (p. 198) 'How to Stop Drunkenness', *North British Review*, Feb. 1855.

[8] (p. 198) *Bolton Chronicle* (Bolton), 1 July 1865, p. 7.

[9] (p. 199) e.g. Dr. Pankhurst, *Alliance News*, 3 Oct. 1885, p. 633.

[10] (p. 199) Goldwin Smith, *Alliance News*, 9 May 1868, p. 148.

[11] (p. 199) *Alliance News*, 22 Jan. 1870, p. 28.

[12] (p. 199) Quo. from Leatham, *Alliance News*, 4 Feb. 1865, p. 37; cf. Bright, *3 Hansard 175*, c. 1405 (8 June 1864).

[13] (p. 199) J. D. Hilton, *James Hayes Raper* (1898), p. 29; C. Fairfield, *Some Account of George William Wilshere, Baron Bramwell* (1898), p. 272.

[14] (p. 200) *Morning Star*, 12 Apr. 1860, p. 4; S.C.H.L. on Intemperance, fourth report, *Parl. Papers* 1878 (338), XIV, Q. 345.

[15] (p. 200) Goldsmid, *3 Hansard 220*, cc. 13–16 (17 June 1874); Chamberlain, in *The Times*, 7 Apr. 1893, p. 11.

[16] (p. 201) Quo. from 'Municipal Drink Traffic', *Fabian Tract Nº 86* (1898), p. 5; for Lawson, see *3 Hansard 211*, c. 457 (8 May 1872).

[17] (p. 201) Seymer, *3 Hansard 171*, c. 292 (3 June 1863); *The Times*, quo. by Brebner, 'Laissez Faire & State Intervention in Nineteenth-Century Britain', *Journal of Economic History*, Supplement VIII (1948), p. 64. *Bee-Hive*, 12 Mar. 1864, 4 June 1864, 20 May 1871, p. 9; see also correspondence and editorials during September & October 1865, and letter from J. H. Randall in *ibid.*, 24 Nov. 1866, p. 7. See also my 'Sunday Trading Riots of 1855', *Historical Journal*, 1965.

[18] (p. 202) *Alliance Weekly News*, 31 May 1856, p. 178.

[19] (p. 202) F. R. Lees, *Alliance Prize Essay* (3rd edn, 1857), pp. 18, 20.

[20] (p. 202) W. Wilks, *The Two Last Speeches . . .* (U.K.A. 1864), p. 9.

[21] (p. 202) F. R. Lees, *op. cit.*, p. 19.

[22] (p. 202) Dawson Burns, in *Poole & Bournemouth Herald*, 7 Aug. 1879.

[23] (p. 203) J. Bentham, *Introduction to the Principles of Morals & Legislation* (Ed. Harrison, Oxford, 1948), p. 420.

[24] (p. 203) Livesey, *Alliance Weekly News*, 17 Mar. 1860, p. 960; A. V. Dicey, *Law & Public Opinion*, pp. 173, 175, 187–8, 219.

[25] (p. 204) Pope, *Alliance News*, 28 Oct. 1865, p. 337; F. W. Newman, *Alliance News*, 16 June 1866, p. 190; *Lecture on the Action and Reaction between Churches and the Civil Government* (1860), p. 4; F. R. Lees, *Prize Essay*, p. 31.

[26] (p. 204) *Meliora*, II, No. 8, p. 344.

[27] (p. 204) F. R. Lees, *Prize Essay*, p. 30.

[28] (p. 204) Gladstone, quo, in W. Hoyle, *Our National Resources*, p. 110; cf. U.K.A. *13th Annual Report, 1864–5*, p. 39. For Lees on the gaslamp, see F. Lees, *Life of Dr. Frederic Richard Lees*, p. 228.

[29] (p. 205) F. R. Lees, *Prize Essay*, p. 30.

[30] (p. 205) U.K.A. Monthly Papers, *Liberty & the Liquor Traffic* (1859), p. 4.

[31] (p. 205) *Alliance News*, 6 Jan. 1872, p. 13.

[32] (p. 205) F. R. Lees, *Prize Essay*, pp. 26–7.

[33] (p. 205) *Alliance Weekly News*, 7 May 1859, p. 781; cf. R. Owen, *A New View of Society*, p. 17; T. H. Green, 'Principles of Political Obligation', in T. H. Green, *Works*, II, pp. 345–6. See also M. Arnold, *Culture & Anarchy* (Ed. J. Dover Wilson, Cambridge, 1950), p. 192; F. W. Newman, 'The Moral Influence of Law' (1860) in his *Miscellanies*, II, p. 94.

[34] (p. 206) *Bradford Observer* 18 Nov. 1841, p. 3; F. W. Newman, *The Right and Duty of the State to Control the Drink Traffic* (1875), p. 2; Earl of Harrington, *The Maine-Law* (1858), p. 20. For the bar-parlour, see *Alliance*, 19 May 1855, p. 364.

[35] (p. 206) *Tait's Magazine*, quo. in *The Friend*, Jan. 1856, p. 15.

[36] (p. 206) *Meliora*, II, No. 8, p. 345 (*c.* 1861).

[37] (p. 206) F. R. Lees, *Prize Essay*, p. 27.

[38] (p. 206) *Meliora*, XI, No. 44, pp. 295, 303 (*c.* 1868).

[39] (p. 207) F. R. Lees, *Prize Essay*, pp. 30–1.

[40] (p. 207) *Alliance News*, 8 May 1875, p. 296; 12 June 1880, p. 377.

[41] (p. 207) *Pall Mall Gazette*, 22 Aug. 1885, p. 13; cf. Dr. Pankhurst, *ibid.*, p. 9. For Pankhurst on local option, see *Alliance News*, 3 Oct. 1885, p. 633.

[42] (p. 207) N. Annan, *Leslie Stephen*, p. 272.

[43] (p. 208) *The Times*, 10 Nov. 1868, p. 4; *Liverpool Daily Post*, 11 Nov. 1868.

[44] (p. 208) R. C. . . . Contagious Diseases Act, *Parl. Papers* 1871 (C. 408, 408–I), XIX, Q. 19,999; see also G. P. Gooch, *Life of Lord Courtney* (1920), pp. 228, 278, 287–8.

[45] (p. 208) [G. Vasey], *Individual Liberty, Legal, Moral, & Licentious* (1867), p. 25. See also Balliol College, Oxford, *T. H. Green MSS.*, MS. note by C. A. F[yffe], pp. 4–5.

[46] (p. 209) J. S. Mill, *Liberty* (Everyman edn, 1960), p. 73.

[47] (p. 209) Quotations from T. H. Green, 'Liberal Legislation & Freedom of Contract', in T. H. Green, *Works*, III, pp. 383–4; T. Hardy, *The Mayor of Casterbridge* (Pan Books, 1955), p. 258; Newman, *Alliance News*, 31 May 1884, p. 342; see also *Alliance Weekly News*, 7 May 1859; *ibid.*, 3 Apr. 1858, p. 562.

[48] (p. 209) H. L. A. Hart, *Law, Liberty and Morality* (1963), p. 33.

[49] (p. 209) Quotations from Rev. J. T. Baylee, in S.C.H.C. Public-Houses, *Parl. Papers* 1854 (367), XIV, Q. 235; N. Card, *ibid.*, Q. 1954. See also J. S. Mill, *Principles of Political Economy* (Ed. W. J. Ashley, 1909), p. 957.

[50] (p. 209) Quotations from *T. H. Green MSS.*: Green to Harcourt, n.d. (presumably draft of Green's reply to Harcourt's MS. letter of 7 Jan. 1873); 'Liberal Legislation and Freedom of Contract', *Works* III, p. 385; see also *ibid.*, p. 375.

[51] (p. 210) [G. Vasey], *op. cit.*, p. 126; cf. *Alliance News*, 11 Jan. 1873, p. 24.

[52] (p. 210) Harcourt in *Alliance News*, 4 Jan. 1873, p. 12; T. H. Green in *Oxford Chronicle*, 4 Jan. 1873, p. 3.

[53] (p. 210) U.K.A. *No Case against the U.K.A. and the Permissive Bill*, p. 69.

[54] (p. 210) Quo. from J. S. Mill, *Liberty*, p. 120; cf. *ibid.*, p. 155. Matthew Arnold, *Culture & Anarchy*, pp. 145–6.

[55] (p. 210) T. H. Green, 'Liberal Legislation', p. 386.

[56] (p. 210) Advertisements in *Alliance News*, 12, 19, 26 Mar; 9, 16, 23 Apr; 14, 28 May 1881. *British Temperance Advocate*, Mar. 1881, p. 457; for Mill's death, see *Alliance News*, 17 May 1873, p. 309; quotation from *ibid.*, 24 May 1873, p. 330. Green's obituary is in *Alliance News*, 1 Apr. 1882, p. 193.

[57] (p. 211) *National Temperance Chronicle*, Oct.–Dec. 1846 (three leaders).

[58] (p. 211) J. Dunlop, *Autobiography*, p. 361.

[59] (p. 211) University College, London, *Brougham MSS.*: Father Mathew to Brougham, 27 July 1853.

[60] (p. 211) Father Mathew, quo. in *Archbishop Manning & the Permissive Bill* (U.K.A. 1871), concluding quotation. I am not convinced by Father Augustine, *Footprints of Father Mathew*, pp. 529–31.

[61] (p. 212) *Weekly Record*, 21 Feb. 1857, p. 63; cf. J. H. Timberlake, *Prohibition & the Progressive Movement, 1900–1920* (Harvard, 1963), p. 144.

[62] (p. 212) *Alliance*, 28 Apr. 1855, p. 342.

[63] (p. 212) *Alliance Weekly News*, 9 Aug. 1856.

[64] (p. 212) Quo, in H. Carter *English Temperance Movement*, p. 119.

[65] (p. 212) Times, quo. in *Alliance News*, 7 Nov. 1863, p. 356.

[66] (p. 212) David Morris, in *Alliance Weekly News*, 25 July 1857; Livesey, in *Weekly Record*, 12 Sept. 1857, p. 322.

[67] (p. 213) Quotations from Bishopsgate Institute, *Howell Collection*, No. 4114 ('A Busy and a Strenuous Life'), p. 55; E. Hodder, *Shaftesbury*, II (1886), p. 483; cf. Sheffield Public Library, *H. J. Wilson Collection*, M.D. 2477–11: H. J. Wilson to his sister Rebekah; W. E. Adams, *Memoirs of a Social Atom*, II, p. 617; G. Howell, 'Autobiography of a Toiler' (Bishopsgate Institute, *Howell Collection*, No. 4114), p. 63; J. Dunlop, *Autobiography*, pp. 360–1.

[68] (p. 213) Taylor, *Temperance Star*, 2 Sept. 1870, p. 3; cf. A. Swift, *Half a Century of Temperance Work in St. Ives* (St. Ives, 1889), p. 19.

[69] (p. 213) Quo. in F. Lees, *Dr. Frederic Richard Lees*, p. 81; cf. *ibid.*, p. 118.

[70] (p. 213) Joseph Taylor, *Temperance Star*, 2 Sept. 1870, p. 3.

[71] (p. 213) For Lees' personality, see—in addition to F. Lees' biography—*Reasoner*, 1 Apr. 1855, p. 1; 'J.N.', 'Frederic Richard Lees 1815–1897', in *Alliance News*, Mar. 1915.

[72] (p. 214) Quo. from N.T.L. *MS. Minutes*, 11 July 1862. For regretful temperance reformers, see Samuel Bowly, in M. Taylor, *Memorials of Samuel Bowly* (Gloucester, 1884), p. 41; T. Whittaker, in *Weekly Record*, 27 Feb. 1858, p. 69; on the whole dispute, see Anon., *Impressions of the 'Gough-Lees Controversy'* . . . by *an Outsider* (1858), *passim.* On the 1862 situation, see Dawson Burns, *Temperance History*, I, p. 414; Anon., *A Chapter of Temperance History* (1863).

[73] (p. 214) Quotations from N.T.L. *Minutes*, 3 Dec. 1858; *Weekly Record*, 7 Feb. 1863, p. 66. See also N.T.L. *MS. Minutes*, 28 Feb. 1857, 17 Sept. 1858. For Sunday closing, see B.T.L. *General Purposes Committee Minutes*, 18 June 1861; N.T.L. *MS. Minutes*, 27 June 1862, 7 Nov. 1862.

[74] (p. 215) Quo. in H. Carter, *English Temperance Movement*, p. 120.

[75] (p. 215) Livesey, quotations from *Alliance Weekly News*, 25 July 1857; H. Carter, *op. cit.*, p. 98. See also *British Temperance Advocate*, 1 Sept. 1855; *Alliance Weekly News*, 7 Apr. 1860, p. 972.

[76] (p. 215) University Coll. London, *Brougham MSS.*: Livesey to Brougham, 15 July 1864.

[77] (p. 216) Quotations from H. Carter, *English Temperance Movement*, pp. 116, 111.
[78] (p. 216) *Drunkenness Committee*, QQ. 1032ff.
[79] (p. 216) Quo. in H. Carter, *op. cit.*, p. 122.
[80] (p. 217) Quotations from T. H. Barker & J. Livesey, *True Policy Vindicated* (Manchester, 1870), pp. 3–4, 7, 11; *Temperance Record*, 21 Sept. 1872, p. 453.
[81] (p. 217) Quo. in H. Carter, *op. cit.*, p. 175.
[82] (p. 217) *Ibid.*, p. 112; cf. H. J. Hanham, *Elections & Party Management* (1959), p. 119.
[83] (p. 218) For parliamentary discussion of Livesey's comments, see *3 Hansard 229*, c. 1824 (14 June 1876); *3 Hansard 244*, c. 664 (11 Mar. 1879); *3 Hansard 303*, c. 387 (10 Mar. 1886).
[84] (p. 218) Quo. in F. Lees, *Dr. Frederic Richard Lees*, p. 189.

Chapter 10. Prohibitionists and Their Tactics: 1853–1872 [pp. 219–246].

[1] (p. 220) W. Bagehot, 'Lord Palmerston at Bradford', in his *Collected Works* (Ed. N. St. J. Stevas), III (1968), p. 281; Ernest Jones, *People's Paper*, 28 Aug. 1852, p. 1.
[2] (p. 220) W. R. D. Adkins, *Our County* (1893), p. 28.
[3] (p. 220) W. Lawson, *Wit & Wisdom* (2nd edn, 1886), p. 58; cf. *ibid.*, p. 25.
[4] (p. 221) *Alliance News*, 21 Oct. 1871, p. 667.
[5] (p. 221) Anon., *Inquiry into the Causes of the Present Long-Continued Depression in the Cotton Trade* (3rd edn, 1869), p. 12; F. W. Newman, *Reasoner*, 6 Jan. 1858, p. 5; cf. *Alliance News*, 31 Mar. 1883, pp. 194–5. For the productivity of temperance donations, see N.T.L. *Annual Report, 1892–3*, p. 24.
[6] (p. 221) Quotations from *Economist*, 7 July 1855, p. 728; *Alliance Weekly News*, 7 May 1859, p. 781.
[7] (p. 222) Churchill, *Alliance News*, 2 Apr. 1870, p. 109.
[8] (p. 222) National Library of Scotland, Edinburgh, *Combe MSS.* 7365, f. 89: Lovett to Combe, 25 Nov. 1857.
[9] (p. 222) Brazier, *Alliance News*, 30 July 1870, p. 246.
[10] (p. 223) Quo. from *Alliance News*, 9 July 1870, p. 220; see also *ibid.*, 18 June 1870, p. 197.
[11] (p. 223) W. Lovett, *Life & Struggles*, p. 437; C. F. G. Masterman, *The Condition of England* (1909), p. 142.
[12] (p. 223) *3 Hansard 171*, c. 311 (3 June 1863); see also H. Cantril, *Gauging Public Opinion* (Princeton, 1944), p. 3; L. W. Doob, *Public Opinion & Propaganda* (New York, 1948), p. 151; I am most grateful to Dr. David Butler, Nuffield College, Oxford, for help on this point.
[13] (p. 224) Quotations from Card, in S.C.H.C. on Public-houses, *Parl. Papers* 1854 (367), XIV, Q. 1954; Pope, in his letter to Stanley, 26 Sept. 1856, printed in *The Stanley-Pope Discussion* (Manchester, n.d., 1856); *Alliance News*, 13 June 1863, p. 188. See also the parody of the song 'A Good Time Coming', in *The Coal Hole Companion*, 3rd ser., part 9 (n.d.), pp. 6–8; and the verses entitled 'Father Mathew', in *ibid.*, 2nd ser., part 5, pp. 18–20; fourth collection, pp. 26–8. Louis James kindly referred me to these items, which are in the Bodleian Library's *James Johnson Collection*, chapbooks, box 9.
[14] (p. 224) Blatchford, *Alliance News*, 14 Aug. 1902, p. 522. For prohibitionist support for the north, see W. Farish, *Autobiography* (privately printed, 1889), pp. 117–18; cf. *Meliora*, IV, No. 16, p. 384; V, No. 18, p. 192.
[15] (p. 224) Sylvia Pankhurst, *Life of Emmeline Pankhurst* (1935), p. 25; cf. G. B. Shaw, 'Epistle Dedicatory to A. B. Walkley', in his *Man & Superman* (Constable edn, 1930), p. xv.
[16] (p. 225) I. G. Sieveking, *Memoir . . . of Francis W. Newman* (1909), p. 139.
[17] (p. 225) H. J. Hanham, 'The General Election of 1868. A Study in the Bases of Mid-Victorian Politics' (Cambridge unpublished Ph.D. thesis, 1953), p. III-6.
[18] (p. 226) Figures from *A Full Report of the Proceedings of the Ministerial Conference on the Suppression of the Liquor Traffic . . . Manchester . . . June 9th, 10th, and 11th, 1857.*
[19] (p. 226) J. G. Shaw, *William Gregson*, pp. 172–3.
[20] (p. 226) P. Mathias, 'The Brewing Industry, Temperance & Politics', *loc. cit.*, p. 108.

[21] (p. 227) *Alliance News*, 28 Oct. 1865, p. 344.

[22] (p. 227) W. J. M. Mackenzie, 'Pressure Groups in British Government', *British Journal of Sociology*, 1955, p. 143.

[23] (p. 228) S.C.H.C. on Public-houses, *Parl. Papers* 1854 (367), XIV, QQ. 3957, 3589.

[24] (p. 228) University College London, *Brougham MSS.*: Pope to Brougham, 14 Oct. 1859, 29 Oct. 1860; cf. Pope to Brougham, 30 Aug. 1861.

[25] (p. 229) U.K.A. *17th Annual Report, 1868–9*, p. 7; H. Carter, *English Temperance Movement*, p. 171.

[26] (p. 229) *Daily News*, 9 May 1872, p. 4.

[27] (p. 230) Quotations from *3 Hansard 229*, cc. 1838–9 (14 June 1876); J. Bowles, *Reflections on the Political & Moral State of Society at the Close of the Eighteenth Century* (1800), p. 153; cf. J. D. Stewart, *British Pressure Groups* (Oxford, 1958), pp. 121, 138.

[28] (p. 230) Pope, *Alliance News*, 21 Oct. 1871, p. 666; cf. *New Statesman*, 27 June 1969, p. 899.

[29] (p. 231) W. H. Macintosh, 'The Agitation for the Disestablishment of the Church of England in the Nineteenth-Century (Excluding Wales), with special reference to the Minutes & Papers of the Liberation Society' (Oxford Univ. unpublished D.Phil. thesis 1955), p. 218. I am most grateful to Dr. Macintosh for allowing me to consult his thesis.

[30] (p. 231) B. R. Mitchell & P. Deane, *Abstract of British Historical Statistics*, p. 367.

[31] (p. 231) P. Mathias, 'The Brewing Industry, Temperance, & Politics', *loc. cit.*, p. 111.

[32] (p. 231) G. B. Wilson, *Alcohol & the Nation*, p. 332.

[33] (p. 232) H. J. Hanham, *Elections and Party Management*, p. 140; R. T. McKenzie, *British Political Parties* (2nd edn, 1963), p. 162; cf. Royden Harrison, 'The British Working Class & the General Election of 1868', *International Review of Social History*, 1960, p. 452.

[34] (p. 232) G. W. E. Russell, *Sir Wilfrid Lawson*, p. 74; cf. *3 Hansard 196*, c. 645 (12 May 1869); *3 Hansard 278*, c. 1283 (27 Apr. 1883).

[35] (p. 233) For the duplicated letters, see Bodleian Library, Oxford, *J. Johnson Collection* (Temperance 2); for Alliance deputations, see Alliance House, London, *U.K.A. Executive Committee Minute Book 1871–3*, minutes for 8 Nov., 20 Dec., 1871; 28 June, 29 Nov. 1871.

[36] (p. 233) National Temperance League, *MS. Minutes*, 17 Apr. 1863, 16 Mar. 1865; B.T.L. *General Purposes Committee MS. Minutes*, 10 Nov. 1859. For the collectors, see N.T.L. *MS. Minutes*, 16 Jan. 1857, 30 Apr. 1858, 21 May 1858, 21 Jan. 1859, 1 May 1863; see also B.T.L. *General Purposes Committee MS. Minutes*, 7 & 21 Nov. 1865. For the tea meeting, see N.T.L. *MS. Minutes*, 29 Nov. 1866. For conversaziones, see University College London, *Brougham MSS.*: H. Solly to Lord Lyttelton, 28 May 1864; H. Solly, '*These Eighty Years*', II, p. 215.

[37] (p. 234) Quotation from *J. Johnson Collection* (Temperance 2), Pope's duplicated letter dated 3 Oct. 1859. For an example of close supervision, see *U.K.A. Executive Committee MS. Minute Book 1871–3*, minutes for 19 Feb. 1873. See also the dispute with J. W. Kirton, in *ibid.*, minutes for 23 Sept. 1872.

[38] (p. 235) T. H. Barker, *Temperance Advocacy* (Manchester, 1859) p. 12; cf. 'J.N.', 'Frederic Richard Lees', *loc. cit.*, p. 13.

[39] (p. 235) F. R. Lees, *Prize Essay*, p. 12.

[40] (p. 236) J. Butler, *Personal Reminiscences of a Great Crusade*, p. 402.

[41] (p. 236) B.M. *Add. MSS.* 43677 (Cobden Papers), f. 49: Cobden to Collet, 5 June 1854.

[42] (p. 236) *Alliance Weekly News*, 12 Dec. 1857; U.K.A. *20th Annual Report, 1871–2*, p. 64.

[43] (p. 236) A. Sinclair, *Prohibition*, p. 129; cf. J. Dunlop, *Autobiography*, p. 249.

[44] (p. 236) Quotation from *Alliance Weekly News*, 13 Feb. 1858, p. 535; for uninspired editorship, see *Brougham MSS.*, M. D. Hill to Brougham, 8 Apr. 1859; cf. G. W. Hastings to Brougham, 16 July 1858.

[45] (p. 236) Cecil, in *Saturday Review*, 11 June 1864, p. 709; all Cecil's *Saturday Review* articles are identified in J. F. A. Mason's article in *Bulletin of the Institute of Historical Research*, May 1961, pp. 41ff.; cf. Osborne, *3 Hansard 215*, c. 1639 (7 May 1873); Giles, *3 Hansard 286*, c. 1450–1 (2 Apr. 1884).

[46] (p. 236) Quotation from *Alliance Weekly News*, 2 Feb. 1856, p. 111. For Bright, see his *Diaries* (1930), pp. 317, 413.

[47] (p. 237) *Alliance Weekly News*, 30 July 1859, p. 829.

[48] (p. 237) *Alliance Weekly News*, 31 Aug. 1861, p. 1265.

[49] (p. 237) *The Era*, 7 Nov. 1858, p. 9.

[50] (p. 237) John, Lord Campbell, *Lives of the Chancellors*, VIII (1869), p. 251; I owe this reference to Mr. W. E. S. Thomas, of Christ Church, Oxford.

[51] (p. 237) *The Times*, 19 Aug. 1835, p. 2. The debate on this clause is not reported in *Hansard.*

[52] (p. 237) *Brougham MSS.*: Pope to Brougham, 14 Oct. 1859; cf. *Trans.* of the N[ational] A[ssociation] for the P[romotion] of S[ocial] S[cience], 1859 (1860), p. 34.

[53] (p. 238) *Brougham MSS.*: Lyndhurst to Brougham, 22 Oct. 1860.

[54] (p. 238) U.K.A. *9th Annual Report*, *1861*, p. 2; see also *Alliance Weekly News*, 31 Aug. 1861, p. 1264; 24 Aug. 1861, p. 1261.

[55] (p. 238) *Brougham MSS.*: Hastings to Brougham, 12 May 1862; cf. *The Shield*, 24 Oct. 1874.

[56] (p. 238) Quotation from *Alliance News*, 1 Oct. 1864, p. 317; see also *Alliance News*, 24 Oct. 1863, p. 341; *Church of England Temperance Magazine*, 1 Dec. 1866, p. 373; U.K.A. *17th Annual Report*, *1868–9*, p. 22. For the N.A.P.S.S. in the 1880s, see B. Rodgers, 'The Social Science Association 1857–1886', *Manchester School of Economic & Social Studies*, XX (Sept. 1952), p. 305–6.

[57] (p. 239) *Alliance*, 23 Sept. 1854, p. 93.

[58] (p. 239) U.K.A. *4th Annual Report*, *1856*, p. 21; *8th Annual Report*, *1860*, p. 4; W. R. Lambert, *op. cit.*, p. 267; for the percentages, see the figures in *ibid.*, pp. 305–7.

[59] (p. 239) *Alliance Weekly News*, 13 Oct. 1855, p. 47.

[60] (p.240) U.K.A. *14th Annual Report*, *1865–6*, p. 7.

[61] (p. 240) U.K.A. *Executive Committee Minute Book 1873–5*, entry for 22 Oct. 1873; for 1868, see U.K.A. *16th Annual Report*, *1867–8*, p. 33.

[62] (p. 240) Lawson, in U.K.A. *Executive Committee Minute Book 1871–3*, minutes for 23 Sept. 1872; Kimberley, quo. in U.K.A. *20th Annual Report*, *1871–2*, p. 38; cf. *ibid.*, p. 46. For Owen, see U.K.A. *Executive Committee Minute Book 1871–3*, minutes for 19 Feb. 1873. See also *3 Hansard 212*, c. 984 (11 July 1872); *Alliance News*, 7 Sept. 1872, p. 647; 19 Oct. 1872, pp. 734–9.

[63] (p. 241) Quotations from *Alliance News*, 19 Oct. 1872, pp. 734, 736–7; 7 Sept. 1872, p. 648 (Whitworth); 16 Oct. 1875, p. 657 (Cossham).

[64] (p. 241) U.K.A. *17th Annual Report*, *1868–9*, p. 5; cf. U.K.A. *Executive Committee Minute Book 1873–5*, minutes for 25 June 1873. See also *Alliance Weekly News*, 11 Apr. 1857, p. 359.

[65] (p. 241) *The Times*, quo. in *Alliance News*, 7 Nov. 1863, p. 356; B.M. *Add. MSS.* 44535 (Gladstone Papers), f. 93: Gladstone to George Melly, 24 July 1865. I owe this latter reference to Professor John Vincent.

[66] (p. 241) H. J. Hanham, *Elections & Party Management*, p. 124.

[67] (p. 242) On American parties, see American Political Science Association, 'Towards a more responsible two-party system. A Report of the Committee on Political Parties'. *American Political Science Review* 1950 (supplement), p. 20.

[68] (p. 242) *Alliance Weekly News*, 7 Feb. 1857; *Staffordshire Advertiser*, 28 Mar. 1857, p. 8.

[69] (p. 242) *Alliance Weekly News*, 20 Dec. 1856, p. 295.

[70] (p. 242) *Ibid.*, 23 Aug. 1856, p. 227.

[71] (p. 242) *Alliance News*, 1 July 1865, p. 204.

[72] (p. 243) *Temperance Star*, 4 June 1869, p. 183.

[73] (p. 243) Lawson, *3 Hansard 229*, c. 897 (17 May 1876); for sympathy with the Liberal party, see U.K.A. *22nd Annual Report*, *1873–4*, p. 6; for Bright see B.M. *Add. MSS.* 43389 (Bright Papers), ff 290–4, 300, 312: Lawson to Bright, 15 Sept. 1878, 1 Nov. 1878, 2 Jan. 1879.

[74] (p. 243) *Alliance News*, 2 Jan. 1902, p. 5.

[75] (p. 243) *Weekly Record*, 14 May 1859, p. 191.

[76] (p. 244) Quotations from F. W. Newman, *The Permissive Bill More Urgent than any Extension of the Franchise* (U.K.A. 1865), p. 11; T. H. Barker, in T. H. Barker & J. Livesey, *True Policy Vindicated. A Friendly Correspondence* (U.K.A., Manchester, 1870), p. 6.

[77] (p. 244) Bishopsgate Institute, *Howell Collection*, No. 4114: 'A Busy & A Strenuous Life', p. 55; cf. W. H. Macintosh, *op. cit.*, pp. 51, 95.

[78] (p. 244) W. S. Fowler, *A Study in Radicalism & Dissent*, p. 26; E. G. Sandford (Ed.), *Memoirs of Archbishop Temple* (1906), I, p. 481; cf. A. Taylor, *Life of George M. Murphy* (1888), pp. 41–2.

[79] (p. 244) *Globe*, 27 June 1855; *The Times*, 15 June 1855; *Marx & Engels on Britain* (Moscow, 1953), p. 415; for the 'temperance' account of these riots, see *Meliora*, Apr. 1868, p. 14 (probably written by Dawson Burns).

[80] (p. 245) Cross, *3 Hansard 253*, c. 912 (25 June 1880); R. C. Liquor Licensing Laws, *Parl. Papers* 1897 (C. 8355), XXXIV, QQ. 1682ff.; see also my 'Sunday Trading Riots of 1855', *Historical Journal*, 1965, pp. 238–9.

[81] (p. 245) Marylebone, *Alliance*, 9 Dec. 1854, p. 181; Southampton, *Alliance Weekly News*, 20 Dec. 1856, p. 295.

[82] (p. 245) *Alliance Weekly News*, 21 Mar. 1857, p. 347; see also election supplement for 4 Apr. 1857; cf. *Staffordshire Advertiser*, 28 Mar. 1857, p. 7.

[83] (p. 245) *Alliance Weekly News*, 11 Apr. 1857, p. 359.

[84] (p. 245) *Weekly Record*, 4 Apr. 1857, p. 116; 11 Apr. 1857, p. 124.

[85] (p. 246) *Staffordshire Sentinel*, 23 Apr. 1859, pp. 4, 6; *Staffordshire Advertiser*, 30 Apr. 1859, p. 5; *Alliance Weekly News*, 7 May 1859, p. 781.

[86] (p. 246) *Alliance Weekly News*, 7 May 1859, p. 780; cf. U.K.A. *7th Annual Report, 1859*, p. 11.

[87] (p. 246) *Alliance Weekly News*, 21 May 1859, p. 789; cf. *Weekly Record*, 14 May 1859, p. 190.

[88] (p. 246) Royden Harrison, *Before the Socialists. Studies in Labour & Politics 1861–1881* (1964), pp. 254–5.

Chapter 11. Mounting Temperance Pressure. 1860–1870 [pp. 247–261].

[1] (p. 247) *3 Hansard 23*, c. 1124 (16 May 1834).

[2] (p. 248) *3 Hansard 137*, c. 1801 (26 Apr. 1855); see also G. B. Wilson, *Alcohol & the Nation*, appendix F, tables 1, 11, 12.

[3] (p. 248) For Gladstone's sherry, see J. Morley, *Life of Gladstone* (2 Vol. edn, 1905), I, p. 661; cf. A. A. Reade, *The House of Commons on Stimulants*, p. 5. For Gladstone's comment on 1860–1, see B.M. *Add. MSS.* 44791 (Gladstone Papers), f. 117: Gladstone's autobiographical notes (1897).

[4] (p. 248) B.M. *Add. MSS.* 44135 (Gladstone Papers), f. 80: Cobden to Gladstone, 5 Dec. 1859.

[5] (p. 248) B.M. *Add. MSS.* 44530 (Gladstone Papers), f. 160: Gladstone to Baines, 24 Feb. 1860.

[6] (p. 249) *Alliance Weekly News*, 24 Mar. 1860, p. 965.

[7] (p. 249) *3 Hansard 157*, c. 1304 (26 Mar. 1860); cf. *Morning Star*, 10 Apr. 1860, p. 4; 12 Apr. 1860, p. 4.

[8] (p. 249) J. T. Mills, *John Bright & the Quakers* (1935), II, pp. 75–6; cf. *3 Hansard 156*, c. 1594 (23 Feb. 1860); *ibid.*, c. 1864 (27 Feb. 1860); *Weekly Record*, 7 Apr. 1860, p. 162; *The Times*, 21 Feb. 1890, p. 10.

[9] (p. 249) *Alliance Weekly News*, 12 May 1860, p. 993; cf. U.K.A. *8th Annual Report, 1860*, p. 16.

[10] (p. 249) B.M. *Add. MSS.* 44393 (Gladstone Papers), f. 126: S. Laing to Gladstone, 17 Feb. 1860; B.M. *Add. MSS.* 44530 (Gladstone Papers), f. 174: Gladstone to the Vice-Chancellor of Oxford, 17 Mar. 1860.

[11] (p. 252) *Alliance News*, 8 Mar. 1862, p. 77; cf. J. D. Hilton, *James Hayes Raper* (1898).

[12] (p. 252) Asquith, quo. in G. W. E. Russell, *Sir Wilfrid Lawson*, p. 383; Lawson, *4 Hansard 70*, c. 137 (20 Apr. 1899).

[13] (p. 252) *4 Hansard 80*, c. 772 (13 Mar. 1900); *3 Hansard 208*, c. 785 (3 Aug. 1871).

[14] (p. 252) Disraeli, *3 Hansard 222*, c. 185 (9 Feb. 1875); cf. H. W. Lucy, *A Diary of Two Parliaments. The Disraeli Parliament 1874–1880* (2nd edn, 1885), pp. 100–1.

[15] (p. 253) *3 Hansard 221*, c. 1299 (4 Aug. 1874); B.M. *Add. MSS*. 43389 (Bright Papers), f. 300: Lawson to Bright, 1 Nov. 1878; *3 Hansard 243*, c. 1000 (17 Dec. 1878).

[16] (p. 253) Quo. in W. H. Dawson, *Richard Cobden and Foreign Policy* (1926), p. 71, citing Cobden to Peel, 23 June 1846.

[17] (p. 254) Granville, in Lord E. Fitzmaurice, *The Life of Granville George Leveson Gower. Second Earl Granville, K.G. 1815–1891* (1905), II, p. 176.

[18] (p. 254) G. P. Gooch, *Life of Lord Courtney*, p. 620; cf. T. Roosevelt, *Autobiography* (1913), p. 96.

[19] (p. 254) For the debate, see *3 Hansard 175*, cc. 1390ff. (8 June 1864); for Roebuck, see *Leader Collection*, Sheffield University Library: Leader to the Sheffield Licensed Victuallers, 16 June 1865 (187 III 283); I owe this reference to Professor John Vincent.

[20] (p. 255) J. Vincent, *Formation of the Liberal Party*, p. xxiii; for Wales, see W. R. Lambert, *op. cit*., pp. 266, 298ff., 405.

[21] (p. 255) Quotation from B. & P. Russell (Eds.), *The Amberley Papers* (1937), I, p. 498, cf. p. 491; for a biography of Cossham, see *Temperance Star*, 28 Aug. 1868. For Carlisle, see *Alliance News*, 15 July 1865, p. 220; *Carlisle Express*, 11 July 1865, p. 3; *Carlisle Examiner* (Carlisle), 15 July 1865, p. 2; *Carlisle Journal* (Carlisle), 14 July 1865, p. 4; 28 July 1865.

[22] (p. 255) Lowe, *3 Hansard 182*, cc. 147–8 (13 Mar. 1866); cf. *3 Hansard 178*, c. 1431 (3 May 1865). *Alliance News*, 3 Nov. 1866, p. 344.

[23] (p. 255) Bishopsgate Institute, *Howell Collection:* George Howell Letterbook No. 2, p. 423: Howell to Malthouse, 11 Jan. 1867; *Bee-Hive*, 17 Nov. 1866, p. 7; A. D. Bell, 'The Reform League from its Origins to the Reform Act of 1867' (Oxford Univ. unpublished D. Phil. thesis, 1961), p. 388, appendix 1, & pp. 97–8. I am most grateful to Dr. Bell for allowing me to read his thesis.

[24] (p. 255) *Howell Collection*, George Howell Letterbook No. 2: Howell to Sir Wilfrid Lawson, Sen., 5 Nov. 1866; Letterbook No. 3: Howell to Sir Wilfrid Lawson, Sen., 5 June 1867; Sir Wilfrid died a week later.

[25] (p. 255) Quotation from U.K.A. *16th Annual Report, 1867–8*, p. 33. See also R. Lowe, *Speeches & Letters on Reform* (2nd edn, 1867), p. 150, speech on 26 Apr. 1866; cf. University College London, *Brougham MSS.*: Hastings to Brougham, 26 May 1865; U.K.A. *16th Annual Report, 1867–8*, p. 33.

[26] (p. 256) U.K.A. *17th Annual Report, 1868–9*, p. 6.

[27] (p. 256) *Alliance News*, 14 Nov. 1868, p. 365.

[28] (p. 256) U.K.A. *16th Annual Report, 1867–8*, p. 32; cf. *Alliance News*, 4 July 1868, p. 212.

[29] (p. 256) *Alliance News*, 17 Oct. 1868, p. 330.

[30] (p. 256) *Bolton Chronicle*, 14 Nov. 1868, p. 7; cf. *Alliance News*, 24 Oct. 1868, p. 343; *Bolton Chronicle*, 3 Oct. 1868, p. 2.

[31] (p. 259) The analysis is based on the officials listed in U.K.A. *14th Annual Report, 1865–6*; C.E.T.S *2nd Annual Report, 1864*; C[entral] A[ssociation] for S[topping] the S[ale] of I[ntoxicating] L[iquors] on S[undays], *1st Annual Report, 1867*; N.T.L. *Annual Report, 1865–6*; B.T.L. *Register, 1866*, p. 4. For the number and location of U.K.A. meetings, see *Alliance News*, 1873.

[32] (p. 260) Bruce, *3 Hansard 196*, c. 674 (12 May 1869); Hughes, *3 Hansard 194*, c. 560 (3 Mar. 1869).

[33] (p. 260) Gladstone, *Alliance News*, 17 Oct. 1868, p. 329; St. Mary of the Angels, Bayswater, *Manning Papers*: Gladstone to Manning, 29 Oct. 1868. I am most grateful to Cormac Rigby, to Mgr. Derek Worlock, now Bishop of Portsmouth, and Fr. Bernard Fisher, now chaplain at Southampton University—for help in gaining access to this collection. See also H. J. Hanham, *Elections & Party Management*, p. 202.

[34] (p. 260) *Brewers Journal*, 15 Mar. 1869.

[35] (p. 260) Lawson, *Wit & Wisdom*, p. 69; cf. J. F. Glaser, 'Nonconformity & Liberalism, 1868–1885. A Study in English Party History' (Harvard Univ. Ph.D. thesis, 1948), pp. 538–42.

[36] (p. 261) G. W. E. Russell, *Lawson*, p. 87; *Alliance News*, 29 Oct. 1870, p. 349.

[37] (p. 261) Kent County Record Office U 951 F 27/3: *Political Journals of Lord Brabourne*, p. 66: H. A. Bruce to Knatchbull-Hugessen, 11 Sept. 1870 (copy). B.M. *Add. MSS*. 44428

(Gladstone Papers), f. 178: Bishop Fraser to Gladstone, 5 Nov. 1870; B.M. *Add. MSS.* 44539 (Gladstone Papers), f. 69: Gladstone to Fraser, 8 Nov. 1870 (copy).

Chapter 12. The Government Response: 1871–1872 [pp. 262–278].

[1] (p. 262) *Political Journals of Lord Brabourne*, f. 64.

[2] (p. 263) B.M. *Add. MSS.* 44301 (Gladstone Papers), f. 172: Lowe to Gladstone, 26 Dec. 1870; B.M. *Add. MSS.* 44086 (Gladstone Papers), f. 175: Bruce to Gladstone, 22 Dec. 1870; cf. B.M. *Add. MSS.* 44087 (Gladstone Papers), f. 4: Bruce to Gladstone, 12 Jan. 1871.

[3] (p. 263) Quotation from H. A. Bruce, *Letters of the Rt. Hon. Henry Austin Bruce, G.C.B.* (Oxford, privately printed, 1902), I, pp. 256–7; cf. *3 Hansard 203*, c. 187 (13 July 1870); W. R. Lambert, *op. cit.*, p. 288. For Bruce on municipalization, see B.M. *Add. MSS*, 44087 (Gladstone Papers), f. 6: Bruce to Gladstone, 16 Jan. 1871; but see also *3 Hansard 253*, cc. 1377–8 (2 July 1880). For Shaftesbury, see Broadlands Papers (consulted at the National Register of Archives), *Lord Shaftesbury's Diary*, 19 Nov. 1868; I quote from this diary by permission of the trustees of the Broadlands Archives.

[4] (p. 263) H. A. Bruce, *Letters*, I, pp. 318–19; for Bruce's advisers, see Kent County Record Office U 951 F 29: *Lord Brabourne's Political Anecdotes*, p. 195.

[5] (p. 263) *Ibid.* p. 178.

[6] (p. 263) *3 Hansard 205*, c. 1091 (3 Apr. 1871); for the cabinet agenda, see B.M. *Add. MSS.* 44638 (Gladstone Papers), f. 129 (2 Nov. 1870); *Add. MSS.* 44639 (Gladstone Papers), f. 4 (25 Jan. 1871).

[7] (p. 264) For attendance, *Christian World*, 7 Apr. 1871; *Birmingham Daily Post* (Birmingham), 4 Apr. 1871, p. 8; for the speech, *Manchester Examiner & Times* (Manchester), 6 Apr. 1871, p. 5; see also *Licensed Victuallers Guardian*, 8 Apr. 1871, p. 128; *Standard*, 12 July 1872.

[8] (p. 264) *3 Hansard 205*, c. 1074 (3 Apr. 1871).

[9] (p. 265) *Ibid.*, c. 1082.

[10] (p. 265) Quotations from *3 Hansard 205*, cc. 1087, 1090, 1091 (3 Apr. 1871).

[11] (p. 265) *3 Hansard 205*, c. 1097 (3 Apr. 1871).

[12] (p. 266) *Brewers Guardian*, 24 Apr. 1871.

[13] (p. 266) Candelet, *Licensed Victuallers Guardian*, 15 Apr. 1871; for the Yorkshire brewers, *Brewers Journal*, 15 Feb. 1871, pp. 30–1; 15 Mar. 1870, p. 57. See also *Brewers Guardian*, 1 May 1871.

[14] (p. 266) For attacks on the Country Brewers, see *Brewers Journal*, 15 Jan. 1870, p. 3; 15 Nov. 1871, p. 256. For the free-trade brewers, see *ibid.*, 15 May 1871, p. 124.

[15] (p. 266) B. L. Crapster, *British Liquor Industry*, pp. 177–9; for the petitions, see U.K.A. *19th Annual Report, 1870–1*, p. 24.

[16] (p. 266) *Manchester Guardian*, 20 Apr. 1871, p. 7; cf. Mr. Birks, *Sheffield & Rotherham Independent*, 25 Apr. 1871, p. 7; *Birmingham Daily Post*, 22 Apr. 1871, p. 5; *Brewers Journal*, 15 May 1871, p. 119; *The Times*, 6 May 1871, p. 11; 8 May 1871, p. 12.

[17] (p. 266) For complaints, see *Brewers Journal*, 15 Mar. 1870, p. 45; *Licensed Victuallers Guardian*, 29 Apr. 1871, 24 June 1871; 6 Jan. 1872, p. 12; *Wine Trade Review*, 15 Oct. 1871; 15 Nov. 1871; *Morning Post*, 19 June 1871, p. 4; *Licensed Victuallers Guardian*, 22 Apr. 1871.

[18] (p. 267) *Pall Mall Gazette*, 1 Apr. 1871; G. E. Buckle (Ed.), *The Letters of Queen Victoria. Second Series, II: 1870–1878* (1926), p. 133; cf. *ibid.*, p. 126 (8 Apr. 1871); P.R.O. 30/29/52 (Granville Papers): Bright to Granville, 29 May 1871.

[19] (p. 267) *Quarterly Review*, Oct. 1871, pp. 569–71; 1873, pp. 543, 549; see also *The Times*, 17 Apr. 1871, p. 6; *Weekly Dispatch*, 23 Apr. 1871, p. 12; 18 June 1871, p. 7.

[20] (p. 267) Quotation from *Brewers Guardian*, 4 Dec. 1871; see also Candelet, in *Lord Bramwell on Liberty, & Other Speeches* (1883), p. 22; Earl of Wemyss, *Socialism at St. Stephen's, 1886 & 1887* (n.d.), p. 49.

[21] (p. 267) *Ashton Reporter*, 29 Apr. 1871, p. 7; for Sheffield, see *Sheffield & Rotherham Independent*, 2 May 1871, p. 7. For Applegarth, *Daily News*, 20 Jan. 1872, p. 6; Hartwell, *Alliance News*, 8 July 1871, p. 434; *Bee-Hive*, 3 June 1871.

[22] (p. 267) *Liverpool Daily Post*, 15 May 1871, p. 7; *Liverpool Daily Courier* (Liverpool),

13 Sept. 1872, p. 5; 28 Oct. 1872, p. 5; 4 Nov. 1872, p. 5. For Manchester, see *Manchester Guardian*, 9 Apr., 2 July 1872.

[23] (p. 268) Walmsley, *Preston Guardian*, 8 July 1871, p. 10; for Catholics, see *Weekly Register*, 8 Apr. 1871; *Catholic Opinion*, 15 Apr. 1871, p. 33; *Morning Advertiser*, 17 May 1871, p. 3; for the priests' petition, see *Universe*, 1 July 1871, p. 6.

[24] (p. 268) Manning, *Alliance News*, 6 May 1871, p. 287.

[25] (p. 268) *Temperance Record*, 13 May 1871, p. 217; cf. *ibid.*, 22 Apr. 1871, p. 181; 29 Apr. 1871, p. 193.

[26] (p. 269) S. Haughton, *A Memoir of James Haughton* (Dublin, 1877), p. 272; cf. F. W. Newman, speech of 1871 reprinted in *Alliance News*, 31 Mar. 1883, p. 195; H. Carter, *English Temperance Movement*, pp. 162–3. For Baines, see *Temperance Record*, 6 May 1871, p. 207; for Morley, *Western Daily Press*, 3 Apr. 1871, p. 3.

[27] (p. 269) Quotation from H. Carter, *op. cit.*, pp. 254–5. On the Alliance attitude generally, see *Manchester Examiner & Times*, 19 Apr. 1871, p. 7; 22 Apr. 1871, p. 6; *Alliance News*, 13 May 1871, p. 306; 21 Oct. 1871, p. 667.

[28] (p. 269) Bruce quotations from *Morning Advertiser*, 17 May 1871, p. 3; *3 Hansard 206*, c. 948 (17 May 1871); cf. *Alliance News*, 20 May 1871, p. 318; *Temperance Record*, 6 May 1871, p. 214.

[29] (p. 269) Bruce, *Alliance News*, 15 Nov. 1895, p. 743; cf. Mundeila, *Morning Advertiser*, 7 Oct. 1871, p. 3; R. N. Fowler, *3 Hansard 207*, c. 194 (16 June 1871); Anstruther, *Alliance News*, 6 May 1871.

[30] (p. 269) *Temperance Record*, 4 Mar. 1871, p. 99; 5 Aug. 1871, p. 363; 18 Mar. 1871, p. 123.

[31] (p. 269) McCarthy, *Fortnightly Review*, 1 Aug. 1871, p. 179; Bruce, *3 Hansard 206*, c. 949 (17 May 1871).

[32] (p. 270) G. O. Trevelyan, *Five Speeches on the Liquor Traffic* (1872), pp. 29, 10. See also U.K.A. *No Case against the U.K.A. & the Permissive Bill*, p. 75.

[33] (p. 271) B.M. *Add. MSS.* 44348 (Gladstone Papers), f. 123: Glyn to Gladstone, 5 Sept. 1871; for Gladstone at Whitby, see *The Standard*, 4 Sept. 1871.

[34] (p. 271) Bruce, *Alliance News*, 6 May 1871, p. 288; cf. J. Ruskin, 'Fors Clavigera', letter 9 (Sept. 1871), in *Works* (Ed. Cook & Wedderburn), XXVII, p. 148.

[35] (p. 271) Derby, *Morning Post*, 5 June 1871, p. 4; *Brewers Journal*, 15 Jan. 1872, p. 2; Stephens, *Ashton Reporter*, 9 Mar. 1872, p. 3.

[36] (p. 271) *The Times*, 4 Apr. 1872, p. 5; see also *Preston Guardian*, 28 Aug. 1872, p. 8; *Morning Post*, 22 May 1872, p. 4; 11 May 1871.

[37] (p. 271) Quotations from *Manchester Guardian*, 16 Apr. 1872, p. 6; Ethel Drus (Ed.), 'A Journal of Events during the Gladstone Ministry, 1868–74', (by John, first Earl of Kimberley), *Camden Miscellany* XXI, 1958, p. 30 (20 Apr. 1872).

[38] (p. 272) *3 Hansard 210*, c. 1324 (16 Apr. 1872).

[39] (p. 272) *Morning Advertiser*, 29 May 1872, p. 3; 21 Dec. 1872, p. 3; 26 Apr. 1872; 2 May 1872.

[40] (p. 273) *Morning Advertiser*, 4 July 1872; cf. *ibid.*, 5 Apr., 21 Dec. 1872.

[41] (p. 273) Richards, *Morning Advertiser*, 4 July 1872, p. 3; Vousley, *ibid.*, 25 July 1872, p. 3.

[42] (p. 273) *Temperance Star*, 9 Aug. 1872, p. 4; *British Temperance Advocate*, 1 May 1872, p. 935, cf. *ibid.*, 1 July 1872, p. 953; see also *Onward*, June 1872, p. 95; Sept. 1872, p. 142.

[43] (p. 274) *Alliance News*, 27 Apr. 1872, p. 319; cf. J. L. & B. Hammond, *James Stansfeld* (1932), pp. 174, 177.

[44] (p. 274) *3 Hansard 211*, c. 477 (8 May 1872); but see also the speeches of T. E. Smith, F. W. Powell and Bruce, *3 Hansard 212*, c. 958 (11 July 1872).

[45] (p. 274) Dalrymple, *3 Hansard 199*, c. 1241 (4 Mar. 1870).

[46] (p. 274) Bruce, *3 Hansard 212*, c. 969 (11 July 1872); Lawson, *ibid.*, c. 981. See also J. S. Mill, *Representative Government* (Everyman edn, 1960), pp. 235–9.

[47] (p. 274) *3 Hansard 212*, c. 1002.

[48] (p. 275) Quotations from Henley, *3 Hansard 212*, c. 1981 (27 July 1872); Hoare, *ibid.*, c. 1984 (27 July 1872); Harcourt, *ibid.*, c. 1901 (26 July 1872).

[49] (p. 275) *Licensed Victuallers Guardian*, 23 Nov. 1872, p. 386.

[50] (p. 275) *Weekly Dispatch*, 25 Aug. 1872; *Reynolds' Newspaper*, 25 Aug., 8 Sept., 22 Sept., 6 Oct. 1872; cf. Edwin Mason, *Licensed Victuallers Guardian*, 21 Dec. 1872, p. 418. See also *Lloyd's Weekly London Newspaper*, 29 Sept. 1872; 21 Apr. 1872, p. 6; 21 July 1872, p. 1; 28 July 1872, p. 6.

[51] (p. 276) For Taylor, see *Sheffield Daily Telegraph*, 27 Aug. 1872, p. 3; see also *Sheffield Independent*, 10 July 1872, p. 4; 19 July 1872, p. 3; 27 July 1872, p. 7.

[52] (p. 276) Cheltenham, *Licensed Victuallers Gazette*, 24 Aug. 1872, p. 140; Maidstone, *Morning Advertiser*, 20 Aug. 1872, p. 2; Exeter, *Licensed Victuallers Guardian*, 24 Aug. 1872; *Western Times*, 27 Aug. 1872; Wolverhampton, *Licensed Victuallers Guardian*, 24 Aug. 1872. For Liverpool, see *Liverpool Daily Courier*, 13 Sept. 1872, p. 5; 28 Oct. 1872, p. 5; for Coventry, see *Licensed Victuallers Guardian*, 31 Aug. 1872, p. 293. For Oxford, see *ibid.*, 21 Sept. 1872, p. 317. For Ipswich, see *ibid.*, 21 Dec. 1872, pp. 420–1.

[53] (p. 276) Stephens, *Ashton Reporter*, 26 Oct. 1872, p. 3; see also *ibid.*, 9 Nov. 1872.

[54] (p. 277) *3 Hansard 220*, c. 244 (22 June 1874); cf. H. Carter, *English Temperance Movement*, p. 159; *Alliance News*, 23 Feb. 1889, p. 151; 8 Aug. 1890, p. 154.

[55] (p. 277) Chamberlain, *Alliance News*, 13 July 1894, p. 441.

[56] (p. 277) Quotations from *Alliance News*, 13 July 1894, p. 445; U.K.A. *Annual Report, 1965–6*, p. 5; *Alliance News*, 20 May 1871, p. 318; cf. James Whyte, *ibid.* 28 Jan. 1898, p. 63; R. Butt, *The Power of Parliament* (1967), p. 226. For Cossham, see *Alliance News*, 16 Oct. 1875, p. 657. For Reid, see S. J. Reid (Ed.), *Memoirs of Sir Wemyss Reid 1842–1885* (1905), pp. 197–8.

[57] (p. 277) *Aberdare Family Collection*, Gladstone to Bruce, 13 Nov. 1874.

[58] (p. 278) P.R.O. 30/29/65 (Granville Papers) note from Bruce dated Feb. 1873; cf. B.M. *Add. MSS.* 44439 (Gladstone Papers), f. 141b (8 July 1873); see also *3 Hansard 220*, cc. 683ff. (30 June 1874). For statistics, see G. B. Wilson, *Alcohol & the Nation*, pp. 332, 430–1.

[59] (p. 278) Bodleian Library, Oxford, *MS. Eng. Misc.* c. 37 (Misc. Acland Papers), ff. 34–5: Aberdare to Acland, 29 Jan. 1882.

[60] (p. 278) B.M. *Add. MSS.* 43535 (Ripon Papers), f. 193: Ripon to Bruce, 22 Sept. 1891. For Green, *Alliance News*, 1 May 1880, p. 279; 5 Feb. 1881, p. 93; 11 Feb. 1882, p. 83; Courtney, in G. P. Gooch, *Courtney*, p. 293; Churchill, *3 Hansard 343*, c. 1705 (29 Apr. 1890).

[61] (p. 278) *Aberdare Family Papers:* Gladstone to Bruce, 13 Nov. 1874; Gladstone to Lady Aberdare, 25 Mar. 1895; cf. Campbell-Bannerman, quo. in *Alliance News*, 23 Nov. 1899, p. 776.

Chapter 13. Liberalism and the Drink Question [pp. 279–296].

[1] (p. 279) H. Carter, *English Temperance Movement*, p. 145; R. C. K. Ensor, *England 1870–1914*, pp. 20–2.

[2] (p. 280) *3 Hansard 211*, c. 457 (8 May 1872).

[3] (p. 280) See H. Carter, *op. cit.* pp. 187–8.

[4] (p. 280) *3 Hansard 220*, c. 235 (22 June 1874).

[5] (p. 281) The Home Secretary is quo. in *Devon & Cornwall Temperance Journal*, Mar. 1868, p. 34; for undoctrinaire Tories, see Paul Smith, *Disraelian Conservatism & Social Reform* (1967), p. 43.

[6] (p. 281) E. Burke, 'Reflections on the French Revolution', *Works* (Boston, U.S.A., 1865 edn), III, p. 359.

[7] (p. 281) See the letter of a 'town clergyman' in *The Times*, 25 Sept. 1871, p. 4.

[8] (p. 281) Cf. J. L. Hammond, *Gladstone & the Irish Nation* (1938), p. 518.

[9] (p. 281) *The Times*, 11 Jan. 1873, p. 7; *Alliance News*, 6 May 1871, p. 288.

[10] (p. 281) Bruce, *3 Hansard 212*, c. 969 (11 July 1872); Selwyn Ibbetson, *3 Hansard 205*, c. 1097 (3 Apr. 1871); Cross, *3 Hansard 207*, c. 191 (16 June 1871); Sandon, *3 Hansard 206*, c. 944 (17 May 1871); Selwyn Ibbetson, *3 Hansard 212*, c. 969 (11 July 1872).

[11] (p. 282) U.K.A. *20th Annual Report, 1871–2*, p. 39.

[12] (p. 282) *Preston Guardian*, 28 Aug. 1872, p. 8.

[13] (p. 282) B.M. *Add MSS.* 44348 (Gladstone Papers), f. 184.

[14] (p. 282) *The Times*, 25 Oct. 1872, p. 8.

[15] (p. 282) Paul Smith, *op. cit.*, p. 101.

[16] (p. 282) *Ibid.* p. 132; cf. the discussion of 'over-legislation' in *Bee-Hive*, 10 Aug. 1872, p. 2.

[17] (p. 283) J. D. Clayton, 'Mr. Gladstone's Leadership of the Parliamentary Liberal Party: 1868–1874' (Oxford unpublished D.Phil. thesis, 1960), pp. 249–50.

[18] (p. 283) Paul Smith, *op. cit.*, pp. 128–9; A. Sinclair, *Prohibition*, p. 157.

[19] (p. 283) Disraeli, *3 Hansard 208*, c. 1110 (8 Aug. 1871); *3 Hansard 215*, c. 1365 (1 May 1873). For Lawson, see *3 Hansard 220*, c. 234 (22 June 1874). For Disraeli's drinking habits, see R. T. Shannon, *Gladstone & the Bulgarian Agitation* (1963), p. 132; G. J. Holyoake, *Bygones Worth Remembering*, II, pp. 43–4; University College London, *John Bright Collection*: John Bright to his wife, 17 Mar. 1868.

[20] (p. 283) *3 Hansard 218*, c. 134 (20 Mar. 1874); cf. his Greenwich speech, in *The Times* 29 Jan. 1874, p. 5 & the speech of Morgan, *3 Hansard 219*, c. 132 (11 May 1874); see also Bruce, *3 Hansard 220*, cc. 683–4 (30 June 1874).

[21] (p. 283) H. J. Hanham, *Elections & Party Management*, pp. 222–5.

[22] (p. 284) B. L. Crapster, *British Liquor Industry*, pp. 256, 263.

[23] (p. 284) *3 Hansard 191*, c. 156 (24 Mar. 1868).

[24] (p. 284) J. R. Vincent, 'The Electoral Sociology of Rochdale', *Econ. Hist. Rev.*, Aug. 1963, p. 83; J. R. Vincent, *Pollbooks*, pp. 17, 65.

[25] (p. 284) The gradualness of the shift in allegiance is well described in B. L. Crapster, *British Liquor Industry* pp. 255–8; cf. J. A. Thomas, *The House of Commons 1832–1901* (Cardiff, 1939), pp. 4–7, 14–16.

[26] (p. 284) Christ Church, Oxford, *Salisbury MSS.*: special correspondence, W. H. Smith to Salisbury, 26 July 1887; cf. *ibid.*, A. J. Balfour to Chamberlain, 20 May 1886; C. J. Valentine M.P. to Salisbury, 20 May 1886; R. Blake, *Disraeli* (1966), p. 538.

[27] (p. 284) H. J. Hanham, *Elections & Party Management*, p. 225; Sir. A. West, *Recollections 1832–1886* (Nelson edn), p. 339–40.

[28] (p. 284) *3 Hansard 273*, c. 49 (28 July 1882).

[29] (p. 285) B. L. Crapster, *British Liquor Industry*, p. 433; cf. J. A. Thomas, *British House of Commons*, pp. 4–6, 14–16.

[30] (p. 285) H. Carter, *English Temperance Movement*, p. 186.

[31] (p. 285) H. Carter, *op. cit.*, p. 190.

[32] (p. 286) Quotation from *Memoirs of the Life of Mr. Ambrose Barnes* (Publications of the Surtees Society, L: 1867) p. 196; I owe this reference to Mr. K. V. Thomas. For dissenting attacks on Anglican drunkenness, see M. Scrivener, *A Treatise Against Drunkenness* (1680), p. 85; for Manchester, see T. Walker, *A Review of Some of the Political Events which have occurred in Manchester during the last Five Years* (1794), pp. 41–2.

[33] (p. 286) R. F. Wearmouth, *Methodism & the Working-class Movements of England. 1800–1850* (1937), p. 77.

[34] (p. 286) E. P. Thompson, *The Making of the English Working Class* (1963), p. 463.

[35] (p. 286) For drink-free feasts, see *British & Foreign Temperance Herald*, May 1833, pp. 64–5 (at Brampton); B.M. *Add. MSS.* 27796 (Place Papers), f. 36 (at Evesham); for the Blackburn election, see *ibid.*, ff. 154–6; cf. *3 Hansard 27*, cc. 310–11 (27 Mar. 1835).

[36] (p. 286) J. B. Braithwaite, *J. J. Gurney*, I, pp. 155–6, 479; D. E. Swift, *Joseph John Gurney. Banker, Reformer, & Quaker* (Middletown, 1962), pp. 95–6, 101; C. Buxton, *T. F. Buxton*, pp. 357, 422; *Memorials of William Foster*, II, p. 91, cited in *Alliance News*, 12 Aug. 1865, p. 253.

[37] (p. 287) *The League*, 6 Apr. 1844, p. 445.

[38] (p. 287) Vincent quotation from *York Herald*, 16 Dec. 1848. For Vincent's candidature at York, see *York Herald*, 22 July 1848, p. 7; *Yorkshire Gazette* (York), 27 May 1848; N. Gash, *Politics in the Age of Peel* (1953), pp. 111–12.

[39] (p. 287) W. Lovett, *Life and Struggles*, p. 413; Joseph Arch, *Life*, p. 329.

[40] (p. 287) *Lord Shaftesbury's Diary*, 2 Aug. 1847; for other evangelicals, see R. I. & S. Wilberforce, *Life of William Wilberforce*, I, p. 383; S. Meacham, *Henry Thornton of*

Clapham. 1760–1815 (Harvard, 1964), pp. 67–8. See also H. J. Hanham, *Elections and Party Management*, p. 92.

[41] (p. 287) M. Ostrogorski, *Democracy & the Organisation of Political Parties* (Tr. F. Clarke, 1902), I, pp. 440, 332.

[42] (p. 287) Lloyd George, *Alliance News*, 28 Jan, 1898, p. 65. See also J. R. Vincent, *Formation of the Liberal Party*, p. 58.

[43] (p. 287) H. J. Hanham, 'Liberal Organisations for Working Men 1860–1914', *loc. cit.*, pp. 5–7; M. Ostrogorski, *op. cit.*, I, p. 346; M. Duverger, *Political Parties*, pp. 25–6.

[44] (p. 288) For Cobden's personal drinking habits, see B.M. *Add. MSS.* 43668 (Cobden Papers), f. 37: Cobden to Livesey, 10 Oct. 1849 (copy), and *Metropolitan Temperance Intelligencer & Journal*, 6 May 1843, p. 140. For his political motives in supporting teetotalism, see B.M. *Add. MSS.* 43653 (Cobden Papers), f. 151: Cobden to Ashworth, 13 Dec. 1849; B. M. *Add. MSS.* 43651 (Cobden Papers), f. 3: Cobden to Bright, 29 Apr. 1859. See also his speech at Leeds, *Freeholder*, 1 Jan. 1851, p. 5.

[45] (p. 288) Quo. from G. W. E. Russell, *Portraits of the Seventies* (1916), p. 177. For Bright's own drinking habits, see J. T. Mills, *John Bright*, II, pp. 26, 73, 75–6.

[46] (p. 288) *3 Hansard 174*, c. 1024 (14 Apr. 1864). See also Sussex County Record Office, *Cobden Collection No. 20*: Cobden to Gilpin, 29 July 1860.

[47] (p. 288) *Weekly Record*, 4 Apr. 1857, p. 116; *Temperance Spectator*, 1 June 1865, p. 87; Sussex County Record Office, *Cobden Papers No. 8:* W. N. Molesworth to Cobden, 6 Feb. 1865, 11 Feb. 1865.

[48] (p. 289) Quotations from *Alliance News*, 16 Dec. 1876, p. 813; Sir E. W. Watkin, *Alderman Cobden of Manchester* (n.d.), p. 203; Cobden favoured the permissive principle in Sunday closing—see *Weekly Record*, 25 Apr. 1863, p. 191.

[49] (p. 289) Quotations from University College, London, *John Bright Collection*: John Bright to his wife, 10 May 1873; J. T. Mills, *op. cit.*, II, p. 25; cf. p. 76. See also Friends' House Library, Euston, *MS. Box 10* (3), 7: Bright to Hannah Sturge, 24 Sept. 1873. For Bright on municipal control, see his *A Scheme of Licensing Reform & Compensation for Closing Public-Houses* (1883), p. 11; *Alliance News*, 15 Feb. 1868, p. 54.

[50] (p. 289) M. Ostrogorski, *op. cit.*, I, p. 189.

[51] (p. 289) Hartington, discussed in J. L. Hammond, *Gladstone & the Irish Nation*, p. 391; cf. J. Vincent, *Formation of the Liberal Party*, p. 13; J. Kent, *The Age of Disunity* (1966), p. 145.

[52] (p. 289) B.M. *Add. MSS.* 43882 (Dilke Papers), f. 12: Lord Edmond Fitzmaurice to Dilke. I owe this reference to Mrs. Gillian Sutherland, Newnham College, Cambridge.

[53] (p. 290) Raper, *Weekly Record*, 27 Dec. 1862, p. 526; S. Haughton, *Memoir of James Haughton*, p. 222.

[54] (p. 291) The following divisions have been analysed, with the aid of Dod's *Parliamentary Companion.* For 1864 prohibitionists—the divisions on the Liverpool Licensing Bill (17 Feb. 1863), the Sunday Closing Bill (6 May 1864), the ballot (21 June 1864), the borough franchise (11 May 1864), abolition of university tests (16 Mar. 1864) and abolition of church rates (29 Apr. 1863). For the 1870 prohibitionists—the divisions on the ballot (16 Mar. 1870), repeal of the C.D. Acts (24 May 1870), abolition of game laws (20 July 1870), repeal of university tests (23 May 1870), motion against going into committee on the Education Bill (24 June 1870), Irish Church disestablishment (23 Mar. 1869), for repeal of the Ecclesiastical Titles Bill (23 Feb. 1871), on army regulation (3 July 1871), Sunday closing (21 June 1871), on making it a crime to persistently follow blacklegs (30 Mar. 1871) and on making the individual liable to be charged with the crime of picketing (30 Mar. 1871). For the 1876 prohibitionists—the Licensing Boards Bill (17 May 1876), the Animal Cruelty (Anti-Vivisection) Bill (2 May 1877), the Sunday opening of museums (8 June 1877), the death penalty (12 June 1877), the extension of the county franchise (7 July 1875), the removal of women's disabilities (7 Apr. 1875), the motion for extending Lubbock's Bank Holiday Act (24 Feb. 1875) and for repealing the C.D. Acts (19 July 1876).

[55] (p. 291) J. M. Robertson, *The Meaning of Liberalism* (1912), p. 10.

[56] (p. 291) Disraeli, *3 Hansard 215*, c. 1365 (1 May 1873); Earl Grey in 1819, quo. in A. Bullock & M. Shock, *The Liberal Tradition* (1956), p. 6; cf. K. R. Minogue, *The Liberal Mind* (1963), p. 1.

[57] (p. 292) Newman, 'The Drink Traffic and the Permissive Bill', *Fraser's Magazine*, Feb. 1872 (U.K.A. reprint), p. 18; Gladstone, quo. in Rt. Hon. Sir H. Maxwell, *Half a Century of Successful Trade* (1907), p. 32 (letter dated 27 Aug. 1894). For railway drink facilities, see *3 Hansard 261*, c. 471 (23 May 1881) and N.T.L. *Annual Report, 1881–2*, p. 26. See also Viscount Gladstone, *After Thirty Years* (1928), p. 33.

[58] (p. 292) Gladstone in 1888, *The Times*, 28 May 1888, p. 8; in 1894, *The Times*, 16 Sept. 1894, p. 4. See also Gladstone's letter to John Hilton, *ibid.*, 29 Sept. 1894, p. 11; Sir A. West, *Private Diaries* (Ed. H. G. Hutchinson, 1922), pp. 149–50.

[59] (p. 292) Quotations from *The Times*, 16 Sept. 1894, p. 4; 5 Oct. 1895, p. 8 (letter to National Temperance Congress). For changes in the drink industry during the 1880s see C. C. Martin, Jr., 'The British Liquor Licensing Act of 1904 and its Historical Background' (North Carolina unpublished Ph. D. thesis, 1953), pp. 195–9 (microfilm copy); G. J. Holyoake, *Bygones Worth Remembering* (1905), II, p. 196; A. Bullock & M. Shock, *The Liberal Tradition* (1956), pp. 189, 210. On the tied-house system, see D. M. Knox, 'The Development of the Tied House System in London', *Oxford Economic Papers*, N.S., X, No. 1. See also H. Parris, *Constitutional Bureaucracy* (1969), p. 272.

[60] (p. 293) R. Lowe, 'A New Reform Bill', *Fortnightly Review*, 1 Oct. 1877, p. 441.

[61] (p. 293) Magee, *Alliance News*, 11 May 1872, p. 357; *3 Hansard 211*, c. 86 (2 May 1872); cf. comment in *Daily Telegraph*, 3 May 1872, p. 4; *Sheffield Daily Telegraph* (Sheffield), 6 May 1872.

[62] (p. 293) G. W. E. Russell, *Sir Wilfrid Lawson*, p. 82; cf. *Church of England Temperance Chronicle*, 1 Aug. 1876, p. 139.

[63] (p. 293) *Alliance News*, 11 May 1872, p. 352; cf. F. W. Newman, *Alliance News*, 15 Mar. 1873, p. 166.

[64] (p. 294) Quotations from *Alliance News*, 7 Sept. 1872, p. 642; T. Carlyle, *Miscellaneous Essays* III (Ashburton edn), p. 595; *Alliance News*, 12 Feb. 1881, p. 106; Carlyle's correspondence with the U.K.A. in 1872 was dated 18 Apr. & 22 Apr.; cf. U.K.A. *20th Annual Report, 1871–2*, p. 62.

[65] (p. 294) Quotations from *Alliance News*, 26 Oct. 1872, p. 759; 12 Dec. 1885, p. 805 (John Morley).

[66] (p. 294) S. Webb, 'Twentieth Century Politics: a Policy of National Efficiency', *Fabian Tract No. 108* (1901), p. 4; R. Cobden, *Speeches on Public Policy* (1870), I, p. 363; G. P. Gooch, *Courtney*, p. 462. See also G. M. Young, *Portrait of an Age* (1960 edn), p. 115; *The Times*, 26 July 1872, p. 9; B. Crick, *In Defence of Politics* (revised Pelican edn, 1964), pp. 124, 126; *Northern Liberator* (Newcastle), 28 Apr. 1838. This aspect of Liberalism is further discussed in B. Harrison and P. Hollis, 'Chartism, Liberalism & the Life of Robert Lowery', *Eng. Hist. Rev.*, July 1967, pp. 524–6.

[67] (p. 294) Cf. *Alliance News*, 13 July 1878, p. 440.

[68] (p. 295) Sussex County Record Office, *Cobden Papers No. 20:* Bright to Cobden, 24 Oct. 1861; cf. E. R. Jones, *The Life & Speeches of Joseph Cowen M.P.* (1885), p. 277.

[69] (p. 295) Quotations from S. Webb, *Fabian Tract No. 108*, p. 4; cf. G. J. Holyoake, in A. Reid (Ed.), *Why I Am A Liberal* (n.d.), p. 57; G. J. Holyoake, 'Impatience in Politics', *Nineteenth Century*, Aug. 1877, pp. 31, 41. See also J. R. Vincent, *Pollbooks*, p. 50; J. Morley, *Recollections* (1917), I, pp. 21–2.

[70] (p. 295) *New Moral World*, 15 May 1841, p. 304; H. S. Sutton, *The Evangel of Love*, p. 185; cf. *ibid.*, pp. 157, 178, 184; F. W. Newman to E. Sargent, 11 Feb. 1876 in Boston (U.S.A.) Public Library, *Newman-Sargent Collection* (photostat copies).

[71] (p. 295) P. T. Winskill, *Temperance Movement & its Workers*, IV, p. 213; cf. Thomas Spencer, *British & Foreign Temperance Intelligencer*, 1 Jan. 1873, p. 515.

[72] (p. 296) *Wakefield Journal & Examiner* (Wakefield), 24 Nov. 1854, p. 5.

[73] (p. 296) M. D. Hill, quo. in R. & F. Hill, *The Recorder of Birmingham* (1878), p. 276; cf. Pope, in *The Stanley-Pope Discussion*, Pope's letter dated 26 Sept. 1856.

[74] (p. 296) J. M. McKerrow, *Memoir of William McKerrow, D.D.* (1881), p. 259; cf. *Freeman*, 10 May 1872, p. 225; National Library of Scotland, Edinburgh: *Combe MSS.* 7294, f. 41: Samuel Lucas to George Combe, 23 Jan. 1848.

[75] (p. 296) e.g. *Freeman*, 19 May 1871, p. 243.

[76] (p. 296) B. Webb, *My Apprenticeship*, p. 143; cf. E. T. Davies, *Religion in the Industrial Revolution in South Wales*, p. 53.

[77] (p. 296) A. J. P. Taylor, *The Trouble Makers* (1957), p. 170; cf. R. H. Tawney, *Religion & the Rise of Capitalism* (Pelican edn, 1961), p. 226.

Chapter 14. Drink and English Society in the 1870s [pp. 297–318].

[1] (p. 298) H. W. Dickinson, *The Water Supply of Greater London* (Leamington, 1954), pp. 118–21; cf. G. Kitson Clark, *The Making of Victorian England* (1962), p. 81; T. F. Reddaway, *art. cit.*, pp. 118–19.

[2] (p. 298) Statistics from W. A. Robson, 'The Public Utility Services', in H. J. Laski, W. I. Jennings & W. A. Robson (Eds.), *A Century of Municipal Progress 1835–1935* (1935), p. 313; S. D. Simon, *A Century of City Government* (1938), p. 350.

[3] (p. 298) B. D. White, *History of the Corporation of Liverpool 1835–1914* (Liverpool, 1951), p. 32; C. Wilkins, *History of Merthyr Tydfil* (Merthyr, 1908), pp. 434–6; H. Mayhew, *London Labour*, III, p. 246.

[4] (p. 299) Quotations from *Lord Shaftesbury's Diary*, 18 July 1850; Mowatt, *3 Hansard 119*, c. 223 (6 Feb. 1852); cf. *3 Hansard 116*, c. 331 (29 Apr. 1851); Asa Briggs, *History of Birmingham*, II, (1952) p. 75.

[5] (p. 299) Quotation from A. Redford & I. S. Russell, *History of Local Government in Manchester* (1940), II, p. 184; cf. *ibid.*, p. 333; C. Wilkins, *op. cit.*, pp. 434–6; B. D. White, *op. cit.*, p. 57–8; A. Briggs, *op. cit.*, p. 75; S. D. Simon, *op. cit.*, p. 350.

[6] (p. 299) Shaftesbury, *3 Hansard 208*, c. 1762 (17 Aug. 1871); cf. Manning, in *The Times*, 7 Aug. 1879, p. 11; for rural conditions, see *3 Hansard 314*, c. 1098 (5 May 1887), Cremer; for public schools, see W. Sterry, *Annals of . . . Eton* (1898), pp. 40, 280; Sir C. Oman, *Memories of Victorian Oxford* (2nd edn, 1941), p. 31.

[7] (p. 299) For Chadwick, see *Drunkenness Committee*, Q. 325; University College, London, *Chadwick MSS.*: Chadwick to Lawson, 17 Apr. 1875 (draft); Lawson to Chadwick, 17 Apr. 1875.

[8] (p. 300) Quotations from *Weekly Record*, 2 June 1866, p. 260; 16 Apr. 1859, p. 149. See also *ibid.*, 14 July 1866. For the N.T.L. see its *MS. Minutes*, 26 Apr. 1861, 19 June 1863. For drink manufacturers contributing towards drinking fountains, see *Weekly Record*, 24 Sept. 1859, p. 362.

[9] (p. 300) Shaftesbury, *Morning Star*, 1 June 1860, p. 6; *Alliance Weekly News*, 18 Aug. 1860, p. 1049; see also Dawson Burns, *Temperance History*, I, p. 441; II, p. 179.

[10] (p. 300) E. H. Whetham, 'The London Milk Trade, 1860–1900', *Econ. Hist. Rev.*, Dec. 1964, pp. 374, 377–8; S. G. Kendall, *Farming Memoirs of a West Country Yeoman* (1944), p. 14; C. Booth, *Life & Labour in London. Second Series*, III, p. 173. For consumption figures see F. W. Hirst, *Gladstone as Financier & Economist* (1931), p. 90; J. M. Blackman, in T. C. Barker *et al.*, *Our Changing Fare*, p. 41; see also Sir W. Crawford & H. Broadley, *op. cit.*, pp. 15, 208, 284.

[11] (p. 301) F. Engels, *The Condition of the Working Class in England* (Oxford, 1958), p. 99; S.C.H.C. Public-Houses, *Parl. Papers* 1852–3 (855), XXXVII, Q. 8091; on 1851, see *Parl. Papers* 1852 (1485), XXVI, p. 150; cf. *National Temperance Chronicle*, July 1851, p. 102. These sources contradict *Fortunes Made in Business*, II (1884), p. 422. See also Father Augustine, *op. cit.*, p. 291; Joseph Barker, in *National Reformer*, 17 Aug. 1861, p. 1.

[12] (p. 301) G. J. Holyoake, *Social Means of Promoting Temperance* (1859), pp. 17–18; cf. 'viator' in *Sheffield Daily Telegraph*, 18 July 1872, p. 3.

[13] (p. 301) On Perry, see F. Atkin, *Reminiscences*, p. 103; R. Seager, *op. cit.*, pp. vi, 58–69; Beckett, in P. T. Winskill, *Temperance Movement & its Workers*, IV, p. 45; see advertisements in *Weekly Record*, 3 Sept. 1859, p. 343—30/– for a dozen 20 oz. pints; & *British Temperance Advocate*, 15 Aug. 1839, p. 95.

[14] (p. 301) Charles Booth, *Life and Labour in London. Second Series*, III, p. 130.

[15] (p. 301) See the attack in *Weekly Record*, 13 Dec. 1862, p. 506.

[16] (p. 301) *Standard*, 6 Aug. 1868, p. 4. For further details see my D.Phil. thesis, diagrams 39, 41.

[17] (p. 302) B.M. *Add. MSS.* 43654 (Cobden Papers), f. 298: Cobden to Henry Ashworth, 26 Mar. 1864; for chancellors, see *3 Hansard 112*, c. 1014 (5 July 1850); *3 Hansard 174*, c. 558 (7 Apr. 1864).

[18] (p. 302) *The Times*, 16 Aug. 1847, p. 5.

[19] (p. 302) S.C.H.C. Import Duties, *Parl. Papers* 1840 (601), V, Q. 2787.

[20] (p. 302) W. Daniell, *Warminster Common*, (1850), p. 33; J. B. Braithwaite, *J. J. Gurney*, I, p. 471. On the *soirée*, see *Temperance Penny Magazine*, Dec. 1836, p. 195; cf. *Weekly Record*, 28 Mar. 1863, p. 140; see also *Oxford English Dictionary* (Ed. Murray), IX, Pt. 1 (ii), p. 377.

[21] (p. 302) e.g. in *Moral Reformer*, 1 Aug. 1832, p. 246; *Preston Temperance Advocate*, Feb. 1837, p. 14; *Livesey's Moral Reformer*, 13 Jan. 1838, p. 10.

[22] (p. 302) *Oxford English Dictionary*, IX Pt. 2, p. 124; cf. G. M. Young (Ed.), *Early Victorian England*, I, pp. 97–8.

[23] (p. 303) *Parl. Papers* 1840 (601), V, QQ. 2742ff., 2787; Lovett, in S.C.H.C. Public Libraries, *Parl. Papers* 1849 (548), XVII, Q. 2767.

[24] (p. 303) *Penny Cyclopaedia*, 1842, XXIV, p. 312; *Parl. Papers* 1840 (601), V, QQ. 2809–2810.

[25] (p. 303) G. J. Holyoake, *Sixty Years of an Agitator's Life*, I, p. 205; *Social Means oj Promoting Temperance*, pp. 19–20. For similar complaints from temperance reformers, see J. Pearce, *Livesey*, p. cxlv; Samuel Bowly, in *National Temperance Chronicle*, 1 May 1856, p. 267.

[26] (p. 303) e.g. *Leeds Temperance Society Minute Book*, 28 Jan. 1848; cf. *Pall Mall Gazette*, 8 July 1885, p. 5.

[27] (p. 303) *Alliance News*, 30 Mar. 1889, p. 245.

[28] (p. 304) *Weekly Record*, 25 Apr. 1863, p. 191; P. T. Winskill & J. Thomas, *op. cit.*, pp. 75–6; cf. *Parl. Papers* 1877 (418), XI, Q. 8278; *Parl. Papers* 1877 (171), XI, Q. 28. For Layard, see P.R.O. 30/29/74 (Granville Papers): Layard's confidential memorandum dated 4 Nov. 1869, f. 48. There is a good account of London eating-houses and chop-houses in Charles Knight, *London*, IV (1843), pp. 310–13. For further figures on coffee-houses, see my D.Phil. thesis, diagrams 35, 37–41. For Pearce, see R. C. Liquor Licensing Laws, *Parl. Papers* 1898 (8694), XXXVI, QQ. 33, 664–7.

[29] (p. 304) *National Temperance Chronicle*, Oct. 1844, p. 251.

[30] (p. 304) S.C.H.L. on Intemperance, *Parl. Papers* 1877 (418), XI, Q. 9156.

[31] (p. 305) O'Connor, *Northern Star*, 31 Aug. 1844, p. 1; cf. *ibid.*, 14 Nov. 1846, p. 4; Bull, in *Preston Chronicle*, 14 Feb. 1835.

[32] (p. 305) *People's Paper*, 30 Sept. 1854; for middle-class housewives, see G. M. Carstairs, *This Island Now* (Penguin edn, 1964), p. 62; cf. S.C.H.C. Habitual Drunkards, *Parl. Papers* 1872 (242), IX, Q. 2313.

[33] (p. 305) Quotations from *Morning Chronicle*, 6 Jan. 1851, p. 5; *3 Hansard 278*, c. 1328 (27 Apr. 1883); Pease, in S.C.H.L. on Intemperance, *Parl. Papers* 1877 (418), XI, Q. 8490; J. M. Robertson, *op. cit.*, p. 77 discusses the situation in 1912.

[34] (p. 306) J. Manners, *A Plea for National Holy Days* (2nd edn, 1843), pp. 7, 16; *Lord Shaftesbury's Diary*, 30 Dec. 1842.

[35] (p. 306) H. G. Hutchinson, *Life of Sir John Lubbock* (1914), I, p. 125.

[36] (p. 306) M. Hodgson (Birkbeck College London), *Workers' Holidays 1840–1900* (unpublished cyclostyled notes); H. G. Hutchinson, *op. cit.*, I, p. 195; II, p. 79.

[37] (p. 306) W. Wilberforce, *Practical View*, p. 453.

[38] (p. 306) W. V. Harcourt & T. H. Barker, *Mistakes & Fallacies respecting Temperance Legislation* (U.K.A. 1868), letter dated 30 June 1868.

[39] (p. 307) For Brown & Todd, see B. W. Richardson, in R. V. French (Ed.), *United Temperance Mission . . .* (Newport, 1879), pp. 197–9; & F. R. Lees, *Inquiry into the Reasons & Results of the Prescription of Intoxicating Liquors . . .* (1866), pp. 96ff., 36.

[40] (p. 307) Kettle, in W. Logan, *op. cit.*, p. 158; for ailing individuals, see Benjamin Parsons, *Anti-Bacchus* (1840), pp. 30–1; Joseph Barker, *Autobiography* (1880), pp. 205–7.

[41] (p. 307) E. Hodder, *Shaftesbury*, II, p. 443.

[42] (p. 307) J. Higginbottom, *Alcohol, Medical Men, Publicans & their Victims* (Nottingham, n.d.), pp. 2, 8; Dawson Burns, *Temperance History*, I, p. 212.

[43] (p. 307) B.M. *Add. MSS.* 43656 (Cobden Papers), f. 316: Cobden to Sturge, 18 Dec. 1852.

[44] (p. 307) Lallemand and Perrin are discussed in B. W. Richardson, *On Alcohol* (7th edn, 1875), pp. 64–5; on Bowly, see M. Taylor, *Samuel Bowly*, p. 162; for Richardson, see F. Lees, *Dr. Frederic Richard Lees*, p. 252.

[45] (p. 308) Fawcett Library, *Josephine Butler Collection:* Josephine Butler to Mrs. H. J. Wilson, 10 Nov. ?1875 (Box 1, envelope D.6.); R. Blake, *Disraeli*, p. 564.

[46] (p. 308) P. T. Winskill, *Temperance Movement & its Workers*, III, p. 218; IV, p. 76.

[47] (p. 308) G. Bourne, *Change in the Village*, p. 77.

[48] (p. 308) W. Pilkington, *Facts About the Origin of the Teetotal Principle & Pledge* (1894), p. 40.

[49] (p. 308) Quotation from J. Livesey, *Malt Lecture*, p. 18; see also F. R. Lees, in *A Correct Outline of the Public Discussion between Mr. Thomas Furneaux Jordan . . . & F. R. Lees* (2nd edn, Leeds, 1839), p. 31; cf. W. Logan, *Early Heroes*, p. 170; *Morning Chronicle*, 22 Oct. 1849, p. 5; 29 Oct. 1849, p. 5.

[50] (p. 308) R. G. McCarthy, *Drinking & Intoxication*, p. 10.

[51] (p. 309) Elihu Burritt, *A Walk from London to John O'Groats* (New York, 1864), p. 239; cf. *National Reformer*, 5 Apr. 1862, p. 1. See also my comments in *Past & Present*, Apr. 1965, pp. 101–2.

[52] (p. 309) Elihu Burritt, *op. cit.*, p. 175; E. Hodder, *Shaftesbury*, III, p. 308.

[53] (p. 309) *3 Hansard 166*, c. 782 (10 Apr. 1862); *3 Hansard 314*, cc. 1094–1102 (5 May 1887).

[54] (p. 309) Quotations from Holyoake, in A. A. Reade, *The House of Commons on Stimulants* (1885), p. 5; Lovett, in S.C.H.C. on Public Libraries, *Parl. Papers* 1849 (548), XVII, Q. 2783.

[55] (p. 309) Dunlop quotation from Jabez Burns, *Retrospect*, p. 162; for Hartwell, see *Bee-Hive*, 3 June 1871; for Leicester, *Alliance News*, 22 Oct. 1903, p. 715; P. T. Winskill, *Temperance Movement*, II, p. 259; for Howell, see Bishopsgate Institute, *Howell Collection*, No. 4110: *Autobiography* (rough draft), pp. 63–4.

[56] (p. 309) Commercial travellers, *Western Temperance Herald*, 1 Nov. 1865, p. 168; dinner-parties, J. Dunlop, *Autobiography*, p. 374 (30 May 1854).

[57] (p. 310) J. C. Drummond & A. Wilbraham, *op. cit.*, p. 106; cf. S.C.H.C. Wine Duties, *Parl. Papers* 1852 (495), XVII, Q. 1248.

[58] (p. 310) G. R. Porter, *The Progress of the Nation* (1851 edn), p. 675; see also R. Fulford, *The Prince Consort* (1949), p. 101; R. Blake, *Disraeli* (1966), p. 74; for gout rests, R. Nevill, *The World of Fashion* (1923), p. 234; Rev. J. C. Atkinson, *Forty Years in a Moorland Parish* (1891), pp. 30–1. On smoking, see Frances, Countess of Warwick, *Life's Ebb & Flow* (n.d.), p. 77; G. L. Apperson, *The Social History of Smoking* (1914), p. 157; R. Nevill, *The World of Fashion*, p. 272.

[59] (p. 310) On funerals, *The Times*, 14 Dec. 1849, p. 4; 15 Dec. 1849, p. 4; 18 Dec. 1849, p. 5; 19 Dec. 1849, p. 3; cf. *Morning Chronicle*, 2 Jan. 1850, p. 4; 17 May 1850, p. 4; see also Lord's Day Observance Society, *Occasional Paper*, Jan. 1874, p. 334; Mrs. Bosanquet, quo. in A. Wilson & H. Levy, *Burial Reform & Funeral Costs* (1938), p. 75.

[60] (p. 310) R. G. Wilberforce, *Life of Samuel Wilberforce*, II, p. 5; for teetotal harvest-homes, see *New British & Foreign Temperance Intelligencer*, 24 Nov. 1836, p. 383; *London Temperance Intelligencer*, 14 Oct. 1837, p. 395; see also Anon., *Practical Suggestions for the Celebration of Parochial Harvest Homes in Norfolk & Suffolk* (Norwich, n.d.), pp. 10–11, 31–2.

[61] (p. 311) Quotation from *Preston Temperance Advocate*, Sept. 1835, p. 68; see also A. J. C. Hare, *The Story of My Life* (1896), I, p. 234; A. Blomfield (Ed.), *Memoir of C. J. Blomfield* (1863), I, p. 105; A. R. Ashwell, *Life of Samuel Wilberforce*, I, p. 331.

[62] (p. 311) For Manning, see A. E. Dingle & B. H. Harrison, 'Cardinal Manning as Temperance Reformer', *Historical Journal*, 1969. For drinking habits among the clergy, see H. A. Bruce, *Lectures & Addresses* (n.d.), p. 24; the wheel has now come full circle—see M. Stacey, *Tradition & Change. A Study of Banbury* (1960), p. 72; see also H. D. Rawnsley, *Harvey Goodwin, Bishop of Carlisle* (1896), pp. 133–5; I owe this latter reference to Cormac

Rigby; Rev. E. Monro, *The 'Navvies' and How to Meet Them* (1857), p. 10; I owe this reference to Rev. Dr. Brian Heeney, University of Alberta, Edmonton.

[63] (p. 311) *Banbury Guardian*, 1 Feb. 1849, p. 2.

[64] (p. 311) J. Buckle, *The Wesleyan Centenary Hall Spirit Vaults Exposed* (n.d.). Information on Banbury kindly provided by Barrie Trinder; see also his 'The Radical Baptists', *Cake & Cockhorse*, Jan. 1965, pp. 180, 183; on Castle Donnington, see J. M. Lee, 'The Rise & Fall of a Market Town. Castle Donnington in the Nineteenth Century', *Trans. Leicestershire Archaeological Society*, 1956, p. 63; on Newcastle-under-Lyme, see F. Bealey, 'Municipal Politics in Newcastle-under-Lyme 1872–1914', *loc. cit.*, p. 67.

[65] (p. 313) J. Livesey, in J. Pearce, *Livesey*, p. 76. The local directories are analysed more fully in my D.Phil. thesis, tables 32–4, and diagrams 35–41. The following sources have been used in making these calculations. For Ripon, Pigot's *National Commercial Directory, 1834*, pp. 897–900; *Kelly's P.O. Directory W/Riding, Yorks, 1871*, pp. 674–7. For Northampton, *Pigot's Commercial Directory, 1823–4*, pp. 426–8; *Kelly's P.O. Directory, 1869*, pp. 172–231. For Banbury, *Pigot's Commercial Directory 1823–4*, pp. 435–7; *Kelly's P.O. Directory for Oxon., 1869*, pp. 829–34. For Preston, Pigot & Co, *National Commercial Directory, 1834*, pp. 512–20; Kelly's *P.O. Directory for Lancashire, 1864*, pp. 358–76. For Whitby, Pigot & Co, *National Commercial Directory, 1834*, pp. 1003–7; Kelly's *P.O. Directory N. & E. Riding, Yorks, 1872*, pp. 292–8.

[66] (p. 314) W. H. Beveridge, *Unemployment. A Problem of Industry* (3rd edn, 1912), pp. 46–7; cf. D. S. Thomas, *Social Aspects of the Business Cycle* (New York, 1925), pp. 127–32. For drinking between the wars, see A. J. P. Taylor, *England 1914–1945* (Oxford, 1965), p. 307.

[67] (p. 314) C. H. Denyer, *art. cit.*, p. 46; G. W. E. Russell, *Collections & Recollections II* (1909 edn), p. 300; D. M. Knox, 'The Development of the London Brewing Industry, 1830–1914' (Oxford unpublished B.Litt. thesis, 1956), pp. 11–13; J. Burnett, 'The History of Food Adulteration in Great Britain in the Nineteenth Century, with special reference to Bread, Tea & Beer' (London Univ. unpublished Ph.D. thesis, 1958), p. 51; J. A. Banks, *Prosperity & Parenthood*, p. 68. For the unreliability of *per capita* consumption figures, see my bibliography, in *International Review of Social History*, XII (1967), Part 2, pp. 207ff.

[68] (p. 314) C. Booth, *Life & Labour in London. Second Series*, III, p. 119.

[69] (p. 315) All these figures are from G. B. Wilson, *Alcohol & the Nation*, pp. 434–6.

[70] (p. 315) Judicial statistics for 1870, *Parl. Papers* 1871 (C. 442), LXIV, pp. 25ff. The figures for offences between 1857 and 1876 are from the Judicial Statistics, *Parl. Papers* 1857–8 (2407), LVII, p. ix; 1859 (2508), XXVI, p. xii; 1860 (2692), LXIV, p. xii; 1861 (2860), LX, p. xiii; 1862 (3025), LVI, p. xvi; 1865 (3534), LII, p. xvii; 1867 (3919), LXVI, p. xvi; 1873 (C. 871), LXX, p. xix; 1877 (C. 1871), LXXXVI, p. xix. The figures for 1860, 1864, 1870 and 1876 come from Judicial Statistics, *Parl. Papers* 1861 (2860), LX, p. 32; 1865 (3534), LII, pp. 25–31; 1871 (C. 442), LXIV, p. 32; 1877 (C. 1871), LXXXVI, pp. 25ff. For London arrest figures, see S.C.H.L. on Intemperance, first report, *Parl. Papers* 1877 (171), XI, p. 342.

[71] (p. 315) G. B. Wilson, *Alcohol & the Nation*, pp. 437ff.

[72] (p. 316) Bruce, *3 Hansard 211*, c. 489 (8 May 1872); Roebuck, *Sheffield & Rotherham Independent*, 15 Nov. 1856. For other literary evidence that sobriety was extending, see Gladstone, in *Alliance Weekly News*, 24 Mar. 1860, p. 965; Lovett, in S.C.H.C. Public Libraries, *Parl. Papers* 1849 (548), XVII, Q. 2767; Charles Dickens, *A Tale of Two Cities* (Everyman edn, 1964), p. 80; James Grant, *Lights & Shadows of London Life* (1842), I, p. 171; *3 Hansard 112*, c. 1014 (5 July 1850); *3 Hansard 174*, c. 558 (7 Apr. 1864). For the difficulty of getting statistics on the number of teetotalers, see my bibliography, *loc. cit.*, pp. 209–10. For estimates of the proportion of reclaimed drunkards, see *National Temperance Chronicle*, Mar. 1845, p. 340; Aug. 1849, p. 506; *London Teetotal Magazine*, Nov. 1840, p. 378; *British Temperance Advocate*, 15 Aug. 1841, p. 85; *National Temperance Magazine*, Sept. 1844, p. 395; *National Temperance Advocate*, III (1847), supplement, p. 8.

[73] (p. 316) *National Temperance Chronicle*, Aug. 1849, p. 506; N.T.L. *Annual Report, 1856*, pp. 24–6.

[74] (p. 316) *Bristol Temperance Herald*, July 1844, p. 50; P. Burne, *Teetotaler's Companion*, p. 350; *National Temperance Magazine*, June 1844, p. 256.

[75] (p. 316) *Preston Temperance Advocate*, supplement for Apr. 1835; *Bristol Temperance Herald*, Apr. 1851, p. 59; B.M. *Add. MSS.* 44188 (Gladstone Papers), f. 42: Newman Hall to Gladstone, 11 May 1865.

[76] (p. 317) *Temperance Spectator*, 1 May 1861, p. 74; N.T.L. *Annual Report 1860–1*, p. 19; Robert Highet, *Rechabite History* (Manchester, 1936), p. 501.

[77] (p. 317) *Saturday Review*, 25 Dec. 1858, p. 641.

[78] (p. 317) Baines reported Tweedie's estimate in parliament; his speech is quo. in N.T.L. *Annual Report 1860–1*, p. 19; for Newman Hall, see B.M. *Add. MSS.* 44188 (Gladstone Papers), f. 42: Newman Hall to Gladstone, 11 May 1865; T. H. Barker, in *Temperance Spectator*, 1 May 1861, p. 74.

[79] (p. 317) Cf. L. J. Macfarlane, *The British Communist Party. Its Origin & Development until 1929* (1966), p. 285.

Chapter 15. The Drink Trade and English Society in the 1870s [pp. 319–347].

[1] (p. 319) Porter, in S.C.H.C. Wine Duties, *Parl. Papers* 1852 (495), XVII, Q. 3817. See also L. Cust, *History of Eton College* (1899), p. 185; P. Grosskurth, *John Addington Symonds. A Biography* (1964), p. 31; F. D. How, *Six Great Schoolmasters* (2nd edn, 1905), pp. 105, 144; I owe these three references to Cormac Rigby; cf. S.C.H L. . . . Acts for the Sale of Beer . . . *Parl. Papers* 1850 (398), X, Q. 429. Salisbury, *3 Hansard 306*, c. 185 (22 June 1886).

[2] (p. 320) G. R. Porter, *The Progress of the Nation* (3rd edn, 1851), p. 522.

[3] (p. 320) This paragraph is based on H. Roberts, *The Improvement of the Dwellings of the Labouring Classes* (1859); J. N. Tarn, 'Some Pioneer Suburban Housing Estates', *Architectural Review*, May 1968; N. Pevsner, 'Model Houses for the Working Classes', *ibid.*, May 1943.

[4] (p. 321) *Scottish Temperance Review*, 1848, pp. 264, 266.

[5] (p. 321) T. Whittaker, *Life's Battles*, p. 66.

[6] (p. 321) S.C.H.L. on Intemperance, *Parl. Papers* 1877 (418), XI, Q. 8272.

[7] (p. 322) H. Mayhew, *London Labour*, III, p. 257; for a public apology, see E. Morris, *History of the Temperance & Teetotal Societies in Glasgow* (Glasgow, 1855), p. 41.

[8] (p. 322) J. C. Farn, *Reasoner*, 14 Oct. 1857, p. 229.

[9] (p. 322) J. Ruskin, 'Fors Clavigera', in *Works*, XXIX, letter 73 (Jan. 1877), p. 23. See also my 'Religion & Recreation in Nineteenth Century England', *loc. cit.*, *passim.*

[10] (p. 323) S. Hobhouse, *Joseph Sturge* (1919), p. 173; R. Balgarnie, *Sir Titus Salt*, p. 110; T. Beggs, *John Guest*, p. 224; *British Temperance Advocate*, 1 Oct. 1857, p. 119; J. Livesey, in J. Pearce, *Livesey*, p. 29. For drinksellers' opposition to parks see, e.g., S.C.H.C. on Public-Houses, *Parl. Papers* 1854 (367), XIV, Q. 3529.

[11] (p. 323) Quotations from *Athenaeum*, 31 Jan. 1857, p. 151; H. Pelling, *Popular Politics & Society in Late-Victorian Britain* (1968), p. 179; cf. *ibid.*, p. 2. See also R. D. Altick, *The English Common Reader* (Chicago, 1957), p. 230; S.C.H.C. Habitual Drunkards, *Parl. Papers* 1872 (242), IX, Q. 832; for Oxford, see *Temperance Star*, 19 Aug. 1870, p. 3; for Newcastle, see F. Bealey, 'Municipal Politics in Newcastle-under-Lyme 1872–1914', *loc. cit.*, p. 70.

[12] (p. 324) Frederic Harrison, *Sundays & Festivals* (1867), p. 5; see also Gladstone, *Oldham Chronicle* (Oldham), 21 Dec. 1867. W. S. Jevons, 'Amusements of the People', in his *Methods of Social Reform* (2nd edn, 1904), p. 22; for Prince Albert, see A. R. Ashwell, *Life of Samuel Wilberforce*, I, p. 224.

[13] (p. 325) M. Miliband (Ed.), *The Observer of the Nineteenth Century* (1966), p. 152; *Morning Chronicle*, 2 Sept. 1850, p. 5; cf. L. Faucher, 'Études sur L'Angleterre', in *Revue des Deux Mondes*, 1843, IV, p. 1005. There is a good account of the music-hall's origins in C. D. Stuart & A. J. Park, *The Variety Stage* (1895). For statistics, see R. Mander & J. Mitchenson, *British Music Hall* (1965), p. 19, & S.C.H.C. on Theatrical Licences and Regulations, *Parl. Papers* 1866 (373), XVI, p. 307; cf. *Morning Chronicle*, 8 Nov. 1849; University College London, *Brougham MSS.*: James Bishop to Brougham, 22 Dec. 1862; S.C.H.C. on Public-Houses, *Parl. Papers* 1852–3 (855), XXXVII, Q. 3826. For twentieth-century developments, see T. Burke, *English Inns* (1944), p. 36.

[14] (p. 325) *Parl. Papers* 1866 (373), XVI, Q. 4750; E. Hodder, *Shaftesbury*, III, p. 106; *Bee-Hive*, 25 Oct. 1862, p. 1. For customer-entertainers, see W. Howitt, *The Rural Life of England* (1838), II, p. 236; W. M. Noble, *Life Story of Thomas Horrocks* (1890), pp. 12–13. For Charrington, see G. Thorne, *The Great Acceptance*, pp. 107ff.

[15] (p. 325) Ministerial Conference on Suppression of the Liquor Traffic, *Full Report 1857* (Manchester), p. 24; cf. S.C.H.C. on Public-Houses, *Parl. Papers* 1854 (367), XIV, Q. 1301.

[16] (p. 326) *Morning Chronicle*, 2 Sept. 1850; S.C.H.C. Public-Houses, *Parl. Papers* 1854 (367), XIV, Q. 1301.

[17] (p. 326) 'Lord' George Sanger, *Seventy Years a Showman*, p. 132.

[18] (p. 328) Derby Temperance Society, *9th Annual Report, 1845*, p. 8; cf. Fairlop, *British & Foreign Temperance Intelligencer*, 6 July 1839, p. 259; Crawshawbooth fair, *British Temperance Advocate*, 1 July 1858, p. 81. For Shrewsbury show, see J. M. J. Fletcher, *Mrs. Wightman of Shrewsbury*, p. 96. See also N.T.L. *MS. Minutes*, 1 Oct. 1858, 13 Sept. 1861.

[19] (p. 329) Quotations from *British & Foreign Temperance Intelligencer*, 28 Aug. 1841, p. 278; *Weekly Record*, 11 July 1857, p. 244; J. Dunlop, *The Universal Tendency to Association in Mankind Analyzed & Illustrated* (1840), p. 187.

[20] (p. 330) *New British & Foreign Magazine & Monthly Chronicle*, Apr. 1841, p. 108.

[21] (p. 330) e.g. *Banbury Advertiser*, 28 July 1855; rival recreations were provided for Grimsbury Wake by two drinking places.

[22] (p. 330) J. Lawson, *Pudsey*, p. 57; cf. S. Bamford, *Early Days*, p. 148.

[23] (p. 330) *Leeds Temperance Society MS. Minute Book*, 10 Sept. 1840. For respectable Londoners, see T. Sparks [*alias* Charles Dickens], *Sunday Under Three Heads* (1836), p. 17.

[24] (p. 330) W. Hazlitt, 'On Going a Journey', in P. P. Howe (Ed.), *Complete Works*, VIII (1931), p. 187; Mill, *3 Hansard 187*, c. 821 (20 May 1867). See also G. J. Holyoake, *Social Means of Promoting Temperance*, p. 21. S.C.H.C. on Public-Houses, *Parl. Papers* 1852–3 (855), XXXVII, Q. 8717.

[25] (p. 330) W. Howitt, *The Rural Life of England*, II, p. 257.

[26] (p. 331) Quotation from M. Rutherford, *The Revolution in Tanner's Lane*, p. 264; Sheffield, *Bee-Hive*, 15 June 1867. See also *Morning Chronicle*, 8 Nov. 1849, p. 4.

[27] (p. 331) W. E. Adams, *Memoirs of a Social Atom*, II, p. 468. See also B. Harrison & P. Hollis, 'Chartism, Liberalism & the Life of Robert Lowery', *loc. cit.*, p. 520.

[28] (p. 331) *Weekly Record*, 5 May 1860, pp. 203–4.

[29] (p. 332) J. L. & B. Hammond, *James Stansfeld* (1932), p. 147; see also Sir E. Cook, *Florence Nightingale* (1914), I, p. 276.

[30] (p. 332) R. C. . . . Recruiting, *Parl. Papers* 1867 (3752), XV, Q. 1408. See also Lord Stanmore, *Sidney Herbert, Lord Herbert of Lea. A Memoir* (1906), II, pp. 362ff.

[31] (p. 332) For 1864, see R. C. . . . Contagious Diseases Act, *Parl. Papers* 1871 (C. 408, 408–I), XIX, Q. 18,152; for Aldershot, *The Shield*, 18 Apr. 1870, pp. 52–3.

[32] (p. 333) S.C.H.C. Contagious Diseases Act (1866) *Parl. Papers* 1868–9 (306), VII, Q. 592.

[33] (p. 333) R. C. Liquor Licensing Laws, *Parl. Papers* 1899 (9075), XXXIV, Q. 71,736; [A. Weston], *Temperance Work in the Royal Navy* (1879), pp. 1–19.

[34] (p. 333) *3 Hansard 37*, c. 180 (9 Mar. 1837).

[35] (p. 333) S.C.H.C. . . . Venereal Disease: *Parl. Papers* 1867–8 (4031), XXXVII, Q. 607; see also *ibid.*, Q. 1023.

[36] (p. 333) R. C. Contagious Diseases Act: *Parl. Papers* 1871 (C. 408, 408–I), XIX, Q. 3845; cf. *ibid.*, QQ. 4090, 4186.

[37] (p. 334) Lees, quo. in J. Robinson, *The Social, Mental & Moral Condition of the British Workman* (Blyth, 1859), p. 18; cf. T. Beggs, *op. cit.*, pp. 26–8; *Devon & Cornwall Temperance Journal*, May 1868, p. 73; *Staunch Teetotaler*, July 1867, p. 109.

[38] (p. 334) W. Cooke Taylor, *Notes of a Tour in the Manufacturing Districts of Lancashire* (2nd edn, 1842), p. 134.

[39] (p. 334) J. Simmons, *Railways of Britain* (1965 paperback edn), p. 87, referring to the Stockton & Darlington railway.

[40] (p. 335) Wellington, quo. in C. B. Patterson, *Angela Burdett-Coutts and the Victorians* (1953), p. 116. For French publicans, see P. A. Mann, 'Changing Outlines of 1848', *Amer.*

Hist. Rev., 1963, p. 941; I owe this reference to Dr. Walsh. For the effect of closing stage-routes on publicans, see S.C.H.C. Public-Houses, *Parl. Papers* 1852–3 (855), XXXVII, QQ. 7399, 7401; *The Era*, 26 May 1839, p. 414; *Rechabite Magazine*, III (1848), p. 281; Charles Knight, *London*, IV (1843), p. 313.

[41] (p. 335) For the effect of the railway in one rural area, Mere, Wilts, see Various, *The Story of Mere* (Gillingham, 1958), p. 48; J. F. Rutter, *1890: Jubilee of the Mere Temperance Society*, pp. 11–12. See also C. Roberts, *The Radical Countess* (Carlisle, 1962), pp. 61–7; J. G. Shaw, *William Gregson*, pp. 173–4. For Leeds trams, see G. C. Dickinson, 'The Development of Surburban Road Passenger Transport in Leeds, 1840–95', *Journal of Transport History*, IV, No. 4 (Nov. 1960), p. 215.

[42] (p. 336) Geo. Stephenson, in *Temperance Monthly Visitor* (Norwich), Oct. 1860, p. 79; *Rechabite Magazine*, 1848, p. 281; E. E. Dodd, *Bingley. A Yorkshire Town through Nine Centuries* (Bingley, 1958), p. 168; *Devon & Cornwall Temperance Journal*, Nov. 1868, p. 180.

[43] (p. 336) S.C.H.C. Import Duties, *Parl. Papers* 1840 (601), V, Q. 2817; H. Solly, '*These Eighty Years*', II, p. 288; cf. Lovett, *Bee-Hive*, 6 June 1868, p. 4.

[44] (p. 336) For the ironmoulders, see S. Maccoby, *English Radicalism. 1832–1852* (1935), p. 407; Hartwell, *Bee-Hive*, 3 June 1871; Stephens, *Ashton Reporter*, 13 Apr. 1867, pp. 6–7.

[45] (p. 337) Quotations from F. W. Peaples, *History of the . . . Bolton Co-operative Society Ltd . . .* (1909), pp. 65–6; I owe this reference to Mr. T. W. Mason of St. Antony's College, Oxford; *Oldham Chronicle*, 21 Dec. 1867; cf. *3 Hansard 178*, c. 1500 (4 May 1865); *3 Hansard 229*, c. 1853 (14 June 1876). For Middlesbrough, see Lady F. Bell, *op. cit.*, p. 178.

[46] (p. 337) B.M. *Add. MSS.* 35149 (Place Papers), f. 259: Place to Coates, 22 Dec. 1833; *Bee-Hive*, 14 Mar. 1863, p. 4.

[47] (p. 337) H. Solly, '*These Eighty Years*', II, pp. 256, 299.

[48] (p. 338) For the Working Men's Club & Institute Union, see University College, London, *Brougham MSS.*: Solly to Brougham, 13 Dec. 1862; *Weekly Record*, 5 Oct. 1867, p. 474; 26 Oct. 1867, p. 517; H. Solly, *Working Men's Clubs & Alcoholic Drinks* (1872), *passim;* H. J. Hanham, *Elections & Party Management*, p. 103. For the Birmingham debating society, see its valuable *MS. Minutes 1858–1886* (2 Vols.), in Birmingham Public Library, ref. nos. 103138–9. Mrs. Corke, of Leamington Historical Association, kindly referred me to this source.

[49] (p. 338) H. Robinson, *Britain's Post Office* (1953), p. 285; 'Will You Try It?', *London Temperance Tracts, 1839*, p. 4.

[50] (p. 339) Quotation from *3 Hansard 70*, c. 1250 (17 July 1843); see also *Temperance Penny Magazine*, Oct. 1837, pp. 146–7; Jan. 1838, p. 5; Sept. 1839, p. 132; H. Mayhew, *London Labour*, III, pp. 252, 249. For the ballast-heavers, see *3 Hansard 120*, c. 783; for Wakley, see *ibid.*, cc. 786–7 (6 Apr. 1852).

[51] (p. 339) Lady F. Bell, *op. cit.*, p. 348; *Lord Shaftesbury's Diary*, 7 Mar. 1883; cf. *3 Hansard 268*, c. 1925 (2 May 1882); *3 Hansard 276*, cc. 1569–82 (6 Mar. 1883).

[52] (p. 339) [T. Wright], *The Great Unwashed* (1868), pp. 201ff.

[53] (p. 339) For public-house museums, see C. E. Lawrence, 'Public-House Museums', *The Ludgate*, 1895; The *Graphic*, 8 Dec. 1928, p. 410. For secularists, see S. Budd, in B. R. Wilson (Ed.), *Patterns of Sectarianism* (1967), p. 385.

[54] (p. 340) Lord Avebury, *Essays & Addresses. 1900–1903* (1903), p. 95; Gladstone, *3 Hansard 158*, c. 1056 (10 May 1860); cf. *3 Hansard 149*, c. 266 (16 Mar. 1858).

[55] (p. 340) D. M. Knox, *Development of the London Brewing Industry, 1830–1914*, pp. 2–4, 138–40; J. Vaizey, *The Brewing Industry. 1886–1951* (1960), pp. 4–5; J. Baxter, 'The Organisation of the Brewing Industry', (London unpublished Ph.D. thesis, 1945), pp. 62–4, 105–8, 111–13, 151–5.

[56] (p. 340) B. Webb, *My Apprenticeship*, p. 41; B. L. Crapster, *British Liquor Industry*, pp. 241–2, 244–6; cf. *3 Hansard 278*, c. 684 (19 Apr. 1883).

[57] (p. 340) For friction with publicans, see R. C. Poor Laws, *Parl. Papers* 1834 (44), XXIX, Appendix A, Part III, p. 26A; cf. *Drunkenness Committee*, Q. 321. For temperance and poor law reform, *3 Hansard 22*, c. 1160 (23 Apr. 1834); *Mirror of Parliament*, 1834, III, p. 1989 (3 June 1834). For outdoor relief, see *Drunkenness Committee*, Q. 318.

[58] (p. 341) *Brougham MSS.*: M. D. Hill to Brougham, 19 May 1861; for Queen Victoria

see *Bristol Temperance Herald*, Feb. 1846, p. 10; for the C.O.S. see *Brewers Journal*, 15 May 1871, p. 123; *Temperance Record*, 6 May 1871, p. 207.

[59] (p. 341) *National Temperance Chronicle*, July 1852, p. 314.

[60] (p. 341) Macclesfield: *Macclesfield Courier & Herald* (Macclesfield), 5 Dec. 1857; Charrington, G. Thorne, *The Great Acceptance*, pp. 21–2, 211–13.

[61] (p. 342) Binney, in Dawson Burns, *Temperance History*, I, p. 326; sabbatarianism, *Scottish Temperance Review*, 1848, pp. 536–7; *3 Hansard 100*, cc. 458–9 (12 July 1848); London City Mission, *Metropolitan Temperance Intelligencer & Journal*, 3 Feb. 1844, p. 34; 30 Aug. 1845, p. 273; Fremlin, *Kent Messenger*, 19 Mar. 1910; Hartington, *3 Hansard 244*, c. 739 (11 Mar. 1879).

[62] (p. 342) J. Pearce, *Livesey*, p. 28; cf. Livesey's *New Year's Address to the People of Preston* (1875, copy in Harris Library, Preston).

[63] (p. 342) Quotation from Banbury Public Library, *Potts Collection*, 1831, p. 6; I owe this reference to Barrie Trinder. See also Robert Lowe, *Fortnightly Review*, 1 Jan. 1877, pp. 3–4. For the drink trade's representation in local government, see E. P. Hennock's excellent discussion in H. J. Dyos (Ed.), *The Study of Urban History*, pp. 323–4; also F. Bealey, 'Municipal Politics in Newcastle-under-Lyme 1835–72', *North Staffordshire Journal of Field Studies*, III (1963), p. 72; 'Municipal Politics in Newcastle-under-Lyme, 1872–1914', *ibid.*, V (1965), pp. 66–7. For brewers and the police, see H. Parris, 'The Home Office and the Provincial Police in England and Wales—1856–1870', *Public Law*, 1961, p. 251.

[64] (p. 342) The rest of this paragraph leans heavily on B. L. Crapster, *British Liquor Industry*, pp. 177–95.

[65] (p. 343) Bright, *Alliance News*, 15 Feb. 1868, p. 54; *ibid.*, 27 Mar. 1880, p. 195.

[66] (p. 343) *3 Hansard 29*, c. 215 (2 July 1835); *3 Hansard 47*, c. 1252 (3 June 1839). As for publicans and the electorate after 1832, the proportion fell at Leicester. The pollbooks used in this cursory analysis are all in the Bodleian Library, Oxford. To establish conclusively the relationship between the 1832 Reform Act and publican influence in the constituencies, far more research would be needed. The pollbooks used here have been selected solely for their accessibility: many more are available in London and elsewhere.

[67] (p. 343) *Weekly Record*, 18 Apr. 1857, p. 129.

[68] (p. 343) H. A. Taylor, 'Politics in Famine-Stricken Preston', *Trans. Historic Society of Lancashire & Cheshire*, 1955, p. 133; C. O'Leary, *The Elimination of Corrupt Practices in British Elections. 1868–1911* (1962), p. 56.

[69] (p. 343) Bruce, *3 Hansard 194*, c. 652 (4 Mar. 1869); cf. Lowe, *3 Hansard 187*, c. 792 (20 May 1867).

[70] (p. 344) Baines, *3 Hansard 54*, c. 681 (28 May 1840); cf. Osborne, *3 Hansard 121*, c. 792 (19 May 1852).

[71] (p. 344) B. L. Crapster, *British Liquor Industry*, p. 232.

[72] (p. 344) *3 Hansard 268*, c. 1337 (24 Apr. 1882); cf. *3 Hansard 281*, c. 193 (3 July 1883); Dean Close, *The Times*, 29 July 1865; cf. *3 Hansard 269*, c. 758 (15 May 1882); but compare *3 Hansard 280*, c. 952–3 (19 June 1883).

[73] (p. 344) *3 Hansard 120*, c. 770 (5 Apr. 1852).

[74] (p. 344) Gladstone, *3 Hansard 193*, c. 1448 (18 July 1868); cf. Brotherton, *3 Hansard 104*, c. 828 (25 Apr. 1849).

[75] (p. 345) Pope, *Alliance News*, 3 Feb. 1872, p. 98; the Alliance address is quo. in James Haughton, *A Plea for Teetotalism & the Maine Liquor Law* (1855), p. 172.

[76] (p. 345) R. Wraith & E. Simpkins, *Corruption in Developing Countries* (1963), p. 38.

[77] (p. 345) *Temperance Penny Magazine*, Aug. 1847, p. 117 (Bath); Manchester & Salford Temperance Society, *2nd Annual Report*, p. 12; *British & Foreign Temperance Intelligencer*, 26 June 1841, p. 202 (Bury St. Edmund's); *Bristol Temperance Herald*, Aug. 1852, p. 115 (Bristol & Bath); for Bradford in 1841, see *British & Foreign Temperance Intelligencer*, 5 June 1841, p. 182; see also *ibid.*, 19 June 1841, p. 194; 10 July 1841, p. 217. For Caine, see *Liverpool Daily Post*, 16 Oct. 1868; note also R. Firth's efforts at Hull in 1841, *Hull Temperance Pioneer* (Hull), 1 July 1841, p. 51.

[78] (p. 346) National Temperance League, *Annual Report, 1860–1*, p. 19.

[79] (p. 346) M. Ostrogorski, *Democracy & the Organisation of Political Parties*, I, p. 466; H. J. Hanham, *Elections & Party Management*, pp. 281–3.

[80] (p. 347) Lowe, *3 Hansard 215*, c. 676 (7 Apr. 1873); cf. *3 Hansard 214*, c. 17 (6 Feb. 1873).

Chapter 16. Assessments [pp. 348–386].

[1] (p. 349) Pope, *Plymouth & Devonport Weekly Journal*, 12 Sept. 1861; cf. Dawson Burns, *Poole & Bournemouth Herald* (Poole), 7 Aug. 1879; Livesey, *Moral Reformer*, 1 Apr. 1831, p. 117; cf. Livesey's argument in *Alliance Weekly News*, 17 Mar. 1860, p. 960.

[2] (p. 349) Quotations from J. Livesey, *A Letter to J. Wilson Patten* (1855), p. 11; R. & F. Hill, *The Recorder of Birmingham*, p. 277; see also *National Temperance Advocate*, Jan. 1848, p. 2.

[3] (p. 349) *Weekly Record*, 7 Feb. 1863, p. 66.

[4] (p. 349) A. Young, *Enquiry into the State of the Public Mind amongst the Lower Classes: and on the Means of Turning it to the Welfare of the State* (1798), p. 30; Bruce, *3 Hansard 205*, c. 1075 (3 Apr. 1871); Rolleston, quo. in *Alliance News*, 19 Oct. 1872, p. 739; cf. Lady F. Bell, *At the Works*, p. 349; Adam Smith, *op. cit.*, I, p. 342. For Salisbury, see C. C. Martin, 'The British Liquor Licensing Act of 1904', p. 216.

[5] (p. 350) R. Williams, 'Laissez Faire', *Fraser's Magazine*, Jan. 1870, p. 76.

[6] (p. 350) *Mirror of Parliament*, 1832, II, p. 2358 (31 May 1832); *3 Hansard 12*, c. 733 (7 May 1832).

[7] (p. 351) Quotations from *Alliance News*, 1 Mar. 1879, p. 135; M. Rutherford, *Autobiography*, p. 80; *Manchester Examiner & Times*, 1 Feb. 1871 (Lawson).

[8] (p. 351) Bowly, *Bristol Temperance Herald*, July 1849, p. 98; see also Lawson, *3 Hansard 203*, c. 172 (13 July 1870).

[9] (p. 351) *National Temperance Advocate*, 15 June 1843, p. 66.

[10] (p. 352) *3 Hansard 71*, c. 88 (1 Aug. 1843).

[11] (p. 352) Grindrod, *Alliance News*, 12 June 1880, p. 381.

[12] (p. 353) Rev. Father Augustine, *Footprints of Father Mathew*, p. 293.

[13] (p. 353) *Record*, 28 Aug. 1871, p. 2.

[14] (p. 353) Quotations from Henry Carter, *English Temperance Movement*, p. 21; F. R. Lees, introduction to P. T. Winskill, *Temperance Movement & its Workers* (1892), I, p. xiv; cf. the study of the feminist movement, in J. A. & O. Banks, 'Feminism & Social Change—a Case Study of a Social Movement', in G. K. Zollschan & W. Hirsch (Eds.), *Explorations in Social Change* (1964).

[15] (p. 354) Dawson Burns, *Temperance History* (1889), II, p. 409, 412; F. R. Lees, introduction to P. T. Winskill, *op. cit.*, I, pp. xiv, xxiv.

[16] (p. 354) G. J. Holyoake, *Social Means of Promoting Temperance*, p. 20; cf. Thomas Hodgskin, in *Economist*, 10 Nov. 1855, p. 1235; William Bunton in *Banbury Advertiser*, 6 Mar. 1855. Livesey, quo. in *Western Temperance Herald*, 1 July 1868, p. 100.

[17] (p. 355) C. Dickens, *Letters* (Nonesuch edn, 1938), I, p. 563: Dickens to Theodore Compton, 26 Jan. 1844; E. Chadwick, *Sanitary Report* (Ed. M. W. Flinn, Edinburgh, 1965), p. 203. Morley, quo. in J. L. & B. Hammond, *James Stansfeld*, p. 134; cf. Kay Shuttleworth in *3 Hansard 220*, c. 22 (17 June 1874), & the quotation from Dickens in *Brewers Journal*, 15 Oct. 1871, p. 241. For the cotton famine, see *Weekly Record*, 21 Feb. 1863, p. 87.

[18] (p. 356) J. C. Farn, *Reasoner*, 28 Oct. 1857, p. 245; I owe this reference to Mrs. Susan Budd, Department of Sociology, Southampton University.

[19] (p. 356) H. Mayhew, *London Labour*, I, p. 25; J. G. Kohl, *England, Ireland & Scotland* (1844), pp. 54–5; cf. Cruikshank, quo. in *Bristol Temperance Herald*, Dec. 1850, p. 184.

[20] (p. 356) Cf. E. Lemert, *Alcohol & the North West Coast Indians* (Univ. of California publications in Culture & Society, II, No. 6, Berkeley, 1954), pp. 364–5.

[21] (p. 357) P. Collins, 'Dickens & Popular Amusements', *Dickensian*, Jan. 1965.

[22] (p. 357) Quotations from H. Parris, *Constitutional Bureaucracy* (1969), p. 275; J. Manton, *Elizabeth Garrett Anderson* (1965), p. 180, referring to the campaign against the C.D. Acts. For Wilberforce, see R. I. & S. Wilberforce, *Life of William Wilberforce*, III, pp. 203–4.

[23] (p. 358) Quotation from M. E. Loane, *Neighbours and Friends* (1910), p. 57; cf. S. Reynolds, *A Poor Man's House* (1911), pp. 246–7, 265–6. See also M. E. Loane, *The Next Street But One* (1907), pp. 78, 106; *From Their Point of View* (1908), p. 92.

[24] (p. 358) G. D. H. Cole, *Chartist Portraits*, p. 186.

[25] (p. 358) W. Acton, *Prostitution* (2nd edn, 1870), p. 267.

[26] (p. 358) *British & Foreign Temperance Intelligencer*, 9 Apr. 1842, p. 113; *Weekly Record*, 15 Mar. 1877, p. 162.

[27] (p. 359) Quotation from *Temperance Spectator*, Aug. 1859, p. 113; see also T. Wright, *Some Habits & Customs of the Working Classes, by a Journeyman Engineer* (1867), p. 148.

[28] (p. 359) J. Dunlop, *Autobiography*, p. 279 (19 Nov. 1846).

[29] (p. 359) N.T.L. *MS. Minutes*, 3 Feb. 1860; J. Livesey, *Malt Lecture*, p. 32; cf. *British Temperance Advocate*, 29 June 1839, p. 73. For the magistrates' social connexions see 'Town Clergyman' in *The Times*, 25 Sept. 1871, p. 4, & 'a country Magistrate' in *ibid.*, 28 Sept. 1871, p. 10. See also R. Blake, *Disraeli*, p. 307.

[30] (p. 360) *British Temperance Advocate*, 1 Nov. 1860, p. 121.

[31] (p. 360) Quo. in P. Thompson, *Socialists, Liberals & Labour* (1967), p. 192; cf. R. Skidelsky, *Politicians & the Slump* (1967), *passim.*

[32] (p. 360) *The Times*, 31 Oct. 1868, p. 9.

[33] (p. 360) Quotations from J. Pearce, *Livesey*, p. 57; G. P. Gooch, *Courtney*, p. 186; cf. R. C. Macridis, 'The Immobility of the French Communist Party', *Journal of Politics*, XX (1958), pp. 633–4.

[34] (p. 361) S.C.H.C. Contagious Diseases Acts, *Parl. Papers* 1881 (351), VIII, QQ. 4327ff.; cf. *ibid.*, QQ. 4860–2.

[35] (p. 361) Herbert, in *Poole & Bournemouth Herald*, 7 Aug. 1879; for the Crimean War, see A. C. F. Beales, *The History of Peace* (1931), p. 98.

[36] (p. 362) B. Trinder, *The Methodist New Connexion in Dawley & Madeley* (Wesley Historical Society West Midlands Branch Occasional Publications No. 1, 1968), p. 9; for the Vicar of Wendover, see W. R. Fremantle, *Memoir of the Rev. Spencer Thornton A.M.*, pp. 175ff.; for Manning, see *Universe*, 19 Aug. 1871, p. 2.

[37] (p. 362) For Welsh Sunday closing, see W. R. Lambert, *op. cit.*, p. 337. See also C. Booth, *Life & Labour in London. Third Series*, IV, p. 15 (Barclay's); *First Series*, I, p. 114.

[38] (p. 363) Quotations from B.M. *Add. MSS.* 44428 (Gladstone Papers), f. 178: Fraser to Gladstone, 5 Nov. 1870; G. Kitson Clark, *The Making of Victorian England*, p. 64. For modern social surveys, see F. Zweig, *The Worker in an Affluent Society* (1961), pp. 130–1; D. E. Allen, *British Tastes* (Panther edn, 1969), pp. 89, 143–4, 162–3. For drunkenness arrests in 1875, see G. B. Wilson, *Alcohol & the Nation*, p. 440; correlation coefficient 0.3819, significant at the 2% level. For temperance reformers on London, see W. Reid, *Robert Kettle*, p. 13; Livesey, *Preston Temperance Advocate*, July 1834, p. 53; Hoyle, in S.C.H.L. on Intemperance, third report, *Parl. Papers* 1877, XI (418), Q. 8404. For London licensing statistics, see Royal Commission on Liquor Licensing Laws, *Parl. Papers* 1898, XXXVII (C. 8696), pp. 44ff. For London's drinking habits, see G. Dodd, *The Food of London* (1856), p. 404; P. Mathias, *Brewing Industry*, p. 378.

[39] (p. 363) J. S. Mill, 'Essays on Economics & Society', in J. S. Mill, *Collected Works*, V (Toronto, 1967), p. 427.

[40] (p. 363) H. Mayhew, *London Labour*, III, p. 265.

[41] (p. 364) *Alliance Weekly News*, 4 Feb. 1860, p. 938.

[42] (p. 364) E. Rathbone, 'Changes in Public Life', in Ray Strachey (Ed.), *Our Freedom & its Results* (1936), pp. 72–3.

[43] (p. 364) W. James, *Varieties of Religious Experience*, p. 340.

[44] (p. 365) J. Ruskin, 'Fors Clavigera', Letter 1 (Jan. 1871), in *Works* (Ed. Cook & Wedderburn), XXVII, p. 13; F. Engels, *Working Class*, p. 143.

[45] (p. 365) e.g. R. A. Cross, quo. in *Brewers Guardian*, 15 Jan. 1872, p. 28; cf. the exchange of letters in *The Friend*, July 1855, p. 128; Aug. 1855, p. 147. For the attitude of countrymen, see G. Bourne, *Change in the Village* (1912 edn), p. 66.

[46] (p. 365) J. Livesey, *Malt Lecture*, p. 29.

[47] (p. 366) Quotation from T. Clarkson, *History . . . of the Abolition of the African Slave Trade* (1839 edn), p. 613. For Lord Salisbury, see R. M. Macleod, 'The Edge of Hope:

Social Policy & Chronic Alcoholism 1870–1900', *Journal of the History of Medicine an Allied Sciences*, Vol. 22, No. 3 (July 1967), *passim.*

[48] (p. 366) Marx & Engels, *Correspondence 1846–1895* (1934), p. 374: Marx & Engels to Bebel, Liebknecht, Bracke *et al.*, Sept. 1879.

[49] (p. 366) Quotation from F. R. Lees, 'Life of William Hoyle', in Hoyle's *Wealth & Social Progress* (Manchester, 1887), p. 268; Hoyle's speech is in *Alliance News* 28 Oct. 1876, p. 690; for Wilson, see H. R. Hodgson, *The Society of Friends in Bradford* (Bradford, 1926), p. 49; Marx & Engels, *op. cit.*, p. 374; cf. M. Richter, *art. cit.*, 1956, p. 469; E. Wertheimer, *Portrait of the Labour Party* (1929), p. 141. On 'small-scale success systems' see John Foster's interesting comments in H. J. Dyos (Ed.), *The Study of Urban History*, p. 294.

[50] (p. 367) E. Duckershoff, *How the English Workman Lives* (1899), pp. 55, 87; C. V. Butler, *Social Conditions in Oxford* (1912), p. 223.

[51] (p. 367) Lord Macaulay, 'History of England', in *Works* (Edinburgh edn, 1896), I, pp. 77–8.

[52] (p. 367) Quotation from *Bristol Temperance Herald*, Aug. 1838, p. 58; for Trevelyan, see *ibid.*, May 1853, p. 70. For coalheavers & ballastheavers, see Spriggs, in *Morning Chronicle*, 8 July 1850, p. 6; also Cassell & Janson in *Teetotal Times & Essayist*, Feb. 1850, p. 17.

[53] (p. 368) B. Parsons, *Anti-Bacchus* (1840), p. iii; T. Okey, *A Basketful of Memories* (1930), p. 149.

[54] (p. 368) B. Parsons, *op. cit.*, p. 53; see also A. W. Coats, 'Changing Attitudes to Labour in the Mid-Eighteenth Century', *Econ. Hist. Rev.*, 1958–9, pp. 35–6.

[55] (p. 368) 1871 Census, *Parl. Papers* 1873 (872–I), LXXI, Part II, pp. 81ff.

[56] (p. 368) J. Morley, *Richard Cobden*, p. 40.

[57] (p. 368) Quotations from dustjacket to M. H. C Hayler, *Vision of a Century*, & p. 195.

[58] (p. 369) H. Carter, *English Temperance Movement*, pp. 14, 234, 239.

[59] (p. 370) *National Temperance Chronicle*, Oct. 1847, p. 153; Oct. 1848, p 345.

[60] (p. 370) *Temperance Star*, 8 Oct. 1869, p. 7; see also V. Brittain, *Pethick-Lawrence. A Portrait* (1963), p. 206.

[61] (p. 371) Muntz, *3 Hansard 215*, c. 1652 (7 May 1873); cf. *3 Hansard 251*, c. 492 (5 Mar. 1880). For protest votes, see *3 Hansard 215*, cc. 1619–21, 1636 (7 May 1873); cf. Lawson, *3 Hansard 223*, c. 1779 (28 Apr. 1875).

[62] (p. 371) Viscount Bury, *3 Hansard 211*, c. 497 (8 May 1872); Bruce, *3 Hansard 215*, c. 1658 (7 May 1873).

[63] (p. 371) Bass, *Weekly Record*, 19 Sept. 1863, p. 415; for Bright, see W. S. Jevons, *Methods of Social Reform* (1883), p. 247.

[64] (p. 371) Quotation from *Weekly Times*, 23 Apr. 1871; cf. *Church of England Temperance Chronicle*, 1 July 1876, pp. 125–6. For Huss, see W. F. Bynum's valuable 'Chronic Alcoholism in the first half of the nineteenth century', *Bulletin of the History of Medicine*, 1968, pp. 170, 180; I owe this reference to Mr. R. D. French, of the Dept. of History, University of Princeton.

[65] (p. 372) Cf. Ladies' National Association, *15th Annual Report, 1884*, p. 73; Manchester Central Library, *George Wilson Collection:* Cobden to George Wilson, 16 July 1842.

[66] (p. 372) Quo. from Dawson Burns' letter to *Christian World*, 14 Apr. 1871, p. 227; *Alliance News*, 8 Sept. 1883, p. 568.

[67] (p. 372) Quotations from Leif Jones, *Why Leave the Straight Road? A Warning to Temperance Reformers* (U.K.A. 1914), p. 5; U.K.A. *Nationalisation of the Drink Traffic* (Manchester, 1915), p. 4.

[68] (p. 372) Quotations from G. B. Wilson, *Nationalisation of the Drink Traffic. Ought the Churches to Advocate it?* (1915), p. 5; B.M. *Add. MSS.* 44250 (Gladstone Papers), f. 151: Manning to Gladstone, 5 Feb. 1874; I owe the latter reference to Mr. A. E. Dingle.

[69] (p. 372) T. H. Barker, *Civil Rights & Social Duties* (1871), p. 11; cf. U.K.A. *19th Annual Report, 1870–1*, p. 89; M. H. C. Hayler, *Vision of a Century*, p. 195.

[70] (p. 373) Quotations from 'The Drunkard's Catechism', in Bodleian Library, Oxford, *Firth Collection* c. 22 (ballads & drinking songs), p. 181; *3 Hansard 206*, c. 927 (17 May 1871), on Bradford; U.K.A. *Principles & Policy of the Alliance* (Manchester, 1859), p. 16. I owe the first of these references to Louis James. For the drink trade's responses, see

Licensed Victuallers Guardian, 7 Sept. 1872; cf. letter from 'XXX' in *ibid.*, 5 Oct. 1872, p. 332.

[71] (p. 373) *Alliance News*, 9 May 1868, p. 148.

[72] (p. 374) *Devon & Cornwall Temperance Journal*, 1 June 1870, p. 81.

[73] (p. 374) Quotations from M. Gilbert (Ed.), *Plough My Own Furrow* (1965), p. 214; James Haughton, *A Plea for Teetotalism & the Maine Liquor Law*, p. 178; cf. Dawson Burns' letter in *The Friend*, 1 Feb. 1866, p. 35.

[74] (p. 374) Lawson, *Alliance News*, 17 Oct. 1868, p. 330; *Church of England Temperance Chronicle*, 1 July 1876, p. 126.

[75] (p. 374) *Alliance News*, 14 Oct. 1871, p. 661.

[76] (p. 374) R.S.P.C.A. *17th Annual Report, 1843*, p. 38.

[77] (p. 374) Card, S.C.H.C. Public-Houses, *Parl. Papers* 1854 (367), XIV, Q. 1967; cf. U.K.A. *Public Inauguration Proceedings* (1853), clause 3 of initial declaration.

[78] (p. 375) U.K.A. *3rd Annual Report, 1855*, p. 13.

[79] (p. 375) U.K.A. *Inaugural Hymn, 26th October 1853*.

[80] (p. 375) Barker, *Alliance News*, 18 Mar. 1876, p. 180; Beggs, in Viscount Ingestre (Ed.), *Meliora . . . Second Series* (1853), p. 231; U.K.A. *No Case against the United Kingdom Alliance and the Permissive Bill* (n.d.), p. 58.

[81] (p. 375) U.K.A. *Full Report of the Speeches Delivered at the Annual Public Meeting . . . Manchester . . . October 26th, 1870*, p. 31.

[82] (p. 376) *Weekly Record*, 27 Dec. 1862, pp. 525–6.

[83] (p. 376) Quotation from Mr. Rice, *3 Hansard 126*, c. 546 (26 Apr. 1853). For drinking among policemen, see S.C.H.L. on Intemperance, second report, *Parl. Papers* 1877 (271), XI, QQ. 3450, 6443–50; cf. E. C. Midwinter, *Law and Order in Early Victorian Lancashire* (York, 1968), p. 26. See also H. E. Manning, S.C.H.C. Sale of Liquor on Sunday Bill . . . *Parl. Papers* 1867–8 (402), XIV, Q. 2386; G. Thorne, *The Great Acceptance*, p. 69.

[84] (p. 376) Mayne, S.C.H.C. Sale of Liquors on Sunday Bill, *Parl. Papers* 1867–8 (402), XIV, Q. 275; Chamberlain, S.C.H.L. Intemperance, *Parl. Papers* 1877 (171), XI, Q. 2281.

[85] (p. 376) S.C.H.L. Intemperance, first report, *Parl. Papers* 1877 (271), XI, Q. 5240; fourth report, *Parl. Papers* 1878 (338), XIV, Q. 3887; *Leeds Mercury*, 19 July 1834; cf. J. L. & B. Hammond, *Lord Shaftesbury* (1939 edn), p. 213.

[86] (p. 377) For illicit stills, see 13th Report of the Commissioners of Her Majesty's Inland Revenue, *Parl. Papers* 1870 (C. 82), XX, pp. 82–3; for betting, see Lady F. Bell, *At the Works*, p. 352; H. Mayhew, *London Labour*, I, p. 16.

[87] (p. 377) K. C. Wheare, *Federal Government* (4th edn, 1963), p. 164.

[88] (p. 377) Salisbury, *3 Hansard 211*, c. 89 (2 May 1872); see also 'Municipal Drink Traffic'. *Fabian Tract No. 86* (6th edn, 1909), p. 5. For Scotland, see G. B. Wilson, *Alcohol & the Nation*, p. 121.

[89] (p. 377) Speech at Alliance banquet, Manchester: *Alliance News*, 22 Apr. 1865, p. 125; cf. Matthew Arnold, *Culture & Anarchy*, p. 135.

[90] (p. 377) For Bessbrook, *3 Hansard 278*, c. 1356 (27 Apr. 1883); W. H. Marwick, 'Some Quaker Firms of the Nineteenth-Century', *Journal of the Friends' Historical Society*, 1956–8, pp. 250–1; S. E. Williams, *Bessbrook, A Temperance Experiment* (n.d., c. 1908), *passim*. For Saltaire, see Rev. R. Balgarnie, *Sir Titus Salt*, pp. 226–7.

[91] (p. 378) Richardson, S.C.H.L. Intemperance, fourth report, *Parl. Papers* 1878 (338), XIV, Q. 4607. Lawson, *3 Hansard 206*, c. 952 (17 May 1871); Manning, sermon at SS. Mary & Joseph's Poplar, in Westminister Cathedral Archives: scrapbook of newspaper articles on Manning.

[92] (p. 378) J. S. Mill, *Representative Government* (Everyman edn, 1960), pp. 183 4; cf. E. Williams, *Capitalism & Slavery*, *passim*.

[93] (p. 379) Krause, S.C.H.C. Contagious Diseases Acts: *Parl. Papers* 1881 (351), VIII, Q. 7848; Josephine Butler, *Parl. Papers* 1871 (C. 408, 408–I), XIX, Q. 12,863; for her Manchester speech, see *The Shield*, 28 Mar. 1870, p. 27.

[94] (p. 379) Cf. J. B. Christoph, *Capital Punishment & British Politics* (1962), p. 186.

[95] (p. 379) T. Billington-Greig, *The Militant Suffrage Movement. Emancipation in a Hurry* (n.d., *c.* 1910), pp. 173, 212; cf. W. Godwin, *Political Justice* (2nd edn, 1796), I, p. 294.

[96] (p. 380) Quotations from M. Arnold, *Culture & Anarchy*, p. 12; S. M. Elkins, *Slavery*

(Chicago, 1959), p. 161; G. W. E. Russell, *Sir Wilfrid Lawson*, p. 151, cf. D. Donald, *Lincoln Reconsidered. Essays on the Civil War Era* (New York, 1956), p. 36.

[97] (p. 380) E. R. Jones, *The Life & Speeches of Joseph Cowen M.P.*, pp. 287–8; Thorold Rogers, *Alliance News*, 17 Oct. 1874, p. 675.

[98] (p. 381) *Weekly Record*, 28 June 1862, p. 273.

[99] (p. 381) E. R. Jones, *Joseph Cowen*, p. 344; Fawcett Library, *Josephine Butler Collection:* Josephine Butler to her husband, n.d. (1872). See also M. Duverger, *Political Parties*, pp. 190–1; Rt. Hon. Lord Pethick-Lawrence, *Fate Has Been Kind* (n.d.), p. 68; Emmeline Pankhurst, *My Own Story* (1914), p. 234.

[100] (p. 381) Cecil, *Saturday Review*, 17 Sept. 1864, p. 358; cf. Aydelotte, 'The House of Commons in the 1840s', *History*, June–Oct. 1954, pp. 257–8.

[101] (p. 382) F. M. Cornford, *Microcosmographia Academica* (6th edn, 1966), p. 20.

[102] (p. 382) Quo. in W. F. Connell, *The Educational Thought & Influence of Matthew Arnold* (1950), p. 148; cf. Fowler, *A Study in Radicalism & Dissent*, p. 119; A. Miall, *Life of Edward Miall* (1884), p. 146.

[103] (p. 383) *The Times*, 7 Apr. 1893, pp. 11, 9; S. Webb, *Fabian Tract No. 108* (1901), p. 4. See also J. R. Vincent, *Pollbooks*, p. 45; cf. J. R. Gusfield, *Symbolic Crusade*, pp. 166, 177–80.

[104] (p. 383) Quotations from H. Carter, *op. cit.*, p. 116; D. Donald, *op. cit.*, p. 36; cf. F. Parkin, *Middle Class Radicalism*, p. 38.

[105] (p. 383) *Alliance News*, 18 Feb. 1860, p. 945.

[106] (p. 383) T. Clarkson, *op. cit.*, p. 614; cf. *ibid.*, pp. 247–8.

[107] (p. 383) S. Webb, *Fabian Tract No. 108* (1901), p. 4.

[108] (p. 383) *Weekly Record*, 24 Mar. 1860, p. 143; see also U.K.A. *Nationalisation of the Drink Trade* (Manchester, 1915), p. 5.

[109] (p. 384) Pope, *Alliance News*, 28 May 1870, p. 175; Barker, *Civil Rights & Social Duties* (1871), p. 15; cf. Jonathan Grubb, in *The Friend*, 1 July 1867, p. 162.

[110] (p. 384) Gladstone, *3 Hansard 203*, cc. 745–6 (22 July 1870); cf. *Saturday Review*, 30 July 1870, p. 130.

[111] (p. 384) Quo. in *Clem Attlee. The Granada Historical Records Interview* (Panther Books, 1967), p. 47.

[112] (p. 385) For Alliance counter-attack, see *Alliance News*, 14 Apr. 1893, p. 249; cf. J. Whyte, *The United Kingdom Alliance Vindicated* (Manchester, n.d. ?1901), p. 45. For Chamberlain's attacks on the Alliance see *The Times*, 7 Apr. 1893, p. 11; *Alliance News*, 23 Feb. 1889, p. 151; 8 Aug. 1890, p. 514; 22 July 1892, p. 468; 13 July 1894, p. 441.

[113] (p. 385) Cossham, *Alliance News*, 16 Oct. 1875, p. 657; A. G. Gardiner, *Life of George Cadbury* (1923), pp. 305–6.

[114] (p. 386) See the excellent discussion in F. Goguel, *France Under the Fourth Republic* (New York, 1952), pp. 152–3.

Chapter 17. The End [pp. 387–405].

[1] (p. 387) L[ondon] W[orking] M[en's] A[ssociation], *Address & Rules* (n.d.) [B.M. shelfmark 8138 a 55], pp. 2, 6; cf. W. Lovett, *Life & Struggles*, p. 94.

[2] (p. 388) *Northern Star*, 23 Apr. 1842, p. 1.

[3] (p. 388) Millington, in *ibid.*, 7 May 1842, p. 2; Cluer, in *Journal of the N.B.F.T.S.*, 20 July 1839, p. 249. See also *Jackson's Oxford Journal*, 6 July 1842; I owe this reference to Mr. Raphael Samuel; also, *British & Foreign Temperance Intelligencer*, 3 Dec. 1842, p. 490. For W. S. Ellis, see *English Chartist Circular*, II, No. 145, p. 371; cf. 'Davie Roberts', in H. Solly, *James Woodford, Carpenter & Chartist* (1881), I, p. 150.

[4] (p. 388) Quotations from *Plymouth, Devonport & Stonehouse Herald* (Plymouth), 18 Mar. 1843; *Ashton Reporter*, 28 Oct. 1871.

[5] (p. 389) Boston Public Library, *Vincent-Garrison Correspondence* (photostat copies), Vincent to Garrison, 11 July 1876; for Vincent's last speeches see *Barrow Times*, 7 Dec. 1878; *Barrow Herald*, 7 Dec. 1878, p. 5.

[6] (p. 389) Lowery, *Carlisle Journal* (Carlisle), 8 Oct. 1838; L.W.M.A. *Address & Rules*, p. 2; cf. Vincent, *Leicestershire Mercury* (Leicester), 3 Apr. 1841.

[7] (p. 389) Goschen's words, used of the Tories, *3 Hansard 182*, c. 1969 (23 Apr. 1866); cf. J. A. Hobson, *Imperialism. A Study* (1948 edn), p. 101.

[8] (p. 389) J. S. Mill, *Liberty*, pp. 116–17; cf. J. A. & O. Banks, *Feminism & Family Planning* (Liverpool, 1964), p. 117.

[9] (p. 389) *Anti-Bread Tax Circular*, 21 Apr. 1841, pp. 5–6; 26 May 1841, p. 23; *Nonconformist*, 18 June 1845, p. 434; A. R. Schoyen, *Chartist Challenge*, p. 73; A. Briggs (Ed.), *Chartist Studies*, pp. 183–4; T. Whittaker, *Life's Battles, passim.*

[10] (p. 389) *Red Republican*, 5 Oct. 1850, p. 122.

[11] (p. 390) O'Connor's complaints, *Northern Star*, 30 Nov. 1839, p. 1; 31 Aug. 1839, p. 6; 24 Feb. 1838; cf. G. Bourne, *Change in the Village*, p. 177; Joseph Arch, *Life*, p. 243.

[12] (p. 390) e.g. *3 Hansard 52*, c. 1311 (23 Mar. 1840); *3 Hansard 54*, c. 337 (19 May 1840).

[13] (p. 390) J. Clay, *30th & 31st Chaplain's Reports of the Preston House of Correction* (1855), pp. 57–8.

[14] (p. 390) Ashley, *3 Hansard 67*, c. 65 (28 Feb. 1843).

[15] (p. 390) E. L. Woodward, *The Age of Reform* (1938), p. 120.

[16] (p. 391) Father Augustine, *Footprints of Father Mathew*, pp. 162–3, 290, 298; for Russell, see *National Temperance Chronicle*, Jan. 1845, p. 298.

[17] (p. 391) Peel, *3 Hansard 61*, c. 447 (11 Mar. 1842); Gladstone, *3 Hansard 170*, c. 213 (16 Apr. 1863); cf. *3 Hansard 278*, c. 1281 (27 Apr. 1883).

[18] (p. 391) L.W.M.A. *Address & Rules*, p. 3.

[19] (p. 391) *Ashton Reporter*, 9 Mar. 1872, p. 3; contrast Vincent, *ibid.*, 18 Mar. 1871, p. 3; 28 Oct. 1871; 12 Oct. 1872.

[20] (p. 391) *Red Republican*, 5 Oct. 1850, p. 122.

[21] (p. 392) *People's Paper*, 16 June 1855; cf. *ibid.*, 23 May 1857, p. 1; Bronterre O'Brien's *Social Reformer*, 15 Sept. 1849, p. 44; J. Saville, *Ernest Jones*, p. 160.

[22] (p. 392) *Manchester Examiner & Times* (Manchester), 24 Aug. 1868, p. 3.

[23] (p. 392) F. Engels, *Working Class*, pp. 143–4; for a similar analysis, see Oastler, quo. in N. Smelser, *op. cit.*, p. 284. See also H. Mayhew, *London Labour*, II, pp. 325–7.

[24] (p. 393) Quotations from F. Engels, *Working Class*, pp. 11, 111, 106, 116, 142, 139.

[25] (p. 393) J. L. & B. Hammond, *The Age of the Chartists*, pp. 144, 146; S. & B. Webb, *Liquor Licensing*, p. 128.

[26] (p. 393) e.g. P. Laslett, *The World We Have Lost* (1965), p. 75.

[27] (p. 393) T. S. Ashton, 'The Standard of Life of the Workers in England', *Journal of Economic History*, Supplement IX (1949), p. 33.

[28] (p. 394) M. G. Field, 'Alcoholism, Crime & Delinquency in Soviet Society', in S. M. Lipset & N. J. Smelser (Eds.), *Sociology. The Progress of a Decade* (Englewood Cliffs, 1961), p. 577; cf. my 'Religion & Recreation in 19th Century England', *loc. cit.*, pp. 119–22.

[29] (p. 394) First and last quotations from K. Marx, *Economic & Philosophic MSS of 1844* (Moscow, 1959), pp. 121–2; others from Marx and Engels, *Works* (2 Vol. edn, Moscow 1962), I, pp. 56, 44; cf. p. 41.

[30] (p. 394) Cobden, *3 Hansard 120*, c. 25 (23 Mar. 1852); *3 Hansard 123*, cc. 1324–5 (13 Dec. 1852); *Freeholder*, 1 Jan. 1851, p. 5.

[31] (p. 394) Quotations from Marx and Engels, *Works*, I, p. 381; II, pp. 99, 102; Marx and Engels, *Correspondence 1846–1895* (1934), pp. 115–16: Engels to Marx, 7 Oct. 1858 See also Marx and Engels, *Works*, II, pp. 99, 102.

[32] (p. 395) *Ibid.*, p. 147 (Marx to Engels, 9 Apr. 1863), p. 461 (Engels to Sorge, 7 Dec. 1889).

[33] (p. 396) Robert Owen, S.C.H.C. Police of the Metropolis, *Parl. Papers* 1816 (510), V, p. 234; see also Robert Owen, in *Crisis*, 15 June 1834, p. 83; R. Owen, *A New View of Society* (Everyman edn, 1927), pp. 31, 66–8. Sidney Webb to Beatrice Potter, 30 Jan. 1892, *Passfield Papers*—I owe this reference to Mr. Royden Harrison, of Warwick University; cf. B. Webb, *My Apprenticeship*, p. 238. For the temperance views of Labour leaders, see P. Thompson, *Socialists, Liberals & Labour*, pp. 116, 126, 162; *Alliance News*, 29 Sept. 1883, 1 Nov. 1884 (Pankhurst); 22 Oct. 1903, p. 709 (Crooks). For Hardie, see his enthusiastic letter on temperance teaching in schools, 31 Mar. 1885—in Clydebank Public Library. I am most grateful to the Librarian for sending me a photostat of this letter.

[34] (p. 396) Burns, *The Times*, 9 June 1890, p. 10; Tillett, *Alliance News*, 4 Dec. 1891, p. 793; 22 Jan. 1892, p. 53; Sidney Webb to Beatrice Potter 30 Jan. 1892, *Passfield Papers*. I owe this latter reference to Mr. Royden Harrison.

[35] (p. 396) Quo. from J. Whyte, *The United Kingdom Alliance Vindicated* (n.d., c. 1901) p. 59; for Snowden, see *Blackburn Labour Journal*, Aug. 1901.

[36] (p. 396) P. Snowden, *Socialism & Teetotalism* (I.L.P. 1909), p. 2; *Socialism & the Drink Question*, pp. 27, 83; D. J. Shackleton, 'Working Men & Temperance Reform' (repr. from *Alliance News*, n.d. ?1907) pp. 6, 10.

[37] (p. 396) Henderson, *4 Hansard 185*, cc. 117–18 (27 Feb. 1908); Hardie, *4 Hansard 194*, cc. 988ff. (20 Oct. 1908); Crooks, *4 Hansard 187*, c. 1506 (30 Apr. 1908); cf. P. Snowden, *4 Hansard 187*, c. 1180ff. (28 Apr. 1908).

[38] (p. 396) E. Wertheimer, *Portrait of the Labour Party*, p. 94.

[39] (p. 396) J. H. Roberts, foreword (18 Jan. 1905) to H. Quelch & J. H. Roberts, *Would Universal Total Abstinence Reduce Wages? A Report of a Public Debate. Carlisle 29th November 1904* (1905).

[40] (p. 396) Quotations from P. Snowden, *Socialism & Teetotalism*, p. 7; foreword to V. W. Garratt, *Labour & the Liquor Traffic* (n.d.), p. 3.

[41] (p. 396) V. W. Garratt, *op. cit.*, p. 5; *Labour & the Liquor Trade. Report of the Special Committee . . . to inquire into the Question of the Liquor Trade* (Labour Party, 1923), p. 21; cf. A. Greenwood, *Publicans & Politics* (Labour Campaign for the Public Ownership & Control of the Liquor Trade, n.d.), pp. 1–3, 8; H. Russell Smart, *Socialism & Drink* (Labour Press Society, Manchester, n.d.), p. 4.

[42] (p. 397) J. Livesey, *Preston Temperance Advocate*, July 1834, p. 49; cf. R. A. Jameson, *Would Universal Teetotalism Lower Wages?* (Glasgow, n.d.), pp. 9–10; J. S. Gavin, *Poverty. Its Cause & Cure* (Manchester, 1898), p. 21.

[43] (p. 397) Joseph Arch, *Life*, p. 243; T. Burt, 'Methodism & the Northern Miners', *Primitive Methodist Quarterly Review*, July 1882, pp. 395–6.

[44] (p. 397) P. Snowden, *End This Colossal Waste. A Neglected Palliative for Unemployment* (U.K.A. 1936), p. 16.

[45] (p. 397) For Hardie, see S. Pankhurst, *Suffragette Movement* (1931), p. 205; G. Blaxland, *J. H. Thomas. A Life for Unity* (1964), pp. 212–13; N. Dennis, F. Henriques & C. Slaughter, *Coal is Our Life* (1956), p. 92.

[46] (p. 397) P. Thompson, *Socialists, Liberals & Labour*, pp. 209–10; cf. A. J. P. Taylor, *The Trouble-Makers*, p. 106.

[47] (p. 397) *The Life of Robert Owen, Written By Himself* (1857), I, p. 58.

[48] (p. 397) Information from Sheffield Police Records, *Register of Arrests 1863–4*, sample of 515 individuals (all those arrested from 1 Jan. to 20 Apr. 1863, and from 24 Feb. 1864 to 1 June 1864).

[49] (p. 398) Joseph Arch, *Life*, p. 245; cf. *ibid.*, pp. 36, 245. John Burns, *Labour & Drink* (cheap edn, 1904), p. 31.

[50] (p. 398) R. Blatchford, *Merrie England* (1894), pp. 113–14, 158–9; H. Quelch, 'Socialism & Temperance Reform', in his *Literary Remains* (Ed. E. B. Bax, 1914), p. 198. See also G. K. Chesterton, 'Temperance & the Great Alliance', in *True Temperance Monographs* (True Temperance Association, 1921), p. 34.

[51] (p. 399) H. Quelch, 'Socialism & Temperance Reform', *loc. cit.*, p. 196; H. Russell Smart, *Socialism & Drink* (Manchester, n.d.), p. 14.

[52] (p. 399) *Ibid.*, p. 7; cf. H. Quelch & J. H. Roberts, *op. cit.*, pp. 10–11, 20–1; R. Blatchford, *Britain for the British* (1902), p. 127.

[53] (p. 399) *Keighley News* (Keighley), 5 Jan. 1895, p. 7.

[54] (p. 399) J. A. Hobson, 'The Economics of the Temperance Movement', *Commonwealth*, June 1896, p. 209.

[55] (p. 399) R. Blatchford, *Britain for the British*, p. 131; cf. F. C. Watts, 'Socialism & Temperance', *Social-Democrat*, 15 Apr. 1904, p. 212; P. Snowden, *Socialism & the Drink Question*, pp. 93, 98, 103.

[56] (p. 400) R. Blatchford, *Britain for the British*, p. 123; cf. J. Arch, *Life*, p. 36.

[57] (p. 400) *Keighley News*, 5 Jan. 1895, p. 7.

[58] (p. 400) Speech reported in *Labour Leader*, 3 Apr. 1908, p. 222.

[59] (p. 400) Quotation from *Labour Leader*, 6 Mar. 1908, p. 152; see also *ibid.*, 8 May 1908, p. 296.

[60] (p. 401) *Labour and Drink*, p. 10.

[61] (p. 401) R. A. Jameson, *Would Universal Teetotalism Lower Wages?* (Glasgow, n.d.), pp. 3, 5, 10; cf. L.W.M.A. *Address from the London Trades' Committee, appointed to watch the Parliamentary Inquiry into Combinations, to the Working Classes* (1838), pp. 4–5; J. A. Hobson, 'The Economics of the Temperance Movement', *loc. cit.*, p. 211; H. Quelch & J. H. Roberts, *op. cit.*, p. 13; William Pearson, in *Alliance News*, 21 Aug. 1902, p. 537.

[62] (p. 401) For drink and industry, see R. A. Jameson, *op. cit.*, pp. 12–13; for women, G. Blaiklock, *Temperance in Relation to the Labour Problem* (2nd edn, 1910), pp. 11–12; for the home market, see P. Snowden, *End This Colossal Waste*, p. 14; Joseph Livesey, *Preston Temperance Advocate*, July 1834, p. 49. For discussion of employment opportunities in the drink industry, see J. A. Hobson, 'The Economics of the Temperance Movement', *loc. cit.*; J. S. Gavin, *op. cit.*, pp. 11ff.; P. Snowden, *Socialism & the Drink Question*, p. 106; cf. P. Mathias, *Brewing Industry*, p. 35.

[63] (p. 401) H. Quelch, 'Boots or Beer? And the Economic Necessity of Waste', *Social-Democrat*, XII, No. 6 (15 June 1908), p. 246.

[64] (p. 402) S. Reynolds, *A Poor Man's House* (1911), pp. 263–4; Bax, quo. in M. D. O'Brien, *Socialism & Infamy* (privately printed, 1909), p. 23; Olivier, in *Fabian Essays* (Ed. Bernard Shaw, 1948), p. 109.

[65] (p. 402) Tillett, quo. in B. L. Crapster, *British Liquor Industry*, p. 112; E. Carpenter, *Love's Coming-of-Age* (2nd edn, 1903), pp. 11–12, 138ff.

[66] (p. 402) E. Carpenter, 'Morality Under Socialism', *Albany Review*, Sept. 1907, p. 639. M. L. Pendered, 'The Psychology of Amusement in its Relation to Temperance Reform', *Socialist Review*, June 1909, pp. 285, 288, 291.

[67] (p. 403) *Labour & the Liquor Trade*, p. 2; cf. Charles Booth, *Life & Labour in London. Third Series*, VII, p. 21; *Final Volume* (1903), p. 103.

[68] (p. 403) Harry Quelch, 'Socialism & Temperance Reform', *loc. cit.*, pp. 196–8; cf. *Justice*, 21 Nov. 1908, p. 6; Charles Booth, *Life & Labour in London. First Series*, I, pp. 115–16; *Final Volume*, p. 112.

[69] (p. 403) *Alliance News*, 9 Dec. 1898, p. 804; the tract was 'Municipal Drink Traffic', *Fabian Tract No. 86*.

[70] (p. 403) E. Wertheimer, *op. cit.*, p. 57; cf. *ibid.*, p. 81.

[71] (p. 403) *Labour & the Liquor Trade*, pp. 21, 20.

[72] (p. 404) Mrs. Humphry Ward, *Robert Elsmere* (2 Vol. edn, 1911), I, p. 57; Macdonald, *3 Hansard 219*, c. 1093 (5 June 1874); cf. *3 Hansard 225*, c. 70 (16 June 1875).

[73] (p. 404) R. Blatchford, *Merrie England*, p. 157; H. Quelch, 'Socialism & Temperance Reform', *loc. cit.*, p. 197; Mond, *5 Hansard 161*, c. 2491 (20 Mar. 1923). For trade unions in the first world war, see A. Bullock, *Life of Ernest Bevin*, I (1960), p. 51; cf. G. Bourne, *Change in the Village*, p. 70.

[74] (p. 404) C. Booth, *Life & Labour in London. First Series*, I, p. 147.

[75] (p. 404) *Ibid.*, II, p. 19.

[76] (p. 404) Chamberlain, *The Times*, 7 Dec. 1894, p. 10; Horner, *Keighley News*, 22 Dec. 1894, p. 4.

[77] (p. 404) *People's Paper*, 16 June 1855.

[78] (p. 405) *Alliance News*, 14 Aug. 1902, p. 522.

[79] (p. 405) J. A. Hobson, 'The Economics of the Temperance Movement', *loc. cit.*, p. 319; Harry Quelch, 'Socialism & Temperance Reform', *loc. cit.*, p. 198. Grayson, *4 Hansard 194*, c. 495 (15 Oct. 1908); *ibid.*, cc. 631–4 (16 Oct. 1908).

Index of Authors

The figures in this index denote the page of the reference notes on which an author's work is first cited.

Index of Authors

Index of Authors

Index of Authors

General Index

Every effort has been made to ensure the usefulness of this index. The most important references appear in bold type; individuals appear under the name by which they are best known (thus 'Disraeli', not 'Beaconsfield'). Footnotes which present the full details of particular works are indexed separately in the 'Index of Authors' above. The book's major themes are brought out in the more general headings, of which the following are the most important:

Alcoholic drinks
Brewers
Commons, House of
Conservative party
Counter-attractions
Doctors
Drink customs
Drink industry
Drink interest
Drinking places
Drunkenness
Education
Elections
Franchise reform
Free licensing movement
Industrialization
Liberal party
Licensing legislation
Local government
Magistrates
Monarchy
Newspapers
Nonconformists
Oratory
Parliamentary inquiries
Permissive Bill
Philanthropy
Poverty
Pressure groups
Recreation
Reformers
Religion
Riots
Rural life
Schisms
Social class
State, the
Sunday
Taxation
Temperance
Thrift
Time
Transport
United Kingdom Alliance
Violence
Women

General Index

General Index

General Index

General Index

General Index

General Index

Garratt, V. W., socialist writer, 396
Garrett, Rev. Charles (1823–1900), Wesleyan minister, 166, 181
Garrett, Elizabeth (1836–1917), doctor, 357
Gaskill, James (1800–70), prohibitionist, 226
Gathorne-Hardy, G., 1st Earl of Cranbrook (1814–1906), 214, 280
George III (1738–1820), 87
George IV (1762–1830), 45, 46
George V (1865–1936), 157
George and Blue Boar, Holborn, 51
George, St., 62
German Democratic Society, 53
Gilbey, Messrs., 250, 292
Giles, John (1795–1877), pioneer teetotaler, 126, 165
Gilpin, Charles (1815–74), Liberal politician, 259, 385
Gin, *see* Alcoholic Drinks
Gin palace, *see* Drinking Places
Ginger beer, 38, 300–1
Ginshops, *see* Drinking Places
Gladstone, W. E. (1809–98), Liberal statesman; coalwhippers and, 338, 352; compensation and, 292; drinking habits, 248; electoral corruption and, 344; free licensing and, 20, **248–51,** 263, 275, 281, **292**; Gothenburg scheme and, 292; Licensing Act (1872) and, 263, 277–8, **282–3**; nonconformists and, 384; pressure groups and, 34; publicans and, 266, 275, 292
taxation and; beer, 251; malt, 62, 82, 284; spirits, 62, 111, 302, 361–2, 390, 391; tea, 302
temperance movement and; affinities, 50, 191; friction, 249, **292,** 364, 365
United Kingdom Alliance and, 204, 241, 260
mentioned, 34, 70, 74, 158, 256, 270–1, 336, 340
Glasgow, 51, 95, 96, 104, 303
Glassblowers, 309
Glyn, G. G. (1824–87), Liberal whip, 270, 282
God, 172, 380
Godfrey's Cordial, 41
Godwin, William (1756–1836), philosopher, 91, 387
Golden Jubilee, 253
Golden Lane Brewery, 70
Gooch, G. P. (1873–1968), historian, 254
Gooch, Sir Thomas, 5th baronet (1767–1851), politician, 77
Good Templars, International Order of, 132, 170, 241
Gordon, Mary, suffragette, 90
Gosse, Sir Edmund William (1849–1928), author, 187
Gossip, 25, 47, 52, 321
Gothenburg scheme, *see* Local Government
Gough, J. B. (1817–86), American temperance orator; lecturing style, **212–213**; Lees and, 214; National Temperance League and, 30, 232, 370; reclamation of, 115, 130; other references, 145, 154, 191, 195, 294, 362
Goulburn, Henry (1784–1856), statesman, 75, 76, 78, 80
Gout, 41, 92, 308, 310
Grace, W. G. (1848–1915), cricketer, 308, 331
Grace Abounding, 130
Grains, 58
Grand Hotel, Scarborough, 335
Grayson, Victor, socialist pioneer, 400, 405
Great Yarmouth, Norfolk, 80
Green, Thomas Hill (1836–82), philosopher; state, attitudes to the, 205, **207–10,** 246; temperance and, **208**, 278, 373; other references, 23, 130, 189, 204, 351
Greenock, Renfrewshire, 104
Greeting, modes of, 42
Gregson, William (1822–90), temperance advocate, 148, 154, 164, 226
Greig, Mr., temperance lecturer, 155
Grey, Charles, 2nd Earl (1764–1845), Whig statesman, 291
Grey, Sir George (1799–1882), Liberal statesman, 251, 254, 262, 376
Grey, Henry G. G., 3rd Earl (1802–94), Liberal statesman, 78, 274
Grier, Rev. R. M. (1834–94), clergyman, 163
Grindrod, R. B. (1811–83), medical temperance advocate, 112, 134, 173, 192, 307, 352
Grosjean, Frederick, London teetotal pioneer, 140
Grosvenor Hotel, London, 335
Grosvenor, Lord Robert, 1st baron Ebury (1801–93), prominent evangelical, 244
Grubb, Edward (1811–91), temperance lecturer, 128, 142, 144, 146, 158, 211
Grundy, Isaac, Preston temperance pioneer, 120
Guest, John (1799–1880), Rotherham brassfounder, 323
Guinness, 59
Guizot, François (1787–1874), French historian and statesman, 202

Gull, Sir William (1816–90), doctor, 308
Gurney, Joseph John (1788–1847), Quaker; and elections, 286, 345; other references, 39, 94, 107, 137, 166, 302
Guthrie, Thomas (1803–73), Scottish Free Church minister, 137, 167

Hales, Stephen (1677–1761), physiologist, 90
Halifax, Yorks., 323
Hall, John Vine (1774–1860), pioneer teetotaler, 116
Hall, Newman (1816–1902), Congregationalist minister, 166, 181, 317
Hall, Richard (1815–81), Cumbd. farmer, 224
Hamilton, Lord Claud (1813–84), Conservative M.P., 157
Hammond, J. L. and B., historians, 81, 393
Hanbury, brewers, 59, 65, 71
Hanbury, Cornelius (1796–1869), chemist and anti-spirits leader, 107
Hanbury, R. C. (1823–?), Liberal brewer-politician, 238, 300
Handloom weavers, 117, 118, 125, 139, 367
Hanham, Professor H. J., 284
Harcourt, Sir W. G. G. V. V. (1827–1904), Liberal statesman; Licensing Act (1872) and, 275, 281, 284; Local Veto and, **210**, 243; other references, 45, 89, 287, 306, 402
Hardie, J. Keir (1856–1915), socialist pioneer, 162, 396, 397
Hargreaves, William (c. 1804–74), prohibitionist, 255
Harney, G. J. (1817–97), Chartist, 391
Harper, Canon, Selby clergyman, 184, 362
Harrington, Charles S., 5th Earl of (1784–1862), prohibitionist, 203, 206, 220
Harrison, Frederic (1831–1923), author and positivist, 324
Harrison, G. W. (1805–60), Wakefield temperance leader, 156, 158, 167
Harrison, James, Preston surgeon, 120, 137
Harrow School, 319, 356
Hartington, S. C. Cavendish, Marquess of (1833–1908), Whig statesman, later 8th Duke of Devonshire, 289, 342
Hartwell, Robert, Chartist compositor, 267, 309, 336
Harvest-beer, *see* Alcoholic Drinks
Harvest-homes, 310
Harvey, Alderman William (1787–1870), prohibitionist, 225–6, 257
Hastings, George, temperance reformer, 151
Hastings, G. W. (1825–?), lawyer and social reformer, 238
Hatters, 39
Haughton, James (1795–1873), corn dealer, 156, 165, 268, 290
Hawker, R. S. (1803–75), clergyman, 310
Hawkers, 54
Hawtrey, E. C. (1789–1862), Provost of Eton, 319
Hazlitt, W. (1778–1830), essayist, 330
Head, Sir George (1782–1855), assistant commissary-general, 127–8
Hell, 117, **172**, 372, 373, 378
Henderson, Arthur (1863–1935), Labour statesman, 396
Henley, Robert E., 2nd Baron (1789–1841), lawyer, 107
Henry VII (1457–1509), 88
Herapath, Mr., maltster, 74
Herbert, Auberon (1838–1906), political philosopher, 27, 251, 281
Herbert, Sidney, 1st Baron Herbert of Lea (1810–61), Liberal statesman, 332
Heron, Sir Robert (1765–1854), Whig politician, 80
Hervey, Lord, 107
Hetherington, Henry (1792–1849), Chartist, 91, 140, 184
Heys, Robert, dissenting minister, 179
Heyworth, Lawrence (1786–1872), temperance reformer, 101, 259
Hibernian Temperance Society, 103
Higginbottom, John (1788–1876), teetotal doctor, 156, 307
Highbury Barn, London, 323
Hildyard Arms, Holderness, 54
Hill, Matthew Davenport (1792–1872), Recorder of Birmingham; United Kingdom Alliance and, **198**, **221**, 226, 237, 296; *mentioned*, 166, 180, 203, 340, 349
Hill, Octavia (1838–1912), philanthropist, 320, 323
Hilton, John (1820–1908), prominent prohibitionist, 225, 243
Hindley, Charles, Whig M.P., 307
Hinton Charterhouse, Som., 163
Hoare, brewers, 59
Hoare, Sir Henry A. (1824–?), Liberal M.P., 275
Hoare, William, brewer, 341
Hobson, J. A. (1858–1940), economist, 27, 253, 389, 399, 405
Hockings, John, Birmingham temperance advocate, **129–30**, 155, 308, 321

General Index

General Index